ANALYZING AND SECURING SOCIAL NETWORKS

ANALYZING AND SECURING SOCIAL NETWORKS

Bhavani Thuraisingham • Satyen Abrol
Raymond Heatherly • Murat Kantarcioglu
Vaibhav Khadilkar • Latifur Khan

CRC Press
Taylor & Francis Group
Boca Raton London New York

CRC Press is an imprint of the
Taylor & Francis Group, an **informa** business
AN AUERBACH BOOK

CRC Press
Taylor & Francis Group
6000 Broken Sound Parkway NW, Suite 300
Boca Raton, FL 33487-2742

Printed on acid-free paper
Version Date: 20160226

International Standard Book Number-13: 978-1-4822-4327-7 (Hardback)

Library of Congress Cataloging-in-Publication Data

Names: Thuraisingham, Bhavani M., author.
Title: Analyzing and securing social networks / Bhavani Thuraisingham, Satyen
Abrol, Raymond Heatherly, Murat Kantarcioglu, Vaibhav Khadilkar, and
Latifur Khan.
Description: Boca Raton : Taylor & Francis Group, 2016. | Includes
bibliographical references and index.
Identifiers: LCCN 2015042961 | ISBN 9781482243277
Subjects: LCSH: Online social networks--Security measures. | Web usage
mining. | Data protection. | Computer crimes--Prevention. | Privacy, Right
of.
Classification: LCC HM742 .T538 2016 | DDC 006.7/54--dc23
LC record available at http://lccn.loc.gov/2015042961

Visit the Taylor & Francis Web site at
http://www.taylorandfrancis.com

and the CRC Press Web site at
http://www.crcpress.com

We dedicate this book to Dr. Robert Herklotz, formerly of the Air Force Office of Scientific Research, for his tireless contributions and support of cybersecurity research.

Contents

SECTION I Supporting Technologies

SECTION II   *Aspects of Analyzing and Securing Social Networks*

SECTION III   *Techniques and Tools for Social Network Analytics*

SECTION IV   Social Network Analytics and Privacy Considerations

SECTION V Access Control and Inference for Social Networks

SECTION VI　Social Media Integration and Analytics Systems

SECTION VII   *Social Media Application Systems*

SECTION VIII   Secure Social Media Systems

SECTION IX   Secure Social Media Directions

Preface

BACKGROUND

Recent developments in information systems technologies have resulted in the computerization of many applications in various business areas. Data has become a critical resource in many organizations, and therefore, efficient access to data, sharing the data, extracting information from the data, and making use of the information has become an urgent need. As a result, there have been many efforts at not only integrating the various data sources scattered across several sites, but extracting information from these databases in the form of patterns and trends has also become important. These data sources may be databases managed by database management systems, or they could be data warehoused in a repository from multiple data sources.

The advent of the World Wide Web (WWW) in the mid-1990s has resulted in even greater demand for effective management of data, information, and knowledge. During this period, the consumer service provider concept has been digitized and enforced via the web. This way, we now have web-supported services where a consumer may request a service via the website of a service provider and the service provider provides the requested service. This service could be making an airline reservation or purchasing a book from the service provider. Such web-supported services have come to be known as web services. Note that services do not necessarily have to be provided through the web. A consumer could send an e-mail message to the service provider and request the service. Such services are computer-supported services. However, much of the work on computer-supported services has focused on web services.

The services paradigm has evolved into providing computing infrastructures, software, databases, and applications as services. For example, just as we obtain electricity as a service from the power company, we can obtain computing as a service from service providers. Such capabilities have resulted in the notion of cloud computing. The emergence of such powerful computing technologies has enabled humans to use the web not only to search and obtain data but also to communicate, collaborate, share, and carry out business. These applications have resulted in the design and development of social media systems, more popularly known as online social networks. During the past decade, developments in social media have exploded, and we now have several companies providing various types of social media services.

As the demand for data and information management increases, there is also a critical need for maintaining the security of databases, applications, and information systems. Data and information have to be protected from unauthorized access as well as from malicious corruption. With the advent of the cloud and social media, it is even more important to protect the data and information as the cloud is usually managed by third parties and social networks are used and shared by over a billion individuals. Therefore, we need effective mechanisms to secure the cloud and social networks.

This book will review the developments in social media and discuss concepts, issues, and challenges in analyzing and securing such systems. We also discuss the privacy violations that could occur when users share information. In addition to the concepts, we will discuss several experimental systems and infrastructures for analyzing and securing social media that we have developed at The University of Texas at Dallas.

We have written two series of books for CRC Press on data management, data mining and data security. The first series consists of 10 books. Book 1 (*Data Management Systems: Evolution and Interoperation*) focused on general aspects of data management and also addressed interoperability and migration. Book 2 (*Data Mining: Technologies, Techniques, Tools, and Trends*) discussed data mining. It essentially elaborated on Chapter 9 of Book 1. Book 3 (*Web Data Management and Electronic Commerce*) discussed web database technologies and discussed e-commerce as an application area. It essentially elaborated on Chapter 10 of Book 1. Book 4 (*Managing and Mining Multimedia Databases for the Electronic Enterprise*) addressed both multimedia database management and multimedia data mining. It elaborated on both Chapter 6 of Book 1 (for multimedia database management) and Chapter 11 of Book 2 (for multimedia data mining). Book 5 (*XML, Databases, and the Semantic Web*) described XML technologies related to data management. It elaborated on Chapter 11 of Book 3. Book 6 (*Web Data Mining and Applications in Business Intelligence and Counter-terrorism*) elaborated on Chapter 9 of Book 3.

Book 7 (*Database and Applications Security: Integrating Data Management and Information Security*) examines security for technologies discussed in each of our previous books. It focuses on the technological developments in database and applications security. It is essentially the integration of information security and database technologies. Book 8 (*Building Trustworthy Semantic Webs*) applies security to semantic web technologies and elaborates on Chapter 25 of Book 7. Book 9 (*Secure Semantic Service-Oriented Systems*) is an elaboration of Chapter 16 of Book 8. Book 10 (*Developing and Securing the Cloud*) is an elaboration of Chapters 5 and 25 of Book 9.

Our second series of books at present consists of four books. Book 1 is *Design and Implementation of Data Mining Tools*. Book 2 is *Data Mining Tools for Malware Detection*. Book 3 is *Secure Data Provenance and Inference Control with Semantic Web*. Book 4 (the current book) is *Analyzing and Securing Social Networks*. For this series, we are converting some of the practical aspects of our work with students into books. The relationships among our texts will be illustrated in the Appendix.

DATA, INFORMATION, AND KNOWLEDGE

In general, data management includes managing databases, interoperability, migration, warehousing, and mining. For example, the data on the web has to be managed and mined to extract information and patterns and trends. Data could be in files, relational databases, or other types of databases such as multimedia databases. Data may be structured or unstructured. We repeatedly use the terms *data*, *data management*, and *database systems* and *database management systems* in this book. We elaborate on these terms in the appendix. We define data management systems to be systems that manage the data, extract meaningful information from the data, and make use of the information extracted. Therefore, data management systems include database systems, data warehouses, and data mining systems. Data could be structured data such as those found in relational databases, or it could be unstructured such as text, voice, imagery, and video.

There have been numerous discussions in the past to distinguish between data, information, and knowledge. In some of our previous books on data management and mining, we did not attempt to clarify these terms. We simply stated that data could be just bits and bytes, or it could convey some meaningful information to the user. However, with the web and also with increasing interest in data, information and knowledge management as separate areas, in this book we take a different approach to data, information, and knowledge by differentiating between these terms as much as possible. For us, data is usually some value like numbers, integers, and strings. Information is obtained when some meaning or semantics is associated with the data, such as *John's salary is 20K*. Knowledge is something that you acquire through reading and learning, and as a result understand the data and information and take actions. That is, data and information can be transferred into knowledge when uncertainty about the data and information is removed from someone's mind. It should be noted that it is rather difficult to give strict definitions of data, information, and knowledge. Sometimes we will also use these terms interchangeably. Our framework for data management discussed in the appendix helps clarify some of the differences. To be consistent with the terminology in our previous books, we will also distinguish between database systems and database management systems. A database management system is that component which manages the database containing persistent data. A database system consists of both the database and the database management system.

FINAL THOUGHTS

The goal of this book is to explore security and privacy issues for social media systems as well as to analyze such systems. For much of the discussion in this book, we assume that social media data is represented using semantic web technologies. We also discuss the prototypes we have developed for social media systems whose data are represented using semantic web technologies. These experimental systems have been developed at The University of Texas at Dallas. We have used the material in this book together with the numerous references listed in each chapter for a graduate-level course at The University of Texas at Dallas on analyzing and securing social media. We have also provided several experimental systems developed by our graduate students.

It should be noted that the field is expanding very rapidly with billions of individuals that are now part of various social networks. Therefore, it is important for the reader to keep up with the developments of the prototypes, products, tools, and standards for secure social media. Security cannot be an afterthought. Therefore, while the technologies for social media are being developed, it is important to include security at the outset.

Acknowledgments

We thank the administration at the Erik Jonsson School of Engineering and Computer Science at The University of Texas at Dallas for giving us the opportunity to direct the Cyber Security Research and Education Center. We also thank Rhonda Walls, our project coordinator, for proofreading and editing the chapters. Without her hard work, this book would not have been possible. We thank many people who have supported our work or collaborated with us.

- The Air Force Office of Scientific Research for funding our research. Without this support, we would never have been able to gain the knowledge to write this book.
- Dr. Victor Piotrowski from the National Science Foundation for funding our capacity building work on assured cloud computing.
- Our colleagues Drs. Kevin Hamlen, Zhiqiang Lin, Kamil Sarac, and Alvaro Cardenas at The University of Texas at Dallas for discussions on secure cloud computing.
- Our collaborators at Kings College, University of London, the University of Insubria, Italy, and Purdue University for our work on cloud-based assured information sharing. In particular, we would like to thank Drs. Elena Ferrari and Barbara Carminati of the University of Insubria, Italy, Dr. Maribel Fernandez and the late Dr. Steve Barker of Kings College London, and Dr. Elisa Bertino from Purdue University for their collaboration.
- The following people for their technical contributions to various chapters in this book: Nathan McDaniel from The University of Texas at Dallas for his contributions to Chapter 2; Jack Lindamood from Facebook for his contributions to the chapters in Section IV; Dr. Elena Ferrari and Dr. Barbara Carminati from the University of Insubria, Italy, for their contributions to Chapters 19 and 20; Dr. Tyrone Cadenhead from Blue Cross Blue Shield for his contributions to Chapters 21, 22, and 25 (part of his PhD thesis); Dr. Neda Alipanah from the University of California, San Diego, for her contributions to Chapter 24 (part of her PhD thesis); Dr. Farhan Husain from Amazon for his contributions to Chapter 25 (part of his PhD thesis); Dr. Mehedy Masud from the University of the United Arab Emirates for his contributions to Chapters 26 and 27; Dr. Ryan Layfield from Amazon for his contributions to Chapter 29 (part of his PhD thesis); Gunasekar Rajasekar for his contributions to Chapter 30; Arindam Khaled from Mississippi State University for his contributions to Chapter 32; Drs. Tyrone Cadenhead, Jyothsna Rachapalli, and Kevin Hamlen for their contributions to Chapter 33; and Dr. Chris Yang from Drexel University for his contributions to Chapter 34 and to whom we owe much of the work in this chapter.

Permissions

CHAPTER 8: CONFIDENTIALITY, PRIVACY, AND TRUST FOR SOCIAL MEDIA DATA

From Thuraisingham, B., Tsybulnik, N., and Alam, A. Administering the semantic web: Confidentiality, privacy, and trust management. *International Journal of Information Security and Privacy* 1(1): 18–34, 2007. © 2007, IGI Global. Reprinted with permission of the publisher.

CHAPTER 10: TWEETHOOD: A SOCIAL MEDIA ANALYTICS TOOL

From Abrol, S. and Khan, L. TweetHood: Agglomerative clustering on fuzzy *k*-closest friends with variable depth for location mining. In: *IEEE Second International Conference on Social Computing (SocialCom)*, pp. 153–160, Minneapolis, 2010. © IEEE. Reprinted with permission of the publisher.

CHAPTER 11: TWEECALIZATION: LOCATION MINING USING SEMISUPERVISED LEARNING

From Abrol, S., Khan, L., and Thuraisingham, B. Tweecalization: Efficient and intelligent location mining in Twitter using semi-supervised learning. In: *8th IEEE International Conference on Collaborative Computing: Networking, Applications and Worksharing*. Pittsburgh, 2012. © ICST/EAI. Reprinted with permission of the publisher.

CHAPTER 12: TWEEQUE: IDENTIFYING SOCIAL CLIQUES FOR LOCATION MINING

From Abrol, S., Khan, L., and Thuraisingham, B. Tweeque: Spatio-temporal analysis of social networks for location mining using graph partitioning. In: *ASE International Conference on Social Informatics (Social Informatics 2012)*. Washington, DC, 2012. © IEEE. Reprinted with permission of the publisher.
From Abrol, S. and Khan, L. TweetHood: Agglomerative clustering on fuzzy *k*-closest friends with variable depth for location mining. In: *IEEE Second International Conference on Social Computing (SocialCom)*, pp. 153–160, Minneapolis, 2010. © IEEE. Reprinted with permission of the publisher.

CHAPTER 13: UNDERSTANDING NEWS QUERIES WITH GEO-CONTENT USING TWITTER

From Abrol, S. and Khan, L. TWinner: Understanding news queries with geo-content using Twitter. In: *6th ACM Workshop on Geographic Information Retrieval*, p. 10. Zurich, 2010. © 2010, Associaton for Computing Machinery, Inc. Reprinted with permission of the publisher.

CHAPTER 14: OUR APPROACH TO STUDYING PRIVACY IN SOCIAL NETWORKS

From Heatherly, R., Kantarcioglu, M., and Thuraisingham, B. Preventing private information inference attacks on social networks, *IEEE Transactions on Knowledge and Data Engineering* 25(8), 1849–1862, 2013. © 2013, IEEE. Reprinted with permission of the publisher.

CHAPTER 15: CLASSIFICATION OF SOCIAL NETWORKS INCORPORATING LINK TYPES

From Carminati, B., Ferrari, E., Heatherly, R., Kantarcioglu, M., and Thuraisingham, B.M. A semantic web based framework for social network access control. In: Carminati, B. and Joshi, J., editors, *SACMAT*, pp. 177–186. ACM, New York, 2009. © 2009, Association for Computing Machinery, Inc. Reprinted with permission of the publisher.

CHAPTER 23: SOCIAL GRAPH EXTRACTION, INTEGRATION, AND ANALYSIS

From Abrol, S., Khan, L., Khadilkar, V., Cadenhead, T. Design and implementation of SNODSOC: Novel class detection for social network analysis, *Proceedings of the 2012 International Conference on Intelligence and Security Informatics*, pp. 215–220, 2012. © IEEE. Reprinted with permission of the publisher.

CHAPTER 24: SEMANTIC WEB-BASED SOCIAL NETWORK INTEGRATION

From Khadilkar, V., Kantarcioglu, M., and Thuraisingham, B.M. StormRider: Harnessing "Storm" for social networks. In: *Proceedings of World Wide Web (WWW) Conference (Companion Volume)*, Lyon, France, pp. 543–544, 2012. Reprinted with permission of the authors.

From Khadilkar, V., Kantarcioglu, M., Thuraisingham, B.M., and Castagna, P. Jena–HBase: A distributed, scalable and efficient RDF triple store. In: *Proceedings of International Semantic Web Conference (Posters & Demos)*, Boston, 2012. Reprinted with permission of the authors.

From Alipanah, N., Parveen, P., Khan, and Thuraisingham, B.M. Ontology-driven query expansion using map/reduce framework to facilitate federated queries. In: *Proceedings of International Conference on Web Services (ICWS)*, Washington, DC, pp. 712–713, 2011. Reprinted with permission of the authors.

CHAPTER 25: EXPERIMENTAL CLOUD QUERY PROCESSING SYSTEM FOR SOCIAL NETWORKS

From Husain, M.F., McGlothlin, J.P., Masud, M.M., Khan, L.R., and Thuraisingham, B.M. Heuristics-based query processing for large RDF graphs using cloud computing. *IEEE Transactions on Knowledge and Data Engineering* 23(9): 1312–1327, 2011. Reprinted with permission of the authors.

CHAPTER 26: SOCIAL NETWORKING IN THE CLOUD

From Abrol, S., Khan, L., Khadilkar, V., Cadenhead, T. Design and implementation of SNODSOC: Novel class detection for social network analysis, *Proceedings of the 2012 International Conference on Intelligence and Security Informatics*, pp. 215–220, 2012. © 2012 IEEE. Reprinted with permission from the publisher.

From Khadilkar, V., Kantarcioglu, M., and Thuraisingham, B.M. StormRider: Harnessing "Storm" for social networks. In: *Proceedings of World Wide Web (WWW) Conference (Companion Volume)*, Lyon, France, pp. 543–544, 2012. Reprinted with permission of the authors.

From Khadilkar, V., Kantarcioglu, M., Thuraisingham, B.M., and Castagna, P. Jena–HBase: A distributed, scalable and efficient RDF triple store. In: *Proceedings of International Semantic Web Conference (Posters & Demos)*, Boston, 2012. Reprinted with permission of the authors.

From Alipanah, N., Parveen, P., Khan, and Thuraisingham, B.M. Ontology-driven query expansion using map/reduce framework to facilitate federated queries. In: *Proceedings of International*

Conference on Web Services (ICWS), Washington, DC, pp. 712–713, 2011. Reprinted with permission of the authors.

CHAPTER 28: TEMPORAL GEOSOCIAL MOBILE SEMANTIC WEB

From Thuraisingham, B., Khan, L., Kantarcioglu, M., Khadilkar, V. Design of a temporal geosocial semantic web for military stabilization and reconstruction operations. In: *Proceedings of the ACM SIGKDD Workshop on CyberSecurity and Intelligence Informatics*, pp. 63–74, 2009. © 2009 Association for Computing Machinery, Inc. Reprinted with permission of the publisher.

CHAPTER 29: SOCIAL MEDIA AND BIOTERRORISM

From Layfield, R., Kantarcioglu, M., and Thuraisingham, B. Simulating bioterrorism through epidemiology approximation. In: *IEEE International Conference on Intelligence and Security Informatics, 2008 (ISI 2008)*, June 17–20, pp. 82–87, 2008. © 2008 IEEE. Reprinted with permission of the publisher.

CHAPTER 30: STREAM DATA ANALYTICS FOR MULTIPURPOSE SOCIAL MEDIA APPLICATIONS

From Abrol, S., Rajasekar, G., Khan, L.; Khadilkar, V., Nagarajan, S., McDaniel, N., and Ganesh, G. Real-time stream data analytics for multi-purpose social media applications. In: *Information 2015, IEEE International Conference on Reuse and Integration (IRI)*, 1315 Aug. 2015, pp. 25–30. © 2015 IEEE. Reprinted with permission of the publisher.

CHAPTER 31: SECURE CLOUD QUERY PROCESSING WITH RELATIONAL DATA FOR SOCIAL MEDIA

Figure 1 and Tables 1, 2 from Thuraisingham, B.M., Khadilkar, V., Gupta, A., Kantarcioglu, M., and Khan, L. Secure data storage and retrieval in the cloud. *Proceedings of CollaborateCom*, pp. 1–8, 2010. Reprinted with permission of the author.

CHAPTER 32: SECURE CLOUD QUERY PROCESSING FOR SEMANTIC WEB-BASED SOCIAL MEDIA

Figures 1–4, Tables 1, 2 from Khaled, A., Husain, M.F., Khan, L., Hamlen, K.W., and Thuraisingham, B.M. A token-based access control system for RDF data in the clouds. In: *Proceedings of the 2010 IEEE Second International Conference on Cloud Computing Technology and Science (CloudCom)*, Indianapolis, IN, pp. 104–111, December 2010. © 2010 IEEE. Reprinted with permission of the publisher.

CHAPTER 33: CLOUD-CENTRIC ASSURED INFORMATION SHARING FOR SOCIAL NETWORKS

Figures 1–14, Tables 1–3, and text from Thuraisingham, B.M., Khadilkar, V., Rachapalli, J., Cadenhead, T., Kantarcioglu, M., Hamlen, K.W., Khan, L., and Husain, M.F. Cloud-centric assured information sharing. In: *Proceedings of the Pacific Asia Workshop on Intelligence and Security Informatics (PAISI)*, Kuala Lumpur, Malaysia, May 29, 2012, pp. 1–26, Lecture Notes in Computer Science 7299, 2012. © Springer-Verlag Berlin Heidelberg 2012. Reprinted with permission of Springer Science+Business Media.

CHAPTER 34: SOCIAL NETWORK INTEGRATION AND ANALYSIS WITH PRIVACY PRESERVATION

Figures 1–4, Tables 1–3, and text from Yang, C. and Thuraisingham, B. A generalized approach for social network integration and analysis with privacy preservation. In: *Data Mining and Knowledge Discovery for Big Data: Methodologies, Challenge and Opportunities,* Volume 1 (ed., Wesley Chu), Springer-Verlag, Berlin, 2014, 259–280. © Springer-Verlag Berlin Heidelberg 2014. Reprinted with permission of Springer Science+Business Media.

1 Introduction

1.1 OVERVIEW

While social networks have been around since at least the 1930s, the advent of the World Wide Web (WWW) resulted in the development of online social networks (OSNs). OSNs are online applications that allow their users to connect by means of various link types. Since its inception in the mid-1990s, social networks have provided a way for users to interact, reflecting the social networks or social relations among people, for example, those who share interests and/or activities. Initially, critics regarded social media as a fad, a temporary fashion. But today, social media has demonstrated exponential growth, making it the most popular activity platform on the WWW.

The number of individuals who use social media such as Twitter and Facebook has increased exponentially. For example, it is stated in Internetlivestats.com that the number of tweets a day has risen from around 100 million in early 2011 to more than 500 million in early 2015. The number of Facebook users is now more than a billion. Additional prominent social networks such as LinkedIn and Google+ have also emerged. As the increase in popularity of social networking is on a constant rise, new uses for the technology are constantly being observed. Two major technologies that have been developed for OSNs are (i) data mining technologies for analyzing these networks and extracting useful information such as location, demographics, and sentiments of the network participants, and (ii) security and privacy technologies that ensure the privacy of the participants of the network as well as provide controlled access to the information posted and exchanged by the participants. Our book will discuss both aspects of OSNs.

The organization of this chapter is as follows. Aspects of analyzing social networks will be discussed in Section 1.2. Aspects of securing social networks, including privacy issues, will be discussed in Section 1.3. The organization of this book is provided in Section 1.4. Next steps are discussed in Section 1.5. Figure 1.1 illustrates the contents of this chapter.

It should be noted that we have used the terms *social media* and *social networks* interchangeably throughout this book. Social media is the more generic term that we use to refer to social networks. That is, while social networks are networks that are used for users to collaborate and share information, social media includes the shared information represented in the form of text, images, audio, video, and animation, among others. We also refer to social media systems and applications as just social media. In addition, we use the terms *data analytics* and *data mining* interchangeably.

1.2 ANALYZING SOCIAL NETWORKS

Social networks have been analyzed since their inception in at least the 1930s. The analysis at that time was carried out manually using statistical techniques. The development of OSNs in the mid-1990s and early 2000s, as well as the development of data mining and analytics techniques over the past two decades, has resulted in numerous analytics tools for OSNs. These include determining the friends of individuals, as well as leaders of groups, and analyzing the sentiments of the OSN members and extracting their information. Figure 1.2 illustrates various types of social media analytics approaches.

With respect to analyzing OSNs, our work has focused on mining and extracting demographics information of the members. While our techniques can be applied to any type of demographics information (e.g., age, gender, and location), we have focused in particular on mining for location and related attributes of individuals. At the forefront of emerging trends in social networking sites is the concept of *real time* and *location based*. So what makes location-based social media services

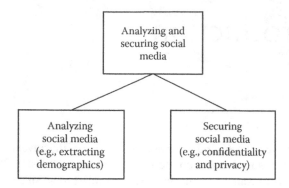

FIGURE 1.1   Analyzing and securing social media.

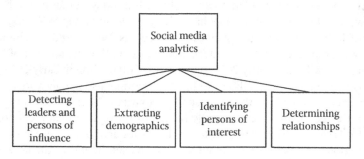

FIGURE 1.2   Social media analytics.

so important? We briefly describe three situations where knowing the location of a user has a direct impact on that user.

Privacy and Safety. Gowalla is a location-based social networking website that allows users to *check-in* at places in their local vicinity, either through a dedicated mobile application or through the mobile website. As a reward, users will sometimes receive items from check-ins. This is achieved through the use of dedicated applications available on smartphones or by logging on to Gowalla's mobile website. Posting such an update publishes your current location to the user and can prove to be an invitation to get your house robbed. In addition to this, knowing the location of the user makes it easier for spammers to attack the user in a more personalized manner.

Trustworthiness. Social media may be a source but is it a reliable one? Time, in partnership with CNN, discussed the impact of Twitter on the coverage of developments after the Iran elections in 2009. On June 12, Iran held its presidential elections between incumbent Ahmadinejad and rival Mousavi. The result, a landslide victory for Ahmadinejad led to violent riots across Iran, charges of voting fraud, and protests worldwide. Even as the government of that country was evidently restricting access to opposition websites and text messaging, on Twitter a separate uprising took place, as tweets marked with the hashtag #cnnfail began tearing into the cable news network for devoting too few resources to the controversy in Iran. US State Department officials reached out to Twitter and asked them to delay a network upgrade that was scheduled for the night of June 15. This was done to protect the interests of Iranians and assess the sentiment of the public about the Iran elections. In such cases, it was important for the US State Department to be able to trust the location of the user. Another major area where trustworthiness of the user's location is important is when companies use social media to obtain location-based opinion of products. Companies worldwide, from Burger King to Ford, are using social media to target customers.

Advertising and Marketing. Here, we talk about two broad aspects on how location-based social media can affect companies in doing business in a better manner. OSNs connect people at low cost; this can be beneficial for entrepreneurs and small businesses looking to expand their contact bases. These networks often act as a customer relationship management tool for companies selling products and services. Companies can also use OSNs for advertising in the form of banners and text ads. Since businesses operate globally, OSNs can make it easier to keep in touch with contacts around the world. Having highlighted the importance of the location of the user in social media, it is important to understand that it is not provided explicitly by users for a number of reasons. Some users are concerned about their privacy and security; others do not find any incentive in sharing their location. The end result is the impeded growth of location-based services in the present world scenario. Social networking companies have shifted their focus from building relationships to identifying temporal and spatial patterns in messages. Twitter has introduced a feature whereby users can find location-based trending topics. But this is still not sufficient as, first, it only covers users who mention their locations explicitly and, secondly, the topic of search is limited to the trending topics.

But to mine the location of the user is not an easy task in itself. In our work, we have shown that traditional text-based location extraction techniques do not perform well in the domain of OSNs. The presence of multiple locations mentioned in the text makes it difficult to identify a single location that serves the purpose of the page focus for the messages. Additionally, we observe a lack of relationship between the location of the user and the location mentioned in the text. Secondly, the high running time associated with such mining techniques makes them unusable in practical scenarios. In the first part of the book, we address the identification of the location of the user on social networking sites based on the location of that user's closest friends. We discuss the system we have developed called TweetHood, which outperforms the typical gazetteer-based approach in both accuracy and running time. Specifically, our book will discuss the challenges faced in identifying the location of the user and describes the various algorithms that we have developed in tackling the problem.

1.3   SECURING SOCIAL NETWORKS

Security and privacy are emerging as critical for the utility of OSNs. For example, members of social networks may want to give access to their personal data only to certain friends, while others may have access to their nonpersonal data such as analysis of sports games or movies. Therefore, one needs flexible access control models for OSNs. In addition, it may be possible to infer unauthorized information from the legitimate responses received to queries posed to OSNs. Therefore, one needs to develop techniques to handle such security violations that come to be known as the inference problem. Another major concern with social media mining and analytics is that private information about individuals can be extracted from the public information they post. As a result, privacy violations may occur due to data analytics in OSNs. Finally, various members of OSNs place different trust values on their online friends. Therefore, trust management is also an important aspect of OSNs. Figure 1.3 illustrates the various security, privacy, and trust aspects of OSNs. We have conducted considerable research on security and privacy for OSNs. Below we provide a general discussion and an overview of our work in this area.

As part of their offerings, many OSNs, such as Facebook, allow people to list details about themselves that are relevant to the nature of the network. For instance, Facebook is a general-use social network; thus, individual users list their favorite activities, books, and movies. Conversely, LinkedIn is a professional network; because of this, users specify details that are related to their professional life (i.e., reference letters, previous employment, etc.). This personal information allows social network application providers a unique opportunity. Direct use of this information could be

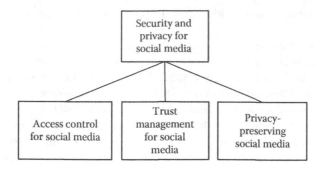

FIGURE 1.3 Security and privacy for OSNs.

useful to advertisers for direct marketing. However, in practice, privacy concerns can prevent these efforts. This conflict between desired use of data and individual privacy presents an opportunity for social network data mining—that is, the discovery of information and relationships from social network data. The privacy concerns of individuals in a social network can be classified into one of two categories: privacy after data release and private information leakage. Privacy after data release has to do with the identification of specific individuals in a data set subsequent to its release to the general public or to paying customers for specific usage. Perhaps the most illustrative example of this type of privacy breach (and the repercussions thereof) is the AOL search data scandal. In 2006, AOL released the search results from 650,000 users for research purposes. However, these results had a significant number of *vanity* searches—searches on an individual's name, social security number, or address—that could then be tied back to a specific individual.

Private information leakage, conversely, is related to details about an individual that are not explicitly stated, but, rather, are inferred through other details released or related to individuals who may express that trait. A trivial example of this type of information leakage is a scenario where a user, say John, does not enter his political affiliation because of privacy concerns. However, it is publicly available that he is a member of the College Democrats. Using this publicly available information regarding a general group membership, it is easily guessable what John's political affiliation is. We note that this is an issue both in live data (i.e., currently on the server) and in any released data. This book focuses on the problem of private information leakage for individuals as a direct result of their actions as being part of an online social network. We model an attack scenario as follows: Suppose Facebook wishes to release data to Electronic Arts for their use in advertising games to interested people. However, once Electronic Arts has this data, they want to identify the political affiliation of users in their data for lobbying efforts. This would obviously be a privacy violation of hidden details. We explore how the online social network data could be used to predict some individual private trait that a user is not willing to disclose (e.g., political or religious affiliation) and explore the effect of possible data sanitization approaches on preventing such private information leakage, while allowing the recipient of the sanitized data to do inference on nonprivate traits. To protect privacy, we sanitize both details and link details, that is, delete some information from a user's profile and remove links between friends. We then study the effect this has on combating possible inference attacks. Additionally, we present a modification of the naïve Bayes classification algorithm that will use details about a node, as well as the node's link structure, to predict private details. We then compare the accuracy of this new learning method against the accuracy of the traditional naïve Bayes classifier.

While mining OSNs and at the same time protecting the privacy of individual is becoming critical for developing useful OSNs, controlling access to OSNs is also becoming a major concern. However, most current OSNs implement very basic access control systems by simply making a user decide which personal information is accessible by other members by marking a given item as public, private, or accessible by their direct contacts. To give more flexibility, some OSNs enforce variants of these settings, but the principle is the same. For instance, besides the basic settings, social media such as Bebo and Facebook support the option *selected friends*; Last.fm, the option *neighbors* (i.e., the set of users having musical preferences and tastes similar to mine); Facebook, Friendster, and Orkut, the option *friends of friends*; and Xing, the options *contacts of my contacts* (second-degree contacts), as well as *third-degree contacts* and *fourth-degree contacts*. It is important to note that all these approaches have the advantage of being easily implemented; however, they lack flexibility. In fact, the available protection settings do not allow users to easily specify their access control requirements in that they are either too restrictive or too loose. Furthermore, existing solutions are platform specific and they are difficult to implement for various different OSNs. To address some of these limitations, we have designed and developed an extensible, fine-grained OSN access control model based on semantic web technologies.

Our main idea is to encode social network-related information by means of an ontology. In particular, we suggest to model the following five important aspects of OSNs using semantic web ontologies: (i) user's profiles, (ii) relationships among users (e.g., Bob is Alice's close friend), (iii) resources (e.g., online photo albums), (iv) relationships between users and resources (e.g., Bob is the owner of the photo album), and (v) actions (e.g., post a message on someone's wall). By constructing such an ontology, we model the Social Network Knowledge Base (SNKB). The main advantage in using an ontology for modeling OSN data is that relationships among many different social network concepts can be naturally represented using OWL (Web Ontology Language). Furthermore, by using reasoning, many inferences about such relationships could be done automatically. Our access control enforcement mechanism is then implemented by exploiting this knowledge. In particular, the idea is to define security policies as rules, whose antecedents state conditions on SNKB and consequents specify the authorized actions. In particular, we propose to encode the authorizations implied by security policies by means of an ontology, obtaining the Security Authorization Knowledge Base (SAKB). Thus, security policies have to be translated as rules whose antecedents and consequents are expressed on the ontology. To achieve this goal, we use the Semantic Web Rule Language (SWRL). As consequents, the access control policies can be enforced by simply querying the authorizations, that is, the SAKB. The query can be easily directly implemented by the ontology reasoner by means of instance-checking operations, or can be performed by a SPARQL query, if the ontology is serialized in the Resource Description Framework. In this book, we focus on how to model such a fine-grained social network access control system using semantic web technologies. We also assume that a centralized reference monitor hosted by the social network manager will enforce the required policies. Since our approach depends on extensible ontologies, it could be easily adapted to various OSNs by modifying the ontologies in our SNKB. Furthermore, as we discuss in details later in the book, semantic web tools allow us to define more fine-grained access control policies than the ones provided by current OSNs. Therefore, in our book of security and privacy of OSNs, we will also discuss the design and implementation of an access control model for a semantic web-based social network system.

1.4   OUTLINE OF THE BOOK

This book is divided into nine sections as illustrated in Figure 1.4. Section I describes supporting technologies and consists of four chapters. Chapter 2 provides an overview of social networks, while concepts in data security and privacy are discussed in Chapter 3. Chapter 4 describes data mining techniques. These three chapters form the core supporting technologies for the work discussed in this book. Chapter 5 describes some technologies such as cloud computing and semantic web that are needed for several chapters in this book.

Section II consists of three chapters that describe some basics of analyzing and securing social networks. Chapter 6 describes aspect of analyzing and securing social networks. Chapter 7 describes the representation of social networks using semantic web technologies. Chapter 8 describes confidentiality, security, and privacy aspects of social networks.

Section III consists of five chapters that describe our design and implementation of various social network analytics tools. In particular, we have focused on location mining for social networks. Our

Developing an Educational Infrastructure for Analyzing and Securing Social Media	Layer 9
Multilevel Secure Online Social Networks	Secure Social
Integrity Management and Data Provenance for Social Media	Media Directions
Unified Framework for Analyzing and Securing Social Media	

Attacks on Social Media and Data Analytics Solutions	Layer 8
Social Network Integration and Analysis with Privacy Preservation	Secure Social
Cloud-Centric Assured Information Sharing for Social Networks	Media Systems
Secure Cloud Query Processing for Semantic Web-Based Social Media	
Secure Cloud Query Processing with Relational Data for Social Media	

Stream Data Analytics for Multipurpose Social Media Applications	Layer 7
Social Media and Bioterrorism	Social Media
Temporal Geosocial Mobile Semantic Web	Application
Graph Mining for Insider Threat Detection	Systems

Social Networking in the Cloud	Layer 6
Experimental Cloud Query Processing System for Social Networks	Social Media
Semantic Web-Based Social Network Integration	Integration and
Social Graph Extraction, Integration, and Analysis	Analytics Systems

Implementing an Inference Controller for Social Media Data	Layer 5
Inference Control for Social Media	Access Control
Implementation of an Access Control System for Social Networks	and Inference for
Access Control for Social Networks	Social Networks

Sanitization of Social Network Data for Release to Semitrusted Third Parties	Layer 4
Social Network Classification through Data Partitioning	Social Network
Extending Classification of Social Networks through Indirect Friendships	Analytics and
Classification of Social Networks Incorporating Link Types	Privacy
Our Approach to Studying Privacy in Social Networks	Considerations

Understanding News Queries with Geo-Content Using Twitter	Layer 3
Tweeque: Identifying Social Cliques for Location Mining	Techniques
Tweecalization: Location Mining Using Semisupervised Learning	and Tools for
TweetHood: A Social Media Analytics Tools	Social Network
Developments and Challenges in Location Mining	Analytics

Confidentiality, Privacy, and Trust for Social Media Data	Layer 2
Semantic Web-Based Social Network Representation and Analysis	Aspects of Analyzing and
Analyzing and Securing Social Networks	Securing Social Networks

Cloud Computing and Semantic Web Technologies	Layer 1
Data Mining Techniques	Supporting
Data Security and Privacy	Technologies
Social Networks: A Survey	

FIGURE 1.4 Framework for the book.

techniques are generic enough to be applicable to extracting various demographics data in addition to location of the social network users. Chapter 9 discusses the challenges in location mining for OSNs. Chapter 10 describes our patented technology called TweetHood that is a location mining tool. TweetHood is at the heart of our OSN analytics research. While TweetHood has been implemented for Twitter, it can extract information and identify demographics data such as location for any social network or database. Chapter 11 describes a tool called Tweecalization, which extends TweetHood. Tweecalization is a location mining system that uses semisupervised learning. Chapter 12 describes our tool called Tweeque, which identifies social cliques for location mining. Chapter 13 describes aspects of understanding news queries with geo-content using Twitter.

Section IV consists of five chapters that describe privacy aspects of social networks. In particular, we describe our research on applying various data analytics techniques to extract sensitive attributes of users. Chapter 14 describes our approach to studying privacy in social networks. Chapter 15 describes classification of OSNs by incorporating link types. Chapter 16 describes extending classification of social networks through indirect friendships. Chapter 17 describes social network classification through data partitioning. Chapter 18 describes the sanitization of social network data for release to semitrusted third parties.

Section V consists of four chapters that describe access control and inference control for social networks. Chapter 19 describes the design of our access control techniques applied to social networks represented using semantic web technologies. Implementation of our system is discussed in Chapter 20. Chapter 21 describes inference control for social networks, while Chapter 22 describes the adaptation of our inference controller developed for provenance data represented as graphs to social media data also represented as graphs.

Section VI consists of four chapters that describe the experimental systems we have designed or developed on analyzing and securing social networks. Chapter 23 describes aspects of social graph extraction, integration, and analysis. Chapter 24 describes a cloud-based semantic web query-processing system for social media data. Chapter 25 describes various experimental cloud-based semantic web technologies that can be applied to social networks. Chapter 26 describes a social network system operating in the cloud.

Section VII consists of four chapters and describes the social media application systems we have developed. Chapter 27 describes graph mining for insider threat detection in social media. Chapter 28 describes a temporal geosocial mobile semantic web for military stabilization and reconstruction. Aspects of social media for bioterrorism applications are discussed in Chapter 29. A real-time stream analytics system for multipurpose social media applications is discussed in Chapter 30.

Section VIII consists of five chapters and describes the secure social media systems we have developed. Chapter 31 describes secure cloud query processing for social media data presented as relational data, while Chapter 32 describes secure cloud query processing for social media data represented as semantic web graphs. Cloud-centric assured information sharing for social media applications is discussed in Chapter 33. Privacy-preserving social network integration and analysis is discussed in Chapter 34. Finally, we address one of the most important topics in social media research—attacks on social media systems. We are hearing about an increasing number of malicious attacks on social media systems. Furthermore, such systems are being exploited to steal information from computers and networks. We discuss both aspects in Chapter 35 and also discuss solutions using data analytics techniques.

Section IX consists of four chapters and describes some of our exploratory work as well as provides directions. Chapter 36 provides a unified framework for social media analytics, security, and privacy. We discuss integrity and data provenance aspects for social networks in Chapter 37. Chapter 38 provides some directions toward developing a multilevel secure social media system. Chapter 39 describes an education program and infrastructure for secure social media that we are developing.

The book is concluded in Chapter 40. Each part begins with an introduction and ends with a conclusion. The book is also augmented with an Appendix that describes data management and the relationship among our texts. We have included this Appendix in all of our books to provide the context. Mapping of the chapters to the framework is illustrated in Figure 1.5.

Developing an Educational Infrastructure for Analyzing and Securing Social Media Chapter 39	*Layer 9* *Secure Social* *Media Directions*
Multilevel Secure Online Social Networks Chapter 38	
Integrity Management and Data Provenance for Social Media Chapter 37	
Unified Framework for Analyzing and Securing Social Media Chapter 36	
Attacks on Social Media and Data Analytics Solutions Chapter 35	*Layer 8* *Secure Social* *Media Systems*
Social Network Integration and Analysis with Privacy Preservation Chapter 34	
Cloud-Centric Assured Information Sharing for Social Networks Chapter 33	
Secure Cloud Query Processing for Semantic Web-Based Social Media Chapter 32	
Secure Cloud Query Processing with Relational Data for Social Media Chapter 31	
Stream Data Analytics for Multipurpose Social Media Applications Chapter 30	*Layer 7* *Social Media* *Application* *Systems*
Social Media and Bioterrorism Chapter 29	
Temporal Geosocial Mobile Semantic Web Chapter 28	
Graph Mining for Insider Threat Detection Chapter 27	
Social Networking in the Cloud Chapter 26	*Layer 6* *Social Media* *Integration and* *Analytics* *Systems*
Experimental Cloud Query Processing System for Social Networks Chapter 25	
Semantic Web-Based Social Network Integration Chapter 24	
Social Graph Extraction, Integration, and Analysis Chapter 23	
Implementing an Inference Controller for Social Media Data Chapter 22	*Layer 5* *Access Control* *and Inference for* *Social Networks*
Inference Control for Social Media Chapter 21	
Implementation of an Access Control System for Social Networks Chapter 20	
Access Control for Social Networks Chapter 19	
Sanitization of Social Network Data for Release to Semitrusted Third Parties Chapter 18	*Layer 4* *Social Network* *Analytics and* *Privacy* *Considerations*
Social Network Classification through Data Partitioning Chapter 17	
Extending Classification of Social Networks through Indirect Friendships Chapter 16	
Classification of Social Networks Incorporating Link Types Chapter 15	
Our Approach to Studying Privacy in Social Networks Chapter 14	
Understanding News Queries with Geo-Content Using Twitter Chapter 13	*Layer 3* *Techniques* *and Tools* *for* *Social Network* *Analytics*
Tweeque: Identifying Social Cliques for Location Mining Chapter 12	
Tweecalization: Location Mining Using Semisupervised Learning Chapter 11	
TweetHood: A Social Media Analytics Tools Chapter 10	
Developments and Challenges in Location Mining Chapter 9	
Confidentiality, Privacy, and Trust for Social Media Data Chapter 8	*Layer 2* *Aspects of* *Analyzing and* *Securing* *Social Networks*
Semantic Web-Based Social Network Representation and Analysis Chapter 7	
Analyzing and Securing Social Networks Chapter 6	
Cloud Computing and Semantic Web Technologies Chapter 5	*Layer 1* *Supporting* *Technologies*
Data Mining Techniques Chapter 4	
Data Security and Privacy Chapter 3	
Social Networks: A Survey Chapter 2	

FIGURE 1.5   Chapters mapped to the framework.

1.5   NEXT STEPS

This chapter has provided an introduction to the book, which is on analyzing and securing social networks. We first provided an overview of social network analysis and then described aspects of social media analytics, security, and privacy. This is essentially a discussion of the contents of this book. It should be noted that while social networks have been studied for many decades, OSNs have proliferated since the advent of the WWW. Various data analytics tools are being developed for analyzing such networks. Furthermore, more recently, privacy violations that could occur due to the analysis of the social networks, as well as approaches to securing social networks, have been investigated. This book describes both analysis of as well as security and privacy for social networks.

Because massive amounts of data have to be managed and analyzed in social networks, there is also an opportunity to make various inferences, such as sentiment analysis and influence detection. There are numerous data analytics tools that are emerging that can make associations between different individuals in social networks as well as study their behavior and motives. Such associations could be highly sensitive but extremely lucrative to businesses. Therefore, one has to balance the trade-offs between utility and privacy. Furthermore, due to the massive quantities of dynamic data present in social media that are often heterogeneous in nature (e.g., video or images), social media data is also often considered to be big data. Therefore, big data management and analytics techniques are being applied to social media data. As progress is made on big data analytics, we also need to be aware of the potential problems that can occur due to violations of privacy. Furthermore, it is important to provide access to the social networks only to authorized individuals. We believe that the results presented in this book provide insights toward analyzing and securing social networks so that the readers are armed with the necessary background knowledge to design and develop analytics and security tools that will be critical for the utility of OSNs.

The best way to understand social networks is to use them. Therefore, we would encourage the readers to join social networks, and post messages and share information in a responsible manner. Furthermore, it would be useful to experiment with the various social networks by carrying out analytics and developing access control techniques. There are also excellent conferences that are emerging that are devoted entirely to social networks. These include the Institute of Electrical and Electronics Engineers/Association for Computing Machinery (ACM) International Conference on Advances in Social Network Analysis and Mining (ASONAM). Furthermore, several conferences in data security and data mining also have special sessions and tracks in social networks. These include the IEEE Conference on Data Mining (ICDM) and the ACM Conference on Data and Applications Security and Privacy (CODASPY). Attending these conferences, reading the proceedings, and interacting and collaborating with the expert researchers, practitioners, and users of social media systems are an excellent way to learn about this very important field.

As stated earlier, it should be noted that this book has focused mainly on topics such as analyzing social media, the privacy implications of social media analytics, and securing social media. There are many other topics in social media that we have not discussed in this book. These include the usage of social media, related ethics issues, and also using social media to promote oneself or a product. There are a few books that have been written on these topics, and our goal is to focus on topics within our expertise and experience.

It should also be noted that we have used the terms *social media* and *social network* interchangeably throughout this book. Social media is the more generic term that we use to refer to social networks. That is, while social networks are networks that are used for users to collaborate and share information, social media includes the shared information represented in the form of text, images, audio, video, and animation, among others. We also refer to social media systems and applications as just social media. In addition, we use the terms *data analytics* and *data mining* interchangeably.

Section I

Supporting Technologies

INTRODUCTION TO SECTION I

To analyze social media systems and to secure them, we need to ensure that several supporting technologies have to work together. These include social media technologies, data analytics technologies, data security technologies, and cloud computing and semantic web technologies. We will discuss these supporting technologies in Section I.

Section I consists of four chapters: Chapters 2 through 5. Chapter 2 will provide an overview of the various social networks that have emerged during the past decades. We then select a few networks (e.g., Facebook. LinkedIn, Google+, and Twitter) and discuss some of their essential features. In Chapter 3, we will provide an overview of discretionary security policies in database systems. We will start with a discussion of access control policies, including authorization policies and role-based access control. Then, we will discuss administration policies. We will briefly discuss identification and authentication. We will also discuss auditing issues and views for security. In Chapter 4, we will first provide an overview of the various data mining tasks and techniques, and then discuss some of the popular techniques such as support vector machines and association rule mining. Chapter 5 will introduce the notion of the cloud and semantic web technologies. We will first discuss concepts in cloud computing, including aspects of virtualization. Next, we will discuss technologies for the semantic web, including eXtensible Markup Language (XML), Resource Description Framework (RDF), ontologies, and Web Ontology Language (OWL). This will be followed by a discussion of security issues for the semantic web. Finally, we will discuss cloud computing frameworks based on semantic web technologies.

2 Social Networks
A Survey

2.1 INTRODUCTION

While the concept of social networks has existed for several decades, it is only during the past decade with the advent of the World Wide Web that the concept of electronic social networks has emerged. Today, such electronic social networks are commonly used between several hundred millions of individuals on a daily basis. These social networks connect numerous communities so that they can communicate and share various personal and business-related information. We are conducting extensive research on analyzing and securing such social networks. This chapter provides a survey of social networks and then discusses a selection of social networks that we are using to conduct our experiments.

Almost a fourth of the world has a registered Facebook account. Although Facebook is currently the largest social network, it does not come anywhere near to dominating the market. There are more than 200 popular social networks. Half of those have more than a million active users, and at least 20 of them have more than 100 million active users. Facebook and Google+ are thus far the only social networks to surpass 1 billion users with Tencent QQ, a primarily Chinese social network, coming close. Evolving from bulletin board systems and chat rooms, social networks vary as much in function as genre or topic.

Where there once was an online forum for every niche subject, there is now a growing social network to replace it. Since 1999, an average of more than five new social network sites have been established every year. Most sites have an age limit, but are open to the general public. There are a few exceptions that claim themselves elite and are based on *invitation only* policies. Social networks represent communities focused on specific languages, learning, images, music, video, business and professional interaction, the elite, and any other collaboration dreamt by humans.

This chapter provides a survey of the various social networks and the capabilities of some of the major social networks. Our survey is described in Section 2.2. Selected social networks are discussed in Section 2.3. The chapter is summarized in Section 2.4. Figure 2.1 illustrates the social networks we have discussed in this chapter.

2.2 SURVEY OF SOCIAL NETWORKS

This section provides an overview of a sample of the various social media sites that have been developed to date. It should be noted that since some of the social networks we have referenced are not operational today, we have cited references from Wikipedia. Such Wikipedia references have been provided in this book only if we are unable to find other suitable references.

Classmates (http://www.classmates.com/) was established in 1995 by Randy Conrads as a means to reunite classmates, and has more than 50 million registered users. By linking together people from the same school and class year, Classmates.com profits from providing individuals with a chance to "walk down memory lane" and get reacquainted with old classmates that have also registered with the site. With a minimum age limit of 18 years, registration is free and anyone may search the site for classmates that they may know. Purchasing a gold membership is required to communicate with other members through the site's e-mail system. User e-mail addresses are private, and communication for paying

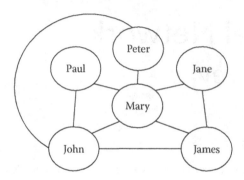

FIGURE 2.1   Social networks.

members is handled through a double-blind e-mail system. This ensures that only paying members can make full use of the site, allowing unlimited communication and orchestration of events like reunions.

Bolt (http://bolt3.com/bolt-social-network/) has operated since 1996 under three separate ownerships. Battling bankruptcy and copyright infringement, Bolt has been revamped twice after being shut down with little notice. Although controversial during its earlier years, Bolt pioneered many things as a community, such as e-cards, music sharing, and Internet radio. Bolt gained much of its success and popularity in 2003 from *American Idol*'s second season, promoting them as their official site for organizing quizzes, voting, and regular blog activity. Though *American Idol* dropped its sponsorship of Bolt after 1 year, they have proven to raise enough interest to stay around for almost 20 years. Their first shutdown was in 2006 after one decade of dedicated user service. They shut down again in 2008; however, after rebranding twice, Bolt is still around.

AsianAvenue (http://www.asianave.com/) was established in 1997 in New York, as a social network for those of Asian or partly Asian descent. It is part of the ethnic trifecta along with BlackPlanet and MiGente. The AsianAvenue community played a large role in identifying and fighting ads during the 1998 Olympics that "promoted racial stereotypes." In the past, AsianAvenue has promoted famous Chinese athletes and partnered with Monster.com. They have grown to more than 1.5 million users, and would probably have more if they had not charged members for previously free features for more than a year. AsianAvenue was also one of the first social networking sites to provide a feature allowing members to view their page's history. This is to say that a member could see who has viewed their site, making a user's browsing history public, not private.

Gapyear (https://www.gapyear.com/) is a UK-based social network established in 1998 by Tom Griffiths. This social network, along with its associated magazine starting in 2000, aim to provide community information and connections for planning a youth's year off taken just before college to better themselves. Travel advice, volunteer jobs, destinations, and general backpacking information are only a few things discussed among this community.

Fotki (http://www.fotki.com/us/en/) is a photo-sharing social network that was established in 1998. It boasts 1.6 million users in more than 200 countries. Although it was originally established by Dmitri Don primarily as a photo-sharing platform, Fotki has grown as a Web 2.0 service engine to support video sharing and audio comments on uploaded content. Fotki supports many languages and provides unlimited storage to paid, premium members.

Open Diary (https://en.wikipedia.org/wiki/Open_Diary) was the first online blogging community geared specifically to sharing of diaries. It was created by Bruce Ableson in 1998 and shut down in early 2014. OpenDiaries provided both public and private diary options for users. OpenDiaries suffered at the hands of two major hacking attempts in 2004 and

2008. These attempts led to the loss of 11 weeks' worth of diary entries and more than 2000 user names and passwords. Even though OpenDiaries provided free e-mail accounts and a continuous supply of public journals from all seven continents, the service disruption and security breach caused by the hacking attempts caused subscribers and funds to dwindle. This directly caused OpenDiaries to shut down after 16 years.

Care2 (http://www.care2.com/) is a social network based in Redwood City, California, established by Randy Paynter. In 1998, it started to create a community interested in activism. To make an impact, Care2 connects individuals with organizations and select businesses with similar concerns and issue bias. They also host online petitions and related news articles. In accordance to their beliefs, Care2 asks for users to supply their level of activism involvement along with all the standard profile information when they register. Care2 currently has almost 10 million registered users.

BlackPlanet (http://www.blackplanet.com/) was established in 1999 by Omar Wasow. BlackPlanet is run out of New York, along with AsianAvenue and MiGente. BlackPlanet has 20 million registered users of mostly black descent with the goal of strengthening the black community. The community of users has grown to promote racial separatism and gang activity. BlackPlanet was utilized by Senator Barack Obama in 2007 to gain support for votes in 2008. In 2009, BlackPlanet introduced mobile support for smartphones to their community.

VampireFreaks (http://vampirefreaks.com/), created in 1999 by Jet Berelson, is a niche social network for the gothic community. The community is encouraged to share stories of love, music, and fashion. VampireFreaks offers online music and clothing stores. They have almost 2 million users and affectionately refer to user-created groups as *cults*. Paying members have the ability to selectively revoke unwanted users from VampireFreaks and all associated resources.

HR (http://www.hr.com/) is the largest social network dedicated to human resource professionals. With more than 200,000 users, HR has been dedicated to sharing knowledge from their base in Aurora, Canada, since 1999. Among the resources provided are newsletters, webcasts, and case studies aimed at providing news for best practices and online certification needed to succeed in their jobs. HR also provides outreach programs to their partners, and hosts related virtual summits.

LiveJournal (http://www.livejournal.com/) was launched by Danga Interactive, owned by Brad Fitzpatrick, in 1999. LiveJournal was bought by Six Apart in 2005 and Russian SUP Media in 2007. Though most LiveJournal users are in the United States, LiveJournal has become the dominant diary/journal network for Russia. LiveJournal attempts to not limit user content unless necessary, such as in cases of harassment or copyright infringement. Because of this, LiveJournal has also been forced to persevere through many lawsuits, often in relation to their refusal to take down content labeled for adults only that others may find offensive or obscene. Barring a minor distributed denial-of-service incident in 2011, LiveJournal provides adequate service to all free users. Paying members gain the additional ability to post on their journals through text or voice calls. These members also gain additional storage and priority update access when writing their journals on the website.

Makeoutclub (http://makeoutclub.com/) or MOC was designed in 1999 by Gibby Miller. It was originally intended as an honest attempt to bridge the gaps in social stigma and bring more people together. MOC focused on providing music and entertainment news, while introducing a couple of features that would become standard operating procedure for social networks of the future. MOC introduced interest-related profiles, and although stated to be a way to make friends, it would often be accused of being a dating site at heart. With more than 150,000 users, MOC has continued to evolve along with other popular social networks, though more popular with many subcultures instead of the mainstream populace.

CyWorld (https://en.wikipedia.org/wiki/Cyworld) is the Facebook of South Korea. Since its launch in 1999, it has always provided the newest advancements in social networks. CyWorld failed to meet the international market before Facebook, which launched their services in Korea in 2009. Facebook took many users who wished to communicate with international friends away from CyWorld. They were also beat out of the Japanese market by Mixi. Despite their failed international expansion, CyWorld still holds more than 24 million users, which is almost 50% of South Korea's population.

Kiwibox (http://www.kiwibox.com/) is a 2.4 million user base social network developed by three students from Carnegie Mellon in 1999. It expanded its access to mobile phones in 2008. Kiwibox remains a popular nightclub and hotspot event organizer for teenagers around New York City.

Advogato (https://en.wikipedia.org/wiki/Advogato) is a small (with less than 15,000 users) social network of advocates for free software development created in 1999. The trust metric is an attack-resistant mechanism whereupon users are passively rated by each other on the basis of their relationships online and actions toward others. This robust mechanism was first used by Advogato and then released under a free software license. Tim Berners-Lee, known as the father of semantic web to some, noted Advogato as an early prominent adopter of friend of a friend or FOAF for distributing Resource Description Framework (RDF) Universal Resource Identifiers (URI) for users.

FriendsReunited (https://www.friendsreunited.com/) was created by Steve and Julie Pankhurst in 2000 in the spirit of the successful Classmates social network. The UK knockoff, created in the Pankhurst living room, would attract more than 20 million users and end up selling for more than £5 million. Following its introduction to the UK market, Facebook would grow a thousand times faster than FriendsReunited, but only after 8 years of solid profitable growth.

Habbo (https://www.habbo.com/) is the largest Finnish social networking service and has more than 300 million active users. Established in 2000, Habbo provides little in the way of what is considered standard for social networks nowadays. Habbo simply provides instant messaging services, but it does it through a series of hotels. Part of each user profile is the design of an avatar and personal hotel room. Users can then join a hotel and walk around exploring the hotel grounds while chatting with other users. Habbo has expanded to include its own currency that can be used to buy pets, play games, and decorate their hotel room.

deviantART (http://www.deviantart.com/) is the largest online art community at 25 million users posting more than 140,000 submissions every day. Founded in 2000 out of Hollywood, California, deviantART originally attracted skin artists. Modified skins for music players like Winamp were very popular at the time. deviantART would expand to include every type of artist who would *deviate* from original works and become a *deviant* by making it their own somehow. As other social networks became available, deviantART was one of the first to integrate sharing across them. deviantART would also become a place for original artists to share and sell their work.

Mixi (https://en.wikipedia.org/wiki/Mixi) is a social network limited to those with a Japanese phone number. In 2000, the Mixi Corporation, under the guidance of Kenji Kasahara, put to use the application (app) developed by Batara Eto. Mixi is now used by more than 24 million Japanese to meet people with common interests. Unlike Facebook, Mixi users protested and succeeded in keeping the terms of use policy aligned with keeping all material rights with the user who posted it, instead of handing over all rights without compensation. Mixi also has popular apps for sharing music and video across popular forms of media sharing.

DXY (https://www.crunchbase.com/organization/dxy) is a Chinese social network established in 2000. DXY is a community of more than 3 million health-care professionals, such as doctors and physicians, with the established goal of sharing research, notifying others of conferences, purchasing the newest drugs on the market, and continuing education in practicing fields.

English, baby! (http://www.englishbaby.com/) is a social network that shows just how much faster the Internet can help unify the world by connecting everyone. Established in Portland, Oregon, in 2000, English, baby! connects students and teachers for those learning English as a second language. More than 1.6 million users have joined this network and more than 25% of them reside in China. With a $5 monthly fee, users gain access to unlimited usage of video and mp3 footage featuring popular English-speaking celebrities. Even without the membership fee, users can talk with each other online and ask for help from teachers as needed. The concept for this social network was started by John Hayden, who attempts to create the effect of traveling through English-speaking countries with his line of media featuring celebrities such as professional athletes and Olympic gold medalists.

Partyflock (http://partyflock.nl/) is a social network similar to Kiwibox. It is the largest Dutch social network for house and electronic music. More than 300,000 people use Partyflock to find and talk about the newest artists and where the coolest concerts are. Starting in 2001, Partyflock has grown to be the biggest online community for the dance scene in the Netherlands. They also provide a subforum for English speakers to post, so they do not miss out on local music events.

CozyCat (http://www.cozycat.net/) is a hobbyist social network for Asian women, mostly in Singapore. CozyCat is host to mostly reviews for beauty products and shopping tips. After being established in 2001, CozyCat grew to about 150,000 users. They also have a smart-phone app that allows users to search the community for products by scanning bar codes in store. Membership to become a user, or *Cotter* as they are sometimes referred to, is free and CozyCat is run on donations with large funding coming from Hong Kong. CozyCat also encourages their community to participate in charity work often associated with helping young women in poor Asian provinces.

Athlinks (http://www.athlinks.com/) was established in 2001 and is another niche social network that is geared specifically to competitive endurance runners. They claim to have the "most comprehensive database of endurance race results and events anywhere in the world." This social network allows users to connect with other competitors, keep race logs, share logs, and keep track of the most popular gear and newest races. Chronotrack acquired Athlinks in 2013 and currently has more than 125,000 users.

iWiW (https://en.wikipedia.org/wiki/IWiW), short for international who is who, is one of the first *invitation only* social networks started in 2002 in Hungary. With more than 4 million users, iWiW is by no means exclusive, but it requires accurate information from each user that is invited, including but not limited to place of residence and schools attended. iWiW was purchased by a large Hungarian telemarketing company in 2006, causing many users to leave with concerns of their personal information being sold by the telemarketing Mega Conglomerate. iWiW is only available in Hungarian and still remains very popular with introduction of mobile apps and many internetwork games similar to Facebook apps.

Hub Culture (https://hubculture.com/) was started in 2002 by Stan Stalnaker, and is possibly the first exclusive online social network. With a strictly controlled list of only 20,000 members at any one time, Hub Culture promises to provide only the best and most suitable group of individuals among all fields of expertise to foster the best business and social connections. In 2008, Hub Culture created what is believed to be the first publicly traded digital currency called Ven. Millions of Ven are traded each year among the members of Hub Culture and are primarily used in the few dozen existing Hub Pavilions worldwide.

Fotolog (http://www.fotolog.com/) is Web 2.0 photo blogging social network released in 2002. Fotolog is very popular in South America and is free to use with advertising support.

Free members are allowed one picture upload per day and 20 comments. Paying members gain gold camera access and can upload six photos per day and have 200 comments. Many Fotologs have been dedicated to users' favorite stars and idols. Fotolog is also heavily backed by investments from BV Capitol.

Friendster (https://en.wikipedia.org/wiki/Friendster) was launched in 2002 by Jonathan Abrams as a generic social network, still predating Facebook. Based in Malaysia, Friendster is a social network made primarily of Asian users. MySpace and Facebook would become rivals of Friendster. However, Friendster was redesigned and launched as a gaming platform in 2011 where it would grow to its current user base of more than 115 million. Friendster filed many of the fundamental patents related to social networks. Eighteen of these patents were acquired by Facebook in 2011 during their explosive international growth.

Travellerspoint (http://www.travellerspoint.com/) is a social network launched in 2002 by creators Samuel and Peter Daams. Travellerspoint has a community of more than 300,000 users who maintain information about common travel locations. Among the available information is a traveler's guide, photos, maps, forums, blogs, and travel help applications, all maintained and monitored by the community.

Last.fm (http://www.last.fm/) is an audio recommender system with a user base of 30 million. After being established in 2002, Last.fm provided audio streaming and automatic recommendations based on other users in the network. Last.fm has primarily operated in the United States, United Kingdom, Germany, and Australia due to Digital Millennium Copyright Act (DMCA) prohibitions. Since their acquisition by CBS in 2007, Last.fm has slowly restricted its free use policy. Many countries were charged a €3 per month fee for their services starting in 2009. In 2010, custom radio stations created by users were eliminated. And in 2014, Last.fm and its remaining community were integrated into Spotify and YouTube radio, finally eliminating Last.fm's original audio streaming functionality altogether.

WAYN (http://www2.wayn.com/), or Where Are You Now, is a social travel network in the United Kingdom. This social network contains 20 million users based on the idea of finding the best place nearby to have a good drink and a good drinking buddy. Founded in 2003, WAYN grew largely due to word of mouth despite the criticism for e-mail harvesting and spam from the parent company.

LinkedIn (https://www.linkedin.com/nhome/) is the largest business-oriented social network in existence, currently with more than 260 million users. Launched in 2003, LinkedIn has changed hands 11 times and grown an excess of 170 million dollars in profit. In the spirit of fostering professional networking, LinkedIn supports more than 20 languages and creates a complex social web of business connections. This network allows users to find the key people they may need to make introductions into the office of the job they may desire. Users can also track friends and colleagues during times of promotion and hiring to congratulate them if they choose. In 2008, LinkedIn introduced their mobile app as well as the ability for users to not only endorse each other, but also to specifically attest to individual skills that they may hold and have listed on the site. LinkedIn is currently considered the de facto source of professional networking by many worldwide.

MySpace (https://myspace.com/) was launched in 2003 by Brad Greenspan. With its focus on music-related news, MySpace grew as the prominent social network among young teenagers until being overtaken by Facebook in 2008 in terms of volume and popularity. Many would consider it the precursor to Facebook in this regard. Until 2013, MySpace faced a general decline in member traffic when it was purchased by pop idol Justin Timberlake and rebranded. MySpace currently supports more than 30 million users with a shared Bulletin Board system. Each bulletin board provides space for users to post music, links, pictures, and embedded video for others to peruse.

Delicious (https://delicious.com/) was created in 2003 by Joshua Schachter as social book-marking service. Delicious is a network of more than 9 million users who share and group their bookmarks. The network organizes sites into stacks based on tags given to book-marks by the users who share them. This allows social networks to form and friend connections to be made over similar bookmark interests.

CouchSurfing (https://www.couchsurfing.com/), named after the term that it supports, is a network of people who wish to travel in the cheapest way possible, while sleeping on someone else's couch. Launched in 2003, CouchSurfing is a network of more than 3 million users who wish to use or provide a spare room, floor, or couch for a passerby traveler. Information is optional, though encouraged to provide trustworthy accommodations between hosts and guests meeting through the site. Most travelers aim to work out some sort of nonmonetary compensation for their short stay with their host.

hi5 (http://www.hi5.com/) is a social network developed by Ramu Yalamanchi in 2003 in San Francisco, California. All of the normal social network features were included like friend networks, photo sharing, profile information, and groups. In 2009, hi5 was redesigned as a purely social gaming network with a required age of 18 years for all new and existing users. Several hundred games were added, and Application Programming Interfaces (APIs) were created that include support for Facebook games. This popular change boosted hi5's user base to more than 80 million. hi5 was then acquired by Tagged in 2011.

Orkut (https://en.wikipedia.org/wiki/Orkut) was a social network almost identical to Facebook that launched in 2004 and closed at the end of September 2014. Orkut obtained more than 100 million users, most of which resided in India and Brazil. Orkut was very successful under its ownership by Google. Orkut was shut down to end with a profit, as other social networks like Facebook and Google+ had created an expansion stalemate. Google moved to have Google+ take over the job that Orkut was providing, as Google+ was the larger of their two social network products.

Facebook (https://www.facebook.com/) has become the largest social network user base since its launch in February 2004. Created by Mark Zuckerberg at Harvard College, Facebook quickly expanded to all of Boston and Stanford University. Now with more than a billion and a half users, Facebook continues to profit off advertising and selling user-created content and information. Facebook has had a number of revisions to its user interface since it was released. Since the major 2011 revamp, Facebook provides personal timelines to complement a user's profile. Timelines show chronological placement of photos, videos, links, and other updates made by a user and their friends. Though a user can customize their timeline and what content and profile information is shared with individual users, Facebook networks rely heavily on people posting publically and tagging people in photos. A user can also always untag themselves, but tagging is a very common practice that places people and events together. On the basis of profile information and browsing history, Facebook has invaded the social network scene with constant bombardments of advertisement and friend/app recommendations, changing the future for revenue streams everywhere.

Twitter (https://twitter.com/) was launched in 2006 by Jack Dorsey, Evan Williams, Biz Stone, and Noah Glass in San Francisco, California. Twitter's original idea that led to the infamous 140 character limit was to design a system for individuals to share SMS messages with a small group of people. Tweets were always designed to be short and inconsequential. By 2013, Twitter had 200 million users sending 500 million tweets a day.

Foursquare (https://foursquare.com/), released in 2009, relies on location-based social networking. Users gain points for visiting locations and can view the points of their friends. Tags and short reviews are also attached to physical locations by many of the 20 million users. These attachments, in collusion with a user's preferences, provide a local selection of places of interests.

Google+ (https://plus.google.com/) was released in 2011, well after Facebook, and is the only social network to rival their user base with more than a billion users. When it was first released, Google+ tried to limit its group with private user invites. They were bombarded with new user account requests and had more than 10 million registered users in the first 2 weeks of their launch. The main feature of Google+ is Circles. Circles allow networks to center around ideas and products. Circles are also the way that streaming content is shared between people. By being part of the same circle, people create focused social networks. Google+ has also integrated support for games and popular media sources like YouTube.

Stage 32 (https://www.stage32.com/welcome/14/) is a social network released in 2012 by Richard Botto for creative arts professionals. Stage 32 caters to providing news from Hollywood, linking users in the entertainment industry and educating new talent. With more than 300,000 users, Stage 32 provides one of many niche groups with the social interaction they need.

Poolwo (https://en.wikipedia.org/wiki/Poolwo) is one of the newest social networking sites, set up by Shashi Tharoor in India at the start of 2014. With only 12,000 users, the site is still growing and provides international support.

Flickr (https://www.flickr.com/) is a photo-sharing website that was created in 2004. It was acquired by Yahoo in 2005. It has tens of millions of members sharing billions of images. Photos and videos can also be accessed via Flickr.

YouTube (https://www.youtube.com/) is a video-sharing website created in 2005 and acquired by Google in 2006. Members as well as corporations and organizations post videos of themselves as well as various events and talks. Movies and songs are also posted on this website.

2.3   DETAILS OF FOUR POPULAR SOCIAL NETWORKS

This section discusses four of the most popular social media systems that have influenced our culture a great deal. They are Facebook, Google+, Twitter, and LinkedIn.

2.3.1   FACEBOOK

Timeline. Your timeline is you on Facebook. It is a chronological representation of you from birth until your death, or present day if you are still using Facebook. It would not just show you everything since the day you joined Facebook, but also photos and other content that may be generated by you or your friends that have a date associated with them will appear in your timeline, even if they happened to be posted before you joined Facebook. Timeline will display many things, including photos, events, friends, places, status updates, and more.

Timelines are populated by categorical additions. By choosing from five different categories, a user's life can be broken up into pieces that can be more meaningfully analyzed by the algorithms run by Facebook. These categories include Work and Education, Family and Relationships, Living, Health and Wellness, and Milestones and Experiences. Each category contains four to seven subcategories. Users have granular control over who sees what content related to them, but less so about what they see in relation to other people.

Social Experiments. Facebook and other social networks perform social experiments with their users. Facebook's timeline feature was originally released as one such experiment. Without telling the users that were part of the experiment, because informing them would affect the outcome, Facebook filtered some individuals' timeline feeds. They prevented user content from showing up on the recent activities of some friends to test if emotions were contagious. Their findings were that emotions were indeed contagious in nature. With users who were shown happy content and denied sad content, it was found that they made more happy posts in response. The same correlation showed for those in the sad category of that experiment. The fact still remains that some users were denied immediate access to content that they may have found important or relevant.

Other Communication. Facebook has a variety of other ways to communicate than just timelines and friend updates. Users can send private messages to each other, similar to an internal mail server. Most people are aware of being able to use this feature to communicate with those on their friends list; however, though less publicized, Facebook also has a harder-to-find feature that allows private messages to be sent to those not connected to them through friends or acquaintances.

Facebook also has a built-in instant message client. Users can see any one of their friends that are logged into a web browser or mobile device and send live messages to each other. Though not immediately obvious, it is possible, at least between two web clients, to send files directly through Facebook as well. Facebook has silently supported the evolution and spread of various emojis in their communication option. The full list of such emojis has been user documented, but Facebook chooses to let people find them by themselves.

Interest Lists are Facebook's version of Twitter lists. An Interest List is a named list of things created by a user. For example, a user may create a top 10 favorite foods Interest List. Posts by the user and friends will automatically be included into the list based on the things that were included in the Interest List.

Security and Privacy. Because Facebook has such a generalized privacy policy, they can get away with handling user information in almost any way that they see fit. They are often accused of selling user information and not fully deleting accounts after users choose to remove them. There is some truth and reason behind the accusations, but Facebook has done many things to improve security in recent years.

Facebook has provided users with a detailed list of open sessions under their account name and given them the ability to revoke them at will. This is to say that, if an unauthorized person accesses a user's account or the user forgets to log out of a computer, they can force that particular connection to close. Location and time of access are listed for each open session, so a user can easily determine if their account is being accessed from somewhere unexpected.

When viewed through a web browser, Facebook supports https. This protocol is considered secure; however, it is not supported by mobile devices. Data transmitted by Facebook to mobile devices has been proven to be in plain text, meaning if it is intercepted it is easily human readable. However, GPS (Global Positioning System) coordinates and information about your friends require special permission. Default access granted to any Facebook app includes user ID, name, profile picture, gender, age range, locale, networks, list of friends, and any information set as public. Any of this information can be transmitted between devices at any time without a user's express permission, and, in the case of mobile devices, in plain, unencrypted text. Facebook has partially solved this problem by releasing a separate app for messaging. It provides more granular control for mobile device permissions, such as contact syncing and specific profile information. The only problem with this solution is that it relies on every user to not only know about and download the separate app, but to also carefully take the considerable amount of time to properly read through and set all the new permissions properly.

When content, like individual photos, are deleted by a user, they are not immediately removed. Facebook uses a cloud service called Akamai to help cache user content for faster access. Content deletion simply causes Facebook to stop serving the cached link from Akamai, and outside access seems to disappear and looks like it has been deleted. Full data deletion can be complicated and takes time, possibly days or weeks, to be fully removed.

Many complaints have been made that deleting messages, photos, and posts does not actually delete the content but simply hides it. Inspection of deletion protocols for

Facebook yield that this should not be the case. Redundant deletion protocols are currently being developed. It should be noted, however, that other people, like friends, have their own privacy settings. This means that anything a user posts on a friend's wall, or if a user comments on something they did not originally post, is able to be viewed by others in accordance with the person's wall that it appears on. If a user has all of their content set to friends only, but posts on a friend's wall that has their privacy set to public for everything, that individual post is publicly available including search engines.

Users can tag and be tagged in photos. This links a person to the event or moment depicted in the photo. The option to untag one's self is available, but the tagging event cannot be prevented. Regardless of a user's privacy settings, there will always exist a logged event that they were tagged in a photo, even if they remove it afterwards.

Facebook for Minors. Minors are offered some important security features. The scope of these features is small and basically only serves to limit surface of exposure for the minor. The key idea is that there is no true public option for minors. In all cases that the *public* setting is used in permissions, a minor's profile and posted information is only visible to friends of friends. The amount and specificity of rules pertaining to how tags, posts, and profile information is spread to this limited network is vast. However, such rules are easily undermined in that a minor's profile is still in the public domain, meaning it can be seen and friend access requested by anyone on the entire Internet.

With no secondary system to protect minors from unwanted or misleading profile friend requests, it is still easily possible for them to click *accept* unwittingly or by accident. Facebook provides additional information urging safe protocol for interactions online, and tools to block and report misconduct by other users. These resources are not guaranteed to be used, and a smarter-than-average person with ill intent would not raise enough alarm to provoke the use of misconduct prevention tools. Without the option to review additions to friend networks by a responsible adult, a single action can put potentially hundreds of unwanted people into that outer *friends of friends* category in a minor's Facebook profile.

2.3.2 GOOGLE+

Circles. Circles are the heart of Google+. Circles generate content for users and help organize and segregate with whom information is shared. A user makes circles by placing other Google+ users into them. This is done through an interface built very similarly to Gmail and Google maps. The interface is built of mostly Java and JavaScript. Google+ makes use of the cross-browser framework known as Closure. HTML5 is used to "maintain pretty-looking URLs." This is in direct opposition to the JavaScript-powered AJAX of the Closure framework. The conflict is handled on the basis of how the page being rendered is accessed. If a static URL is accessed inside the Google+ domain, HTML5 is used server side to render the page. However, if a page is accessed in a dynamic fashion, that is, a user click browsing through friend profiles, then JavaScript is used client side to render the page.

When circles create content for a user, it is accumulated and displayed on their Stream. A user's Stream is a prioritized list of any content from that user's circles that they have decided to display. A user can control how much of a Circle's content is included in their Stream. The settings choices are all, none, some, or most. The all-inclusive/exclusive options speak for themselves, but the algorithms for deciding what is included in the some and most categories have neither been divulged nor reverse engineered. For Circles set to include none of their content in the user's Stream, or any Circle for that matter, all of that Circle's content can be individually viewed by clicking on that Circle.

Circles can also be shared, either with individual users or other circles. This action takes place as a single time share. This means that there is no syncing after the share takes places. A user may share a Circle as many times as they please, especially if frequent updates are made and they want their network to stay up to date. The lack of synchronous updates without sharing a Circle again means that it is simply very easy for others to have incorrect information about Circles that change on a regular basis. Even at a very seldom basis of change, it is not necessarily habitual for someone to continuously share circles again after making changes to them.

Pages. Google+ Pages are essentially profiles for businesses, organizations, publications, or other entities that are not related to a single individual. They can be added to Circles like normal users and share updates to user Streams in the same way. The real distinction is that Pages do not require a legal given name to be attached to the associated Google account. This requirement is generally enforced for Google+ profiles, and entities not making use of a Page instead are liable to be deleted.

Other Services. Google+ has a large amount of additional support owing to its high level of integration with Google accounts, both in design and implementation. Relevant information is shared from Gmail. Available services include games, messenger, photo editing and saving, mobile upload and diagnostics, apps, calendars, and video streaming.

Google+ integrates with Google's video-streaming application, Hangouts. Hangouts is free and supports up to 10 simultaneous users in a session. Hangouts can be used as a conference call solution or to create instant webcasts. Hangouts serves a similar function to programs like Skype; however, the background approach is completely different.

Whereas Skype uses P2P (peer-to-peer) to accomplish a connection between individuals, Hangouts does not. Hangouts is based on many technologies, including XMPP, Jingle, RTP, ICE, STUN, and SRTP. This cumulative approach attempts to reduce transmission lag to below 100 milliseconds. This low-latency approach is not without its drawbacks. The cloud computational requirements for Hangouts sessions are immense, which from a user standpoint is null when the service is being provided for free. Hangouts sessions have, in many cases, taken large amounts of resources on host machines to keep this stable connection. Even on modern medium- to high-quality machines, Hangouts can render the CPU cycles to a crawl as it eats up system resources.

Controversy. Before adding appropriate privacy controls, Google+ was criticized for having limited options for mandatory public gender disclosure. Masking this gross oversight, Google claimed the mandatory gender identification was for automatic injection of pronouns like *he* or *she* in profile descriptions.

Shortly after the release of Google+, it was banned in Iran and China through censorship. Despite the censorship, several native-speaking Chinese spammed Obama election pages on Google+ in early 2012. This was explained to be a temporary mistake on China's part to uphold its own censorship.

Google+ has slowly revised their requirement of a legal name as a display name for users. As of July 2014, any name can be used. This has caused many issues with YouTube, who conversely raised the requirement for commenter of videos to have a Google account. This has created many glitches with older videos without comments and commenters who do not have a registered Google account.

2.3.3 TWITTER

140 Character Limit. Twitter was originally designed to work with text messages. This is why the 140 character limit was put into the original design, to comply with text message rates. Twitter's original design was to create a service that a person could send a text to, and that text would not only be available online but it would then be able to resend that text to other people using the service.

Twitter has evolved to incorporate many different sources of media. Online video and photo viewing without redirection to third-party sites was added in 2010. In 2013, Twitter added its own music service as an iPhone app. Despite Twitter's continued expansion of supported content, the language used in modern tweets along with some other helpful additions has continued to adhere to the 140 character limit.

Many modern URLs are much longer than 140 characters. URL shorteners have made it possible to link these longer URLs well within the confines of a tweet. At first, users simply linked third-party shortened links to save space. Then, Twitter started supporting these URL shorteners themselves. Finally, in June 2011, Twitter bought its own domain, t.co, for automatically shortening URLs in tweets before allowing them to post. Twitter currently rehosts images and videos, and does its own in-house URL mapping and shortening in the name of reducing tweet size and serving content to users faster.

Redesign. When Twitter was first implemented, tweets were handled by a server running Ruby on Rails and stored tweets in a shared MySQL database. Rails was a good initial choice. It seemed to be a scalable solution for writing agile web applications. As the number of Twitter users grew tremendously fast and the number of tweets being made skyrocketed past the throughput of the system, the MySQL database could not keep up. Read and write errors prevented tweets from being handled properly.

From 2009 to 2011, all Rails components were slowly replaced with Scala implementations of their code. Scala is a functional language that reduces to Java, but is syntactically reminiscent of C. Upon completing the full redesign, Twitter was able to increase its tweet throughput by 50 times what it was handling with the original design.

In 2010, during the middle of this major redesign, Twitter added trending topics. Trending topics can be local or global. Trending topics represent tags that appear at a much higher rate than the average tag for a specific region.

Security. Until 2007, there existed a vulnerability where, if an attacker knew the phone number for an account, fake tweets could be made for that person using SMS spoofing. Twitter remedied this by offering PINs for authenticating text messages. In 2009, a Twitter administrator had their password cracked with a dictionary attack. This resulted in illegal tweets being sent, and company finances stolen and leaked to the public. Until 2010, there existed a bug that allowed followers to be added to other users' accounts without their knowledge or permission. This breach resulted in legal action from the Department of Justice and forced reevaluation of Twitter's security protocol for users' information. In the same year, there was a cross-site scripting attack stemming from colored tweet text allowing both user account infection and self-replication. Twitter still currently fights against Twitterbots. These bots do not represent real people and automatically comb tweets, respond, and even falsely add to famous persons' follower counts.

2.3.4 LinkedIn

Professional. LinkedIn is unique in that it aims to be professional and make professional connections in all of its social networks, and every aspect of the company and its service revolves around money. Users cannot upload their resumes directly to LinkedIn. Instead, a user adds skills and work history to their profile. Other users inside that social network can verify and endorse each attribute. This essentially makes a user's presence on LinkedIn only as believable as the people they connect with.

LinkedIn provides a professional environment to search for companies and research who inside a company's social network might be able to make the introduction you want. If a user wishes to do much more, they better be ready to hand over some money. If a user wants to apply for a job listing or message someone not directly in their network of contacts, then they must pay a subscription fee. If a user wants to simply make use of any job-finding abilities, then they will have to spend at least $30–50 per month. The upgraded accounts still have limitations on the number of searches, mails, and introductions they can use. This system almost ensures that a user will have to spend for more than just one month to search for a job in this fashion. Users can always pay for larger limitations. However, even if you pay $500 per month to LinkedIn, you still face hard-capped limitations on all activities that you gain access to.

Those looking for jobs are not the only ones who have to pay. Recruiters and named businesses are also required to pay, and they are the ones providing the content that makes LinkedIn a valuable resource that people might even pay for. LinkedIn is one of the most traded social networks. Since its creation, it has been traded 11 times. The last buyout was for more than 200 times its original value.

Economic Graph. The economic graph is the ideal goal of the company in decades to come. The idea is to fully map out the entire world's economy. By adding transparency to actors and the skills involved at every node within the economy, it is the desire of the company to make the world economy more efficient. Galene is the name given to the search engine allowing access to this ever-growing graph.

2.4 SUMMARY AND CONCLUSION

This chapter has provided an overview of the various social networks that have emerged during the past decades. We then selected a few networks (e.g., Facebook. LinkedIn, Google+, and Twitter) and discussed some of their essential features. These social networks are being used by several hundreds of millions of individuals on a daily basis for personal, professional, and business purposes.

Our work has analyzed these social networks for applications such as marketing, security, and law enforcement. Furthermore, we have also developed various access control policies to secure such social networks. Finally, we have studied the privacy implementation of these social networks where people can infer highly sensitive information from the public data posted by the users of the social networks.

We believe that we are still in the first generation with respect to these social networks. As progress is made on technologies such as machine learning, security and privacy, and big data management, we will see such networks being used for almost all aspects of life and living.

3 Data Security and Privacy

3.1 INTRODUCTION

As we stated in Chapter 1, secure social media integrates social media technologies with security technologies. We discussed social media systems in Chapter 2 of this book. In this chapter, we will discuss security technologies. In particular, since much of the discussion in this book is on social data analytics and security, we will provide a fairly comprehensive overview of access control in data management systems. In particular, we will discuss security policies and enforcing the policies in database systems. Our focus will be on discretionary security policies. We will also discuss data privacy aspects. More details of secure data management can be found in Ferrari and Thuraisingham (2000) and Thuraisingham (2005a).

The most popular discretionary security policy is the access control policy. Access control policies were studied for operating systems back in the 1960s and then for database systems in the 1970s. The two prominent database systems, System R and INGRES, were the first to investigate access control for database systems (see Griffiths and Wade, 1976; Stonebraker and Wong, 1974). Since then, several variations of access control policies have been reported. Other discretionary policies include administration policies. We also discuss identification and authentication under discretionary policies. Note that much of the discussion in this chapter will focus on discretionary security in relational database systems. Many of the principles are applicable to other systems such as object database systems, distributed database systems, and cloud data management systems.

Before one designs a secure system, the first question that must be answered is, what is the security policy to be enforced by the system? Security policy is essentially a set of rules that enforce security. Security policies include mandatory security policies and discretionary security policies. Mandatory security policies are the policies that are *mandatory* in nature and should not be bypassed. Discretionary security policies are policies that are specified by the administrator or anyone who is responsible for the environment in which the system will operate.

By policy enforcement, we mean the mechanisms to enforce the policies. For example, back in the 1970s, the relational database system products, such as System R and INGRES, developed techniques such as the query modification mechanisms for policy enforcement (see, e.g., Griffiths and Wade, 1976; Stonebraker and Wong, 1974). The query language SQL (Structured Query Language) has been extended to specify security policies and access control rules. More recently, languages such as XML (eXtensible Markup Language) and RDF (Resource Description Framework) have been extended to specify security policies (see, e.g., Bertino et al., 2002; Carminati et al., 2004).

In Section 3.2, we introduce discretionary security including access control and authorization models for database systems. We also discuss role-based access control systems. In Section 3.3, we discuss ways of enforcing discretionary security, including a discussion of query modification. We also provide an overview of the various commercial products. In Section 3.4, we discuss data privacy. The chapter is summarized in Section 3.5. The discussion in this chapter will provide an overview of essentially the basics of discretionary security focusing primarily on relational database systems. Figure 3.1 illustrates the concepts discussed in this chapter.

3.2 SECURITY POLICIES

The organization of this section is as follows. In Section 3.2.1, we will provide an overview of access control policies. Administration policies will be discussed in Section 3.2.2. Issues in identification

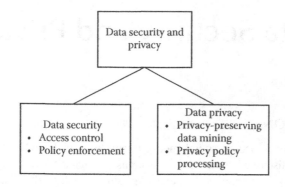

FIGURE 3.1   Data security and privacy.

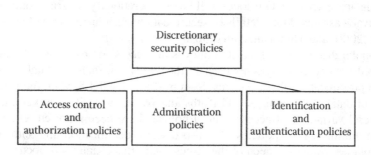

FIGURE 3.2   Discretionary security policies.

and authentication will be discussed in Section 3.2.3. Auditing a database management system will be discussed in Section 3.2.4. Views as security objects will be discussed in Section 3.2.5. Figure 3.2 illustrates various components of discretionary security policies.

3.2.1   ACCESS CONTROL POLICIES

Access control policies were first examined for operating systems. The essential point here is that, can a process be granted access to a file? Access could be *read* access or *write* access. Write access could include access to modify, append, or delete. These principles were transferred to database systems such as Ingres and System R. Since then, various forms of access control policies have been studied. Notable among those are the role-based access control policies that are now implemented in several commercial systems. Note that access control policies also include mandatory policies. Figure 3.3 illustrates the various access control policies.

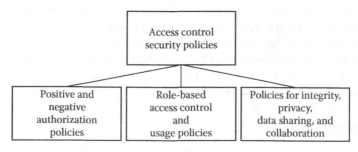

FIGURE 3.3   Access control security policies.

3.2.1.1 Authorization-Based Access Control Policies

Many of the access control policies are based on authorization policies. Essentially, what this means is that users are granted access to data based on authorization rules. In this section, we will discuss various types of authorization rules. Note that in the book chapter by Ferrari and Thuraisingham (2000), a detailed discussion of authorization policies is provided.

Positive authorization: Early systems focused on what is now called positive authorization rules. Here, user John is granted access to relation EMP or user Jane is granted access to relation DEPT. These are access control rules on relations. One can also grant access to other entities such as attributes and tuples. For example, John has read access to attribute Salary and write access to attribute Name in relation EMP. Write access could include append, modify, or delete access.

Negative authorization: The question is, if John's access to an object is not specified, does this mean John does not have access to that object? In some systems, any authorization rule that is not specified is implicitly taken to be a negative authorization, while in other systems negative authorizations are explicitly specified. For example, we could enforce rules such as, John does not have access to relation EMP or Jane does not have access to relation DEPT.

Conflict resolution: When we have rules that are conflicting, then how do we resolve the conflicts? For example, we could have a rule that grants John read access to relation EMP. However, we can also have a rule that does not grant John read access to the salary attribute in EMP. This is a conflict. Usually, a system enforces the least privilege rule in which case John has access to EMP except for the salary values.

Strong and weak authorization: Systems also enforce strong and weak authorizations. In the case of strong authorization, the rule holds regardless of conflicts. In the case of weak authorization, the rule does not hold in case of conflict. For example, if John is granted access to EMP and it is a strong authorization rule and the rule where John is not granted access to salary attribute is a weak authorization, there is a conflict. This means the strong authorization will hold.

Propagation of authorization rules: The question here is, how do the rules get propagated? For example, if John has read access to relation EMP, then does it automatically mean that John has read access to every element in EMP? Usually, this is the case unless we have a rule that prohibits automatic propagation of an authorization rule. If we have a rule prohibiting the automatic propagation of a rule, then we must explicitly enforce authorization rules that specify the objects that John has access to.

Special rules: In our work on mandatory policies, we have explored extensively the enforcement of content- and context-based constraints. Note that security constraints are essentially the security rules. Content- and context-based rules are rules where access is granted depending on the content of the data or the context in which the data is displayed. Such rules can also be enforced for discretionary security. For example, in the case of content-based constraints, John has read access to tuples only in DEPT D100. In the case of context- or association-based constraints, John does not have read access to names and salaries taken together; however, he can have access to individual names and salaries. In the case of event-based constraints, after the election, John has access to all elements in relation EMP.

Consistency and completeness of rules: One of the challenges here is ensuring the consistency and completeness of constraints. That is, if the constraints or rules are inconsistent, then do we have conflict resolution rules that will resolve the conflicts? How can we ensure that all of the entities (such as attributes, relations, or elements) are specified in access

> **Authorization rules:**
>
> • John has read access to employee
>   relation.
> • John does not have write access
>   to department relation.
> • Jane has read access to name values
>   in employee relation.
> • Jane does not have read access
>   to department relation.

FIGURE 3.4   Authorization rules.

control rules for a user? Essentially what this means is, are the rules complete? If not, what assumptions do we make about entities that do not have either positive or negative authorizations specified on them for a particular user or a class of users?

We have discussed some essential points with respect to authorization rules. Some examples are given in Figure 3.4. In the next section, we will discuss a very popular access control policy (i.e., role-based access control) that is now implemented in commercial systems.

3.2.1.2   Role-Based Access Control

Role-based access control has become one of the more popular access control methods (see Sandhu et al., 1996). This method has been implemented in commercial systems, including Trusted Oracle. The idea here is to grant access to users depending on their roles and functions.

The essential idea behind role-based access control, also known as RBAC, is as follows. Users need access to data depending on their roles. For example, a president may have access to information about his/her vice presidents and the members of the board, while the chief financial officer may have access to the financial information and information on those who report to him. A director may have access to information about those working in his division, while the human resources director will have information on personal data about the employees of the corporation. Essentially, role-based access control is a type of authorization policy that depends on the user role and the activities that go with the role.

Various research efforts on role hierarchies have been discussed in the literature. There is also a conference series called SACMAT (Symposium on Access Control Models and Technologies) that evolved from role-based access control research efforts. For example, how does access get propagated? Can one role subsume another? Consider the role hierarchy illustrated in Figure 3.5. This means if we grant access to a node in the hierarchy, does the access propagate upwards? That is, if a department manager has access to certain project information, does that access get propagated to the parent node, which is a director node? If a section leader has access to employee information in his/her section, does the access propagate to the department manager who is the parent in the role hierarchy? What happens to the child nodes? That is, does access propagate downwards? For example, if a department manager has access to certain information, then do his subordinates have access to that information? Are there cases where the subordinates have access to data that the department manager does not have? What happens if an employee has to report to two supervisors, one his department manager and the other his project manager? What happens when the department manager is working on a project and has to report to his project leader who also works for him?

Role-based access control has been examined for relational systems, object systems, distributed systems, and now some of the emerging technologies such as data warehouses, knowledge management systems, semantic web, e-commerce systems, and digital libraries. Furthermore, object models have been used to represent roles and activities (see, e.g., *Proceedings of the IFIP Database*

FIGURE 3.5   Role hierarcy.

Security Conference Series). This is an area that will continue to be discussed, and the Association for Computing Machinery's SACMAT is a venue for publishing high-quality papers on this topic.

More recently, Sandhu et al. have developed yet another access control-like model, and that is the Usage Control Model, which they refer to as UCON (see, e.g., the work reported in Park and Sandhu, 2004). The UCON model attempts to integrate three policies: trust management, access control, and rights management. The idea is to provide control on the usage of objects. While the ideas are somewhat preliminary, this model shows a lot of promise.

3.2.2   ADMINISTRATION POLICIES

While access control policies specify access that specific users have to the data, administration policies specify who is to administer the data. Administration duties would include keeping the data current, making sure the metadata is updated whenever the data is updated, and ensuring recovery from failures and related activities.

Typically, the database administrator (DBA) is responsible for updating, say, the metadata, the index, and access methods, and also ensuring that the access control rules are properly enforced. The System Security Officer (SSO) may also have a role. That is, the DBA and SSO may share the duties between them. The security-related issues might be the responsibility of the SSO, while the data-related issues might be the responsibility of the DBA. Some other administration policies being considered include assigning caretakers. Usually, owners have control of the data that they create and may manage the data for its duration. In some cases, owners may not be available to manage the data, in which case they may assign caretakers.

Administration policies get more complicated in distributed environments, especially in a web environment. For example, in web environments, there may be multiple parties involved in distributing documents, including the owner, the publisher, and the users requesting the data. Who owns the data? Is it the owner or the publisher? Once the data has left the owner and arrived at the publisher, does the publisher take control of the data?

There are many interesting questions that need to be answered as we migrate from a relational database environment to a distributed and perhaps a web environment. These also include managing

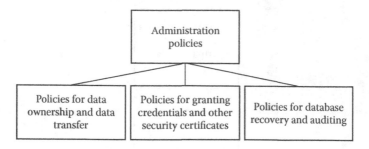

FIGURE 3.6   Administration policies.

copyright issues, data quality, data provenance, and governance. Many interesting papers have appeared in recent conferences on administration policies. Figure 3.6 illustrates various administration policies.

3.2.3   IDENTIFICATION AND AUTHENTICATION

For the sake of completeness, we discuss identification and authentication as part of our discussion on discretionary security. By identification, we mean users must identify themselves with their user ID and password. Authentication means the system must then match the user ID with the password to ensure that this is indeed the person he is purporting to be. A user may also have multiple identities depending on his roles. Identity management has received a lot of attention (see Bertino, 2006).

Numerous problems have been reported with the password-based scheme. One is that hackers can break into the system and get the passwords of users and then masquerade as the user. In a centralized system, the problems are not as complicated as in a distributed environment. Now, with the World Wide Web and e-commerce applications, financial organizations are losing billions of dollars when hackers masquerade as legitimate users.

More recently, biometrics techniques are being applied. These include face recognition and voice recognition techniques to authenticate the user. These techniques are showing a lot of promise and are already being used. We can expect widespread use of biometric techniques as face recognition technologies advance.

3.2.4   AUDITING A DATABASE SYSTEM

Databases are audited for multiple purposes. For example, they may be audited to keep track of the number of queries posed, the number of updates made, the number of transactions executed, and the number of times the secondary storage is accessed so that the system can be designed more efficiently. Databases can also be audited for security purposes. For example, have any of the access control rules been bypassed by releasing information to the users? Has the inference problem occurred? Has privacy been violated? Have there been unauthorized intrusions?

Audits create a trail, and the audit data may be stored in a database. This database may be mined to detect any abnormal patterns or behaviors. There has been a lot of work in using data mining for auditing and intrusion detection. Audit trail analysis is especially important these days with e-commerce transactions on the web. An organization should have the capability to conduct an analysis and determine problems like credit card fraud and identity theft.

3.2.5   VIEWS FOR SECURITY

Views as a mechanism for security have been studied a great deal both for discretionary security and mandatory security. For example, one may not want to grant access to an entire relation especially

EMP			
SS#	Ename	Salary	D#
1	John	20K	10
2	Paul	30K	20
3	Mary	40K	20
4	Jane	20K	20
5	Bill	20K	10
6	Larry	20K	10
1	Michelle	30K	20

Rules:
John has read access to V1.
Johh has write access tot V2.

V1. View EMP (D# = 20)		
SS#	Ename	Salary
2	Paul	30K
3	Mary	40K
4	Jane	20K
1	Michelle	30K

V2. View EMP (D# = 10)		
SS#	Ename	Salary
1	John	20K
5	Bill	20K
6	Larry	20K

FIGURE 3.7 Views for security.

if it has, say, 25 attributes such as health-care records, salary, travel information, or personal data. Therefore, the DBA could form views and grant access to the views. Similarly, in the case of mandatory security, views could be assigned security levels.

Views have problems associated with them, including the view update problem (see Date, 1990). That is, if the view is updated, then we need to ensure that the base relations are updated. Therefore, if a view is updated by John, and John does not have access to the base relation, then can the base relation still be updated? That is, do we create different views for different users and then the DBA merges the updates on views as updates on base relations? Figure 3.7 illustrates views for security.

3.3 POLICY ENFORCEMENT AND RELATED ISSUES

The organization of this section is as follows. SQL extensions for security are discussed in Section 3.3.1. In Section 3.3.2, we discuss query modification. The impact of discretionary security on other database functions will be discussed in Section 3.3.3. Note that we will focus on relational database systems. Figure 3.8 illustrates the various aspects involved in enforcing security policies. These include specification, implementation, and visualization.

Policy enforcement mechanisms:
Query modification algorithm
Rule processing to enforce the access control rules
Theorem proving techniques to determine if policies are violated
Consistency and completeness checking of policies

FIGURE 3.8 Policy enforcement.

3.3.1 SQL Extensions for Security

This section discusses policy specification. While much of the focus will be on SQL extensions for security policy specification, we will also briefly discuss some of the emerging languages. Note that SQL was developed for data definition and data manipulation for relational systems. Various versions of SQL have been developed, including SQL for objects, SQL for multimedia, and SQL for the web. That is, SQL has influenced data manipulation and data definition a great deal during the past 20 years (see SQL, 1992).

As we have stated, SQL is a data definition and data manipulation language. Security policies could be specified during data definition. SQL has GRANT and REVOKE constructs for specifying grant and revoke access to users. That is, if a user John has read access to relation EMP, then one could use SQL and specify something like GRANT JOHN EMP READ, and if the access is to be revoked, and then we need something like REVOKE JOHN EMP READ. SQL has also been extended with more complex constraints such as granting John read access to a tuple in a relation and granting Jane write access to an element in a relation.

In Thuraisingham and Stachour (1989), we specified SQL extensions for security assertions. These assertions were for multilevel security. We could use similar reasoning for specifying discretionary security policies. For example, consider the situation where John does not have read access to names and salaries in EMP taken together, but he can read names and salaries separately. One could specify this in SQL-like language as follows:

```
GRANT JOHN READ
EMP.SALARY
GRANT JOHN READ
EMP.NAME
NOT GRANT JOHN READ
Together (EMP.NAME, EMP.SALARY).
```

If we are to grant John read access to the employees who earn less than 30K, then this assertion is specified as follows:

```
GRANT JOHN READ
EMP
Where EMP.SALARY < 30K
```

Note that the assertions we have specified are not standard assertions. These are some of our ideas. We need to explore ways of incorporating these assertions into the standards. SQL extensions have also been proposed for role-based access control. In fact, products such as Oracle's trusted database product enforce role-based access control. The access control rules are specified in an SQL-like language.

Note that there are many other specification languages that have been developed. These include XML, RDF, and related languages for the web and the semantic web. Semantic web is essentially an intelligent web. Figure 3.9 illustrates specification aspects for security policies.

Policy specification:

SQL extensions to specify security policies

Rule-based languages to specify policies

Logic programming languages such as Prolog to specify policies

---

FIGURE 3.9   Policy specification.

3.3.2 Query Modification

Query modification was first proposed in the INGRES project at the University of California at Berkeley (see Stonebraker and Wong, 1974). The idea is to modify the query based on the constraints. We have successfully designed and implemented query modification for mandatory security (see Dwyer et al., 1987; Thuraisingham, 1987; Thuraisingham et al., 1993). However, much of the discussion in this section will be on query modification based on discretionary security constraints. We illustrate the essential points with some examples.

Consider a query by John to retrieve all tuples from EMP. Suppose that John only has read access to all the tuples where the salary is less than 30K and the employee is not in the Security department. Then, the query is

```
Select * from EMP
Will be modified to
Select * from EMP
Where salary <30K
And Dept is not Security
```

where we assume that the attributes of EMP are, say, name, salary, age, and department.

Essentially what happens is that the *where* clause of the query has all the constraints associated with the relation. We can also have constraints that span across multiple relations. For example, we could have two relations EMP and DEPT joined by Dept #. Then, the query is modified as follows:

```
Select * from EMP
Where EMP.Salary < 30K
And EMP.D# = DEPT.D#
And DEPT.Name is not Security
```

We have used some simple examples for query modification. The detailed algorithms can be found in Dwyer et al. (1987) and Stonebraker and Wong (1974). The high-level algorithm is illustrated in Figure 3.10.

Query modification algorithm:

Input: query, security constraints
Output: modified query

For constraints that are relevant to the query, modify the where clause of the query via a negation.

For example: if salary should not be released to Jane and if Jane requests information from employee, then modify the query to retrieve information from employee where attribute is not salary.

Repeat the process until all relevant constraints are processed.

The end result is the modified query.

FIGURE 3.10 Query modification algorithm.

3.3.3   DISCRETIONARY SECURITY AND DATABASE FUNCTIONS

In Section 3.3.2, we discussed query modification, which is essentially processing security constraints during the query operation. Query optimization will also be affected by security constraints. That is, once the query is modified, then the query tree has to be built. The idea is to push selections and projection down in the query tree and carry out the join operation later.

Other functions are also affected by security constraints. Let us consider transaction management. Bertino et al. have developed algorithms for integrity constraint processing for transactions management (see Bertino and Musto, 1988). We have examined their techniques for mandatory security constraint processing during transaction management. The techniques may be adapted for discretionary security constraints. The idea is to ensure that the constraints are not violated during transaction execution.

Constraints may be enforced on the metadata. For example, one could grant and revoke access to users to the metadata relations. Discretionary security constraints for metadata could be handled in the same way they are handled for data.

Other database functions include storage management. The issues in storage management include developing appropriate access methods and index strategies. One needs to examine the impact of the security constraints on the storage management functions. That is, can one partition the relations based on the constraints and store them in such a way that the relations can be accessed efficiently? We need to develop secure indexing technologies for database systems. Some work on secure indexing for geospatial information systems is reported in Atluri and Chun (2004).

Databases are audited to determine whether any security violation has occurred. Furthermore, views have been used to grant access to individuals for security purposes. We need efficient techniques for auditing as well as for view management.

In this section, we have examined the impact of security on some of the major database functions, including query management, transaction processing, metadata management, and storage management. We need to also investigate the impact of security on other functions such as integrity constraint processing and fault tolerant computing. Figure 3.11 illustrates the impact of security on the database functions.

Secure database functions:

Query processing: enforce access control rules during query processing; inference control; consider security constraints for query optimization.

Transaction management: check whether security constraints are satisfied during transaction execution.

Storage management: develop special access methods and index strategies that take into consideration the security constraints.

Metadata management: enforce access control on metadata. Ensure that data is not released to unauthorized individuals by releasing the metadata.

Integrity management: ensure that integrity of the data is maintained while enforcing security.

FIGURE 3.11   Security impact on database functions.

3.4   DATA PRIVACY

Data privacy is about protecting sensitive information of individuals. While different definitions of privacy have been proposed, the most common definition is that a person decided what information is to be released about him or her. While data privacy has been studied for decades, especially with statistical databases, with the advent of the World Wide Web and the efforts on applying data mining for counter-terrorism applications, there has been increasing interest in this topic during the past 15 years. Much research has been reported on balancing the need between privacy and security. The first effort on privacy-preserving data mining was reported in Agrawal and Srikant (2000). Several other efforts on this topic have followed since the early 2000s (Kantarcioglu and Clifton, 2004). In addition, treating the privacy problem as a variation of the inference problem was studied in Thuraisingham (2005b).

With the developments in big data technologies, there is significant interest in data privacy. For example, a National Science Foundation workshop (2014) on Big Data Security and Privacy was held in September 2014 and the results have been reported. An interagency workshop on data privacy was also held in February 2015. With advancements in technology, such as data analytics and the interest in data privacy among the policy makers, lawyers, and social scientists, we can expect significant developments in protecting the privacy of individuals as well as ensuring their security.

3.5   SUMMARY AND DIRECTIONS

In this chapter, we have provided an overview of discretionary security policies in database systems. We started with a discussion of access control policies, including authorization policies and role-based access control. Then, we discussed administration policies. We briefly discussed identification and authentication. We also discussed auditing issues and views for security. Next, we discussed policy enforcement. The major issue in policy enforcement is policy specification, policy implementation, and policy visualization. We discussed SQL extensions for specifying policies and provided an overview of query modification. We also briefly discussed how policy visualization might be used to integrate multiple policies. We focused mainly on relational databases systems.

There is still a lot of work to be done. For example, much work is still needed on role-based access control for emerging technologies such as digital libraries and the semantic web. We need administration policies to manage multiparty transactions in a web environment. We also need biometric technologies for authenticating users. Digital identity is becoming an important research area especially with cloud systems.

Security policy enforcement is a topic that will continue to evolve as new technologies emerge. We have advanced from relational to object to multimedia to web-based data management systems. Each system has some unique features that are incorporated into the security policies. Enforcing policies for the various systems will continue to be a major research focus. We also need to carry out research on the consistency and completeness of policies. Policy visualization may help toward this.

Policy management in the cloud is an active area of research. Our work includes access control as well as policy-based information sharing in the cloud. The experimental systems we have developed on security policy enforcement in the cloud are discussed throughout this book.

REFERENCES

Agrawal, R. and Srikant, R. Privacy-preserving data mining. *SIGMOD Conference*, pp. 439–450, 2000.

Atluri, V. and Chun S. An authorization model for geospatial data. In: *IEEE Transactions on Dependable and Secure Computing* 1(4): 238–254, 2004.

Bertino, E., Digital identity management and protection. In: *Proceedings of the 2006 International Conference on Privacy, Security and Trust, Ontario, Canada*, 2006.

Bertino, E. and Musto, D. Integrity constraint processing during transaction processing. *Acta Informatica* 26(1–2): 25–57, 1988.

Bertino, E., Castano, S., Ferrari, F., and Mesiti, M. Protection and administration of XML data sources. *Data and Knowledge Engineering* 43(3): 237–260, 2002.

Carminati, B. et al. Security for RDF. In: *Proceedings of the DEXA Conference Workshop on Web Semantics*, Zaragoza, Spain, August 2004.

Date, C. *An Introduction to Database Systems*. Addison-Wesley, Reading, MA, 1990.

Dwyer, P. et al. Multilevel security for relational database systems. *Computers and Security* 6(3): 252–260, 1987.

Ferrari, E. and Thuraisingham, B. Secure database systems. In: *Advances in Database Management* (Editors: M. Piatini and O. Diaz). Artech House, UK, 2000.

Griffiths P. and Wade, B. An authorization mechanism for a relational database system. *ACM Transactions on Database Systems* 1(3): 242–255, 1976.

Kantarcioglu, M. and Clifton, C. Privacy-preserving distributed mining of association rules on horizontally partitioned data. *IEEE Transactions on Knowledge and Data Engineering* 16(9): 1026–1037, 2004.

National Science Foundation Workshop. Available at http://csi.utdallas.edu/events/NSF/NSF-workhop-Big -Data-SP-Feb9-2015_FINAL.pdf, 2014.

Park, J. and Sandhu, R. The UCON usage control model. *ACM Transactions on Information and Systems Security* 7(1): 128–174, 2004.

Sandhu R. et al. Role-based access control models. *IEEE Computer* 29(2): 38–47, 1996.

SQL. Available at en.wikipedia.org/wiki/SQL. American National Standards Institute, Draft, Maynard, MN, 1992.

Stonebraker, M. and Wong, E. Access control in a relational database management system by query modification. In: *Proceedings of the ACM Annual Conference*. ACM Press, New York, 1974.

Thuraisingham, B. Security checking in relational database management systems augmented with inference engines. *Computers and Security* 6(6): 479–492, 1987.

Thuraisingham, B. *Database Security, Integrating Database Systems and Information Security*. CRC Press, Boca Raton, FL, 2005a.

Thuraisingham, B. Privacy constraint processing in a privacy-enhanced database management system. *Data Knowledge and Engineering Journal* 55(2): 159–188, 2005b.

Thuraisingham, B. and Stachour, P. SQL extensions for security assertions. *Computer Standards and Interface Journal* 11(1), 1989.

Thuraisingham, B., Ford, W., and Collins, M. Design and implementation of a database inference controller. *Data and Knowledge Engineering* 11(3): 5–14, 1993.

4 Data Mining Techniques

4.1 INTRODUCTION

We have used data mining and analytics techniques in several of our efforts in social media. For example, in Section II, we discuss algorithms for location-based data mining that will extract the location of the various social media (e.g., Twitter) users. These algorithms can be extended to extract other demographics data. Our prior research has also developed data mining tools for sentiment analysis. In Section III, we illustrate how the various data mining techniques can be applied on social media data to extract sensitive information about the various individuals and consequently violate privacy. While we have described the various data mining techniques we have developed or utilized, in this chapter we provide some background information about general data mining techniques so that the reader can have an understanding of the field.

Data mining outcomes (also called tasks) include classification, clustering, forming associations, and detecting anomalies. Our tools have mainly focused on classification as the outcome, and we have developed classification tools. The classification problem is also referred to as supervised learning in which a set of labeled examples is learned by a model, and then a new example with unknown labels is presented to the model for prediction.

There are many prediction models that have been used, such as Markov model, decision trees, artificial neural networks (ANNs), support vector machines (SVMs), association rule mining (ARM), and many others. Each of these models has its strengths and weaknesses. However, there is a common weakness among all of these techniques, which is the inability to suit all applications. The reason that there is no such ideal or perfect classifier is that each of these techniques is initially designed to solve specific problems under certain assumptions.

In this chapter, we discuss the data mining techniques that have been commonly used. Specifically, we present the Markov model, SVM, ANN, ARM, the problem of multiclassification, and image classification, which is an aspect of image mining. In our research and development, we propose hybrid models to improve the prediction accuracy of data mining algorithms in various applications, namely, intrusion detection, social media analytics, World Wide Web (WWW) prediction, and image classification (Awad, 2009).

The organization of this chapter is as follows. In Section 4.2, we provide an overview of various data mining tasks and techniques. The techniques that are relevant to the contents of this book are discussed in Sections 4.3 through 4.8. In particular, neural networks, SVMs, Markov models, and ARM, and some other classification techniques, will be described. The chapter is summarized in Section 4.9.

4.2 OVERVIEW OF DATA MINING TASKS AND TECHNIQUES

Before we discuss data mining techniques, we provide an overview of some of the data mining tasks (also known as data mining outcomes). Then, we will discuss the techniques. In general, data mining tasks can be grouped into two categories: predictive and descriptive. Predictive tasks essentially predict whether an item belongs to a class or not. Descriptive tasks in general extract patterns from the examples. One of the most prominent predictive tasks is classification. In some cases, other tasks such as anomaly detection can be reduced to a predictive task such as whether a particular situation is an anomaly or not. Descriptive tasks in general include making associations and forming clusters.

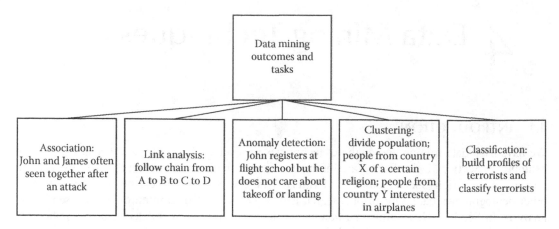

FIGURE 4.1   Data mining tasks.

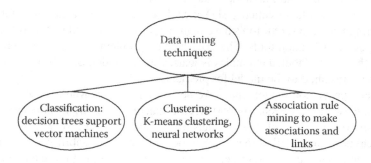

FIGURE 4.2   Data mining techniques.

Therefore, classification, anomaly detection, making associations, and forming clusters are also thought to be data mining tasks.

Next, the data mining techniques can be either be predictive or descriptive, or both. For example, neural networks can perform classification as well as clustering. Classification techniques include decision trees, SVM, and memory-based reasoning. ARM techniques are used in general to make associations. Link analysis can also make associations between links and predict new links. Clustering techniques include K-means clustering. An overview of the data mining tasks (i.e., the outcomes of data mining) is illustrated in Figure 4.1. The techniques (e.g., neural networks or SVMs) are illustrated in Figure 4.2.

4.3   ARTIFICIAL NEURAL NETWORKS

ANN is a very well-known, powerful, and robust classification technique that has been used to approximate real-valued, discrete-valued, and vector-valued functions from examples (Mitchell, 1997). ANNs have been used in many areas such as interpreting visual scenes, speech recognition, and learning robot control strategies. An ANN simulates the biological nervous system in the human brain. The nervous system is composed of a large number of highly interconnected processing units (neurons) working together to produce our feelings and reactions. ANNs, like people, learn by example. The learning process in the human brain involves adjustments to the synaptic connections between neurons. Similarly, the learning process of ANN involves adjustments to the node weights. Figure 4.3 presents a simple neuron unit, which is called a perceptron. The perceptron

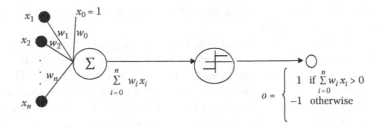

FIGURE 4.3 Perceptron.

input, x, is a vector or real-valued input. w is the weight vector whose value is determined after train-ing. The perceptron computes a linear combination of an input vector x as follows:

$$o(x_1,...,x_n) = \begin{cases} 1 & \text{if } w_0 + w_1x_1 + \cdots + w_nx_n > 0 \\ -1 & \text{otherwise} \end{cases} \tag{4.1}$$

Notice that w_i corresponds to the contribution of the input vector component x_i of the percep-tron output. Also, in order for the perceptron to output a 1, the weighted combination of the inputs $\left(\sum_{i=1}^{n} w_i x_i \right)$ must be greater than the threshold w_0.

Learning the perceptron involves choosing values for the weights $w_0 + w_1x_1 + ... + w_nx_n$. Initially, random weight values are given to the perceptron. Then, the perceptron is applied to each training example updating the weights of the perceptron whenever an example is misclassified. This process is repeated many times until all training examples are correctly classified. The weights are updated according to the following rule:

$$\begin{cases} w_i = w_i + \delta w_i \\ \delta w_i = \eta(t-o)x_i \end{cases} \tag{4.2}$$

where η is a learning constant, o is the output computed by the perceptron, and t is the target output for the current training example.

The computation power of a single perceptron is limited to linear decisions. However, the per-ceptron can be used as a building block to compose powerful multilayer networks. In this case, a more complicated updating rule is needed to train the network weights. In this work, we employ an ANN of two layers, and each layer is composed of three building blocks (see Figure 4.4). We use

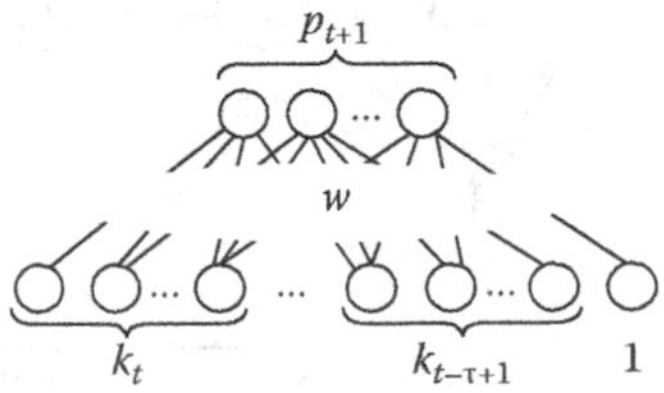

FIGURE 4.4 Artificial neural network.

the back-propagation algorithm for learning the weights. The back-propagation algorithm attempts to minimize the squared error function.

A typical training example in WWW prediction is $<[k_{t-\tau+1},\ldots,k_{t-1}, k_t]^T, d>$, where $[k_{t-\tau+1},\ldots,k_{t-1}, k_t]^T$ is the input to the ANN and d is the target web page. Notice that the input units of the ANN in Figure 4.5 are τ previous pages that the user has recently visited, where k is a web page ID. The output of the network is a Boolean value, not a probability. We will see later how to approximate the probability of the output by fitting a sigmoid function after ANN output. The approximated probabilistic output becomes $o' = f(o(I) = p_{t+1}$, where I is an input session and $p_{t+1} = p(d|k_{t-\tau+1},\ldots,k_t)$. We choose the sigmoid function (Equation 4.3) as a transfer function so that the ANN can handle nonlinearly separable data sets (Mitchell, 1997). Notice that in our ANN design (Figure 4.5), we use a sigmoid transfer function (Equation 4.3) in each building block. In Equation 4.3, I is the input to the network, O is the output of the network, W is the matrix of weights, and σ is the sigmoid function.

$$\begin{cases} o = \sigma(w.I) \\ \sigma(y) = \dfrac{1}{1+e^{-y}} \end{cases} \tag{4.3}$$

$$E(W) = \frac{1}{2}\sum_{k\in D}\sum_{i\in outputs}(t_{ik} - o_{ik})^2 \tag{4.4}$$

$$\begin{cases} w_{ji} = w_{ji} + \delta w_{ji} \\ \delta w_{ji} = -\eta\dfrac{\partial E_d}{\partial w_{ji}} \end{cases} \tag{4.5}$$

$$\delta w_{ji}(n) = -\eta\frac{\partial E_d}{\partial w_{ji}} + \alpha\delta w_{ji}(n-1) \tag{4.6}$$

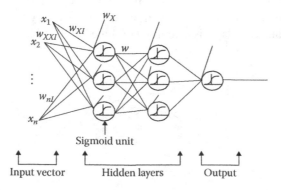

FIGURE 4.5   Design of ANN used in our implementation.

We implement the back-propagation algorithm for training the weights. The back-propagation algorithm employs gradient descent to attempt to minimize the squared error between the network output values and the target values of these outputs. The sum of the error over all of the network output units is defined in Equation 4.4. In Equation 4.4, the *outputs* is the set of output units in the network, D is the training set, and t_{ik} and o_{ik} are the target and the output values associated with the ith output unit and training example k. For a specific weight w_{ji} in the network, it is updated for each training example as in Equation 4.5, where η is the learning rate and w_{ji} is the weight associated with the ith input to the network unit j (for details, see Mitchell, 1997). As we can see from Equation 4.5, the search direction δw is computed using the gradient descent, which guarantees convergence toward a local minimum. To mitigate that, we add a momentum to the weight update rule such that the weight update direction $\delta w_{ji}(n)$ depends partially on the update direction in the previous iteration $\delta w_{ji}(n-1)$. The new weight update direction is shown in Equation 4.6, where n is the current iterations and α is the momentum constant. Notice that in Equation 4.6, the step size is slightly larger than in Equation 4.5. This contributes to a smooth convergence of the search in regions where the gradient is unchanging (Mitchell, 1997).

In our implementation, we set the step size η dynamically based on the distribution of the classes in the data set. Specifically, we set the step size to large values when updating the training examples that belong to low distribution classes and vice versa. This is because when the distribution of the classes in the data set varies widely (e.g., a data set might have 5% positive examples and 95% negative examples), the network weights converge toward the examples from the class of larger distribution, which causes a slow convergence. Furthermore, we adjust the learning rates slightly by applying the momentum constant (Equation 4.6) to speed up the convergence of the network (Mitchell, 1997).

4.4 SUPPORT VECTOR MACHINES

SVMs are learning systems that use a hypothesis space of linear functions in a high dimensional feature space, trained with a learning algorithm from optimization theory. This learning strategy, introduced by Vapnik et al. (Vapnik, 1995, 1998, 1999; Cristianini and Shawe-Taylor, 2000), is a very powerful method that has been applied in a wide variety of applications. The basic concept in SVM is the hyperplane classifier, or linear separability. To achieve linear separability, SVM applies two basic ideas—margin maximization and kernels, that is, mapping input space to a higher dimension space, feature space.

For binary classification, the SVM problem can be formalized as in Equation 4.7. Suppose we have N training data points $\{(x_1,y_1), (x_2,y_2), \ldots, (x_N,y_N)\}$, where $x_i \in R^d$ and $y_i \in \{+1, -1\}$. We would like to find a linear separating hyperplane classifier as in Equation 4.8. Furthermore, we want this hyperplane to have the maximum separating margin with respect to the two classes (see Figure 4.6).

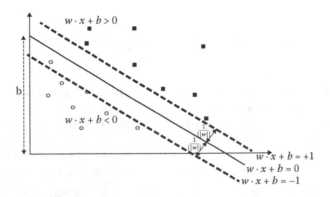

FIGURE 4.6 Linear separation in SVM.

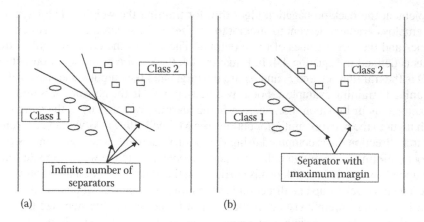

(a)   (b)

FIGURE 4.7   SVM separator that causes the maximum margin.

The functional margin, or the margin for short, is defined geometrically as the Euclidean distance of the closest point from the decision boundary to the input space. Figure 4.7 gives an intuitive explanation of why margin maximization gives the best solution of separation. In Figure 4.7a, we can find an infinite number of separators for a specific data set. There is no specific or clear reason to favor one separator over another. In Figure 4.7b, we see that maximizing the margin provides only one thick separator. Such a solution proves to achieve the best generalization accuracy, that is, prediction for the unseen (Vapnik, 1995, 1998, 1999).

$$\begin{cases} \text{minimize } (w,b) \dfrac{1}{2} w^T w \\ \\ \text{subject to } y_i (w \cdot x_i - b) \ge 1 \end{cases} \tag{4.7}$$

$$f(x) = \text{sign}(w \cdot x - b) \tag{4.8}$$

$$\text{maximize } L(w,b,\alpha) = \frac{1}{2} w^T w - \sum_{i=1}^{N} \alpha_i y_i (w \cdot x_i - b) + \sum_{i=1}^{N} \alpha_i \tag{4.9}$$

$$f(x) = \text{sign}(wx - b) = \text{sign}\left(\sum_{i=1}^{N} \alpha_i y_i (x \cdot x_i - b) \right) \tag{4.10}$$

Notice that Equation 4.8 computes the sign of the functional margin of point x in addition to the prediction label of x; that is, the functional margin of x equals $wx - b$.

The SVM optimization problem is a convex quadratic programming problem (in w, b) in a convex set (Equation 4.7). We can solve the Wolfe dual instead as in Equation 4.9 with respect to α, subject to the constraints that the gradient of $L(w, b, \alpha)$ with respect to the primal variables w and b vanish and $\alpha_i \ge 0$. The primal variables are eliminated from $L(w, b, \alpha)$ (see Cristianini and Shawe-Taylor, 2000, for more details). When we solve α_i, we can get $w = \sum_{i=1}^{N} \alpha_i y_i x_i$ and we can classify a new

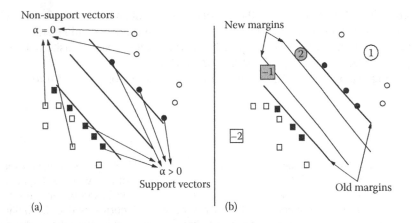

FIGURE 4.8   (a) Values of α_i for support vectors and non-support vectors. (b) Effect of adding new data points on the margins.

object x using Equation 4.10. Note that the training vectors occur only in the form of dot product, and that there is a Lagrangian multiplier α_i for each training point, which reflects the importance of the data point. When the maximal margin hyperplane is found, only points that lie closest to the hyperplane will have $\alpha_i > 0$, and these points are called *support vectors*. All other points will have $\alpha_i = 0$ (see Figure 4.8a). This means that only those points that lie closest to the hyperplane give the representation of the hypothesis/classifier. These most important data points serve as support vectors. Their values can also be used to give an independent boundary with regard to the reliability of the hypothesis/classifier (Bartlett and Shawe-Taylor, 1999).

Figure 4.8a shows two classes and their boundaries, that is, margins. The support vectors are represented by solid objects, while the empty objects are non-support vectors. Notice that the margins are only affected by the support vectors; that is, if we remove or add empty objects, the margins will not change. Meanwhile, any change in the solid objects, either adding or removing objects, could change the margins. Figure 4.8b shows the effects of adding objects in the margin area. As we can see, adding or removing objects far from the margins, for example, data point 1 or −2, does not change the margins. However, adding or removing objects near the margins, for example, data point 2 or −1, has created new margins.

4.5   MARKOV MODEL

Some recent and advanced predictive methods for web surfing are developed using Markov models (Pirolli et al., 1996; Yang et al., 2001). For these predictive models, the sequences of web pages visited by surfers are typically considered as Markov chains, which are then fed as input. The basic concept of the Markov model is that it predicts the next action depending on the result of previous action or actions. Actions can mean different things for different applications. For the purpose of illustration, we will consider actions specific for the WWW prediction application. In WWW prediction, the next action corresponds to prediction of the next page to be traversed. The previous actions correspond to the previous web pages to be considered. On the basis of the number of previous actions considered, Markov models can have different orders.

$$pr(P_k) = pr(S_k) \tag{4.11}$$

$$pr(P_2|P_1) = pr(S_2 = P_2|S_1 = P_1) \tag{4.12}$$

$$pr(P_N|P_{N-1},\ldots,P_{N-k}) = pr(S_N = P_N|S_{N-1} = P_{N-1},\ldots,S_{N-k} = P_{N-k}) \tag{4.13}$$

The zeroth-order Markov model is the unconditional probability of the state (or web page) (Equation 4.11). In Equation 4.11, P_k is a web page and S_k is the corresponding state. The first-order Markov model (Equation 4.12) can be computed by taking page-to-page transitional probabilities or the n-gram probabilities of $\{P_1, P_2\}, \{P_2, P_3\}, ..., \{P_{k-1}, P_k\}$.

In the following, we present an illustrative example of different orders of Markov model and how it can predict.

Example

Imagine a website of six web pages, P1, P2, P3, P4, P5, and P6. Suppose we have user sessions as in Table 4.1. Table 4.1 depicts the navigation of many users of that website. Figure 4.9 shows the *first-order Markov model*, where the next action is predicted based on only the last action performed, that is, last page traversed, by the user. States S and F correspond to the initial and final states, respectively. The probability of each transition is estimated by the ratio of the number of times the sequence of states was traversed and the number of times the anchor state was visited. Next to each arch in Figure 4.8, the first number is the frequency of that transition and the second number is the transition probability. For example, the transition probability of the transition (P2 to P3) is 0.2 because the number of times users traverse from page 2 to page 3 is 3, and the number of times page 2 is visited is 15 (i.e., 0.2 = 3/15).

Notice that the transition probability is used to resolve prediction. For example, given that a user has already visited P2, the most probable page she visits next is P6. That is because the transition probability from P2 to P6 is the highest.

Notice that that transition probability might not be available for some pages. For example, the transition probability from P2 to P5 is not available because no user has visited P5 after P2. Hence, these transition probabilities are set to zeros. Similarly, the Kth-order Markov model is where the prediction is computed after considering the last Kth action performed by the users

---

TABLE 4.1

Collection of User Sessions and Their Frequencies

Session	Frequency
P1,P2,P4	5
P1,P2,P6	1
P5,P2,P6	6
P5,P2,P3	3

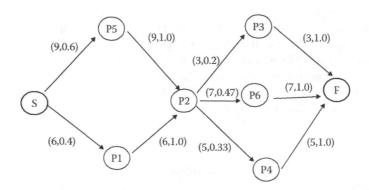

FIGURE 4.9   First-order Markov model.

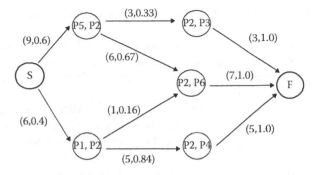

FIGURE 4.10 Second-order Markov model.

(Equation 4.13). In WWW prediction, the Kth-order Markov model is the probability of user visit to P_kth page given its previous $k - 1$ page visits.

Figure 4.10 shows the second-order Markov model that corresponds to Table 4.1. In the second-order model, we consider the last two pages. The transition probability is computed in a similar fashion. For example, the transition probability of the transition (P1, P2) to (P2, P6) is 0.16 = 1 × 1/6 because the number of times users traverse from state (P1, P2) to state (P2, P6) is 1 and the number of times pages (P1, P2) is visited is 6 (i.e., 0.16 = 1/6). The transition probability is used for prediction. For example, given that a user has visited P1 and P2, she most probably visits P4 because the transition probability from state (P1, P2) to state (P2, P4) is greater than the transition probability from state (P1, P2) to state (P2, P6).

The order of Markov model is related to the sliding window. The Kth order Markov model corresponds to a sliding window of size $K - 1$.

Notice that there is another concept that is similar to the sliding window concept, which is *number of hops*. In this chapter, we use *number of hops* and sliding window interchangeably.

In WWW prediction, Markov models are built on the basis of the concept of *n*-gram. The *n*-gram can be represented as a tuple of the form $<x_1, x_2, ..., x_n>$ to depict sequences of page clicks by a population of users surfing a website. Each component of the *n*-gram takes a specific page ID value that reflects the surfing path of a specific user surfing a web page. For example, the *n*-gram $<P_{10}, P_{21}, P_4, P_{12}>$ for some user U states that the user U has visited the pages 10, 21, 4, and finally page 12 in a sequence.

4.6 ASSOCIATION RULE MINING (ARM)

Association rules is a data mining technique that has been applied successfully to discover related transactions. The association rules technique finds the relationships among item sets based on their co-occurrence in the transactions. Specifically, ARM discovers the frequent patterns (regularities) among those items sets. For example, what are the items purchased together in a superstore? In the following, we briefly introduce ARM. For more details, see Agrawal et al. (1993) and Agrawal and Srikant (1994).

Assume we have m items in our database; define $I = \{i_1, i_2, ..., i_m\}$ as the set of all items. A transaction T is a set of items such that $T \subseteq I$. Let D be the set of all transactions in the database. A transaction T contains X if $X \subseteq T$ and $X \subseteq I$. An association rule is an implication of the form $X \to Y$, where, $X \subset I$, $Y \subset I$, and $X \cap Y = \phi$. There are two parameters to consider a rule: confidence and support. A rule $R = X \to Y$ holds with confidence c if $c\%$ of the transactions of D that contain X also contain Y (i.e., $c = pr(Y|X)$). The rule R holds with support s if $s\%$ of the transactions in D contain X and Y (i.e., $s = pr(X,Y)$). The problem of mining association rules is defined as follows: given a set of transactions D, we would like to generate all rules that satisfy a confidence and a support greater than a minimum confidence (σ), minconf, and minimum support (ϑ), minsup. There are several efficient algorithms proposed to find association rules such as the AIS algorithm (Agrawal et al.,

1993; Agrawal and Srikant, 1994), SETM algorithm (Houtsma and Swanu, 1995), and AprioriTid (Liu et al., 1999).

In the case of web transactions, we use association rules to discover navigational patterns among users. This would help to cache a page in advance and reduce the loading time of a page. Also, discovering a pattern of navigation helps in personalization. Transactions are captured from the clickstream data captured in web server logs.

In many applications, there is one main problem in using ARM. First, a problem with using global minimum support (minsup), because rare hits, that is, web pages that are rarely visited, will not be included in the frequent sets because it will not achieve enough support. One solution is to have a very small support threshold; however, we will end up with very large frequent item sets, which are computationally difficult to handle. Liu et al. (1999) propose a mining technique that uses different support thresholds for different items. Specifying multiple thresholds allow rare transactions that might be very important to be included in the frequent item sets. Other issues might arise depending on the application itself. For example, in case of WWW prediction, a session is recorded for each user. The session might have tens of clickstreams (and sometimes hundreds, depending on the duration of the session). Using each session as a transaction will not work because it is rare to find two sessions that are frequently repeated (i.e., identical); hence, it will not achieve even a very high support threshold, minsup. There is a need to break each session into many subsequences. One common method is to use a sliding window of size w. For example, suppose we use a sliding window $w = 3$ to break the session $S = <A,B,C,D,E,F>$; then, we will end up with the subsequences $S' = \{<A,B,C>, <B,C,D>, <C,D,E>, <D,E,F>\}$. The total number of subsequences of a session S using window w is length(S) − w. To predict the next page in an active user session, we use a sliding window of the active session and ignore the previous pages. For example, if the current session is $<A,B,C>$, and the user references page D, then the new active session becomes $<B,C,D>$, using a sliding window 3. Notice that page A is dropped, and $<B,C,D>$ will be used for prediction. The rationale behind this is because most users go back and forth while surfing the web, trying to find the desired information, and it may be most appropriate to use the recent portions of the user history to generate recommendations/predictions (Mobasher et al., 2001).

Mobasher et al. (2001) propose a recommendation engine that matches an active user session with the frequent item sets in the database and predicts the next page the user most probably visits. The engine works as follows. Given an active session of size w, the engine finds all the frequent item sets of length $w + 1$ satisfying some minimum support, minsup, and containing the current active session. Prediction for the active session A is based on the confidence (ψ) of the corresponding association rule. The confidence (ψ) of an association rule $X \rightarrow z$ is defined as $\psi(X \rightarrow z) = \sigma(X \cup z)/\sigma(X)$, where the length of z is 1. Page p is recommended/predicted for an active session A, iff

$$\forall V, R \text{ in the frequent itemsets,}$$

$$\text{length}(R) = \text{length}(V) = \text{length}(A) + 1\wedge$$

$$R = A \cup \{p\} \wedge$$

$$V = A \cup \{q\} \wedge$$

$$\psi(A \rightarrow p) > \psi(A \rightarrow q)$$

The engine uses a cyclic graph called Frequent Item Set Graph. The graph is an extension of the lexicographic tree used in the tree projection algorithm of Agrawal et al. (2001). The graph is organized in levels. The nodes in level *l* have item sets of size of *l*. For example, the sizes of the nodes (i.e., the size of the item sets corresponding to these nodes) in levels 1 and 2 are 1 and 2, respectively. The root of the graph, level 0, is an empty node corresponding to an empty item set. A node *X* in level *l* is linked to a node *Y* in level *l* + 1 if $X \subset Y$. To further explain the process, suppose we have the following sample web transactions involving pages 1, 2, 3, 4, and 5 as in Table 4.2. The Apriori algorithm produces the item sets as in Table 4.3, using a minsup = 0.49. The Frequent Item Set Graph is shown in Figure 4.11.

Suppose we are using a sliding window of size 2, and the current active session A = <2,3>. To predict/recommend the next page, we first start at level 2 in the Frequent Item Set Graph, and extract all the item sets in level 3 linked to A. From Figure 4.11, the node {2,3} is linked to {1,2,3} and {2,3,5} nodes with confidence:

$$\psi(\{2,3\} \to 1) = \sigma(\{1,2,3\}/\sigma(\{2,3\}) = 5/5 = 1.0$$
$$\psi(\{2,3\} \to 5) = \sigma(\{2,3,5\}/\sigma(\{2,3\}) = 4/5 = 0.8$$

and the recommended page is 1 because its confidence is larger. Notice that, in recommendation engines, the order of the clickstream is not considered; that is, there is no distinction between a session <1,2,4> and <1,4,2>. This is a disadvantage of such systems because the order of pages visited might bear important information about the navigation patterns of users.

TABLE 4.2
Sample Web Transaction

Transaction ID	Items
T1	1,2,4,5
T2	1,2,5,3,4
T3	1,2,5,3
T4	2,5,2,1,3
T5	4,1,2,5,3
T6	1,2,3,4
T7	4,5
T8	4,5,3,1

TABLE 4.3
Frequent Item Sets Generated by the Apriori Algorithm

Size 1	Size 2	Size 3	Size 4
{2}(6)	{2,3}(5)	{2,3,1}(5)	{2,3,1,5}(4)
{3}(6)	{2,4}(4)	{2,3,5}(4)	
{4}(6)	{2,1}(6)	{2,4,1}(4)	
{1}(7)	{2,5}(5)	{2,1,5}(5)	
{5}(7)	{3,4}(4)	{3,4,1}(4)	
	{3,1}(6)	{3,1,5}(5)	
	{3,5}(5)	{4,1,5}(4)	
	{4,1}(5)		
	{4,5}(5)		
	{1,5}(6)		

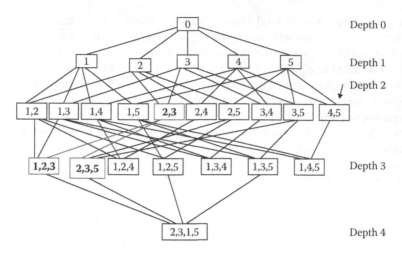

FIGURE 4.11   Frequent item set graph.

4.7   MULTICLASS PROBLEM

Most classification techniques solve the binary classification problem. Binary classifiers are accumulated to generalize for the multiclass problem. There are two basic schemes for this generalization, namely, one-versus-one and one-versus-all. To avoid redundancy, we will present this generalization only for SVM.

One-versus-One. The one-versus-one approach creates a classifier for each pair of classes. The training set for each pair classifier (i,j) includes only those instances that belong to either class i or j. A new instance x belongs to the class upon which most pair classifiers agree. The prediction decision is quoted from the majority vote technique. There are $n(n-1)/2$ classifiers to be computed, where n is the number of classes in the data set. It is evident that the disadvantage of this scheme is that we need to generate a large number of classifiers, especially if there are a large number of classes in the training set. For example, if we have a training set of 1000 classes, we need 499,500 classifiers. On the other hand, the size of the training set for each classifier is small because we exclude all instances that do not belong to that pair of classes.

One-versus-All. One-versus-all creates a classifier for each class in the data set. The training set is preprocessed such that for a classifier j, instances that belong to class j are marked as class (+1) and instances that do not belong to class j are marked as class (−1). In the one-versus-all scheme, we compute n classifiers, where n is the number of pages that users have visited (at the end of each session). A new instance x is predicted by assigning it to the class that its classifier outputs the largest positive value (i.e., maximal marginal), as in Equation 4.15. We can compute the margin of point x as in Equation 4.14. Notice that the recommended/predicted page is the sign of the margin value of that page (see Equation 4.10).

$$f(x) = wx - b = \sum_{i}^{N} \alpha_i y_i (x \cdot x_i - b) \qquad (4.14)$$

$$\text{Prediction}(x) = \arg\max_{1 \le c \le M} f_c(x) \qquad (4.15)$$

In Equation 4.15, M is the number of classes, $x = <x_1, x_2, ..., x_n>$ is the user session, and f_i is the classifier that separates class i from the rest of the classes. The prediction decision in Equation 4.15 resolves to the classifier f_c that is the most distant from the testing example x. This might be explained as f_c has the most separating power, among all other classifiers, of separating x from the rest of the classes.

The advantage of this scheme (one-versus-all), compared with the one-versus-one scheme, is that it has fewer classifiers. On the other hand, the size of the training set is larger for one-versus-all than for a one-versus-one scheme because we use the whole original training set to compute each classifier.

4.8 IMAGE MINING

4.8.1 Overview

Along with the development of digital images and computer storage technologies, huge amounts of digital images are generated and saved every day. Applications of digital image have rapidly penetrated many domains and markets, including commercial and news media photo libraries, scientific and nonphotographic image databases, and medical image databases. As a consequence, we face a daunting problem of organizing and accessing these huge amounts of available images. An efficient image retrieval system is highly desired to find images of specific entities from a database. The system expected can manage a huge collection of images efficiently, respond to users' queries with high speed and deliver a minimum of irrelevant information (high precision), as well as ensure that relevant information is not overlooked (high recall).

To generate such kinds of systems, people tried many different approaches. In the early 1990s, because of the emergence of large image collections, content-based image retrieval (CBIR) was proposed. CBIR computes relevance based on the similarity of visual content/low-level image features such as color histograms, textures, shapes, and spatial layout. However, the problem is that visual similarity is not semantic similarity. There is a gap between low-level visual features and semantic meanings. The so-called semantic gap is the major problem that needs to be solved for most CBIR approaches. For example, a CBIR system may answer a query request for a "red ball" with an image of a "red rose." If we undertake the annotation of images with keywords, a typical way to publish an image data repository is to create a keyword-based query interface addressed to an image database. If all images came with a detailed and accurate description, image retrieval would be convenient based on current powerful pure text search techniques. These search techniques would retrieve the images if their descriptions/annotations contained some combination of the keywords specified by the user. However, the major problem is that most of images are not annotated. It is a laborious, error-prone, and subjective process to manually annotate a large collection of images. Many images contain the desired semantic information, even though they do not contain the user-specified keywords. Furthermore, keyword-based search is useful especially to a user who knows what keywords are used to index the images and who can therefore easily formulate queries. This approach is problematic, however, when the user does not have a clear goal in mind, does not know what is in the database, and does not know what kind of semantic concepts are involved in the domain.

Image mining is a more challenging research problem than retrieving relevant images in CBIR systems. The goal of image mining is to find an image pattern that is significant for a given set of images and helpful to understand the relationships between high-level semantic concepts/descriptions and low-level visual features. Our focus is on aspects such as feature selection and image classification. It should be noted that image mining and analytics is important for social media as the members post numerous images. These images could be used to embed messages that could penetrate into computing systems. Such social media attacks are discussed in Section IX. Images in social media could also be analyzed to extract various demographics such as location.

4.8.2 Feature Selection

Usually, data saved in databases is with well-defined semantics, such as numbers or structured data entries. In comparison, data with ill-defined semantics is unstructured data. For example, images, audio, and video are data with ill-defined semantics. In the domain of image processing, images are represented by derived data or features such as color, texture, and shape. Many of these features have multivalues (e.g., color histogram and moment description). When people generate these derived data or features, they generally generate as many features as possible, since they are not aware which feature is more relevant. Therefore, the dimensionality of derived image data is usually very high. Actually, some of the selected features might be duplicated or may not even be relevant to the problem. Including irrelevant or duplicated information is referred to as noise. Such problems are referred to as the "curse of dimensionality." Feature selection is the research topic for finding an optimal subset of features. In this chapter, we will discuss this curse and feature selection in detail.

We developed a wrapper-based simultaneous feature weighing and clustering algorithm. Clustering algorithm will bundle similar image segments together and generate a finite set of visual symbols (i.e., blob token). On the basis of histogram analysis and χ^2 value, we assign features of image segments different weights instead of removing some of them. Feature weight evaluation is wrapped in a clustering algorithm. In each iteration of the algorithm, feature weights of image segments are reevaluated on the basis of the clustering result. The reevaluated feature weights will affect the clustering results in the next iteration.

4.8.3 Automatic Image Annotation

Automatic image annotation is research concerned with object recognition, where the effort is concerned with trying to recognize objects in an image and generate descriptions for the image according to semantics of the objects. If it is possible to produce accurate and complete semantic descriptions for an image, we can store descriptions in an image database. On the basis of a textual description, more functionality (e.g., browse, search, and query) of an image database management system could be implemented easily and efficiently by applying many existing text-based search techniques. Unfortunately, the automatic image annotation problem has not been solved in general, and perhaps this problem is impossible to solve.

However, in certain subdomains, it is still possible to obtain some interesting results. Many statistical models have been published for image annotation. Some of these models took feature dimensionality into account and applied singular value decomposition or principal component analysis to reduce dimension. However, none of them considered feature selection or feature weight. We propose a new framework for image annotation based on a translation model. In our approach, we applied our weighted feature selection algorithm and embedded it in image annotation framework. Our weighted feature selection algorithm improves the quality of visual tokens and generates better image annotations.

4.8.4 Image Classification

Image classification is an important area, especially in the medical domain, because it helps in managing large medical image databases and has great potential on diagnostic aid in a real-world clinical setting. We describe our experiments for the image CLEF medical image retrieval task. Sizes of classes of CLEF medical image data set are not balanced, which is a serious problem for all classification algorithms. To solve this problem, we resample data by generating subwindows. The K nearest neighbor (KNN) algorithm, distance weighted KNN, fuzzy KNN, nearest prototype classifier, and evidence theory–based KNN are implemented and studied. Results show that evidence-based KNN has the best performance based on classification accuracy.

4.9 SUMMARY

In this chapter, we first provided an overview of the various data mining tasks and techniques and then discussed some of the techniques that we will utilize in this book. These include neural networks, SVM, and ARM. We have utilized a combination of these techniques together with some other techniques in the literature, as well as our own techniques, to develop data analytics techniques for social media. These techniques are discussed in Sections III, V, VI, VII, and VIII.

Numerous data mining techniques have been designed and developed, and many of them are being utilized in commercial tools. Several of these techniques are variations of some of the basic classification, clustering, and ARM techniques. One of the major challenges today is to determine the appropriate techniques for various applications. We still need more benchmarks and performance studies. In addition, the techniques should result in fewer false positives and negatives. While there is still much to be done, the progress over the last decade is extremely promising.

REFERENCES

Agrawal, R., Imielinski, T., and Swami, A. Mining association rules between sets of items in large database. In: *Proceedings of the ACM SIGMOD Conference on Management of Data*, Washington, DC, May, pp. 207–216, 1993.

Agrawal, R. and Srikant, R. Fast algorithms for mining association rules in large database. In: *Proceedings of the 20th International Conference on Very Large Data Bases*, San Francisco, pp. 487–499, 1994.

Agrawal, R., Aggarawal, C., and Prasad, V. A tree projection algorithm for generation of frequent item sets. *Journal of Parallel and Distributed Computing Archive* 61(3): 350–371, 2001.

Awad, M., Khan, L., Thuraisingham, B., and Wang, L. *Design and Implementation of Data Mining Tools*. CRC Press, Boca Raton, FL, 2009.

Bartlett, P. and Shawe-Taylor, J. Generalization performance of support vector machines and other pattern classifiers. In: *Advances in Kernel Methods—Support Vector Learning*. MIT Press, Cambridge, MA, pp. 43–54, 1999.

Cristianini, N. and Shawe-Taylor, J. *Introduction to Support Vector Machines*, 1st Ed. Cambridge University Press, Cambridge, pp. 93–122, 2000.

Houtsma, M. and Swanu, A. Set-oriented mining of association rules in relational databases. In: *Proceedings of the Eleventh International Conference on Data Engineering*, Washington, DC, pp. 25–33, 1995.

Liu, B., Hsu, W., and Ma, Y. Mining association rules with multiple minimum supports. In: *Proceedings of the Fifth ACM SIGKDD International Conference on Knowledge Discovery and Data Mining*, San Diego, CA, pp. 337–341, 1999.

Mitchell, T.M. Artificial Neural Networks. In: *Machine Learning*, McGraw-Hill, Boston, 1997.

Mobasher, B., Dai, H., Luo, T., and Nakagawa, M. Effective personalization based on association rule discovery from web usage data. In: *Proceedings of the ACM Workshop on Web Information and Data Management (WIDM01)*, pp. 9–15, 2001.

Pirolli, P., Pitkow, J., and Rao, R. Silk from a sow's ear: Extracting usable structures from the web. In: *Proceedings of 1996 Conference on Human Factors in Computing Systems (CHI-96)*, Vancouver, British Columbia, Canada, pp. 118–125, 1996.

Vapnik, V.N. *The Nature of Statistical Learning Theory*, 1st Ed. Springer-Verlag, New York, 1995.

Vapnik, V.N. *Statistical Learning Theory*. Wiley, New York, 1998.

Vapnik, V.N. *The Nature of Statistical Learning Theory*, 2nd Ed. Springer-Verlag, New York, 1999.

Yang, Q., Zhang, H., and Li, T. Mining web logs for prediction models in WWW caching and prefetching. In: *The 7th ACM SIGKDD International Conference on Knowledge Discovery and Data Mining KDD*, August 26–29, pp. 473–478, 2001.

5 Cloud Computing and Semantic Web Technologies

5.1 INTRODUCTION

Chapters 2, 3, and 4 have discussed concepts in social networks, data security and privacy, and data mining. These three supporting technologies lay the foundations for the concepts discussed in this book. For example, Section II describes social network analytics where we integrate data mining with social network technologies. Section III describes access control for social networks and privacy violations that could occur in social networks due to data mining. That is, we integrate social networks, data mining, and data privacy in Section III. Security aspects are discussed in Section IV. In this chapter, we discuss two additional technologies that we have used in several of the chapters in this book. They are cloud computing and semantic web technologies. While these two technologies are not foundational technologies, for Sections III, IV, and V of this book, an understanding of these technologies is essential for the experimental systems we have developed, to be discussed in Sections VI, VII, and VIII.

Cloud computing has emerged as a powerful computing paradigm for service-oriented computing. Many of the computing services are being outsourced to the cloud. Such cloud-based services can be used to host the various social networks. Another concept that is being used for a variety of applications is the notion of the semantic web. A semantic web is essentially a collection of technologies to produce machine-understandable web pages. These technologies can also be used to represent any type of data, including social media data. We have based many of our analytics and security investigation on social networks represented using semantic web data.

The organization of this chapter is as follows. Section 5.2 discusses cloud computing concepts. Semantic web concepts are discussed in Section 5.3. Semantic web and security concepts are discussed in Section 5.4. Cloud computing frameworks based on the semantic web are discussed in Section 5.5. The chapter is concluded in Section 5.6. Figure 5.1 illustrates the concepts discussed in this chapter.

5.2 CLOUD COMPUTING

5.2.1 OVERVIEW

The emerging cloud computing model attempts to address the growth of web-connected devices and handle massive amounts of data. Google has now introduced the MapReduce framework for processing large amounts of data on commodity hardware. Apache's Hadoop Distributed File System (HDFS; http://hadoop.apache.org/) is emerging as a superior software component for cloud computing, combined with integrated parts such as MapReduce (Dean and Ghemawat, 2004). Clouds such as HP's Open Cirrus Testbed are utilizing HDFS. This, in turn, has resulted in numerous social networking sites with massive amounts of data to be shared and managed. For example, we may want to analyze multiple years of stock market data statistically to reveal a pattern or to build a reliable weather model based on several years of weather and related data. To handle such massive amounts of data distributed at many sites (i.e., nodes), scalable hardware and software components are needed. The cloud computing model has emerged to address the explosive growth of web-connected devices, and handle massive amounts of data. It is defined and characterized by massive scalability and new Internet-driven economics.

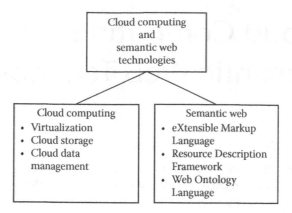

FIGURE 5.1 Cloud computing and semantic web technologies.

In this chapter, we will discuss some preliminaries in cloud computing and the semantic web. We will first introduce what is meant by cloud computing. While various definitions have been proposed, we will adopt the definition provided by the National Institute of Standards and Technology (NIST). This will be followed by a service-based paradigm for cloud computing. Next, we will discuss the various key concepts, including virtualization and data storage in the cloud. We will also discuss some of the technologies such as Hadoop and MapReduce.

The organization of this section is as follows. Cloud computing preliminaries will be discussed in Section 5.2.2. Virtualization will be discussed in Section 5.2.3. Cloud storage and data management issues will be discussed in Section 5.2.4. Cloud computing tools will be discussed in Section 5.2.5. Figure 5.2 illustrates the components addressed in this section.

5.2.2 PRELIMINARIES

As stated in Wikipedia (http://en.wikipedia.org/wiki/Cloud_computing), cloud computing delivers computing as a service, while in traditional computing it is provided in the form of a product. Therefore, users pay for the services based on a pay-as-you-go model. The services provided by a cloud may include hardware services, systems services, data services, and storage services. Users of the cloud need not know where the software and data are located; that is, the software and data services provided by the cloud are transparent to the user. The NIST has defined cloud computing as follows (http://csrc.nist.gov/publications/nistpubs/800-145/SP800-145.pdf):

> Cloud computing is a model for enabling ubiquitous, convenient, on-demand network access to a shared pool of configurable computing resources (e.g., networks, servers, storage, applications, and services) that can be rapidly provisioned and released with minimal management effort or service provider interaction.

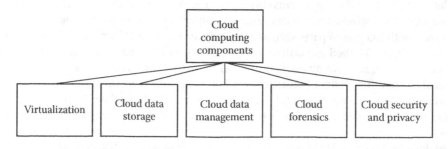

FIGURE 5.2 Cloud computing components.

The cloud model is composed of multiple deployment models and service models. These models are described next.

Cloud Deployment Models. There are multiple deployment models for cloud computing. These include the public cloud, community cloud, hybrid cloud, and the private cloud. In a public cloud, the service provider typically provides the services over the World Wide Web that can be accessed by the general public. Such a cloud may provide free services or pay-as-you-go services. In a community cloud, a group of organizations get together and develop a cloud. These organizations may have a common objective to provide features such as security and fault tolerance. The cost is shared among the organizations. Furthermore, the cloud may be hosted by the organizations or by a third party. A private cloud is a cloud infrastructure developed specifically for an organization. This could be hosted by the organization or by a third party. A hybrid cloud consists a combination of public and private clouds. This way, in a hybrid cloud, an organization may use the private cloud for highly sensitive services, while it may use the public cloud for less sensitive services and take advantage of what the World Wide Web has to offer. Khadilkar et al. (2012a) have stated that the hybrid cloud is the deployment model of the future. Figure 5.3 illustrates the cloud deployment models.

Service Models. As stated earlier, cloud computing provides a variety of services. These include Infrastructure as a Service (IaaS), Platform as a Service (PaaS), Software as a Service (SaaS), and Data as a Service (DaaS). In IaaS, the cloud provides a collection of hardware and networks for use by the general public or organizations. The users install operating systems and software to run the applications. The users will be billed according to the resources they utilize for their computing. In PaaS, the cloud provider will provide to their users the systems software such as operating systems (OSs) and execution environments. The users will load their applications and run them on the hardware and software infrastructures provided by the cloud. In SaaS, the cloud provider will provide the applications for the users to run. These applications could be, say, billing applications, tax computing applications, and sales tools. The cloud users access the applications through cloud clients. In the case of DaaS, the cloud provides data to the cloud users. Data may be stored in data centers that are accessed by the cloud users. Note that while DaaS was used to denote Desktop as a Service, more recently it denotes Data as a Service. Figure 5.4 illustrates the service models.

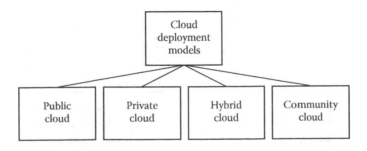

FIGURE 5.3   Cloud deployment models.

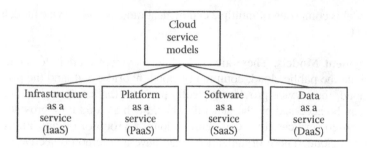

FIGURE 5.4   Cloud service models.

5.2.3 Virtualization

Virtualization essentially means creating something virtual and not actual. It could be hardware, software, memory, or data. The notion of virtualization has existed for decades with respect to computing. Back in the 1960s, the concept of virtual memory was introduced. This virtual memory gives the application program the illusion that is has contiguous working memory. Mapping is developed to map the virtual memory to the actual physical memory.

Hardware virtualization is a basic notion in cloud computing. This essentially creates virtual machines hosted on a real computer with an OS. This means while the actual machine may be running a Windows OS, through virtualization it may provide a Linux machine to the users. The actual machine is called the host machine, while the virtual machine is called the guest machine. The term *virtual machine monitor*, also known as the *hypervisor*, is the software that runs the virtual machine on the host computer.

Other types of virtualization include OS level virtualization, storage virtualization, data virtualization, and database virtualization. In OS level virtualization, multiple virtual environments are created within a single OS. In storage virtualization, the logical storage is abstracted from the physical storage. In data virtualization, the data is abstracted from the underlying databases. In network virtualization, a virtual network is created. Figure 5.5 illustrates the various types of virtualizations.

As we have stated earlier, at the heart of cloud computing is the notion of hypervisor or the virtual machine monitor. Hardware virtualization techniques allow multiple OSs (called guests) to run concurrently on a host computer. These multiple OSs share virtualized hardware resources. Hypervisor is not a new term; it was first used in the mid-1960s in the IBM 360/65 machines. There are different types of hypervisors; in one type, the hypervisor runs on the host hardware and manages the guest OSs. Both VMware and XEN, which are popular virtual machines, are based on this model. In another model, the hypervisor runs within a conventional

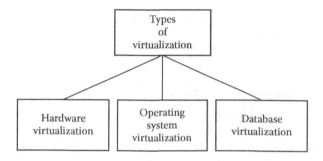

FIGURE 5.5   Types of virtualization.

OS environment. Virtual machines are also incorporated into embedded systems and mobile phones. Embedded hypervisors have real-time processing capability. Some details of virtualization are provided on the VMWare website (http://www.vmware.com/virtualization/virtualiza tion-management.html).

5.2.4   CLOUD STORAGE AND DATA MANAGEMENT

In a cloud storage model, the service providers store massive amounts of data for customers in data centers. Those who require storage space will lease the storage from the service providers who are the hosting companies. The actual location of the data is transparent to the users. What is presented to the users is virtualized storage; the storage managers will map the virtual storage with the actual storage and manage the data resources for the customers. A single object (e.g., the entire video database of a customer) may be stored in multiple locations. Each location may store objects for multiple customers. Figure 5.6 illustrates cloud storage management.

Virtualizing cloud storage has many advantages. Users need not purchase expensive storage devices. Data could be placed anywhere in the cloud. Maintenance such as backup and recovery are provided by the cloud. The goal is for users to have rapid access to the cloud. However, because the owner of the data does not have complete control of his data, there are serious security concerns with respect to storing data in the cloud.

A database that runs on the cloud is a cloud database manager. There are multiple ways to utilize a cloud database manager. In the first model, for users to run databases on the cloud, a Virtual Machine Image must be purchased. The database is then run on the virtual machines. The second model is the Database as a Service model; the service provider will maintain the databases. The users will make use of the database services and pay for the service. An example is the Amazon Relational Database Service (http://aws.amazon.com/rds/), which is an SQL database service and has a MySQL interface. A third model is the cloud provider, which hosts a database on behalf of the user. Users can either utilize the database service maintained by the cloud or they can run their databases on the cloud. A cloud database must optimize its query, storage, and transaction processing to take full advantage of the services provided by the cloud. Figure 5.7 illustrates cloud data management.

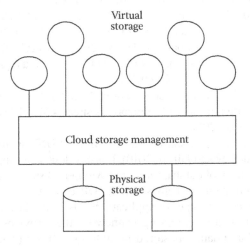

FIGURE 5.6   Cloud storage management.

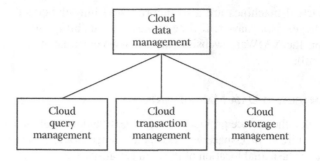

FIGURE 5.7   Cloud data management.

5.2.5   CLOUD COMPUTING TOOLS

Processing large volumes of provenance data require sophisticated methods and tools. In recent years, cloud computing tools, such as cloud-enabled NoSQL systems, MongoDB, CouchDB, and frameworks such as Hadoop offer appealing alternatives and great promises for systems with high availability, scalability, and elasticity (Anderson et al., 2010; Cattell, 2011; Chodorow and Dirolf, 2010; White, 2010). In this section, we will briefly survey these systems and their applicability and usefulness for processing large-scale data sets.

 Apache Hadoop. Apache Hadoop is an open source software framework that allows batch-processing tasks to be performed on vast quantities of data (White, 2010). Hadoop uses the HDFS, a Java-based open source distributed file system that employs the Google File System as its underlying storage mechanism. HDFS provides several advantages such as data replication and fault tolerance (Ghemawat et al., 2003). HDFS uses a master/slave architecture that consists of a single NameNode process (running on the master node) and several DataNode processes (usually one per slave node).

 MapReduce. A MapReduce job consists of three phases: (i) A "map" phase in which each slave node performs some computation on the data blocks of the input that it has stored. The output of this phase is a key–value pair based on the computation that is performed. (ii) An intermediate "sort" phase in which the output of the map phase is sorted based on keys. (iii) A "reduce" phase in which a reducer aggregates various values for a shared key and then further processes them before producing the desired result.

 CouchDB. Apache CouchDB is a distributed, document-oriented database that can be queried and indexed in a MapReduce fashion (Anderson et al., 2010). Data is managed as a collection of Javascript object notation (JSON) documents (Crockford, 2006). Users can access the documents with a web browser, via HTTP as well as querying, combining, and transforming documents with JavaScript.

 HBase. Apache HBase is a distributed, versioned, column-oriented store modeled after Google's Bigtable, written in Java. Organizations such as Mendeley, Facebook, and Adobe are using HBase (George, 2011).

 MongoDB. MongoDB is an open source, schema-free (JSON) document-oriented database written in C++ (Chodorow and Dirolf, 2010). It is developed and supported by 10gen and is part of the NoSQL family of database systems. MongoDB stores structured data as JSON-like documents with dynamic schemas (MongoDB calls the format BSON), making the integration of data in certain types of applications easier and faster.

 Hive. Apache Hive is a data warehousing framework that provides the ability to manage, query, and analyze large data sets stored in HDFS or HBase (Thusoo et al., 2010). Hive provides basic tools to perform Extract–Transfer–Load (ETL) operations over data, project structure onto the extracted data, and query the structured data using an SQL-like language called HiveQL. HiveQL performs query execution using the MapReduce paradigm, while allowing advanced Hadoop programmers to plug in their custom built MapReduce programs to perform advanced analytics not supported by the language. Some of the design goals of Hive include dynamic scale-out, user-defined analytics, fault tolerance, and loose coupling with input formats.

Apache Cassandra. Apache Cassandra is an open source distributed database management system (Hewitt, 2010). Apache Cassandra is a fault-tolerant, distributed data store that offers linear scalability, allowing it to be a storage platform for large high-volume websites. Cassandra is designed to handle big data workloads across multiple nodes with no single point of failure. Its architecture is based on the understanding that system and hardware failures can and do occur.

5.3   SEMANTIC WEB

While the current web technologies facilitate the integration of information from a syntactic point of view, there is still a lot to be done to handle the different semantics of various systems and applications. That is, current web technologies depend a lot on the "human-in-the-loop" for information management and integration. Tim Berners-Lee, the father of the World Wide Web, realized the inadequacies of current web technologies and subsequently strived to make the web more intelligent. His goal was to have a web that would essentially alleviate humans from the burden of having to integrate disparate information sources, as well as to carry out extensive searches. He then came to the conclusion that one needs machine-understandable web pages and the use of ontologies for information integration. This resulted in the notion of the semantic web (Berners-Lee et al., 2001). The web services that take advantage of semantic web technologies are semantic web services.

A semantic web can be thought of as a web that is highly intelligent and sophisticated so that one needs little or no human intervention to carry out tasks such as scheduling appointments, coordinating activities, searching for complex documents, as well as integrating disparate databases and information systems. While much progress has been made toward developing such an intelligent web, there is still a lot to be done. For example, technologies such as ontology matching, intelligent agents, and markup languages are contributing a lot toward developing the semantic web. Nevertheless, one still needs the human to make decisions and take actions. Since the 2000s, there have been many developments on the semantic web. The World Wide Web consortium (W3C; www .w3c.org) is specifying standards for the semantic web. These standards include specifications for XML (eXtensible Markup Language), RDF (Resource Description Framework), and interoperability.

Figure 5.8 illustrates the layered technology stack for the semantic web. This is the stack that was developed by Tim Berners-Lee. Essentially, the semantic web consists of layers where each layer takes advantage of the technologies of the previous layer. The lowest layer is the protocol

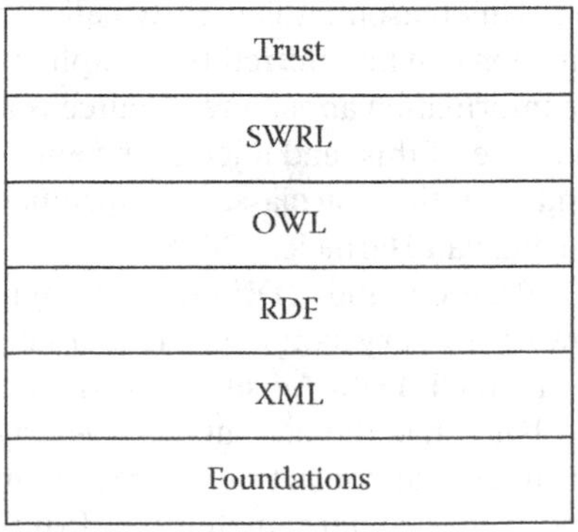

Trust
SWRL
OWL
RDF
XML
Foundations

FIGURE 5.8   Technology stack for the semantic web.

layer, and this is usually not included in the discussion of the semantic technologies. The next layer is the XML layer. XML is a document representation language. While XML is sufficient to specify syntax, semantics such as "the creator of document D is John" is difficult to specify in XML. Therefore, the W3C developed RDF, which uses XML syntax. The semantic web community then went further and came up with a specification of ontologies in languages such as OWL (Web Ontology Language). Note that OWL addresses the inadequacies of RDF. To reason about various policies, the semantic web community has come up with web rules language such as SWRL (Semantic Web Rule Language). Next, we will describe the various technologies that constitute the semantic web.

XML. XML is needed due to the limitations of HTML (Hypertext Markup Language) and complexities of SGML (Standard Generalized Markup Language). XML is an extensible markup language specified by the W3C and designed to make the interchange of structured documents over the Internet easier. An important aspect of XML used to be Document Type Definitions (DTDs), which define the role of each element of text in a formal model. XML schemas have now become critical to specifying the structure of data. XML schemas are also XML documents (Bray et al., 1997).

RDF. The Resource Description Framework (RDF) is a standard for describing resources on the semantic web. It provides a common framework for expressing this information so it can be exchanged between applications without loss of meaning. RDF is based on the idea of identifying things using web identifiers (called Uniform Resource Identifiers, or URIs), and describing resources in terms of simple properties and property values (Klyne et al., 2004).

The RDF terminology T is the union of three pairwise disjoint infinite sets of terms: the set U of URI references, the set L of literals (itself partitioned into two sets, the set L_p of plain literals and the set L_t of typed literals), and the set B of blanks. The set $U \cup L$ of names is called the vocabulary.

Definition 5.1: RDF Triple

An RDF triple (s, p, o) is an element of $(U \cup B) \times U \times T$. An RDF graph is a finite set of triples.

An RDF triple can be viewed as an arc from s to o, where p is used to label the arc. This is represented as $s \xrightarrow{p} o$. We also refer to the ordered triple (s, p, o) as the subject, predicate, and object of a triple.

RDF has a formal semantics that provides a dependable basis for reasoning about the meaning of an RDF graph. This reasoning is usually called entailment. Entailment rules state which implicit information can be inferred from explicit information. In general, it is not assumed that complete information about any resource is available in an RDF query. A query language should be aware of this, and tolerate incomplete or contradicting information. The notion of class and operations on classes are specified in RDF though the concept of RDF schema (Antoniou and van Harmelen, 2008).

SPARQL. SPARQL (Simple Protocol and RDF Query Language) (Prud'hommeaux and Seaborne, 2006) is a powerful query language. It is a key semantic web technology and was standardized by the RDF Data Access Working Group of the W3C. SPARQL syntax is similar to SQL, but it has the advantage whereby it enables queries to span multiple disparate data sources that consist of heterogeneous and semistructured data. SPARQL is based around graph pattern matching (Prud'hommeaux and Seaborne, 2006).

Definition 5.2: Graph Pattern

A SPARQL graph pattern expression is defined recursively as follows:

1. A triple pattern is a graph pattern.
2. If P_1 and P_2 are graph patterns, then the expressions $(P_1$ AND $P_2)$, $(P_1$ OPT $P_2)$ and $(P_1$ UNION $P_2)$ are graph patterns.
3. If P is a graph pattern, V a set of variables and $X \in U \cup V$, then $(X$ GRAPH $P)$ is a graph pattern.
4. If P is a graph pattern and R is a built-in SPARQL condition, then the expression $(P$ FILTER $R)$ is a graph pattern.

OWL. The OWL (McGuinness and Van Harmelen, 2004) is an ontology language that has more expressive power and reasoning capabilities than RDF and RDF Schema (RDF-S). It has additional vocabulary along with a formal semantics. OWL has three increasingly expressive sublanguages: OWL Lite, OWL DL, and OWL Full. These are designed for use by specific communities of implementers and users. The formal semantics in OWL is based on Description Logics (DL), which is a decidable fragment of first-order logics.

Description Logics. DL is a family of knowledge representation (KR) formalisms that represent the knowledge of an application domain (Baader, 2003). It defines the concepts of the domain (i.e., its terminology) as sets of objects called classes, and it uses these concepts to specify properties of objects and individuals occurring in the domain. A description logic is characterized by a set of constructors that allow one to build complex concepts and roles from atomic ones.

ALCQ. A DL language, ALCQ consists of a countable set of individuals *Ind*, a countable set of atomic concepts *CS*, a countable set of roles *RS*, and the concepts built on *CS* and *RS* as follows:

$$C,D := A|\neg A|C \sqcap D|C \sqcup D|\exists R.C|\forall R.C|(\leq nR.C)|(\geq nR.C)$$

where $A \in CS$, $R \in RS$, C and D are concepts and n is a natural number. Also, individuals are denoted by $a, b, c,....$ (i.e., lowercase letters of the alphabet).

This language includes only concepts in negation normal form. The complement of a concept $\neg(C)$ is inductively defined, as usual, by using the law of double negation, de Morgan laws, and the dualities for quantifiers. Moreover, the constants $\top$ and $\perp$ abbreviate $A \sqcup \neg A$ and $A \sqcap \neg A$, respectively, for some $A \in CS$.

An interpretation I consists of a nonempty domain, Δ^I, and a mapping, $.^I$, that assigns
- To each individual $a \in Ind$ an element $a^I \in \Delta^I$
- To each atomic concept $A \in CS$ a set $A^I \subseteq \Delta^I$
- To each role $R \in RS$ a relation $R^I \subseteq \Delta^I \times \Delta^I$

The interpretation extends then on concepts as follows:

$$\neg A^I = \Delta^I \backslash A^I$$

$$(C \sqcup D)^I = C^I \cup D^I$$

$$(C \sqcap D)^I = C^I \cap D^I$$

$$(\exists R.C)^I = \{x \in \Delta^I | \exists y \, ((x,y) \in R^I \wedge y \in C^I)\}$$

$$(\forall R.C)^I = \{x \in \Delta^I | \forall y\ ((x,y) \in R^I \Rightarrow y \in C^I)\}$$

$$(\leq R.C)^I = \{x \in \Delta^I | \#\{y | ((x,y) \in R^I \land y \in C^I)\} \leq n\}$$

$$(\geq R.C)^I = \{x \in \Delta^I | \#\{y | ((x,y) \in R^I \land y \in C^I)\} \geq n\}$$

We can define the notion of a knowledge base and its models. An ALCQ knowledge base is the union of
1. A finite terminological set (TBox) of inclusion axioms that have the form $T \sqsubseteq C$, where C is called inclusion concept
2. A finite assertional set (ABox) of assertions of the form $a{:}C$ (concept assertion) or $(a,b){:}$ R (role assertion), where R is called assertional role and C is called assertional concept.

We denote the set of individuals that appear in KB by $Ind(KB)$. An interpretation I is a model of
- An inclusion axiom $T \sqsubseteq C (I \vDash T \sqsubseteq C)$ if $C^I = \Delta^I$
- A concept assertion $a{:}C (I \vDash a{:}C)$ if $a^I \in C^I$
- A role assertion $a,b{:}\ R (I \vDash (a,b){:}\ R)$ if $(a^I, b^I) \in R^I$

Let K be the ALCQ knowledge base of a TBox, T, and an ABox, A. An interpretation I is a model of K if $I \vDash \phi$ for every $\phi \in T \cup A$. A knowledge base K is consistent if it has a model. Moreover, for φ an inclusion axiom or an assertion, we say that $K \vDash \varphi$ (in words, K entails φ) if for every model I of $K, I \vDash \varphi$ also holds.

The consistency problem for ALCQ is ExpTime-complete. The entailment problem is reducible to the consistency problem as follows.

Let K be an ALCQ knowledge base and d be an individual not belonging to $Ind(K)$. Then,
- $K \vDash T \sqsubseteq C$ iff $K \cup \{d{:}\ \neg C\}$ is inconsistent and
- $K \vDash a{:}C$ iff $K \cup \{a{:}\ \neg C\}$ is inconsistent.

This shows that an entailment can be decided in ExpTime. Moreover, the inconsistency problem is reducible to the entailment problem, and so deciding an entailment is also an ExpTime-complete problem.

Inferencing. The basic inference problem for DL is checking a knowledge base consistency. A knowledge base K is consistent if it has a model. The additional inference problems are as follows:
- *Concept satisfiability.* A concept C is satisfiable relative to K if there is a model I of K such that $C^I \neq \varnothing$.
- *Concept subsumption.* A concept C is subsumed by concept D relative to K if, for every model I of K, $C^I \sqsubseteq D^I$.
- *Concept instantiation.* An individual a is an instance of concept C relative to K if, for every model I of K, $a^I \in C^I$.

All these reasoning problems can be reduced to KB consistency. For example, concept C is satisfiable with regard to the knowledge base K if $K \cup C(a)$ is consistent, where a is an individual not occurring in K.

SWRL. The SWRL extends the set of OWL axioms to include horn-like rules, and it extends the horn-like rules to be combined with an OWL knowledge base (Horrocks et al., 2004).

Definition 5.3: Horn Clause

A horn clause C is an expression of the form $D_0 \leftarrow D_1 \cap \dots \cap D_n$, where each D_i is an atom. The atom D_0 is called the head and the set $D_1 \cap \dots \cap D_n$ is called the body. Variables that occur in the body at most once and do not occur in the head are called unbound variables; all other variables are called bound variables.

The proposed rules are of the form of an implication between an antecedent (body) and a consequent (head). The intended meaning can be read as follows: whenever the conditions specified in the antecedent hold, the conditions specified in the consequent must also hold. Both the antecedent (body) and consequent (head) consist of zero or more atoms. An empty antecedent is treated as trivially true (i.e., satisfied by every interpretation), so the consequent must also be satisfied by every interpretation. An empty consequent is treated as trivially false (i.e., not satisfied by any interpretation), so the antecedent must not be satisfied by any interpretation.

Multiple atoms are treated as a conjunction, and both the head and body can contain conjunction of such atoms. Note that rules with conjunctive consequents could easily be transformed (via Lloyd–Topor transformations) into multiple rules each with an atomic consequent. Atoms in these rules can be of the form $C(x)$, $P(x,y)$, SameAs (x,y), or DifferentFrom(x,y), where C is an OWL description, P is an OWL property, and x,y are either variables, OWL individuals, or OWL data values.

5.4   SEMANTIC WEB AND SECURITY

We first provide an overview of security issues for the semantic web and then discuss some details on XML security, RDF security, and secure information integration, which are components of the secure semantic web. As more progress is made on investigating these various issues, we hope that appropriate standards would be developed for securing the semantic web. Security cannot be considered in isolation. Security cuts across all layers.

For example, consider the lowest layer. One needs secure TCP/IP, secure sockets, and secure HTTP. There are now security protocols for these various lower-layer protocols. One needs end-to-end security. That is, one cannot just have secure TCP/IP built on untrusted communication layers; we need network security. The next layer is XML and XML schemas. One needs secure XML. That is, access must be controlled to various portions of the document for reading, browsing, and modifications. There is research on securing XML and XML schemas. The next step is securing RDF. Now with RDF, not only do we need secure XML, but we also need security for the interpretations and semantics. For example, under certain contexts, portions of the document may be Unclassified, while under certain other contexts the document may be Classified.

Once XML and RDF have been secured, the next step is to examine security for ontologies and interoperation. That is, ontologies may have security levels attached to them. Certain parts of the ontologies could be Secret, while certain other parts may be Unclassified. The challenge is how does one use these ontologies for secure information integration? Researchers have done some work on the secure interoperability of databases. We need to revisit this research and then determine what else needs to be done so that the information on the web can be managed, integrated, and exchanged securely. Logic, proof, and trust are at the highest layers of the semantic web. That is, how can we trust the information that the web gives us? Next, we will discuss the various security issues for XML, RDF, ontologies, and rules.

XML Security. Various research efforts have been reported on XML security (see, e.g., Bertino and Ferrari, 2002). We briefly discuss some of the key points. The main challenge is whether to give access to all the XML documents or to parts of the documents. Bertino et al. have developed authorization models for XML. They have focused on access control policies and on dissemination policies. They also considered push-and-pull architectures. They specified the policies in XML. The policy specification contains information about which users can access which portions of the documents. In Bertino and Ferrari (2002), algorithms for access control and computing views of the results are presented. In addition, architectures for securing XML documents are also discussed. In Bertino et al. (2004) and Bhatti et al. (2004), the authors go further and describe how XML documents may be published on the web. The idea is for owners to publish documents, subjects request access to the documents, and untrusted publishers give the subjects the views of the documents they are authorized to see. The W3C is specifying standards for XML security. The XML security project is focusing on providing the implementation of security standards for XML. The focus is on XML–Signature Syntax and Processing, XML–Encryption Syntax and Processing, and XML Key Management. While the standards are focusing on what can be implemented in the near term, much research is needed on securing XML documents.

RDF Security. RDF is the foundation of the semantic web. While XML is limited in providing machine-understandable documents, RDF handles this limitation. As a result, RDF provides better support for interoperability as well as searching and cataloging. It also describes contents of documents as well as relationships between various entities in the document. While XML provides syntax and notations, RDF supplements this by providing semantic information in a standardized way (Antoniou and van Harmelen, 2008).

The basic RDF model has three components: resources, properties, and statements. Resource is anything described by RDF expressions. It could be a web page or a collection of pages. Property is a specific attribute used to describe a resource. RDF statements are resources together with a named property plus the value of the property. Statement components are subject, predicate, and object. Thus, for example, if we have a sentence of the form "John is the creator of xxx," then xxx is the subject or resource, property or predicate is "creator," and object or literal is "John." There are RDF diagrams very much like, say, the entity relationship diagrams or object diagrams to represent statements. It is important that the intended interpretation be used for RDF sentences. This is accomplished by RDF schemas. Schema is sort of a dictionary and has interpretations of various terms used in sentences.

More advanced concepts in RDF include the container model and statements about statements. The container model has three types of container objects: bag, sequence, and alternative. A bag is an unordered list of resources or literals. It is used to mean that a property has multiple values but the order is not important. A sequence is a list of ordered resources. Here, the order is important. Alternative is a list of resources that represent alternatives for the value of a property. Various tutorials in RDF describe the syntax of containers in more detail. RDF also provides support for making statements about other statements. For example, with this facility, one can make statements of the form, "The statement A is false," where A is the statement "John is the creator of X." Again, one can use object-like diagrams to represent containers and statements about statements. RDF also has a formal model associated with it. This formal model has a formal grammar. The query language to access RDF document is SPARQL. For further information on RDF, we refer to the excellent discussion in the book by Antoniou and van Harmelen (2008).

Now to make the semantic web secure, we need to ensure that RDF documents are secure. This would involve securing XML from a syntactic point of view. However, with RDF, we also need to ensure that security is preserved at the semantic level. The issues include the security implications of the concepts resource, properties, and statements. That is, how is access control ensured? How can statements and properties about statements be protected? How can one provide access control at a finer grain of granularity? What are the security properties of the container model? How can bags, lists, and alternatives be protected? Can we specify security policies in RDF? How can we resolve semantic inconsistencies for the policies? What are the security implications of statements about statements? How can we protect RDF schemas? These are difficult questions, and we need to start research to provide answers. XML security is just the beginning. Securing RDF is much more challenging (see also Carminati et al., 2004).

Security and Ontologies. Ontologies are essentially representations of various concepts in order to avoid ambiguity. Numerous ontologies have been developed. These ontologies have been used by agents to understand the web pages and conduct operations such as the integration of databases. Furthermore, ontologies can be represented in languages such as RDF or special languages such as OWL. Now, ontologies have to be secure. That is, access to the ontologies has to be controlled. This means that different users may have access to different parts of the ontology. On the other hand, ontologies may be used to specify security policies just as XML and RDF have been used to specify the policies. That is, we will describe how ontologies may be secured and how ontologies may be used to specify the various policies.

Secure Query and Rules Processing. The layer above the secure RDF layer is the secure query and rule processing layer. While RDF can be used to specify security policies (see, e.g., Carminati et al., 2004), the web rules language developed by W3C is more powerful to specify complex policies. Furthermore, inference engines were developed to process and reason about the rules (e.g., the Pellet engine developed at the University of Maryland). One could integrate ideas from the database inference controller that we have developed (see Thuraisingham et al., 1993) with web rules processing to develop an inference or privacy controller for the semantic web. The query-processing module is responsible for accessing the heterogeneous data and information sources on the semantic web. Researchers are examining ways to integrate techniques from web query processing with semantic web technologies to locate, query, and integrate the heterogeneous data and information sources.

5.5 CLOUD COMPUTING FRAMEWORKS BASED ON SEMANTIC WEB TECHNOLOGIES

In this section, we introduce a cloud computing framework that we have utilized in the implementation of our systems for social networking applications, some of which are discussed in this book. In particular, we will discuss our framework for RDF integration and provenance data integration.

RDF Integration. We have developed an RDF-based policy engine for use in the cloud for social networking applications. The reasons for using RDF as our data model are as follows: (i) RDF allows us to achieve data interoperability between the seemingly disparate sources of information that are catalogued by each agency/organization separately. (ii) The use of RDF allows participating agencies to create data-centric applications that make use of the integrated data that is now available to them. (iii) Since RDF does not require the use of an explicit schema for data generation, it can be easily adapted to ever-changing user requirements. The policy engine's flexibility is based on its accepting high-level policies and executing them as rules/constraints over a directed RDF graph representation of the provenance and its associated data. The strength of our policy engine is that it can handle any type of policy that could be represented using RDF technologies, horn logic rules (e.g., SWRL), and OWL constraints. The power of these semantic web technologies can be successfully harnessed in cloud computing environment to provide the user with capability to efficiently store and retrieve data for data-intensive applications. Storing RDF data in the cloud brings a number of new features such as scalability and on-demand services, resources and services for users on demand, ability to pay for services and capacity as needed, location independence, guarantee quality of service for users in terms of hardware/CPU performance, bandwidth, and memory capacity. We have examined the following efforts in developing our framework for RDF integration.

In Sun and Jin (2010), the authors adopted the idea of Hexastore and considered both RDF data model and HBase capability. They stored RDF triples into six HBase tables (S_PO, P_SO, O_SP, PS_O, SO_P, and PO_S), which covered all combinations of RDF triple patterns. They indexed the triples with HBase-provided index structure on row key. They also proposed a MapReduce strategy for SPARQL Basic Graph Pattern (BGP) processing, which is suitable for their storage schema. This strategy uses multiple MapReduce jobs to process a typical BGP. In each job, it uses a greedy method to select join key and eliminates multiple triple patterns. Their evaluation result indicated that their approach worked well against large RDF data sets. In Husain et al. (2009), the authors described a framework that uses Hadoop to store and retrieve large numbers of RDF triples. They described a schema to store RDF data in the HDFS. They also presented algorithms to answer SPARQL queries. This made use of Hadoop's MapReduce framework to actually answer the queries. In Huang et al. (2011), the authors introduced a scalable RDF data management system. They introduced techniques for (i) leveraging state-of-the-art single node RDF store technology, and (ii) partitioning the data across nodes in a manner that helps accelerate query processing through locality optimizations. In Papailiou et al. (2012), the authors presented H2RDF, which is a fully distributed RDF store that combines the MapReduce processing framework with a NoSQL distributed data store. Their system features unique characteristics that enable efficient processing of both simple and multijoin SPARQL queries on virtually unlimited number of triples. These include join algorithms that execute joins according to query selectivity to reduce processing, and include adaptive choice among centralized and distributed (MapReduce-based) join execution for fast query responses. They claim that their system can efficiently answer both simple joins and complex multivariate queries, as well as scale up to 3 billion triples using a small cluster consisting of nine worker nodes. In Khadilkar et al. (2012b), the authors designed a Jena–HBase framework. Their HBase-backed triple store can be used with the Jena framework. Jena–HBase provides end users with a scalable storage and querying solution that supports all features from the RDF specification.

Provenance Integration. While our approach for assured information sharing in the cloud for social networking applications is general enough for any type of data, we have utilized provenance data as an example. We will discuss the various approaches that we have examined in our work on provenance data integration. More detailed of our work can be found in Thuraisingham (2015).

In Ikeda et al. (2011), the authors considered a class of workflows that they call generalized map and reduce workflows. The input data sets are processed by an acyclic graph of map and reduce functions to produce output results. They also showed how data provenance (lineage) can be captured for map and reduce functions transparently. In Chebotko et al. (2013), the authors explored and addressed the challenge of efficient and scalable storage and querying of large collections of provenance graphs serialized as RDF graphs in an Apache HBase database. In Park et al. (2011), they proposed RAMP (Reduce and Map Provenance) as an extension to Hadoop that supports provenance capture and tracing for workflows of MapReduce jobs. The work discussed in Abraham et al. (2010) proposed a system to show how HBase Bigtable-like capabilities can be leveraged for distributed storage and querying of provenance data represented in RDF. In particular, their ProvBase system incorporates an HBase/Hadoop backend, a storage schema to hold provenance triples, and a querying algorithm to evaluate SPARQL queries in their system. In Akoush et al. (2013), the authors' research introduced HadoopProv, a modified version of Hadoop that implements provenance capture and analysis in MapReduce jobs. Their system is designed to minimize provenance capture overheads by (i) treating provenance tracking in map and reduce phases separately, and (ii) deferring construction of the provenance graph to the query stage. The provenance graphs are later joined on matching intermediate keys of the map and reduce provenance files.

5.6 SUMMARY AND DIRECTIONS

This chapter has introduced the notion of the cloud and semantic web technologies. We first discussed concepts in cloud computing, including aspects of virtualization. We also discussed the various service models and deployment models for the cloud, and provided a brief overview of cloud functions such as storage management and data management. Next, we discussed technologies for the semantic web, including XML, RDF, ontologies, and OWL. This was followed by a discussion of security issues for the semantic web. Finally, we discussed cloud computing frameworks based on semantic web technologies. More details on cloud computing and semantic web can be found in Thuraisingham (2007, 2013).

Our discussion of cloud computing and semantic web will be useful in understanding some of the chapters in this book. For example, we have discussed experimental social network systems that function in a cloud. We have also discussed access control for social networks represented using semantic web technologies. Finally, we have discussed assured information sharing in the cloud for social networking applications. These topics will be discussed in Sections II and III of this book.

REFERENCES

Abraham, J., Brazier, P., Chebotko, A., Navarro, J., and Piazza, A. Distributed storage and querying techniques for a semantic web of scientific workflow provenance. In: *Proceedings Services Computing (SCC), 2010 IEEE International Conference on Services Computing*, 2010.

Akoush, S., Sohan, R., and Hopper, A. HadoopProv: Towards provenance as a first class citizen in MapReduce. In: *Proceedings of the 5th USENIX Workshop on the Theory and Practice of Provenance*, 2013.

Anderson, C., Lehnardt, J., and Slater, N. *CouchDB: The Definitive Guide*. O'Reilly Media, Sebastopol, CA, 2010.

Antoniou, G. and Van Harmelen, F. *Semantic Web Primer*. MIT Press, Boston, 2008.

Baader, F. *The Description Logic Handbook: Theory, Implementation, and Applications*, Cambridge University Press, Cambridge, 2003.

Berners-Lee, T., Hendler, J., and Lasilla, O. The semantic web. *Scientific American*, May 2001.

Bertino, E. and Ferrari, E. Secure and selective dissemination of XML documents. *ACM Transactions on Information and System Security (TISSEC)* 5(3): 290–331, 2002.

Bertino, E., Guerrini, G., and Mesiti, M. A matching algorithm for measuring the structural similarity between an XML document and a DTD and its applications. *Information Systems* 29(1): 23–46, 2004.

Bhatti, R., Bertino, E., Ghafoor, A., and Joshi, J. XML-based specification for Web services document security. *Computer* 37(4): 41–49, 2004.

Bray, T., Paoli, J., Sperberg-McQueen, C.M., Maler, E., and Yergeau, F. Extensible markup language (XML). *World Wide Web Journal* 2(4), 1997.

Carminati, B., Ferrari, E., and Thuraisingham, B.M. *Using RDF for Policy Specification and Enforcement*. *Proceedings of the 15th International Workshop on Database and Expert Systems Applications*, 163–167, 2004.

Cattell, R. Scalable SQL and NoSQL data stores. *ACM SIGMOD Record* 39(4): 12–27, 2011.

Chebotko, A., Abraham, J., Brazier, P., Piazza, A., Kashlev, A., and Lu, S. Storing, indexing and querying large provenance data sets as RDF graphs in Apache HBase. *IEEE International Workshop on Scientific Workflows*, Santa Clara, CA, 2013.

Chodorow, K. and Dirolf, M. *MongoDB: The Definitive Guide*. O'Reilly Media, Sebastopol, CA, 2010.

Crockford, D. *The Application/JSON Media Type for Javascript Object Notation (JSON)*, 2006.

Dean, J. and Ghemawat, S. MapReduce: Simplified data processing on large clusters. Available from http://research.google.com/archive/mapreduce.html, 2004.

George, L. *HBase: The Definitive Guide*. O'Reilly Media, Sebastopol, CA, 2011.

Ghemawat, S., Gobioff, H., and Leung, S.-T. The Google file system. *ACM SIGOPS Operating Systems Review* 37(5): 29–43, 2003.

Hewitt, E. *Cassandra: The Definitive Guide*. O'Reilly Media, Sebastopol, CA, 2010.

Horrocks, I., Patel-Schneider, P.F., Boley, H., Tabet, S., Grosof, B., and Dean, M. SWRL: A semantic web rule language combining OWL and RuleML. W3C member submission, 2004.

Huang, J., Abadi, D.J., and Ren, K. Scalable SPARQL querying of large RDF graphs. In: *Proceedings of the VLDB Endowment*, vol. 4, no. 11, 2011.

Husain, M.F., Doshi, P., Khan, L., and Thuraisingham, B. Storage and retrieval of large RDF graph using Hadoop and MapReduce. *Cloud Computing*, 2009.

Ikeda, R., Park, H., and Widom, J. Provenance for generalized map and reduced workflows. Stanford InfoLab, 2011.

Khadilkar, V., Octay, K.Y., Kantarcioglu, M., and Mehrotra, S. Secure data processing over hybrid clouds. *IEEE Data Engineering Bulletin* 35(4): 46–54, 2012a.

Khadilkar, V., Kantarcioglu, M., Castagna, P., and Thuraisingham, B. Jena–HBase: A distributed, scalable and efficient RDF triple store. Technical report available from http://ceur-ws.org/Vol-914/paper_14.pdf, 2012b.

Klyne, G., Carroll, J.J., and McBride, B. Resource description framework (RDF): Concepts and abstract syntax. *W3C Recommendation* 10, 2004.

McGuinness, D.L. and Van Harmelen, F. OWL Web Ontology Language overview. *W3C Recommendation*, 2004.

Papailiou, N., Konstantinou, I., Tsoumakos, D., and Koziris, N. H2RDF: Adaptive query processing on RDF data in the cloud. In: *Proceedings of the 21st International Conference Companion on World Wide Web*, 2012.

Park, H., Ikeda, R., and Widom, J. *Ramp: A System for Capturing and Tracing Provenance in MapReduce Workflows*. Stanford InfoLab, 2011.

Prud'hommeaux, E. and Seaborne, A. SPARQL query language for RDF. W3C working draft, 2006.

Sun, J. and Jin, Q. Scalable RDF store based on HBase and MapReduce. In: *Proceedings 2010 3rd International Conference on Advanced Computer Theory and Engineering (ICACTE)*, vol. 1, pp. V1–633, 2010.

Thuraisingham, B. *Building Trustworthy Semantic Webs*. CRC Press, Boca Raton, FL, 2007.

Thuraisingham, B. *Developing and Securing the Cloud*. CRC Press, Boca Raton, FL, 2013.

Thuraisingham, B. *Secure Data Provenance and Inference Control with Semantic Web*. CRC Press, Boca Raton, FL, 2015.

Thuraisingham, B., Ford, W., Collins, M., and O'Keeffe, J. Design and implementation of a database inference controller. *Data and Knowledge Engineering* 11(3): 271–297, 1993.

Thusoo, A., Sarma, J.S., Jain, N., Shao, Z., Chakka, P., Zhang, N., Antony, S., Liu, H., and Murthy, R. Hive—A petabyte scale data warehouse using Hadoop. In: *Proceedings Data Engineering (ICDE), 2010 IEEE 26th International Conference on Data Engineering (ICDE)*, 2010.

White, T. *Hadoop: The Definitive Guide*. O'Reilly Media, Sebastopol, CA, 2010.

CONCLUSION TO SECTION I

Section I has provided an overview of the supporting technologies for social media. In particular, we provided a survey of social media systems, data mining, data security, and cloud computing and semantic web technologies.

Chapter 2 provided an overview of the various social networks that have emerged during the past decades. We then selected a few networks (e.g., Facebook, LinkedIn, Google+, and Twitter) and discussed some of their essential features.

In Chapter 3, we provided an overview of discretionary security policies in database systems. We started with a discussion of access control policies, including authorization policies and role-based access control. Then, we discussed administration policies. We briefly discussed identification and authentication. We also discussed auditing issues and views for security.

In Chapter 4, we first provided an overview of the various data mining tasks and techniques, and then discussed some of the popular techniques such as neural networks, support vector machines, and association rule mining.

Chapter 5 introduced the notion of the cloud and semantic web technologies. We first discussed concepts in cloud computing, including aspects of virtualization. Next, we discussed technologies for the semantic web, including XML (eXtensible Markup Language), RDF (Resource Description Framework), ontologies, and OWL (Web Ontology Language). This was followed by a discussion of security issues for the semantic web. Finally, we discussed cloud computing frameworks based on semantic web technologies.

Section II

Aspects of Analyzing and Securing Social Networks

INTRODUCTION TO SECTION II

Now that we have discussed the supporting technologies for analyzing and securing social media, in Section II we will explore various aspects of analytics and the security of such systems. In particular, we will examine the data mining tasks for social media systems, as well as discuss confidentiality, privacy, and trust for such systems. We will also discuss the representation and reasoning of social networks using semantic web technologies.

Section II consists of three chapters: Chapters 6 through 8. Chapter 6 will give the reader a feel for the various applications of social media analytics. These applications range from detecting communities of interest to determining political affiliations. We also address security and privacy aspects. Chapter 7 will discuss aspects of representing and reasoning about social networks represented as Resource Description Framework (RDF) graphs. Chapter 8 will discuss confidentiality, privacy, and trust for social networks. Confidentiality policies will enable the members of the network to determine what information is to be shared with their friends in the network. Privacy policies will determine what a network can release about a member, provided that these policies are accepted by the member. Trust policies will provide a way for members of a network to assign trust values to the others.

6 Analyzing and Securing Social Networks

6.1 INTRODUCTION

Online social networks (OSNs) have gained a lot of popularity on the Internet and become a hot research topic attracting many professionals from diverse areas. Since the advent of OSN sites like Facebook, Twitter, and LinkedIn, OSNs continue to influence and change every aspect of our lives. From politics to business marketing, from celebrities to newsmakers, everyone is hooked on the phenomenon. Facebook is used to connect with friends and share various personal and professional data, as well as photos and videos. LinkedIn is entirely a professional network that is used to connect to colleagues. Google+ is similar to Facebook, while Twitter is a free social networking and microblogging service that enables users to send and read messages known as tweets. Tweets are text posts of up to 140 characters displayed on the author's profile page and delivered to the author's subscribers who are known as *followers*. Each network has its own set of advantages, and the networks make money mainly through advertising since the services they provide are largely free of charge, unless of course one wants to get premium service in networks such as LinkedIn.

Much of our work on social media analytics has focused on Twitter and analyzing the tweets. Adrianus Wagemakers, the founder of the Amsterdam-based Twopcharts, analyzed Twitter (Wasserman, 2012) and reported that there were roughly 72 million active Twitter accounts. As of the first quarter of 2015, that number had grown to around 236 million. San Antonio-based market research firm Pear Analytics (Kelly, 2009) analyzed 2000 tweets (originating from the United States and in English) during a 2-week period from 11:00 am to 5:00 pm (CST) and categorized them as

- News
- Spam
- Self-promotion
- Pointless babble
- Conversational
- Pass-along value

Tweets with news from mainstream media publications accounted for 72 tweets or 3.60% of the total number (Kelly, 2009). Realizing the importance of Twitter as a medium for news updates, the company emphasized news and information networking strategy in November 2009 by changing the question it asks users for status updates from "What are you doing?" to "What's happening?"

So what makes Twitter so popular? It is free to use, highly mobile, very personal, and very quick (Grossman, 2009). It is also built to spread, and spread fast. Twitter users like to append notes called hashtags—#theylooklikethis—to their tweets, so that they can be grouped and searched for by topic; especially interesting or urgent tweets tend to get picked up and retransmitted by other users, a practice known as retweeting, or RT. And Twitter is promiscuous by nature: tweets go out over two networks, the Internet and SMS, the network that cell phones use for text messages, and they can be received and read on practically anything with a screen and a network connection (Grossman, 2009). Each message is associated with a time stamp, and additional information such as user location and details pertaining to his or her social network can be easily derived.

Much of our work on social media analytics has focused on analyzing tweets. In particular, we have analyzed tweets for detecting suspicious people and analyzing sentiments. Also, many of the

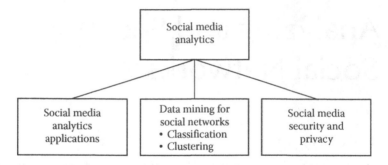

FIGURE 6.1   Social media analytics.

experimental systems we have developed have focused on social media data represented using seman-tic web technologies. Our work has also examined Facebook and studied the information people post, and determined whether one could extract sensitive attributes of the users. We have also used semantic web-based representations of social networks in our work on social network access control. Our work on analyzing tweets is discussed in Section III, while our work on privacy aspects and access control is discussed in Sections IV and V. The experimental systems we have developed are discussed in Sections VI, VII, and VIII. In Section II, we discuss some of the basics for social media analytics and security. Specifically, we discuss semantic web-based representation and reasoning of social networks in Chapter 7, while confidentiality, privacy, and trust management in social networks are discussed in Chapter 8. In this chapter, we set the stage to discuss both social media analytics and security.

The organization of this chapter is as follows. In Section 6.2, we discuss various applications of social media analytics. These include determining persons of interest and extracting demographics data. Applying various data mining techniques for social network analysis (SNA) is discussed in Section 6.3. Security and privacy aspects are discussed in Section 6.4. The chapter is summarized in Section 6.5. Figure 6.1 illustrates the contents of this chapter.

6.2   APPLICATIONS IN SOCIAL MEDIA ANALYTICS

This section lists several social media analytics tasks, including detecting associations, analyzing sentiments, and determining the leaders. Figure 6.2 illustrates the various applications.

Extracting Demographics. In this task, the social media data are analyzed and demograph-ics data such as location and age are extracted. If a social media user has already specified his or her location, then there is no further work to do here. Otherwise, one simple way to extract location is to check the locations of one's friends and then determine the location with the assumption that one lives near one's friends. The age attribute can be extracted

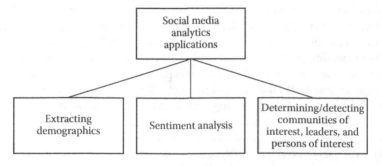

FIGURE 6.2   Social media analytics applications.

by checking LinkedIn to see when a person graduated and then compute the age. It should be noted that there could be deviations from the norm, and so there is a potential for false positives and negatives.

Sentiment Analysis. Here, one analyzes the tweets and extracts words such as "I like pizza" or "I dislike chocolates." The idea here is to analyze the tweets of the various individuals and determine what the sentiments are toward a particular item such as pizza or chocolate, or a topic such as sports or music.

Detecting Communities of Interest. Certain people in a network will have similar goals and interests. Therefore, from the posts in Facebook, one can connect the various people with similar interests so that they can form a community. The analysis here will be to extract the individuals of similar interests and connect them.

Determining Leaders. In this application, one analyzes the network to see the numbers of connections that a person has and also the strength of the relationships. If many people are connected to a person or follow a person, then that person will emerge as a leader. There are obvious leaders such as celebrities and politicians, and nonobvious leaders who can be extracted by analyzing the network.

Detecting Persons of Interest. If, say, communicating with a person from a particular country makes a person suspicious, then that person could be a person of interest. This way, the person can be investigated further. Often, persons of interest are not straightforward to find, like communicating with a person from a particular country. Therefore, the challenge is to extract the hidden links and relationships through data analytics techniques.

Determining Political Affiliation. The idea here is to determine the political affiliations of individuals even though they have not specified explicitly whether he or she is a liberal or a conservative. In this case, one can examine the political leaders they admire (e.g., Margaret Thatcher or Hillary Clinton) and whether they go to church or not, and make a determination as to whether the person is a liberal or a conservative.

The above examples are just a few of the applications. There are numerous other applications such as determining gender biases, detecting suspicious behavior, and even predicting future events. These SNA techniques use various analytics tools that carry out association rule mining, clustering, classification, and anomaly detection, among others. We discuss how the various data mining techniques are applied for SNA in the next section.

6.3   DATA MINING TECHNIQUES FOR SNA

Chapter 3 provided an overview of some of the data mining techniques that we have used in our work, as well as some other techniques that have been proposed for SNA. In this section, we will examine how various data mining techniques are being applied for SNA. The objective of these techniques is to extract the nuggets for the various applications such as determining demographics and detecting suspicious behavior. Figure 6.3 illustrates the various data mining techniques that are being applied for SNA.

Association Rule Mining. Association rule mining techniques extract rules from vast quantities of information. These rules determine items that are purchased together or people who are seen together. Therefore, within the context of SNA, association rule mining techniques will extract rules that specify the people who have a strong relationship to each other.

Classification. Classification techniques will determine classes from a set of predefined criteria. Applying such techniques for SNA, one can form communities of interest. For example, one community may consist of individuals who like tennis, while another community may consist of individuals who like golf. Note that there is a predefined criterion where a person likes sports if he/she plays the sport and he/she also watches the sport.

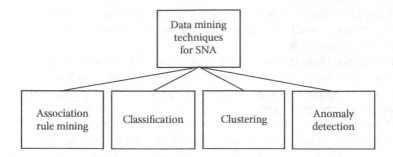

FIGURE 6.3   Data mining techniques for SNA

Clustering. Clustering techniques will form groups when there are no predefined criteria. Therefore, by analyzing the data, one extracts patterns, such as people who live in the northeast smoke mostly cigarettes, while people who live in the southwest smoke mostly cigars.

Anomaly Detection. Anomaly detection techniques determine variations to the norm. For example, everyone in John's social network likes watching spy movies except Paul and Jane.

Web Mining. Web mining techniques have a natural application for SNA. This is because the World Wide Web (WWW) can be regarded as a network where the nodes are the web pages and links are the links between the web pages. Therefore, web structure mining determines how the web pages are connected to each other, while web content mining will analyze tube contents of the WWW. Web log mining will analyze the visits to a web page. Similarly, one can mine the social graphs and extract the structure of the graph. The contents of the graphs (i.e., the data) can be mined to extract the various patterns. One can also mine the visits to, say, a Facebook page, which is analogous to web log mining.

This section has briefly discussed how the data mining techniques can be applied to analyze social networks. In Sections III and IV, we will discuss the various data mining techniques, some of which we have developed ourselves and applied for SNA.

6.4   SECURITY AND PRIVACY

As stated earlier, while part of our book focuses on social media analytics, another part focuses on security and privacy for social media. Owing to data mining, users can access information about the various members of social networks and extract sensitive information. This could include financial data, health data, and travel data that an individual may want to keep private. Additional sensitive information that can be extracted includes political affiliations and gender preferences, as well as drinking and smoking habits. Our work in Section IV discusses various privacy violations that occur in social media data due to data mining and analytics. We have applied various data analytics techniques and have shown how private information can be inferred.

Another aspect of security is confidentiality. That is, access to sensitive information in social media has to be controlled. Users should have the option to grant access to only certain friends. Furthermore, one may place more trust in some friends. In Section V of this book, we will discuss access control for social networks represented using semantic web technologies. We will also discuss additional experimental systems, including inference control in social networks and cloud-based assured information sharing. In Chapter 8, we will elaborate more on confidentiality, privacy, and trust. Figure 6.4 illustrates security and privacy for social networks.

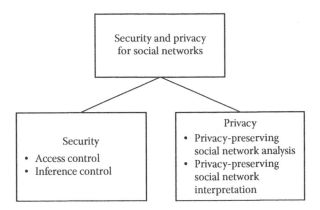

FIGURE 6.4   Security and privacy for social networks.

6.5   SUMMARY AND DIRECTIONS

This chapter has given the reader a feel for the various applications of social media analytics. These applications range from detecting communities of interest to determining political affiliations. We have also addressed security and privacy aspects. While we have not made any assumption about the representation of social networks in this chapter, much of the work we have carried out on analyzing social networks assumes that these networks are represented using semantic web technologies. In Chapter 7, we will discuss representation and analysis resonation of social networks using semantic web technologies. In Chapter 8, we will discuss security and privacy aspects of social networks represented using semantic web technologies.

Much of our work on SNA has been on extracting demographics information in general and location extraction in particular. Therefore, in Section III of this book, we will discuss location mining for social networks. In particular, we will discuss the extraction locations of twitter users. In Section IV, we will study the privacy violations that can occur due to SNA. Access control for social networks will be discussed in Section V, while experimental systems are discussed in Sections VI and VII.

REFERENCES

Grossman, L. Iran protests: Twitter, the medium of the movement. Retrieved January 26, 2013, from *Time World*. Available at http://www.time.com/time/world/article/0,8599,1905125,00.html, June 17, 2009.

Kelly, R. Twitter study reveals interesting results about usage. San Antonio, Texas. Retrieved January 26, 2013, from *Pear Analytics*. Available at http://www.pearanalytics.com/wp-content/uploads/2009/08/Twitter-Study-August-2009.pdf, August 12, 2009.

Wasserman, T. Twitter user ID numbers cross into the billions. Retrieved February 5, 2013, from *Mashable*. Available at http://mashable.com/2012/12/11/twitter-1-billionth-user-id/, December 11, 2012.

7 Semantic Web-Based Social Network Representation and Analysis

7.1 INTRODUCTION

Managing complex networks, whether they are social networks, transportation networks, crime networks, terrorist networks, or communication networks, has become a major challenge. Such networks may have millions of nodes (or even a few billion) with an even larger number of edges. The nodes and edges are dynamic, and may have multiple versions. Essentially, these networks transform into large dynamic graph structures. There is an urgent need to manage these graph structures and analyze them to determine suspicious behavior in various individuals. Furthermore, semantic web technologies are being applied to represent the graph structures. One of the prominent ontologies that has been developed based on Resource Description Framework (RDF) is Friend of a Friend (FOAF), which has been used to build a very large social network. We need techniques to extract graph structures from multimodal data, integrate the graph structures, and mine/analyze the structures and extract patterns.

One of the major tasks in social network analysis is to represent the network. Typically, social networks are represented using graphs. One needs to come up with a way to electronically represent these graphs. Another task is to build the network. For example, in social networks such as Facebook, one can build a graph where the nodes are the people in the network and the links are the relationships between the people (e.g., friendships). In many situations, we may need to build a network from vast amounts of data, both structured and unstructured. The data could emanate from various databases as well as e-mails, blogs, and web pages. Therefore, we need to use various analytics techniques to extract the nuggets from the various data sources and then build the network. Once the network is developed, then we can carry out analysis to extract information such as communities of interest and those who are leaders of the network. One can also specify various policies such as security and privacy policies for the network. Sections III through V will focus on analytics, privacy, and security for social networks. In these parts, we will provide the basics for social network representation, analysis, and security and privacy.

This chapter focuses on social network representation and analysis. While various representation schemes have been proposed, including relational databases and matrices, we focus on semantic web representations for the networks. We focus on semantics web representation due to the representation and reasoning power of semantic networks. Various articles have been published on using semantic web for representing and reasoning about social networks. One such effort is the work of Peter Mika for his PhD thesis at Veer University in the Netherlands. In Section 7.2, we have summarized his work (Mika, 2007). We have also developed experimental systems based on semantic web data for social network representation. Therefore, we will also discuss our approach to resonating and reasoning about social networks, which we have utilized for many of our experimental systems.

The organization of this chapter is as follows. Semantic web-based representations and reasoning of social networks, as examined by Mika, are discussed in Section 7.2. Our approach to social network representation and reasoning is discussed in Section 7.3. The chapter is summarized in Section 7.4. Figure 7.1 illustrates the contents of this chapter.

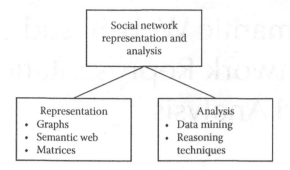

FIGURE 7.1   Social network representation and analysis.

7.2   SOCIAL NETWORK REPRESENTATION

As stated by Mika (2007), social network analysis (SNA) is the study of social networks among a set of actors. The focus is on the relationships between the actors and not on the actors themselves; for example, some relationships and actors are more important than others. Data collection and analysis are major aspects of SNA. One needs to collect data, build a graph to represent the data, and analyze the graph. In the early days, one used manual processes that consisted of filling questionnaires and analyzing the data using statistical methods. With the advent of the World Wide Web (WWW), current methods are automated, where entities and relationships are extracted from massive amounts of data.

Social scientists have influenced the field since the 1930s; for example, Morenos's concept diagram where sociograms visualized a collection of nodes and links. Today, we have the WWW that is a collection of nodes and links where the nodes are the web pages and the links represent the relationships between the web pages. Social networks are represented as graphs. Mathematical representations of a graph are typically a matrix where a 1 represents a link between two nodes and a 0 represents the absence of a link between two nodes. One can add weights to the links to represent the strength of the relationships. There has been a general observation for quite a while that people are separated by six steps. Furthermore, it is stated that most people have about two coauthors, while very few have more than 20 coauthors (Mika, 2007). SNA has carried out various tasks. These include finding the in-degree and out-degree of the vertices, as well as finding the hub and clusters. Questions to be answered include important people in the network, the person with the most relationships, and the pair with the strongest relationship. Figure 7.2 illustrates a social network represented as a graph, while Figure 7.3 shows a matrix representation of a social graph.

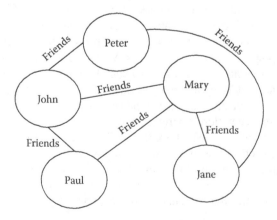

FIGURE 7.2   Example social graph.

	John	Mary	Jane	Paul	Peter
John	1	1	0	1	1
Mary	1	1	1	1	0
Jane	0	1	1	0	1
Paul	1	1	0	1	0
Peter	1	0	1	0	1

FIGURE 7.3 Matrix representation of a social graph.

The recent social networks integrate both networking (i.e., communications with friends) and the ability to share videos, photographs, and images. The semantic web technologies lend themselves well to facilitate such sharing of data as well as for representing the nodes and links of a network. The FOAF project is an early social network system that utilizes semantic web technologies for representation and analysis. As stated by Mika, "the FOAF project has created a web of machine-readable pages describing people, the links between them, and the things they create and do; it defines an open, decentralized technology for connecting social websites, and the people they describe." Details of FOAF can be found at http://www.foaf-project.org/. Figure 7.4 gives an example of FOAF.

Mika has developed one of the early comprehensive semantic web-based social media systems call Flink. In semantic web representations, RDF graphs and Web Ontology Language (OWL) are used to represent the nodes and links. Description logic-based reasoning tools are used to analyze the social networks to extract the nuggets. As stated by Mika, Flink is a social network that exploits FOAF for the purposes of social intelligence. He described social intelligence to be "semantics-based integration and analysis of social knowledge extracted from electronic sources under diverse ownership or control." He goes on to state that "Flink extracts knowledge about the social networks of the community and consolidates what is learned using a common semantic representation, namely the FOAF."

The architecture of Flink can be divided into three layers that carry out metadata acquisition, storage, and visualization. The metadata acquisition layer utilizes a web mining component that carries out data analytics and extracts nuggets, such as finding topics of interest. The storage layer manages the data. The data is managed by RDF data management systems such as Sesame or JENA. Flink uses Sesame for data management. The visualization layer has a browser and supports the display of the data. Flink uses a component called JUNG to carry out SNA, such as finding clusters to identify communities. In summary, Flink essentially represents the data extracted from various pieces of data in RDF managed by Sesame, builds a network, and analyzes the network using JUNG.

```
•  <foaf:Person rdf:about="#me"
   xmlns:foaf="http://xmlns.com/foaf/0.1/">

   <foaf:name>Dan Brickley</foaf:name>

   <foaf:mbox_sha1sum>241021fb0e6289f92815fc210f9e9
   137262c252e</foaf:mbox_sha1sum>

   <foaf:homepage rdf:resource="http://danbri.org/" />
   <foaf:img rdf:resource="/images/me.jpg" />

   </foaf:Person>
```

FIGURE 7.4 FOAF example.

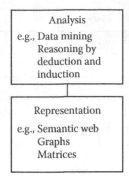

FIGURE 7.5   Social network representation and analysis.

We have utilized a similar architecture for a number of the systems we have designed and developed. The general idea is to apply web analytics techniques and extract the nuggets from the various pieces of data such as blogs, e-mails, and databases; build a network from the various pieces of nuggets extracted; and analyze the networks to answer important problems such as detecting communities and determining user sentiments. If the network is already developed in the case of social networks such as Facebook, the goal is to represent these networks in a graph structure, including using semantic web technologies for representation and analyzing the networks to extract the nuggets. Figure 7.5 illustrates the concepts behind SNA, which is essentially a summary of the approach by Mika.

7.3   OUR APPROACH TO SOCIAL NETWORK ANALYSIS

We have designed and developed tools and techniques to analyze and mine RDF graphs extracted from unstructured data to determine patterns and trends. These tools are discussed in Section VI of this book. Our technical approach mainly consists of extracting entities, reasoning about the entities, extracting RDF graphs, and analyzing the graphs. We have also developed techniques for managing very large RDF graphs. Our approach is illustrated in Figure 7.6.

We have designed a layered approach to social network analysis, which is, in many ways, similar to the approach by Mika discussed in Section 7.2. The first task is to extract the entities from the large quantities of data. These entities have to be integrated to form a network. Reasoning has to be carried out to address incomplete and inconsistent information. Ontologies may be used to facilitate this reasoning. Subsequently, the entities and the relationships have to be represented as RDF graphs. Finally, social network analysis is carried out on the RDF graphs. Therefore, the layers of our architecture are entity extraction and integration, ontology-based heuristics reasoning, and RDF representation and analysis. Finally, the RDF graphs extracted and integrated may be massive. Therefore, we need techniques for managing very large RDF graphs. These layers are illustrated in Figure 7.6.

7.4   SUMMARY AND DIRECTIONS

Social networks are usually represented as graphs. This chapter has focused on representing social networks as RDF graphs. We first discussed Peter Mika's work on representing and reasoning about RDF graphs, then social network representation, and finally discussed our approach. We have designed a layered architecture for social network analysis that includes entity extraction and integration, ontology-based heuristic reasoning, RDF graph analysis, and managing very large RDF graphs. Several of the systems we have designed or developed are based on this layered architecture. These systems are discussed in Sections VI through VIII of this book.

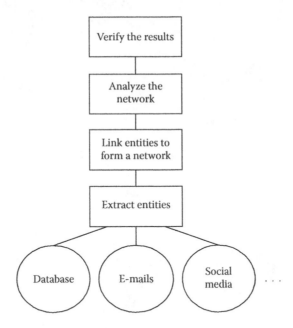

FIGURE 7.6   Our approach to social network analysis.

As stated earlier, the goal of Section II is to set the stage so that the reader has an understanding of the chapters that follows. While Chapter 6 discussed the basics of analyzing and securing social networks, in this chapter we have discussed aspects of semantic web-based representations and reasoning of social networks. In Chapter 8, we will focus on confidentiality, privacy, and trust management for social networks represented using semantic web technologies.

REFERENCE

Mika, P. *Social Networks and the Semantic Web*. Springer, New York, 2007.

REFERENCE

8 Confidentiality, Privacy, and Trust for Social Media Data

8.1 INTRODUCTION

Security has many dimensions, including confidentiality, privacy, trust, availability, and dependability, among others. Our work has examined the confidentiality, privacy, and trust (CPT) aspects of security for social media data represented using semantic web technologies and how they relate to each other. Confidentiality is essentially secrecy. Privacy deals with not disclosing sensitive data about individuals. Trust is about the assurance one can place on the data or on an individual. For example, even though John is authorized to get salary data, can we trust John not to divulge this data to others? Even though the website states that it will not give out social security numbers of individuals, can we trust the website? Our prior work has designed a framework called CPT based on semantic web technologies that provide an integrated approach to addressing confidentiality, privacy, and trust (Thuraisingham et al., 2007). In this chapter, we will revisit CPT and discuss how it relates to social media data. Later, in Sections VI through VIII of this book, we will discuss the design and implementation of social media systems we have carried out with respect to privacy, access control, and inference control.

The organization of this chapter is as follows. Our definitions of confidentiality, privacy, and trust, as well as the current status on administering the semantic web will be discussed in Section 8.2. This will be followed by a discussion of our proposed framework for securing the social media data that we call CPT (confidentiality, privacy, and trust) in Section 8.3. Next, we will take each of the features, confidentiality, privacy, and trust, and discuss various aspects as they relate to social media in Sections 8.4 through 8.6, respectively. An integrated architecture for CPT as well as inference and privacy control will be discussed in Section 8.7. Relationship to social media data is discussed in Section 8.8. Finally, the chapter is summarized and future directions are given in Section 8.9. Figure 8.1 illustrates the concepts of this chapter.

8.2 TRUST, PRIVACY, AND CONFIDENTIALITY

In this section, we will discuss aspects of the security and privacy relationship to the inference problem with respect to social media data. In particular, confidentiality, privacy, trust, integrity, and availability will be briefly defined with an examination of how these issues specifically relate to the trust management and inference problem. Confidentiality is preventing the release of unauthorized information. One view of privacy is to consider it to be a subset of confidentiality in that it is the prevention of unauthorized information being released with regard to an individual. However, much of the recent research on privacy, especially relating to data mining, addresses the following aspect: how can we mine and extract useful nuggets about groups of people while keeping the values of the sensitive attributes of an individual private? That is, even though we can make inferences about groups, we want to maintain individual privacy. For example, we want to protect the fact that John has cancer. However, the fact that people who live in Dallas, Texas, are more prone to cancer is something we make public. More details on privacy and its relationship to data mining can be found in Agrawal and Srikant (2000) and Kantarcioglu and Clifton (2003).

Integrity of data is the prevention of any modifications made by an unauthorized entity. Availability is the prevention of unauthorized omission of data. Trust is a measure of confidence in data correctness and legitimacy from a particular source. Integrity, availability, and trust are

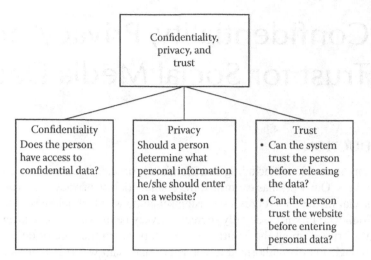

FIGURE 8.1 Confidentiality, privacy, and trust.

all very closely related in the sense that data quality is of particular importance, and all require individuals or entities processing and sending information to not alter the data in an unauthorized manner. If confidentiality, privacy, trust, integrity, and availability are all guaranteed, a system can be considered secure. Thus, if the inference problem can be solved such that unauthorized information is not released, the rules of confidentiality, privacy, and trust will not be broken. A technique such as inference can either be used to aid or impair the cause of integrity, availability, and trust. If correctly used, inference can be used to infer trust management policies. Thus, inference can be used for good or bad purposes. The intention is to prevent inferred, unauthorized conclusions and to use inference to apply trust management.

8.2.1 Current Successes and Potential Failures

The World Wide Web Consortium (www.w3c.org) has proposed encryption techniques for securing XML documents. Furthermore, logic, proof, and trust belong to one of the layers of the semantic web. However, by trust, in that context, what is meant is whether the semantic web can trust the statements such as data and rules. In our definition, by trust, we mean to what extent we can believe that the user and the website will enforce the confidentiality and privacy policies as specified. Privacy has been discussed by the semantic web community. The main contribution of this community is developing the Platform for Privacy Preferences (P3P).

P3P requires the web developer of the server to create a privacy policy, validate it, and then place it in a specific location on the server, as well as write a privacy policy in English. When the user enters the website, the browser will discover the privacy policy, and if the privacy policy matches the user's browser security specifications, then the user can simply enter the site. If the policy does not match the user's specifications, then the user will be informed of the site's intentions and the user can then choose to enter or leave.

While this is a great start, it is lacking in certain areas. One concern is the fact that the privacy policy must be placed in a specific location. If a website, for example, a student website on a school's server, is to implement P3P and cannot place it in a folder directly from the school's server, then the user's browser will not find the privacy policy.

Another problem with P3P is that it requires the data collector on the server side to follow exactly what is promised in the privacy policy. If the data collections services on the server side decide to abuse the policy and instead do other things not stated in the agreement, then no real consequences occur. The server's privacy policy can simply choose to state that it will correct the problem upon discovery; however, if the user never knows it until the data is shared publicly, correcting it to show the data is private will simply not solve the problem. Accountability should be addressed, where it is not the server's decision but rather the lawmaker's decision. When someone breaks a law or does not abide by contractual agreements, we do not turn to the accused and ask what punishment they deem necessary. Instead, we look to the law and apply each law when applicable.

Another point of contention is trust and inference. Before beginning any discussions of privacy, a user and a server must evaluate how much the other party can be trusted. If neither party trusts each other, how can either party expect the other to follow a privacy policy? Currently, P3P only uses tags to define actions; it uses no web rules for inference or specific negotiations regarding confidentiality and privacy. With inference, a user can decide if certain information should not be given because it would allow the distrusted server to infer information that the user would prefer to remain private or sensitive.

8.2.2 MOTIVATION FOR A FRAMEWORK

While P3P is a great initiative to approaching the privacy problem for users of the semantic web, it becomes obvious from the above discussion that more work must be continued on this process. Furthermore, we need to integrate confidentiality and privacy within the context of trust management. A new approach to be discussed later must be used to address these issues such that the user can establish trust, preserve privacy and anonymity, and ensure confidentiality. Once the server and client have negotiated trust, the user can begin to decide what data can be submitted that will not violate his/her privacy. These security policies, one each for trust, privacy, and confidentiality, are described with web rules. Describing policies with web rules can allow an inference engine to determine what is in either the client or server's best interest and help advise each party accordingly. Also with web rules in place, a user and server can begin to negotiate confidentiality. Thus, if a user does not agree with a server's privacy policies but would still like to use some services, a user may begin negotiating confidentiality with the server to determine if the user can still use some services but not all (depending on the final conclusion of the agreement). The goal of this new approach is to simulate real-world negotiations, thus giving semantics to the current web and providing much needed security.

8.3 CPT FRAMEWORK

In this section, we will discuss a framework for enforcing CPT for the semantic web. We first discuss the basic framework where rules are enforced to ensure confidentiality, privacy, and trust. In the advanced framework, we include inference controllers that will reason about the application and determine whether confidentiality, privacy, and trust violations have occurred.

8.3.1 ROLE OF THE SERVER

In the previous section, focus was placed on the client's needs; now, we will discuss the server's needs in this process. The first obvious need is that the server must be able to evaluate the client to grant specific resources. Therefore, the primary goal is to establish trust regarding the client's identity and, based on this identity, grant various permissions to specific data. Not only must the server be able to evaluate the client, but also be able to evaluate its own ability to grant permission with standards and metrics. The server also needs to be able to grant or deny a request appropriately without giving away classified information, or, instead of giving away classified information, the server may desire to give a cover story. Either scenario, a cover story or protecting classified resources, must be completed within the guidelines of a stated privacy policy in order to guarantee a client's confidentiality. One other key aspect is that all of these events must occur in a timely manner such that security is not compromised.

8.3.2 CPT PROCESS

Now that the needs of the client and server have been discussed, focus will be placed on the actual process of our system CPT. First, a general overview of the process will be presented. After the reader has garnered a simple overview, this chapter will continue to discuss two systems, basic CPT and advanced CPT, based on the general process previously discussed. The general process of CPT is to first establish a relationship of trust and then negotiate privacy and confidentiality policies. Figure 8.2 shows the general process.

Notice that both parties partake in establishing trust. The client must determine the degree to which it can trust the server in order to decide how much trust to place in the resources supplied by the server and also to negotiate privacy policies. The server must determine the degree to which it can trust the client in order to determine what privileges and resources it can allow the client to access, as well as how to present the data. The server and client will base their decisions of trust on the credentials of each other. Once trust is established, the client and server must come to an agreement of privacy policies to be applied to the data that the client provides the server. Privacy must follow trust because the degree to which the client trusts the server will affect the privacy degree. The privacy degree affects what data the client chooses to send. Once the client is comfortable with the privacy policies negotiated, the client will then begin requesting data. On the basis of the initial trust agreement, the server will determine what and when the client views these resources. The client will make decisions regarding confidentiality and what data can be given to the user based on its own confidentiality requirements and confidentiality degree. It is also important to note that the server and client must make these decisions, and then configure the system to act upon these decisions. The basic CPT system will not advise the client or server in any way regarding the outcomes of any decisions. Figure 8.3 illustrates the communication between the different components.

8.3.3 ADVANCED CPT

The previous section discussed the basic CPT system; the advanced CPT system is an extension of the basic system. The advanced CPT system is outlined in Figure 8.4, which incorporates three new entities not found in the basic system. These three new entities are the Trust Inference Engine (TIE), the Privacy Inference Engine (PIE), and the Confidentiality Inference Engine (CIE). The first step of sending credentials and establishing trust is the same as the basic system, except that both parties consult with their own TIE. Once each party makes a decision, the client receives the privacy policies from the server and then uses these policies in configuration with PIE to agree, disagree, or negotiate. Once the client and server have come to an agreement about the client's privacy, the

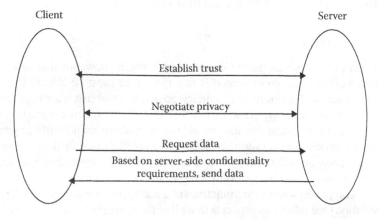

FIGURE 8.2 Basic framework for CPT.

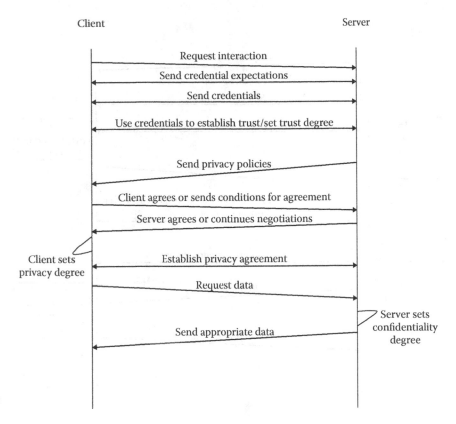

FIGURE 8.3 Communication between the components for basic CPT.

client will send a request for various resources. On the basis of the degree of trust that the server has assigned to a particular client, the server will determine what resources it can give to the client. However, in this step, the server will consult the CIE to determine what data is preferable to give to the client, and what data, if given, could have disastrous consequences. Once the server has made a conclusion regarding data the client can receive, it can then begin transmitting data over the network.

8.3.4 Trust, Privacy, and Confidentiality Inference Engines

With regard to trust, the server must realize that if it chooses to assign a certain percentage of trust, then this implies that the client will have access to the specific privileged resources and can possibly infer other data from granted permissions. Thus, the primary responsibility of the trust inference engine is to determine what information can be inferred and if this behavior is acceptable. Likewise, the client must realize that the percentage of trust it assigns to the server will affect permissions of viewing the site, as well as affect how data given to the client will be processed. The inference engine in the client's scenario will guide the client regarding what can or will occur based on the trust assignment given to the server.

Once trust is established, the privacy inference engine will continue the inference process. It is important to note that the privacy inference engine only resides on the client side. The server will have its own privacy policies; however, these policies may not be acceptable to the client. It is impossible for the server to evaluate each client and determine how to implement an individual privacy policy without first consulting the client. Thus, the privacy inference engine is unnecessary on the server's side. The privacy inference engine must guide the client in negotiating privacy policies.

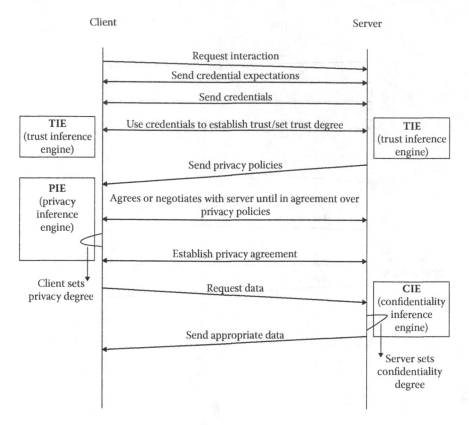

FIGURE 8.4 Communication between components for advanced CPT.

To guide the client through negotiations, the inference engine must be able to determine how the server will use the data the client gives it, as well as who else will have access to the submitted data. Once this is determined, the inference engine must evaluate the data given by the client to the server. If the inference engine determines that this data can be used to infer other data that the client would prefer to remain private, the inference engine must warn the client and then allow the client to choose the next appropriate measure of either sending or not sending the data.

Once the client and server have agreed on the privacy policies to be implemented, the client will naturally begin requesting data and the server will have to determine what data to send based on confidentiality requirements. It is important to note that the confidentiality inference engine is located only on the server side. The client has already negotiated its personal privacy issues and is ready to view the data, thus leaving the server to decide what the next appropriate action is. The confidentiality inference engine must first determine what data will be currently available to the client, based on the current trust assignment. Once the inference engine has determined this, the inference engine must explore what policies or data can be potentially inferred if the data is given to the client. The primary objective of the confidentiality inference engine is to ponder how the client might be able to use the information given to it and then guide the server through the process of deciding a client's access to resources.

8.4   OUR APPROACH TO CONFIDENTIALITY MANAGEMENT

While much of our previous work focused on security control in relational databases, our work discussed in this book focuses on extending this approach to social media data. The social network is augmented by an inference controller that examines the policies specified as ontologies and rules,

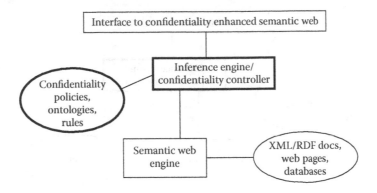

FIGURE 8.5 Confidentiality controller for the semantic web.

and utilizes the inference engine embedded in the web rules language, reasons about the applications, and deduces the security violations via inference. In particular, we focus on the design and implementation of an inference controller where the data is represented as Resource Description Framework (RDF) documents.

It should be noted that before the work discussed in this book, we designed and developed a preliminary confidentiality controller in 2005. Here, we utilized two popular semantic web technologies in our prototype, called Intellidimension RDF Gateway (http://www.intellidimension .com/) and Jena (http://jena.sourceforge.net/). RDF Gateway is a database and integrated web server utilizing RDF and built from the ground up rather than on top of existing web servers or databases (http://www.w3.org/TR/rdf-primer/). It functions as a data repository for RDF data and also as an interface to various data sources, external or internal, that can be queried. Jena is a Java application programming package to create, modify, store, query, and perform other processing tasks on RDF/XML documents from Java programs. RDF documents can be created from scratch, or preformatted documents can be read into memory to explore various parts. The node–arc–node feature of RDF closely resembles how Jena accesses an RDF document. It also has a built-in query engine designed on top of the RDF Query Language (RDFQL) that allows querying documents using standard RDFQL query statements. Our initial prototype utilized RDFQL, while our current work has focused on Simple Protocol and RDF Query Language (SPARQL) queries.

By using these technologies, we specify the confidentiality policies. The confidentiality engine ensures that the policies are enforced correctly. If we assume the basic framework, then the confidentiality engine will enforce the policies and will not examine security violations via inference. In the advanced approach, the confidentiality engine will include what we call an inference controller. Figure 8.5 illustrates an inference/confidentiality controller for the semantic web that has been the basis of our book.

8.5 PRIVACY FOR SOCIAL NETWORKS

As discussed in Chapter 3, privacy is about protecting information about individuals. Furthermore, an individual can specify, say, to a web service provider, the information that can be released about him or her. Privacy has been discussed a great deal in the past, especially when it relates to protecting patients' medical information. Social scientists and technologists have been working on privacy issues. However, privacy has received enormous attention during the past year. This is mainly because of the advent of the web, the semantic web, counterterrorism, and national security. For example, to extract information about various individuals and perhaps prevent or detect potential terrorist attacks, data mining tools are being examined. We have heard much about national security versus privacy in the media. This is mainly because people are now realizing that to handle

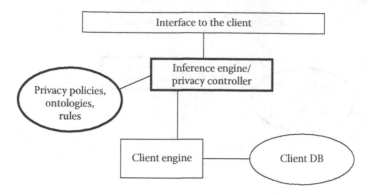

FIGURE 8.6   Privacy controller for the semantic web.

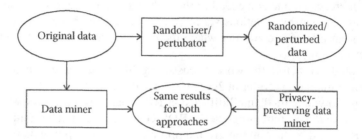

FIGURE 8.7   Privacy control for social network mining and analysis.

terrorism, the government may need to collect data about individuals and mine the data to extract information. Data may be in relational databases or it may be text, video, or images. This is causing a major concern with various civil liberties unions (Thuraisingham, 2003).

From a technology policy of view, a privacy controller could be considered to be identical to the confidentiality controller we have designed and developed. The privacy controller is illustrated in Figure 8.6. However, it is implemented at the client side. Before the client gives out information to a website, it will check whether the website can divulge aggregated information to the third party and subsequently result in privacy violations. For example, the website may give out medical records without the identity so that the third party can study the patterns of flu or other infectious diseases. Furthermore, at some other time, the website may give out the names. However, if the website gives out the link between the names and diseases, then there could be privacy violations. The inference engine will make such deductions and determine whether the client should give out personal data to the website.

As we have stated earlier, privacy violations could also result due to data mining and analysis. In this case, the challenge is to protect the values of the sensitive attributes of an individual and make public the results of the mining or analysis. This aspect of privacy is illustrated in Figure 8.7. A CPT framework should handle both aspects of privacy. Our work on privacy aspects of social networks addresses privacy violations that could occur in social networks due to data analytics.

8.6   TRUST FOR SOCIAL NETWORKS

Researchers are working on protocols for trust management. Languages for specifying trust management constructs are also being developed. In addition, there is research on the foundations of trust management. For example, if A trusts B and B trusts C, then can A trust C? How do you share the data and information on the semantic web and still maintain autonomy? How do you propagate trust? For example, if A trusts B, say, 50% of the time and B trusts C 30% of the time, then what value do you assign for A trusting C? How do you incorporate trust into semantic interoperability? What are the quality of service primitives for trust and negotiation? That is, for certain situations, one may need 100% trust while for certain other situations, 50% trust may suffice (Yu and Winslett, 2003).

Another topic that is being investigated is trust propagation and propagating privileges. For example, if you grant privileges to A, what privileges can A transfer to B? How can you compose privileges? Is there an algebra or calculus for the composition of privileges? Much research still needs to be done here. One of the layers of the semantic web is logic, proof, and trust. Essentially, this layer deals with trust management and negotiation between different agents, and examining the foundations and developing logics for trust management. Some interesting work has been carried out by Finin and colleagues (Denker et al., 2003; Finin and Joshi, 2002; Kagal et al., 2003). For example, if given data A and B, can someone deduce classified data X (i.e., $A + B \rightarrow X$)? The inference engines will also use an inverse inference module to determine whether classified information can be inferred if a user employs inverse resolution techniques. For example, if given data A and the user wants to guarantee that data X remains classified, the user can determine that B, which combined with A implies X, must remain classified as well (i.e., $A + ? \rightarrow X$; the question mark results with B). Once the expert system has received the results from the inference engines, it can conclude a recommendation and then pass this recommendation to the client or server who will have the option to either accept or reject the suggestion.

8.7 INTEGRATED SYSTEM

To establish trust, privacy, and confidentiality, it is necessary to have an intelligent system that can evaluate the user's preferences. The system will be designed as an expert system to store trust, privacy, and confidentiality policies. These policies can be written using a web rules language with foundations of first-order logic. Traditional theorem provers can then be applied to the rules to check for inconsistencies and alert the user (Antoniou and van Harmelen, 2008). Once the user approves of all the policies, the system can take action and properly apply these policies during any transaction occurring on a site. Also, the user can place percentages next to the policies in order to apply probabilistic scenarios. Figure 8.8 gives an example of a probabilistic scenario occurring with a trust policy.

In Figure 8.8, the user sets the trust degree to 59%. Because the user trusts another person at 59%, only policies 5 through 8 will be applied. Figure 8.9 shows some example policies. These example policies will be converted into a web rules language, such as the Semantics Web Rules Language (http://www.w3.org/Submission/SWRL/) and enforced by the trust engine. Figure 8.10 illustrates an integrated architecture for ensuring confidentiality, privacy, and trust for the semantic web. The web server and the client have trust management modules. The web server has a confidentiality engine, whereas the client has a privacy engine. The inference controller, to be discussed in Section V, is the first step toward an integrated CPT system with XML, RDF, and web rules technologies. Some details of the modules are illustrated in Figure 8.11.

Trust degree = 59%	
90	Policy1
75	Policy2
70	Policy3
60	Policy4
50	Policy5
35	Policy6
10	Policy7
0	Policy8

FIGURE 8.8 Trust probabilities.

Policy1: **if** A **then** B **else** C
Policy2: **not** A **or** B
Policy3: A **or** C
Policy4: A **or** C **or** D **or not** E
Policy5: **not** (A **or** C)

FIGURE 8.9 Example policies.

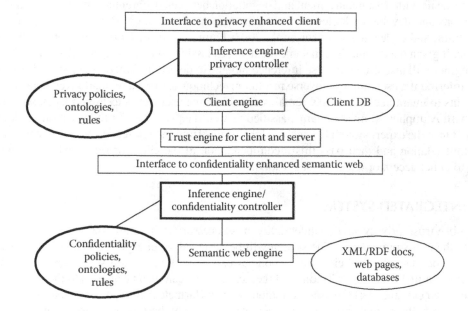

FIGURE 8.10 Integrated architecture for confidentiality, privacy, and trust.

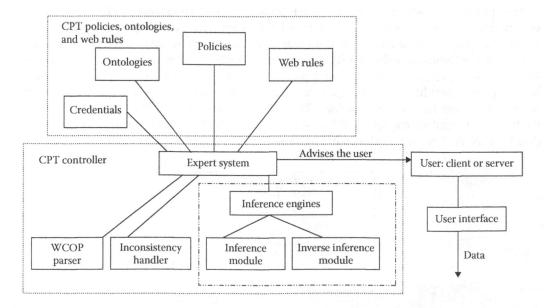

FIGURE 8.11 Modules of CPT controller.

In Figure 8.11, ontologies, CPT policies, and credentials are given to the expert system such that the expert system can advise the client or server who should receive access to what particular resource and how these resources should further be regulated. The expert system will send the policies to the web rules, credentials, ontologies, and policies (WCOP) parser to check for syntax errors and validate the inputs. The information contained within the dashed box is a part of the system that is only included in the Advanced TP&C system. The inference engines (e.g., TIE, PIE, and CIE) will use an inference module to determine if classified information can be inferred.

8.8   CPT WITHIN THE CONTEXT OF SOCIAL NETWORKS

CPT are crucial services that must be built into a social network. Confidentiality policies will enable the members of the network to determine what information is to be shared with their friends in the network. Privacy policies will determine what a network can release about a member provided that these policies are accepted by the member. Trust policies will provide a way for members of a network to assign trust values to the others. For example, a member may not share all the data with his/her friends in the network unless he trusts the friends. Similarly, a network may enforce certain privacy policies, and if one does not approve of these policies or not trust the network, then he or she may not join the network. Therefore, we see that many of the concepts discussed in the previous sections are directly applicable to social networks.

If the social networks are represented using semantic web technologies such as RDF graphs, then the reasoning techniques inherent in technologies such as RDF and Web Ontology Language (OWL) can be used to reason about the policies and determine whether any information should be shared with members. In addition to CPT policies, social networks also have to deal with information-sharing policies; that is, member John of a network may share data with member Jane, provided that Jane does not share with member Mary. We have carried out an extensive investigation of assured information sharing in the cloud, and are extending this work to social media data. Our experimental systems on this topic will be discussed in Sections V, VII, and VIII. Figure 8.12 illustrates the adaptation of the CPT framework for social media data.

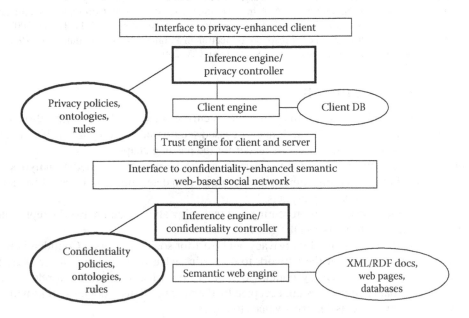

FIGURE 8.12   CPT for social media data.

8.9   SUMMARY AND DIRECTIONS

This chapter has provided an overview of security and privacy considerations with respect to inference. We first discussed a framework for enforcing confidentiality, privacy, and trust for the semantic web. Next, we described our approach to confidentiality and inference control. Then, we discussed privacy for the semantic web. This was followed by a discussion of trust management as well as an integrated framework for CPT. Finally, we discussed how we can adapt the CPT framework for social media data.

While the discussion in this chapter provides a high-level discussion of CPT with semantic web technologies that may represent social network data, the discussion in this book has focused in detail on confidentiality and privacy. There are many directions for further work. We need to continue with the research on confidentiality and privacy, as well as trust for the semantic web representing social media data, and subsequently develop the integrated framework for CPT. Finally, we need to formalize the notions of CPT and build a security model. One very productive area of research would be to enhance our framework for secure social networks discussed in Section V of this book, and incorporate both privacy and trust models into this framework. That is, we need a unifying framework for incorporating confidentiality, privacy, trust, and information-sharing policies for social media data. Such a framework is discussed in Section IX.

REFERENCES

Agrawal, R. and Srikant, R. Privacy-preserving data mining. In: *SIGMOD Conference*, pp. 439–450, 2000.
Antoniou, G. and van Harmelen, F. *A Semantic Web Primer*. MIT Press, Cambridge, MA, 2008.
Denker, G. et al. Security for DAML web services: Annotation and matchmaking. In: *Proceedings of the International Semantic Web Conference*, Sanibel Island, FL, 2003.
Finin, T. and Joshi, A. Agents, trust, and information access on the semantic web. *ACM SIGMOD* (4): 30–35, 2002.
Kagal, L., Finin, T., and Joshi, A. A policy based approach to security for the semantic web. In: *Proceedings of the International Semantic Web Conference*, Sanibel Island, FL, 2003.
Kantarcioglu, M. and Clifton, C. Assuring privacy when big brother is watching. In: *Proceedings of Data Mining Knowledge Discover (DMKD)*, pp. 88–93, 2003.
Thuraisingham, B. Data mining, national security and privacy. *ACM SIGKDD*, January 2003.
Thuraisingham, B., Tsybulnik, N., and Alam, A. Administering the semantic web: Confidentiality, privacy, and trust management. *International Journal of Information Security and Privacy* 1(1): 18–34, 2007.
Yu, T. and Winslett, M. A unified scheme for resource protection in automated trust negotiation. In: *Proceedings of IEEE Symposium on Security and Privacy*, Oakland, CA, 2003.

CONCLUSION TO SECTION II

Section II has described aspects of analyzing and securing social media. We first discussed the various social media analytics tasks, and then discussed security and privacy for such systems. The main goal of this section is to motivate the reader for the ensuing chapters.

Chapter 6 gave the reader a feel for the various applications of social media analytics. These applications ranged from detecting communities of interest to determining political affiliations. We also addressed security and privacy aspects.

Chapter 7 discussed aspects of representing and reasoning about social networks represented as Resource Description Framework (RDF) graphs.

Chapter 8 discussed confidentiality, privacy, and trust for social networks. Confidentiality policies will enable the members of the network to determine what information is to be shared with their friends in the network. Privacy policies will determine what a network can release about a member, provided that these policies are accepted by the member. Trust policies will provide a way for members of a network to assign trust values to others.

Section III

Techniques and Tools
for Social Network Analytics

INTRODUCTION TO SECTION III

Now that we have provided an overview of the various aspects of analyzing and securing social media, we are now ready to delve into some of the technical details of location mining for social networks. We have carried out an extensive investigation of this topic and have developed systems based on our algorithms. We will discuss novel algorithms that we call TweetHood, Tweecalization, and Tweeque, and a system called TWinner.

Section III consists of five chapters: Chapters 9 through 13. Chapter 9 will discuss aspects of location mining for social networks. Such approaches would enable, say, law enforcement to determine where the members of the network are if they have committed a crime. We will first discuss the importance of location mining and then provide an overview of the related efforts on this topic. This will be followed by a discussion of the challenges in location mining. Some aspects of geospatial proximity and friendship were then discussed. Finally, we provide an overview of our contributions to location mining. Chapter 10 describes TweetHood, an algorithm for agglomerative clustering on fuzzy k closest Friends with variable depth. Graph-related approaches are the methods that rely on the social graph of the user while deciding on the location of the user. We describe three such methods that show the evolution of the algorithm currently used in TweetHood. These algorithms are as follows: (i) a simple majority algorithm with variable depth, (ii) k closest friends with variable depth, and (iii) fuzzy k closest friends with variable depth. We will also provide experimental results for the algorithms. In Chapter 11, we will argue that the location data of users on social networks is a rather scarce resource and only available to a small portion of the users. This creates a need for a methodology that makes use of both labeled and unlabeled data for training. In this case, the location concept serves the purpose of class label. Therefore, our problem is a classic example for the application of semisupervised learning algorithms. We will describe a semisupervised learning method for label propagation, which we call Tweecalization. Chapter 12 will describe the effects of migration and propose a set of algorithms that we call Tweeque. In particular, we will discuss the effect of migration and temporal data mining aspects. Then, we will discuss social clique identification algorithms and provide our experimental results. Chapter 13 will describe an application of our location mining work, and we describe the development of a system that focuses on understanding the intent of a user search query. In particular, we discuss a system called TWinner that examines the application of social media in improving the quality of web searches.

9 Developments and Challenges in Location Mining

9.1 INTRODUCTION

One of the critical applications of social network analysis is to extract demographics information. Such information can be used to determine whether a person is suspicious, and if so, their education, age, and location. Often people may specify incorrect information about their personal data. Even in LinkedIn, which is supposed to be used for professional applications such as finding jobs, people sometimes may post false data. Therefore, we need to determine whether the information on social networks is incorrect, and if so, determine the correct information.

We have developed algorithms that will determine various types of demographics data. Our initial work was on determining the locations of Twitter users. We have subsequently designed a system that will extract demographics data from various social networks. That is, our techniques will integrate multiple social networks, identify a person, and then extract demographics data.

Section III consists of several chapters that focus on location mining. Specifically, we will describe multiple algorithms for location mining and its importance. The organization of this chapter is as follows. In Section 9.2, we will discuss key aspects of location mining and its importance. Section 9.3 describes efforts in location mining. Section 9.4 describes challenges in location mining. Aspects of geospatial proximity and friendships are discussed in Section 9.5. Our contributions to location mining are discussed in Section 9.6. The chapter is summarized in Section 9.7. Figure 9.1 illustrates the contents of this chapter.

9.2 KEY ASPECTS OF LOCATION MINING

Importance of Location. The advances in location acquisition and mobile communication technologies empower people to use location data with existing online social networks (OSNs). The dimension of location helps bridge the gap between the physical world and online social networking services (Cranshaw et al., 2010). The knowledge of location allows the user to expand his or her current social network, explore new places to eat, etc. Just like time, location is one of the most important components of user context, and further analysis can reveal more information about an individual's interests, behaviors, and relationships with others. In this section, we look at the reasons that make location such an important attribute.

Privacy and Security. Location privacy is the ability of an individual to move in public space with the expectation that under normal circumstances, their location will not be systematically and secretly recorded for later use (Blumberg and Eckersley, 2009). It is no secret that many people apart from friends and family are interested in the information users post on social networks. This includes identity thieves, stalkers, debt collectors, con artists, and corporations wanting to know more about the consumers. Sites and organizations like http://pleaserobme.com/ are generating awareness about the possible consequences of oversharing. Once collected, this sensitive information can be left vulnerable to access by the government and third parties. And, unfortunately, the existing laws give more emphasis to the financial interests of corporations than to the privacy of consumers.

Trustworthiness. Trustworthiness is another reason that makes location discovery so important. It is well known that social media had a big role to play in the revolutionary wave of

FIGURE 9.1   Location mining.

demonstrations and protests that occurred in the Arab world termed the *Arab Spring* to accelerate social protest (Kassim, 2012; Sander, 2012). The Department of State has effectively used social networking sites to gauge the sentiments within societies (Grossman, 2009). Maintaining a social media presence in deployed locations also allows commanders to understand potential threats and emerging trends within the regions. The online community can provide a good indicator of prevailing moods and emerging issues. Many vocal opposition groups will likely use social media to air grievances publicly. In such cases and others similar to these, it becomes very important for organizations (like the US State Department) to be able to verify the correct location of the users posting these messages.

Marketing and Business. Finally, let us discuss the impact of social media in marketing and garnering feedback from consumers. First, social media facilitates marketers to communicate with peers and customers (both current and future). It is reported that 93% of marketers use social media (Stelzner and Mershon, 2012). It provides significantly more visibility for the company or the product, and helps spread the message in a relaxed and conversational way (Lake, n.d.). The second major contribution of social media toward business is getting feedback from users. Social media allows the ability to get the kind of quick feedback inbound marketers require to stay agile. Large corporations from Wal-Mart to Starbucks are leveraging social networks beyond your typical posts and updates to get feedback on the quality of their products and services, especially ones that have been recently launched on Twitter (March, 2012).

Understanding News Intent. It is November 12, 2009, and John is a naïve user who wants to know the latest on the happenings related to the shootings that occurred at the army base in Fort Hood. John opens his favorite search engine site and enters *Fort Hood*, expecting to see the news. But, unfortunately, the search results that he sees are a little different from what he had expected. First, he sees a lot of timeless information such as Fort Hood on maps, the Wikipedia article on Fort Hood, the Fort Hood homepage, etc., clearly indicating that the search engine has little clue as to what the user is looking for. Secondly, among the small news bulletins that get displayed on the screen, the content is not organized and the result is that he has a hard time finding the news for November 12, 2009.

Companies like Google, Yahoo, and Microsoft are battling to be the main gateway to the Internet (NPR, 2004). Since a typical way for Internet users to find news is through search engines, and a rather substantial portion of the search queries is news related where the user wants to know about the latest on the happenings at a particular geo-location, it thus becomes necessary for search engines to understand the intent of the user query, based on the limited user information available to it and also the current world scenario.

The impact of Twitter on news can be understood further by its coverage of two very crucial recent events: the July 2008 earthquake in Southern California and the turbulent aftermath of Iran's elections in June 2009.

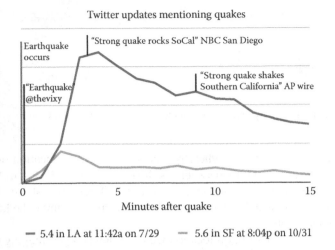

Twitter updates mentioning quakes

— 5.4 in LA at 11:42a on 7/29   — 5.6 in SF at 8:04p on 10/31

FIGURE 9.2 Twitter message graph after the Southern California earthquakes. (From Stone, B. Twitter as news-wire. Retrieved January 26, 2013, from *Twitter Blog*: http://blog.twitter.com/2008/07/twitter-as-news-wire.html, July 29, 2008.)

Figure 9.2 illustrates the beginning of the earthquake followed seconds later by the first Twitter update from Los Angeles. About 4 minutes later, official news began to emerge about the quake. By then, *Earthquake* was trending on Twitter Search with thousands of updates and more on the way. Many news agencies get their feed from a news wire service such as the Associated Press (AP). "Strong quake shakes Southern California" was pushed out by AP about 9 minutes after people began *tweeting* primary accounts from their homes, businesses, doctor's appointments, or wherever they were when the quake struck (Stone, 2008).

The second example would be that of the elections in Iran in 2009. Time, in partnership with CNN, discussed the impact of Twitter on the coverage of developments after the Iran elections of 2009 (Grossman, 2009). On June 12, 2009, Iran held its presidential elections between incumbent Ahmadinejad and rival Mousavi. The result, a landslide for Ahmadinejad, led to violent riots across Iran, charges of voting fraud, and protests worldwide. Even as the government of that country was evidently restricting access to opposition websites and text messaging, on Twitter, a separate uprising took place, as tweets marked with the hashtag *#cnnfail* began tearing into the cable news network for devoting too few resources to the controversy in Iran. US State Department officials reached out to Twitter and asked them to delay a network upgrade that was scheduled for Monday (June 15) night. This was done to protect the interests of Iranians using the service to protest the presidential election that took place on June 12, 2009.

9.3 EFFORTS IN LOCATION MINING

In this section, we first review the related research in the fields of location mining from semistructured text such as web pages and then from OSNs such as Twitter and Facebook. Also, we survey a wide range of existing work for determining intent from search queries. It is important to understand that the location of the user is not easily accessible owing to security and privacy concerns, thus impeding the growth of location-based services in the present world scenario. By conducting experiments to find the locations of 1 million users, we found that only 14.3% specify their locations explicitly.

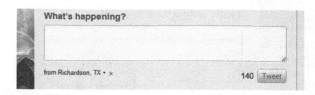

FIGURE 9.3   Feature introduced by Twitter to provide location with messages.

Twitter introduced a feature in 2010 whereby users can associate a location (identified from the Internet Protocol [IP] address) with their tweets as shown in Figure 9.3. But, unfortunately, a very small fraction of users make use of this service. Martin (2010) reports that only 0.23% of the total tweets were found to be geo-tagged. That leaves us with the option to mine the location of the user, which is not an easy task in itself.

There has been a lot of prior work on location identification and geo-tagging of documents and web pages. Social networking, on the other hand, is still a very new field of computer science, and little work has been carried out toward identifying the location of users based on their social activity. In this section, we do a brief survey of the previous works.

The problem of geographic location identification and disambiguation has been dealt with mostly using two approaches. One approach involves the concepts of machine learning and natural language processing (NLP), and the other approach involves the use of data mining with the help of gazetteers. In NLP and machine learning, a lot of previous work has been carried out on the more general topic of named entity recognition (NER). Most of the work makes use of structured and well-edited text from news articles or sample data from conferences.

Most research works rely on NLP algorithms and less on machine learning techniques. The reason for this is that machine learning algorithms require training data that is not easy to obtain. Also, their complexity makes them less efficient as compared with the algorithms using the gazetteers.

Other researchers use a five-step algorithm, where the first two steps of the algorithm are reversed. First, only terms appearing in the gazetteer are shortlisted. Next, they use NLP techniques to remove the non-geo terms. Li et al. (2002) report a 93.8% precision on news and travel guide data.

McCurley (2001) analyzes the various aspects of a web page that could have a geographic association, from its Uniform Resource Locator (URL), the language in the text, phone numbers, zip codes, etc. Names appearing in the text may be looked up in White Pages to determine the location of the person. His approach is heavily dependent on information like zip codes, etc., and is hence successful in the United States, where it is available for free, but is difficult to obtain for other countries. Their techniques rely on heuristics and do not consider the relationship between geo-locations appearing in the text.

The gazetteer-based approach relies on the completeness of the source and, hence, cannot identify terms that are not present in the gazetteer. But, on the other hand, they are less complex than NLP, and machine learning techniques are hence faster.

Amitay et al. (2004) present a way of determining the page focus of web pages using the gazetteer approach and after using techniques to prune the data. They are able to correctly tag individual name place occurrences 80% of the time and are able to recognize the correct focus of the pages 91% of the time. However, they have a low accuracy for the geo/non-geo disambiguation.

Lieberman et al. (2007) describe the construction of a spatio-textual search engine using the gazetteer and NLP tools, a system for extracting, querying, and visualizing textual references to geographic locations in unstructured text documents. They use an elaborate technique for removing the stop words, using a hybrid model of part-of-speech (POS) and named entity recognition (NER) tagger. POS helps identify the nouns, and the NER tagger annotates them as person, organization, and location. They consider the proper nouns tagged as locations. But this system does not work well for text where the name of a person is ambiguous with a location. For example, Jordan might mean Michael Jordan, the basketball player, or it might mean the location. In that case, the NER tagger might remove Jordan, considering it to be the name of a person. For removing geo–geo ambiguity, they use the pair strength algorithm. Pairs of feature records are compared to determine whether or not they give evidence to each other, based on the familiarity of each location, frequency of each location, as well as their document and geodesic distances. They do not report any results for accuracy of the algorithm, so comparison and review is not possible.

The most relevant related work in social networks using the content-based approach is the one proposed in Cheng et al. (2010) to estimate the geo-location of a Twitter user. For estimating the city-level geo-location of a Twitter user, they consider a set of tweets from a set of users belonging to a set of cities across the United States. They estimate the probability distribution of terms used in these tweets, across the cities considered in their data set. They report accuracy in placing 51% of Twitter users within 100 miles of their actual location.

Hecht et al. (2011) performed a simple machine learning experiment to determine whether they can identify a user's location by only looking at what that user tweets. They concluded that a user's country and state can be estimated with decent accuracy, indicating that users implicitly reveal location information, with or without realizing it. The approach used by them only looks to predict the accuracy at the country and state levels, and the accuracy figures for the state level are in the 30s, and hence are not very promising.

It is vital to understand here that identifying the location mentioned in documents or messages is very different from identifying the location of the user. That is, even if the page focus of the messages is identified correctly, that may not be the correct location of the user. For example, people express their opinions on political issues around the world all the time. The catastrophic earthquake in Haiti led to many messages having references to that country. Another example is that of the volcano in Iceland that led to flights being canceled worldwide. In addition, the time complexity of text-based geo-tagging messages is very large, making it unsuitable for real-time applications like location-based opinion mining. Thus, as we shall show in later sections, the geo-tagging of user messages is an inaccurate method and has many pitfalls.

Recently, some work has been carried out in the area of establishing the relation between geo-spatial proximity and friendship. In Backstrom et al. (2010), the authors performed extensive experiments on data collected from Facebook and came up with a probabilistic model to predict the location. They show that their algorithm outperforms the IP-based geo-location method. Liben-Nowell et al. (2005) focused their research on LiveJournal and established the fact that the probability of befriending a particular person is inversely proportional to the number of closer people.

A major drawback of all the previous location extraction algorithms, including the ones discussed above, is that they do not consider time as a factor. Migration is an important social phenomenon with a significant fraction of people in the United States changing cities every year. It is, therefore, very important to design algorithms that use some intelligent criteria for distinguishing between the current location of a user from different locations he or she may have lived in in the past.

Geographic Information Retrieval. Geographic information retrieval is a well-discussed topic in the past, where a lot of research has been done to establish a relationship between the location of the user and the type of content that interests him or her. Researchers have analyzed the influence of a user's location on the type of food he or she eats, the sports he or she follows, the clothes he or she wears, etc. But it is important to note here that most of the previous research does not take into account the influence of *time* on the preferences of the user.

Liu and Birnbaum (2008) did a similar geo-analysis of the impact of the location of the source on the viewpoint presented in the news articles. Sheng et al. (2008) discussed the need for reordering the search results (like food, sports, etc.) based on user preferences obtained by analyzing the user's location. Other previous research attempts (Backstrom et al., 2008; Zhuang et al., 2008) focused on establishing the relationship between the location obtained from the IP address and the nature of the search query issued by the user. In our work, we do not take the location of the user into consideration, since it may not be very accurate in predicting the intent of the user.

Hassan et al. (2009) focused their work on establishing a relationship between the geographic information of the user and the query issued. They examined millions of web search queries to predict the news intent of the user, taking into account the query location confidence, location type of the geo-reference in the query, and the population density of the user location. But they did not consider the influence of the time at which the user issued the query, which can negatively affect the search results for news intent. For example, a query for *Fort Hood* 5 months before November 2009 would have less news intent and more information intent than a query made in second week of November 2009 (after the Ft. Hood shootings took place).

Twitter acts as a popular social medium for Internet users to express their opinions and share information on diverse topics ranging from food to politics. A lot of these messages are irrelevant from an information perspective, and are either spam or pointless babble. Another concern while dealing with such data is that it consists of a lot of informal text, including words such as *gimme*, *wassup*, etc., and need to be processed before traditional NLP techniques can be applied to them.

Nagarajan et al. (2009) explore the application of restricted relationship graphs or Resource Description Framework (RDF) and statistical NLP techniques to improve named entity annotation in challenging informal English domains. Sheth and Nagarajan (2009), Sheth et al. (2002), and Nagarajan et al. (2009) aimed at characterizing what people are talking about, how they express themselves, and why they exchange messages.

9.4 CHALLENGES IN LOCATION MINING

9.4.1 OVERVIEW

As discussed previously, many efforts are being made on the part of social networking companies to incorporate location information in communication. Twitter, in 2009, acquired Mixer Labs (Parr, 2009), a maker of geo-location web services, to boost its location-based services campaign and compete with geo-savvy mobile social networking sites like Foursquare and Gowalla. Nowadays, on logging into your Twitter account, you are given the option to add location (city level) to your messages.

But still, these efforts are not paying dividends, simply for several security and privacy reasons. And there is no incentive for users. We conducted an experiment and found that of 1 million users on Twitter, only 14.3% actually share their location explicitly. Since the location field is basically a text field, many times the information provided is not very useful (Hecht et al., 2011). The various problems in using the location provided by the user himself or herself include the following:

- *Invalid geographical information*: Users may provide locations that are not valid geographic information and hence cannot be geo-coded or plotted on a map. Examples include *Justin Bieber's heart*, *NON YA BISNESS!!*, and *looking down on u people*.
- *Incorrect locations that may actually exist*: At times a lot of users may provide information that is not meant to be a location but is mapped to an actual geographical location. Examples include *Nothing* in Arizona, or *Little Heaven* in Connecticut.
- *Provide multiple locations*: There are other users who provide several locations, and it becomes difficult for the geo-coder to single out a unique location. Examples include *CALi bOY $TuCC iN V3Ga$*, who apparently is a California boy stuck in Las Vegas, Nevada.
- *Absence of finer granularity*: Hecht et al. (2011) report that almost 35% of users just enter their country or state, and there is no reference to the finer-level location such as city or neighborhood.

Hence, explicitly mentioned locations are rare and maybe untrustworthy in certain cases where the user has mal-intent. That leaves us with the question, can the location be mined from implicit information associated with the users like the content of messages posted by them and the nature of their social media network?

A commonly used approach to determine the location of the user is to map the IP address to geographic locations using large gazetteers such as hostip.info. Figure 9.4 shows a screenshot where a user is able to determine his or her location from the IP address by using the hostip.info website (http://www.hostip.info/). But Mitchell (2013) argues that using the IP address for location identification has its limitations:

- IP addresses may be associated with the wrong location (e.g., the wrong postal code, city or suburb within a metropolitan area).
- Addresses may be associated only with a very broad geographic area (e.g., a large city, or a state). Many addresses are associated only with a city, not with a street address or latitude/longitude location.
- Some addresses will not appear in the database and therefore cannot be mapped (often true for IP numbers not commonly used on the Internet).

Additionally, only the hosting companies (in this case, the social networking sites) have access to the user's IP address, whereas we want to design algorithms that are generic so that any third-party people can implement and use them. And since most Twitter users have public profiles, such analysis of user profiles is very much possible.

FIGURE 9.4 Hostip.info allows user to map IP addresses to geo-locations.

In this section, we will first discuss the problems related to mining location from text and why we find it to be a rather unreliable way for location determination. Second, we discuss the challenges associated with the social graph network-based location extraction technique.

9.4.2 What Makes Location Mining from Text Inaccurate?

Twitter, being a popular social media site, is a way by which users generally express their opinions, with frequent references to locations including cities, countries, etc. It is also intuitive in such cases to draw a relation between such locations mentioned in the tweets and the place of residence of the user. In other words, a message from a user supporting the Longhorns (football team for the University of Texas at Austin) is most likely from a person living in Austin, Texas, United States, than from someone in Australia.

Twitter's Noisy and Unique Style—Unstructured Data. As previously mentioned, the identification of the location of a user from the messages is a very different task from identification of the locations in web pages or other media. Twitter messages consist of text that is unstructured and more often than not have grammatical and spelling errors. And these characteristics distinguish microtext from traditional documents or web pages (Dent and Paul, 2011; Rosa and Ellen, 2009). Therefore, it becomes more difficult to identify the location from them. Figure 9.5 shows one such tweet (Twitter, 2013).

Presence of Multiple Concept Classes. The other major issue that one faces in identification of a location concept is that unlike other sources of information like web pages, news articles, etc., Twitter messages consist of multiple concept classes; that is, several locations may be mentioned in the messages collected from a single user. In such a case, identification of a single location that acts as a page focus can be a difficult problem. Figure 9.6 shows one such tweet, where the user is actually from Serbia but the message mentions multiple locations (Serbia, Brazil, and France).

Geo/Geo Ambiguity and Geo/Non-Geo Ambiguity. Even if the algorithm is able to identify words that are possible candidates for location concepts, we still need to disambiguate them correctly. There are two types of ambiguities that exist: geo/non-geo and geo/geo ambiguities (Amitay et al., 2004; Brunner and Purves, 2008; Smith and Crane, 2001; Volz et al., 2007).

Geo/non-geo ambiguity: Geo/non-geo ambiguity is the case of a place name having another, nongeographic meaning, for example, Paris might be the capital of France or might refer to the socialite actress Paris Hilton. Another example is Jordan, which could refer to the Arab kingdom in Asia or Michael Jordan, the famous basketball player.

FIGURE 9.5 Example of a tweet containing slang and grammatically incorrect sentences.

FIGURE 9.6 Example of a tweet containing multiple locations.

Lancaster Los Angeles County CA US	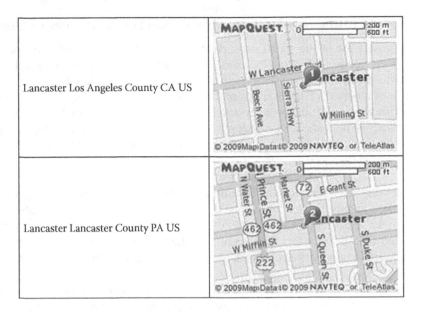
Lancaster Lancaster County PA US	

FIGURE 9.7   Geo/geo ambiguity as shown by the MapQuest API.

> *Geo/geo ambiguity*: Geo/geo ambiguity arises from two places having the same name but different geographic locations; for example, Paris is the capital of France and is also a city in Texas. Another example is Amsterdam, which could refer to the capital and largest city of the Netherlands, or to a city located in Montgomery County, New York, United States. Figure 9.7 shows an example of geo/geo ambiguity arising from a query for *Lancaster* (MapQuest, 2009).
>
> **Location in Text Is Different from Location of User.** Unlike location mining from web pages, where the focus of the entire web page is a single location (Amitay et al., 2004) and we do not care about the location of the author, in social networking sites the case is very different. In OSNs, when we talk about location, it could mean two things. The first is the location of the user (which we are trying to predict) and the other, the location in a message. And, in some cases, these two could be two totally different locations. Figure 9.8 shows one such tweet in which the person talks about a football game between Brazil and France, but it is actually from Hemel Hempstead, Hertfordshire, United Kingdom.

As is evident, the content-based approach may prove to be inaccurate in cases where the user talks about news-making incidents in other parts of the world. Another example is for Haiti. Haiti was a popular geo-reference in tweets after the earthquake in 2010. In another case, someone who talks about going to Venice for a vacation is not necessarily Italian.

FIGURE 9.8   Tweet from a user who is actually from Hemel Hempstead, Hertfordshire, United Kingdom, but talks about a football game between Brazil and France. (From Twitter. Twitter search. Retrieved February 2, 2013, from *Twitter*: https://twitter.com/search, February 2, 2013.)

9.4.3 TECHNICAL CHALLENGES IN LOCATION MINING FROM SOCIAL NETWORK OF USER

This approach makes use of the social network of the user. Here, the social network of the user comprises followers (people following the user) and following (people he or she is following). This approach gives us an insight on a user's close friends and the celebrities he or she is following. Intuitively, most of a person's friends are from the same country and, also, a person is more likely to follow celebrities that are from his or her own country. In other words, an American's friends are mostly Americans, and he or she has a higher probability of following President Barack Obama than Asian users. There are certain technical challenges that need to be solved before we can mine the location from the social network.

Small Percentage of Users Reveal Location, Others Provide Incorrect Locations. As stated earlier in this chapter, only a small percentage of the users with public profiles are willing to share their location on Twitter for privacy and security reasons. And since the location field is just a text field, there are others who provide location(s) that are not valid geographic information, or are incorrect but may actually exist, or consist of several locations.

Special Cases: Spammers and Celebrities. It is necessary to identify spammers and celebrities since they cannot be dealt in the same way as other users because of the differences in the properties associated with their social graphs. At the country level, it is not always safe to assume that a person always follows celebrities from his own country. Queen Rania of Jordan advocates for global education and thus has followers around the world. In such cases, judging the location of a user based on the celebrities he or she is following can lead to inaccurate results.

Defining the Graph. We need to come up with an objective function that captures *friendship* in the best manner for constructing the graphs for application of the algorithms.

Geographical Mobility: Predicting Current Location. Social migration is a very important phenomenon. And a significant percentage of users move from one county to another. It is therefore crucial for us to design algorithms that do temporal analysis and are able to separate out the most recent location from previous locations.

9.5 GEOSPATIAL PROXIMITY AND FRIENDSHIP

We hypothesize that there is a direct relation between geographical proximity and probability of friendship on Twitter. In other words, even though we live in the Internet age, where distances actually do not matter and people can communicate with other people across the globe, users tend to bring people from their offline friends into their online world. The relationship between friendship and geographic proximity in OSNs has been studied in detail previously also in Backstrom et al. (2010) for Facebook and in Liben-Nowell et al. (2005) for LiveJournal. We performed our own set of experiments to understand the nature of friendships on Twitter, and study the effect of geographical proximity on friendship.

We formulated 10 million friendship pairs in which the location of both users is known. It is important to understand that our initial definition of friendship on Twitter is that A and B are friends if A follows B or B follows A. We divided the edge distance for the pairs into buckets of 10 miles. We determined the cumulative distribution function, to observe the probability as a continuous curve. Figure 9.9a shows the results of our findings. It is interesting to note that only 10% of the pairs have the users within 100 miles and 75% of the users are at least 1000 miles from each other. That is, the results are contrary to the hypothesis we proposed and to the findings of Backstrom et al. (2010) for Facebook and Liben-Nowell et al. (2005) for LiveJournal. Next, we study the nature of relationships on Twitter and find it to be very different from other OSNs like Facebook, LiveJournal, etc.

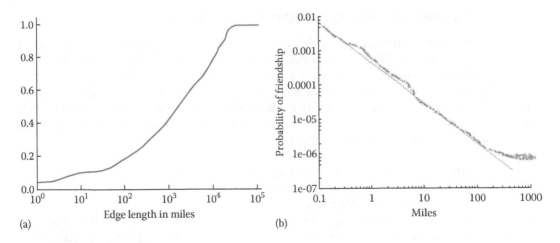

FIGURE 9.9 (a) Cumulative distribution function to observe the probability as a continuous curve and (b) probability versus distance for 10^{12} Twitter user pairs.

We make several interesting observations that distinguish Twitter from other OSNs like Facebook and LiveJournal:

- A link from A to B (A following B) does not always mean there is an edge from B to A (B follows A back).
- A link from A to B (A following B), unlike Facebook or LinkedIn, does not always indicate friendship, but sometimes means that A is interested in the messages posted by B.
- If A has a public profile (which is true for a large majority of profiles), then he or she has little control over who follows him or her.
- Twitter is a popular OSN used by celebrities (large follower-to-following ratio) to reach their fans and spammers (large following-to-followers ratio) to promote businesses.

These factors make us redefine the concept of friendship on Twitter to make it somewhat stricter. Two users, A and B, are friends if and only if A is following B and B also follows A back.

To put it plainly, from the earlier set of friends for a user A, we are taking a subset, called associates of A, which are more likely to be his or her actual friends than the other users. By ensuring the presence of a two-way edge, we ensure that the other user is neither a celebrity (since celebrities do not *follow back* fans) nor a spammer (because no one wants to follow a spammer!). And a two-way edge also means that the user A knows B, and thus B is not some random person following A. And finally, the chances of A being interested in messages of B and vice versa without them being friends are pretty slim.

We rerun the earlier experiments to study the relation between association probability and geographic distance.

We form 10^{12} user pairs and identify the geographical distance between them. And then, we divide the data set into buckets of 0.1 miles and determine what percentage of them actually have an edge (are friends). Figure 9.9b shows the probability of friendship versus the distance (in miles) distribution. The results for Twitter are very similar to those for LiveJournal (Liben-Nowell et al., 2005) and Facebook (Backstrom et al., 2010). The curve follows the power law having a curve of the form $a(x + b)^{-c}$ with exponent of -0.87 and for distances >1000 miles becomes a straight line.

9.6   OUR CONTRIBUTIONS TO LOCATION MINING

We make an important contribution in the field of identifying the current location of a user through the social graph of the user. This section (Section III) describes in detail three techniques for location mining from the social graph of the user, and each one is based on a strong theoretical framework of machine learning. We demonstrate how the problem of identification of the location of a user can be mapped to a machine learning problem. We conducted a variety of experiments to show the validity of our approach, and how it outperforms previous approaches and the traditional content-based text mining approach in accuracy.

- We performed extensive experiments to study the relationship between geospatial proximity and friendship on Twitter, and show that with increasing distance between two users, the probability of friendship decreases.
- The first algorithm, TweetHood, looks at the k closest friends of the user and their locations for predicting the user's location. If the locations of one or more friends are not known, the algorithm is willing to go further into the graph of that friend to determine a location label for him. The algorithm is based on the k nearest neighbor approach, a supervised learning algorithm commonly used in pattern recognition (Coomans and Massart, 1982).
- The second approach described, Tweecalization, uses label propagation, a semisupervised learning algorithm, for determining the location of a user from his or her social network. Since only a small fraction of users explicitly provide a location (labeled data), the problem of determining the location of users (unlabeled data) based on the social network is a classic example of a scenario where the semisupervised learning algorithm fits in.
- For our final approach, Tweeque, we did an analysis of the social phenomenon of migration, and describe why it is important to take time into consideration when predicting the most current location of the user.
- Tweeque uses graph partitioning to identify the most current location of the user by taking migration as the latent time factor. The proposed efficient semisupervised learning algorithm provides us with the ability to intelligently separate out the current location from the past locations.
- All the three approaches outperform the existing content-based approach in both accuracy and running time.
- We developed a system, TWinner, that makes use of these algorithms and helps the search engine to identify the intent of the user query, whether he or she is interested in general information or the latest news. Second, TWinner adds additional keywords to the query so that the existing search engine algorithm understands the news intent and displays the news articles in a more meaningful way.

9.7   SUMMARY AND DIRECTIONS

Identifying the location of social media users would enable, say, law enforcement to determine where the users are if they have committed a crime. On the other hand, we may want to protect the location of innocent users. We first discussed the importance of location mining and then provided an overview of the related efforts on this topic. This was followed by a discussion of the challenges in location mining. Some aspects of geospatial proximity and friendship were then discussed. Finally, we provided an overview of our contributions to location mining to be discussed in Chapters 10 through 13.

We have developed four techniques for location mining. They are TweetHood, Tweecalization, Tweeque, and TWinner. These techniques use different data mining algorithms to extract the location of Twitter users. As we have mentioned, we can apply the techniques to other social media systems as well as databases. In addition, we can also adapt these techniques to extract other demographics information. We will discuss our location mining algorithms in the following chapters.

REFERENCES

Amitay, E., Har'El, N., Sivan, R., and Soffer, A. Web-a-where: Geotagging web content. In: *27th Annual International ACM SIGIR Conference on Research and Development in Information Retrieval*, 2004.

Backstrom, L., Kleinberg, J., Kumar, R., and Novak, J. Spatial variation in search engine. In: *Proc. 17th International World Wide Web Conference*, 2008.

Backstrom, L., Sun, E., and Marlow, C. Find me if you can: Improving geographical prediction with social and spatial proximity. In: *Proceeding of the 19th International Conference on World Wide Web*. ACM, New York, 2010.

Blumberg, A. and Eckersley, P. On location privacy, and how to avoid losing it forever. Retrieved from Electronic Frontier Foundation: https://www.eff.org/wp/locational-privacy, 2009.

Brunner, T.J. and Purves, R.S. Spatial autocorrelation and toponym ambiguity. In: *2nd ACM International Workshop on Geographic Information Retrieval (GIR '08)*, pp. 25–26. ACM, New York, 2008.

Cheng, Z., Caverlee, J., and Lee, K. You are where you tweet: A content-based approach to geo-locating Twitter users. In: *19th ACM International Conference on Information and Knowledge Management*, pp. 759–768. ACM, New York, 2010.

Coomans, D. and Massart, D.L. Alternative k-nearest neighbour rules in supervised pattern recognition: Part 1. k-Nearest neighbour classification by using alternative voting rules. *Analytica Chimica Acta* 136: 15–27, 1982.

Cranshaw, J., Toch, E., Hong, J., Kittur, A., and Sadeh, N. Bridging the gap between physical location and online social networks. In: *ACM ASE International Conference on Social Informatics*. ACM, New York, 2010.

Dent, K. and Paul, S. Through the twitter glass: Detecting questions in micro-text. In: *Workshop on Analyzing Microtext at the 25th AAAI Conference on Artificial Intelligence*, 2011.

Grossman, L. *Iran Protests: Twitter, the Medium of the Movement*. Retrieved January 26, 2013, from Time World: http://www.time.com/time/world/article/0,8599,1905125,00.html, June 17, 2009.

Hassan, A., Jones, R., and Diaz, F. A case study of using geographic cues to predict query news intent. In: *17th ACM SIGSPATIAL International Conference on Advances in Geographic Information Systems*, pp. 33–41. ACM, New York, 2009.

Hecht, B., Hong, L., Suh, B., and Chi, H.E. Tweets from Justin Bieber's heart: The dynamics of the location field in user profiles. In: *Annual ACM Conference on Human Factors in Computing Systems*, pp. 237–246, 2011.

Kassim, S. *Twitter Revolution: How the Arab Spring Was Helped By Social Media*. Retrieved February 11, 2013, from Policymic: http://www.policymic.com/articles/10642/twitter-revolution-how-the-arab-spring-was-helped-by-social-media, July 2012.

Lake, L. *Understanding the Role of Social Media in Marketing*. Retrieved February 11, 2013, from About.com: http://marketing.about.com/od/strategytutorials/a/socialmediamktg.htm.

Li, H., Srihari, R., Niu, C., and Li, W. Location normalization for information extraction. In: *19th International Conference on Computational Linguistics; Volume 1*, pp. 1–7. Association for Computational Linguistics, Stroudsburg, PA, 2002.

Liben-Nowell, D., Novak, J., Kumar, R., Raghavan, P., and Tomkins, A. Geographic routing in social networks. *National Academy of Sciences of the United States of America* 102(33): 11623–11628, 2005.

Lieberman, M.D., Samet, H., Sankaranarayanan, J., and Sperling, J. STEWARD: Architecture of a spatio-textual search engine. In: *15th Annual ACM International Symposium on Advances in Geographic Information Systems*, p. 25, 2007.

Liu, J. and Birnbaum, L. Localsavvy: Aggregating local points of view about news issues. In: *First ACM International Workshop on Location and the Web*, 2008.

MapQuest. Geocoding web service. Retrieved February 03, 2013, from MapQuest Developers Blog: http://devblog.mapquest.com/2009/10/19/batch-geocoding-and-static-map-custom-icons-in-beta/, October 19, 2009.

March, J. How to turn social feedback into valuable business data. Retrieved February 11, 2013, from Mashable: http://mashable.com/2012/02/27/social-data-insights/, February 27, 2012.

Martin, B. Twitter geo-fail? Only 0.23% of tweets geotagged. Retrieved 2013, from *TNW: The Next Web*: http://thenextweb.com/2010/01/15/twitter-geofail-023-tweets-geotagged/, 2010.

McCurley, K. Geospatial mapping and navigation of the web. In: *10th ACM International Conference on World Wide Web*, pp. 221–229. ACM, New York, 2001.

Mitchell, B. Does IP address location (geolocation) really work? Retrieved February 1, 2013, from *About.com*: http://compnetworking.about.com/od/traceipaddresses/f/ip_location.htm, 2013.

Nagarajan, M., Baid, K., Sheth, A., and Wang, S. Monetizing user activity on social networks—Challenges and experiences. In: *IEEE/WIC/ACM International Joint Conference on Web Intelligence and Intelligent Agent Technology*. IEEE Computer Society, Washington, DC, 2009.

NPR. The search engine wars. Retrieved February 12, 2013, from *NPR*: http://www.npr.org/programs/morning/features/2004/apr/google/, April 12, 2004.

Parr, B. Twitter buys mixer labs to boost location features. Retrieved January 30, 2013, from *Mashable*: http://mashable.com/2009/12/23/breaking-twitter-buys-mixer-labs-to-boost-location-features/, 2009.

Rosa, K.D. and Ellen, J. Text classification methodologies applied to micro-text in military chat. In: *Machine Learning and Applications, IEEE ICMLA'09*, pp. 710–714, 2009.

Sander, T. Twitter, Facebook and YouTube's role in Arab Spring (Middle East Uprisings). Retrieved February 11, 2013, from *Social Capital Blog*: http://socialcapital.wordpress.com/2011/01/26/twitter-facebook-and-youtubes-role-in-tunisia-uprising/, updated: October 12, 2012.

Sheng, C., Hsu, W., and Lee, M.L. Discovering geographical-specific interests from web click data. In: *First International Workshop on Location and the Web*. ACM, New York, 2008.

Sheth, A., Bertram, C., Avant, D., Hammond, B., Kochut, K., and Warke, Y. Managing semantic content for the Web. *IEEE Internet Computing* 6(4): 80–87, 2002.

Sheth, A. and Nagarajan, M. Semantics-empowered social computing. *IEEE Internet Computing* 13: 76–80, 2009.

Smith, D.A. and Crane, G. Disambiguating geographic names in a historical digital library. In: *5th European Conference on Research and Advanced Technology for Digital Libraries*, pp. 127–136, 2001.

Stelzner, M. and Mershon, P. How B2B marketers use social media: New research. Retrieved February 11, 2013, from *Social Media Examiner*: http://www.socialmediaexaminer.com/b2b-social-media-marketing-research/, April 24, 2012.

Stone, B. Twitter as news-wire. Retrieved January 26, 2013, from *Twitter Blog*: http://blog.twitter.com/2008/07/twitter-as-news-wire.html, July 29, 2008.

Twitter. Twitter search. Retrieved February 2, 2013, from *Twitter*: https://twitter.com/search, February 2, 2013.

Volz, R., Kleb, J., and Mueller, W. Towards ontology-based disambiguation of geographical identifiers. In: *Proc. 16th International Conference on World Wide Web* 8–12, 2007.

Zhuang, Z., Brunk, C., and Giles, C.L. Modeling and visualizing geo-sensitive queries based on user clicks. In: *First ACM International Workshop on Location and the Web*, 2008.

10 TweetHood
A Social Media Analytics Tool

10.1 INTRODUCTION

In Chapter 9, we discussed the importance of location mining and the challenges we are faced with in extracting the accurate locations of social media users. While extracting the location may result in privacy violations, especially if a user wants to keep his/her location private, it has numerous benefits such as locating the whereabouts of a criminal. We have developed several algorithms that can extract the location of a user. In this chapter, we will describe our first algorithm that we have called TweetHood.

Simply put, TweetHood is an algorithm that determines the location of a Twitter user based on where his or her friends are living. While this is an overly simplified description of an algorithm, it is based on the premise that you are like your friends. We describe several clustering algorithms that we have developed to extract the location of Twitter users. As we have mentioned in Chapter 9, we have used Twitter as the data was available for us to use. Our techniques are applicable to any social network, including Facebook, Google+, and LinkedIn, provided we have access to the data.

In Section VII, we describe a comprehensive social media system we have developed that has TweetHood at its heart. This social media system is a triple-purpose system that can be used for national security applications, as well as marketing and law enforcement applications. In the future, we can extend our system for many more applications, including health care, finance, and epidemiology. The organization of this chapter is as follows. In Section 10.2, we will discuss a collection of TweetHood algorithms. Experimental results are provided in Section 10.3. The chapter is summarized in Section 10.4. Figure 10.1 illustrates the concepts of this chapter. Our algorithms can also be found in Abrol et al. (2009) and Abrol and Khan (2010).

10.2 TWEETHOOD

10.2.1 OVERVIEW

TweetHood is an algorithm for agglomerative clustering on fuzzy k closest friends with variable depth. Graph-related approaches are the methods that rely on the social graph of the user while deciding on the location of the user. In this chapter, we describe three such methods that show the evolution of the algorithm currently used in TweetHood. Figure 10.2 shows an undirected graph with a depth $d = 2$ used to represent the social network of a user.

Each node in the graph represents a user and an edge represents friendship. The root represents the user U whose location is to be determined, and F_1, F_2,..., F_n represents the n friends of the user. Each friend can have his or her own network, like F_2 has a network comprising of m friends F_{21}, F_{22},..., F_{2m}.

The organization of this section is as follows. A simple majority algorithm with variable depth is presented in Section 10.2.2. Our second algorithm, given in Section 10.2.3, is k closest friends with variable depth. The third algorithm to be presented is fuzzy k closest friends with variable depth, in Section 10.2.4.

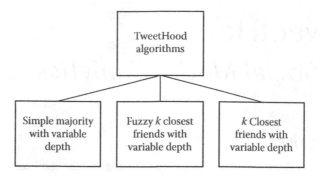

FIGURE 10.1   TweetHood algorithms.

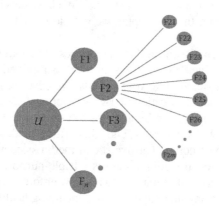

FIGURE 10.2   Undirected graph for a user U showing his friends.

10.2.2   SIMPLE MAJORITY WITH VARIABLE DEPTH

A naïve approach for solving the location identification problem would be to take a simple majority on the locations of friends (followers and following) and assign it as the label of the user. Since a majority of friends will not contain a location explicitly, we can go further into exploring the social network of the friend (friend of a friend). For example, in Figure 10.2, if the location of friend F_2 is not known, instead of labeling it as *null*, we can go one step further and use F_2's friends in choosing the label for it. It is important to note here that each node in the graph will have just one label (single location).

Algorithm 10.1: Simple_Majority (userId, depth)

   Input: User ID of the user and the current depth
   Output: Location of the user
   1: If (*Twitter_Location(userId)*! = *null*)
   2:          then return (*Twitter_Location(userId)*);
   3: Else If (*depth* = 0)
   4:          then return *null*;
   5: Else {
   6:          *All_Friends*[] = *Get_Friends(userId)*;
   7:          For each friend in *All_Friends*[]
   8:                  *Location*[i] = *Simple_Majority*($All_{Friends[i]}$, *depth* − 1);

```
 9:           Aggregate (Location[]);
10:           Boost (Location[]);
11:           Return Max_Location(Location[]);
12:     }
```

The algorithm Simple_Majority (userId, depth) is divided into several steps, as shown in Algorithm 10.1. In steps 1 and 2, we check for the explicitly specified location, and if it is present, the node is given that label. At step 3, if the algorithm on being called recursively has reached a depth of 0 and is unable to find a location, the algorithm returns *null* to the calling method. It is important to note here that the above two conditions specify the boundary conditions of the recursive function. If either of the two conditions is not met, then we try to determine the location on the basis of the simple majority of the labels of the friends. In step 6, we collect the list of all friends of the user. Next, for each of the friends, we determine the location by recursively calling Simple_ Majority with the friend's user ID and decreasing the depth by 1. Once we have the locations for all friends, in step 6 we perform an aggregation of the locations to obtain unique locations. Next, we perform the boosting of the concepts in which a more specific concept is boosted by a more general concept. That is, the state concepts boost all the city concepts in which the city belongs to that state. Similarly, the country-level concepts boost the state- and city-level concepts. Finally, the algorithm chooses the one with the maximum frequency and assigns it to the node.

10.2.3   *k* CLOSEST FRIENDS WITH VARIABLE DEPTH

As Twitter has a high majority of users with public profiles, a user has little control over the people following him or her. In such cases, considering spammers, marketing agencies, etc., deciding on the user's location can lead to inaccurate results. Additionally, it is necessary to distinguish the influence of each friend when deciding the final location. We further modify this approach and just consider the *k* closest friends of the user.

Algorithm 10.2: Closeness (userId, friendId)

Input: User ID of the user and user ID of the friend
Output: CF, the closeness between the user and the friend
1: $CF = 0$; //initialize
2: $All\_Friends1[] = Get\_Friends\ (userId)$;
3: $All\_Friends2[] = Get\_Friends\ (friendId)$;
4: $CF = Common_{Friends}\ (All_{Friends1}[], All_{Friends2}[])$;
5: If $(SR > N_{spammer})$//spammer
6:          then $CF = 0$;
7: If $(Followers\ (friendId) > N_{celebrity})$
8:          then $CF = CF \times \dfrac{\left|All_{Friends_1}\right|}{Followers\ (friendId)}$;
9: Return CF;

Before we explain the *k*_Closest_Friends () algorithm, let us define closeness among users. Closeness among two people is a subjective term, and we can implement it in several ways including number of common friends, semantic relatedness between the activities (verbs) of the two users collected from the messages posted by each one of them, etc. On the basis of the experiments we conducted, we adopted the number of common friends as the optimum choice because of the low time complexity and better accuracy. Algorithm 10.2 illustrates the detailed explanation of the closeness algorithm. The algorithm takes as input the IDs of the user and the friend, and returns the closeness measure. In steps 2 and 3, we calculate the IDs of both the user and his or her friend. Next, we calculate their common friends and assign it as CF. In certain cases, we need to take care of spammers and celebrities. The algorithm has zero tolerance toward spammers. A spammer is typically identified by the vast difference between the number of users he or she is following and the number of users following him or her back. We define the spam ratio (SR) of a friend as

$$SR(friendId) = \frac{Following\,(friendId)}{Followers\,(friendId)} \tag{10.1}$$

If SR is found to be greater than a threshold $N_{spammer}$, we identify the friend as a spammer and set CF as 0. Finally, we would like to control the influence of celebrities in deciding the location of the user because of the previously mentioned problems. However, it is also important to note here that, in certain cases, the celebrities he or she is following are our best bet in guessing the user's location. In step 6, we abbreviate the closeness effect a celebrity has on a user.

Algorithm 10.3 shows the steps involved in the k_Closest_Friends (userId, depth). Steps 1 through 7 remain the same as that of the Simple_Majority (userId, depth). Next, we call the method k-CF (userId, AllFriends [], k). The method returns an array consisting of userids of k closest friends of the user along with their pairwise closeness to the user as described in Algorithm 10.2. In the next step, for each of the k closest friends, we determine the location by recursively calling k_Closest_ Friends () with the friend's user ID and decreasing the depth by 1. Once we have all locations of k closest friends, supported by their individual closeness as specified by Algorithm 10.2, we aggregate and boost the scores of the concepts and the concept with the maximum weight is returned.

Algorithm 10.3: k_Closest_Friends (userId, depth)

> **Input:** User ID of the user and the current depth
> **Output:** Location of the user
> 1: If *Twitter_Location(userId)! = null)*
> 2:   then return *Twitter_Location(userId)*;
> 3: Else If *(depth = 0)*
> 4:   then return *null*;
> 5: Else {
> 6:   *All_Friends[] = Get_Friends(userId)*;
> 7:   *k_ClosestFriends[][2] = k_CF(userdId, Friends[], k)*;
> 8:   For each friend in *k_ClosestFriends[i][]*
> 9:   *Location[i][1] = k_ClosestFriends(k_ClosestFriends[i], depth − 1)*;
> 10:   *Location[i][2] = k_ClosestFriends[i][2]*;
> 11:   Aggregate (*Location* []);
> 12:   Boost (*Location* []);
> 13:   Return *Max_Location(Location[][])*;
> 14:   }

10.2.4 FUZZY k CLOSEST FRIENDS WITH VARIABLE DEPTH

As mentioned previously, in Simple_Majority () and k_Closest_Friends (), each node in the social graph has a single label, and at each step, the locations with lower probabilities are not propagated to the upper levels of the graph. The disadvantage of this approach is that first, it tells us nothing about the confidence of the location identification of each node; and second, for instances where there are two or more concepts with similar score, only the location with highest weight is picked up, while the rest are discarded. This leads to higher error rates.

The idea behind the fuzzy *k* closest friends with variable depth is the fact that each node of the social graph is assigned multiple locations of which each is associated with a certain probability. And these labels get propagated throughout the social network; no locations are discarded whatsoever. At each level of depth of the graph, the results are aggregated and boosted similar to the previous approaches so as to maintain a single vector of locations with their probabilities.

Algorithm 10.4: Fuzzy_*k*_Closest_Friends (userId, depth)

Input: User ID of the user and the current depth
Output: Location of the user
1: If *Twitter_Location(userId)*! = *null)*
2:             then return [*Twitter_Location(userId)*, 1.0];
3: Else If (*depth* = 0)
4:             then return [*null*, 1.0];
5: Else {
6:             *All_Friends*[] = *Get_Friends*(userId);
7:             *k_ClosestFriends*[][2] = *k_CF(userdId, Friends*[], *k*);
8:             For each friend in *k_ClosestFriends*[*i*][]
9:                     Location[*i*][1] = *k_ClosestFriends*(*k_ClosestFriends*[*i*], *depth* − 1);
10:                    Location[*i*][2] = *k_ClosestFriends*[*i*][2];
11:            Aggregate (*Location* []);
12:            Boost (*Location* []);
13:            Return *Max_Location(Final_Location*[][]);
14:    }

Algorithm 10.4 shows the steps involved in the algorithm. The initial input to the algorithm is the userid of the user and the maximum depth. In step 1, at any depth of recursion, the algorithm tries to determine the explicitly specified location. If the location is mentioned explicitly, then it is returned with confidence 1.0. Otherwise, on reaching a depth of 0, if the algorithm is not able to find the location, it returns *null* with a confidence 1.0. If the location is not mentioned explicitly, then the algorithm tries to determine it on the basis of the locations of the *k* closest friends of the user. In step 5, we collect the list of all the friends of the user comprising the people he or she is following and the people following him or her. Next, we call the method *k*-CF (userId, AllFriends [], *k*) described in the *k*_Closest_Friends () algorithm. In the next step, for each of the *k* closest friends, we determine the list of locations, each associated with a probability, by recursively calling *k*_Closest_Friends () with the friend's user ID and decreasing the depth by 1. Once we have all location–probability distribution of *k* closest friends, supported by their individual closeness as specified by Algorithm 10.2, we aggregate and boost the scores of the concepts as discussed in the Simple_Majority () algorithm. The method finally returns a vector of location concepts with individual probabilities.

10.3 EXPERIMENTS AND RESULTS

10.3.1 DATA

For the experiments, we randomly choose 1000 users from all different countries and cities who explicitly mention their location. But to the algorithms, we do not mention the same. It is important to note here, for uniformity, that we ensure that each has at least 50 friends so that the 50 closest friends approach can be applied.

Our evaluation is designed with the following goals in mind. First, we aim to compare the accuracy of different approaches both at the city as well as the country level, and show the effectiveness of TweetHood. Second, we want to show the trade-off between accuracy and time as a function of depth. Finally, we wish to show the effect the choice of number of closest friends (*k*) has on accuracy and time. For all experiments, we choose the gazetteer-based approach discussed in the Appendix as the baseline.

10.3.2 EXPERIMENT TYPE 1: ACCURACY VERSUS DEPTH

Figure 10.3 shows accuracy as a function of depth for the city-level location identification for the agglomerative clustering on fuzzy *k* closest friends. We make two key observations. First, with increasing depth, the accuracy increases monotonically. This is obvious because for *null* nodes, we are willing to go further and thus eventually find a label. However, the accuracy does not increase significantly after depth = 3.

Second, for a major portion, choosing *k* = 10 gives us the highest accuracy as compared with the other values of *k*. The baseline gazetteer-based approach has a fairly low accuracy of 35.6% compared with our approach.

Next, we study the effect of increasing the depth on country-level location identification for agglomerative clustering on fuzzy *k* closest friends (Figure 10.4). The observations are very similar to the city-level identification; that is, for depth > 3, the accuracy saturates. But here, the choice of

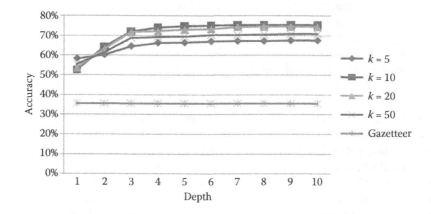

FIGURE 10.3   Accuracy versus depth at the city level for TweetHood.

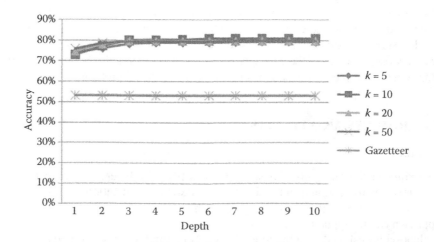

FIGURE 10.4   Accuracy versus depth at the country level for TweetHood.

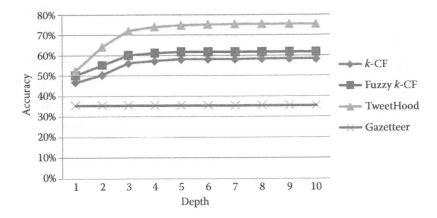

FIGURE 10.5 Accuracy versus depth for various algorithms compared with TweetHood.

k does not affect the accuracy as significantly as it did for the city-level identification. And understandably, the accuracy for the country level is higher than for the city level, and at $k = 10$, depth $= 3$, it is found to be 80.1%.

Figure 10.5 shows the comparison of various algorithms proposed by us on the city-level location identification. It is important to note here that on the basis of previous experiments, we conclude that $k = 10$ is the optimal value for future experiments. The key observations to make here are that the introduction of an agglomeration of concepts actually brings about great improvement in accuracy because in some cases, just choosing the maximum value does not produce the correct result; the proximity of concepts and the threshold have to be taken into account.

10.3.3 EXPERIMENT TYPE 2: TIME COMPLEXITY

Now, we discuss the average running time for the determination of the location of a single user. First, we compare the execution time for the various algorithms as a function of depth. As expected, the time increases exponentially with increasing depth (Figure 10.6).

The other observation we make is that the time complexity increases as we go from k closest friends to fuzzy k closest friends to agglomerative fuzzy k closest friends. This happens because of the increased overhead in the calculations and additional iterations performed to choose the cluster of concepts. But even then, for depth < 4, the time is less than that for the baseline gazetteer approach in which the searching of gazetteer proves to be expensive on time.

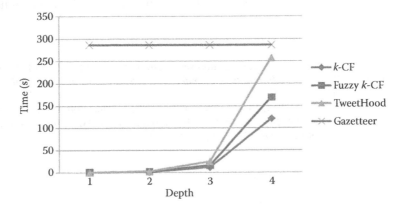

FIGURE 10.6 Time versus depth for various algorithms compared with TweetHood.

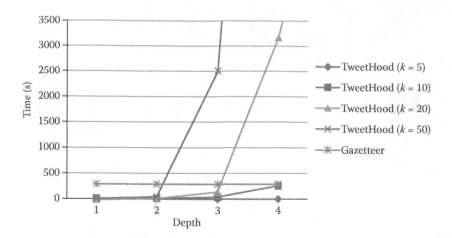

FIGURE 10.7   Time versus depth for different values of *k*.

Finally, we discuss the effect of increasing *k* on the time complexity of the algorithm (Figure 10.7). The increase is still exponential; however, with the greater value of *k*, the greater is the slope. In fact, we have just shown that even for depth = 4, the graph for *k* = 50 becomes too large to be considered for practical use.

10.4   SUMMARY AND DIRECTIONS

As we have discussed, TweetHood is an algorithm for agglomerative clustering on fuzzy *k* closest friends with variable depth. Graph-related approaches are the methods that rely on the social graph of the user while deciding on the location of the user. In this chapter, we have described three such methods that show the evolution of the algorithm currently used in TweetHood. These algorithms are (i) a simple majority algorithm with variable depth, (ii) *k* closest friends with variable depth, and (iii) fuzzy *k* closest friends with variable depth. We have also provided experimental results for the algorithms.

Now that we have provided our collection of innovative TweetHood algorithms, we will next discuss the additional algorithms we have developed. These algorithms are Tweecalization, Tweeque, and TWinner. Tweecalization is a semisupervised learning method for label propagation. Tweeque identifies social cliques. It is based on the premise that people are constantly on the move, changing homes, and going from one city to another. TWinner examines the application of social media in improving the quality of web search and predicting whether the user is looking for news or not.

REFERENCES

Abrol, S. and Khan, L. TweetHood: Agglomerative clustering on fuzzy *k*-closest friends with variable depth for location mining. In: *IEEE Second International Conference on Social Computing (SocialCom)*, pp. 153–160, Minneapolis, 2010.

Abrol, S., Khan, L., and Al-Khateeb, T.M. MapIt: Smarter searches using location driven knowledge discovery and mining. In: *1st SIGSPATIAL ACM GIS 2009 International Workshop on Querying and Mining Uncertain Spatio-Temporal Data (QUeST)*, Seattle, 2009.

11 Tweecalization
Location Mining Using Semisupervised Learning

11.1 INTRODUCTION

In Chapter 9, we discussed the importance of location mining and the challenges we are faced with in extracting the accurate locations of social media users. In Chapter 10, we discussed our collection of TweetHood algorithms for extracting the location of Twitter users. In particular, we have described three methods that show the evolution of the algorithm currently used in TweetHood. These algorithms are as follows: (i) a simple majority algorithm with variable depth, (ii) k closest friends with variable depth, and (iii) fuzzy k closest friends with variable depth. We have also provided experimental results for the algorithms. In this chapter, we propose a semisupervised learning method for label propagation. This algorithm is called Tweecalization.

Our algorithm is based on the premise that we need a methodology that makes use of both labeled and unlabeled data for training in determining the location. That is, the location concept serves the purpose of class label. Therefore, the data mining techniques then reduce to a semisupervised learning algorithm.

As stated earlier, with respect to analyzing OSNs, our work has focused on mining and extracting demographics information of the members. While our techniques can be applied to any type of demographics information (e.g., age, gender, location), we have focused in particular on mining for location and related attributes of individuals. We have also discussed the importance of extracting the location of social media users.

The organization of this chapter is as follows. We provide an overview of Tweecalization in Section 11.2. Aspects of trustworthiness and similarity measure relevant to Tweecalization are discussed in Section 11.3. Experimental results are provided in Section 11.4. The chapter is summarized in Section 11.5. Figure 11.1 illustrates the concepts discussed in this chapter. Our algorithms can also be found in Abrol et al. (2012).

11.2 TWEECALIZATION

Graph-related approaches are the methods that rely on the social graph of the user while deciding on the location of the user. As observed earlier, the location data of users on social networks is a rather scarce resource and only available to a small portion of the users. This creates a need for a methodology that makes use of both labeled and unlabeled data for training. In this case, the location concept serves the purpose of class label. Therefore, our problem is a classic example for the application of semisupervised learning algorithms. In this chapter, we propose a semisupervised learning method for label propagation based on the algorithm proposed by Zhu and Ghahramani (2002) and surveyed in Bengio (2006) with strong theoretical foundation, where labeled data act like sources that push out labels through unlabeled data.

Before we begin explaining the algorithm, we briefly describe the theoretical framework that lies beneath the label propagation and how it is different from the k nearest neighbor (k-NN) approach. The labeled propagation algorithm is based on transductive learning. In this environment, the data set is divided into two sets. One is the training set, consisting of the labeled data. On the basis of this labeled data, we try to predict the class for the second set, called the test or validation data

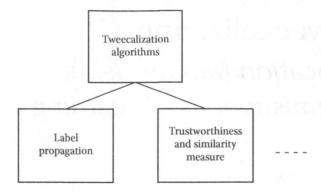

FIGURE 11.1   Tweecalization algorithms.

consisting of unlabeled data. On the other hand, the k-NN approach is based on the inductive learning in which, based on the training set, we try to determine a prediction function that attempts to determine the class for the test set correctly. The major disadvantage with the k-NN approach is that in certain cases, predicting the model based on the test set becomes a difficult task. For example, in our case, if we try to determine the number of neighbors we need to consider for optimal accuracy based on some users (from training data), this approach may not always produce the best results for other users. Hence, finding a value of k that works best for all instances of users seems a rather impossible task.

Chapelle et al. (2006) propose something called the *semisupervised smoothness assumption*. It states that if two points x_1 and x_2 in a high-density region are close, then so should be the corresponding outputs y_1 and y_2 (see also Bengio, 2006). This assumption implies that if two points are linked by a path of high density (e.g., if they belong to the same cluster), then their outputs are likely to be close. If, on the other hand, they are separated by a low-density region, then their outputs need not be close.

We divide the data set into two parts. The first part consists of the labeled data (U_1, L_1) ... (U_l, L_l) of the form (user, location) where $\{L_1 ... L_l\} \in \{C_1 ... C_p\}$ (C_k is a location concept as discussed previously). The second part of the data set has the unlabeled data (U_{l+1}, L_{l+1}) ... (U_{l+u}, L_{l+u}). The pair (U_{l+u}, L_{l+u}) corresponds to the user whose location is to be determined.

Algorithm 11.1: Label Propagation (User, Depth)

> **Input:** User and the depth of the graph
> **Output:** Location vector of the user
> 1: Compute the friends of user for maximum depth
> 2: Calculate the similarity weight matrix W
> 3: Calculate the diagonal matrix D
> 4: Initialize $L^{(0)}$
> 5: Until $L^{(t)}$ converges
> 6: $L^{(t)} = D^{-1} \times W \times L^{(t-1)}$
> 7: $L_1^{(t)} = L_1^{(t-1)}$
> 8: Return $L_i^{(\infty)}[n + 1]$

First, we need to construct a weight matrix W of dimensions $(n + 1) \times (n + 1)$, where W_{ij} is the measure of similarity between the two users U_i and U_j.

11.3 TRUSTWORTHINESS AND SIMILARITY MEASURE

Just like any other machine learning technique, in label propagation also, the single most important thing is the way we define similarity (or distance) between two data points or, in this case, users. All the existing graph-based techniques, including those of Abrol and Khan (2010) and Backstrom et al. (2010), either build a probabilistic model or simply look at the location of friends to predict the location. In other words, these techniques are unintelligent and have the common flaw that not all friends are equally credible when suggesting locations for the primary user. We introduce the notion of trustworthiness for two specific reasons. First, we want to differentiate between various friends when propagating the labels to the central user and, second, to implicitly take into account the social phenomenon of migration and thus provide a simple yet intelligent way of defining similarity between users.

Trustworthiness (TW) is defined as the fraction of friends who have the same label as the user himself. So, if a user, John Smith, mentions his location to be Dallas, Texas, and 15 out of his 20 friends are from Dallas, we say that the trustworthiness of John is 15/20 = 0.75. It is worthwhile to note here that users who have lived all their lives in a single city will have a large percentage of their friends from the same city and hence will have a high trustworthiness value. On the other hand, someone who has lived in several places will have a social graph consisting of people from all over, and hence such a user should have little say when propagating labels to users with unknown locations. For users without a location, TW is zero.

Friendship similarity between two people is a subjective term, and we can implement it in several ways, including the number of common friends, semantic relatedness between the activities (verbs) of the two users collected from the messages posted by each one of them, etc. On the basis of the experiments we conducted, we adopted the number of common friends as the optimum choice because of the low time complexity and better accuracy. We first calculate the common friends between users U_i and U_j and assign it as CF.

$$CF_{ij} = \text{Common\_Friends}(U_i, U_j) \tag{11.1}$$

The similarity between two users, SIM_{ij}, is a function of trustworthiness and friendship similarity and can be represented as

$$SIM_{ij} = \alpha \times \text{Max}\{TW(U_i), TW(U_j)\} + (1 - \alpha) \times CF_{ij} \tag{11.2}$$

where TW is the individual trustworthiness of the two users and α is an arbitrary constant whose value is between 0 and 1. Typically, α is chosen to be around 0.7 for the trustworthiness measure to have the decisive say in the final similarity measure.

Next, we use the Gaussian distribution function to calculate the weight W_{ij}. If the number of events is very large, then the Gaussian distribution function may be used to describe physical events. The Gaussian distribution is a continuous function that approximates the exact binomial distribution of events. Since the number of common friends can vary a lot, we use the Gaussian distribution. The Gaussian distribution shown is normalized so that the sum over all values of CF gives a probability of 1.

$$W_{ij} = e^{\frac{SIM^2}{2\sigma^2}} \tag{11.3}$$

However, there are certain special cases we need to take care of. Spammers and celebrities tend to be misleading while predicting the location of a user. The algorithm has zero tolerance toward spammers. A spammer is typically identified by the high ratio of the number of users he or she is following, and the number of users following him or her back. We define the spam ratio (Ω_{ij}) of two users U_i and U_j as

$$\Omega_{ij} = \max\left\{\frac{\text{Following}(U_i)}{\text{Followers}(U_i)}, \frac{\text{Following}(U_j)}{\text{Followers}(U_j)}\right\} \quad (11.4)$$

And if Ω_{ij} is found to be greater than a threshold N_{spammer}, either of the two users is a spammer and set W_{ij} as 0, to isolate the spammer.

Finally, we would like to control the influence of celebrities in deciding the location of the user because of previously discussed problems. However, it is also important to note here that in certain cases, the celebrities the user is following are our best bet in guessing the user's location. If Followers(U_j) is greater than the threshold $N_{\text{celebrity}}$, then U_j is identified as a celebrity and the existing similarity it has with any user U_i gets abbreviated by a factor β, which is a function of number of followers of U_j and increases monotonically with the number of followers.

$$W_{ij} = \beta(U_i) \times W_{ij} \quad (11.5)$$

It is important to note here that the similarity weight matrix W is symmetric in nature for all i and j except if U_i is a celebrity. In such a case, the weight W_{ij} will be much less than the calculated value, as mentioned before.

Another data structure that we define is the $(n + 1) \times (n + 1)$ diagonal matrix D, used for normalization

$$D_{ii} = \sum_{j=1}^{n+1} W_{ij} \quad (11.6)$$

And finally, we define the location label matrix L of dimensions $(n + 1) \times p$, where p is the number of distinct location concepts. Initialize $L(0)$ as

$$L_{ij}^{(0)} = 1; \text{ if at } j, \; L_i = \text{concept class of } U_i$$

$$0; \text{ otherwise} \quad (11.7)$$

Thus, initially, the bottom u rows consist of only zeroes. After all the matrices have been initialized, we begin to iterate. Thus, at step t of the iteration,

$$L^{(t)} = D^{-1} \cdot W \cdot L^{(t-1)} \quad (11.8)$$

$$L_l^{(t)} = L_l^{(t-1)} \; / / \text{ Clamp the labeled data} \quad (11.9)$$

At each step of the iteration, all unlabeled users receive a location contribution from their respective neighbors, proportional to the normalized similarity weight of the existing edge between the two. In this algorithm, we ensure that the labeled vertices are clamped to the users and do not change. It can be easily shown here that as the number of iterations, t, becomes large, L converges to a definite value (α approaches zero).

$$\alpha = L^{(t)} - L^{(t-1)} = (D^{-1} \cdot W)^{(t)} \cdot L^{(0)} - (D^{-1} \cdot W)^{(t-1)} \cdot L^{(0)} \qquad (11.10)$$

$$\alpha = (D^{-1} \cdot W)^{(t-1)} \cdot L^{(0)} \cdot [D^{-1} \cdot W - I] \qquad (11.11)$$

Because the matrix $D^{-1}W$ is a square matrix, each of whose rows consists of nonnegative real numbers, with each row summing to 1, it follows that as $t \to \infty$, $(D^{-1}W)^{(t-1)} \to 0$, and hence L converges to a fixed value. The worst-case running time of the algorithm is $O(n^3)$.

Now we discuss the impact of increasing the depth on the accuracy and running time of the algorithm. By increasing the depth, we include the friends of friends of the user also in our set of data points. The direct advantage of this is that we have more labeled data points in our set, thereby having a positive impact on the accuracy. Next, inclusion of more data points (users) leads to the discovery of implicit *friendship* relationships between users that may not be specified otherwise. The only disadvantage that is associated with increasing the depth is the increase in the running time of the algorithm.

In the next section, we evaluate the quality of the algorithms mentioned in the previous sections and describe how Tweecalization outperforms the other approaches.

11.4 EXPERIMENTS AND RESULTS

Data. For the experiments, we randomly choose 1000 users from different countries and cities who explicitly mention their location and treat it as ground truth. It is important to note here, for uniformity, that we ensure that each has at least 10 friends so that the k closest friends approach used in TweetHood can be applied. Figure 11.2 shows the friend distribution for the data set of 1000 users. We see that almost 45% of the users have 20 to 100 people as their friends.

Second, all processes are run offline; that is, we store all the relevant information about the user like location, friend count, friends IDs, etc., on the local machine and then run the algorithm. Hence, the entire process is done offline, barring the geo-coding process, which is used to convert the explicitly mentioned locations to a standard format.

Evaluation Method. Our evaluation is designed with the following goals in mind. First, we aim to compare the accuracy of different approaches both at the city and the country level, and show the effectiveness of Tweecalization in comparison with TweetHood and the

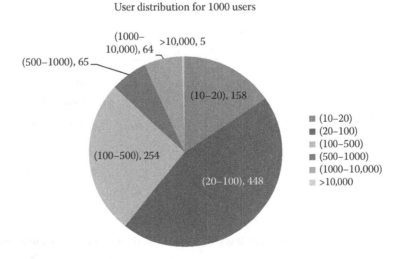

FIGURE 11.2   User distribution for the data set.

gazetteer-based location mining technique. Second, we want to show the trade-off between accuracy and time as a function of depth. Finally, we show how running time increases for different algorithms with increasing depth. For all experiments, we choose the gazetteer-based approach discussed in the previous sections as the baseline.

Experiment Type 1: Accuracy versus Depth. For this set of experiments, the *Y* axis represents the accuracy in percentage and the *X* axis shows the depth.

Figure 11.3 shows the accuracy as a function of the depth for the city-level location identification for the agglomerative clustering (described in Chapter 10) on label propagation (Tweecalization), compared with agglomerative clustering on fuzzy *k* closest friends (TweetHood). We make two key observations. First, with increasing depth, the accuracy increases monotonically for both algorithms. As mentioned earlier, the reason for this is that by increasing depth in Tweecalization, we ensure that we are adding more labeled data to our training set. Secondly, adding more data points leads to identification of new associations between nodes; that is, we can find new friendships that may not be otherwise specified by the user himself or herself. On the other hand, for TweetHood, this is obvious because for *null* nodes, we are willing to go further and thus eventually find a label. The second key observation we make for this experiment is that the accuracy does not increase significantly after depth = 3 for both algorithms. On further analysis, we find that the possibility of an implicit friendship existing between a user and node decreases with increasing depth of the graph, and hence in such cases the increasing depth has little effect on the label propagation algorithm.

For depth <4, the accuracy value increases linearly with depth and is recorded to be 75.5% for Tweecalization at *d* = 3. The baseline gazetteer-based approach has a fairly low accuracy of 35.6% compared with our approach.

Next, we study the effect of increasing the depth on country-level location identification for the two algorithms. Figure 11.4 shows the accuracy versus depth comparison for different algorithms. The observations are very similar to the city-level identification; that is, for depth >4, the accuracy saturates. The accuracy for Tweecalization at depth = 4 is reported to be 80.10% compared with 78.4% for TweetHood. And understandably, the accuracy for country level is higher than that for the city level, because in certain cases the algorithm chooses the incorrect city, even though the country for both is the same.

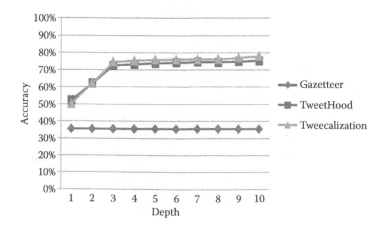

FIGURE 11.3 Accuracy versus depth at city level for various algorithms compared with Tweecalization.

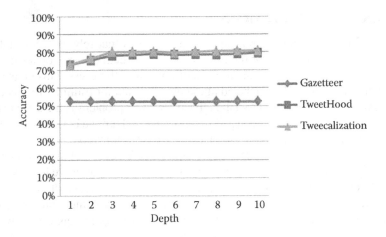

FIGURE 11.4   Accuracy versus depth at country level for Tweecalization.

Experiment Type 2: Time Complexity. For this set of experiments, the *Y* axis represents the time in seconds for various algorithms and the *X* axis shows the depth.

Figure 11.5 shows the average running time for various algorithms for the determination of the location of a single user as a function of depth. The key observations to make here are that for TweetHood, the time increases exponentially with increasing depth. Tweecalization, on the other hand, shows much better scalability because of a running time that is cubic in the size of friends. The increase in running time for Tweecalization is so insignificant in comparison with TweetHood that it appears as a straight line close to the *X* axis. At depth = 4, the average running time recorded for TweetHood was 258.19 seconds as compared with 0.624 seconds for Tweecalization. The average running time for the content-based approach is found to be 286.23 seconds. But for depth <4, both TweetHood and Tweecalization outperform the traditional gazetteer-based location mining technique. This highlights the major contribution of Tweecalization, which is increased scalability with increasing depth for higher accuracy.

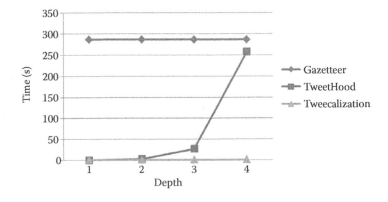

FIGURE 11.5   Time versus depth for various algorithms compared with Tweecalization.

11.5   SUMMARY AND DIRECTIONS

As we have stated, graph-related approaches are the methods that rely on the social graph of the user while deciding on the location of the user. The location data of users on social networks is a rather scarce resource and only available to a small portion of the users. This creates a need for a methodology that makes use of both labeled and unlabeled data for training. In this case, the location concept serves the purpose of class label. Therefore, our problem is a classic example for the application of semisupervised learning algorithms. In this chapter, we have described a semisupervised learning method for label propagation that we call Tweecalization.

Now that we have provided our collection of innovative TweetHood algorithms as well as our Tweecalization algorithm, we will next discuss the additional algorithms we have developed. These algorithms are Tweeque and TWinner. Tweeque identifies social cliques. It is based on the premise that people are constantly on the move, changing homes, and going from one city to another. TWinner examines the application of social media in improving the quality of web search and predicting whether the user is looking for news or not.

REFERENCES

Abrol, S. and Khan, L. TweetHood: Agglomerative clustering on fuzzy k-closest friends with variable depth for location mining. In: *IEEE Second International Conference on Social Computing (SocialCom)*, pp. 153–160. Minneapolis, 2010.

Abrol, S., Khan, L., and Thuraisingham, B. Tweecalization: Efficient and intelligent location mining in Twitter using semi-supervised learning. In: *8th IEEE International Conference on Collaborative Computing: Networking, Applications and Worksharing*. Pittsburgh, 2012.

Backstrom, L., Sun, E., and Marlow, C. Find me if you can: Improving geographical prediction with social and spatial proximity. In: *19th ACM International Conference on World Wide Web*, 2010.

Bengio, Y.O. *Label Propagation and Quadratic Criterion. Semi-supervised Learning.* MIT Press, Cambridge, MA, 2006.

Chapelle, O., Scholkopf, B., and Zien, A. *Semi-supervised Learning*, MIT, http://olivier.chapelle.cc/ssl-book/ssl_toc.pdf, 2006.

Zhu, X. and Ghahramani, Z. Learning from labeled and unlabeled data with label propagation. Technical Report CMU-CALD-02-107, Carnegie Mellon University, Pittsburgh, 2002.

12 Tweeque
Identifying Social Cliques for Location Mining

12.1 INTRODUCTION

In Chapter 9, we discussed the importance of location mining and the challenges we are faced with in extracting the accurate locations of social media users. In Chapter 10, we discussed our collection of TweetHood algorithms for extracting the location of Twitter users. In particular, we have described three methods that show the evolution of the algorithm currently used in TweetHood. These algorithms are as follows: (i) a simple majority algorithm with variable depth, (ii) k closest friends with variable depth, and (iii) fuzzy k closest friends with variable depth. We have also provided experimental results for the algorithms. In Chapter 11, we enhanced our location extraction algorithms and proposed a semisupervised learning method for label propagation. This algorithm is called Tweecalization.

This chapter describes the effects of migration. People migrate from city to city, state to state, and country to country all the time. Therefore, our algorithms may be affected by such migration. That is, how does one extract the location of a person when he or his friends may be continually migrating? Toward this end, we have proposed a set of algorithms that we call Tweeque. That is, Tweeque takes into account the migration effect. In particular, it identifies social cliques for location mining.

The organization of this chapter is as follows. In Section 12.2, we discuss the effect of migration. Temporal data mining aspects are discussed in Section 12.3. Social clique identification algorithms are discussed in Section 12.4. Experimental results are given in Section 12.5. Location prediction algorithms are discussed in Section 12.6. Agglomerative hierarchical clustering algorithms are discussed in Section 12.7. Mining unstructured text is discussed in Section 12.8. The chapter is summarized in Section 12.9. Figure 12.1 illustrates the contents of this chapter. Our algorithms can also be found in Abrol and Khan (2009).

12.2 EFFECT OF MIGRATION

Now we come to our second hypothesis, which focuses on an important aspect of social life in the present world. People are constantly on the move, changing homes, going from one city to another. In this chapter, we shall discuss some experiments and studies that show that a significant percentage of people move every year, and it becomes necessary to do temporal analysis to be able to predict the user's current location correctly.

The first set of experiments is performed on data collected by the US Census Bureau (Geographical Mobility/Migration, 2009), a series of tables that describe the movement of people in the United States. The tables include data on why people moved, types of moves, and the distance moved.

Figure 12.2 shows the findings regarding the migration trend in the past 5 years in the United States reported by the US Census Bureau for people aged older than 1 year moving from one county to another. We observe that the migration rate varies between 4% and 6%. This means 12 to 17 million people of those surveyed change counties each year. And that is a significant number to be ignored.

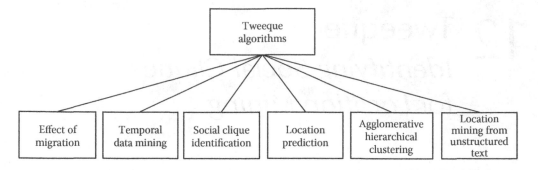

FIGURE 12.1 Tweeque algorithms.

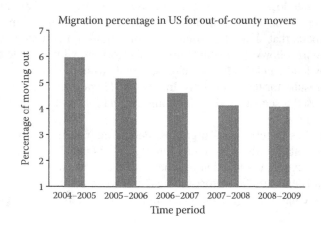

FIGURE 12.2 Fraction of people in the United States that move out of counties by year.

To understand the long-term or cumulative effect of this migration, especially for online social network users, we collected demographic information, including age, hometown, and current location, for more than 300,000 public profiles on Facebook for users with hometown in the United States. Figure 12.3 shows the distribution of users based on age whose current location is the same as their hometown. It is interesting to note that only 28% to 37% users are living in their hometown. The rest of all the users have shown some form of migration, leaving their hometown.

Next, we try to link the migration effect to the users on Twitter using data from the US census for the year 2008–2009 and the Twitter age demographics studied by Pingdom (Report, 2012).

First, we study the migration rate as a function of age, dividing the age groups into buckets of 10 years. There are two key observations that we make from the graph in Figure 12.4. First, we see a distinguishably high migration rate of more than 9% for users in the age groups from 20 to 29 years. This is consistent with our intuition that after the completion of high school, people have a tendency to move out of their hometowns for college or jobs. The second observation is that the migration rate decreases with increasing age. This is also intuitive, since as we grow older there are increased chances of employment stability and people with families preferring to settle down.

The second part in linking is the study of demographics. Figure 12.5 shows the graph for the age distribution for Twitter users as surveyed by Pingdom (Report, 2012). The interesting observation is that 25–34 year olds make up a third of the Twitter population. On the basis of these two observations, we conclude that Twitter users have a high tendency to migrate.

To summarize this section, we make two key observations from Facebook data indicating that 63% to 72% are in a different city than their hometowns. Second, by doing age-based analysis of

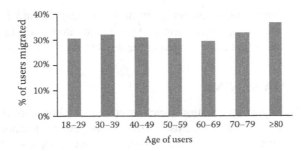

FIGURE 12.3 Percentage of Facebook users with current location the same as their hometown.

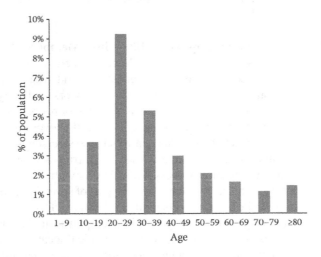

FIGURE 12.4 Intercounty migration rate in the United States as a function of age.

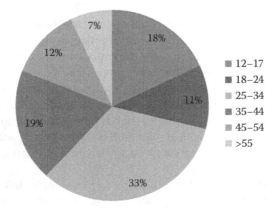

FIGURE 12.5 Distribution of Twitter users according to age.

US census data, we found that a high percentage of users between 20 and 34 years have done an intercounty migration. Thus, geographical migration is a very important factor to be taken into consideration by any algorithm that aims to predict the current location of the user successfully.

12.3 TEMPORAL DATA MINING

That leaves us with some important questions, such as how do we know from a bunch of locations which one is the most current location of the user? How do we perform temporal analysis of friendships? The first half of the next section discusses how we can indirectly infer the most current location of a user, and the second half describes the algorithm that helps us.

Doing temporal analysis would have been much easier if we had a time stamp attached to each friendship to indicate when it was formed in the real world. Then, we would just need to look at the most recent friends to determine the current location. But, unfortunately, that does not happen, so we have to come up with a way of inferring the time the friendship was created. To do that, we make two very simple social science observations.

Observation 1: Apart from Friendship, What Else Links Members of a Social Clique?
We begin by making a very simple observation. Man is a social animal, and wherever he goes he has a strong tendency to form new friendships. And friendship seldom occurs alone; it is usually in groups known as cliques in social networking theory. Let us start by giving a definition of a clique. A clique is an inclusive group of people who share interests, views, purposes, patterns of behavior, or ethnicity. In social network theory, as well as in graph theory, a clique is a subset of individuals in which every person is connected to every other person. For example, I have a clique consisting of friends I made at school; John has a group at the office where mostly everyone is friends with everyone. An interesting observation to make here is that an individual may be part of several cliques, for example, a reference group formed while he or she was in high school, one formed in college, another one after he started working in a company, and so on. Apart from friendship, what is the attribute that links members of a clique? It is their individual locations. All members of a clique were or are at a particular geographical location at a particular instant of time, like college, school, a company, etc.

Observation 2: Over Time, People Migrate. The second observation is based on the study from the previous section that, over the course of time, people have a tendency to migrate. In other words, over time the locations of members of a clique will change.

On the basis of these two social science observations, we propose a new social science theory. We hypothesize that if we can divide the social graph of a particular user into cliques as defined above and check for location-based purity of the cliques, we can accurately separate out his or her current location from other locations. Among the different groups formed for a user, owing to migration studied in the previous section, the most current group will show the maximum purity. Migration is our latent time factor, as with passing time the probability of people migrating increases. So, what happens if a user does not migrate but his or her friends move? A scenario in which the user does not move but his or her friends show signs of migration is rare; however, nonetheless, we shall have new people moving in, and as the user will not lead a lonely life, new groups will be formed with a high percentage of location-based purity.

Let us try to understand the intuition behind it using an example. John Smith did his schooling in Dallas and then moved to Austin for college and got a job in, say, Seattle. Now, if we divide John's friends into groups, we expect to find groups of friends formed in school, college, and at work. But if we look at the locations of the users in the school group, then we shall find that owing to the prominent long-term effects of migration, most the school friends in the group would also have moved from Dallas. Similarly, after finishing college in Austin, a significant percentage of his college friends would show signs of migration owing to job relocation and family reasons. But because his friendship at work in Seattle is very new, the possibility of migration decreases and the chance that all the members of the group are in the same physical location increases. And we are likely to observe a pure group where most of the users have their location as Seattle.

12.4   SOCIAL CLIQUE IDENTIFICATION

Now that we have proposed our social theory, in this subsection, we address the problem of identifying all the social cliques of a user, U, as defined in the previous section. We construct the entire set of a user's friends as graph $G = (V, E)$, with each friend represented as a node in the graph. Two users who are friends with each other are connected by an edge. Now, the goal is to partition the graph into k nonoverlapping social cliques represented by $\pi = C_1, C_2, ..., C_k$.

Finding all the cliques in a graph is an NP-complete problem. The Bron–Kerbosch algorithm (Bron and Kerbosch, 1973) is a recursive backtracking procedure that augments a candidate clique by considering one vertex at a time, either adding it to the candidate clique or to a set of excluded vertices that cannot be in the clique but must have some nonneighbor in the eventual clique. Variants of this algorithm can be shown to have worst-case running time of $O(3^{n/3})$. Since the running time is infeasible for practical applications where locations for millions of users have to be determined, we need to come up with something that is at least polynomial in running time.

We reformulate the problem to a graph partition problem. Graph partition focuses on determining a partition of the friends such that the cut (the total number of edges between two disjoint sets of nodes) is minimized. Even though the cut minimization can be solved efficiently, the outcome is partitions consisting of single nodes. Thus, we employ an often used variant, called the normalized cut, which is defined as

$$\text{Normalized cut } (\pi) = \sum_{i=1}^{k} \frac{\text{Cut}(Ci, \overline{C_i})}{\text{Vol}(C_i)} \qquad (12.1)$$

where $\overline{C_i}$ is the complement of the partition C_i and Vol (C_i) is the volume of a set of vertices. C_i is the total weight of the edges incident to it:

$$\text{Vol }(C_i) = \sum_{x \in C_i, y \in V} w(x, y) \qquad (12.2)$$

To obtain an optimal cut, the goal is to minimize the objective function specified in Equation 12.1, so as to minimize the number of edges between partitions (numerator), while the denominator ensures that we do not end up with single node partitions.

Computing a cut that minimizes the equation in question is an NP-hard problem. We employ the Shi–Malik algorithm, introduced by Jianbo Shi and Jitendra Malik (2000), commonly used for image segmentation. We can find in polynomial time a cut $\left(C_i, \overline{C_i}\right)$ of small normalized weight Ncut $\left(C_i, \overline{C_i}\right)$ using this algorithm.

Let us now describe the Ncut algorithm. Let D be an $N \times N$ diagonal matrix with d on its diagonal, and W be an $N \times N$ symmetrical matrix with $W(i, j) = w_{ij}$.

After some algebraic manipulations (Shi and Malik, 2000), we get

$$\min_{(C_i, \overline{C_i})} \text{Ncut}(C_i, \overline{C_i}) = \min_y \frac{y^T(D-W)y}{y^T Dy} \tag{12.3}$$

subject to the constraints:

- $y_i \in \{1, -b\}$, for some constant $-b$, and
- $1: y^t D1 = 0$

Minimizing $\dfrac{y^T(D-W)y}{y^T Dy}$ subject to the constraints above is NP-hard. It is important to note here that the expression on the right side in Equation 12.3 is the Rayleigh quotient (Shi and Malik, 2000). To make the problem tractable, we relax the constraints on y, and allow it to take just real values. The relaxed problem has the same solution as the generalized eigenvalue problem for the second smallest generalized eigenvalue

$$(D - W)x = \lambda Dx \tag{12.4}$$

Algorithm 12.1: Social Clique $(G\ (V, E))$

Input: Graph $G = (V, E)$, for a user U where V denotes friends of a user and E represents friendship between them.
Output: Social cliques, $\pi = C_1, C_2,..., C_k$
1: Given a weighted graph $G = (V, E)$, compute the weight of each edge, and construct the adjacency matrix W and diagonal matrix, D.
2: Define the unnormalized graph Laplacian matrix as $L = D - W$.
3: Solve $L \cdot x = \lambda D \cdot X$ for eigenvectors with the smallest eigenvalues.
4: Use the eigenvector with the second smallest eigenvalue to bipartition the graph.
5: Decide if the current partition should be subdivided, and recursively repartition the segmented parts if necessary.

Algorithm 12.1 outlines the steps involved in partitioning the user's friends' graph $G = (V, E)$ into social cliques, represented by $\pi = C_1, C_2,..., C_k$, as defined earlier. In step 1 of the algorithm, we compute the diagonal matrix as described earlier with

$$d_i = \sum_{j=1}^{n} w_{ij} \tag{12.5}$$

Next, we determine the unnormalized Laplacian matrix for the graph

$$L = D - W \tag{12.6}$$

In step 3, we solve the eigenproblem $Lx = \lambda Dx$ and choose the eigenvector with the second smallest eigenvalue to bipartition the graph.

We repeat the iterations involving steps 1 through 4 until we reach a point where no more partitions are necessary. But how do we decide that? To answer that question, we need to first define the weight of the edge between vertices.

Defining Weight. To ensure that we capture the phenomenon of social cliques, we have to be very careful as to how we define the weight of the edge between two users. For our work, we define the weight between two users i and j as

$$w(i, j) = w_{\text{edge}}(i, j) + \alpha \times w_{\text{mutf}}(i, j) \tag{12.7}$$

where w_{edge} is positive if i and j are friends, and is less than 0 otherwise. The presence of w_{edge} controls the membership of each cluster to ensure that it consists of only users who are friends among themselves. If two users are not friends, then we penalize the weight between them, often causing the score to become less than zero.

w_{mutf} is the number of mutual friends that i and j share. On the other hand, α is an arbitrary constant whose value depends on the number of friends i and j have, and lies between 0 and 1. The presence of w_{mutf}, in the overall similarity, guarantees that friends who are closer (have more mutual friends) have a higher probability of staying in the same clique.

It is important to note that the contribution of w_{edge} to the overall similarity score is significantly larger than that of the w_{mutf}. This is done to ensure that the formation of each cluster is consistent with the definition of a social clique.

Let us try to answer our earlier question, "When do we stop?" In our case, we iterate till we reach a point, where the similarity measure of the nearest user clusters is negative. It can be easily shown that the complexity of the algorithm is $O(n^3)$.

Purity-Based Voting Algorithm. Once we have obtained clusters that are consistent with the definition of social cliques, we have to decide on the current location of the user. As mentioned previously, we check for purity of the individual clusters to determine the current location.

Before we begin explaining the algorithm, let us first define a location concept.

Location concept: A location concept L of a user U is the location of the user in the format {city} X /{state} Y /{country} Z. And for each location depending on the level of detail, either of X, Y or/ and Z can be null.

We propose a purity-based voting algorithm to determine the final location (Algorithm 12.2). The idea is that each cluster casts its vote on what the current location should be. First, each cluster decides which location it is going to vote in favor of. This is computed by doing a simple majority of all the locations inside the cluster.

Algorithm 12.2: Purity Voting (π)

Input: $\pi = C_1, C_2, \ldots, C_k$, group of all clusters with location concepts
Output: Vector (L, S): concepts and score vector
1: For each cluster, $C_i \in \pi$
2:          Location (C_i) = Simple_Majority (C_i)
3:          Purity_Vote $(C_i) = \dfrac{|U_{\text{max}}|}{|C_i|}$
4: Aggregate (Location (C_i), Purity_Vote(C_i))
5: Boost (Location (C_i), Purity_Vote(C_i))
6: Return Max_Location(Final_Location (L, S))

And the power of the vote for each cluster is dependent on the purity of the cluster and the number of members in the cluster. In other words, for each cluster, we calculate purity, Purity (C_i), defined as

$$\text{Purity\_Vote}(C_i) = \frac{|U_{\max}|}{|C_i|} \tag{12.8}$$

where $U_{\max} = U_i$, such that $U_i \in C_i$ AND Location (U_i) = Max_Location (C_i).

After we have calculated Purity_Vote(C_i) for each of the clusters, we have a list of location concepts, each of which is supported by a cluster. It is important to note here that several cliques may support a single location concept. Intuitively, when a user moves to a location, we can expect a user to belong to more than one social clique (probably one from work and another consisting of his friends).

Next, we perform aggregation of the locations to obtain unique locations. Finally, we perform the boosting of the concepts in which a more specific concept is boosted by a more general concept. That is, the state concepts boost all the city concepts in which the city belongs to that state. Similarly, the country-level concepts boost the state- and city-level concepts.

12.5   EXPERIMENTS AND RESULTS

Data. For the experiments, we randomly choose 10,000 users from all different countries and cities who explicitly mention their location. But to the algorithms, we do not mention the same. Figure 12.6 shows the friend distribution for the data set of 10,000 users. We see that almost 45% of the users have 20 to 100 people as their friends.

Second, all processes are run offline; that is, we store all the relevant information about the user like location, friend count, friends ids, etc., on the local machine and then run the algorithm. Hence, the entire process is done offline, barring the geo-coding process, which is used to convert the explicitly mentioned locations to a standard format.

Social Clique Identification. Before we begin evaluating our location prediction approach, we first need to assess the correctness of our algorithm to form social cliques.

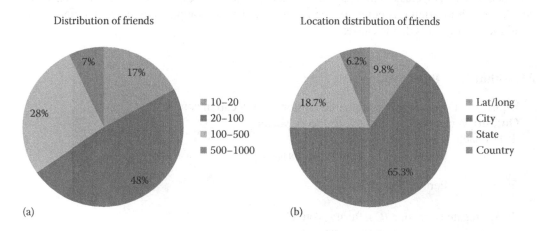

FIGURE 12.6   (a) User distribution for the data set according to number of friends. (b) Distribution of users according to granularity of location specified by them.

TABLE 12.1
Social Clique Evaluation

Total Users	Average No. of Clusters per User	Average Size of Cluster	Accuracy
1000	15	7	88.32%

To do so, we handpicked a group of 1000 known Twitter users, and performed graph partitioning to form social cliques for each of them. We then asked annotators to manually look into each group and verify the correctness of the group. The annotators made use of other resources such as the user's other social networking pages (Facebook, LinkedIn, etc.) to determine where the friend met the user and whether the cliques actually made sense. The users chosen by us are from a wide range of demographics, including men, women, young and old, and people from different countries and cultures.

The way we evaluated the algorithm was by looking at each partition and then identifying the number of data points (friends) that the annotator thought did not belong to that particular partition. Table 12.1 shows the results of the experiments. The graph partitioning algorithm is found to have a very promising accuracy, and hence can be used to obtain social cliques.

12.6   LOCATION PREDICTION

Now that we have established the correctness of the social clique formation algorithm, we would like to evaluate the location prediction algorithm.

Table 12.2 shows the results of the experiments we performed. The algorithm is able to correctly predict the current city of the user with an accuracy of 76.3% as compared with 72.1% for TweetHood and 75.5% for Tweecalization. The average size of a city group is 1.82, meaning that after the threshold is reached and the agglomeration of location concepts stops, the average location concept contains, on average, two city concepts.

The accuracy for the algorithm at the country level is 84.9%, and is much higher than 52.3% for the content-based approach and 80.1% for both TweetHood and Tweecalization.

Next, we study the impact of the number of friends of any user on the accuracy of the algorithm. Figure 12.7 shows the variation of error rate as a function of the number of friends.

It is interesting to observe that, in general, the error rate decreases with the increase in the number of friends. The presence of more friends means that we have more data for a particular user, which works well for the algorithm, allowing it to form clusters that actually conform to the definition of social cliques.

TABLE 12.2
Accuracy Comparison for Tweeque

	City Level	Country Level
Content-based approach	35.6%	52.3%
TweetHood	72.1%	80.1%
Tweecalization	75.5%	80.1%
Tweelocal	76.3%	84.9%

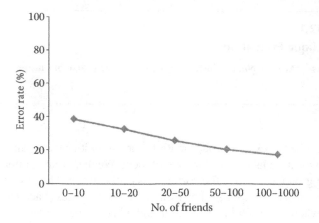

FIGURE 12.7   Error rate for Tweeque as a function of the number of friends of the user.

12.7   AGGLOMERATIVE HIERARCHICAL CLUSTERING

The location prediction algorithms described in Chapters 9 and 10 each return location concepts associated with a score. We could just stop at this point and choose the location concept with the maximum score. But we are missing a crucial aspect of locations.

Up to this point, we have placed little emphasis on the geospatial proximity of the different concepts. That is, we have been treating the concepts purely as labels, with no mutual relatedness. Since the concepts are actual geographical cities, we agglomerate the closely located cities and suburbs in an effort to improve the confidence and thus the accuracy of the system.

At this point, we introduce something called the location confidence threshold (LCT). The idea behind the LCT is to ensure that when the algorithm reports the possible locations, it does so with some minimum level of confidence. The LCT depends on the user itself. The LCT increases with the increasing number of friends for the user, because more friends imply more labeled data. Let us consider that we have p concepts each associated with its respective probability.

Initially, we have all concepts present individually as $\{L_1\}$, $\{L_2\}$,...,$\{L_p\}$. If any concept has a value greater than the LCT, then the program returns that concept as the location and terminates. Otherwise, at the next step, we construct a matrix in which the number in the ith row jth column is an objective function Θ of the distances and cumulative scores between the ith and jth concepts.

$$\Theta_{ij} = \frac{e^{\frac{S}{T}}}{d(i,j)} \tag{12.9}$$

where $S = S_i + S_j$, the combined score of concept clusters $\{L_i\}$ and $\{L_j\}$, is the geographic distance between the two clusters and T is a constant with $0 < T < 1$.

At the first step of agglomeration, we combine two concepts with the highest value of the objective function, Θ, and check if the new concept cluster has a combined score greater than the LCT. If not, then we continue the process, constructing the matrix again, but this time some of the concepts are replaced by concept clusters. And we proceed to choose the two concept clusters that have the maximum value of the objective function Θ. The mean geographic distance between a concept cluster A and a concept cluster B can be defined as

$$d_{AB} = \frac{1}{|A||B|} \sum_{x \in A} \sum_{x \in B} d(x,y) \tag{12.10}$$

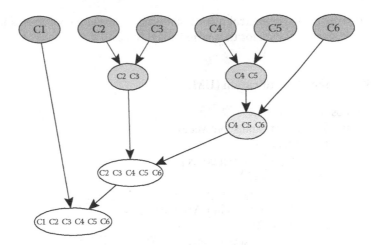

FIGURE 12.8   Illustration to show the agglomerative hierarchical clustering.

Thus, at each step of the agglomeration, we choose the two concept clusters with maximum value of the objective function Θ. If the score of the combined bag of concepts crosses the LCT, we return the bag of concepts as the possible location vector and terminate.

To understand how agglomerative clustering basically works, consider a scenario in which the location prediction algorithm returns an array of location concepts including (Los Angeles, 0.34), (Long Beach, 0.05), (Irvine, 0.17), and many other concepts. Suppose the LCT for the algorithm to return a cluster of concepts is 0.5. Then, if we simply combine location concepts on the basis of just proximity, then initially Los Angeles and Long Beach will get combined (Long Beach is closer to Los Angeles than Irvine); however, since their combined score is not sufficient, in the next iteration Irvine also gets added to the cluster. And the final cluster that is returned is {Los Angeles, Long Beach, Irvine} with a combined score of 0.56. On the other hand, if we use agglomerative clustering with an objective function mentioned previously, Los Angeles and Irvine are combined to yield a location cluster of {Los Angeles, Irvine}, which has a combined score greater than the LCT and is hence returned as the output. Thus, by using agglomerative clustering, we end up being more specific by returning two concepts instead of three, at a small loss of confidence. Figure 12.8 illustrates agglomerative clustering.

12.8   MAPIT: LOCATION MINING FROM UNSTRUCTURED TEXT

In this section, we discuss the content-based approach developed by us (Abrol and Khan, 2009) to identify the location of a user on Twitter upon which we have based the series of algorithms discussed in Chapters 9 through 11. It is important to understand here that a location concept is typically of the format {city} A /{state} B /{country} C. And for each location depending on the level of detail, either of A, B, or/and C can be null.

To determine the location from mining the messages, we devise a score-based identification and disambiguation method Location_Identification. Before running the actual algorithm, we perform preprocessing of data, which involves the removal of all those words from the messages that are not references to geographic locations. For this, we use the conditional random field (CRF) tagger, which is an open source part-of-speech (POS) tagger for English with an accuracy of close to 97% and a tagging speed of 500 sentences per second (Phan, 2006). The CRF tagger identifies all the proper nouns from the text and terms them as keywords $\{K_1, K_2, \ldots, K_n\}$. In the next step, the TIGER (Topologically Integrated Geographic Encoding and Referencing system) data set (TIGER/Line, 2008) is searched to identify the city names from among them. The TIGER data set is an open source gazetteer consisting of topological records and shape files with coordinates for cities, counties, zip codes, street segments, etc., for the entire United States.

Algorithm 12.3: Location_Identification (UM)

> **Input:** *UM*: all messages of user
> **Output:** Vector (C, S): concepts and score vector
> 1: For each keyword, K_i //phase 1
> 2:   For each $C_j \in K_i$ //C_j – street concept
> 3:   For each $T_f \in C_j$
> 4:   type = Type (T_f)
> 5:   If (T_f occurs in UM), then $S_{C_j} = S_{C_j} + S_{type}$
> 6: For each keyword, K_i //phase 2
> 7:   For each $C_j \in K_i$ //C_j – street concept
> 8:   For each $T_f \in C_j$ AND $T_s \in C_l$
> 9:   If ($T_f = T_s$) AND ($C_j = C_l$)
> 10:   type = Type (T_f)
> 11: $S_{C_j} = S_{C_j} + S_{type}$
> 12: Return (C, S)

The algorithm describes the gazetteer-based algorithm. We search the TIGER gazetteer (TIGER/Line, 2008) for the concepts $\{C_1, C_2,\ldots, C_n\}$ pertaining to each keyword. Now our goal for each keyword would be to pick out the right concept among the list; in other words, disambiguate the location. For this, we use a weight-based disambiguation method. In phase 1, we assign the weight to each concept based on the occurrence of its terms in the text. Specific concepts are assigned a greater weight as compared with the more general ones. In phase 2, we check for correlation between concepts, in which one concept subsumes the other. In that case, the more specific concept gets the boosting from the more general concept. If a more specific concept C_i is part of another C_j, then the weight of C_j is added to that of C_i.

Let us try to understand this by looking at an example. City carries 15 points, state 10, and a country name carries 5 points. For the keyword *Dallas*, consider the concept of {city} Dallas / {state} Texas /{country} United States. The concept gets 15 points because Dallas is a city name, and it gets an additional 10 points if Texas is also mentioned in the text. In phase 2, we consider the relation between two keywords. Considering the previous example, if {Dallas, Texas} are the keywords appearing in the text, then among the various concepts listed for *Dallas* would be {city} Dallas /{state} Texas /{country} United States, and one of the concepts for *Texas* would be {state} Texas /{country} United States. Now, in phase 2, we check for such correlated concepts, in which one concept subsumes the other. In that case, the more specific concept gets the boosting from the more general concept. Here, the above-mentioned Texas concept boosts up the more specific Dallas concept. After the two phases are complete, we reorder the concepts in descending order of their weights. Next, each concept is assigned a probability depending on their individual weights.

12.9   SUMMARY AND DIRECTIONS

This chapter has described the effects of migration and proposed a set of algorithms that we call Tweeque. In particular, we discussed the effect of migration and temporal data mining aspects. Then, we discussed social clique identification algorithms and provided our experimental results. This was followed by a discussion of location prediction algorithms, agglomerative hierarchical clustering algorithms, as well as mining unstructured data.

In Chapter 13, as an application of our location mining work, we demonstrate the development of a system that focuses on understanding the intent of a user search query. We call this system TWinner. TWinner examines the application of social media in improving the quality of web search and predicting whether the user is looking for news or not. We go one step beyond the previous research by mining social media data, assigning weights to them, and determining keywords that can be added to the search query to act as pointers to the existing search engine algorithms, suggesting to it that the user is looking for news.

REFERENCES

Abrol, S. and Khan, L. MapIt: Smarter searches using location driven knowledge discovery and mining. In: *1st SIGSPATIAL ACM GIS 2009 International Workshop on Querying and Mining Uncertain Spatio-Temporal Data (QUeST)*. ACM, Seattle, 2009.

Abrol, S. and Khan, L. TWinner: Understanding news queries with geo-content using Twitter. In: *6th ACM Workshop on Geographic Information Retrieval*. p. 10. Zurich, 2010.

Bron, C. and Kerbosch, J. Algorithm 457: Finding all cliques of an undirected graph. *Communications of the ACM* 16(9): 575–577, 1973.

Geographical Mobility/Migration. Retrieved February 03, 2013, from the US Census Bureau: http://www.census.gov/hhes/migration/, 2009.

Phan, X.-H. CRFTagger: CRF English POS Tagger. Retrieved from CRF Tagger: http://crftagger.sourceforge.net, 2006.

Report: Social network demographics in 2012. Retrieved January 22, 2013, from *Pingdom*: http://royal.pingdom.com/2012/08/21/report-social-network-demographics-in-2012/, August 21, 2012.

Shi, J. and Malik, J. Normalized cuts and image segmentation. *IEEE Transactions on Pattern Analysis and Machine Intelligence* 22(8), 888–905, 2000.

TIGER/Line® Shapefiles and TIGER/Line Files. Retrieved 2013, from the US Census Bureau, 2008.

13 Understanding News Queries with Geo-Content Using Twitter

13.1 INTRODUCTION

In Chapter 9, we discussed the importance of location mining and the challenges we are faced with in extracting the accurate locations of social media users. In Chapter 10, we discussed our collection of TweetHood algorithms for extracting the location of Twitter users. In particular, we have described three methods that show the evolution of the algorithm currently used in TweetHood. These algorithms are as follows: (i) a simple majority algorithm with variable depth, (ii) k closest friends with variable depth, and (iii) fuzzy k closest friends with variable depth. We have also provided experimental results for the algorithms. In Chapter 11, we enhanced our location extraction algorithms and proposed a semisupervised learning method for label propagation. This algorithm was called Tweecalization. Chapter 12 described the effects of migration. People migrate from city to city, state to state, and country to country all the time. Therefore, we addressed the problem of how does one extract the location of a person when he or his friends may be continually migrating? We developed a set of algorithms that we call Tweeque. That is, Tweeque takes into account the migration effect. In particular, it identifies social cliques for location mining.

In this chapter, as an application of our location mining work, we demonstrate the development of a system that focuses on understanding the intent of a user search query. We developed a system called TWinner that examines the application of social media in improving the quality of web search and predicting whether the user is looking for news or not. The organization of this chapter is as follows. The application of location mining for improving web searches is discussed in Section 13.2. Approach to assigning weights to tweets is discussed in Section 13.3. Similarity measures are discussed in Section 13.4. Experimental results are discussed in Section 13.5. The chapter is summarized in Section 13.6. Figure 13.1 illustrates the contents of this chapter. Our work that has influenced the subject of this chapter can be found in Abrol and Khan (2009, 2010a,b) and Abrol et al. (2012a,b,c).

13.2 APPLICATION OF LOCATION MINING AND SOCIAL NETWORKS FOR IMPROVING WEB SEARCH

In this chapter, as an application of our location mining work, we demonstrate the development of a system that focuses on understanding the intent of a user search query. TWinner examines the application of social media in improving the quality of web search and predicting whether the user is looking for news or not. We go one step beyond the previous research by mining social media data, assigning weights to them, and determining keywords that can be added to the search query to act as pointers to the existing search engine algorithms, suggesting to it that the user is looking for news.

Since location is an important part of the system as we shall show later, for the system to work efficiently, it is important that the location of the Twitter users and the location mentioned in the tweet be determined accurately.

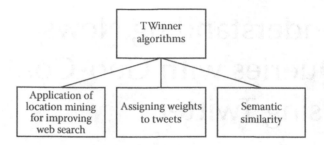

FIGURE 13.1   TWinner algorithms.

It is critical that we determine the news intent.

Determining News Intent. Below, we describe the processes that we undertake to understand the intent of the user query.

Identification of location: In the first step, we attempt to geo-tag the query to a location with certain confidence. For this, we can use any of the systems described in MapIt (Abrol and Khan, 2009), which uses a gazetteer-based mining algorithm to determine the location present in the text of the message.

Frequency–population ratio (FPR): Once the location mentioned in the query has been identified explicitly, the next step is to assign a news intent confidence to the query.

Coming back to the Fort Hood query, once we are able to identify Fort Hood as a unique location, our next task is to identify the intent of the user. Intuition tells us that if something has happened at a place, the likelihood of people talking about it on Twitter will increase manifold.

To understand this concept, we define an index called the FPR for each geographical location. FPR is defined as

$$FPR = \alpha \times N_t + \beta \tag{13.1}$$

where α is the population density factor, N_t is the number of tweets per minute at that instant, and β is the location type constant. The constant α is used taking into consideration the fact that the location of a Twitter user also affects the user's interest in the news. Hassan et al. (2009) in their experiments found out that users from areas with high population density are more interested in current news. We extended these findings to ascertain that people in higher-population-density areas are more likely to tweet about news. Figure 13.2 shows how the percentage of news-related tweets is affected by the population density of the region. The X axis represents the population density in number of persons per square miles, and the Y axis represents the percentage of total tweets that contain news.

The other observation made is that the percentage of news tweets is greatly affected by the location type. For this, we collected a sample of 10,000 Twitter messages having location, and classified them into predetermined location types.

Figure 13.3 shows the outcome of the experiment. We determine that state or country names are more likely to appear in Twitter messages rather than the city names. For each geo-location, we chose the value of the constants α and β in such a way that the FPR for each geo-location is a constant independent of the type and the population density.

Table 13.1 shows some sample geo-locations, the chosen values of α and β, and the resulting FPR ratio for weekdays based on a 1-week time period. It is very important to note here that FPR is a constant on regular days when the geo-location is not in the news or is not a popular topic on Twitter.

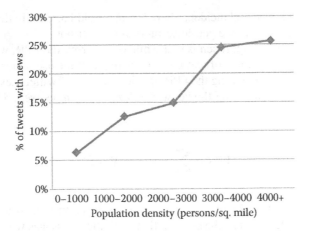

FIGURE 13.2   Percentage of news messages versus the population density of user location in persons per square miles.

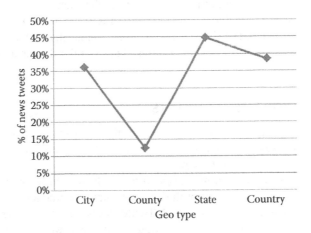

FIGURE 13.3   Percentage of tweets corresponding to type of geo-reference.

TABLE 13.1

Some Sample Locations and Corresponding Estimated α and β Values, and the Frequency Population Ratio

Example of Location	Value of α	Value of β	Frequency Population Ratio (FPR)
Fort Hood (city)	1.2100	2.6315	2.8267
Los Angeles (city)	0.0200	2.6315	2.8677
Collin (county)	0.7490	8.1506	2.8519
Texas (state)	0.0045	2.2702	2.7790
North Dakota (state)	0.2330	2.2702	2.8088
Australia (country)	0.1040	2.5771	2.9051

But in events such as the Fort Hood incident, there is a manifold increase in the FPR. We make use of this feature to determine whether a geo-location is in news or not.

An evident drawback of this approach is that while considering the FPR, we are not taking into account the geographical relatedness of features. For example, if the user enters *Tehran* and is looking for Iran elections, while calculating the FPR, in addition to the Twitter messages for *Tehran*, we need to consider messages containing the keywords *Iran* and *Asia* as well. Therefore, we modify our earlier definition for FPR to

$$\mathrm{FPR} = \sum \mu_i \times (\alpha \times N_t + \beta) \qquad (13.2)$$

where the constant μ_i accounts for the fact that each geo-location related to the primary search query contributes differently. That is, the contribution of Twitter messages with *Fort Hood* (primary search location) will be more than that of messages with *Texas* or *United States of America*.

Now, since we know that FPR for a location is a constant value or lies in a very narrow range in the absence of news-making events, by calculating the FPR for a particular location at any given instance of time and by checking its value, we can determine to a level of certainty whether the area is in the news or not. And if the calculated FPR exceeds the values shown in Table 9.1 by a significant margin, then we can be confident of the news intent of the user.

For example, the calculated value of an average FPR for *Fort Hood* during the week of November 5 to 12 was as high as 1820.7610, which is much higher than the usual 2.8267, indicating that people were talking about Fort Hood on Twitter. And we take that as a pointer that the place is in news.

13.3   ASSIGNING WEIGHTS TO TWEETS

Once we have determined to a certain confidence level the news intent of the user query, the next step is to add certain keywords to the query, which act as pointers to the current search engine algorithm telling it that the user is looking for news.

To begin with, we collect all Twitter messages posted in the last 24 hours containing a reference to either the geo-location (e.g., Fort Hood) or the concepts that subsume it (e.g., Texas, United States of America, etc.). We then assign weights to each Twitter message on the basis of the likelihood of its accuracy in conveying the news. In the following subsections, we describe the various factors that might affect the possibility of a Twitter message having news content.

Detecting Spam Messages. On close observation of the Twitter messages for popular topics, it was noticed that some of the Twitter messages are actually spam messages, where the user has just used the popular keywords so that his or her message reaches out to the people who are looking at this trending topic. In other words, a significant percentage of the Twitter messages are actually spam and carry little or no relevant information. It is thus important to recognize such messages and give lower weight to them. In this section, we briefly describe our method of identifying whether a message is spam or not.

   The methodology we use is based on analyzing the social network of the user posting the message. The social network of a user on Twitter is defined by two factors: (i) the people he or she is following and (ii) the other people following him or her. We hypothesize that the ratio of the number of followers to the number of people he or she is following is very small. The second observation is that a spammer rarely addresses his or her messages to specific people; that is, he or she will rarely reply to messages, retweet other messages, etc. Figure 13.4 shows the profile of a typical spammer. Note that he or she is following 752 people and is being followed by only seven people.

FIGURE 13.4   Profile of a typical spammer.

On the basis of these two hypotheses, we come up with a formula that tags to a certain level of confidence whether the message is spam or not. The spam confidence Z_i is defined as

$$Z_i = \frac{1}{\dfrac{N_p}{N_q} + (\lambda \times N_r)}$$ (13.3)

where N_p and N_q are the number of followers and number of people the user is following, respectively; μ is an arbitrary constant; and N_r is the ratio of number of tweets containing a reply to the total number of tweets.

It is important to note here that the higher the value of the spam confidence, Z_i, the greater is the probability of the message being spam, and therefore its contribution to the total weight is lowered.

On the Basis of User Location. We describe the experiments that we conducted to understand the relationship between Twitter news messages and the location of the user. We performed experiments on two different samples of data each comprising 10,000 tweets, one for tweets about *Fort Hood* and the other on tweets for *Iran*. We grouped the tweets according to the proximity between the topic and the user location. The results of the experiment on Fort Hood are shown in Figure 13.5.

It can be interpreted from the findings that people located in the same state, same country, and also neighboring countries are more likely to talk about a news event as compared with the people located immediately next to the location (within a 10 mile radius) or very far from it (different continent). We use these experiments as the baseline and use the inferences to assign weights for messages on future topics.

Using Hyperlinks Mentioned in Tweets. An interesting observation that we make from our experiments is that 30–50% of the general Twitter messages contain a hyperlink to an external website, and for news Twitter messages, this percentage increases to 70–80%. Closer analysis indicates that first, many popular news websites tweet regularly and, secondly, mostly, people follow a fixed template of writing a short message followed by a link to the actual news article. Figure 13.6 shows the screenshot for a recent Twitter

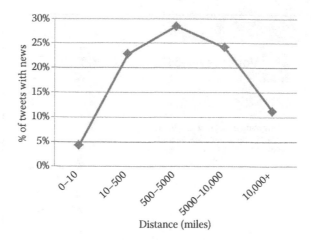

FIGURE 13.5 Relationship between number of tweets to the distance between the Twitter user and query location.

FIGURE 13.6 Results of a Twitter search for *Fort Hood*.

search for *Fort Hood*. Note the high percentage of messages with a hyperlink embedded in them.

So we make use of this pointer in the Twitter message for extra information and crawl the links to analyze the content. Hence, in addition to the previously mentioned two strategies, the weight for the message is also affected by the content of the website mentioned in the message. A weight, which is a function of the factors such as the type of site (news, spam, blog, etc.), the currency of the site, etc., is assigned to each message.

13.4 SEMANTIC SIMILARITY

Now that we have assigned the weights to each Twitter message, it becomes essential for us to summarize them into a couple of the most meaningful keywords. A naïve approach to do this would be to simply take the keywords carrying the maximum weights and modify the query with them.

However, one disadvantage of this approach would be that it would not take into account the semantic similarity of the keywords involved; for example, *shooting* and *killing* are treated as two separate keywords, in spite of their semantic proximity. In this section, we describe a process that in the first step reassigns weights to the keywords on the basis of semantic relatedness, and in the second step picks *k* keywords that are semantically dissimilar but have maximum combined weight.

As mentioned earlier, any two words are rarely independent and are semantically related to each other; for example, *shooting*, *killing*, and *murder* are semantically very similar words. To calculate the same, we use the *New York Times* corpus that contains 1.8 million articles. The semantic similarity, S_{xy}, of two words x and y is defined as

$$S_{xy} = \frac{\max\{\log f(x), \log f(y)\} - \log f(x, y)\}}{\log M - \min\{\log f(x), \ \log f(y)\}} \tag{13.4}$$

where M is the total number of articles searched in *New York Times* corpus; $f(x)$ and $f(y)$ are the number of articles for search terms x and y, respectively; and $f(x, y)$ is the number of articles on which both x and y occur.

Now, we reassign the weight to the ith keyword on the basis of the following formula:

$$W_i^* = W_i + \sum (S_{ij} \times W_j) \tag{13.5}$$

where W_i^* is the new weight of the keyword, W_i is the weight without semantic similarity, S_{ij} is the semantic similarity derived from formula, and W_j is the initial weight of the other words being considered.

After all the n keywords are reassigned a weight, we go to our next step that aims at identifying k keywords that are semantically dissimilar but together contribute maximum weight. In other words, choose words $W_1, W_2,\ldots,W_k$ such that

1. $S_{pq} < S_{\text{threshold}}$, the similarity between any two words, p and q, belonging to the set k is less than a threshold.
2. $W_1 + W_2 +\ldots+ W_k$ is maximum for all groups satisfying condition 1.

It can be easily shown that the complexity of the above-described method is exponential in n. We thus briefly describe three techniques to approximately come up with the k keywords.

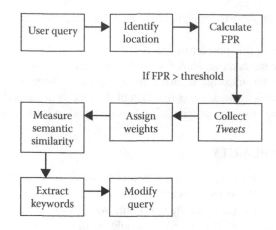

FIGURE 13.7 Architecture of news intent system TWinner.

First, we apply the greedy algorithm approach. For this, we arrange all the words in decreasing order of their weights. We start with the keyword with the maximum weight that is W_1, put it in the basket, and start traversing the array of words. Next, we define an objective function by

$$\Theta_i = \frac{W_i}{E_i} \tag{13.6}$$

where E_i is the sum of semantic similarity of word i with all the words in the basket, and W_i is its own weight. Hence, at each step of the algorithm, we choose a word that maximizes the objective function (Θ).

The second approach is the hill climbing approach. We choose a set of k random words that satisfy the condition 1 mentioned above. Next, we randomly select a word and check if it satisfies the condition of semantic similarity threshold with all the k words. If its weight is more than the weight of the lightest word, we replace the two. We keep repeating the process until the random word selected does not satisfy the condition.

And our final method is that of simulated annealing. The advantage of simulated annealing as compared with hill climbing is that it does not get stuck on local minima. It also takes into consideration the neighborhood, and decides its progress on the basis of an objective function.

Among the three methods described above, simulated annealing produces the most accurate results, but, in general, is slower than the other two. The running time of these methods heavily depends on the value of k. And since for our approach, k is a very small number (usually 2), we can safely adopt simulated annealing to obtain the bag of k words.

These k keywords derived from reassigning the weights after taking semantic similarity into account are treated as special words that act as pointers, making the news intent of the query evident to the current search engine algorithm. The architecture of the TWinner system is illustrated in Figure 13.7.

13.5 EXPERIMENTS AND RESULTS

To see the validity of our hypothesis, we performed experiments to determine two words ($k = 2$) to enhance two queries that returned confidence values of ~1 indicating news intent. The first experiment was conducted to enhance the search query *Fort Hood* entered by a user on November 12, 2009. For this, we collected more than 10,000 Twitter messages for November 12 having the keywords *Fort Hood* or *Texas* in them, and used our approach to determine the keywords. After using

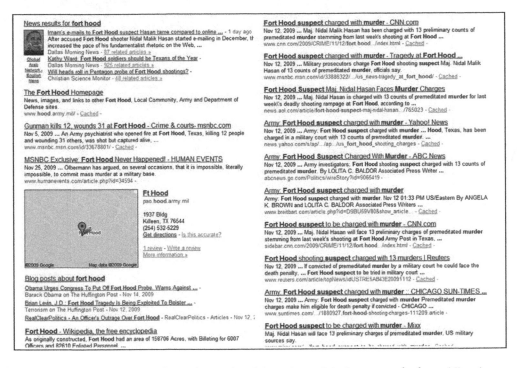

FIGURE 13.8 Contrast in search results produced by using original query and after adding keywords obtained by TWinner.

our methods and assigning weights to the messages, the keywords *murder* and *suspect* were selected by the algorithm to have the cumulative weights. We added these keywords to the search query and observed the impact they had on the results returned by the search engine. The difference in the results is shown in Figure 13.8.

In a similar fashion, we conducted an experiment to enhance the query for *Russia*. We chose all the Twitter messages containing the keyword *Russia* and applied the algorithm to them. The algorithm returned the two words *night* and *explosion*; however, it was interesting to note here that two other sets of words, *club* and *explosion*, also had very similar collective weight. In such a scenario, the algorithm chooses all three words *night*, *club*, and *explosion* to enhance the query.

It can be observed that without using TWinner, the search engine is not sure about the news intent of the user. As a result, it displays results that constitute a short news caption, the homepage of Fort Hood, the maps version, Wikipedia articles, etc. On the right side of Figure 13.8 is an enhanced version of the query obtained after TWinner extracted the keywords *murder* and *suspect*. The impact on the content of the results is clearly visible. The majority of the search results are news oriented and are also in accordance with the date the user issued the query, that is, November 12 (the Twitter data set was also collected for November 12).

13.5.1 TIME COMPLEXITY

One of the apparent concerns raised by the methodology adopted could be the real-time application to search queries. We would like to point out that the process described earlier does not need to be repeated for each query, but instead the search engine can do it on a periodic basis and cache the special keywords corresponding to a particular keyword. And in times of situations like the Fort Hood shootings in November 2009, *Fort Hood* would become a top searched query. The Google Search trends (2009) for November 5 support our assumption, as shown in Figure 13.9.

FIGURE 13.9 Google Search trends for November 5, 2009.

13.6   SUMMARY AND DIRECTIONS

This chapter describes an application of our location mining work, and we describe the development of a system that focuses on understanding the intent of a user search query. In particular, we develop a system called TWinner that examines the application of social media in improving the quality of web search and predicting whether the user is looking for news or not. First, we discuss the application of location mining for improving web search. Then, we discussed an approach to assigning weights to tweets. Similarity measures including TWinner were then described. Finally, we described the experimental results.

Now that we have described our data mining systems for social media data. In Section IV, we describe the privacy violations that could occur due to data mining. We give several examples and then apply a variety of data mining techniques and show how privacy of individuals may be violated.

REFERENCES

Abrol, S. and Khan, L. MapIt: Smarter searches using location driven knowledge discovery and mining. In: *1st SIGSPATIAL ACM GIS 2009 International Workshop on Querying and Mining Uncertain Spatio-Temporal Data (QUeST)*. Seattle, 2009.

Abrol, S. and Khan, L. TweetHood: Agglomerative clustering on fuzzy *k*-closest friends with variable depth for location mining. In: *IEEE Second International Conference on Social Computing (SocialCom)*, pp. 153–160. Minneapolis, 2010a.

Abrol, S. and Khan, L. TWinner: Understanding news queries with geo-content using Twitter. In: *6th ACM Workshop on Geographic Information Retrieval*, p. 10. Zurich, 2010b.

Abrol, S., Khan, L., and Thuraisingham, B. Tweecalization: Efficient and intelligent location mining in twitter using semi-supervised learning. In: *8th IEEE International Conference on Collaborative Computing: Networking, Applications and Worksharing*. Pittsburgh, 2012a.

Abrol, S., Khan, L., and Thuraisingham, B. Tweelocal: Identifying social cliques for intelligent location mining. *Human Journal* 1(3): 116–129, 2012b.

Abrol, S., Khan, L., and Thuraisingham, B. Tweeque: Spatio-temporal analysis of social networks for location mining using graph partitioning. In: *ASE International Conference on Social Informatics (Social Informatics 2012)*. Washington, DC, 2012c.

Hassan, A., Jones, R., and Diaz, F. A case study of using geographic cues to predict query news intent. In: *17th ACM SIGSPATIAL International Conference on Advances in Geographic Information Systems*. ACM, New York, 2009.

CONCLUSION TO SECTION III

Section III has described social network analytics in general and location mining in particular. We discussed the various social media analytics tasks and then described several novel algorithms for location mining, which is an important aspect of social media analytics.

Chapter 9 discussed aspects of location mining for social networks. Such approaches would enable, say, law enforcement to determine where the users are if they have committed a crime. On the other hand, we may want to protect the location of innocent users. We first discussed the importance of location mining and then provided an overview of the related efforts on this topic. This was followed by a discussion of the challenges in location mining. Some aspects of geospatial proximity and friendship were then discussed. Finally, we provided an overview of our contributions to location mining. Chapter 10 described TweetHood, an algorithm for agglomerative clustering on fuzzy k closest friends with variable depth. Graph-related approaches are the methods that rely on the social graph of the user while deciding on the location of the user. We described three such methods that show the evolution of the algorithm currently used in TweetHood. These algorithms are as follows: (i) a simple majority algorithm with variable depth, (ii) k closest friends with variable depth, and (iii) fuzzy k closest friends with variable depth. We have also provided experimental results for the algorithms. In Chapter 11, we argued that the location data of users on social networks is a rather scarce resource and only available to a small portion of users. This creates a need for a methodology that makes use of both labeled and unlabeled data for training. In this case, the location concept serves the purpose of class label. Therefore, our problem is a classic example of the application of semisupervised learning algorithms. We described a semisupervised learning method for label propagation that we call Tweecalization. Chapter 12 described the effects of migration and proposed a set of algorithms that we call Tweeque. In particular, we discussed the effect of migration and temporal data mining aspects. Then, we discussed social clique identification algorithms and provided our experimental results. Chapter 13 described an application of our location mining work, and we described the development of a system that focuses on understanding the intent of a user search query. In particular, we discussed a system called TWinner that examines the application of social media in improving the quality of web searches.

Section IV

Social Network Analytics and Privacy Considerations

INTRODUCTION TO SECTION IV

While Section III focused on social media analytics, in Section IV we will discuss the privacy violations that can result from social media analytics. That is, an adversary can infer highly private attributes of an individual from the public data he posts. Once we know that a social network is vulnerable to such inference attacks, then we can explore ways to handle such a problem.

Section IV consists of five chapters: Chapters 14 through 18. Chapter 14 will begin with the discussion of one of the early full-scale analysis of social networks with a focus on privacy. We will provide several major insights that contribute to the overall concept. We will show that based on simple, preexisting relational classifiers, we are able to use specific information about link types that had previously been ignored, and utilize it to increase our ability to determine hidden information. Chapter 15 will present, for ease of comparison, a summarization of all of our experiments. We believe that it shows that our enhancements to the traditional relational Bayes classifier (rBC), which we call link-type rBC and weighted link-type rBC, are both successful extensions to the well-researched area of classification in social networks. We will show how our extensions have improved on the implementation of the traditional rBC on our data set, and how the overall accuracy compares to similar experiments done on a similar data set in other research work. In Chapter 16, we will show that by intelligently choosing *important* nodes in a subgraph, one is able to increase classification accuracy on real-world social network data. We will present a method of selecting nodes by using weighted graph metrics and a programmatically determinable threshold parameter. Furthermore, we will show that our τ threshold is a useful tool for determining the general increase in graph size versus a desired amount of classification accuracy, and that it may be possible to determine a beneficial value of τ through calculation of the chosen degree metric. In Chapter 17, we will show how the information gain–based partitioning methods may be used to efficiently divide and then classify the data in a social network. In Chapter 18, we will address various issues related to private information leakage in social networks. For unmodified social network graphs, we will show that using details alone, one can predict class values more accurately than using friendship links alone. We wil further show that using friendship links and details together gives better predictability than using details alone. In addition, we will explore the effect of removing details and links in preventing sensitive information leakage.

14 Our Approach to Studying Privacy in Social Networks

14.1 INTRODUCTION

Social networks as an entity unto themselves are a fairly modern concept that has taken advantage of the benefits provided by the Internet to become one of the most popular recent phenomena. In fact, it may not be a stretch to say that the defining technology of the current decade—if not century—is the social network. Not only has Google launched its own (beta) version of a social network in Google+, but also mobile phones natively send data to the existing social networks, and desktop applications come preinstalled on new computers. Even the social network leaders are integrating with each other—Twitter will reproduce your tweets to your Facebook status feed or your LiveJournal blog. However, the utility of social networks has extended far beyond the average Internet user's activities on Facebook. Researchers have created social networks from such unique data sets as Enron's electronic mails, and used them to analyze fraud within that company. It is exactly this ability to use social network analysis—even on data sets that are not conventional social networks—to determine hidden information that makes them so valuable and so dangerous.

If we separate the privacy concerns from the potential gain of information, we see that owing to the unique nature of these networks, one is able to obtain extremely useful information. For example, researchers from the University of Washington and Columbia University mapped the sexual activities of a midwestern high school, and showed the potential of such data sets for epidemiological and sociological research. Furthermore, researchers at the Massachusetts Institute of Technology showed that based on knowledge of the local area, given access to a subset of data in the Facebook network, they were able to accurately determine the sexual orientation of users who had initially not provided this data to the network. Because of this, it is increasingly important to determine methods by which we can efficiently obtain hidden information from these networks. Citing the specific example of counterterrorism, the intelligence community has devoted a considerable amount of time and effort determining the composition of terrorist cells. However, following the attacks of September 11, 2001, these cells have also spent a considerable amount of time and effort attempting to ensure their anonymity. To this end, we offer three different solutions to improve the accuracy of classifiers built on these data sets.

The first is a classification improvement based on the growing nature of link differentiation within social networks. For example, if one considers a Facebook user's edge set, one may find some combination of friends, coworkers, high school acquaintances, college classmates, and family members. Each of these types of links has a different bearing on what a particular user may believe or take part in. Our system of classification adds consideration of these various link types into probability classification. Secondly, we offer a method of classification that considers that there are regional influences within graphs. Not every individual in a graph has the same influence on the entirety of the graph (or a smaller subgraph therein); in high schools there is the *popular clique*, or in technology there are *early adopters*. However, regardless of the domain, it is apparent that there are some people who have a higher regional influence. Finally, we offer a partitioning-based method of classification that separates the data set into multiple groups. Each of these groups is modeled individually, and we perform classification therein.

The previous examples illustrate the conflicting nature of research into social network analysis. While there are certain usages that are obviously important—epidemiology, counterterrorism, or fraud—there are other uses that serve no *greater good* yet violate an individual's privacy. The former

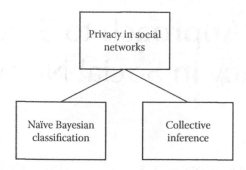

FIGURE 14.1   Our approach to studying privacy in social networks.

offers compelling evidence that analytical techniques for social networks should be improved so that we gain the maximum benefit from their use. The latter indicates that providers of online social networks should provide some mechanisms to protect the information of its users. However, privacy in social networks is divided into two distinct areas: privacy through standard usage of the network and privacy with released data. To solve the former, we provide a method of social network access control that addresses the unique requirements of online social networks. For the latter, we provide two methods of sanitizing social network data for release to a semitrusted third party.

This chapter is organized as follows. In Section 14.2, we provide a brief overview of related works. In Section 14.3, we provide some definitions. In Section 14.4, we provide our analysis. In Section 14.5, we discuss aspects of data gathering. Finally, in Section 14.6, we conclude with a brief discussion of future work. Figure 14.1 illustrates the concepts discussed in this chapter.

14.2   RELATED WORK

In this section, we will give an overview of the current research in the three research domains identified in this work: social network data mining, access controls, and privacy within social networks.

14.2.1   Social Network Data Mining

Other papers have tried to infer private information inside social networks. He et al. (2006) considered ways to infer private information via friendship links by creating a Bayesian network from the links inside a social network. While they crawled a real social network, LiveJournal, they used hypothetical attributes to analyze their learning algorithm. Also, compared with He et al. (2006), we provide techniques that can help with choosing the most effective details or links that need to be removed for protecting privacy. Finally, we explore the effect of collective inference techniques in possible inference attacks.

The Facebook platform's data has been considered in some other research as well. Jones and Hiram Soltren (2005) crawled Facebook's data and analyzed usage trends among Facebook users, employing both profile postings and survey information. However, their paper focuses mostly on faults inside the Facebook platform. They did not discuss attempting to learn unrevealed details of Facebook users, and did no analysis of the details of Facebook users. Their crawl consisted of around 70,000 Facebook accounts.

The area of link-based classification is well studied. Sen and Getoor (2007) compared various methods of link-based classification, including loopy belief propagation, mean field relaxation labeling, and iterative classification. However, their comparisons did not consider ways to prevent link-based classification. Belief propagation as a means of classification is presented by Yedidia et al. (2003). Tasker et al. (2002) present an alternative classification method where they build on Markov networks. However, none of these papers consider ways to combat their classification methods.

Zheleva and Getoor (2009) attempted to predict the private attributes of users in four real-world data sets: Facebook, Flickr, Dogster, and BibSonomy. Their focus is on how specific types of data, namely that of declared and inferred group membership, may be used as a way to boost local and relational classification accuracy. Their defined method of group-based (as opposed to details-based or link-based) classification is an inherent part of our details-based classification, as we treat the group membership data as just another detail, as we do favorite books or movies. In fact, Zheleva and Getoor's work provides substantial motivation for the need for the solution proposed in our work.

14.2.2 PRIVACY IN SOCIAL NETWORKS

Backstrom et al. (2007) considered an attack against an anonymized network. In their model, the network consists of only nodes and edges. Detail values are not included. The goal of the attacker is simply to identify people. Furthermore, their problem is very different than the one considered in this chapter because they ignored details and did not consider the effect of the existence of details on privacy. Hay et al. (2007) and Liu and Terzi (2008) considered several ways of anonymizing social networks. However, our work focuses on inferring details from nodes in the network, not individually identifying individuals. Hay et al. (2007) considered perturbing network data in order to preserve privacy. While their method considered graph structure, it ignored any extra details or traits that a node inside the social network may possess. Liu and Terzi (2008) considered the problem of anonymizing a social graph through making the graph k anonymous. In their approach, they applied k anonymity toward the identification of nodes through measuring the degree of a node. However, in their research, they assumed that the structure and identity of the nodes is the sensitive information, and neither nodes nor links contain any additional information that can be used to distinguish a node. We consider that the graph has considerably more information and that the attributes of nodes, not their identity, are the end goal of an attacker.

Zheleva and Getoor (2007) proposed several methods of social graph anonymization, focusing mainly on the idea that by anonymizing both the nodes in the group and the link structure, one thereby anonymizes the graph as a whole. However, their methods all focused on anonymity in the structure itself. For example, through the use of k anonymity or t closeness, depending on the quasi-identifiers that are chosen, much of the uniqueness in the data may be lost. Through our method of anonymity preservation, we maintain the full uniqueness in each node, which allows more information in the data post-release. Gross et al. (2005) examined specific usage instances at Carnegie Mellon. They also noted potential attacks, such as node reidentification or stalking, that easily accessible data on Facebook could assist with. They further note that while privacy controls may exist on the user's end of the social networking site, many individuals do not take advantage of this tool. This finding coincides very well with the amount of data that we were able to crawl using a very simple crawler on a Facebook network. We extend on their work by experimentally examining the accuracy of some types of the demographic reidentification that they propose before and after sanitization. Menon and Elkan (2010) used dyadic data methods to predict class labels. We show later that while we do not examine the effects of this type of analysis, the choice of technique is arbitrary for anonymization and utility.

14.3 DEFINITIONAL PRELIMINARIES

We begin by describing background information that will be necessary to the understanding of the works described herein. We start with a formal description of a social network and related concepts. We then discuss classification in regards to social networks, and we conclude with a description of the data sets used throughout this work. Our definitions are given in Definitions 14.1 through 14.7.

Social Network Description. While most people have a vague notion of social networks, often in terms of one of the many online providers of such services, formally, we define a social network as follows:

Definition 14.1

A *social network*, $\mathcal{G}$ is a set $\mathcal{G} = \{\mathcal{V}, \mathcal{E}, \mathcal{D}\}$, where $\mathcal{V} = \{v_1, v_2, \ldots, v_n\}$ is a set describing the vertices of the graph, $\mathcal{E} = \{(v_i, v_j), \ldots, (v_y, v_z)\}$ is a set describing the links within the graph, and $\mathcal{D}$ is a set of additional *details* within the social network.   ■

In the context of the Facebook social network, this means that $\mathcal{V}$ is all users of Facebook, $\mathcal{E}$ is all friendship links, and $\mathcal{D}$ is all additional data that is stored about the user. In Chapter 4, we propose methods that utilize additional information within $\mathcal{E}$; however, for a large portion of this work, we focus on various uses of the data contained in $\mathcal{D}$. For this reason, we now highlight specifics regarding $\mathcal{D}$.

Definition 14.2

A *detail type* is a string defined over an alphabet Σ, which corresponds to one of the domain-specific attribute categories. The set of all detail types is referred to by $\mathcal{H}$.

Definition 14.3

A *detail value* is a string defined over an alphabet Σ, which corresponds to a possible response for a given detail type.

Definition 14.4

A *detail* is a single (detail type, detail value) pair that occurs within the data. The set of all unique details is referred to as $\mathcal{J}$.

Definition 14.5

The *detail set*, $\mathcal{D}$, is a set composed of m (v_i, detail) pairs, where $v_i \in \mathcal{V}$.   ■

To continue illustrating these concepts through Facebook, then a detail type is one of the categories a user may enter data under, such as *favorite books*, *hometown*, or *education*. Possible detail values for these types are *Harry Potter and the Deathly Hallows*; *Dallas, Texas*; and *Millsaps College*, respectively.

We further define a set of private details $\mathcal{I}$, where any detail is private if for any $h_m \in \mathcal{H}$, $h_m \in \mathcal{I}$. Consider the following illustrative examples:

$$\mathcal{I} = (\text{political affiliation, religion}) \tag{14.1}$$

$$n_1 = (\text{Jane Doe}) \tag{14.2}$$

TABLE 14.1

Common Notations Used in the Book

Name of Value	Variable
Node numbered i in the graph	n_i
All details of node n_i	D_i
Detail j of node n_i	D_i^j
Friendship link between person n_i and n_k	$F_{i,k}$
Weight of a friend link from n_i to n_j	$W_{i,j}$

$$n_2 = (\text{John Smith}) \tag{14.3}$$

$$D_2 = \{\text{John Smith's details}\} \tag{14.4}$$

$$D_2^4 = (\text{activities, fishing}) \tag{14.5}$$

$$F_{1,2} \in E \tag{14.6}$$

$$F_{2,1} \in E \tag{14.7}$$

That is, we define two *detail types* to be private, a person's political affiliation and their religion (Equation 14.1). Then, say, we have two people, named Jane Doe and John Smith (Equations 14.2 and 14.3). John Smith has specified that one of the activities he enjoys is fishing (Equation 14.5). Also, John and Jane are friends. Note that because our graph is undirected, Equations 14.6 and 14.7 are interchangeable, and only one is actually recorded.

For further clarity, in Table 14.1, we have a reference for many frequently used notations found in the remainder of this chapter. Obviously, the detail types of $\mathcal{I}$ are varied based on an individual's choice. Generally, however, we consider a user's $\mathcal{I}$ to be any details that they do not specify. For experimentation, however, we choose to use only $\mathcal{I} = \{\text{political affiliation}\}$. We use this detail type as our C in all classification methods. Furthermore, we consider only C_{lib} and C_{cons} as possible class values—that is, *Liberal* and *Conservative*.

14.4 ANALYSIS

14.4.1 CLASSIFICATION

At any given time, a data representation of a social network could be incomplete. There are many potential reasons for this issue, including technical limitations of the network or conscious choices of the users therein. As an example of this, Facebook does not have an explicit *sexual orientation* field; however, it does have a *political affiliation* field that many users explicitly leave empty. There are times when this incompleteness interferes with operations within the network. Consider, for instance, if Gearbox Studios pays for their newest game to be marketed on Facebook. There may be 2% of the entire graph that lists *video games* as a *Favorite Activity*. If Facebook only markets to that segment, then there may be a considerable population who miss out on relevant advertisements. To determine other users who may be interested in video games, a fact that could be considered *hidden*, then Facebook may perform *classification* to find additional users to target with marketing.

Definition 14.6

Classification is a mechanism by which one attempts to determine the likelihood of a given event when the information directly related to that event is unknown or only partially known.

$\Lambda_c^{\mathcal{J}_y}$ ($\mathcal{G}$) is the accuracy of a given classifier, c, on detail $\mathcal{J}_y$ using the graph $\mathcal{G}$. This accuracy is given as the ratio of correct classifications to total classifications.

Naïve Bayes Classification. Within this work, the most common type of classifier that will be used is the Bayesian classifier. The details of this classification method are described below.

Definition 14.7

Given a node n_i with m details and p potential classification labels, $C_1,...,C_p$, the probability of being in a class is given by the equation

$$\underset{1 \le x \le p}{\operatorname{argmax}}[P(C_x|D_{1,i},...,D_{m,i})]$$

where argmax $1 \le x \le p$ represents the possible class label that maximizes the previous equation. However, this is difficult to calculate, since $P(C_x)$ for any given value of x is unknown. By applying Bayes' theorem, we have the equation

$$\underset{1 \le x \le p}{\operatorname{argmax}}\left[\frac{P(C_x) \times P(D_{1,i},...,D_{m,i}|C_x)}{P(D_{1,i},...,D_{m,i})}\right]$$

Furthermore, by assuming that all details are independent, we are left with the simplified equation

$$\underset{1 \le x \le p}{\operatorname{argmax}}\left[\frac{P(C_x) \times P(D_{1,i}|C_x) \times ... \times P(D_{m,i}|C_x)}{P(D_{1,i},...,D_{m,i})}\right]$$

Notice, however, that $P(D_{1,i},...D_{m,i})$ is equivalent for all values of C_x, which means that we need only to compare

$$\underset{1 \le x \le p}{\operatorname{argmax}}[P(C_x) \times P(D_{1,i}|C_x) \times ... \times P(D_{m,i}|C_x)] \tag{14.8}$$

to determine a new class label for n_i.

While there are multiple benefits to this method of classification, one of the most important for this work is its reliability in classification, as well as its speed. Further benefits, specifically related to our privacy mechanisms, will be discussed in more detail in Chapter 18.

Collective Inference. One problem with the traditional Bayesian classifier described previously is that they generally consider only the data local to a node, which has led to their being classified as *local* classifiers. Social networks, however, also contain a rich collection of data for the associated links. To leverage this information, *collective inference* is a method of classifying social network data using a combination of node details, such as favorite books and movies, and connecting links in the social graph. Each of these classifiers consists of three components: local classifier, relational classifier, and collective inference algorithm.

Local classifiers are a type of learning method that is applied in the initial step of collective inference. As mentioned previously, social networks can be in various states of *knowledge*. Where this involves the detail to be classified on, this can create situations where after even a number of iterations of a relational classifier, some nodes may not have a classification value. To prevent this, the first step of all collective inference techniques is to determine a *prior* for each node through the use of a local classifier.

Relational classifiers are a separate type of learning algorithm that looks at the link structure of the graph, and uses the labels of nodes in the training set to develop a model that, in turn, is used to classify the nodes in the test set. Specifically, Macskassy and Provost (2007) examined four relational classifiers: class-distribution relational neighbor (cdRN), weighted-vote relational neighbor (wvRN), network-only Bayes classifier (nBC), and network-only link-based classification (nLB).

A problem with relational classifiers is that while we may cleverly divide fully labeled test sets so that we ensure every node is connected to at least one other node in the training set, real-world data may not satisfy this strict requirement. If this requirement is not met, then relational classification will be unable to classify nodes that have no neighbors in the training set. Collective inference attempts to make up for these deficiencies by using both local and relational classifiers in a precise manner to attempt to increase the classification accuracy of nodes in the network. By using a local classifier in the first iteration, collective inference ensures that every node will have an initial probabilistic classification. The algorithm then uses a relational classifier to reclassify nodes.

14.5 DATA GATHERING

We wrote a program to crawl the Facebook network to gather data for our experiments. Written in Java 1.6, the crawler loaded a profile, parsed the details out of the HTML, and stored the details inside a MySQL database. Then, the crawler loaded all friends of the current profile and stored the friends inside the database, both as friendship links and as possible profiles to crawl later. Because of the sheer size of Facebook's social network, the crawler was limited to only crawling profiles inside the Dallas/Fort Worth (DFW) network. This means that if two people share a common friend that is outside the DFW network, this is not reflected inside the database. Also, some people have enabled privacy restrictions on their profile that prevented the crawler from seeing their profile details.* The total time for the crawl was 7 days. Because the data inside a Facebook profile is free-form text, it is critical that the input be normalized. For example, favorite books of *Bible* and *The Bible* should be considered the same detail. Furthermore, there are often spelling mistakes or variations on the same noun.

The normalization method we used was based on a Porter stemmer presented by van Rijsbergen (1980). To normalize a detail, it was broken into words and each word was stemmed with a Porter stemmer, then recombined. Two details that normalized to the same value were considered the same for the purposes of the learning algorithm. Our total crawl resulted in more than 167,000 profiles, almost 4.5 million profile details, and more than 3 million friendship links. In the graph representation, we had one large central group of connected nodes that had a maximum path length of 16. Only 22 of the collected users were not inside this group.

In Table 14.2, we provide some general statistics of our Facebook data set, including the diameter mentioned above. Common knowledge leads us to expect a small diameter in social networks (Watts and Strogatz, 1998). To reconcile this fact with the empirical results of a 16-degree diameter in the graph, note that, although popular, not every person in society has a Facebook account, and

---

* The default privacy setting for Facebook users is to have all profile information revealed to others inside their network.

TABLE 14.2

General Information about the Data

Diameter of the largest component	16
No. of nodes in the graph	167,390
No. of friendship links in the graph	3,342,009
Total no. of listed details in the graph	4,493,436
Total no. of unique details in the graph	110,407
No. of components in the graph	18

even those that do, still do not have friendship links to every person they know. Additionally, given the limited scope of our crawl, it is possible that some connecting individuals may be outside the DFW area.

In Table 14.3, we show the original class likelihood for those details that will be used as experimental class values.

Figures 14.2 and 14.3 show how many people have the specified number of details or friendship links, respectively. For example, the point ($x = 4$, $y = 6100$) in Figure 14.3 means that 6100 people have four friendship links. The point ($x = 4$, $y = 38,979$) in Figure 14.2 means that 38,979 people have four listed details. It is important to note that both figures have a logarithmic Y scale. This shows that the vast majority of nodes in the graph have few details and friendship links. Figure 14.4 shows the number of profiles where the most popular activities were listed. For example, the point ($x = 1$, $y = 2373$) means that the most popular detail of the *Activities* type was listed inside 2373 profiles, while the point ($x = 41,482$) means that the fourth most popular detail was listed 1482 times. Figure 14.4 is actually only part of the graph. The X axis can extend to the point 94,146 but was

TABLE 14.3

Odds of Being Liberal or Conservative

Probability of being liberal	0.45
Probability of being conservative	0.55
Probability of being heterosexual	0.95
Probability of being homosexual	0.05

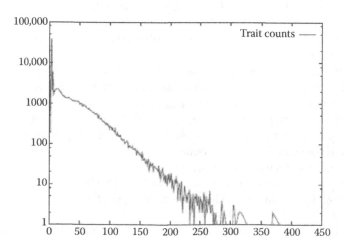

FIGURE 14.2 Frequency of (per person) detail set size.

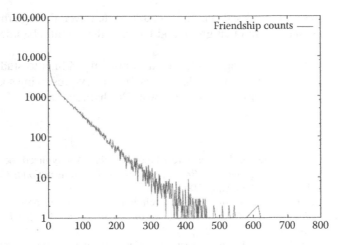

FIGURE 14.3   Frequency of (per person) friendship link set size.

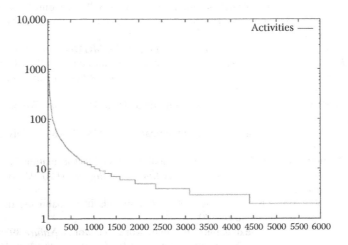

FIGURE 14.4   Frequency of the activities detail.

cut off at 6000 for readability purposes. Combined with the fact that the Y axis has a logarithmic Y scale, this shows that the few most popular details are represented strongly in the data set.

14.6   SUMMARY AND DIRECTIONS

This chapter begins with the discussion of one of the early full-scale analyses of social networks with a focus on privacy. We have provided several major insights that contribute to the overall concept. We show that based on simple, preexisting relational classifiers, we are able to use specific information about link types that had previously been ignored, and use this to increase our ability to determine hidden information. By altering these classifiers, and discovering how to improve their classification ability through the use of this data, we can determine more hidden information than previously expected.

In the next few chapters, we show that through the use of indirect links, we are able to find members of the social network who have a high relative importance to their subregion, and because we propagate this importance to other members of their region, we increase the overall classification accuracy of that network. Finally, we show that by selectively partitioning the network, we can reduce the size of the model that a local classifier is built on; however, through this process, we are able to eliminate excess data within that group and increase the overall classification accuracy of the graph.

Future directions will include using existing data mining algorithms to study data privacy in social networks, as well as developing novel algorithms for privacy-preserving social network analysis. The discussion in this chapter is the first step toward such direction.

REFERENCES

Backstrom, L., Dwork, C., and Kleinberg, J. Wherefore art thou r3579x?: Anonymized social networks, hidden patterns, and structural steganography. In: *Proceedings of the 16th International Conference on World Wide Web*, pp. 181–190. ACM, New York, 2007.

Gross, R., Acquisti, A., and Heinz, J.H. Information revelation and privacy in online social networks. In: *WPES '05: Proceedings of the 2005 ACM Workshop on Privacy in the Electronic Society*, pp. 71–80. ACM Press, New York, 2005.

Hay, M., Miklau, G., Jensen, D., Weis, P., and Srivastava, S. Anonymizing social networks. Technical Report 07-19, University of Massachusetts Amherst, Computer Science Department, March 2007.

He, J., Chu, W., and Liu, V. Inferring privacy information from social networks. In: Mehrotra, S., editor, *Proceedings of Intelligence and Security Informatics*, vol. LNCS 3975, Springer, New York, 2006.

Jones, H. and Hiram Soltren, J. Facebook: Threats to privacy. Technical report, Massachusetts Institute of Technology, Boston, 2005.

Liu, K. and Terzi, E. Towards identity anonymization on graphs. In: *SIGMOD '08: Proceedings of the 2008 ACM SIGMOD International Conference on Management of Data*, pp. 93–106, ACM, New York, 2008.

Macskassy, S.A. and Provost, F. Classification in networked data: A toolkit and a univariate case study. *Journal of Machine Learning Research* 8: 935–983, 2007.

Menon, A.K. and Elkan, C. Predicting labels for dyadic data. *Data Mining and Knowledge Discovery* 21: 327–343, 2010.

Sen, P. and Getoor, L. Link-based classification. Technical report CS-TR-4858, University of Maryland, College Park, MD, February 2007.

Tasker, B., Abbeel, P., and Daphne, K. Discriminative probabilistic models for relational data. In: *Proceedings of the 18th Annual Conference on Uncertainty in Artificial Intelligence (UAI-02)*, pp. 485–492. Morgan Kaufmann, San Francisco, 2002.

van Rijsbergen, C.J., Robertson, S.E., and Porter, M.F. New models in probabilistic information retrieval. Technical report 5587, British Library, 1980.

Watts, D.J. and Strogatz, S.H. Collective dynamics of "small-world" networks. *Nature* 393: 440–442, 1998.

Yedidia, J.S., Freeman, W.T., and Weiss, Y. *Exploring Artificial Intelligence in the New Millennium*. Morgan Kaufmann, San Francisco, 2003.

Zheleva, E. and Getoor, L. Preserving the privacy of sensitive relationships in graph data. In: *1st ACM SIGKDD International Workshop on Privacy, Security, and Trust in KDD (PinKDD 2007)*, 2007.

Zheleva, E. and Getoor, L. To join or not to join: the illusion of privacy in social networks with mixed public and private user profiles. In: *WWW '09: Proceedings of the 18th International Conference on World Wide Web*, pp. 531–540, ACM, New York, 2009.

15 Classification of Social Networks Incorporating Link Types

15.1 INTRODUCTION

Social networks are platforms that allow people to publish details about themselves and to connect to other members of the network through links. Recently, the population of such online social networks has increased significantly. For instance, Facebook now has close to a billion daily active users (see http://newsroom.fb.com/Company-Info/). Facebook is only one example of a social network that is for general connectivity. Other examples of social networks are LinkedIn (professional), Last.fm (music), orkut (social), aNobii (books), and the list continues.

Each of these networks allows users to list details about themselves, and also allows them to not specify details about themselves. However, these hidden details can be important to the administrators of a social network. Most of these sites are free to the end user and are thus advertising supported. If we assume that advertisers want to reach the people most likely to be interested in their products, then identifying those individuals becomes a priority for maintaining much-needed advertisers. However, by just using specifically defined information, the site may be missing a large number of potentially interested users. Taking the specified knowledge from some users and using it to infer unspecified data may allow the site to extend its target audience for particular advertisements.

Of course, the implications of classification in social network data extend far beyond the simple case of targeted advertising. For instance, such ideas could be used for addressing classification problems in terrorist networks. By using the link structure and link types among nodes in a social network with known terrorist nodes, we can attempt to classify unknown nodes as terrorist or nonterrorist. In such a classification process, the type of the link shared among nodes could be really critical in determining the internal success of the classifier. For example, assume that there exist two different individuals, Alice and Bob, who are linked to some known terrorist, Malory. Furthermore, assume that Alice works at the same place as Malory, but they are not friends. (That is, Alice and Malory have a relationship. The type of relationship is *colleague*.) In addition, assume that Malory talks frequently on the phone with Bob and they are friends. (That is, Bob is linked to Malory and the link type is *friend*.) Given such a social network, to our knowledge, all the existing classification methods just use the fact that individuals are linked and they do not use the information hidden in the link types. Clearly, in some cases, one link type (e.g., friendship) can be more important than other link types for increasing the accuracy of the classification process. Therefore, social network classification techniques that consider link types could be very useful for many classification tasks.

To address the above problem, we choose the network-only naïve Bayes classifier (nBC) as our starting point, since it was shown by Macskassy and Provost (2007) that relational naïve Bayes classification combined with collective inference techniques provide an efficient solution with acceptable accuracy in practice. We modify this relational nBC to incorporate the type of the link between nodes into the probability calculations. First, we devise a naïve Bayes classification method in which all link types are equally important and we then redefine this method by adding an additional granularity to the calculation method. To our knowledge, this is one of the early works in using link types for relational naïve Bayes classification.

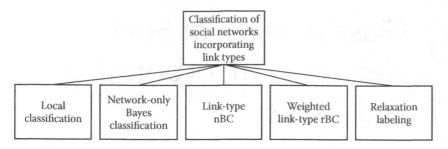

FIGURE 15.1 Classification of social networks incorporating link types.

One feature that is frequently overlooked when classifying in social networks is the richness of data in the link set, $\mathcal{E}$. Consider, for instance, the variety of link types within only Facebook. An individual can have *regular* friends, *best* friends, siblings, cousins, coworkers, and classmates from high school and college. Previous work has either ignored these link types or, worse, used them solely on the basis of whether to include or exclude them from consideration. Here, we show a new classification method that takes advantage of this data. We further show that by intelligently weighting those link types, it is possible to gain even more benefit from the link types.

This chapter is organized as follows. In Section 15.2, we provide a brief overview of the related work. In Section 15.3, we discuss our relational naïve Bayes methods that incorporate link types. In Section 15.4, we show the effectiveness of our learning method on a real-world data set. Finally, in Section 15.5, we conclude with a brief discussion of future work. Figure 15.1 illustrates the concepts discussed in this chapter.

15.2 RELATED WORK

Mika (2007) used iterative classification techniques to improve the accuracy of classification methods of social networks. This approach was mirrored by Macskassy and Provost (2007), who extended the work with a full comparison of several relational classification methods and several collective inference techniques. However, while Macskassy and Provost (2007) began to acknowledge the use of link types, in their experiments using the Internet Movie Database (IMDb) data set, they generated separate relational graphs based on this link type. Unfortunately, they considered only one link type in each experiment. Similarly, Gross et al. (2005) considered the problem of information revelation on the Facebook social network, giving focus to the users' ability to decrease the amount of information they reveal, but highlighted the relatively small number of users who actually do so.

Xu et al. (2008) used hypothetical attributes from the real-world data set of LiveJournal to construct a Bayesian network that they used to analyze their algorithm. However, they did not consider any aspect of link types. Zheleva and Getoor (2007) discussed methods of link re-identification. However, in our data, the links are not explicitly defined and are instead inferred directly from the stated facts. Anonymization of the data that allows us to generate the relationships would make the data meaningless.

Jensen et al. (2004) analyzed the importance of collective inference methods on relational networks. Senator (2005) gave a general review of the past research in link mining and link analysis, and went on to issue a call for a unified framework to support a variety of data representations and for the analysis tools. Getoor and Diehl (2005) offered a survey of the various tasks performed on both hetero- and homogeneous social networks. Sweeney (2005) described several problems and posed a potential solution to naïvely generating a social network from data that did not specifically come from a social network. The author indicated that the use of a form of privacy-enhanced linking in algorithm development can be used to guarantee individual privacy while advancing the cause of technological research.

Chau and Faloutsos (2005) implemented a method of detecting fraudulent transactions in the online auction site eBay. By modeling transaction histories of buyers and sellers, they were able to use characteristic features and design a decision tree that is able to detect fraudulent activities with an 82% accuracy. He et al. (2006) and Xu et al. (2008) used relational Bayesian classification techniques in an attempt to determine private information from a social network. Finally, in Zheleva and Getoor (2009), the authors conducted experiments and built a system to classify both relational and attribute-based models. They then showed the accuracy of their system on a set of constructed data.

15.3   LEARNING METHODS

Currently, classification in social networks is done in a variety of ways. The simplest of these is to use the data about nodes for which the label is known, and to use a simple classification mechanism, such as a naïve Bayes classifier, to classify based on only those attributes that are local to the node being classified. Methods that classify in this manner are considered *local classifiers*.

Another method is referred to as *relational classifiers*. These classification algorithms model the social network data as a graph, where the set of nodes are a specific, homogeneous entity in the representative network. Edges are added based on specific constraints from the original data set. For instance, in Facebook data, the edges are added based on the existence of a friendship link between the nodes. Macskassy and Provost (2007) determine a link between two nodes in their IMDb data set if the two nodes share the same production company. Once this graph structure is created, a classification algorithm is then applied that uses the labels of a node's neighbors to probabilistically apply a label to that node. These algorithms use the theory of *homophily*; that is, that a node is more likely to associate with other nodes of the same type, to perform their calculations.

However, one of the problems with even relational classifiers is that if the labels of a large portion of the network are unknown, then there may be nodes for which we cannot determine a classification. To truly represent homophily, the classified nodes should be used to reassess the classifications of its neighbors. This is the thought behind *collective inference*. These algorithms use a local classifier to create a set of class priors for every node, to ensure that each node has an initial *guess* at a classification. Then, the algorithm uses a relational classifier to generate a probability assignment for each node based on those class priors. This allows us to use a relational classifier and ensure that each node will have a classification. The collective inference algorithm specifies a weighting scheme for each iteration. It also specifies either a number of iterations to run for or to wait for convergence in the classification.

Because we focus our efforts on improving the overall relational classification by increasing the data available for this class of classifiers to use, we use a single local classifier and vary the relational classifiers. Each of these methods is based on the traditional nBC.

Local Classification. As shown by He et al. (2006), using a simple Bayes classifier is an effective method of discerning private information from a social network. Because of this finding and its relatively low computational requirements, we use an nBC. We use the classifier to determine the probability that a particular node, x_i, is of a particular class, c_i, given the entire set of its traits, τ by the formula

$$Pr(x_i = c_i \mid \tau) = \frac{Pr(\tau \mid x_i = c_i)Pr(x_i = c_i)}{Pr(\tau)} = Pr(x_i = c_i) \times \prod_{t_i \in \tau} \frac{Pr(t_i \mid x_i = c_i)}{Pr(t_i)} \qquad (15.1)$$

Network-Only Bayes Classification. This is the first, and most basic, of the three relational classifiers that we examine here. The general nBC assumes that all link types are the same, and that the probability of a particular node's class is influenced by the class of its neighbors. We use the local classifier to assign an inferred prior of each node in the test set.

Since the details of a particular node are factored in when we establish these priors, we do not duplicate this in the nBC calculations. We alter the probability calculations as follows:

$$Pr(x_i = c_i \mid \mathcal{N}) = \frac{Pr(\mathcal{N} \mid x_i = c_i)Pr(x_i = c_i)}{Pr(\mathcal{N})} = Pr(x_i = c_i) \times \prod_{n_i \in \mathcal{N}} \frac{Pr(n_i \mid x_i = c_i)}{Pr(n_i)} \qquad (15.2)$$

This method is a basic classifier, yet Chakrabarti et al. (1998) and Macskassy and Provost (2007) both used nBC to effectively classify nodes on a variety of data sets. Because of their findings, we use this algorithm as the basis for ours.

Link-Type nBC. The next relational classifier that we test is the first to include link types. We noticed that there were no classification algorithms to specify constraints about what type of link two individuals shared, in an important way, for the probability calculations. We believe that including these differences when determining probabilities could be an important and useful extension. For instance, consider Ron Howard. As a writer, director, producer, and actor, he is linked to more than 100 different television shows and movies. However, when classifying whether a movie would be a success, there must be a difference in how important his role in a production is, to calculate his weight on the movie's success.

We represent this by including the link type as an additional parameter to a naïve Bayes classification. Whereas originally we define the probability of any specific node, x_i, to be in a particular class, c_i, to be $Pr(x_i = c_i \mid \mathcal{N})$, that is, the probability of a node being in a class is dependent only on its neighbors, we now define the probability to be $Pr(x_1 = c_1 \mid \mathcal{N}, \mathcal{L})$. That is, the probability of any particular node being in a class is determined by its neighbors, and the set of links that define those neighbors. Thus, we amend the traditional naïve Bayes calculation to be

$$Pr(x_i = c_i \mid \mathcal{N}, \mathcal{L}) = \frac{Pr(\mathcal{N}, \mathcal{L} \mid x_i = c_i)Pr(x_i = c_i)}{Pr(\mathcal{N}, \mathcal{L})}$$

$$= \prod_{n_i \in \mathcal{N}} l_i \in \mathcal{L} \frac{Pr(n_i, l_i \mid x_i = c_i)Pr(x_i = c_i)}{Pr(n_i, l_i)} \qquad (15.3)$$

Weighted Link-Type Relational Bayes Classifier (rBC). The final relational classifier considers that certain link types are indicative of a stronger relationship. For instance, our IMDb data set contains data about all of the crew of a show. This includes the directors, producers, actors, costume designers, grippers, and special-effects technicians. We theorized that not all of these jobs can be equally important. So, we alter our link-type rBC to include weights. To do this, we add the idea of variable weights to the calculation as shown in Equation 15.4:

$$Pr(x_i = c_i \mid \mathcal{N}, \mathcal{L}) = \prod_{\substack{n_i \in \mathcal{N} \\ l_i \in \mathcal{L}}} \left[\frac{w_i}{W} \times \frac{Pr(n_i, l_i \mid x_i = c_i)Pr(x_i = c_i)}{Pr(n_i, l_i)} \right] \qquad (15.4)$$

where w_i is the weight associated with link type l_i and W is the sum of all weights for the network.

Relaxation Labeling. We chose to use relaxation labeling as described by Macskassy and Provost (2007), a method that retains the uncertainty of our classified labels. Relaxation labeling is an iterative process, where at each step $i + 1$ the algorithm uses the probability estimates, not a single classified label, from step i to calculate probability estimates. Furthermore, to account for the possibility that there may not be a convergence, there is a decay rate, called α, set to 0.99 that discounts the weight of each subsequent iteration compared with the previous iterations.

We chose to use relaxation labeling because in the experiments conducted by Macskassy and Provost (2007), relaxation labeling tended to be the best of the three collective inference methods.

We decided to choose the best of the three methods as reported by Macskassy and Provost (2007), and use that to focus on our new relational classifiers.

15.4   EXPERIMENTS

The data used in our experiments was gathered from the IMDb. This decision was made on the basis of the importance of not only having links between members in our social network representation, but also on the ability to specifically define what specific relationship is indicated by them. Although we considered using data from the Facebook online social network, we discovered that while Facebook allows users the ability to specify the relationship type linking friends, most relationships are not defined. Rather than add additional inference operations that could cast doubt on the validity of the relationship types, we chose to use a data set where relationship types are given.

We implemented a crawler using Java 1.6 that crawled the site and parsed information from a selection of pages of all movies. The pages we selected were Full Cast and Crew, Main Details, Company Credits, Business/Box Office, and Awards. We store the data about movies in an RDF (Resource Description Framework) data store, which gives us a table of three-tuples, where each tuple is a single fact about a movie. For instance, the movie *Transformers*, if assigned the IMDb unique ID of tt0418279, would be represented by the tuple <tt0418279, Title, Transformers>. It is important to note that when we record facts about individuals who participate in a movie, we use their IMDb unique ID, so there is no confusion between people who may have the same name.

We then defined two movies to be related if they share at least one individual in the same job. For instance, *Batman Begins* would be related to *The Dark Knight* because they share (as a single instance) Christopher Nolan in the job *Director*. Similarly, *Batman Begins* and *Equilibrium* would be related because they both have Christian Bale as an actor in them, even though he does not play the same role in both films. Additionally, *Batman*, *Batman Begins*, and *Batman and Robin* are all related because they share the same character, Batman. All fields were initially used to create relationships. However, we discovered in experimentation that the use of the two languages and properties <*, Language, English> and <*, Country, USA> resulted in a very tight clique where a majority of movies were all related to each other. As a result of this, we removed those two entries for all movies, to reduce the number of relationships in our data set.

Data Store Alterations. We began with all information stored in a single table in RDF format. In the process of experimentation, we made several alterations to this in order to increase the efficiency of our classification routine.

The first change we made was to create a separate table to store all of the data about those nodes for which we have the earnings property recorded. The motivation for this came from the queries used to generate relationships and the local classifier. To ensure that only relationships among these valid nodes were considered, we either maintained a full list of valid nodes in memory to check against, or used queries with a series of joins. However, both of these steps required that we conduct them each time a relationship was found in every iteration. We chose to implement a preprocessing step that pulls the classification criteria from a configuration file, and inserts all the tuples of nodes that meet the requirements into the valid nodes table. We then used this as our main data store for the remainder of the experiments. Also, the preprocessing step adds a tuple defining the field that the valid nodes table is created on. This allows our implementation to intelligently decide if this preprocessing step needs to be conducted or if it may be skipped in later iterations. As a direct benefit of this step, our local classification step requires considerably less time to run.

The last alteration that we made was an additional preprocessing step to precompute the relationships in our data set. We decided to precompute the relationships because of the time involved in determining them. Each individual test in each experiment spent time rediscovering the same static relationships. To reduce this time, we added a precomputing step that creates a table to maintain a list of all relationships between nodes in our *valid nodes* table. We maintained this as another three-tuple of the form <NodeA, NodeB, <Relationships>>. Each row indicates that there exists at least one type of relationship between NodeA and NodeB. The link types and the values of each link type are stored in a vector. So, for instance, let us use the earlier examples of *Batman Begins* and *The Dark Knight*. We would have an entry of the form <Batman Begins, The Dark Knight, <Director = Christopher Nolan; Actor = Christian Bale>>. This allows us to generate one relationship table that we can then use in various ways in all of our experiments.

Experimental Setup. As our classification criterion, we followed the example by Macskassy and Provost (2007), and used earnings figures in an attempt to determine whether a movie will make in excess of $2 million. We began with a set of 259,937. We then eliminated those movies that do not have a figure recorded for Earnings. This left us with a set of size 5382. Of these nodes, 3324 earned more than $2 million. This gave us a baseline accuracy of 59.9% for simply guessing that each movie will make more than $2 million.

We conducted experiments at each ratio of 10:90, 20:80, ..., 90:10 for training data versus test data. To do this, we randomized the order of the nodes and then constructed the partition at the appropriate spot for the ratio we are testing at the time. Once we had these two random sets, we conducted four experiments using the relaxation labeling method of collective inference. For each test set, we consistently used an nBC as the local classifier, but we varied the relational classifier. We repeated each test 20 times and took an average of all runs for the presented results.

15.5   RESULTS

Our first experiment was aimed at using only the local Bayes classifier with relaxation labeling to establish a baseline accuracy of a nonrelational classifier on our particular data set. As can be seen in Figure 15.2, using local Bayes only initially, increasing the ratio of labeled nodes to unlabeled nodes drastically increases the classification accuracy. However, after 40% of the nodes are labeled, the gains from additional nodes in the training set are minimal. This shows that even though we do not consider any relationships at all, by simply using a method of supervised learning, we can improve on the naïve method of guessing the most populous group. This improvement is evident even in a situation where most of the class values for the nodes are unlabeled.

Our second experiment was conducted to establish a performance baseline of an existing relational classifier on our extended data set. We compared these results to those of Macskassy and Provost (2007), specifically, the *imdb prodco–nBC* results. While our classifier underperformed in comparison with theirs, as shown in Figure 15.3, we still saw improvements on the local Bayes classifier. We believe that the performance degradation in this result is because of overfitting. Consider that their experiment was conducted using only one attribute, the production company, as the determinant of relationships between movies, whereas we considered all attributes to be indicative of relationships. This large number of relationships appears to inject a higher degree of error into our trials as opposed to simply using a single attribute.

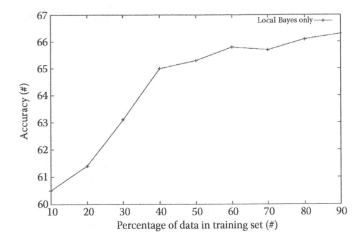

FIGURE 15.2 Local Bayes only.

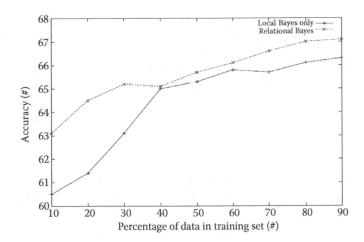

FIGURE 15.3 Relaxation labeling using relational Bayes classifier.

In our third experiment, we used the values for the link types. In this set of tests, we used the probabilities shown in Equation 15.4 to consider the link type as an additional parameter. We see quite clearly in Figure 15.4 that including the link types in the calculations increased our accuracy dramatically. Even when we had the least number of nodes in the training set, we achieved higher than a 10 percentage point increase in accuracy over the generic rBC. We believe that because we gave some difference to the link types, this allowed our classification method to make up for the performance loss in the previous experiments.

In our final series of experiments, we used the weighted link-type rBC. Delen et al. (2007) identified seven components of a movie that they used to design a decision support system for a Hollywood production company. The areas they identified were MPAA Rating, Competition, Star Value, Genre, Special Effects, Sequel, and Number of Screens. Some of these attributes, such as Competition, Special Effects, and Number of Screens, are opinion-based values, and are difficult to quantify for a data set spanning the number of years ours covers. We took their description of Star Power, and considered what current trailers for movies were listed as being an inducement

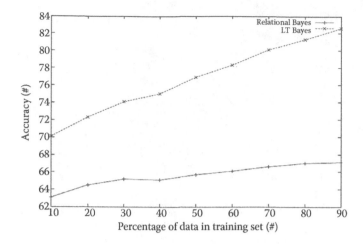

FIGURE 15.4 Relaxation labeling using link-type (LT) relational Bayes classifier.

for the movie. We divided the jobs into three groups. The first group was composed of writers, directors, and actors. The second group was made up of technical crew, that is, editors, costume, wardrobe, camera, and electrical. The third group comprised the remaining roles: producers, production company, special effects studio, etc. To test our division of roles, we conducted individual tests on a 50:50 division into training and test sets. That is, half of the nodes in the data set for these tests were unlabeled. For these tests, we specified a weight of x for the actors, directors, and writers, and a weight of y for the technical crew. The results of this experiment are shown in Table 15.1.

As shown in the table, our assumptions about the importance of respective jobs were confirmed. In those experiments where we increased the weight value of actors, directors, and writers, the accuracy of our classification calculations increased. Similarly, when we increased the weight value of the technical crew, the accuracy decreased from 74.1% to 72% when $x = 0.5$ and from 83.2% to 78.6% when $x = 2$.

With this consideration, we gave all writers, actors, and directors a weight of 2, and specified that technical crew is given a weight of 0.5. We had a default weight of 1.0 for all other jobs, such as animation, music, choreography, etc. We show in Figure 15.5 that using these weights, we achieved substantial performance gains. Even at a relatively low percentage of known data, we were able to accurately classify nodes more than 80% of the time, and at 90% of nodes labeled, our accuracy was slightly higher than 85%. These results indicate an improvement over the results shown by Macskassy and Provost (2007), where the accuracy does not seem to reach higher than 80% for any of the collective inference methods when using the IMDb data set.

We believe that these figures make it apparent that with even a small amount of domain knowledge, we can use that knowledge to devise weights for link types to increase the accuracy of classification algorithms (Figure 15.6).

TABLE 15.1

Summary of Accuracy Weights with Varied Tests

	$y = 0.5$	$y = 2$
$x = 0.5$	74.1	72.0
$x = 2$	83.2	78.6

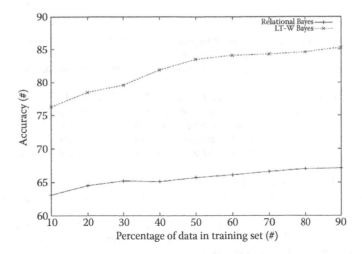

FIGURE 15.5   Relaxation labeling using weighted link-type (LT-W) relational Bayes classifier.

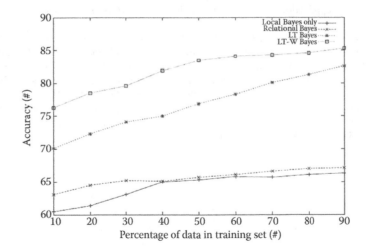

FIGURE 15.6   Comparison of all experiments.

15.6 SUMMARY AND DIRECTIONS

We have presented, for ease of comparison, a summary of all of our experiments in this chapter. We believe that it shows that our enhancements to the traditional rBC, which we call link-type rBC and weighted link-type rBC, are both successful extensions to the well-researched area of classification in social networks. We have shown how our extensions have improved on the implementation of the traditional rBC on our data set, and how the overall accuracy compares to similar experiments done on a similar data set in other research work. We believe that this is a solid foundation for further examination of the inclusion of link types in social network classification research.

In the future, we believe that we need to apply these new calculations to other domains in order to determine when these new methods may be applied or when we must use the more traditional rBC implementation. Also, additional research should be conducted in programmatically determining weights for the weighted link-type rBC, perhaps by using social network metrics.

REFERENCES

Chakrabarti, S., Dom, B., and Indyk, P. Enhanced hypertext categorization using hyperlinks. In: *ACM SIGMOD Record*, vol. 27, pp. 307–318. ACM, New York, 1998.

Chau, D.H. and Faloutsos, C. Fraud detection in electronic auction. In: *European Web Mining Forum (EWMF 2005)*, p. 87. Citeseer, 2005.

Delen, D., Sharda, R., and Kumar, P. Movie forecast guru: A web-based DSS for Hollywood managers. *Decision Support Systems* 43(4): 1151–1170, Elsevier Science, Amsterdam, The Netherlands, 2007.

Getoor, L. and Diehl, C.P. Link mining: A survey. *SIGKDD Explorations Newsletter* 7(2): 3–12, 2005.

Gross, R., Acquisti, A., and Heinz, J.H. Information revelation and privacy in online social networks. In *WPES '05: Proceedings of the 2005 ACM Workshop on Privacy in the Electronic Society*, pp. 71–80. ACM Press, New York, 2005.

He, J., Chu, W., and Liu, V. Inferring privacy information from social networks. In Mehrotra, S., editor, *Proceedings of Intelligence and Security Informatics*, vol. LNCS 3975, Springer-Verlag, Berlin-Heidelberg, 2006.

Jensen, D., Neville, J., and Gallagher, B. Why collective inference improves relational classification. In: *Proceedings of the Tenth ACM SIGKDD International Conference on Knowledge Discovery and Data Mining*, pp. 593–598. ACM, New York, 2004.

Macskassy, S.A. and Provost, F. Classification in networked data: A toolkit and a univariate case study. *Journal of Machine Learning Research* 8: 935–983, 2007.

Mika, P. *Social Networks and the Semantic Web*. Springer, New York, 2007.

Senator, T. Link mining applications: Progress and challenges. *ACM SIGKDD Explorations Newsletter* 7(2): 76–83, 2005.

Sweeney, L. Privacy-enhanced linking. *ACM SIGKDD Explorations Newsletter* 7(2): 72–75, 2005.

Xu, W., Zhou, X., and Li, L. Inferring privacy information via social relations. In: *Data Engineering Workshop, 2008. ICDEW 2008. IEEE 24th International Conference on*, pp. 525–530. IEEE, Cancum, Mexico, 2008.

Zheleva, E. and Getoor, L. Preserving the privacy of sensitive relationships in graph data. In: *1st ACM SIGKDD International Workshop on Privacy, Security, and Trust in KDD (PinKDD 2007)*, 2007.

Zheleva, E. and Getoor, L. To join or not to join: The illusion of privacy in social networks with mixed public and private user profiles. In: *WWW '09: Proceedings of the 18th International Conference on World Wide Web*, pp. 531–540. ACM, New York, 2009.

16 Extending Classification of Social Networks through Indirect Friendships

16.1 INTRODUCTON

Within social network analysis, one of the most frequently referenced properties is that of *homophily*—that is, the tendency of individuals to form direct connections with those who are most like them. However, in some medical research, studies have shown that some behaviors and attitudes, such as smoking cessation, tend to propagate out from a regional focus. This finding contradicts the central assumptions that are used when performing relational classification. One reason for these assumptions is that they allow us to complete full-network calculations within a reasonable number of iterations. However, we seek to merge these two considerations by creating *artificial* links between regional *influencers* and those who follow in their wake.

The utility of social network analysis has long been recognized as important for the fields of epidemiology, counterterrorism, and business applications. The importance of having accurate classification techniques in these areas cannot be understated. By utilizing social network analysis, we are able to perform classification tasks upon nodes in the graph, allowing us to determine whether an individual may be infected with a virus, a potential terrorist, or a likely customer of an industry. Social network analysis techniques are generally based on the principle of homophily; that is, individuals who are in near proximity to one another in the social graph will form relationships to one another. This property is a reflection of the adage "birds of a feather flock together." Through application of this property, modeling of social networks typically relies on only the first-degree neighbors of a node (Macskassy and Provost, 2007). However, medical studies have determined that smoking cessation and obesity networks may benefit from an extended analysis (Christakis and Fowler, 2007, 2008; Rosenquist et al., 2010). Instead, there appear to be nodes that influence those around them, and this influence spreads throughout the nodes in a near, nondirect relation to them.

If we focus on the counterterrorism domain, we frequently see that terrorist cells are decentralized with few direct contacts among members. This presents a unique challenge when attempting to use traditional social network analysis techniques in order to attempt to determine hidden patterns or perform classification tasks on these networks. Collective classification, or collective inference, techniques attempt to propagate information from one side of the social graph to another, which generally results in improved classification accuracy. Generally, these techniques are sufficient to determine classification labels within networks where users are participating in a generally honest manner. For example, in a Facebook data set, one may be reasonably certain that an individual is not attempting to completely hide his relationship with another member of the network. In certain real-world networks where these classification tasks may be life-and-death challenges, such as terrorist detection tasks, the network structure is being actively hidden.

In this scenario, we need to determine who the important individuals are in the graph and attempt to extend their influence by directly connecting them to individuals who are affected by said influence. Standard inference methods do not allow this information to propagate through the graph, instead considering that all links have some predetermined weight. Instead, we utilize network metrics to automatically identify the most important nodes in the graph to improve our node classification tasks.

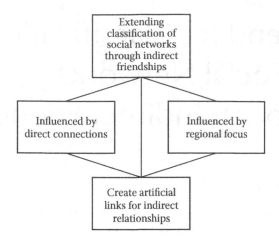

FIGURE 16.1 Extending classification of social networks through indirect friendships.

The organization of this chapter is as follows. In Section 16.2, we discuss related work in the area of social network analysis. In Section 16.3, we give relevant background in social network classification. In Section 16.4, we explain our approach to information propagation. In Section 16.5, we describe the data that we use and the results of experimentation of our method of classification. Lastly, in Section 16.6, we summarize our findings and provide possible avenues for further research. Figure 16.1 illustrates the concepts discussed in this chapter.

16.2   RELATED WORK AND OUR CONTRIBUTIONS

Much work has been conducted in classification tasks in social networks. Macskassy and Provost (2007) conducted thorough analyses on the utility of collective inference techniques and local classifiers. The results indicated in their work form the basis of the selection of our inference methods here.

In the general area of social network data mining, Rosenquist et al. (2010) attempted to discover hidden communities in social network data analysis. Bird et al. (2006) discussed a method of mining a series of text e-mails to create a social network representation and perform an analysis of the data therein. Lu and Getoor (2003) compared multiple researchers' work in link-based classification of network data. This work and those cited therein provide the rationale of our choice in relational classifiers. Similarly, Heatherly et al. (2009b) used link types in conjunction with the above-listed methods to improve the efficiency of standard classifiers.

Getoor and Diehl (2005) presented a survey of various approaches in discovering hidden links within social networks. The major difference between those approaches and ours is that traditional link mining approaches attempt to discover links that exist in real life and do not yet exist in the current state of the network. In our approach, though we add in links for our relational classifier, we do not insinuate that these necessarily represent links that may exist in real life. The links we create are used only to connect highly important nodes for the sake of improved information flow.

While there has been some recent work in dyadic prediction of social networks, we believe that our work contributes in parallel to this work. The primary focus is on using the dyadism in order to predict node labels for social graphs (Menon and Elkan, 2010), while here we attempt to uncover hidden links that could then be used for an arbitrary choice of classifiers to increase prediction accuracy.

While other work has concentrated on the ability to determine hidden links from underlying data within the network, to the best of our knowledge, this is the first work that attempts to use

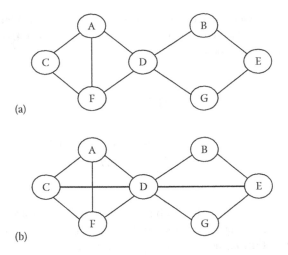

FIGURE 16.2   Graph (a) before and (b) after alteration.

the information hidden several nodes away from a target node in order to identify graph details that may be used to improve classification of this target node. For example, consider Figure 16.2a. Node D is situated at the center of the graph, and has the highest degree centrality. We use network measures such as this in an effort to determine what nodes may have the highest regional influence within a graph, and create links between these important nodes and those that may be influenced by their activities. In the case of Figure 16.2a, node D would be connected to nodes C and E, shown in Figure 16.2b. We further show that by performing these techniques in a real-world social network, we can improve the accuracy of within-network classification tasks.

16.3   DEFINITIONS

The traditional method of social network classification involves the use of a local classifier, a relational classifier, and a collective inference algorithm applied sequentially in an attempt to determine hidden information that is then used in each subsequent step or iteration of the algorithm.

Definition 16.1

A *social network* is represented as a graph, $G = \{V, E, D\}$, where V is the set of nodes in the graph, E is the set of edges connecting those nodes, and D is the set of details containing some personal information about the members of V. Here, an individual detail is a fact that a person releases about himself, such as "v_i's favorite book is *Harry Potter*."

Definition 16.2

A *classification task* is a function $C : V \rightarrow C$. That is, given a node $v \in V$, $C(v) = c_1$ is an assignment of v into class c_1, which is a valid label within the set of all possible classifications C.

The most basic method of classification is local classification. Local classification is a classification task with the additional restriction that $G = \{V, D\}$. That is, the classifier may not take advantage of the information contained within the set of edges, hence the name *local*.

While our proposed technique can work with any classifiers, here we explain only those we used in the experiments shown here. For our purposes, we make use of a naïve Bayes local classifier. This classifier models a classification task as

$$C(v) = \underset{c \in \mathcal{C}}{\text{argmax}}\,[Pr(c \mid \mathcal{D}_v)]$$

$$= \underset{c \in \mathcal{C}}{\text{argmax}} \left[\frac{Pr(\mathcal{D}_v \mid c) \times Pr(c)}{Pr(\mathcal{D}_v)} \right]$$

That is, while we wish to determine the probability of being in a certain class, c, given a specific node, v, and its details, $\mathcal{D}_v$, through application of the Bayes theorem, we wind up with a reduced complexity in calculation. Furthermore, we assume that our detail set is independent. This means that, for example, the probability of an individual liking the *Harry Potter* book series has no effect on whether he likes fishing as an activity.

With this assumption, it is simple to calculate the probability of any node to belong to each valid class within our classification task. The potential class label that maximizes the calculated value—that is, which has the highest probability of being true—is assigned to that class. When using collective inference, this probabilistic assignment is referred to as the *prior*.

Building on top of the local classifier is a relational classifier. Relational classifiers consider the full graph $\mathcal{G}$. However, it is important to note that, generally, while the relational classifier has access to the full set $\mathcal{E}$, due to computability, only the first-degree relations of a node are considered.

In our experiments, we used the network-only Bayes algorithm. We chose this method because of its reliability and accuracy on these data sets from other work performed (Heatherly et al., 2009a). Similarly to the local Bayes classifier, this algorithm uses the naïve independence assumption on links. This means that the likelihood of having a link to one person is no higher or lower because you have a link to another user.

Last is the collective inference algorithm. This algorithm is the method by which local and relational classifiers are used and controls the terminating condition, either a set number of iterations or convergence.

Here, we use the relaxation labeling method of collective inference. This method provided excellent results in previous studies (Heatherly et al., 2009a), and also ensured that the graph is always fully labeled. Relaxation labeling initializes the nodes with a prior by using a chosen local classifier, and then runs repeated instances of the relational classifier until convergence.

16.4 OUR APPROACH

Clearly, it is infeasible for us to determine the exact weight that a group or individual carries with all other members of a social network. Then, our task is to develop a method that will allow us to effectively estimate what nodes could be influenced by what we determine to be *important* nodes for some region of our network.

Definition 16.3

The neighborhood of a node $\mathcal{N}_v = \{u \mid (u,v) \in \mathcal{E}\}$.

The nodes $u \in \mathcal{N}_v$ are also referred to as the *first-degree friends* of v.

Definition 16.4

The *second-degree friends* of a node, v, is the set of nodes $\mathcal{N}_v^2 = \{w \mid u \in \mathcal{N}_v, w \in \mathcal{N}_u, w \notin \mathcal{N}_v\}$.

It is worth noting here that in our definition, $\mathcal{N}_v$ and $\mathcal{N}_v^2$ are necessarily disjoint sets for an arbitrary v.

Third-degree friends are determined in a similar manner to second-degree friends.

We examine the effect of second- and third-degree friends in a real-world social network and attempt to determine if we can increase the classification accuracy of a collective inference classifier on this data set.

To test this, we gauge the effectiveness of several separate factors:

1. The general importance of extended relations in a graph
2. The importance of cohesive groups in near proximity to a node
3. The effective distance of cohesive groups from a node

These questions raise the issue of how to determine groups automatically. Our attempts to determine this importance are based on the use of well-established graph metrics. Specifically, on the basis of previous work in the area, we constrain our examination to two metrics: clustering coefficient and degree centrality. The clustering coefficient is a measure of how tightly grouped a region of the graph is. Generally, it is a measure of how many of a node's friends are also friends. The *clustering coefficient* of a node, n_i, is represented by the following equation:

$$CC_i = \frac{2 \mid \{(j,k) \mid j,k \in \mathcal{N}_i, (j,k) \in \mathcal{E}\} \mid}{d_i(d_i - 1)} \tag{16.1}$$

where d_i is the degree of n_i.

The *degree centrality* of a node is the ratio of how many edges are incident to a node compared with how many are possible. This is represented by the equation

$$DC_i = \frac{d_i}{|\mathcal{V}| - 1} \tag{16.2}$$

where $\mathcal{V}$ is the set of vertices for the graph.

Since it is infeasible to add every possible friendship link of extended degree in the data set, we use a parameter, τ, to define a threshold of the required metric value for propagating the information contained in a node to a target node. That is, for an altered edge set $\mathcal{E}'$, potential edge $(u,v) \in \mathcal{E}'$ if and only if $\frac{DC_u}{Z} > \tau$ and $v \in \mathcal{N}_u^i$, where DC is the arbitrary graph metric chosen for the altered graph, Z is a normalization constant, and i is a given parameter for allowable distance of nodes.

What this measure indicates is that only those nodes that are determined as *important*—according to a predetermined graph metric—will be selected for a region of the graph. If we instead choose a percentage of links to add, then we may be adding links that have a low probability of increasing the overall knowledge inside our graph. However, consider a subgraph, such as that shown in Figure 16.2a, where all shown nodes are members of class label α. Now, consider an example where nodes A and G are labeled β while all other nodes are labeled α. On the basis of the previous metrics, each of these graphs will be treated exactly the same when determining new edges. Intuitively, we reason that there should be some differences when considering them. To reflect this, we alter the traditional graph metrics in an attempt to more indiscriminately determine the flow of information through the graph. We refer to these as class-weighted graph metrics, and alter their equations as follows:

$$
\begin{aligned}
wCC_i &= \frac{|\{(j,k) \mid j,k \in \mathcal{N}_i, (j,k) \in \mathcal{E}, C(j) = C(k)\}|}{d_i(d_i - 1)} \\
&\quad - \frac{|\{(j,k) \mid j,k \in \mathcal{N}_i, (j,k) \in \mathcal{E}, C(j) \neq C(k)\}|}{d_i(d_i - 1)}
\end{aligned}
\tag{16.3}
$$

and

$$
wDC_i = \frac{\left| \mathcal{N}_i(c) \right| - \left| \mathcal{N}_i(\overline{c}) \right|}{|\mathcal{V}| - 1}
\tag{16.4}
$$

where $\mathcal{N}_i(c)$ are the neighbors of n_i who share the same class as n_i, and $\mathcal{N}_i(\overline{c})$ are the neighbors of n_i who are in the opposite class of n_i.

It is important to note that we are not attempting to determine links that represent real-world relationships. Instead, we are attempting to model the flow of information or preferences through the graph in such a way that those individuals who are trendsetters or network influencers have an importance that is reflected in our classification tasks.

16.5   EXPERIMENTS AND RESULTS

16.5.1   DATA

The data that we used for the experiments was pulled from the Dallas/Fort Worth, Texas, network of Facebook in May 2007 and from the Internet Movie Database (IMDb) in September 2007. The data was obtained from the publicly available profiles on Facebook. That is, the profiles had no privacy settings, allowing anyone within the geographic region to see the full details of their profile.

For our experiments, we attempted to determine the political affiliation of nodes within the data set. Specifically, we attempted to determine whether an individual classifies himself as *Conservative* or *Liberal*—which are the two primary affiliations listed in the data. Anyone listing another affiliation, such as *Libertarian* or *Human*, was considered to have listed no affiliation and was removed from the experiments. After removing the nodes that do not list a political affiliation, we were left with 35,000 nodes to examine and approximately 400,000 edges. Of these 35,000, 55% listed their affiliation as Conservative and 45% listed their affiliation as Liberal.

The IMDb data was pulled from all movies available on the site (as of September 2007). Of all available pages, we maintained information regarding the full cast and crew, box office receipts, production company credits, and awards received. Owing to the nature of this network, links were determined *a priori* based on the relationship between two movies. For our analysis, we examined the network with the following link types defined: (i) actors, (ii) directors, (iii) producers, (iv) writers, and (v) all of the previous. These link types were chosen based on the accuracy of classification in previous work (Heatherly et al., 2009b).

16.5.2   EXPERIMENTS

When conducting our experiments, we tested for multiple situations. Because we were using the propagation of information through links, we needed to use relational classifiers to take full advantage of this. For the determination of the priors, we used a local naïve Bayes classifier. Following this step, we used the relaxation labeling method of collective inference, utilizing a network Bayes classifier.

We initially tested these options on the possible second-degree nodes. That is, for our experiments labeled *Neighbor* (Figures 16.3c, 16.4a, 16.5a, and 16.6a), when determining whether to add links to a given node n_i, we used the calculated values for all $n_j \in \mathcal{N}_i$. For each n_j that is included (based on the chosen value of τ), we added a link between n_i and n_k where $n_k \in \mathcal{N}_j$.

To illustrate, using this method of link addition in Figure 16.3a, the new links would be (A, B), (A, G), (B, F), (B, G), (F, G). For the experiments labeled *2nd Degree* (Figures 16.3b and 16.4b), for any node n_i that has a minimal distance of 2 from a node with the allowed τ strength. This is the form of link addition used to illustrate in Figure 16.3b. On the basis of the results in these figures, for the remaining tests, we use this method of link addition.

We then tested for multiple possible values of labeled versus unlabeled data. That is, we divided our data set into a training and testing set with different percentages of labeled data in order to examine our method's effect on graphs that are in various states of knowledge. For each point, we ran 200 experiments using randomly partitioned data. The results of these tests are shown in Figures 16.3 and 16.4. As we can see from these results, the clustering coefficient method of determining importance is more effective than the degree centrality, but both metrics improve upon the base accuracy of a classifier without information propagation.

Additionally, we see from the differences in Figures 16.3b,c and 16.5b,c that while any method of including the second-degree neighbors is effective at increasing the accuracy of a classifier, adding

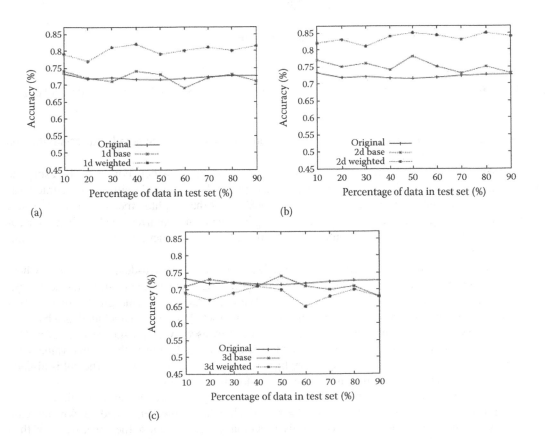

FIGURE 16.3   Clustering coefficient with $\tau = 0.8$ (Facebook). (a) Neighbor; (b) 2nd degree; and (c) 3rd degree.

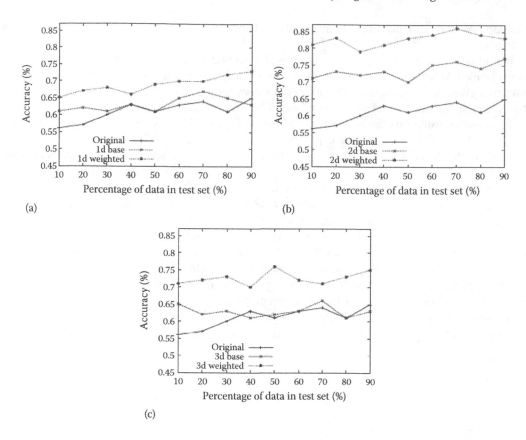

FIGURE 16.4 Clustering coefficient with $\tau = 0{:}90$ (IMDb). (a) Neighbor; (b) 2nd degree; and (c) 3rd degree.

the third-degree nodes (instead of second, not in addition to, it should be noted) causes a reduction in classification accuracy.

Furthermore, we significantly improved the accuracy of our classifier. For example, using the IMDb data set shown in Figure 16.4b, at the 50% data point, the average classification accuracy was 0.83 with a maximum of 0.851 and a minimum of 0.8023 for the weighted metric. The next closest metric was the original clustering coefficient calculation, which had an average classification accuracy of 0.6983, a maximum of 0.710, and a minimum of 0.6891. The other data points show a similar improvement (Figures 16.5 and 16.6).

This observation was further confirmed when we tested using fourth-degree neighbors where the inclusion of fourth-degree neighbors resulted in a dramatic decrease in classification accuracy.

Additionally, we tested on various values of τ. We note that any τ value greater than 1.00 is unattainable by any node in the set, and is the original data set. This point is included as a baseline figure to allow for an examination of the change in accuracy as we vary for other values of τ. This lets us vary the allowed importance of the extended neighborhood. Our tests for reliable values of τ, as shown in Figure 16.7, indicate that for very high values of τ, the clustering coefficient is already able to produce a significantly increased accuracy almost immediately.

Automatic Selection of Parameters. The degree centrality measure, however, required a lower τ to be able to reach its peak accuracy at $0.80 = \tau$. Both classifiers, however, would quickly decrease their accuracy with even lower values of τ. This effect makes sense because the lower we set τ, then more nodes with a lower importance will be linked, until eventually all possible edges are added to the graph.

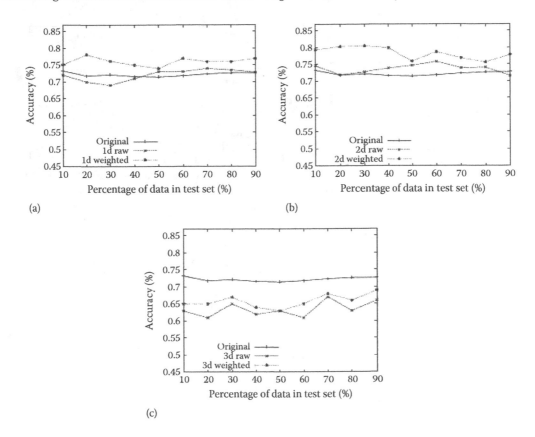

(a)

(b)

(c)

FIGURE 16.5   Degree centrality with $\tau = 0{:}85$ (Facebook). (a) Neighbor; (b) 2nd degree; and (c) 3rd degree.

What these figures indicate to us is that while the inclusion of hidden sources of importance can increase the accuracy of classification tasks in social networks, each metric and each social network requires a specific value of τ to be effective. In a real-world scenario, one will not necessarily be able to use supervised learning techniques in order to pinpoint a specific value of τ.

To resolve this issue, we performed k means clustering on the normalized results of each centrality measure, using two clusters, roughly defined as *important* and *not important*. We established initial centroids at 0.95 and 0.25, in order to weight the clusters to have a wider range of possible values in the *not important* cluster. Once k means reached convergence, we looked at the value of the lowest node in the *important* cluster, and used this value for τ. The results of experiments using this clustering-based assignment of τ are presented in Table 16.1.

To get these figures, we performed the analysis using 50% of the data in the test set and 50% of the data in the training set using the weighted version of our second-degree friends method of link addition. We show the result of the clustering method of choosing τ first for each metric within each data set, and then for the sake of comparison, the best performer from our iterating selection. As can be seen from this figure, use of the clustering method of determining τ provides results very similar to the iterative approach over multiple τ. While the method may not necessarily provide the optimum assignment of τ, the value it provides is very close and is easily computable on many data sets.

Lastly, it is important to note that these changes in accuracy are caused only by changes to the network structure. Because of our choice of local classifier, the local model does not change, and thus the probability of being assigned to the same prior is equal across all experiments. However,

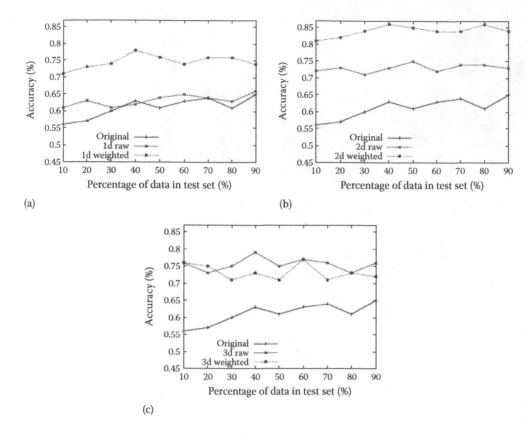

FIGURE 16.6   Degree centrality with $\tau = 0.95$ (IMDb). (a) Neighbor; (b) 2nd degree; and (c) 3rd degree.

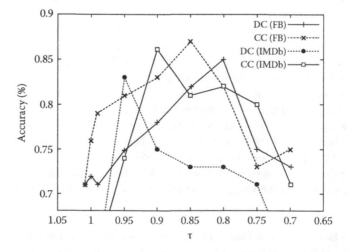

FIGURE 16.7   Experiments with varied values of τ.

TABLE 16.1

***k* Means Clustering Values for τ**

Metric	Value (Method)	Accuracy
	Facebook	
*CC	$\tau = 0.82$ (*k* Means)	0.855
	$\tau = 0.80$ (Iterative)	0.853
*DC	$\tau = 0.85$ (*k* Means)	0.751
	$\tau = 0.85$ (Iterative)	0.759
	IMDb	
*CC	$\tau = 0.89$ (*k* Means)	0.811
	$\tau = 0.90$ (Iterative)	0.832
*DC	$\tau = 0.97$ (*k* Means)	0.873
	$\tau = 0.95$ (Iterative)	0.855

we see here that by choosing additional edges in the graph well, we can improve the classification accuracy of the network classifier.

16.6 SUMMARY AND DIRECTIONS

We have shown here that by intelligently choosing *important* nodes in a subgraph, one is able to increase classification accuracy on real-world social network data. We present a method of selecting nodes by using weighted graph metrics and a programmatically determinable threshold parameter. Furthermore, we show that our τ threshold is a useful tool for determining the general increase in graph size versus a desired amount of classification accuracy, and that it may be possible to determine a beneficial value of τ through calculation of the chosen degree metric.

It is important to note, however, that the data set we used is not sufficient for determining the direction of information flow through a graph. For this, we would need to be able to obtain a data set that allows us to observe changing values over time, which is not available in our Facebook data set. As a direction for future research, obtaining access to data that has changes over time is necessary to determine the actual flows of data through a network. As an additional direction, testing additional graph metrics, or the creation of specific metrics for use in information flow, could be useful for increasing the accuracy of classifiers even more.

REFERENCES

Bird, C., Gourley, A., Devanbu, P., Gertz, M., and Swaminathan, A. Mining email social networks. In: *MSR '06: Proceedings of the 2006 International Workshop on Mining Software Repositories*, pp. 137–143. ACM, New York, 2006.

Christakis, N.A. and Fowler, J.H. The spread of obesity in a large social network over 32 years. *New England Journal of Medicine* 357(4): 370–379, 2007.

Christakis, N.A. and Fowler, J.H. The collective dynamics of smoking in a large social network. *New England Journal of Medicine* 358(21): 2249–2258, 2008.

Getoor, L. and Diehl, C.P. Link mining: A survey. *SIGKDD Explorations Newsletter* 7(2): 3–12, 2005.

Heatherly, R., Kantarcioglu, M., Thuraisingham, B., and Lindamood, J. Preventing private information inference attacks on social networks. Technical Report UTDCS-03-09, Department of Computer Science, The University of Texas at Dallas, 2009a.

Heatherly, R., Kantarcioglu, M., and Thuraisingham, B. Social network classification incorporating link type values. In: *Proceedings of the 2009 IEEE International Conference on Intelligence and Security Informatics*, ISI'09, pp. 19–24. IEEE Press, Piscataway, NJ, 2009b.

Lu, Q. and Getoor, L. Link-based classification. In: *20th International Conference on Machine Learning*, Washington, DC, August 2003.

Macskassy, S.A. and Provost, F. Classification in networked data: A toolkit and a univariate case study. *Journal of Machine Learning Research* 8: 935–983, 2007.

Menon, A.K. and Elkan, C. Predicting labels for dyadic data. *Data Mining and Knowledge Discovery* 21: 327–343, 2010.

Rosenquist, J.N., Murabito, J., Fowler, J.H., and Christakis, N.A. The spread of alcohol consumption behavior in a large social network. *Annals of Internal Medicine* 152(7): 426–433, 2010.

17 Social Network Classification through Data Partitioning

17.1 INTRODUCTION

One consideration for social network providers is that this data will accumulate over time. Because of the highly desirable nature of social network longitudinal data, it is unlikely that a network such as Facebook will ever delete data they obtain. Even if later revisions directly contradict previously entered data, this is still valuable in tracking change in attitudes over time. Because of this, performing calculations and inference on this data will become more difficult over time, because of the size of this data. However, we now show that by intelligently examining this data, we are able to partition the full data into smaller sets, which both increases classification accuracy and reduces the time required for classification.

Each social network allows users to list certain details about their personal or professional lives. While social network administrators can see all of the information that users specify, the data that users hide from the network may also be of interest to these administrators. Most of these sites are free to the end user and are thus advertisement supported. If we assume that advertisers want to reach the people most likely to be interested in their products, then identifying those individuals becomes a priority for maintaining much-needed advertisers. However, by just using specifically defined information, the site may be missing a large number of potentially interested users. Taking the specified knowledge from some users and using it to infer unspecified data may allow the site to extend its target audience for particular advertisements. For example, if Pepsi is using Facebook to advertise a new, grapefruit flavor of Mountain Dew, then one approach is advertising to people who mention that Mountain Dew or grapefruit sodas are their favorite. However, what about people who do not list their drink preferences? We may be able to infer from other activities, such as being a member of video gaming-based groups, that an individual would probably buy the new soda.

We are able to model various methods of human interaction as a social network, and, in some, predictive models are considerably more important than targeted advertising. Consider, for example, counterterrorism goals of classifying whether an individual is involved in terrorist activities or not. We can easily model this as a social network classification task. By using telephone records, e-mail logs, or other similar data sets, we can model almost any human interaction in the form of a social network, as shown in Krebs (2002). As social networks become more popular, more data is stored about each individual and more individuals are joining each social network. The large increases in data provide both a benefit and a detriment to these operations. As a benefit to classification, as there is more information, we are able to define a much more fine-grained model that may improve the classification accuracy. On the other hand, because many social network classification tasks depend on repeated iteration of calculations performed on the entire network, each of these iterations will take considerably more time and memory, as both the number of individuals and the number of connecting links increase.

This chapter is organized as follows. In Section 17.2, we describe previous work in the area of social network data mining. In Section 17.3, we describe all of the metrics that we will use in the subsequent sections. We also define the process of collective inference and describe how it will be used in the classification section of the experiments. In Section 17.4, we detail the specifics of the partitioning schemes we developed. In Section 17.5, we provide the results of our experiments. In Section 17.6, we offer some conclusions and potential future work in this area. Figure 17.1 illustrates the concepts used in this chapter.

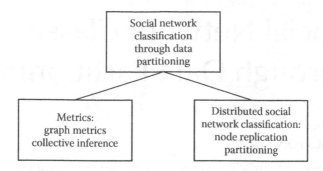

FIGURE 17.1   Social network classification through data partitioning.

17.2   RELATED WORK AND OUR CONTRIBUTIONS

In the general area of social network data mining, Cai et al. (2005) attempted to discover hidden communities in social network data analysis. Bird et al. (2006) discussed a method of mining a series of text e-mails to create a social network representation and perform an analysis of the data therein. Lu and Getoor (2003) compared multiple researchers' work in link-based classification of network data. This work and those cited therein provide the rationale of our choice in relational classifiers. Similarly, Heatherly et al. (2009a,b) used classification tasks similar to those that we have used. However, none of these works considered the impact of growing social network data and the need to efficiently partition the data, and then conducted classification tasks on that partitioned data. Specifically, we focus on the area of distributed mining of social networks. Datta et al. (2006) conducted distributed data mining in a peer-to-peer network to find usage data about the network itself. However, the situation mentioned in our work is different from their scenario; in their research, the assumption is that the data is distributed fully across the system with each site having only minuscule knowledge of the entirety. In our system, the overall social network's data is divided among several data warehouses where we perform classification.

In the area of large-scale, efficient data mining, Papadimitriou and Sun (2008) suggested a map–reduce framework using Hadoop to perform data mining on the petabyte scale. Similarly, Chu et al. (2006) showed that by using Google's MapReduce architecture, it is possible to increase computational efficiency on multicore systems by using traditional single-core learning methods. However, the authors considered a generic data warehouse, and did not consider those unique elements of social networks, such as the link structure, and thus their solutions may not be as effective for processing social network data. To improve on this, we focused specifically on the unique nature of the data in a social network and work to provide a method to divide this data for use at multiple sites or on multiple cores. We also examined potential graph measures that have been studied in social networks to devise methods by which to partition our data sets. Jackson (2008) described the graph metrics that we used in our experiments to divide the data sets. However, he used these metrics as a way of simply measuring aspects of the social network, and used the figures from this to infer information about the network as a whole. We used these to measure specific information about an individual node in the graph, and used that to later partition the graph into several subsets.

Macskassy and Provost (2007) conducted a thorough investigation of the use of collective inference techniques in classifying social network data. We used the results of their experiments in choosing the relational and collective inference techniques we used in the experiments for this work. Furthermore, Neville and Jensen (2002) proposed a series of techniques for mining data specifically from social networks. However, their approach did not consider the need to distribute the data contained in the social networks for ease of calculation.

We provide a reference for the architecture of our system in Figure 17.2. Our goal is to efficiently classify a large amount of social network data without loss of accuracy. To satisfy this goal, we

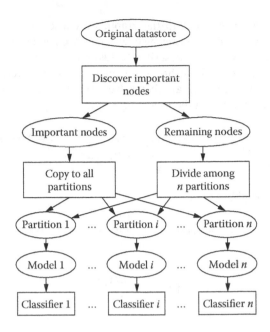

FIGURE 17.2   System architecture.

propose a partitioning technique that can leverage multicore or map–reduce architectures. Using well-known centrality measures, we identify important nodes in the graph. Later, we heuristically allocate important nodes from the original data store to multiple (partitioned) data stores, and then intelligently divide the remaining nodes in the original data store to the partitioned data stores. We then develop in-partition models that we use to perform a given classification task on each partition. In addition, we also utilize the concept of *information gain*-based partitioning. We use information gain on each data set to determine the best single attribute, and define a division on this attribute to be a partitioning scheme unique to each data set, as that attribute may not exist in other data sets.

Obviously, partitioning the data in the social network alone will decrease the time required for classification. However, care must be taken when partitioning. Naïve methods of partitioning may decrease execution time at the expense of accuracy. Our contribution is important because we focus on maintaining efficient classifiers while decreasing execution time. Furthermore, while we focus our work on multicore architectures, we consider partitioning in a way that allows the operations on each processor to operate independently, and in a way that does not rely on any cross-partition communications, which we believe makes them easily applicable to a map–reduce architecture.

17.3 METRICS

17.3.1 Graph Metrics

We begin with a discussion of the graph metrics we use to measure the importance of nodes. We chose these graph metrics because they have been extensively studied in other graph-related applications, such as those by Jackson (2008). By using these as part of a baseline, we can see the effects of division based purely on the structural composition of the graph.

For our work, we model a social network as an undirected graph, $\mathcal{G} = \{\mathcal{V}, \mathcal{E}, \mathcal{A}\}$, where $\mathcal{V}$ is the set of all nodes, $\mathcal{E}$ is the set of all edges, and $\mathcal{A}$ is the set of all attributes. For example, nodes $v_i, v_j \in \mathcal{V}$ are two nodes with an edge, $(v_i, v_j) \in \mathcal{E}$, between them. v_i represents a person named *John Smith* who is 20 years old. That is, $a_i = \{\text{Name} = \text{`JohnSmith'}; \text{Age} = 20\}$, $a_i \in \mathcal{A}$. Furthermore, we use the notation $d(v_i)$ to indicate the degree measure of node v_i, that is, the number of links v_i is involved in.

To measure the importance of nodes in the graph, we chose several metrics as discussed in Jackson (2008). Specifically, we chose clustering coefficient (CC) and degree centrality (DC) for the discussion of our work here.* We briefly describe the two relevant metrics here for completeness.

The CC is a general measure of cliquishness. Given a node v_g, we were interested in how often two friends of v_g, v_j and v_k, where $v_j \neq v_k$, are themselves friends. Specifically, we compute the clustering coefficient for a node v_g through the following formula:

$$CC(v_g) = \frac{\text{COUNT}((v_k, v_j) \in \mathcal{E} | v_k \neq v_j; v_j, v_k \in \mathcal{N}(v_g))}{d(v_g)(d(v_g) - 1)/2} \tag{17.1}$$

where $\mathcal{N}(v_g)$ is the set of neighbors of v_g.

The DC of a node is a simple normalized measure of how many links a node has compared with the highest possible number of neighbors in any graph composed of $|\mathcal{V}|$ nodes. Formally, we calculate this as

$$DC(v_g) = \frac{d(v_g)}{|\mathcal{V}| - 1}$$

We define *information gain* metrics to be a heuristic defined for a specific data set that uses some feature of that data chosen, chosen through information gain, as a method of partitioning the data. For instance, in our Facebook data set, a potential information gain division would be the specific geographic region within the Dallas/Fort Worth area. We could consider each town/city (Dallas, Allen, Plano, etc.) as well as each university (The University of Texas at Dallas, Southern Methodist University, etc.) to be a unique location for this partitioning. For our experiments, we use information gain to compare the ability of various attributes to partition the data set. We choose the attribute with the highest information gain ratio to partition the network. However, both of our data sets contain information that may have multivalued attributes. For example, an individual could list 50 books as their Favorite. Because of this, we use the information gain ratio proposed by Quinlan (1993). First, information gain is calculated as the difference between the entropy of the full data set and the conditional entropy if the data was partitioned on the basis of a particular attribute. To do this, we need to first determine the entropy of the test set for a given attribute A^n (i.e., Favorite Books) by

$$\text{Entropy}(\mathcal{V}_t) = \sum_{i=1}^{|A^n|} -Pr\left(A_i^n\right) \log_2 \left[Pr\left(A_i^n\right) \right]$$

where $\mathcal{V}_t$ is the set of all nodes in the training set, $|A^n|$ is the total number of entries for attribute A^n, and A_i^n is the value of the ith attribute (i.e., *Harry Potter*). We then calculate the information gain (IG) for the attribute under consideration by the equation

$$\text{IG}(\mathcal{V}_t, A^n) = \text{Entropy}(\mathcal{V}_t) - \sum_{A_i \in A^n} \frac{|\mathcal{V}_{t,A^i}|}{|\mathcal{V}_t|} \text{Entropy}\left(\mathcal{V}_{t,A^i}\right)$$

---

* Initial work was also conducted using closeness centrality and betweenness centrality; however, discussions of these metrics are omitted for space, since these metrics performed significantly poorer than CC and DC.

where $A_i \in A^n$ represents a single possible attribute value (i.e., *The Shining* as a favorite book) and $\mathcal{V}_{t,A^i}$ represents a division of the training set based on attribute A^n that contains attribute A_i. We can now calculate the information gain ratio (IGR) by

$$\mathrm{IGR}\left(\mathcal{V}_t, A^n\right) = \frac{IG\left(\mathcal{V}_t, A^n\right)}{-\sum_{k=1}^{|A^i|} \frac{\left|\mathcal{V}_{t,A^k}\right|}{\left|\mathcal{V}_t\right|} \log_2 \left[\frac{\left|\mathcal{V}_{t,A^k}\right|}{\left|\mathcal{V}_t\right|}\right]}$$

We also use a completely random partitioning scheme as a baseline to identify what advantage we would gain just by distributing nodes to partitions uniformly at random and performing classification on these smaller sets. As such, we also do not replicate any nodes for this metric.

17.3.2 COLLECTIVE INFERENCE

Collective inference is a method of classifying social network data using a combination of node details, such as favorite books and movies, and connecting links in the social graph. Each of these classifiers consists of three components: local classifier, relational classifier, and collective inference algorithm.

Local classifiers are a type of learning method that is applied in the initial step of collective inference. Generally, local classifiers build models based on attributes of nodes in the training set. Then, the models are applied to nodes with an unknown label to classify them.

Relational classifiers are a separate type of learning algorithm that looks at the link structure of the graph, and uses the labels of nodes in the training set to develop a model that, in turn, is used to classify the nodes in the test set. Specifically, Macskassy and Provost (2007) examined four relational classifiers: class-distribution relational neighbor (cdRN), weighted-vote relational neighbor (wvRN), network-only Bayes classifier (nBC), and network-only link-based (nLB) classification.

In the wvRN relational classifier, to classify a node n_i, each of its neighbors, n_j, is given a weight. The probability of n_i being in class C_x is the weighted mean of the class probabilities of n_i's neighbors. That is,

$$P\left(n_i = C_x | \mathcal{N}(v_i)\right) = \frac{1}{Z} \sum_{n_j \in \mathcal{N}(v_i)} \left[w_{i,j} \times P(n_j = C_x)\right]$$

where $\mathcal{N}(v_i)$ is the set of neighbors of n_i, and Z is a normalization factor.

A major problem with relational classifiers is that while we may cleverly divide fully labeled test sets so that we ensure every node is connected to at least one other node in the training set, real-world data may not satisfy this strict requirement. If this requirement is not met, then relational classification will be unable to classify nodes that have no neighbors in the training set. Collective inference attempts to make up for these deficiencies by using both local and relational classifiers in a precise manner to try to increase the classification accuracy of nodes in the network. By using a local classifier in the first iteration, collective inference ensures that every node will have an initial probabilistic classification. The algorithm then uses a relational classifier to reclassify nodes.

We choose to use relaxation labeling as described in Macskassy and Provost (2007) because in the experiments conducted by the authors, relaxation labeling tended to be the best of the three collective inference methods.

17.4 DISTRIBUTED SOCIAL NETWORK CLASSIFICATION

17.4.1 NODE REPLICATION TO PARTITIONS

Since the goal of this work is to examine the efficacy of a distributed system for classifying social network data, we developed a multicore algorithm to calculate the standard metrics that can easily be extended to a standard distributed architecture. For DC, we simply distribute the adjacency list for each node to a separate processor. For information gain-based partitioning (IGBP), when calculating the information gain for each attribute, we distribute the processing of each attribute to a separate processor.

Algorithm 17.1: CC_Multicore()

1: **for** $v_i \in \mathcal{V}$ **do**
2: $\mathcal{N}_i \leftarrow \{v_j | (v_i, v_j) \in \mathcal{E}\}$ {first-degree neighbors of v_i}
3: $r_i = \text{FindPossibleTriples}(v_i, \mathcal{N}_i)$
4: **end for**
5: **for** $(v_i, v_j, v_k) \in r_i$ **do** {H is a Hashmap}
6:   IncrementCount(Hash(v_i, v_j, v_k), H)
7: **end for**
8: **for** $v_i \in \mathcal{V}$ {initialize counters}
9: $c_i = 0$
10: **end for**
11: **for** $(k, v) \in H$ **do**
12: **if** $v = 3$ **then**
13: **for** $v_i \in k$ **do**
14:             c_i ++
15: **end for**
16: **end if**
17: **end for**
18: **for** $v_i \in \mathcal{V}$ **do**
19: $CC_i = \text{ClusteringCoefficient}(c_i, \{(v_i, v_j) \in \mathcal{E}\})$
20: **end for**

We give the general algorithm for the multicore CC in Algorithm 17.1. Algorithm 17.1 is the general program flow, where the master processor distributes the list of neighbors to a different processor (lines 2 and 3). When the processors complete, we have a series of return results, where each entry of the result is a node triple. For each triple, we store the number of times that triple has been returned by some processor (line 6) in a hashed data store, called H. After we have gone through all results of the processors, we iterate through the keys in H and if a key has been seen three times, then for each node in the triple, we iterate a counter for that node of how many triples that node is involved in (lines 11 through 17). After this, we distribute the calculation of the CC to other processors, which is a simple application of Equation 17.1.

The FindPossibleTriples (FPT) method gets a list of all the neighbors of a given node, v_i, and then returns a sorted list of all triples of nodes that have a shared friend of v_i. The logic of this is the following: suppose that nodes v_i, v_j, and v_k are a clique. Then, $v_j, v_k \in F_i$; $v_i, v_k \in F_j$; $v_i, v_j \in F_k$. So, the FPT for each of these will return (v_i, v_j, v_k) (assuming $v_i < v_j < v_k$). This means that the main algorithm will have a count of three for this triple, and each node will be listed in at least one cluster for the actual CC calculation.

We began by devising methods by which we could partition the nodes in a social network. As noted in Bearman et al. (2004), there are some nodes in the social network that are large influencers of the remainder of the network. Since these influencers have an effect that may not be simply related to the direct nodes they touch, their effects propagate throughout the graph. To retain this property, we devised methods of keeping these important nodes.

For experiments using the metrics described in Section 17.3, we use the value calculated for each of those metrics to define the *important* nodes. For IGBP, we assume that the major influencers for any particular group stay in that group and will end up in the same partition. Therefore, we do not replicate any nodes. For the completely random partition, we also do not attempt to replicate any nodes.*

The benefit of this is that while the learning model built on each partition for classification has fewer overall nodes to classify, those nodes that are present are, in theory, very indicative of the overall trends in the graph. By making sure that each partition has these nodes, then we can work to ensure that each partition's model is more accurate while maintaining the efficiencies of smaller data sets.

17.4.2 Partitioning

Algorithm 17.2 describes the general partitioning step used for DC and CC, which requires as input the metric M to be used (CC or DC), the replication rate r, and the number of partitions to be used p. We use the metrics described in Section 17.4.1 to partition the data. We do this by taking the specific metric to be used in the experiment and finding the specific numerical value for that metric using algorithms described in Section 17.4.1 (line 1). We then use the replication rate to choose the highest percentage of nodes to replicate across all partitions (lines 3 through 8). Among the remaining nodes, we pick the next node with the highest metric value and add it to the first partition.[†] We then take each of that node's first-degree neighbors and add it to the same partition (lines 12 through 14). We repeat on the remaining nodes in the list, adding each subsequent choice to the partition with the lowest cardinality (lines 14 through 17).

Algorithm 17.2: CC_DC_Partition (M, r, p)

1: $c_i = \{M(v_i)|v_i \in \mathcal{V}\}$ {M is the calculation for the chosen metric}
2: Sort $\mathcal{V}$ {in descending order on c}
3: **for** $i = 1$ to $|\mathcal{V}| \times r$ **do** {replication}
4: **for** $j = 1$ to p **do**
5: $P_j = P_j \cup v_i$
6:   **end for**
7: Remove v_i from $\mathcal{V}$
8: **end for**
9: **while** $\mathcal{V} \neq \varnothing$ **do**{partitioning}
10: $j \leftarrow ARGMIN_{|P_j|} (p_j \in P)$
11: $P_j = P_j \cup v_1$
12: **for all** $v_k \in \mathcal{N}(v_1)$ **do**
13:   $P_k = P_k \cup v_k$
14:   Remove v_k from $\mathcal{V}$
15:   **end for**
16: Remove v_1 from $\mathcal{V}$
17: **end while**

The IGBP is based on the specific nature of the social network and is shown in Algorithm 17.3 and takes as an input only the number of partitions to be used. We first calculate the IGR for each attribute (lines 1 through 5). We then find the attribute that has the highest IGR (line 6). We then pick a random node (line 8) and find the most frequently observed value of the attribute. For some single-valued attributes, this is straightforward. For multivalued attributes, we simply

---

* Used for comparison only.
† The choice of partition could be random without loss of generality.

choose the most frequent value. We then place all the nodes with that value into the partition with the fewest items (lines 12 through 15). We then repeat this with another randomly chosen node.

Algorithm 17.3: DS_Part (p)

```
 1:  h = Entropy (V_t)
 2: for A^n ∈ A do
 3:    i_{A_n} = IG(V_t, A^n)
 4:    c_n = IGR(V_t, A^n)
 5: end for
 6:  c ← ARGMAX_n {c_n}
 7: while V ≠ ∅ do {partitioning}
 8:    v_i ←_R V
 9:    a_i ← ARGMAX_j {Count(a_{i,j}^c)}
10:    j ← ARGMIN_{|P_j|} (p_j ∈ P)
11:    P_j = P_j ∪ v_1
12: for all v_k ∈ {v_k ∈ V | a_i ∈ a_k^c} do
13:    P_k = P_k ∪ v_k
14:    Remove v_k from V
15: end for
16:    Remove v_1 from V
17: end while
```

It is important to note that we do not attempt to maintain an equal number of nodes in each partition. We merely add nodes to a partition with the lowest cardinality in an attempt to keep the partitions roughly balanced in size. On the basis of the information gain calculations, for the Facebook data set, we divide the data based on group memberships (i.e., the group named *Linux*), and for the Internet Movie Database (IMDb) data set, we partition the data based on the decade in which the movie was made.

17.5   EXPERIMENTS

17.5.1   OUR APPROACH

For the experiments, we have identified three major parameters that we vary in our experiments:

1. *Replication rate*: We assume that there are some nodes in the graph that are extremely important for classification tasks. These nodes will be copied to all partitions to increase the accuracy of the classifier. Obviously, if we have too low a replication rate, then we will not get the most benefit from its use; similarly, if we have too high a replication rate, then we will gain no computational benefit from dividing the data into partitions.
2. *Training/test ratio*: This measure indicates the uncertain nature of a variety of released social networks. We vary the percentage of nodes in our training set from 50% to 90%. In this way, we are able to test our partitioned classifiers on a variety of graphs with unknown data.
3. *Number of partitions*: As our goal is to attempt to optimize social network classification for multiprocessor or multicore environments, we divide our data into one through eight partitions. This allows us to test for use on dual- and quad-core computers while overlapping as little work as possible.

When conducting our experiments, we chose to focus on two different situations to identify the ability of our system to accurately classify partitioned data. First, we wished to determine how varying the size of the training set in each partition would affect the accuracy of our distributed classification technique. We do note here that in a real-world scenario, the actual availability of nodes about whom the target data is known versus the number of nodes about whom the target data is being inferred will vary by partition. However, in testing the partitions repeatedly across many test/training divisions, we believe that we accurately indicate the ability of our partitioning and classification scheme. For the sake of brevity, we include here only results from tests where 50%, 60%, 70%, 80%, and 90% of the nodes in each partition are in the training set. By including these, we give the accuracy of our approach on what is frequently the most difficult scenario to model—where the training method has very little information to build the classification model on.

In each of these scenarios, we measured the following:

1. The total run-time required to partition and classify the data
2. The average classification accuracy of the partitioned data

To calculate the classification accuracy for each partition, we report accuracy over 50-fold cross validation runs. We computed the accuracy of each run by averaging the accuracy measurements of each classifier built on a partition. Our second consideration was for the amount of data replicated across all partitions in a test. We established the test set before calculation of the metrics, which means that the nodes in the test set were randomly distributed among the partitions with no attempt made to balance the number of nodes with the unknown class value in each partition.

17.5.2 Data Sources

The Facebook data was collected by a program written to crawl the Facebook network. Written in Java 1.6, the crawler loads a profile, parses the details out of the HTML, and stores the details inside a MySQL database. Then, the crawler loads all friends of the current profile and stores the friends inside the database both as friendship links and as possible profiles to later crawl.

Because of the sheer size of Facebook's entire social network, the crawler was limited to only crawling profiles inside the Dallas/Fort Worth (DFW) network as of July 2008. This means that if two people share a common friend that is outside the DFW network, this is not reflected inside our data set. Also, some people have enabled privacy restrictions on their profile that prevented the crawler from seeing their profile details. For our experiments, we attempted to classify individuals as either *Conservative* or *Liberal* with regard to their *Political Views*. We used only nodes that specify their political views in their Facebook profile. With this additional constraint on the composition of the data, this data set comprised 35,000 nodes.

The second set of data for our experimentation came from the IMDb. This is an online repository of data about movies and television shows with every member of the cast and crew, from directors and actors to grippers and gaffers. We developed a Java 1.6 crawler that downloaded the details of every title (as of November 2008) in five categories: Main Details, Full Cast and Crew, Company Credits, Box Office/Business, and Company Credits. Since the standard classification attribute for IMDb is *Box Office Earnings*, and because there is no entry for this in television episodes, we keep track of only movies. For this data set, we had 26,000 nodes.

17.5.3 Accuracy of the Results

It is important to note that the accuracy for the one-partition entry is the accuracy of classification performed on the entire data set with no partitioning scheme used.

In Figure 17.3, we show the results of the experiments conducted on the Facebook data set. Because of this, all one-partition data points are exactly the same, regardless of replication or

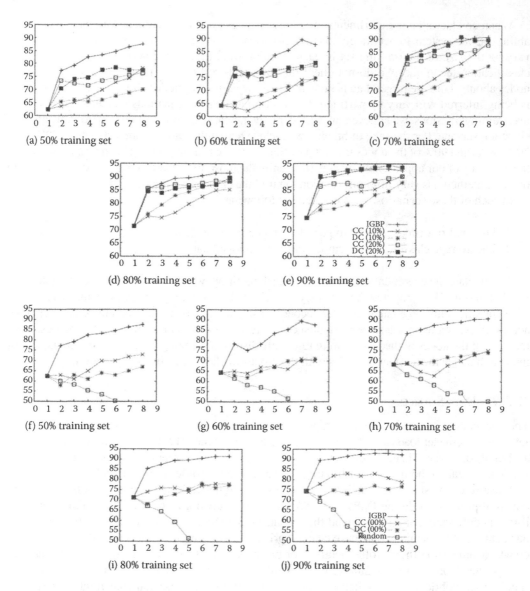

FIGURE 17.3 Facebook accuracy with 10% and 20% node replication (a through e) and random partitioning and 0% node replication (f through j).

partitioning metric, since neither was actually used in that experiment. We include this point on each figure for ease of comparison of the improvement of each method.

Figure 17.3a through e indicates that use of the IGBP heuristic for partitioning provided the greatest increase in accuracy when we used even a single additional partition, and this continued across all tested sizes of the training set. The final difference in accuracies (with a full eight partitions) is most apparent in those experiments where the size of the training set was smallest—that is, with a training set of 50% or 60% (Figure 17.3a and b, respectively). For training sets of 70% (Figure 17.3c), at the eight partitions mark, CC is approximately 2 percentage points away from IGBP in terms of accuracy. At this point, DC has more than a 10% difference in accuracy. For training sets of 80% and 90% (Figure 17.3d and e, respectively) this difference again shrinks, with DC being more accurate at the 80% test and CC being more accurate at 90%.

We see slightly different results for experiments with the 20% replication rate. In the 50% experiment, we again see that domain specific is significantly more accurate than either of the other metrics. However, what we can see from each graph is that the largest jump comes from the change from a single partition to two. We see that there is a significant difference at even the two-partitions entry for the same partitioning metric. This should be attributable only to the greater replication rate, since that is the only difference in the two experiments. One would expect that differences attributable to the random selection of the training set would be less significant over the multiple runs of the experiment we performed. It is important to note that this does not improve the accuracy of the IGBP metric, since, as mentioned previously, there is no node replication for this metric.

Continuing, we found that the wide disparity in classification accuracies found in the earlier experiments does not continue with the 20% replication rate. The CC and DC measures quickly increase their accuracy, while only infrequently classifying more accurately than the IGBP metric, and steadily increase throughout most of the experiments. One interesting finding is that the change from 80% to 90% training set sizes does not increase the classification accuracy of the CC metric as much as it had previously, indicating that for any partitioning of a graph that has few unknowns, it is the worst performing metric we used.

We show the results of our baseline tests in Figure 17.3f through j. We also include the IGBP line for further ease of comparison. The random partition, as shown, far underperforms any of the intelligent partitioning. For the 0% replication rate, the accuracy only increases slightly, compared with those where we replicate nodes, although the accuracy increase is generally fairly stable. It is worth noting here that while we do not use the metrics to find *important* nodes in the graph, we do still use them to determine the order that we pick nodes for partitioning. Since we choose in descending order based on the calculated value for the metric, this explains the reason for the difference between DC and CC for 0% replication.

In Figure 17.4, we see results from the IMDb data set similar to those observed in the Facebook data set. Overall, the IGBP metric outperforms both DC and CC, with only a few incidents where one of the other two obtains a higher classification accuracy (such as two partitions in Figure 17.4c).

One interesting feature of the IMDb data set is that for graphs where there are only a few nodes whose class values are unknown, the classifier is less affected by the replication rate than was shown by the Facebook data set. This may merely be a factor of the different natures of the data sets—Facebook is a dynamic, ever-changing representation of the information about the individuals. IMDb will rarely change older nodes due to updates for newer movies. However, our experiments indicate that even for these diverse types of data sets, increasing the replication rate from 10% to 20% does not hurt the classification accuracies; thus, for the levels we tested, there appears to be no detriment to the replication rate.

We again show the results of random partitioning and 0% node replication in Figure 17.4 with the IGBP line for reference. We get different results from the baseline view on Figure 17.3. In the IMDb data set, the replication does not seem to have as large an impact on the final accuracy as it does for Facebook. The reason for this may be in the nature of the data set. Since IMDb is not specifically a social network, but is merely modeled as one, it is possible the *important nodes* theory does not hold as strictly with this type of data set.

17.5.4 Execution Time

All timing experiments were conducted on an IBM x3500 server with two Intel Xeon quad-core 2.5 GHz processors and 16 GB of RAM. For recording the elapsed time, we used Java 1.6 time-keeping methods. Because our tests are intended to give an indication of what level of time/accuracy trade-off one can expect for dividing social networks, we are interested only in the total run time of an experiment, that is, the total time, including numerical calculation for the division metric—the

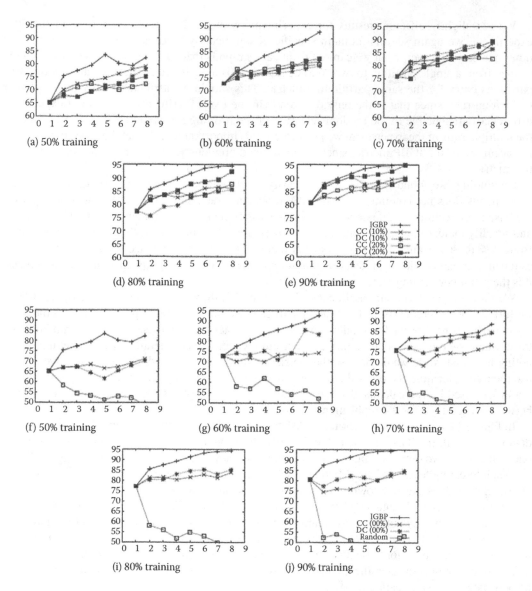

FIGURE 17.4 IMDb accuracy with 10% and 20% node replication (a through e) and random partitioning and 0% node replication (f through j).

time required for the segregation and complete classification of nodes. For these, we did not record the time taken for each classification task, but the real-world time that has elapsed while the threads were performing classification.

When examining the amount of time that it takes to separate each data set as a percentage of the time that it takes to classify the entire original data store (73 minutes for Facebook and 253 minutes for IMDb), we see several trends that make sense. First, using DC as a metric for data set division is always a low-cost option. Furthermore, we see that the IGBP metric has a high overhead for the calculation of information gain. In fact, using the IGBP metric for fewer than five portions actually increases the amount of time that can be taken for classification tasks. The average experiment run time as a percentage of single partition is given in Table 17.1.

TABLE 17.1

Average Experiment Run Time as a Percentage of Single Partition

	Facebook						
	2	**3**	**4**	**5**	**6**	**7**	**8**
CC	1.273	1.211	1.190	1.030	0.934	0.866	0.831
DC	0.943	0.932	0.876	0.831	0.712	0.603	0.519
IGBP	1.430	1.399	1.280	1.058	0.953	0.640	0.416
	IMDb						
CC	1.473	1.348	1.223	1.043	1.006	1.034	0.948
DC	0.853	0.749	0.711	0.634	0.598	0.594	0.475
IGBP	1.834	1.547	1.023	0.955	0.685	0.504	0.448

17.5.5 DISCUSSION OF RESULTS

These results led us to consider the reason for the increase in accuracy through partitioning. To further clarify our results, we broke the tasks down to examine the effects of the local classifier versus the benefit gained by using relaxation labeling—that is, the use of the relational classifier. When calculating the accuracy in all tests, we find the classification accuracy after the local classifier. We then find the classification accuracy at the end of the relaxation labeling step of that experiment. For both data sets, the local classifier accuracy for the IGBP, DC, and CC methods is approximately 85% (plus or minus 4%) of the total accuracy after iterative classification. The local classifier accounts for only 60% of the classification accuracy on the original data set and 54% through the random partitioning method. This means that when only a local classifier, such as naïve Bayes, is used on our partitioned segments, we achieve a higher accuracy without including any of the link structure over the initial data set.

Even though it appears that our partitioning methods have their benefit because they simply build better local classifiers, this is not necessarily true. We can see through the accuracy of the random partitioning that the improved local classification is not achieved through simply modeling on smaller data sets. However, with our methods that intelligently determine group membership, we see improvement not only in local classification accuracy but also overall classification accuracy. We also, however, gain additional classification accuracy through the use of the collective inference mechanism. By combining the information gain partitioning method, the naïve Bayes local classifier, and the relaxation labeling collective inference algorithm, we achieve the greatest accuracy in our social network classification.

17.6 SUMMARY AND DIRECTIONS

Our work indicates that information gain-based partitioning methods may be used to efficiently divide and then classify the data in a social network. While our work does indicate that for small-scale applications or very few divisions, we may spend more time on calculating the segments if we use an IGBP heuristic, we also show that for a more moderate or high number of processors, any segmentation method saves time for the entire classification.

Future work will include applying emerging social network mining techniques as well as developing novel techniques and testing with various data sets. We also need to determine whether our algorithms will scale for very large social networks, and whether there are additional metrics that would be useful to test our algorithms. Finally, we need to develop realistic privacy-preserving social network analytics algorithms.

REFERENCES

Bearman, P.S., Moody, J., and Stovel, K. Chains of affection: The structure of adolescent romantic and sexual networks. *American Journal of Sociology* 110(1): 44–91, 2004.

Bird, C., Gourley, A., Devanbu, P., Gertz, M., and Swaminathan, A. Mining email social networks. In: *MSR'06: Proceedings of the 2006 International Workshop on Mining Software Repositories*, pp. 137–143. ACM, New York, 2006.

Cai, D., Shao, Z., He, X., Yan, X., and Han, J. Mining hidden community in heterogeneous social networks. In: *LinkKDD'05: Proceedings of the 3rd International Workshop on Link Discovery*, pp. 58–65. ACM, New York, 2005.

Chu, C.T., Kim, S.K., Lin, Y.A., Yu, Y., Bradski, G.R., Ng, A.Y., and Olukotun, K. Map–reduce for machine learning on multicore. In: Schölkopf, B., Platt, J.C., and Hoffman, T., editors, *NIPS*, pp. 281–288. MIT Press, Boston, 2006.

Datta, S., Bhaduri, K., Giannella, C., Wolff, R., and Kargupta, H. Distributed data mining in peer-to-peer networks. *Internet Computing, IEEE* 10(4): 18–26, 2006.

Heatherly, R., Kantarcioglu, M., Thuraisingham, B., and Lindamood, J. Preventing private information inference attacks on social networks. Technical Report UTDCS-03-09, Department of Computer Science, The University of Texas at Dallas, Dallas, 2009a.

Heatherly, R., Kantarcioglu, M., and Thuraisingham, B. Social network classification incorporating link type values. In: *Proceedings of the 2009 IEEE International Conference on Intelligence and Security Informatics, ISI'09*, pp. 19–24. IEEE Press, Piscataway, NJ, 2009b.

Jackson, M.O. *Social and Economic Networks*, pp. 34–43. Princeton University Press, Princeton, NJ, 2008.

Krebs, V.E. Mapping networks of terrorist cells. *Connections* 24(3): 43–52, 2002.

Lu, Q. and Getoor, L. Link-based classification. In: *20th International Conference on Machine Learning*, Washington, DC, August 2003.

Macskassy, S.A. and Provost, F. Classification in networked data: A toolkit and a univariate case study. *Journal of Machine Learning Research* 8: 935–983, 2007.

Neville, J. and Jensen, D. Data mining in social networks. In: *National Academy of Sciences Symposium on Dynamic Social Network Analysis*, National Academy Press, Washington, DC, 2002.

Papadimitriou, S. and Sun, J. DisCo: Distributed co-clustering with map-reduce: A case study towards petabyte-scale end-to-end mining. In: *ICDM'08. Eighth IEEE International Conference on Data Mining*, pp. 512–521. IEEE Press, Pisa, Italy, 2008.

Quinlan, J.R. *C4.5: Programs for Machine Learning*. Morgan Kaufmann, San Francisco, 1993.

18 Sanitization of Social Network Data for Release to Semitrusted Third Parties

18.1 INTRODUCTION

The previous four chapters discussed various aspects of privacy on social networks. Chapter 14 discussed our approach to analyzing social networks. Chapter 15 discussed a new classification method that takes advantage of link types. We showed that by intelligently weighting those link types, it is possible to gain even more benefit from the link types. In Chapter 16, we created *artificial* links between regional influencers and those who follow in their wake. In Chapter 17, we showed that by intelligently examining historical social media data, we are able to partition the full data into smaller sets, which both increases classification accuracy and reduces the time required for classification. These approaches have given us an understanding of social network analysis and of their privacy implications so that we can develop privacy-enhanced social network analysis techniques. In this chapter, we will add a new dimension to our work in social network analysis. In particular, we show that even if we hide various links and details in social networks, one can still predict various sensitive and private data.

We have applied various data analytics techniques such as naïve Bayesian analysis, support vector machines (SVM), and other classification techniques to classify various individuals, including their religious beliefs, political beliefs, and gender orientation from the explicit data people post on social networks. We assume that the individuals do not directly post any private information. Therefore, by applying various inference techniques, we show that the private traits can be deduced.

The organization of this chapter is as follows. Learning methods on social networks are discussed in Section 18.2. Aspects of hiding private information are discussed in Section 18.3. Our experiments are discussed in Section 18.4. The chapter is concluded in Section 18.5. Figure 18.1 illustrates the concepts discussed in this chapter.

18.2 LEARNING METHODS ON SOCIAL NETWORKS

18.2.1 Naïve Bayes on Friendship Links

Consider the problem of determining the class detail value of person n_i given their friendship links using a naïve Bayes model; that is, of calculating $P(C_x|\mathcal{N}_i)$. Because there are relatively few people in the training set that have a friendship link to n_i, the calculations for $P(C_x|F_{i,j})$ become extremely inaccurate. Instead, we choose to decompose this relationship. Rather than having a link from person n_i to n_j, we instead consider the probability of having a link from n_i to someone with n_j's details. Thus,

$$P(C_x|F_{i,j}) \approx P(C_x|L_1, L_2, \ldots, L_m) \approx \frac{P(C_x) \times P(L_1|C_x) \times \ldots \times P(L_m|C_x)}{P(L_1, \ldots, L_m)} \qquad (18.1)$$

where L_n represents a link to someone with detail ID_n.

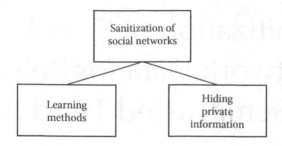

FIGURE 18.1   Sanitization of social network data for release to semitrusted third parties.

18.2.2   WEIGHING FRIENDSHIPS

There is one last step to calculating $P(C_x|\mathcal{N}_i)$. In the specific case of social networks, two friends can be anything from acquaintances to close friends or family members. While there are many ways to weigh friendship links, the method we used is very easy to calculate and is based on the assumption that the more public details two people share, the more private details they are likely to share. This gives the following formula for $W_{i,j}$, which represents the weight of a friendship link from n_i to node n_j:

$$W_{i,j} = \frac{\left|\left(D_i^1,\dots,D_i^n\right) \cap \left(D_j^1,\dots,D_j^m\right)\right|}{\left|D_i\right|} \tag{18.2}$$

Equation 18.2 calculates the total number of details n_i and n_j share divided by the number of details of n_i.

Note that the weight of a friendship link is not the same for both people on each side of a friendship link. In other words, $W_{j,i} \ne W_{i,j}$. The final formula for person i becomes the following, where Z represents a normalization constant and $P(C_x|F_{i,j})$ is calculated by Equation 18.1.

$$\rho(C_x,\mathcal{N}_i) = \frac{1}{Z}\sum_{n_j \in \mathcal{N}_i}\left[P(C_x|F_{i,j}) \times W_{i,j}\right] \tag{18.3}$$

The value $\rho\left(C_x,\mathcal{N}_i\right)$ is used as our approximation to $P(C_x|\mathcal{N}_i)$.

18.2.3   NETWORK CLASSIFICATION

Collective inference is a method of classifying social network data using a combination of node details and connecting links in the social graph. Each of these classifiers consists of three components: a local classifier, a relational classifier, and a collective inference algorithm.

> **Local Classifiers.** Local classifiers are a type of learning method that is applied in the initial step of collective inference. Typically, it is a classification technique that examines details of a node and constructs a classification scheme based on the details that it finds there. For instance, the naïve Bayes classifier we discussed previously is a standard example of Bayes classification. This classifier builds a model based on the details of nodes in the training set. It then applies this model to nodes in the testing set to classify them.
> **Relational Classifiers.** The relational classifier is a separate type of learning algorithm that looks at the link structure of the graph, and uses the labels of nodes in the training set to

develop a model that it uses to classify the nodes in the test set. Specifically, Macskassy and Provost (2007) examine four relational classifiers:

1. Class-distribution relational neighbor (cdRN)
2. Weighted-vote relational neighbor (wvRN)
3. Network-only Bayes classifier (nBC)
4. Network-only link-based classification (nLB)

The *cdRN* classifier begins by determining a reference vector for each class. That is, for each class, C_x, cdRN develops a vector RV_x, which is a description of what a node that is of type C_x tends to connect to. Specifically, $RV_x(a)$ is an average value for how often a node of class C_x has a link to a node of class C_a. To classify node n_i, the algorithm builds a class vector, CV_i, where $CV_i(a)$ is a count of how often n_i has a link to a node of class C_a. The class probabilities are calculated by comparing CV_i with RV_x for all classes C_x.

The *nBC* uses Bayes theorem to classify based only on the link structure of a node. That is, it defines

$$P(n_i = C_x | \mathcal{N}_i) = \frac{P(\mathcal{N}_i | n_i = C_x) \times P(n_i = C_x)}{P(\mathcal{N}_i)}$$

$$= \prod_{n_j \in \mathcal{N}_i} \frac{P(n_j = C_a | n_i = C_x) \times P(n_i = C_x)}{P(n_j)}$$

where $\mathcal{N}_i$ are the neighbors of n_i, and then uses these probabilities to classify n_i.

The *nLB* classifier collects the labels of the neighboring nodes, and by means of logistic regression, uses these vectors to build a model.

In the *wvRN* relational classifier, to classify a node n_i, each of its neighbors, n_j, is given a weight. The probability of n_i being in class C_x is the weighted mean of the class probabilities of n_i's neighbors. That is,

$$P(n_i = C_x | \mathcal{N}_i) = \frac{1}{Z} \sum_{n_j \in \mathcal{N}_i} \left[w_{i,j} \times P(n_j = C_x) \right]$$

where $\mathcal{N}_i$ is the set of neighbors of n_i and $w_{i,j}$ is a link weight parameter given to the wvRN classifier. For our experiments, we assume that all link weights are 1.

18.2.4 COLLECTIVE INFERENCE METHODS

Unfortunately, there are issues with each of the methods described above. Local classifiers consider only the details of the node they are classifying. Conversely, relational classifiers consider only the link structure of a node. Specifically, a major problem with relational classifiers is that while we may cleverly divide fully labeled test sets so that we ensure every node is connected to at least one node in the training set, real-world data may not satisfy this strict requirement. If this requirement is not met, then relational classification will be unable to classify nodes that have no neighbors in the training set. Collective inference attempts to make up for these deficiencies by using both local and relational classifiers in a precise manner to attempt to increase the classification accuracy of nodes in the network. By using a local classifier in the first iteration, collective inference ensures that every node will have an initial probabilistic classification, referred to as a *prior*. The algorithm then uses a relational classifier to reclassify nodes. At each of these steps $i > 2$, the relational classifier uses the fully labeled graph from step $i - 1$ to classify each node in the graph.

The collective inference method also controls the length of time the algorithm runs. Some algorithms specify a number of iterations to run, while others converge after a general length of time. We choose to use relaxation labeling as described in Macskassy and Provost (2007), a method that retains the uncertainty of our classified labels. That is, at each step i, the algorithm uses the probability estimates, not a single classified label, from step $i - 1$ to calculate new probability estimates. Furthermore, to account for the possibility that there may not be a convergence, there is a decay rate, called α, set to 0.99 that discounts the weight of each subsequent iteration compared with the previous iterations. We chose to use relaxation labeling because in the experiments conducted by Macskassy and Provost (2007), relaxation labeling tended to be the best of the three collective inference methods. Each of these classifiers, including a relaxation labeling implementation, is included in NetKit-SRL.* As such, after we perform our sanitization techniques, we allow NetKit to classify the nodes to examine the effectiveness of our approaches.

18.3 HIDING PRIVATE INFORMATION

In this section, we first give the operating definition of privacy for a social network. Next, we discuss how to preserve this privacy through manipulation of both details and links.

18.3.1 FORMAL PRIVACY DEFINITION

Problem 1

Given a graph, $\mathcal{G}$, from a social network, where $\mathcal{I}$ is a subset of $\mathcal{H}$ and $\| \geq 1$, is it possible to minimize the classification accuracy on $\mathcal{I}$ when using some set of classifiers $\mathcal{C}$ while preserving the utility of $\mathcal{H} - \mathcal{I}$?

Definition 18.1

Background knowledge, $\mathcal{K}$, is some data that is not necessarily directly related to the social network, but that can be obtained through various means by an attacker. Examples of background knowledge include voter registration, election results, phone book results, etc.

Definition 18.2

Utility of a graph,

$$\mathcal{U}(\mathcal{G}) = \sum_{ID_x \in (\mathcal{H} - \mathcal{I})} \left[\max_{c \in C} \left(\mathcal{P}_{c(\mathcal{G})}(ID_x) \right) \right] \tag{18.4}$$

where $\mathcal{H} - \mathcal{I}$ are all nonsensitive detail types, and $\mathcal{P}_{c(\mathcal{G})}$ is the accuracy of a classification task using a given classifier c on all arbitrary detail values for a given detail type.

Definition 18.3

A graph is $(\Delta, \mathcal{C}, \mathcal{G}, \mathcal{K})$-private if, for a given set of classifiers $\mathcal{C}$,

$$\max\left[\left(\max_{c \in C} (\mathcal{P}_{c(\mathcal{G}, \mathcal{K})}) - \max_{c' \in C} \left(\mathcal{P}_{c'(\mathcal{K})} \right) \right), 0 \right] = \Delta$$

---

* Available at http://netkit-srl.sourceforge.net/.

That is, if we have any set of given classifiers, C, then the classification accuracy of any arbitrary classifier $c' \in C$ when trained on K and used to classify G to predict sensitive hidden data is denoted by $P_{c'(K)}$. Similarly, $P_{c(G,K)}$ denotes the prediction accuracy of the classifier that is trained on both G and K. Here, Δ denotes the additional accuracy gained by the attacker using G. Ideally, if $\Delta = 0$, this means that the attacker does not gain additional accuracy in predicting sensitive hidden data.

18.3.2 Manipulating Details

Clearly, details can be manipulated in three ways: adding details to nodes, modifying existing details, and removing details from nodes. However, we can broadly classify these three methods into two categories: perturbation and anonymization. Adding and modifying details can both be considered methods of perturbation—that is, introducing various types of *noise* into D in order to decrease classification accuracies. Removing nodes, however, can be considered an anonymization method.

Consider, for instance, the difference in two graphs, G' and G'', which are sanitized versions of G by perturbation and anonymization methods, respectively. In G', there are artificial details within D'. That is, suppose that there is a node $n_i \in G, G', G''$, which has a listed detail of (favorite activities, sports) in our two sanitized data sets. When we consider this instance in G', we are uncertain about its authenticity. Depending on the perturbation method used, the original node could have had no favorite activities, or had an entry of (favorite activities, Dallas Cowboys), which was altered to contain the aforementioned detail.

However, in G'', if we see the detail (favorite activities, sports), then we know the detail was in the original data set by the same node. If the detail does not occur in the sanitized data set, then we have no information about the user's preference for sports. All we know is that it was not listed. Owing to these considerations, our first solution is to attempt to remove details in order to decrease classification accuracy on sensitive attributes. We follow this with an examination of perturbation methods.

Problem 2

Given G and a nonzero set of sensitive details I, determine the set of details $D' \subset D$, where $G' = \{V, E, D - D'\}$ has the most reduction in classification accuracy for some set of classifiers C on the sensitive attributes I for the given number of removals m.

Assume a person n_i has the class value C_2 out of the set of classes C, and this person has public details D_i.

$$\arg\max_y [P(C_y) * P\left(D_i^1 \middle| C_y\right) * \ldots * P\left(D_i^m \middle| C_y\right) \tag{18.5}$$

Equation 18.5 identifies the learned class. Because we globally remove the most representative details, we are able to find this based off of the equation

$$\arg\max_y [\forall C_x \in C : P(D_y | C_x)] \tag{18.6}$$

This allows us to find the single detail that is the most highly indicative of a class and remove it. Experimentally, we later show that this method of determining which details to remove provides a good method of detail selection.

18.3.3 MANIPULATING LINK INFORMATION

The other option for anonymizing social networks is altering links. Unlike details, there are only two methods of altering the link structure: adding or removing links. For the same reasons given in Section 18.3.2, we choose to evaluate the effects of privacy on removing friendship links instead of adding fake links. Consider Equation 18.3 for determining detail type using friendship links. Also assume that there are two possible classes for a node, and the true class is C_1. We want to remove links that increase the likelihood of the node being in class C_1. Please note that we define a node to be in class C_2 if formula 18.7 is positive.

$$\beta(i) = \rho(C_2, \mathcal{N}_i) - \rho(C_1, \mathcal{N}_i) \tag{18.7}$$

Therefore, we would like to maximize the value of $\beta(i)$ as much as possible by removing links.

Define $\beta_j(i)$ as the new value for formula 18.7 if we remove friendship link $F_{i,j}$. We can compute $\beta_j(i)$ as

$$
\begin{aligned}
\beta_j(i) &= \left(\rho(C_2, \mathcal{N}_i) - \frac{P(C_2|F_{i,j}) * W_{j,i}}{Z} \right) \\
&\quad - \left(\rho(C_1, \mathcal{N}_i) - \frac{P(C_1|F_{i,j}) * W_{j,i}}{Z} \right) \\
&= \beta(i) + \frac{(P(C_1|F_{i,j}) - (P(C_2|F_{i,j})) * W_{j,i}}{Z}
\end{aligned}
\tag{18.8}
$$

Because $\beta(i)$ and Z are constants for all $\beta_j(i)$, the best choice for i that maximizes $\beta_j(i)$ becomes one that maximizes $M_j = (P(C_1|F_{i,j})) - (P(C_2|F_{i,j})) * W_{j,i}$.

In our experiments, we order the links for each node based on the M_j values. When we remove links, we remove those with the greatest M_j values.

18.3.4 DETAIL ANONYMIZATION

To combat this type of attack on privacy, we attempt to provide detail anonymization for social networks. By doing this, we believe that we will be able to reduce the value of $\Delta_{\mathcal{G},\mathcal{K}}(C)$ to an acceptable threshold value that matches the desired utility/privacy trade-off for a release of data.

Definition 18.4

A detail generalization hierarchy (DGH) is an anonymization technique that generates a hierarchical ordering of the details expressed within a given category. The resulting hierarchy is structured as a tree, but the generalization scheme guarantees that all values substituted will be an ancestor, and thus at a maximum may be only as specific as the detail the user initially defined.

To clarify, this means that if a user inputs a favorite activity as the Boston Celtics, we could have, as an example, the following DGH:

$$\text{Boston Celtics} \rightarrow \text{NBA} \rightarrow \text{Basketball}$$

This means that to completely anonymize the entry of *Boston Celtics* in a user's details, we replace it with *Basketball*. However, notice that we also have the option of maintaining a bit more specificity (and therefore utility) by replacing it instead with *NBA*. This hierarchical nature will allow us to programmatically determine a more efficient release anonymization, which hopefully ensures that we have a generalized network that is as near optimal as possible. Our scheme's guarantee, however, ensures that at no time will the value *Boston Celtics* be replaced with the value *Los Angeles Lakers*. Alternately, we have some details, such as *Favorite Music*, which do not easily allow themselves to be placed in a hierarchy. Instead, we perform detail value decomposition (DVD) on these details.

Definition 18.5

DVD is a process by which an attribute is divided into a series of representative tags. These tags do not necessarily reassemble into a unique match to the original attribute.

Thus, we can decompose a group such as *Enya* into {ambient, alternative, Irish, new age, Celtic} to describe the group. To generate the DGH and the DVD, we use subject authorities, which, through having large amounts of data, are able to provide either a DGH or a DVD for some particular (set of) detail types.

18.4   EXPERIMENTS

18.4.1   EXPERIMENTAL SETUP

In our experiments, we implemented four algorithms to predict the political affiliation of each user. The first algorithm is called *Details Only*. This algorithm uses Equation 14.8 to predict political affiliation and ignores friendship links. The second algorithm is called *Links Only*. This algorithm uses Equation 18.3 to predict political affiliation using friendship links and does not consider the details of a person. The third algorithm is called *Average*. The Average algorithm predicts a node's class value based on the following equation:

$$P_A(N_i = C_a) = 0.5 * P_D(n_i = C_a) + 0.5 * P_L(n_i = C_a)$$

where P_D and P_L are the numerical probabilities assigned by the Details Only and Links Only algorithms, respectively. The final algorithm is a traditional naïve Bayes classifier, which we used as a basis of comparison for our proposed algorithms.

We define two classification tasks. The first is that we wish to determine whether an individual is politically *Conservative* or *Liberal*. The second classification task is to determine whether an individual is *heterosexual* or *homosexual*. It is important to note that we considered individuals who would also be considered *bisexual* as *homosexual* for this experiment. We began by pruning the total graph of 160,000 nodes down to only those nodes for which we have a recorded political affiliation or sexual organization in order to have reasonable tests for the accuracy of our classifiers and the impact of our sanitization. This reduced our overall set size to 35,000 nodes for our political affiliation tests and to 69,000 nodes for our sexual orientation tests. We then conducted a series of experiments where we removed a number of details and a separate series of experiments where we removed a number of links. We conducted these removing up to 20 details and links, respectively. The results of these initial tests are discussed in Section 18.4.2.

18.4.2   LOCAL CLASSIFICATION RESULTS

Tables 18.1 and 18.2 list the most liberal or conservative details. For example, the most liberal detail, as shown in Table 18.1, is being a member of the group "legalize same sex marriage." Tables 18.3 and 18.4 show the most liberal and conservative details for each detail type.

TABLE 18.1

Sample of the Most Liberal Detail Values

Detail Name	Detail Value	Weight
Group member	Legalize same sex marriage	46.160667
Group member	Every time I find out a cute boy is conservative, a little part of me dies	39.685994
Group member	Equal rights for gays	33.837868
Favorite music	Ani DiFranco	17.368250
Favorite movie	Sicko	17.280959

TABLE 18.2

Sample of the Most Conservative Detail Values

Detail Name	Detail Value	Weight
Group member	George W. Bush is my homeboy	45.88831329
Group member	Bears for bush	30.86484689
Group member	Kerry is a fairy	28.50250433
Favorite movie	End of the Spear	14.53703765

TABLE 18.3

Most Conservative Detail Value for Each Detail

Detail Name	Detail Value	Weight
Activities	College Republicans	5.846955271
Favorite books	Redeeming Love	6.348153362
Favorite movies	End of the Spear	14.53703765
Favorite music	Delirious	18.85227471
Favorite TV shows	Fox News	7.753312932
Grad school	SW Seminary	2.749648395
Group member	George W. Bush is my homeboy	45.88831329
Interests	Hunting and fishing	7.614995442
Relationship status	Married	1.667495517
Religious views	Christian	2.441063037
Sex	Male	1.087798286

In Table 18.5, we show the details that most indicate the *homosexual* classification. In contrast to political affiliation, there are no single details that are very highly correlated with that classification. For example, the three details we have selected here are more highly indicative of being *liberal* than of being *homosexual*. Conversely, we see in Table 18.6 that there are a few categories that are very highly representative of the *heterosexual* classification.

As can be seen from the results, our methods are generally successful at reducing the accuracy of classification tasks. Figure 18.2 show that removing the details most highly connected with a class is accurate across the Details and Average classifiers. Counterintuitively, perhaps, is that the accuracy of our Links classifier is also decreased as we remove details. However, as discussed in Section 18.3.3, the details of two nodes are compared to find a similarity. As we remove details from

TABLE 18.4
Most Liberal Detail Values for Each Detail

Detail Name	Detail Value	Weight
Activities	Amnesty International	4.659100601
Favorite books	Middlesex	4.841749269
Favorite movies	Hedwig and the Angry Inch	24.80050378
Favorite music	Deerhoof	22.94603913
Favorite TV shows	Queer as Folk	9.762900035
Grad school	Computer Science	1.698146579
Group member	Legalize same sex marriage	46.16066789
Interests	Vegetarianism	11.76878725
Looking for	Whatever I can get	1.703651985
Relationship status	In an open relationship	1.617950632
Religious views	Agnostic	3.157564120
Sex	Female	1.103484182

TABLE 18.5
Most Homosexual Detail Value for Each Detail

Detail Name	Detail Value	Weight
Group member	Legalize same sex marriage	1.004393825
Group member	Equal rights for gays	1.000573463
Relationship status	It's complicated	1.005384899

TABLE 18.6
Most Heterosexual Detail Value for Each Detail

Detail Name	Detail Value	Weight
Favorite books	The Bible	24.58371923
Group member	One man, one woman	45.39182390
Relationship status	Married	53.84381923

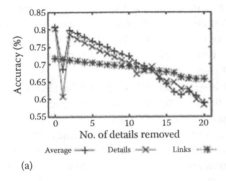
(a)

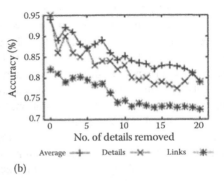
(b)

FIGURE 18.2 Local classification accuracy by number of details removed. (a) Political affiliation and (b) sexual orientation.

the network, the set of *similar* nodes to any given node will also change. This can account for the decrease in accuracy of the Links classifier. Additionally, we noted that there is a severe drop in the classification accuracy after the removal of a single detail. However, when looking at the data, this can be explained by the removal of a detail that is very indicative of the *Conservative* class value. When we remove this detail, the probability of being *Conservative* drastically decreases, which leads to a higher number of incorrect classifications. When we remove the second detail, which has a similar likelihood for the *Liberal* classification, then the class value probabilities begin to trend downward at a much smoother rate.

While we do not see this behavior in Figure 18.2b, we do see a much more volatile classification accuracy. This appears to be a result of the wider class size disparity in the underlying data. Because approximately 95% of the available nodes are *heterosexual* and there are no details that are as highly indicative of sexual orientation as there are of political affiliation, even minor changes can affect the classification accuracy in unpredictable ways. For instance, when we removed five details, we have lowered the classification accuracy; however, for the sixth and seventh details, we see an increase in classification accuracy. Then, we again see another decrease in accuracy when we removed the eighth detail.

When we removed links, we have a generally more stable downward trend, with only a few exceptions in the *Political Affiliation* experiments. While each measure provided a decrease in classification accuracy, we also tested what happens to our data set if we remove both details and links. To do this, we conducted further experiments where we test classification accuracy after removing 0 details and 0 links (the baseline accuracy), 0 details and 10 links, 10 details and 0 links, and 10 details and 10 links. We chose these numbers because after removing 12 links, we found that we were beginning to create a number of isolated groups of few nodes or single, disconnected nodes. Additionally, when we removed 13 details, 44% of our *Political Affiliation* data set and 33% of our *Sexual Orientation* data set had fewer than four details remaining. Since part of our goal was to maintain utility after a potential data release, we chose to remove fewer details and links to support this.

We refer to these sets as 0 details, 0 links; 10 details, 0 links; 0 details, 10 links; 10 details, 10 links removed, respectively. Following this, we want to gauge the accuracy of the classifiers for various ratios of labeled versus unlabeled graphs. To do this, we collect a list of all of the available nodes, as discussed above. We then obtain a random permutation of this list using the Java function built in to the *Collections* class. Next, we divide the list into a test set and a training set, based on the desired ratio.

We focus on multiples of 10 for the accuracy percentages, so we generated sets of 10/90, 20/80, …, 90/10. Additionally, when creating training sets for our *Sexual Orientation* data set, because of the wide difference in the group size for *heterosexual* and *homosexual*, we made sure that we separate out the chosen percentage from the known *heterosexual* and *homosexual* groups independently in order to ensure that we have a diversity in both our training and test sets. For example, in a test where we will have only 10% labeled data, we selected 10% of heterosexual individuals and 10% of homosexual individuals independently to be in our training set. We referred to each set by the percentage of data in the test set. We generated five test sets of each ratio, and ran each experiment independently. We then took the average of each of these runs.

Our results indicate that the Average Only algorithm substantially outperformed traditional naïve Bayes and the Links Only algorithm. Additionally, the average-only algorithm generally performed better than the Details Only algorithm with the exception of the (0 details, 10 links) experiments. Also, as a verification of expected results, the Details Only classification accuracy only decreased significantly when we removed details from nodes, while the (0 details, *) accuracies are approximately equivalent. Similarly, the Links Only accuracies were mostly affected by the removal of links between nodes, while the (*, 0 links) points of interest are approximately equal. The difference in accuracy between (0 details, 0 links) and (10 details, 0 links) can be accounted for by the weighting portion of the Links Only calculations, which depend on the similarity between two nodes.

Figures 18.3 and 18.4 show the results of our classification methods for various labeled node ratios. These results indicate that the Average and Details classifiers generally performed at approximately the same accuracy level. The Links Only classifier, however, generally performed significantly worse except in the case where 10 details and 0 links were removed. In this situation, all three classifiers performed similarly. We see that the greatest variance occurred when we removed details alone. It may be unexpected that the Links Only classifier had such varied accuracies as a result of removing details, but since our calculation of probabilities for that classifier used a measure of similarity between people, the removal of details may have affected that classifier. Additionally, Figures 18.3 and 18.4 also show the results of using SVM as a classification technique. We see here that when we removed no details, the classification accuracy of the SVM had a classification accuracy between our Links Only and Average/Details Only classifiers, with the exception of sets

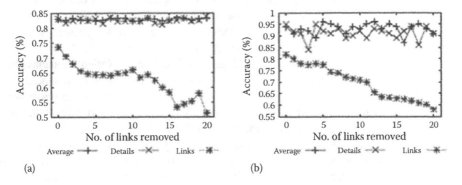

FIGURE 18.3 Local classification accuracy by number of links removed. (a) Political affiliation and (b) sexual orientation.

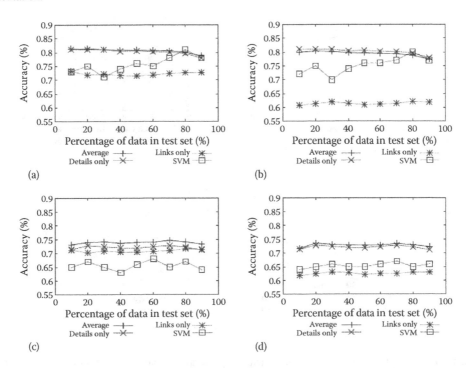

FIGURE 18.4 Local classifier prediction accuracies by percentage of nodes in test set for political affiliation. (a) 0 details, 0 links removed, (b) 0 details, 10 links removed, (c) 10 details, 0 links removed, and (d) 10 details, 10 links removed.

where the graph has a large percentage of unknowns (80% and 90% of the graph is unknown) where the SVM classifier can actually outperform the Details Only/Average classifier. However, once we removed details, the classification accuracy of the SVM dropped much further than the Average/Details Only classifier, and even performed worse than the Links Only classification method.

Next, we examined the effects of removing the links. We removed K links from each node, where $K \in [0, 10]$, and again partitioned the nodes into a test set and training set of equal size. We then tested the accuracy of the local classifier on this test set. We repeated this five times, and then took the average of each accuracy for the overall accuracy of each classifier after K links were removed. For $K \in [1, 6]$, each link removal steadily decreased the accuracy of the classifier. Removing the seventh link had no noticeable effect, and subsequent removals only slightly increased the accuracy of the Links Only classifier. Also, owing to space limitations, for the remainder of the experiments, we show only the results of the Average classifier, as it is generally the best of the three classifiers. When we again examined the performance of the SVM, we saw similar results to what was seen with Details Only and Average. Since the SVM does not include the link structure in its classification, there is no real effect from removing links on this classification method.

It is important to note that, as we can see from Figure 18.5, the Sexual Orientation classifier seems to be more susceptible to problems of incomplete knowledge. We can see in each subfigure, to a far greater degree than in Figure 18.4, that as we decreased the amount of information available to the training method, the Sexual Orientation classifier accuracy decreased considerably. Once again, we believe that this may be explained simply by the fact that there is far less support for the *homosexual* classification, and as such, it is considerably harder to classify without adequate data. Specifically, since there were so few instances of the *homosexual* classification in our data set, when you combine this with the fact that there are no absolute predictors of homosexuality and that the indicators for homosexuality have a very low increased likelihood, if most of the examples of homosexuals are unknown, then classifiers are going to be unable to create an accurate model for prediction.

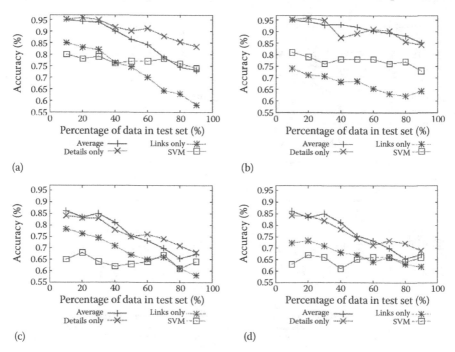

FIGURE 18.5 Local classifier prediction accuracies by percentage of nodes in test set for sexual orientation. (a) 0 details, 0 links removed, (b) 0 details, 10 links removed, (c) 10 details, 0 links removed, and (d) 10 details, 10 links removed.

18.4.3 GENERALIZATION EXPERIMENTS

Each of those details fell into one of several categories: Religion, Political Affiliation, Activities, Books, Music, Quotations, Shows/Movies, and Groups. Owing to the lack of a reliable subject authority, Quotations were discarded from all experiments. To generate the DGH for each Activity, Book, and Show/Movie, we used Google Directories. To generate the DVD for Music, we used the Last.fm tagging system. To generate the hierarchy for Groups, we used the classification criteria from the Facebook page of that group.

To account for the free-form tagging that Last.fm allows, we also stored the popularity for each tag that a particular detail has. This font size is representative of how many users across the system have defined that particular tag for the music type. We then kept a list of tag recurrence (weighted by strength) for each user. For Music anonymization, we eliminated the lowest-scoring tags.

In our experiments, we assumed that the trait *political affiliation* is a sensitive attribute, and C includes a naïve Bayes classifier and the implementation of SVM from Weka.

In Figure 18.6a, we present some initial findings from our domain generalization. We present a comparison of simply using K to guess the most populated class from background knowledge, the result of generalizing all trait types, generalizing no trait types, and when we generalize the best single performing trait type (activities).

We see here that our method of generalization (seen through the All and Activities lines) indeed decreased the accuracy of classification on the data set. Additionally, our ability to classify on non-sensitive attributes (such as gender) were affected by only 2–3% over the course of the experiments (figure omitted for space). Interestingly, while previous work (Lindamood et al., 2009) indicates that Group membership is the dominant detail in classification, we see the most benefit here from generalizing only the Activities detail.

Next, we show that given a desired utility increase, we are able to determine to what level the data set should be anonymized. We see from Figure 18.6b that as we allow more utility gain from our anonymized graph, fewer categories are generalized to any degree. We also see that Groups is most consistently anonymized completely until the allowed utility gain is 20%. Furthermore, we see that the most variable entry is music.

This may be because the nature of the music detail is that it allows us more easily to include or remove details in order to fit a required utility value. Rather than, say, the activities detail type, which has a fixed hierarchy, music has a loosely collected group of tags that we can more flexibly include.

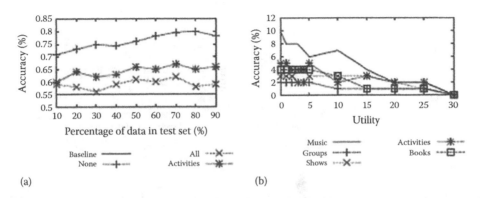

FIGURE 18.6   Generalization results. (a) Effect of generalization on utility and (b) determining anonymization.

18.4.4 COLLECTIVE INFERENCE RESULTS

We note that in the Facebook data, there are a limited number of *groups* that are highly indicative of an individual's political affiliation. When removing details, these were the first to be removed. We assumed that conducting the collective inference classifiers after removing only one detail may generate results that are specific for the particular detail we classify for. For that reason, we continued to consider only the removal of 0 details and 10 details, the other lowest point on the classification accuracy. We also continued to consider the removal of 0 links and 10 links due to the marginal difference between the region (Bird et al., 2006; Brickley and Miller, 2007) and removing 10 links.

For the experiments using relaxation labeling, we took the same varied ratio sets generated for the local classifiers. For each, we stored the predictions made by the Details Only, Links Only, and Average classifiers, and used those as the priors for the NetKit toolkit. For each of those priors, we tested the final accuracy of the cdRN, wvRN, nLB, and nBC classifiers. We did this for each of the five sets generated for each of the four points of interest. We then took the average of their accuracies for the final accuracy.

Figure 18.7 shows the results of our experiments using relaxation labeling. Macskassy and Provost (2007) studied the effects of collective inference on four real-world data sets: Internet Movie Database (IMDb), Cora, WebKB, and Security and Exchange Commission (SEC) filings. While they did not discuss the difference in the local classifier and iterative classification steps of their experiments, their experiments indicated that relaxation labeling almost always performs better than merely predicting the most frequent class. Generally, it performs at near 80% accuracy, which is an increase of approximately 30% in their data sets. However, in our experiments, relaxation labeling typically performed no more than approximately 5% better than predicting the majority class for political affiliation. This is also substantially less accurate than using only our local classifier. We believe that this performance is at least partially because our data set is not densely connected.

Our results in Figure 18.7 indicate that there is very little significant difference in the collective inference classifiers except for cdRN, which performs significantly worse on data sets where there is

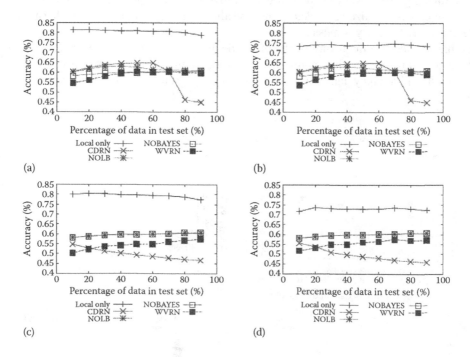

FIGURE 18.7 Prediction accuracy of relaxation labeling using the average local classifier (political affiliation). (a) 0 details, 0 links removed, (b) 10 details, 0 links removed, (c) 0 details, 10 links removed, and (d) 10 details, 10 links removed.

a small training set. These results also indicate that our Average classifier consistently outperforms relaxation labeling on the preanonymized and postanonymized data sets.

Additionally, if we compare Figure 18.7a through d, we see that while the local classifier's accuracy is directly affected by the removal of details and/or links, this relationship is not shown by using relaxation labeling with the local classifiers as a prior. For each pair of figures mentioned, the relational classifier portion of the graph remains constant; only the local classifier accuracy changes. From these, we see that the most *anonymous* graph, meaning the graph structure that has the lowest predictive accuracy, is achieved when we remove both details and links from the graph.

18.5   EFFECT OF SANITIZATION ON OTHER ATTACK TECHNIQUES

We further tested the removal of details as an anonymization technique by using a variety of different classification algorithms to test the effectiveness of our method. For each number of details removed, we began by removing the indicated number of details in accordance with the method as described in Section 18.3. We then performed 10-fold cross validation on this set 100 times, and conducted this for 0–20 details removed. The results of these tests are shown in Figure 18.8a and b. As can be seen from the figure, our technique is effective at reducing the classification of networks for those details that we have classified as sensitive.

While the specific accuracy reduction is varied by the number of details removed and by the specific algorithm used for classification, we see that we do, in fact, reduce the accuracy across a broad range of classifiers. We see that linear regression is affected the least, with an approximately 10% reduction in accuracy. Also, decision trees are affected the most, with a roughly 35% reduction in classification accuracy.

This indicates that through the use of a Bayesian classifier, which makes it easier to identify the individual details that make a class label more likely, we can decrease the accuracy of a far larger set of classifiers.

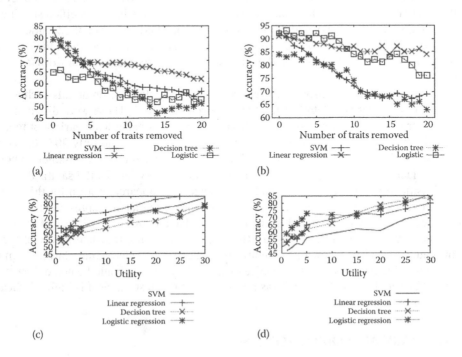

FIGURE 18.8 Classification accuracy using non-Bayesian methods. (a) Political affiliation, (b) sexual orientation, (c) political affiliation (generalization), and (d) sexual orientation (generalization).

TABLE 18.7
Postrelease Utility of g (Classification Accuracy)

Task	Presanitization	Postsanitization
Like to read	84.3	82.9
Like sports	71.7	70.3
College educated	73.1	75.2
Like video games	86.1	88.9

We also see similar results with our generalization method in Figure 18.8c and d. While the specific value of the utility that was defined for naïve Bayes does not exactly hold, we still see that by performing generalization, we are able to decrease classification accuracy across multiple types of classifier.

18.6   EFFECT OF SANITIZATION ON UTILITY

Of course, if the data is to be used by a company, then there must still be some value in the post-sanitization graph. To gauge the utility of the anonymized data set, in Table 18.7 we show the results of various inference tests performed on nonsensitive details. For these tests, we used an SVM and our Bayesian classifiers, as discussed earlier, to run inference and collective inference tasks on each selected detail. We performed each test with 50% of the data in a training set and 50% in a test set. Here, we report the accuracy from running the experiments on random test sets 50 times each from the best-performing classifiers, which were the average Bayesian with nLB. The accuracies were averaged for display here. The postsanitization figures were performed after removing 10 details and 10 links. Please note that this table represents the accuracy of a classifier on these details, *not* what percentage of the graph has this detail. We tested a selection of details with multiple attributes. For example, the *like video games* detail value is specified specifically in the data set (in favorite activities). *College educated* was specified as a level of education (scanned for type of degree and school). *Like to read* and *like sports* were inferred from the existence of books in the *favorite book* category or the existence of a sports team in the *favorite activities* category.

It is important to note, obviously, that when we performed inference on details such as *likes to read*, we did not consider any detail of the type *favorite book* = *. These were discarded for the tests on that type of classification task. Furthermore, the test sets had a wide variety of representative sizes. *Like to read* had 148,000 profiles, while *like video games* had only 30,000. As we can see from these results, sanitization has minimal impact on the accuracy of a classifier on nonsensitive details. In fact, for the *college educated* and *like video games* details, the sanitization method improved classification accuracies by a small percentage. The apparent reason for this is that the details that are representative of nonsensitive attributes and those that are representative of our sensitive attributes are very disjoint. Recall from Table 18.1 that the group *legalize same sex marriage* is highly indicative that a member is liberal. However, this does not translate to any of the tested details. Instead, groups like "1 pwn j00 n h410" are indicative of video game players, "I'm taking up money to buy SEC refs glasses" is indicative of sports fans, etc. It should be noted, however, that the attribute "favorite book = the bible" was removed from this test set, as it is highly indicative of one being a conservative.

18.7   SUMMARY AND DIRECTIONS

We addressed various issues related to private information leakage in social networks. For unmodified social network graphs, we show that using details alone, one can predict class values more accurately than using friendship links alone. We further show that using friendship links and details together gives better predictability than details alone. In addition, we explored the effect of removing details and links in preventing sensitive information leakage. In the process, we discovered situations in which collective inferencing does not improve on using a simple local classification method to identify nodes. When we combined the results from the collective inference implications with the individual results, we began to see that removing details and friendship links together is the best way to reduce classifier accuracy. This is probably infeasible in maintaining the use of social networks. However, we also showed that by removing only details, we greatly reduce the accuracy of local classifiers, which gives us the maximum accuracy that we were able to achieve through any combination of classifiers.

Furthermore, effort should be given to converting this to a method by which a social network provider can protect against multiple attribute leakage, rather than a single attribute. We also assumed full use of the graph information when deciding which details to hide. Useful research could be done on how individuals with limited access to the network could pick which details to hide. Similarly, future work could be conducted in identifying key nodes of the graph structure to see if removing or altering these nodes can decrease information leakage.

REFERENCES

Bird, C., Gourley, A., Devanbu, P., Gertz, M., and Swaminathan, A. Mining email social networks. In: MSR 06: *Proceedings of the 2006 International Workshop on Mining Software Repositories*, pp. 137–143. ACM, New York, 2006.

Brickley, D. and Miller, L. FOAF vocabulary specification 0.91. *RDF Vocabulary Specification*. Available at http://xmlns.com/foaf/0.1, 2007.

Lindamood, J., Heatherly, R., Kantarcioglu, M., and Thuraisingham, B. Inferring private information using social network data. In: *WWW Poster*, ACM, New York, 2009.

Macskassy, S.A. and Provost, F. Classification in networked data: A toolkit and a univariate case study. *Journal of Machine Learning Research* 8: 935–983, 2007.

CONCLUSION TO SECTION IV

In Section IV, we discussed the privacy violations that can result from social media analytics. That is, an adversary can infer highly private attributes of an individual from the public data he posts. Once we know that a social network is vulnerable to such inference attacks, then we can explore ways to handle such a problem.

Chapter 14 began with a discussion of one of the early full-scale analyses of social networks with a focus on privacy. We provided several major insights that contributed to the overall concept. We showed that based on simple, preexisting relational classifiers, we are able to use specific information about link types that had previously been ignored and then utilize it to increase our ability to determine hidden information. Chapter 15 presented, for ease of comparison, a summary of all of our experiments. We believe that it shows that our enhancements to the traditional relational Bayes classifier (rBC), which we call link-type rBC and weighted link-type rBC, are both successful extensions to the well-researched area of classification in social networks. We showed how our extensions have improved on the implementation of the traditional rBC on our dataset, and how the overall accuracy compares to similar experiments done on a similar dataset in other research work. In Chapter 16, we showed that by intelligently choosing *important* nodes in a subgraph, one is able to increase classification accuracy on real-world social network data. We presented a method of selecting nodes by using weighted graph metrics and a programmatically determinable threshold parameter. Furthermore, we showed that our τ threshold is a useful tool for determining the general increase in graph size versus a desired amount of classification accuracy, and that it may be possible to determine a beneficial value of τ through calculation of the chosen degree metric. In Chapter 17, we discussed that information gain-based partitioning methods may be used to efficiently divide and then classify the data in a social network. In Chapter 18, we addressed various issues related to private information leakage in social networks. For unmodified social network graphs, we showed that using details alone, one can predict class values more accurately than using friendship links alone. We further showed that using friendship links and details together gives better predictability than using details alone. In addition, we explored the effect of removing details and links in preventing sensitive information leakage. In the process, we discovered situations in which collective inferencing does not improve on using a simple local classification method to identify nodes.

Section V

Access Control and Inference for Social Networks

INTRODUCTION TO SECTION V

Now we are ready to discuss the heart of security for social networks, and that is access and inference control. We need to develop access control models suitable for such networks. Furthermore, it may be possible for an adversary to infer unauthorized information from the legitimate data posed by members of the networks. Such topics will be discussed in Section V.

Section V consists of four chapters: Chapters 19 through 22. In Chapter 19, we will describe the design of an extensible fine-grained online social network access control model based on semantic web tools. In addition, we will discuss authorization, administration, and filtering policies that are modeled using Web Ontology Language (OWL) and Semantic Web Rule Language (SWRL). The architecture of a framework in support of this model will also be presented. In Chapter 20, we will describe the implementation of an extensible fine-grained online social network access control model based on semantic web tools. In particular, we will discuss the implementation of the authorization, administration, and filtering policies that are modeled using OWL and SWRL. In Chapter 21, we will first describe the design of an inference controller that operates over a semantic web-based provenance graph and protects important provenance information from unauthorized users, and then determine how our techniques could be applied for social networks represented as Resource Description Framework graphs. In Chapter 22, we will describe the implementation of the inference controller for data provenance. The inference controller is built using a modular approach; therefore, it is very flexible in that most of the modules can be extended or replaced by another application module.

19 Access Control for Social Networks

19.1 INTRODUCTION

In the chapters in Section IV, we have shown methods of using data within the social network to improve local and relational classification methods. While the fields of epidemiology and counterterrorism are generally agreed to be important areas for these tasks, a major emergent field is using these data in marketing by partnering with social network providers. This usage has prompted privacy concerns with many users of these social networks. Here, we provide a framework for giving users far greater control over access to their information within the social network. By utilizing semantic web technologies, we are able to propose very granular controls for managing everything from user photos to who is able to send messages or videos to underage children.

Online social networks (OSNs) are platforms that allow people to publish details about themselves and to connect to other members of the network through links. Recently, the popularity of OSNs is increasing significantly. For example, Facebook now claims to have more than a hundred million active users.* The existence of OSNs that include person-specific information creates both interesting opportunities and challenges. For example, social network data could be used for marketing products to the right customers. At the same time, security and privacy concerns can prevent such efforts in practice. Improving the OSN access control systems appears as the first step toward addressing the existing security and privacy concerns related to OSNs. However, most current OSNs implement very basic access control systems, by simply making a user able to decide which personal information is accessible by other members by marking a given item as public, private, or accessible by their direct contacts. To give more flexibility, some OSNs enforce variants of these settings, but the principle is the same. For instance, besides the basic settings, Bebo (http://bebo.com), Facebook (http://facebook.com), and Multiply (http://multiply.com) support the option *selected friends*; Last.fm (http://last.fm) the option *neighbors* (i.e., the set of users having musical preferences and tastes similar to mine); Facebook, Friendster (http://friendster.com), and Orkut (http://www.orkut.com) the option *friends of friends*; Xing (http://xing.com) the options *contacts of my contacts* (second-degree contacts), and *third-* and *fourth-degree contacts*. It is important to note that all these approaches have the advantage of being easily implemented; however, they lack flexibility. In fact, the available protection settings do not allow users to easily specify their access control requirements, in that they are either too restrictive or too loose. Furthermore, existing solutions are platform specific and they are difficult to implement for various different OSNs.

To address some of these limitations, we propose an extensible, fine-grained OSN access control model based on semantic web technologies. Our main idea is to encode social network-related information by means of an ontology. In particular, we suggest to model the following five important aspects of OSNs using semantic web ontologies: (i) user's profiles, (ii) relationships among users (e.g., Bob is Alice's close friend), (iii) resources (e.g., online photo albums), (iv) relationships between users and resources (e.g., Bob is the owner of the photo album), and (v) actions (e.g., post a message on someone's wall). By constructing such an ontology, we model the Social Network Knowledge Base (SNKB). The main advantage of using an ontology for modeling OSN data is that relationships among many different social network concepts can be naturally represented using Web Ontology Language (OWL). Furthermore, by using reasoning, many inferences about such

---

* http://www.facebook.com/press/info.php?statistics.

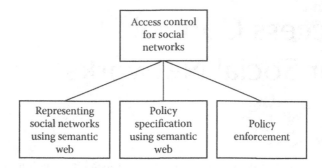

FIGURE 19.1   Access control for social networks.

relationships could be done automatically. Our access control enforcement mechanism is then implemented by exploiting this knowledge. In particular, the idea is to define security policies as rules (see Section 19.4), whose antecedents state conditions on SNKB and consequents specify the authorized actions. In particular, we propose to encode the authorizations implied by security policies by means of an ontology, obtaining the Security Authorization Knowledge Base (SAKB). Thus, security policies have to be translated as rules whose antecedents and consequents are expressed in the ontology. To achieve this goal, we use the Semantic Web Rule Language (SWRL) (Horrocks et al., 2004). As a consequence, the access control policies can be enforced by simply querying the authorizations, that is, the SAKB. The query can be easily directly implemented by the ontology reasoner by means of instance checking operations, or can be performed by a SPARQL query, if the ontology is serialized in Resource Description Framework (RDF). In this chapter, we focus on how to model such a fine-grained social network access control system using semantic web technologies. We also assume that a centralized reference monitor hosted by the social network manager will enforce the required policies. Since our proposed approach depends on extensible ontologies, it could be easily adapted to various OSNs by modifying the ontologies in our SNKB. Furthermore, as we will discuss in detail later in the chapter, semantic web tools allow us to define more fine-grained access control policies than the ones provided by current OSNs.

The chapter is organized as follows. In Section 19.2, we provide a brief discussion of current security and privacy research related to OSNs. In Section 19.3, we discuss how to model social networks using semantic web technologies. In Section 19.4, we introduce a high-level overview of the security policies we support in our framework. In addition to access control policies, we state filtering policies that allow a user (or one of the user's supervisors) to customize the content the user accesses. We also introduce administrator (admin) policies, stating who is authorized to specify access control and filtering policies. In Section 19.5, we introduce the authorization ontology and the SWRL rule encoding of security policies. In Section 19.6, we discuss how security policies could be enforced. Finally, we conclude the chapter in Section 19.7. Figure 19.1 illustrates the concepts of this chapter. Note that our system architecture and the implementation are discussed in Chapter 20.

19.2   RELATED WORK

Past research on OSN security has mainly focused on privacy-preserving techniques to allow statistical analysis on social network data without compromising OSN members' privacy (for discussions on this topic, see Carminati et al., 2008, 2009a,b, 2011). In contrast, access control for OSNs is a relatively new research area. As far as we are aware, the only other proposals of an access control mechanism for OSNs are the works of Kruk et al. (2006), Ali et al. (2007), and Carminati et al. (2009b). The D-FOAF system (Kruk et al., 2006) is primarily a friend of a friend (FOAF) ontology-based distributed identity management system for social networks, where access rights and trust delegation management are provided as additional services. In D-FOAF, relationships are associated with a trust level, which denotes the level of *friendship* existing between the users participating in a given relationship. Although Kruk et al. (2006) discuss only generic relationships, corresponding to the ones modeled by the foaf:knows RDF property in the FOAF vocabulary (Brickley and Miller, 2007), another D-FOAF-related paper (Choi et al., 2006) also considers the case of multiple relationship types. As far as access rights are concerned, they denote authorized users in terms of the minimum trust level and maximum length of the paths connecting the requester to the resource owner. Ali et al. (2007) adopted a multilevel security approach where trust is the only parameter used to determine the security level of both users and resources. In the study by Carminati et al. (2009a), a semidecentralized discretionary access control model and a related enforcement mechanism for controlled sharing of information in OSNs is presented. The model allows the specification of access rules for online resources, where authorized users are denoted in terms of the relationship type, depth, and trust level existing between nodes in the network.

Compared with existing approaches, we use semantic web technologies to represent much richer forms of relationships among users, resources, and actions. For example, we are able to represent access control rules that leverage relationship hierarchies, and by using OWL reasoning tools, we can infer that a *close friend* is also a *friend* and anything that is accessible by a friend could be also accessible by a close friend. In addition, our proposed solution could be easily adapted for very different OSNs by modifying the underlying SNKB. A further discussion on the differences between the proposed framework and the access control mechanism of Carminati et al. (2009b) is provided in Section 19.4.

Semantic web technologies have been recently used for developing various policy and access control languages for domains different from OSNs. For example, Tonti et al. (2003) compared various policy languages for distributed agent-based systems that define authorization and obligation policies. In the study by Finin et al. (2008), OWL was used to express role-based access control policies. Yagüe Valle et al. (2005) proposed a semantic access control model that separates the authorization and access control management responsibilities to provide solutions for distributed and dynamic systems with heterogeneous security requirements. None of these previous works deal with access control issues related to OSNs. Among the existing works, that of Elahi et al. (2008) is the most similar to our proposal. Compared with Elahi et al. (2008), we provide a much richer OWL ontology for modeling various aspects of OSNs. In addition, we propose authorization, administration, and filtering policies that depend on trust relationships among various users.

19.3 MODELING SOCIAL NETWORKS USING SEMANTIC WEB TECHNOLOGIES

19.3.1 TYPE OF RELATIONSHIPS

Recently, semantic web technologies such as RDF and OWL have been used for modeling social network data (Mika, 2007). Although our goal in this chapter is not to propose new semantic approaches for modeling OSN data, we would like to give a brief overview of current approaches for the sake of completeness, by also pointing out other social network information that could be modeled by semantic technologies. In our discussion, we will use Facebook as a running example. At the same time, we would like to stress that our discussion could easily be extended to other social networking frameworks.

In general, we identify five categories of social network data that could be modeled by semantic technologies. These are (i) personal information, (ii) personal relationships, (iii) social network resources, (iv) relationships between users and resources, and (v) actions that can be performed in a social network. In the following, we discuss how these social network data can be represented. In the ensuing subsections, we will discuss aspects of modeling of each of the above four relationships.

19.3.2 Modeling Personal Information

Some of the personal information provided in OSNs such as Facebook can be modeled by using the FOAF ontology (Brickley and Miller, 2007). FOAF is an OWL-based format for representing personal information and an individual's social network. FOAF provides various classes and properties to describe social network data such as basic personal information, online account, projects, groups, documents, and images. However, these basic mechanisms are not enough to capture all the available information. For example, there is no FOAF construct to capture the meaning for *lookingFor* (e.g., John Smith is looking for friendship). Thanks to the extensibility of the RDF/OWL language, this is easily solvable. For example, consider the following case where we capture the information related to an individual with Facebook profile ID 999999 by using a new Facebook ontology written in the RDF/OWL language.* In this example, we assume that *fb* ontology has a property name *lookingFor* to capture the required information.

```
@prefix rdf: <http://www.w3.org/1999/02/22-rdf-syntax-ns>
@prefix foaf: <http://xmlns.com/foaf/0.1/>
@prefix fb: <http://example.org/facebook>
<http://www.facebook.com/profile.php?id = 999999999>
foaf:name "John Smith"
<http://www.facebook.com/profile.php?id = 999999999>
fb:lookingFor "Friendship"
```

As the example suggests, existing ontologies such as FOAF could be easily extended to capture personal information available in OSNs.

19.3.3 Modeling Personal Relationships

Currently, OSNs do not support fine-grained definitions of relationships. For instance, Facebook allows you to specify whether you attended school or work with a friend, but offers no way to express what that truly means, that is, the strength of the relationship. It is this fine-grained structure that we wish to capture. Mika (2007) proposed a reification-based model for capturing relationship strength. Instead, to comply with W3C specifications (World Wide Web Consortium, 1999), we adopt the use of the n-ary relation pattern rather than use simple statement reification, which is a violation of the specification (World Wide Web Consortium, 2006). If we were to violate the specification, then relationships would be modeled using a series of four RDF statements to create an identifier for the relationship. Unfortunately, as a result of that, the SWRL would be unable to understand these relationships. We believe that using a specification-recommended pattern and retaining the ability to use SWRL to do inference on relationships is the best solution.

For the reasons stated above, we choose to model personal relationships using n-ary relation pattern. To comply with n-ary relation specification (World Wide Web Consortium, 2006), we define a *FriendshipRelation* class that has subclasses that denote a general strength of friendship. The root *FriendshipRelation* class implies an unspecific friendship, while the three subclasses, *Family*, *CloseFriend*, and *DistantFriend*, give an indicator of the closeness between people. The *CloseFriend* subclass has a further extension: *BestFriend*.

This basic structure allows us to easily mimic the existing structure of Facebook relationship types. However, as mentioned previously, these relationship types have no predefined meanings. To begin to quantify the meaning of relationship assignments, each instance of *FriendshipRelation* has a data property *TrustValue*. This represents the level of trust that the initiator has with the friend.

As an example, suppose that an individual (e.g., John Smith) defines a relationship with a colleague (e.g., Jane Doe). This creates an instance of the *FriendshipRelation* class with the

---

* We use Turtle notation for representing OWL.

TrustValue data property, which represents the level of trust between the initiator and his friend. The instance also has an object property that links it to the instance of the friend. This instance of the *FriendshipRelation* class is then tied back to John Smith through the use of the *Friendship* object property.

It is important to note that any (unidirectional) relationship in the social network is a single instance of the *FriendshipRelation* class. Thus, to model the standard bidirectional nature of social network relations, we need two instances of this class. However, the simple logical inference that if B is a friend of A, then A is a friend of B cannot be implemented by SWRL, in that this would imply to create a new instance of the Friendship class. Unfortunately, this is outside the realm of SWRL's capability. Thus, this must be taken care of outside of the SWRL framework by an external application. It is also important to note that the *TrustValue* property of relationships is a value that is computed automatically outside the OWL/SWRL component of the social network. This value is used to do various inference tasks further in the network. At the most basic level, where the *TrustValue* is a static number based on the friendship type, this is a trivial component. We assume that there will be a more complicated formula used in calculating the *TrustValue* that may be beyond the bounds of the built-in mathematical operators of SWRL.

We experience a similar difficulty with indirect relationships. To define an inferred relationship, we would once again need to create a new instance of *FriendshipRelation*. We can, however, create these indirect relationships similar to how we maintain symmetry of relationships, detailed above. The only difference in the indirect relationship is that instead of creating an instance of the class *FriendshipRelation*, we create an instance of a separate class, *InferredRelation*, which has no detailed subclasses yet is otherwise identical to the *FriendshipRelation* base class.

19.3.4 MODELING RESOURCES

A typical OSN provides some resources, such as *albums* or *walls*, to share information among individuals. Clearly, RDF/OWL could be used to capture the fact that albums are composed of pictures, and each picture may have multiple people in it. In our framework, we model resources as a class, beginning with a generic *Resource* class. As subclasses to this, we can have, for example, *PhotoAlbum*, *Photo*, and *Message*. Each of these has specific, unique properties and relationships. For instance, *PhotoAlbum* has a name and a description as data properties, and has an object property called *containsPhoto* that links it to instances of *Photo*. These have a name, a caption, and a path to the stored location of the file. Messages have a sender, a receiver, a subject, a message, and a time stamp. We can also create a subclass of messages called *WallMessage*, which is similar to messages in that it has the same data properties but it has additional restrictions such as that a *WallMessage* may only be sent to a single individual.

19.3.5 MODELING USER/RESOURCE RELATIONSHIPS

Current applications such as Facebook assume that the only relationship between users and resources is ownership. However, from an access control point of view, this is not enough. Let us consider, for example, a photograph that contains both John Smith and Jane Doe. Jane took the picture and posted it on the social network. Traditionally, Jane would be the sole admin of that resource. Since the photo contains the image of John (we say that John is *tagged* in the photo), in our model John may have some determination as to which individuals can see the photo.

To model something like a photo album, we can use two classes. The first is a simple *Photo* class that simply has an optional name and caption of the photo, and a required path to the location of the file. A photo is then linked to each person that is listed as being in the photo. A *PhotoAlbum* has a name and a description. *PhotoAlbum* and *Photo* are linked using the *containsPhoto* relationship. The individual owner—the person who uploaded the photos—is indicated by the *ownsAlbum* relationship. Similarly, we can represent other relationships between users and resources.

19.3.6 MODELING ACTIONS

In a social network, actions are the basis of user participation. According to the proposed representation, an action is defined as an object property that relates users, resources, and actions. Moreover, we model hierarchies for actions by means of subproperty. Take, for instance, three generic actions: *Read*, *Write*, and *Delete*. We define a hierarchy in which *Delete* is a subtype of *Write*, which is, itself, a subtype of *Read*. In a nonhierarchical model, if John Smith was able to read, write, and delete a photo, then we would need three authorizations to represent this property. However, as we have defined the hierarchy, with only the authorizations of <"John Smith", Delete, Photo1>, John Smith has all three properties allowed.

We can also extend traditional access restrictions to take advantage of social networking extensions. For instance, the action *Post* can be defined as a subtype of *Write*. So, let us say that we define the actions *Write* to mean that an individual can send a private message to another individual, and that the action *Post* means that an individual can post a message to another's wall so that any of their friends can see it. Then, allowing a user the *Post* action would allow them to see the friend's wall, send them a private message, and write on their wall, but he or she could not delete anything.

19.4 SECURITY POLICIES FOR OSNs

19.4.1 RUNNING EXAMPLE

In the remainder of this chapter, we will use the small network shown in Figure 19.2 to illustrate our access control mechanism. Our running example has four individuals: Alice, Bob, Charlie, and David. Alice, Bob, and Charlie form a clique with different strengths of friendship connecting them. David is a friend only of Bob via the default Friendship type. There is also a *PhotoAlbum* that was uploaded by Alice that contains a single photo that is a picture of Charlie.

As evidenced by recent work on social network security, protecting resources in social networks requires us to revise traditional access control models and mechanisms. However, the approaches proposed thus far have focused only on access control policies, that is, on the problem of regulating the access to OSN resources. We think that this is not enough, in that the complexity of the social network scenario requires the definition of further security policies, besides standard access control policies. In this section, we outline the security policies our framework supports.

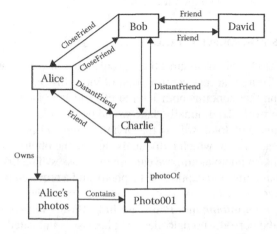

FIGURE 19.2 Portion of an OSN.

19.4.2 Access Control Policies

The framework supports access control policies to regulate how resources can be accessed by OSN participants. In particular, the supported access control policies are defined on the basis of our previous work (Carminati et al., 2009b). Here, authorized users are denoted in terms of the type, depth, and trust level of the relationships existing between nodes in the network. For instance, an access control policy can state that the only OSN participants authorized to access a given resource are those with a direct or indirect friendship relationship with the resource owner, provided that this relationship has a given trust value. However, the access control policies supported by the proposed framework have some notable improvements with regard to those presented by Carminati et al. (2009b). These improvements are mainly due to the fact that our access control policies are defined according to the SNKB described in Section 19.3. This means that the object, subject, and privilege of an access control policy are defined exploiting the semantic modeling of resources, users, and actions. In particular, as will be explained in Section 19.5, access control policies are defined as rules over ontologies representing the concepts introduced in Section 19.3. Thus, rather than access control policies specified over each single participant and resource of an OSN, we are able to specify access control policies directly on the OSN semantic concepts. Indeed, it is possible to specify a generic access control policy stating that the photos can be accessed only by friends, by simply specifying the *Photo* class as a protected object. As such, the access control policy will be applied to all instances of the *Photo* class, that is, to all photos, thus greatly simplifying policy administration. Specifying access control policies over semantic concepts has another benefit in that it is possible to exploit the hierarchy defined over the concepts to automatically propagate access control policies. For example, with respect to resources, if *Photo* has been defined with some subclasses, say *PrivatePhoto* and *HolidaysPhoto*, the previous access control policy can be automatically applied to all the instances belonging to any subclass of *Photo*. Access control policies can be also propagated along other dimensions, that is, according to hierarchies specified in the ontologies of other OSN concepts (e.g., ontologies for relationship types and actions). For example, when the supported relationship ontology defines a hierarchy for the friendship relationship, the previous access control policy is propagated to all OSN participants with which the resource owner has any kind of friendship relationship. A similar propagation arises if the action ontology defines a hierarchy of actions. Note that also in the study by Carminati et al. (2009b), authorized subjects were defined in terms of user relationships rather than by listing specific instances (i.e., person IDs). However, in that work, policy propagation was not possible since no hierarchies were defined over resources, relationships, and actions. Moreover, the semantic modeling we propose in this chapter enables us to specify authorized users not only in terms of the relationships they should have with the resource owner (as in Carminati et al., 2009b), but also in terms of the relationships they should have with the resource. Thus, for example, it is possible to specify an access control policy stating that all OSN participants that are tagged in a photo are authorized to access that photo. The only way to specify this access control policy in the work by Carminati et al. (2009b), as well as in all the other existing models for OSNs, is to explicitly specify a different access control policy for each OSN participant tagged in the photo.

19.4.3 Filtering Policies

In an OSN, users can publish information of very heterogeneous content, ranging from family photos to adult-oriented contents. In this sense, the access control issues arising in OSNs are similar to those we have in the web, where the availability of inappropriate information could be harmful for some users (e.g., young people). To protect users from inappropriate or unwanted contents, we introduce *filtering policies*, by which it is possible to specify which data has to be filtered out when a given user browses the social network pages. By means of a filtering policy, it is, for example, possible to state that from OSN pages fetched by user Alice, all videos that have not been published by

Alice's direct friends have to be removed. Similar to access control policies, filtering policies are defined as rules over ontologies representing the concepts introduced in Section 19.3 (see Section 19.5). This implies that policy propagation is possible also in case of filtering policies. Another relevant aspect of filtering policies is related to the user that specifies the policy (i.e., the grantor). Indeed, in our framework, a filtering policy can be specified in two different ways. According to the first one, a filtering policy is specified by a user to state which information he or she prefers not to access, that is, which data has to be filtered out from OSN pages fetched by the user. Thus, in this case, the grantor and the user to whom the policy applies, that is, the target user, are the same. These policies state user preferences with regard to the contents one wants to access and for that reason are called *filtering preferences*. However, we also support the specification of filtering policies where the target user and the grantor are different. This kind of filtering policies makes the grantor able to specify how the social network pages fetched by target users have to be filtered. By means of these filtering policies, a grantor can *supervise* the content a target user can access. In this case, we refer to the filtering policy as *supervised filtering policy*. This represents an extremely useful feature in open environments like OSNs. For example, parents can specify a supervised filtering policy stating that their children do not have to access those videos published by users who are not trusted by the parents themselves. As it will be made clearer later on, semantic technologies greatly facilitate the specification of this kind of policies.

It is worth noting that both filtering preferences and supervised filtering policies cannot be enforced by simply supporting negative access control policies, that is, policies avoiding access to resources. This is because access control policies and filtering policies have totally different semantics. Indeed, an access control policy is specified by the resource owner to state who is authorized or denied to access his or her resources. Rather, a filtering policy is specified by a supervisor for a target user or by the target users themselves, to specify how resources have to be filtered out when the target user fetches an OSN page. Note that, according to the proposed semantics, this filtering takes place even when the target user is authorized to access the resource; that is, even if the target user satisfies the access control policies specified by the resource owner.

19.4.4 ADMIN POLICIES

Introducing access control and filtering policies in a multiuser environment like OSNs requires determining who is authorized to specify policies, and for which target users and objects. To address this issue, we introduce *admin policies* that enable the security administrator (SA) of the social network to state who is authorized to specify access control and filtering policies. Admin policies have to be flexible enough to model some obvious admin strategies that are common to traditional scenarios (e.g., the resource owner is authorized to specify access control policies for his or her resources) as well as more complex strategies, according to the security and privacy guidelines adopted by the OSN. For instance, the SA could specify an admin policy stating that users tagged in a given resource are authorized to specify access control policies for that resource. Note that, as previously pointed out, the ontology modeling the relationships between users and resources described in Section 19.3 is extremely useful in the specification of such admin policies. Other kinds of admin policies are those related to filtering policies. For instance, by means of an admin policy, an SA could authorize parents to define supervised filtering policies for their young children. This admin policy can be defined by stating that if a user U1 has a relationship of type ParentOf with a user U2, who has an age of less than 16 years (i.e., with the property age less than 16 years), then U1 can state supervised filtering policies where the target user is U1. The SA could further refine this admin policy to specify that the parents can state supervised filtering policies for their young children only for video resources. This would modify the previous admin policy by limiting the scope of the supervised filtering policy the parents are authorized to specify.

19.5   SECURITY POLICY SPECIFICATION

19.5.1   POLICY LANGUAGE

A policy language defines security policies according to three main components: a *subject speci-fication* aiming to specify the entity to which a security policy applies (e.g., users, processes), an *object specification* to identify the resources to which the policy refers to (e.g., files, hardware resources, or relational tables), and an *action specification* specifying the action (e.g., read, write execute, or admin) that subjects can exercise on objects. Moreover, to make easier the task of policy evaluation, policies are enforced through a set of *authorizations*, stating for each subject the rights he or she has on the protected resources. We encode security policies by means of rules. In general, a rule consists of two formulae and an implication operator, with the obvious meaning that if the first formula, called the antecedent, holds then the second formula, called the consequent, must also hold. Thus, we encode each security policy as a *security rule*, that is, a rule whose antecedent represents the conditions stated in the policy subject and object specifications, and the consequent represents the entailed authorizations. Note that since the framework supports different types of security policies, the security rules could entail different types of authorizations. In particular, if the antecedent of a security rule encodes an access control or admin policy, the consequent denotes the entailed access control or admin authorizations. In contrast, if the rule's antecedent encodes a filtering policy (either a filtering preference or a supervised filtering policy), the consequent entails *prohibitions* rather than authorizations, since this policy limits access to resources.

We adopt SWRL to encode security rules. SWRL has been introduced to extend the axioms provided by OWL to also support rules. In SWRL, the antecedent, called the body, and the con-sequent, called the head, are defined in terms of OWL classes, properties, and individuals. More precisely, they are modeled as positive conjunctions of *atoms*. Atoms can be of the following forms: (i) $C(x)$, where C is an OWL description or data range; (ii) $P(x,y)$, where P is an OWL property and x and y could be variables, OWL individuals, or OWL data values; (iii) sameAs(x,y); (iv) differentFrom(x,y); and (v) builtIn$(r,x, ...)$, where r is a built-in predicate that takes one or more arguments and evaluates to true if the arguments satisfy the predicate. More precisely, an atom $C(x)$ holds if x is an instance of the class description or data range C; an atom $P(x,y)$ holds if x is related to y by property P; an atom sameAs(x,y) holds if x is interpreted as the same object as y; an atom differentFrom(x,y) holds if x and y are interpreted as different objects; and builtIn$(r,x, ...)$ holds if the built-in relation r holds on the interpretations of the arguments.

Exploiting SWRL to specify security rules implies that authorizations and prohibitions must be represented in some ontology, thus to be encoded as an SWRL head. For this reason, before present-ing the encoding of a security policy, we first introduce an ontology to model authorizations and prohibitions. We refer to the knowledge base derived by this ontology as SAKB.

19.5.2   AUTHORIZATIONS AND PROHIBITIONS

Since the framework supports three different types of security policies, it has to manage three different types of authorizations, namely access control authorizations, admin authorizations, and prohibitions. In the following, we introduce the proposed ontology for their representations. However, it is relevant to notice that this ontology is strictly related to the ontologies supported by the OSN (see Section 19.3), in that it defines authorizations/prohibitions on the basis of the supported actions and resources. As such, the following does not intend to be the standard ontology for SAKBs; rather, it is the one that we adopt in our framework, based on the semantic modeling presented in Section 19.3. Thus, the discus-sion presented here must be read as a guideline for the definition of an ontology of an SAKB.

19.5.2.1   Access Control Authorizations

The first kinds of authorizations are those entailed by access control policies. In general, an access control authorization can be modeled as a triple (u,p,o) stating that subject u has the right to execute privilege *p* on object *o*. Thus, in some way, an access control authorization represents a relationship *p* between *u* and *o*, meaning that *u* can exercise *p* on *o*. Therefore, we decide to encode an access control authorization for privilege *p* as an instance of an OWL object property, named *p*, defined between the authorized person and the authorized resource. To model all possible access control authorizations, we have to introduce a different object property for each action supported in the OSN (see Section 19.3). It is interesting to note that by properly defining the object property encoding access control authorizations, we can automatically propagate the authorizations on the basis of the classification defined among actions.

Let us consider, for example, the action *Post* and assume it has been defined as subclass of action *Write*. In terms of access control, if the post privilege is authorized to a user, then the write privilege is also authorized. In the proposed framework, the access control authorizations can be automatically inferred provided that object property *Post* has been defined as subproperty of the object property *Write*. We do note that this hierarchy may be different than in traditional access control systems. When we use SWRL, anything that is defined for a superclass will also be defined for its subclasses. However, the reverse is not true. So, when we allow an individual to *Write*, it does not automatically confer the *Post* authority.

19.5.2.2 Prohibitions

Filtering policies state whether the target user is not authorized to access a certain object, in the case of supervised filtering policies, or the target user prefers not to access, in the case of filtering preferences. Similarly to access control authorizations, a prohibition specifies a relationship between a user and the resource the user is not authorized or prefers not to access. For this reason, prohibitions can also be expressed as an object property between *Person* and *Resource* classes. More precisely, a prohibition for the Read privilege is defined as the OWL object property *PRead*. An instance of this object property <John, URI1>:*PRead* states that Bob has not to read resource URI1. Similarly, to access control authorizations, it is possible to specify how prohibitions have to be propagated by simply defining subproperty.

Let us again consider the three basic actions *Read*, *Write*, and *Delete*, and their prohibited versions *PRead*, *PWrite*, and *PDelete*. We again wish to form a hierarchy of actions in a logical order. That is, if an individual is prohibited from *reading* a resource, then this person should also be prohibited from *writing* and *deleting* that resource. To do this, we can simply define *PRead* to be a subtype of *PWrite*, which is a subtype of *PDelete*.

19.5.2.3 Admin Authorizations

Admin authorizations are those authorizations implied by admin policies, which, we recall, have the aim to authorize users to specify access control or filtering policies. Therefore, admin policies entail two types of authorizations: authorizations to specify access control policies, which we simply refer to as *admin authorizations*, and authorizations to specify filtering policies, that is, *admin prohibitions*. In general, an admin authorization can be represented as a triple (u,p,o) stating that user *u* is authorized to specify access control policies for privilege *p* on object *o*. Thus, similarly to authorizations and prohibitions, admin authorizations can also be expressed as an object property between *Person* and *Resource* classes. According to this modeling, we can define the Object property *AdminRead*, whose instances state that a given user is authorized to express access control policies granting the read privilege on a given object. Consider the instance <Bob,URI1>:*AdminRead*, which states that Bob is authorized to specify access control policies granting the read privilege on the URI1 object.

Similarly, to access control authorizations, it is possible to specify how admin authorizations have to be propagated by simply defining subproperty. Let us declare the previously mentioned property *AdminRead* and further create the properties *AdminWrite* and *AdminAll*. We declare *AdminAll* to be a subproperty of both *AdminWrite* and *AdminRead*. Consider our running example where Alice owned a photo. Let us assume that this grants her the *AdminAll* authorization on the photo. If Alice attempts to allow Bob to Read the photo, an action that is restricted to individuals with the *AdminRead* property, then this is allowed via the *AdminAll* property.

In contrast, an admin prohibition can be represented as a tuple (s,t,o,p), which implies that user s (supervisor) is authorized to specify filtering policies for the privilege p applying to the target user t and to object o. Differently from previous authorizations, admin prohibitions cannot be represented as properties in that they do not represent a binary relationship. For that reason, we decide to model admin prohibitions as an OWL class *Prohibition*. This enables us to specify all the components of the prohibition as class properties. More precisely, given an admin prohibition (s,t,o,p), we can model the authorized supervisor to have an object property *Supervisor* between the *Prohibition* and *Person* classes. Similarly, the target user can be represented as an object property *TargetUser* between the *Prohibition* and *Person* classes, and the target object as an object property *TargetObject* between the *Prohibition* and the *Resource* classes. In contrast, the privilege over which the supervisor is authorized to state filtering policies is not represented as an object property. Indeed, to automatically propagate admin prohibitions, we prefer to specify the privilege directly as the class name. Thus, as an example, instances of the *ProhibitionRead* class state admin prohibitions authorizing the specification of filtering policies for the read privilege. By properly defining subclasses, it is possible to automatically infer new admin prohibitions.

Suppose we have a generic *Prohibition* class with the subclasses *PRead* and *PView*. We then create another subclass of each of these as *PAll*. Suppose we have two individuals, John and Jane, and John is Jane's father. In this scenario, John should be allowed to filter what videos his daughter is able to see. That is, we have a prohibition (John, Jane, Video, *PAll*). Now, for any video and any permission, John can disallow those that he wishes.

19.5.3 SECURITY RULES

The proposed framework translates each security policy as an SWRL security rule where the antecedent encodes the conditions specified in the policy (e.g., conditions denoting the subject and object specifications), whereas the consequent encodes the implied authorizations or prohibitions. In particular, since we model security rules as SWRL rules, the SWRL body states policy conditions over the SNKB (i.e., conditions on ontologies introduced in Section 19.3), whereas the SWRL head entails new instances of the SAKB (i.e., instances of the ontology introduced in Section 19.3). As a consequence, the specification of SWRL security rules is strictly bound to the ontologies supported by the OSN to model social network and SAKB. This implies that it is not possible to provide a formalization of generic SWRL rules since these can vary based on the considered ontologies. In contrast, in this section, we aim to present some meaningful examples of possible SWRL security rules defined on top of ontologies adopted in our framework.

We start by considering the admin policy stating that the owner of an object is authorized to specify access control policies for that object. The corresponding SWRL rule defined according to the ontologies presented in the previous sections is the following:

```
Owns(?grantor, ?targetObject) ⇒ AdminAll(?grantor, ?targetObject)
```

The evaluation of the above rule has the result of generating a different instance of the object property *AdminAll* for each pair of user and the corresponding owned resource. It is relevant to note that this authorization is propagated according to the ontology modeling the SAKB. Thus, since the framework exploits the one introduced in Section 19.5.1, the above authorization is propagated also to *AdminRead* and *AdminWrite*.

Another meaningful admin policy for a social network is the one stating that if a user is tagged in a photo, then that user is authorized to specify access control policies for the read privilege on that photo. This can be encoded by means of the following SWRL security rule:

```
Photo(?targetObject) ∧ photoOf(?grantor, ?targetObject)
⇒ AdminRead(?grantor,?targetObject)
```

TABLE 19.1

Examples of SWRL Security Rules

SWRL Rule

(1)   Video(?targetObject,) ∧ ParentOf(Bob,?controlled) ⇒
        PRead(?controlled,?targetObject)

(2)   Owner(Bob,?targetObject) ∧ Photo(?targetObject) ∧
        Friend(Bob,?targetSubject) ⇒ Read(?targetSubject,?targetObject)

(3)   Photo(?targetObject) ∧ photoOf(Alice,?targetObject) ∧
        Friend(Alice,?targetSubject) ⇒ Read(?targetSubject,?targetObject)

(4)   Photo(?targetObject) ∧ Owns(?owner, ?targetObject) ∧
        Friend(?owner, ?targetSubject1) ∧ Friend(?targetSubject1,
        ?targetSubject2) ⇒
        Read(?targetSubject2, ?targetObject)

The above rules are interesting examples stressing how in the proposed framework, it is possible to easily specify admin policies whose implementation in a nonsemantic-based access control mechanism would require complex policy management. Indeed, providing the OSN with ontologies modeling the relationships between users and resources (e.g., modeling ownership or tagging relationships) makes the SA able to specify admin policies by simply posing conditions on the type of the required relationship. In contrast, enforcing these admin policies in a traditional access control mechanism would require implementing complex policy management functionalities, in that it would be required to first determine all possible relationships between users and resources, then to specify admin authorizations for all of them. Rather, in the proposed framework, this task is performed by the reasoner.

Table 19.1 presents some examples of SWRL security rules. The first security rule encodes a filtering policy stating that Bob's children cannot access videos. Once this rule is evaluated, an instance of prohibition for each of Bob's children and video resource is created. In contrast, the second security rule corresponds to an access control policy stated by Bob to limit the read access to his photos only to his direct friend, whereas the third encodes an access control policy specifying that photos where Alice is tagged can be accessed by her direct friends. Finally, the fourth rule specifies that if a person has a photo, then friends of their friends (an indirect relationship) can view that photo.

19.6   SECURITY RULE ENFORCEMENT

19.6.1   OUR APPROACH

Our framework acts like a traditional access control mechanism, where a *reference monitor* evaluates a request by looking for an authorization granting or denying the request. Exploiting this principle in the proposed framework implies retrieving the authorizations/prohibitions by querying the SAKB ontology. Thus, for example, to verify whether a user *u* is authorized to specify access control policies for the read privilege on object *o*, it is necessary to verify if the instance *AdminRead(u,o)* is in the ontology, that is, to perform an instance checking. This implies that before any possible request evaluation, all the SWRL rules encoding security policies have to be evaluated to infer all access control/admin authorizations and all prohibitions. For this reason, before policy enforcement, it is required to execute a preliminary phase, called *policy refinement*. This phase aims to populate the SAKB with the inferred authorizations/prohibitions, by executing all the SWRL rules encoding security policies.

Once authorizations/prohibitions are inferred, security policy enforcement can be carried out. In particular, access control and filtering policies are evaluated upon the submission of an *access request*, whereas admin policies are evaluated when an *admin request* is submitted. In the following, we present both request evaluations by showing how the corresponding policies are enforced.

19.6.2 ADMIN REQUEST EVALUATION

An admin request consists of two pieces of information: the name of the *grantor*, that is, the user who has submitted the admin request, and the access control or filtering policy the grantor would like to specify, encoded as SWRL rule, that is, the *submitted SWRL*. The submitted SWRL has to be inserted in the system only if there exists an admin authorization in the SAKB for the grantor. For example, if the submitted rule requires to specify an access control policy for the read privilege on targetObject, then there must exist an instance of <grantor, targetObject>:*Read*. Note that information about the privilege and the targetObject can be retrieved directly from the submitted SWRL. Thus, in order to decide whether the request above can be authorized or not, a possible way is to query the SAKB to retrieve the corresponding admin authorization, if any. If there exists an instance, then the submitted SWRL can be evaluated; otherwise, the framework denies to the grantor the admin request. An alternative way is to rewrite the submitted SWRL by adding in its body also a condition to verify whether there exists an admin authorization in the SAKB authorizing the specification of the rule. The following example will clarify the underlying idea.

Let us assume that the system receives the following admin request: {Bob, SWRL$_1$}, where SWRL$_1$ is the following:

```
SWRL₁: Owns(Bob,?targetObject) ∧ Photo(?targetObject)
∧ Friend(Bob,?targetSubject) ⇒ Read(?targetSubject,?targetObject)
```

To determine the result of the admin request, the framework has to verify the existence of <Bob,targetObject>:*AdminRead* instance in the SAKB. This check can be incorporated in the body of SWRL$_1$ by simply modifying it as follows:

```
New_SWRL₁:AdminRead(Bob,?targetObject) ∧
Owns(Bob,?targetObject) ∧ Photo(?targetObject) ∧
Friend(Bob,?targetSubject)
⇒ Read(?targetSubject, ?targetObject)
```

Then, New_SWRL$_1$ is evaluated with the consequence that Read access control authorizations will be inserted in SAKB only if Bob is authorized to specify them by an admin policy.

In the case of an admin request submitting a filtering policy, to decide whether the grantor is authorized to specify that policy, a search is required in the *Prohibitions* class (i.e., the subclass corresponding to the action the filtering policy requires to prohibit) for an instance having the property *Grantor* equal to the grantor, and the properties *Controlled* and *TargetObject* equal to the controlled and *TargetObject* specified in the head of the submitted SWRL rule, respectively. Also in this case, we can adopt an approach based on SWRL rewriting.

Let us assume that the framework receives the following admin request: {Bob, SWRL$_2$}, where SWRL$_2$ is the following:

```
SWRL₂: Video(?targetObject) ∧ ParentOf(Bob,?controlled) ⇒
PRead(?controlled,?targetObject)
```

Then, the system can modify the submitted SWRL as

New_SWRL$_2$: PRead(?p) ∧ Grantor(?p,Bob) ∧ Controlled(?p,?controlled) ∧ TargetObject (?p,?targetObject) ∧ Video(?targetObject) ∧ ParentOf(Bob,?control-led) ⇒ PRead(?controlled,?targetObject) whose evaluation has the effect to insert instances of *PRead* property (i.e., read prohibitions) only if there exists an Admin Prohibition (Bob,*c*,*o*,Read), where *c* is Bob's children and *o* is a video resource. Note that this is valid also if the submitted SWRL explicitly specifies the name of the controlled user (e.g., ... ⇒ PRead(Alice,?targetObject)).

19.6.3 ACCESS REQUEST EVALUATION

In general, an access request can be modeled as a triple (u, p, URI), which means that a user u requests to execute the privilege p on the resource located at *URI*. To evaluate this request, the framework has to verify whether there exists an access control authorization granting p on *URI* to requester r. However, since the proposed system also supports filtering policies, the presence of such an authorization does not necessarily imply that r is authorized to access *URI* because there could be a prohibition denying access to the resource to the user. Thus, to evaluate whether an access request has to be granted or denied, it is necessary to perform two queries to the SAKB: the first to retrieve authorizations and the second to retrieve prohibitions. More precisely, if u requires the read privilege *Read*, the system has to query the instances of object property *Read* and *PRead*. In particular, both the queries look for instance <u,URI> (i.e.,<u,URI>:Read and <u,URI>:PRead). Then, access is granted if the first query returns an instance and the second returns the empty set. It is denied otherwise.

Consider again the examples in Sections 19.3 and 19.4 with the addition of a person named Susan. Susan is a friend of Jane and has posted a video that she allows to be seen by all of her friends. However, Jane's father prohibits her from viewing videos. When a request is made by Jane to see Susan's video, authorization and prohibition queries are performed. The authorization query returns a Read permission, but the prohibition query returns a PRead. This means that Jane will be unable to view the video.

19.7 SUMMARY AND DIRECTIONS

In this chapter, we have proposed an extensible fine-grained OSN access control model based on semantic web tools. In addition, we propose authorization, admin, and filtering policies that are modeled using OWL and SWRL. The architecture of a framework in support of this model has also been presented. The implementation of the framework is discussed in the next chapter.

We intend to extend this work toward several directions. A first direction arises from the fact that supporting flexible admin policies could bring the system to a scenario where several access control policies specified by distinct users can be applied to the same resource. Indeed, in our framework, a social network's resources could be related to different users according to the supported ontology. For example, a given photo could be connected to the owner, say Bob, as well as to all users tagged in that photo, say Alice and Carl. According to the semantics of admin policies, it could be the case that some of these tagged users are authorized to specify access control policies for that resource, say only Alice. For example, Alice could have specified that the photos in which she is tagged can be accessed only by her direct friends, whereas Bob could have specified that his photos have to be accessed by his direct friends and colleagues. To enforce access control, the framework has to decide how the specified access control policies have to be combined together. As such, a first important extension of the proposed framework will be the support of a variety of policy integration strategies. As a further important future work, we plan to implement our framework using the ideas discussed in Chapter 20, and test the efficiency of various ways of combining forward and backward chaining-based reasoning for different scenarios.

REFERENCES

Ali, B., Villegas, W., and Maheswaran, M. A trust based approach for protecting user data in social networks. In: *2007 Conference of the Center for Advanced Studies on Collaborative Research (CASCON'07)*, pp. 288–293. Richmond Hill, Ontario, Canada, 2007.

Brickley, D. and Miller, L. FOAF vocabulary specification 0.91. In: *RDF Vocabulary Specification*, November 2007. Available at http://xmlns.com/foaf/0.1, 2007.

Carminati, B., Ferrari, E., and Perego, A. *Security and Privacy in Social Networks*, vol. VII, *Encyclopedia of Information Science and Technology*, 2 Ed., pp. 3369–3376. IGI Publishing, Hershey, PA, 2008.

Carminati, B., Ferrari, E., Heatherly, R., Kantarcioglu, M., and Thuraisingham, B.M. A semantic web based framework for social network access control. In: Carminati, B. and Joshi, J., editors, *SACMAT*, pp. 177–186. ACM, New York, 2009a.

Carminati, B., Ferrari, E., and Perego, A. Enforcing access control in web-based social networks. *ACM Transactions on Information Systems Security* 13(1), 2009b.

Carminati, B., Ferrari, E., Heatherly, R., Kantarcioglu, M., and Thuraisingham, B. Semantic web-based social network access control. *Computers & Security*, 30, 108–115, 2011.

Choi, H.-C., Kruk, S.R., Grzonkowski, S., Stankiewicz, K., Davids, B., and Breslin, J. Trust models for community-aware identity management. *Identity, Reference and the Web Workshop* (IRW 2006), Edinburgh, Scotland, 2006.

Elahi, N., Chowdhury, M.M.R., and Noll, J. Semantic access control in web based communities. In: *The Third International Multi-Conference on Computing in the Global Information Technology, 2008. ICCGI'08*, pp. 131–136. Athens, Greece, 2008.

Finin, T.W., Joshi, A., Kagal, L., Niu, J., Sandhu, R.S., Winsborough, W.H., and Thuraisingham, B.M. R OWL BAC: Representing role based access control in OWL. In: Ray, I. and Li, N., editors, *SACMAT*, pp. 73–82. ACM, New York, 2008.

Horrocks, I., Patel-Schneider, P.F., Boley, H., Tabet, S., Grosof, B., and Dean, M. SWRL: A semantic web rule language combining OWL and RuleML. In: *W3C Member Submission, World Wide Web Consortium*. Available at: http://www.w3.org/Submission/SWRL, 2004.

Kruk, S.R., Grzonkowski, S., Gzella, A., Woroniecki, T., and Choi, H.-C. D-FOAF: Distributed identity management with access rights delegation. In: Mizoguchi, R., Shi, Z., and Giunchiglia, F., editors, *ASWC*, vol. 4185, *Lecture Notes in Computer Science*, pp. 140–154. Springer, Berlin, 2006.

Mika, P. *Social Networks and the Semantic Web*. Springer, London, 2007.

Tonti, G., Bradshaw, J.M., Jeffers, R., Montanari, R., Suri, N., and Uszok, A. Semantic web languages for policy representation and reasoning: A comparison of KAoS, Rei, and Ponder. In: Fensel, D., Sycara, K.P., and Mylopoulos, J., editors. *International Semantic Web Conference*, vol. 2870, *Lecture Notes in Computer Science*, pp. 419–437. Springer, Berlin, 2003.

World Wide Web Consortium. Status for resource description framework (RDF) model and syntax specification. Available at http://www.w3.org/1999/.status/PR-rdf-syntax-19990105/status, 1999.

World Wide Web Consortium. Defining n-ary relations on the semantic web. Available at http://www.w3.org /TR/swbp-n-aryRelations/, 2006.

Yagüe Valle, M., Gallardo, M.-d.-M., and Maña, A. Semantic access control model: A formal specification. In: *ESORICS: European Symposium on Research in Computer Security*. LNCS, Springer-Verlag, Berlin, 2005.

20 Implementation of an Access Control System for Social Networks

20.1 INTRODUCTION

In the previous chapter, we provided a framework for social network access control using semantic web technologies. Here, we show the results of an initial implementation of our framework on synthetic data. As stated in Chapter 19, we have designed an extensible, fine-grained online social network (OSN) access control model based on semantic web technologies. Our main idea is to encode social network-related information by means of an ontology. In particular, we suggest to model the following five important aspects of OSNs using semantic web ontologies: (i) user profiles, (ii) relationships among users (e.g., Bob is Alice's close friend), (iii) resources (e.g., online photo albums), (iv) relationships between users and resources (e.g., Bob is the owner of the photo album), and (v) actions (e.g., posting a message on someone's wall). By constructing such an ontology, we model the Social Network Knowledge Base (SNKB). Our access control enforcement mechanism is then implemented by exploiting this knowledge. In particular, the idea is to define security policies as rules, whose antecedents state conditions on SNKB and consequents specify the authorized actions. We assume that a centralized reference monitor hosted by the social network manager will enforce the required policies. Our architecture is extensible in that we can add modules to carry out functions such as inference control. Furthermore, we can also extend our policies to include information-sharing policies in addition to access control policies. These extensions will be discussed in Section VIII of this book.

The chapter is organized as follows. In Section 20.2, we introduce a high-level overview of the security policies we support in our framework. In addition to access control policies, we state filtering policies that allow a user (or one of the user's supervisors) to customize the content he or she accesses. We also introduce administration policies, stating who is authorized to specify access control and filtering policies. In Section 20.3, we discuss how security policies could be enforced. In Section 20.4, we describe our architecture, which we also refer to as our framework. In Section 20.5, we discuss the experiments we have carried out with our implementation of semantic web-based access control for social networks. Finally, we conclude the chapter in Section 20.6. Figure 20.1 illustrates the topics discussed in this chapter. Our research has been influenced by the work reported by Finin et al. (2008).

20.2 SECURITY IN ONLINE SOCIAL NETWORKS

For a detailed discussion of the use of semantic technologies in OSNs, please refer to our previous work (Carminati et al., 2009a). Here, we will constrain our discussions to those specific topics that influence our implementation of an access control mechanism for resources in an OSN.

In the recent past, Facebook has made significant changes to its method of defining the relationships between friends on the network. Previously, if we had two Facebook users who were friends, John and Jane for instance, either John or Jane could select one of the prechosen friendship types that Facebook allowed, where the other friend would be required to confirm or reject this label of their friendship. Following this, any friend of either John or Jane could see the definition that was

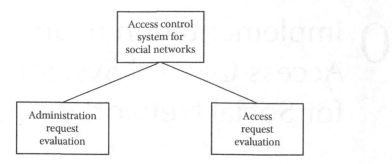

FIGURE 20.1   Access control system for social networks.

applied to this friendship. Now, however, instead of defining link types that are visible to others, each individual has the ability to create meaningful lists. Friends can then be added into as many lists as a user chooses. These lists can then be used to control visibility to status updates, wall posts, etc. However, there is no way to define a hierarchy of these lists. For instance, if one was to create a High School Classmates list and then a College Classmates list, there is no way to create a Classmates list without individually adding each individual person to that third list.

We represent a friendship using the n-ary relation pattern, as specified by the W3C (World Wide Web Consortium, 1999). This means that each friendship is an instance of a class, which we call *FriendshipRelation*. This allows us to maintain separate information about each friendship. Specifically, we maintain a *TrustValue* for each friendship. This allows us to determine a specific strength of a friendship, even when compared to those in the same class. Our implementation supports access control policies to regulate how resources can be accessed by members of an OSN. In particular, the supported access control policies are defined on the basis of our previous work (Carminati et al., 2009b). Here, authorized users are denoted in terms of the type or trust level of the relationships between nodes in the network. For instance, an access control policy can state that the only OSN participants authorized to access a given resource are those with a direct friendship relationship with the resource owner, as long as the relationship also has a certain trust level.

Note, however, that using semantic reasoning can give some improvements over the capabilities discussed in our previous work (Carminati et al., 2009b). This benefit comes from our ability to specify access control policies over semantic concepts in the OSN. For example, as a default, Facebook may specify that photos can only be viewed by direct friends. In the absence of policies defined by individual users, reasoning will default to this general policy. The design of our approach to proving security in OSNs is discussed in Chapter 19. The major aspects include filtering policies, security rule enforcement, administration policy evaluation, and the access request evaluation. In the next section, we will describe our implementation framework.

20.3   FRAMEWORK ARCHITECTURE

In our proposed framework, we plan to build several layers on top of the existing OSN application. We plan to implement our prototype using Java-based open source semantic web application development framework called JENA (http://jena.sourceforge.net/) since it offers an easy-to-use programmatic environment for implementing the ideas discussed in this chapter. Here, we describe each of these layers independently, as well as the motivation behind choosing specific technologies in our framework. While we use specific instances of Facebook as the overarching application utilizing the lower-level semantic layers, any social network application could be modified to use the design we describe here. Figure 20.2 describes our framework. The policies and data are stored as Resource Description Framework (RDF) triples. The reference monitor controls access to the data.

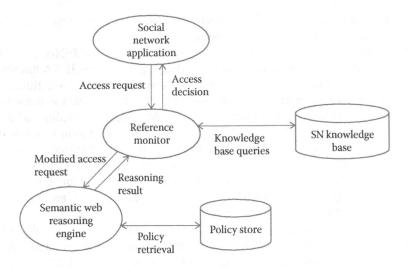

FIGURE 20.2 Framework for social network (SN) access control.

It will carry out functions such as query rewriting. Some key points in the framework are discussed in the ensuing paragraphs. Next, we will discuss the components of the framework.

RDF Data Store. We assume the use of a general RDF triple store to hold the underlying data. In this representation, all facts about an entity are recorded as a triple of the form <Subject, Predicate, Object>. So, suppose we have an individual named John Smith, who is assigned a unique identifier 999999; this would give us the tuple <999999, *foaf:Name*, "John Smith">.

We plan to use a similar format in a separate table to store a list of authorizations so that we do not have to re-infer them each time an authorization is requested. For the data storage system, we plan to use MySQL because of its availability and because of its ease of interface with JENA.

We note here that an RDF data store differs from a relational database in that there is no database method of ensuring that constraints are maintained on the ontology as a whole, such as making sure that a defined *Person* has a name. The database representation of this fact is no different from the nonessential statement that the person lives in Albuquerque. However, we plan to use Web Ontology Language Description Logic (OWL DL) statements to define these constraints, and then allow the RDF/OWL engine to enforce the constraints as described below.

Reasoner. Any reasoner that supports SWRL rules can be used to perform the inferences described in this chapter. However, we chose SweetRules (http://sweetrules.projects.semwebcentral .org/) because it interfaces with JENA and has a rule-based inference engine. This means that we can use both forward and backward chaining in order to improve the efficiency of reasoning for enforcing our access control policies. Forward chaining is an inference method where the engine will begin with the data provided and look at the established inference rules in an attempt to derive further information. This can be used when the system needs to infer permissions on a large scale, such as when a resource is added for the first time.

At this point, there will be a large one-time addition of authorizations to the allowed list of users. However, later, after other friends are added, checking to see if a user has access to a limited number of resources can be done through backward chaining. Basically, in backward chaining, we begin with the desired goal (e.g., to infer whether "John has permission to see the photo album A"), and check whether it is explicitly stated or whether it could be inferred by some other rules in a recursive fashion. Obviously, this will allow a result to be inferred about an individual (e.g., John) without rechecking all other individuals. Mika (2007) proposed a basic general social network, called Flink, based on a semantic data store using a similar framework to that we have proposed, but using several different specific semantic technologies. However, he specified that their implementation, using backward and forward chaining, is efficiently scalable to millions of tuples, which provides an evidence of the viability of our proposed scheme.

RDF/OWL Engine. For the RDF/OWL interface, we chose to use the JENA API. We use this to translate the data between the application and the underlying data store. JENA has several important features that were considered in its use. First, it is compatible with SweetRules. Secondly, it supports OWL DL reasoning, which we could use to verify that the data is consistent with the OWL restrictions on the ontology. The OWL restrictions are simple cardinality and domain/range constraints, such as every person has to have a name and must belong to at least one network. To enforce these constraints, we plan to have the application layer pass the statements to be entered about an individual until all have been collected. We then have JENA insert these statements into the database and then check the new model for consistency. If there are any constraints that have been violated, then we pass this information back to the social network application and have it gather the required information from the user.

In our system, we built several layers on top of a reduced OSN application. We considered the actions of a social network (messages, wall posts, viewing profiles, viewing images, etc.) and examined those that involved the most access requests. For example, if a user, John, was to go to Jane's profile, then in the best case, there is a single check (Are John and Jane friends of an appropriate level?) on permissions. However, when you consider an image, which can easily have a dozen people tagged in it and each of those individuals may specify their own additional constraints to the viewership of that image, then it is easy to see that this will be the more complicated example of permissions inference in a system. In effect, we built our system to test a consistent series of worst-case scenarios to test its ability to handle a testing load.

We implement our prototype using the Java-based open source semantic web application development framework called JENA (http://jena.sourceforge.net/), since it offers an easy-to-use programmatic environment for implementing the ideas discussed in this chapter, as well as generally being a framework that is supported by most semantic products currently available. While we use specific instances of Facebook as the overarching application utilizing the lower-level semantic layers, any social network application could potentially be modified to use the design we describe here. As discussed earlier, the major components of our system are the RDF data store, the Reasoner, and the RDF/OWL engine.

20.4 EXPERIMENTS

Data Generation. As we began our implementation, it was apparent we would need to be able to measure the performance of our implementation on large data sets. Because the size of Facebook (at the time we started the implementation) was approximately 300 million users, we established 350 million as the required number of nodes in our data set, to ensure that our implementation could scale to match the numbers Facebook would soon reach.* Unfortunately, there are no publicly available data sets of this size that we could use. Therefore, we generated our own data set.

That is, we created a data generator that generates n nodes. We began by creating a group of 50 nodes, and generated 50 edges that were distributed randomly across the 50 nodes in the graph. We then chose a random node, n_i, with at least one friend and performed Dijkstra's algorithm to determine if the subgraph was connected. If the subgraph was not connected, then there were j nodes that were not reachable from n_i. We then chose $0 < r_i \leq j$ to be a number of new edges to create. For each edge, we randomly chose a node from the connected subgraph containing n_i and chose a destination node in the disconnected portion of the subgraph. As long as there was a disconnected portion of the subgraph, we continued generating edges. By performing subgraph joins in

---

* It is important to note that at this time, Facebook reports that they have in excess of 450 million users (http://www.facebook.com/press/info.php?statics).

this manner, we were able to generate a social network-like graph while still maintaining randomness and not handpicking which edges would have links between them.

It is important to note at this point that our data store records each link twice. Even though the graph is undirected, there is a link type (used in inference) that is directed. For instance, while the generic *Friend* link type is bidirectional, the specific *BestFriend* link type is not necessarily bidirectional. To maintain this, we recorded each direction of the link with its associated link type. Once the initial subgraph was complete, we iterated through the nodes to assign each edge a link type. We established three generic link types: Friend, Family, and Coworker, and recorded them for each direction of the edge. That is, $(n_i, n_j) \in \mathcal{E}$, if assigned the Friend link type, would have generated the tuples $\{n_i, n_j,$ Friend$\}$, and $\{n_j, n_i,$ Friend$\}$.

We uniformly chose a generic type for each edge that a node is a member of. After this, we then assigned specific subtypes. For 10% of Friend generic link types, we assigned the specific (unidirectional) link type of BestFriend. That is, in the above example, if n_i declared n_j to be a BestFriend, then the tuple $\{n_i, n_j,$ Friend$\}$ would have become $\{n_i, n_j,$ BestFriend$\}$. Note that the second tuple would have remained unchanged at this time.

Next, we used a Pareto distribution over the number of defined Family Members to determine how many relationships would be defined as *ParentOf*. We use a Pareto distribution because while having one or two parents listed is what we may generally think of as reasonable for a child, in today's mixed families, it would not be outside the realm of the believable to have more parents listed for a child. It is also important to note that when a link was defined as ParentOf, its partner tuple was automatically assigned the inverse relationship of ChildOf. That is, suppose that our earlier example was instead $\{n_i, n_j,$ Family$\}$ and $\{n_j, n_i,$ Family$\}$; if n_i was determined to be the parent, in a single step, we would have the amended tuples $\{n_i, n_j,$ ParentOf$\}$ and $\{n_j, n_i,$ ChildOf$\}$.

For the coworker generic link type, we did not further define a specific link type.

For each node, we also defined a security policy. For clarity, we defined three security policies that are chosen uniformly at random:

1. Strict—Only BestFriends and Family can view photos of self and any children; their children may not view any videos.
2. Casual—Anyone can see photos; no restriction on children.
3. ParentStrict—Anyone can see photos of the parent; only family can see photos of their children; children cannot see any videos.

We then generated m resources, where m is a random number less than 4.5 million and more than 750,000, which should allow us to model both more active and more passive social networks. A resource could be either a photo or a video. We weighted the probability of a resource being a photo to 75%. We then drew from a uniform distribution between 1 and 25, inclusive, to represent the number of people to *tag* in a photo. This *tag* indicated a person appearing in the photo, and we viewed this as having a *stake* in the individuals in the network who could see the photo.

It is important here to note several things. The first is that while our uniform distribution may not reflect a true probabilistic model of the realities of photos on a social networking site such as Facebook, the inclusion of larger groups having a stake in photos represents a more difficult inference problem for such a site. The second is that we do not restrict the individuals being tagged in a photo to only those friends of the photo owner. Because this functionality exists in current OSNs, we needed to support this type of tagging. This ability can support photos of events such as weddings, where a person taking a photo may only know a subset of individuals in the photo, but people who view the photo can supply more details as to other individuals who were photographed. We also note at this point that our method generates a graph where the average number of friends that a person has is 102 users.*

---

* As of April 1, 2010, Facebook reports an average of 130 friends.

Event Generation. We next generated a series of events that will be processed in order to examine the effect of using a semantic web-based reasoner for social network access control. We condensed the full set of actions that can be performed in a social network (such as games, posting on walls, or changing one's status) to those that would most strongly affect the ability of a reasoner (adding friends, accessing existing resources, creating new resources, and changing permissions). When creating users, adding friends, or creating new resources, we performed the task as described previously. However, when we accessed an existing resource, a randomly chosen user attempted to access a randomly selected resource.

Experiments. We performed two independent implementations of reasoners. Our first implementation relied on the SweetRules inference engine. We attempted to perform inference on the entire data set. Performing inference in this way took 17 hours to load the initial model into memory, and then several seconds to perform each specific reasoning request. However, we noticed that when our model needed to be updated (through new resources, friends, or a change in security policy), these changes were not reflected in our in-memory model. This caused inference done later to become more and more incorrect.

Because of this, we implemented a reasoning solution using Pellet, which has become a very popular reasoner. Initially, we simply changed the reasoner that we used to Pellet. However, in the initial loading step with Pellet, we received *out of memory* errors and were unable to proceed to the reasoning segment. We then decided that we needed to implement some type of partitioning scheme for the social network. A naïve approach to partitioning would have resulted in some friendship links that spanned partitions. These cross-partition edges would have resulted in one of two things:

1. Reconstructing partitions—Suppose that a partition, P_i, has an user u_a with n friends, $u_1,...,$ u_n who are stored in partitions $P_1,...P_n$, respectively. Remember that we can determine who the friends of u_a are from our *Friends* data store. This ability, however, does not assist us in determining which specific partition their friends are in without an additional index. We must then devote considerable resources to recombining specific partitions in order to be able to effectively infer access permissions.
2. Ignoring links—The other option is that we can simply ignore any friendship links that lead to another partition. This is clearly not a viable option because it will obviously result in far too many invalid access requests.

We then realized that for any individual access request, there are only groups of users whose security policies and friends are important to determining the success or failure of the request: (i) the resource owner, (ii) the person making the access request, and (iii) those individuals tagged in the resource. So, we adopt an amended partitioning scheme. For any access request, we generate a temporary table that contains only the members of the three groups mentioned above, all links involving those individuals, the requestor, and the security policies of all these people.

We then use three methods of measuring trust values and perform experiments to determine how each type affects the time required to perform inference:

- Link type only (LTO) is the method described above, where there is only a link type for each edge.
- Trust value only (TVO) is a method in which we use only a trust value in place of most link types. Note, however, that because of the unique constraints held by a ParentOf/ChildOf relationship, we do still maintain only this link type. We do not maintain other generic or specific link types here, however. We assume that the trust values (which would be assigned by a user) are more specific measures than a defined link type.
- Value/trust hybrid (VTH) is an approach where we retain all generic link type declarations, the ParentOf specific type, and add on top of this a Trust Value. This provides for a finer granularity in a security policy. For instance, instead of just being a BestFriend, a

TABLE 20.1

Time to Conduct Inference (in Seconds)

	Average	Low	High
LTO	0.585	0.562	0.611
TVO	0.612	0.534	0.598
VTH	0.731	0.643	0.811

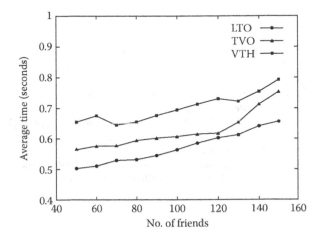

FIGURE 20.3   Average time for inference by number of friends.

specific user can define various security policies, such as only accessible to friends with a trust value greater than 7, where they may declare a BestFriend to be a trust value of 6 or higher. This allows the user to restrict even among best friends or family.

The results of our experiments are provided in Table 20.1. This table shows the average amount of time that it takes to perform inference tasks, as well as the longest time taken and the shortest time taken. Note that this includes the time required to generate the temporary table that is required for the request to be evaluated. Additionally, we ran other series of tests to determine the effect of the number of friends in a graph, as shown in Figure 20.3. For these tests, we generated a subgraph where each person had a specific number of friends, ranging between 50 and 150. We repeated tests using our three types of trust measurement (LTO, TVO, and VTH) and report the average time taken for inference. Again, we see that LTO clearly takes the least time for inference. However, additionally, we can see that there is only a slight increase in the time taken for inference at each additional group of friends. Furthermore, there is only a slight decrease at the point where all members have 50 friends, which indicates that most of the time our inference operation is consumed by the overhead of the inference engine, including our dynamic partitioning method.

20.5   SUMMARY AND DIRECTIONS

In this chapter, we described the implementation of an extensible fine-grained online social network access control model based on semantic web tools. In particular, we discussed the implementation of the authorization, administration, and filtering policies that are modeled using OWL and SWRL. That is, we discussed the implementation of a version of the framework described in Chapter 19 and presented experimental results for the length of time access control can be evaluated using this scheme. Further work could be conducted in the area of determining a minimal set of access policies that could be used in evaluating access requests in a further attempt to increase the efficiency of these requests.

Additionally, we have shown that existing social networks need some form of reasonable data partitioning in order for semantic inference of their access control to be reasonable in its speed and memory requirements, due to constraints on the memory available to perform inference. Additionally, further work can be carried out to determine the best method of representing the individual information of a person in a social network to see whether a hybrid semantic/relational approach or a pure approach offers the best overall system.

REFERENCES

Carminati, B., Ferrari, E., Heatherly, R., Kantarcioglu, M., and Thuraisingham, B.M. A semantic web based framework for social network access control. In: Carminati, B. and Joshi, J., editors, *SACMAT*, pp. 177–186. ACM, New York, 2009a.

Carminati, B., Ferrari, E., and Perego, A. Enforcing access control in web-based social networks. *ACM Transactions on Information Systems Security* 13(1), 2009b.

Finin, T.W., Joshi, A., Kagal, L., Niu, J., Sandhu, R.S., Winsborough, W.H., Thuraisingham, B.M. ROWLBAC: Representing role based access control in *OWL. ACM SACMAT* 2008, pp. 73–82.

Mika, P. *Social Networks and the Semantic Web*. Springer, London, 2007.

World Wide Web Consortium. Status for resource description framework (RDF) model and syntax specification. Available at http://www.w3.org/1999/.status/PR-rdf-syntax-19990105/status, 1999.

21 Inference Control for Social Media

21.1 INTRODUCTION

Inference is the process of forming conclusions from premises. This process is harmful if the user draws unauthorized conclusions from the legitimate responses he or she receives. This problem has come to be known as the inference problem. An inference controller is the device that prevents a user from drawing unauthorized conclusions. We have studied the inference problem extensively in the past. Specifically, we have defined various types of inference strategies and developed inference controllers that handle certain types of inference strategies (Thuraisingham et al., 1993).

Previous work to build an inference controller to protect data confidentiality was described in the late 1980s and early 1990s (Thuraisingham, 1987; Thuraisingham et al., 1993); however, this work was mainly in the area of multilevel secure databases and supported limited reasoning capabilities. Our current work is a substantial improvement over prior efforts with more sophisticated reasoning and policy representation techniques through the use of semantic web technologies (Thuraisingham et al., 2015). We use as our data model the Resource Description Framework (RDF), which supports the interoperability of multiple databases having disparate data schemas. In addition, we express policies and rules in terms of semantic web rules and constraints, and we classify data items and relationships between them using semantic web software tools, such as Pellet, Jena, and Protégé (Carroll et al., 2004; Knublauch et al., 2004; Sirin et al., 2007).

Our previous book focused on classifying and protecting provenance data, which is a kind of metadata that captures the origins of single data items of interest, as well as other relevant information such as data manipulation operations and temporal information (Thuraisingham et al., 2015). Although it is acceptable to represent provenance in any data format, it is sometimes easier to visualize its structure using a directed graph layout. Therefore, we will refer to the provenance data as a directed graph, since a directed graph structure, besides being popular, has many advantages with respect to data modeling in a semantic web environment. The semantic web extends the RDF graph data model to have reasoning capabilities through the use of formal semantics. In our work, we used the reasoning capabilities of the semantic web to support the inference strategies of the inference controller. Furthermore, we presented several new query modification (i.e., rewriting) techniques that can be used to enforce security policies over a provenance graph.

In this chapter, we discuss inference control that employs inference strategies and techniques built around semantic web technologies that can be utilized for inference control in social media. Our work has focused on inference control for provenance data that is represented as RDF graphs. Our methods can be adapted for social network data since such data can also be modeled as RDF graphs. The organization of this chapter is as follows. Our design is discussed in Section 21.2. Query modification is discussed in Section 21.3.1. Specifically, the background in query modification with relational data will be discussed in Section 21.3.2. Query modification for SPARQL queries will be discussed in Section 21.3.3. Implementation aspects are discussed in Section 21.4. The chapter is summarized in Section 21.5. Figure 21.1 illustrates the topics discussed in this chapter.

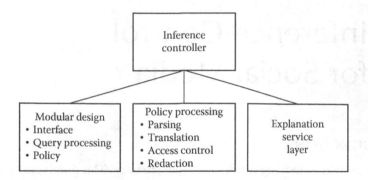

FIGURE 21.1   Architecture of an inference controller.

21.2   DESIGN OF AN INFERENCE CONTROLLER

21.2.1   ARCHITECTURE

The unsolvability of the inference problem was proved by Thuraisingham (1990). Its complexity is an open problem. While there is a need to analyze the complexity classes of the inference problem, still a lot of research has been pivoted around the implementations based on traditional databases. However, since provenance has a logical graph structure, it can also be represented and stored in a graph data model; therefore, it is not limited to any particular data format. Although our focus in this design is on building an inference controller over the graph representation of provenance, our inference controller could be used to protect the case with the traditional database as well. Also, the use of an RDF data model does not overburden our implementation with restrictions, since other data formats are well served by an RDF data model. Furthermore, tools such as the one discussed by Bizer (2003) convert relational data to RDF data.

Our architecture takes a user's input query and returns a response that has been pruned using a set of user-defined policy constraints. We assume that a user could interact with our system to obtain both traditional and provenance data. However, since our focus will be on protecting provenance, we will focus more on the design of the inference controller and the provenance data layers.

In our design, we will assume that the available information is divided into two parts: the actual data and provenance. Both the data and provenance are represented as RDF graphs. The reader should note that we do not make any assumptions about how the actual information is stored. A user may have stored data and provenance in two different triple stores or in the same store. A user application can submit a query for access to the data and its associated provenance, or vice versa. Figure 21.2 shows our design and some modules in our prototype implementation of an inference controller over provenance data. We now present a description of the modules in Figure 21.2.

User Interface Manager. The user interface manager is responsible for processing the user's requests, authenticating the user, and providing suitable responses back to the user. The interface manager also provides an abstraction layer that allows a user to interact with the system. A user can therefore pose either a data query or a provenance query to this layer. The user interface manager also determines whether the query should be evaluated against the traditional data or provenance.

Policy Manager. The policy manager is responsible for ensuring that the querying user is authorized to use the system. It evaluates the policies against a user's query and associated query results to ensure that no confidential information is released to unauthorized users. The policy manager may enforce the policies against the traditional data or against the provenance data. Each data type may have its own policy manager; for example, the traditional data may be stored in a different format from the provenance data. Hence, we may require different implementations of each policy manager.

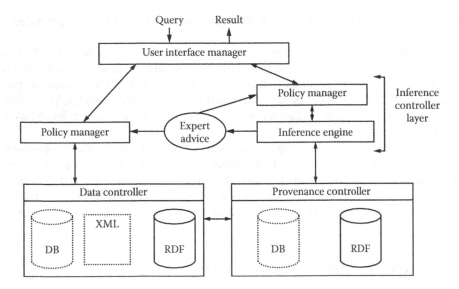

Query   Result

FIGURE 21.2   System modules.

Inference Engine. The inference engine is the heart of the inference controller. The engine is equipped to use a variety of inference strategies that are supported by a particular reasoner. Since there are many implementations of reasoners available, our inference controller offers an added feature of flexibility, whereby we can select from among any reasoning tool for each reasoning task. We can improve the efficiency of the inference controller since each inference strategy (or a combination of strategies) could be executed on a separate processor. An inference engine typically uses software programs that have the capability of reasoning over some data representation, for example, a relational data model or an RDF graph model representation.

Data Controller. The data controller is a suite of software programs that store and manage access to data. The data could be stored in any format, such as in a relational database, in XML files, or in an RDF store. The controller accepts requests for information from the policy manager (or the inference engine layer) if a policy allows the requesting user access to the data item. This layer then executes the request over the stored data and returns results back to the policy layer (or inference engine layer) where it is reevaluated on the basis of a set of policies.

Provenance Controller. The provenance controller is used to store and manage provenance information that is associated with data items that are present in the data controller. In the case when we select a graph representation of provenance, the provenance controller stores information in the form of logical graph structures in any appropriate data representation format. This controller also records the ongoing activities associated with the data items stored in the data controller. This controller takes as input a graph query and evaluates it over the provenance information. This query evaluation returns a subgraph back to the inference controller layer where it is reexamined using a set of policies.

21.3   INFERENCE CONTROL THROUGH QUERY MODIFICATION

21.3.1   QUERY MODIFICATION

The query modification technique has been used in the past to handle discretionary security and views (Stonebraker, 1975). This technique has been extended to include mandatory security in Dwyer et al. (1987). In our design of the query processor, this technique is used by the inference engine to modify the query depending on the security constraints, the previous responses released, and real-world information. When the modified query is posed, the response generated will not violate security.

Consider the architecture for the inference controller discussed in Section 21.2. The inference engine has access to the knowledge base, which includes security constraints, previously released responses, and real-world information. Conceptually, one can think of the database as part of the knowledge base. We illustrate the query modification technique with examples. The actual implementation of this technique could adapt any of the proposals given in Gallaire and Minker (1978) for deductive query processing.

We have conducted extensive investigation on applying query modification for processing security policies (also known as constraints) to determine whether any unauthorized inferences can be deduced by the user (Thuraisingham et al., 1993). Our inference controller will then sanitize the data and give the results to the user. Much of our prior work has built inference controllers on top of relational databases. In our current work, we have developed inference controllers for semantic web data.

21.3.2 Query Modification with Relational Data

Security policies are rules (or constraints) that assign confidential values (or scores) to data items. We have several options available to help us implement these rules in a semantic web environment. A policy can be handled by TBox at design time, by a query modification module at run time, and by a release knowledge base, which tracks the release of provenance.

In this section, we will discuss query modification with relational data. We have obtained this information from our prior work. Figure 21.3 illustrates inference control through query modification.

Query Modification. We could modify the query according to the access control rules; for example, retrieve all employee information where salary <30,000 and Dept is not Security.

Query Modification Algorithm
- Inputs: query, access control rules
- Output: modified query
- Algorithm:
  - Given a query Q, examine all the access control rules relevant to the query.
  - Introduce a Where clause to the query that negates access to the relevant attributes in the access control rules.

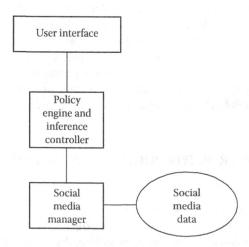

FIGURE 21.3 Inference control through query modification.

Example 21.1

> *Rules:* John does not have access to Salary in EMP and Budget in DEPT.
> *Query:* Join the EMP and DEPT relations on Dept #.
> *Modify Query:* Join EMP and DEPT on Dept # and project on all attributes except Salary and Budget.
> *Output:* is the resulting query.

Security Constraints/Access Control Rules/Security Policies
- Simple constraint: John cannot access the attribute Salary of relation EMP.
- Content-based constraint: If relation MISS contains information about missions in the Middle East, then John cannot access MISS.
- Association-based constraint: Ship's location and mission taken together cannot be accessed by John; individually each attribute can be accessed by John.
- Release constraint: After X is released, Y cannot be accessed by John.
- Aggregate constraint: Ten or more tuples taken together cannot be accessed by John.
- Dynamic constraint: After the mission, information about the mission can be accessed by John.

Security Constraints for Health Care
- Simple constraint: Only doctors can access medical records.
- Content-based constraint: If the patient has AIDS, then this information is private.
- Association-based constraint: Names and medical records taken together are private.
- Release constraint: After medical records are released, names cannot be released.
- Aggregate constraint: The collection of patients is private; individually, patient information is public.
- Dynamic constraint: After the patient dies, information about him becomes public.

21.3.3 SPARQL QUERY MODIFICATION

RDF is increasingly used to store information as assertions about a domain. This includes both confidential and public information. SPARQL has been selected as a query language that extracts data from RDF graphs. Since confidential data is accessed during the querying process, we need to filter SPARQL queries so that only authorized information is released with respect to some confidentiality policy. Our aim is to rewrite the SPARQL queries so that the results returned are compliant with the confidential policies.

A considerable amount of work has been carried out in the area of databases that apply query modification techniques over the SQL querying language. These traditional approaches use rewrite procedures to modify the Where clause so that additional restrictions are added according to some constraints in the set of policies. More recently, the work by Oulmakhzoune et al. (2012) described a query modification technique based on RDF/SPARQL. However, their techniques deal with privacy and do not take inference control into consideration. Our focus will be on applying similar query modification techniques to SPARQL queries.

We design security mechanisms that control the evaluation of SPARQL queries in order to prevent the disclosure of confidential provenance information. Our approach is to modify the graph patterns in the SPARQL query by adding filters and/or property functions that evaluate over a triple pattern. These approaches may return answers different from the user's initial query intent. It may be necessary to decide on appropriate actions in these cases. We propose two approaches that may be followed. The first approach checks the query validity against that of the initial query and notifies the user that the query validity is not guaranteed. The second approach takes into consideration that a feedback about the validity of a query result may lead the user to draw undesirable inferences.

In some cases, it may be possible to return only the answers that we know comply with the policy constraints. In other cases, it may be necessary to replace a restricted subgraph satisfying a query according to some transformation rules that leaves the released knowledge base consistent with the policy constraints. Yet another approach may be to lie; this is similar to polyinstantiation in multilevel secure databases where users at different clearance levels see different versions of reality.

21.3.4 QUERY MODIFICATION FOR ENFORCING CONSTRAINTS

Approaches for modifying the graph patterns in a SPARQL query make use of different techniques, for example, SPARQL filters and property functions, graph transformations, and match/apply pattern. To determine the type of triple with respect to a security classification, the inference engine would use a domain ontology to determine the concept each data item belongs to, as well as a query modification based on a SPARQL BGP (basic graph pattern matching) transformation.

SPARQL Query Filter. The SPARQL specification provides another technique for modifying a graph pattern (Prud'hommeaux et al., 2006). SPARQL FILTERs restrict solutions to those for which the filter expression evaluates to TRUE. We will briefly discuss how to rewrite a SPARQL query by applying SPARQL filters. The following is a SPARQL query requesting the age of a patient.

```
PREFIX med: http://cs.utdallas.edu/semanticweb/Prov-AC/medical#
SELECT ?patient
WHERE {?patient med:age ?age}
```

After query modification, we restrict the query to only patients with age greater than 18 years.

```
PREFIX  med: http://cs.utdallas.edu/semanticweb/Prov-AC/medical#
SELECT ?patient
WHERE { ?patient med:age ?age
      FILTER (?age> 18)
}
```

Property Paths. A property path is a possible route through a graph between two graph nodes. A trivial case is a property path of length exactly 1, which is a triple pattern. A property path expression (or just *path*) is similar to a regular expression string but over properties, not characters. Table 21.1 describes regular path expressions and their descriptions.

Property Path Queries. These queries allow us to modify the property of a triple pattern (note that the property can be a directed label edge or a directed path between a subject and object). One important application is supporting regular expressions. We intend to build constraints over the paths in a graph pattern as a way of reducing leakages that cause the inference problem. We write a code that can execute in accordance to the content of a user query. The code can examine various aspects of a user query, such as the literal text of a triple or triple patterns, and take immediate actions to ensure the appropriate policy constraints are intact. The following is an example of using regular expressions as part of the BGP of a SELECT query over a provenance graph, which uses the Open Provenance Model (OPM) vocabulary.

```
{
med:Doc_n_4  gleen:Subgraph("([opm:WasDerivedFrom]*/
      [opm:WasGeneratedBy]/
      [opm:WasControlledBy])" ?x).
}
```

TABLE 21.1

Regular Path Expressions and Descriptions

Expression	Description
Uri\	A URI or a prefixed name. A path of length one.
^elt	Reverse path (object to subject).
(elt)	A group path *elt*, brackets control precedence.
elt1/elt2	A sequence path of *elt*1, followed by *elt*2.
elt1 ^ elt2	Shorthand for *elt*1 ^ *elt*2, that is *elt*1 followed by reverse *elt*2.
elt1|elt2	An alternative path of *elt*1, or *elt*2 (all possibilities are tried).
elt*	A path of zero or more occurrences of *elt*.
elt+	A path of one or more occurrences of *elt*.
elt?	A path of zero or one *elt*.
elt {n,m}	A path between n and m occurrences of *elt*.
elt{n}	Exactly n occurrences of *elt*. A fixed length path.
elt{n,}	n or more occurrences of *elt*.
elt{,n}	Between 0 and n occurrences of *elt*.
!uri	A path matching a properly that is not URI (negated property set)
!(uri$_1$|...|uri$_N$)	A path matching a property that is not any of uri$_1$, ..., uri$_N$ (negated property set).

This query pattern would give access to the artifacts, processes, and agents on the path to John's record. This query is written using the Gleen regular expression library (Detwiler et al., 2008). The Gleen library (Detwiler et al., 2008) provides two useful functions, OnPath and Subgraph. The OnPath function can be used to locate all of the resources in a graph that stand in a particular relationship pattern to a query resource by returning the set of reachable resources. The Subgraph function returns the set of resources and properties traversed on paths to these results.

Overview of Query Modification. An overview of a query modification for SPARQL could be as follows:

1. Iterate over the graph patterns.
2. Identify the sub(t), obj(t), pred(t) for each triple t in a graph pattern.
3. If a sub(t), obj(t) or pred(t) is confidential, then isolate t or transform it.
4. Create a new query with modified graph patterns.

Graph Transformation of a SPARQL Query BGP. SPARQL is based around graph pattern matching, and a SPARQL query BGP is a graph pattern (i.e., a set of triples) (Prud'hommeaux et al., 2006).

Definition 21.1

(Graph pattern) A SPARQL graph pattern expression is defined recursively as follows:

1. A triple pattern is a graph pattern.
2. If P_1 and P_2 are graph patterns, then the expressions (P_1 AND P_2), (P_1 OPT P_2), and (P_1 UNION P_2) are graph patterns.
3. If P is a graph pattern and R is a built-in SPARQL condition, then the expression (P FILTER R) is a graph pattern.
4. If P is a graph pattern, V is a set of variables, and $X \in U \cup V$, then (X GRAPH P) is a graph pattern.

In a SPARQL query-rewriting process, a BGP is replaced with an updated graph pattern. A graph transformation rule takes the original BGP as its LHS (left hand side) and specifies another pattern as the RHS (right hand side). ∎

Example 21.2: Hide the Surgery of a Patient

```
{
med:Doc_n_4 gleen:OnPath("([opm:WasDerivedFrom]*/
        [opm:WasGeneratedBy])" ?x).
}
```

This pattern matches a path where an entry in the patient's record, which is optionally derived from other versions of the patient's record, is created as a result of some process. That process is the surgery. This pattern, when it is the LHS of a graph transformation rule, could be replaced by another pattern, the RHS of the rule, so that the surgery is not disclosed. A possible RHS pattern would be the following:

```
{
med:Doc_n_4 gleen:OnPath("([opm:WasDerivedFrom])" ?x).
}
```

This pattern would only return the previous version of the patient's record without any entry that some version of the record had a path to the surgery.

Match Pattern/Apply Pattern. In Oracle Database (2012), a data access constraint is described using two graph patterns: a match pattern and an apply pattern. A match pattern determines the type of access restriction to enforce and binds one or more variables to the corresponding data instances accessed in the user query.

Example 21.3: A Data Access Constraint Using Match and Apply Patterns

```
Match: {?contract pred:hasContractValue ?cvalue}
Apply: {?contract pred:hasManageremp:Andy}
```

This example ensures that the *hasContractValue* of a contract can be accessed only if *Andy* is the manager of the contract being accessed. The important feature in Example 21.3 is that a variable defined in the match pattern is used in the corresponding apply pattern to enforce the access restrictions on the identified resources.

Processing Rules: There is a difference between a query engine that simply queries an RDF graph but does not handle rules, and an inference engine that also handles rules. In the literature, this difference is not always clear. The complexity of an inference engine is a lot higher than that of a query engine. The reason is that rules permit us to make sequential deductions. In the execution of a query, these deductions are to be constructed. This is not necessary in the case of a query engine. Note that there are other examples of query engines that rely on a formal model for directed labeled graphs such as DQL and RQL (Fikes et al., 2002; Karvounarakis et al., 2002).

Rules also support a logic base that is inherently more complex than the logic in the situation without rules. For an RDF query engine, only the simple principles of entailment on graphs are necessary. RuleML is an important effort to define rules that are usable for the World Wide Web. The inference web is a recent realization that defines a system for handling different inference engines on the semantic web (McGuinness and Pinheiro da Silva, 2004).

Enforcing Constraints by Graph Rewriting: Graph rewriting, also called graph transformation, is a technique for creating a new graph out of an original graph by using some automatic machine. This is usually a compilation abstraction, where the basic idea is that the state of a computation can be represented as a graph, and further steps in the computation are then represented as transformation rules on the graph (Ehrig, 2006; Rozenberg and Ehrig, 1997).

Graph rewriting came out of the logic and database theory, where graphs are treated as database instances, and rewriting operations as a mechanism for defining queries and views. Popular graph rewriting approaches include the double-pushout approach, single-pushout approach, and algebraic approach (Ehrig et al., 1991). The approach we describe is similar to the one for the single-pushout approach. A graph rewriting system consists of a set of rewrite rules of the form $p: L \to R$, with L being a graph pattern (or LHS of the rule) and R being the replacement graph (or RHS of the rule). A graph rewrite rule is applied to the original graph by searching for an occurrence of the pattern graph and replacing the found occurrence by the existence of the replacement graph.

21.4   APPLICATION TO SOCIAL MEDIA DATA

As discussed in Chapters 19 and 20, social media data can be represented as RDF graphs. Therefore, the ideas presented in the previous sections apply for such social graphs. The security policies may also be represented as RDF or in a language such as Semantic Web Rule Language (SWRL). These policies include access control policies and information-sharing policies. For example, if a person divulges his religious beliefs, then his political affiliation would be inferred. Therefore, if a person wants to keep his political affiliations private, then his religious beliefs should not be posted on his social media website.

We can build the inference controller on top of the access control architecture that we described in Chapter 20. We illustrate such an inference controller in Figure 21.4. The inference engine is essentially the policy engine that controls access and handles unauthorized access via inference. Social media data is represented as RDF graphs, and the policies and knowledge may be specified using combinations of SWRL, RDF, and OWL (Web Ontology Language). When a user queries, say in SPARQL, the policy engine examines the knowledge base, which could include provenance data and the policies, and modify the query. The modified query is posed against the RDF-based social media database. Much of the discussion in the previous sections and the implementation of the inference controller to be discussed in Chapter 22 apply to RDF-based social media data.

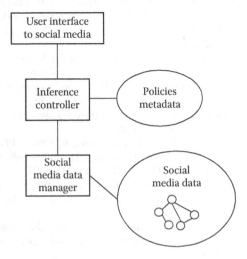

FIGURE 21.4   Inference controller for social media.

21.5 SUMMARY AND DIRECTIONS

In this chapter, we first described the design of an inference controller that operates over a semantic web-based provenance graph and protects important provenance information from unauthorized users. Since our social networks discussed in Chapters 19 and 20 are also represented by semantic web technologies, the techniques we have developed apply to such social media data. Previous work to build an inference controller to protect data confidentiality was described in the late 1980s and early 1990s; however, this work was mainly in the area of multilevel secure databases and supported limited reasoning capabilities. Our current work is a substantial improvement over prior efforts with more sophisticated reasoning and policy representation techniques through the use of semantic web technologies. We used RDF as our data model as it supports the interoperability of multiple databases having disparate data schemas. In addition, we expressed policies and rules in terms of semantic web rules and constraints, and we classify data items and relationships between them using semantic web software tools.

Next, we discussed inference control through query modification. Query modification has also been referred as query rewriting. In this approach, the inference controller takes a user query, and modifies the query according to the policies and gives a sanitized result to the query. We provided background information on query modification for relational data and aspects of modifying SPARQL queries. While moving to SPARQL queries from relational queries is the first step toward handling inferences for next-generation inference controllers, our ultimate goal is to process queries with sophisticated logic-based reasoners that use machine learning approaches. This way, we can handle many more inference strategies than we have discussed in this book. As stated earlier, as the inference strategies become more complex, we need to keep the scalability of the query-processing techniques in mind. That is, while the data management system should release only authorized responses, users will need performance requirements to be met. Therefore, developing scalable inference controllers is one of our major goals.

REFERENCES

Bizer, C. D2R MAP—A database to RDF mapping language. In: *WWW (Posters)*, Budapest, Hungary, 2003.

Carroll, J., Dickinson, I., Dollin, C., Reynolds, D., Seaborne, A., and Wilkinson, K. Jena: Implementing the semantic web recommendations. In: *Proceedings of the 13th International World Wide Web Conference on Alternate Track Papers & Posters*, ACM, New York, 2004.

Detwiler, L., Suciu, D., and Brinkley, J. Regular paths in SparQL: Querying the NCI thesaurus. In: *AMIA Annual Symposium Proceedings, American Medical Informatics Association*, Washington, DC, 2008.

Dwyer, P., Jelatis, G.D., and Thuraisingham, B.M. Multilevel security in database management systems. *Computers & Security* 6(3): 252–260, 1987.

Ehrig, H. *Fundamentals of Algebraic Graph Transformation*. Springer-Verlag, New York, 2006.

Ehrig, H., Korff, M., and Lowe, M. Tutorial introduction to the algebraic approach of graph grammars based on double and single pushouts. In: Erhig H., Kreowski, H.-J., and Rozenberg, G., editors. *Graph Grammars and Their Application to Computer Science*. Springer-Verlag, Berlin, 1991.

Fikes, R., Hayes, P., and Horrocks, I. DQL—A query language for the semantic web. Knowledge Systems Laboratory, Report DR-05, Stanford University, 2002.

Gallaire, H. and Minker, J., *Logic and Data Bases*, Plenum Press, New York, 1978.

Karvounarakis, G., Alexaki, S., Christophides, V., Plexousakis, D., and Scholl, M. RQL: A declarative query language for RDF. In: *ACM WWW*, pp. 592–603. Honolulu, HI, 2002.

Knublauch, H., Fergerson, R., Noy, N., and Musen, M. The Protege OWL plugin: An open development environment for semantic web applications. *ISWC 2004, LCNS* 3298, pp. 229–243. Springer-Verlag, Berlin-Heidelberg, 2004.

McGuinness, D.L. and Pinheiro da Silva, P. Explaining answers from the semantic web: The inference web approach. *ISCW 2003, Web Semantics: Science, Services and Agents on the World Wide Web* 1(4), Elsevier, Sanibel Island, FL, 2004.

Oracle Database. Fine-grained access control for RDF data. Available at http://docs.oracle.com/cd/E11882_01/appdev.112/e25609.pdf, 2012.

Oulmakhzoune, S., Cuppens-Boulahia, N., Cuppens, F., Morucci, S. Privacy policy preferences enforced by SPARQL query rewriting. *ARES* 335–342, 2012.

Prud'hommeaux, E., Seaborne, A. et al. SPARQL query language for RDF. W3C working draft, 20, 2006.

Rozenberg, G. and Ehrig, H. *Handbook of Graph Grammars and Computing by Graph Transformation*, vol. 1. World Scientific Publishing, Singapore, 1997.

Sirin, E., Parsia, B., Grau, B., Kalyanpur, A., and Katz, Y. Pellet: A practical OWL-DL reasoner. *Web Semantics: Science, Services and Agents on the World Wide Web* 5(2), 2007.

Stonebraker, M. Implementation of integrity constraints and views by query modification. In: *SIGMOD Conference*, 1975.

Thuraisingham, B.M. Security checking in relational database management systems augmented with inference engines. *Computers & Security* 6(6): 479–492, 1987.

Thuraisingham, B. Recursion theoretic properties of the inference problem. Presented at the Computer Security Foundations Workshop, Franconia, NH, June 1990 (also MITRE Report), 1990.

Thuraisingham, B., Cadenhead, T., Kantarcioglu, M., Khadilkar, V. *Secure Data Provenance and Inference Control with Semantic Web*. CRC Press, Boca Raton, FL, 2015.

Thuraisingham, B. and Ford, W., Collins, M., and O'Keeffe, J. Design and implementation of a database inference controller. *Data & Knowledge Engineering* 11(3), 1993.

22 Implementing an Inference Controller for Social Media Data

22.1 INTRODUCTION

Traditionally, we protect data using policies, such as access control policies and sanitization-based policies. However, current mechanisms for enforcing these policies do not operate over data that takes the form of a directed graph (Braun et al., 2008). Additionally, users can infer sensitive information from the results returned by performing frequent queries over a provenance graph. We are particularly interested in any conclusion formed from premises where the conclusion is formed without any expressed or prior approval from anyone or any organization that controls or processes the premises or information from which the conclusion is formed. We also refer to the process of forming these conclusions from the premises as inference. When the information inferred is something unauthorized for the user to see, we say that we have an instance of the inference problem. This problem is always present in systems that contain both public and private information. The inferred knowledge could depend on data obtained from a knowledge base, or it could depend on some prior knowledge possessed by the user in addition to the information obtained from the knowledge base (Thuraisingham et al., 1993).

The inferred knowledge obtained from a knowledge base alone could be used to reveal what is and what is not in a knowledge base. For example, if a user asks for information relating to a patient's x-ray procedure, any response could indicate whether the patient had an x-ray or not. In general, a positive answer to a query discloses what is in a knowledge base, while a negative answer could have more than one interpretation. For example, a user could interpret a negative answer to mean that the answer is not in the knowledge base, or the user could interpret that it is in the knowledge base, but the knowledge base chooses not to reveal the correct answer to the query. These two interpretations could also depend on whether the knowledge base uses a closed-world or an open-world assumption (Reiter, 1977). Normally, an open-world assumption indicates that data is incomplete or it could be somewhere else in the system and is not restricted to a particular file or location. In a closed-world assumption, data is complete and a negative answer to a query usually indicates that the data is not present in the knowledge base. We assume an open-world assumption; in particular, a user should not be able to distinguish, with accuracy, between the presence of facts hidden by the inference controller and the absence of facts that are available elsewhere.

Our main focus is on classifying and protecting social media data presented as Resource Description Framework (RDF) graphs. However, our initial implementation of the inference controller was for provenance data, which is present in numerous domains including for social media data. Our inference controller can be adapted for social media data since our social networks are represented as RDF graphs. The semantic web extends the RDF graph model to have inferencing capabilities by using formal semantics. It is this inferencing service that we use to support the inference strategies of the inference controller. Furthermore, we have shown how to perform new query modification techniques to enforce the security policies over a provenance graph that can be extended for social media graphs discussed in Chapters 19 and 20.

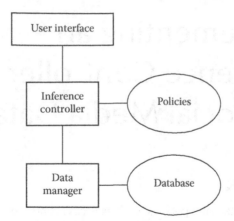

FIGURE 22.1 Implementing an inference controller for social media data.

A semantic reasoner enables us to infer logical consequences from a set of axioms. It provides a richer set of mechanisms that enables us to draw inferences from a provenance graph encoded using Web Ontology Language (OWL) vocabulary. We can specify the inference rules by means of an ontology language. Reasoners often use first-order predicate logic to perform reasoning. The inference proceeds by forward chaining and backward chaining.

The organization of this chapter is as follows. In Section 22.2, we will discuss inference and provenance to motivate the reader. We will also provide use cases. Our implementation is discussed in Section 22.3. Developing generators is discussed in Section 22.4, and a medical example is provided as a use case in Section 22.5. Implementing constraints is the subject of Section 22.6. The chapter is summarized in Section 22.7. Figure 22.1 illustrates the contents of this chapter.

22.2 INFERENCE AND PROVENANCE

22.2.1 EXAMPLES

Rules of inference can be used to infer a conclusion from a premise to create an argument. It is important to point out that a set of rules can be used to infer any valid conclusion if it is complete. A set of rules is sound if no invalid conclusion is drawn. Some rules may be redundant, and thus a sound and complete set of rules need not include every rule when arriving at a conclusion. As stated earlier, when the conclusion is not something authorized to be seen by a user, we have a security leak and a case of the inference problem.

A rule can be invoked in forward chaining or backward chaining:

- In a forward-chaining mode, we are given some set of statements and we use the rules to deduce new statements. In principle, repeated application of forward chaining will find all facts that can be deduced by the inference rule from some initial set of facts from a knowledge base.

Example 22.1

Consider the following two rules:

1. (med:HeartSurgery opm:wasControlledBy ?X) → (X rdf:type med:Surgeon)
2. (med:Results_n_1 opm:Used med:Doc_n_6) ∧ (med:Results_n_1 opm:wasControlledBy ?X) → (X rdf:type med:Surgeon)

If our knowledge base contains the following triples:

<med:HeartSurgery_n_1><opm:Used><med:Doc_n_5>
<med:Doc_n_6><opm:WasGeneratedBy><med:HeartSurgery_n_1>
<med:Doc_n_6><opm:wasDerivedFrom><med:Doc_n_5>
<med:Results_n_1><opm:Used><med:Doc_n_6>
<med:Results_n_1><opm:WasControlledBy><med:Surgeon_n_1>
<med:HeartSurgery_n_1><opm:WasControlledBy><med:Surgeon_n_1>

We can conclude that ?X is a Surgeon, by using the last triple in the above knowledge base. The triple (med:Surgeon_n_1 rdf:type med:Surgeon) would then be added to the knowledge base. Note that the execution of rule 2 would also add this triple to the knowledge base.

- In backward chaining, we are given some expression and we determine all of the antecedents that must be satisfied in order for the given consequent expression to be true.

Example 22.2

Consider the following rules:

1. (med:HeartSurgery opm:wasControlledBy ?X) → (X rdf:type med:Surgeon)
2. (med:Results_n_1 opm:Used med:Doc_n_6) ∧ (med:Results_n_1 opm:wasControlledBy ?X) → (X rdf:type med:Surgeon)

If we want to satisfy rule 1, the reasoner would conclude that med:HeartSurgery opm:wasControlledBy ?X. Given the statement

<med:HeartSurgery_n_1><opm:WasControlledBy><med:Surgeon_n_1>

this derivation will cause the reasoner to produce med:Surgeon_n_1 as the answer to the question

(X rdf:type med:Surgeon)

22.2.2 APPROACHES TO THE INFERENCE PROBLEM

Different approaches can be employed for building an inference controller. For example, we can use state-of-the-art machine learning techniques to build a learner that automatically learns to recognize complex patterns and make intelligent decisions based on some explicit data. We can also build an inference controller that uses semantic web technologies equipped with reasoners, which perform inferences over the data in the knowledge base. In this section, we will illustrate some approaches of our inference controller that are based on the use of semantic web technologies.

Aggregation problem is a special case of the inference problem—collection of data elements is Secret but the individual elements are Unclassified.

$$A \cup B \cup C \subseteq \text{Secret}$$

We could enforce this rule by checking if there are any sensitive concepts in the provenance KB or the Released KB.

$$A \cap B \cap C \subseteq \text{Secret}$$

$$\geq 10R.(A \cap B \cap C)$$

If we know that at least 10 persons have a property, then classify KB.

Association problem is when attributes A and B taken together are Secret, but individually they are Unclassified.

Example 22.3: *A* and *B* and *C* → Secret

We could encode this as an SWRL (Semantic Web Rule Language) rule, then check the provenance KB or the Released KB if there is anything secret.

> (med:Doc_n_6 opm:wasDerivedFrom med:Doc_n_5)
> ∧ (med:Doc_n_6 opm:wasGeneratedBy med:HeartSurgery_n_1)
> ∧ (med:HeartSurgery_n_1 opm:WasControlled)By med:Surgeon_n_1)
> →
> (med:HeartSurgery_n_1 med:Classification Secret)

If we consider the surgery operation to be sensitive, we can classify it as Secret. Similarly, the resulting version of the patient's record that was generated by this operation should be considered secret as well.

> (med:Doc_n_6 opm:wasDerivedFrom med:Doc_n_5)
> ∧ (med:Doc_n_6 opm:wasGeneratedBy med:HeartSurgery_n_1)
> ∧ (med:HeartSurgery_n_1 opm:WasControlled)By med:Surgeon_n_1)
> →
> (med:Doc_n_6 med:Classification Secret)

Example 22.4

Something that is in all three classes is private:

$$A \cap B \cap C \subseteq \text{Secret}$$

Example 22.5

If at most one individual is in all three classes, then classify KB:

$$\leq 1R.(A \cap B \cap C)$$

Domain Restriction. We can put a range restriction on a qualified value for a property as Secret. For example, a property whose value is something with nine digits is Sensitive. Note that a Social Security number (SSN) contains nine digits; therefore, if something with nine digits is released, then we need to classify the KB. Similarly, we could specify that something with 16 digits is a credit card number.

Statistical Reasoning. In statistical reasoning, we are given the summary data; the object is to learn macroproperties about a population.

Example 22.6

If at most one heart surgeon is on duty during a patient's visit, and we reveal the following triple to a user:

> <med:HeartSurgery_n_1><opm:WasControlledBy><_:b>

then the user can conclude that the surgeon on duty performed the operation on the patient.

Machine Learning Techniques. Chang et al. (1998) approached the inference problem with a parsimonious downgrading framework using decision trees. The assumption is that when Low needs information for purposes such as performance and functionality, High must decide whether to give (i.e., downgrade) information to Low. In other words, when High wishes to downgrade a set of data to Low, it may be necessary, because of inference channels, to trim the set. Basically, decision trees are used to form rules from the downgraded data High makes available to Low. Remember that we can use the nonsensitive attributes of an individual to arrive at (i.e., predict) the sensitive attribute, using rules that are trained on similar individuals (occurring in previous released data). In parsimonious downgrading, a cost measure is assigned to the potential downgraded information that is not sent to Low. The idea is to determine if the loss of functionality (to Low) associated with (High) not downgrading this data is worth the extra confidentiality. Decision trees assist in analyzing the potential inference channels in the data that one wishes to downgrade. The authors assign penalty functions to this parsimonious downgrading in order to minimize the amount of information that is not downgraded, and compare the penalty costs to the extra confidentiality that is obtained.

Other approaches covered by our inference engine include the following:

- *Handling inference during database design.* This approach is considered rather static. It depends mainly on schema design and integrity constraints. It was also pointed out that it is not very convenient to keep changing the database schema in response to each user's query.
- *Handling inference during query processing.* The bulk of the research mostly focuses on query modification mainly because queries are dynamic.

22.2.3 INFERENCES IN PROVENANCE

A user can infer sensitive information from the results returned from performing frequent queries over a provenance graph. We are particularly interested in any conclusion formed from premises, where the conclusion is formed without any expressed or prior approval from anyone or any organization that controls or processes the premises or information from which the conclusion is formed. Furthermore, our goal is to examine the inference problem that occurs with provenance data. We need automated software tools to discover and evaluate the interesting patterns and semantic associations in a provenance store. The amount of information generated by recording fine-grained provenance is an important but time-consuming work for security analysts. We can record the provenance using a semantic web language so that intelligent agents and reasoners can automate the inference without compromising the semantics of the underlying provenance.

Implicit Information in Provenance. A provenance document contains both data items and their relationships formulated as a directed graph. An intermediate node on a path in this graph may contain sensitive information such as the identity of an agent who filed an intelligence report, and thus we need efficient tools for querying and inference as well. Also, we need to support large provenance graphs, and the ability to query this graph so that we can build user views that filter user queries.

Security policies (i.e., security constraints) are used to determine who can access a document and under what conditions access is to be granted. In intelligence, it may be necessary to guard one's methods and sources; hence, an access control policy could limit access to the source of a report to sister agencies. However, these policies are limited to creating views and do not take into account implicit information in the provenance, and we need to develop policies that scale with the provenance data. We need to build large data stores for provenance. Provenance can be recorded in any knowledge representation language, for example, RDF, Resource Description Framework Schema (RDFS), and OWL. Using these languages allows us to later perform inference over the provenance graph. Therefore, we could determine the implicit information over the provenance graph.

22.2.4 Use Cases of Provenance

The use cases for provenance can be found at UseCases For Provenance Workshop (http://wiki.esi .ac.uk/UseCasesForProvenanceWorkshop).

Another useful source for use cases can be found at http://www.w3.org/2005/Incubator/prov /wiki/Use_Cases. This gives the initial use cases gathered by W3C incubator group.

For a list of security issues in provenance by the W3C group, see http://www.w3.org/2005 /Incubator/prov/wiki/Security_issues_in_provenance_use_cases.

Use cases are also available at the URLs http://lists.w3.org/Archives/Public/public-xg-prov /2010Jan/0014.html and http://arxiv.org/PS_cache/arxiv/pdf/1002/1002.0433v1.pdf.

We construct use cases involving who/why/when/where queries. We may not know the answers to these queries for a particular domain, so revealing the provenance could be our best source for these answers. On the other hand, we may need to protect the who/when/where/why of a particular resource or node in a provenance graph. We present case studies in this section in order to illustrate what we want to achieve when we apply semantic web technologies to provenance information. In particular, we will discuss some of the use cases using a toy hospital example. While we will try to keep these use cases as close to our medical domain as possible, we also discuss use cases in other domains.

Data Discovery. This encompasses the provenance of observing and capturing patient activities at all stages in a visit and operation.

A physician must rely on the historical information in a patient's record, such as who or what causes a record to be in its current state. Also, the contents of the record can change with time, which can result in a temporal fine-grained capture of the provenance information for decision processes.

Data Set Documentation. This allows physicians to retrieve the current and most up-to-date snapshot of a patient's record as well as its origin. This documentation supports further processing of the record by emergency personnel and drug dispensary units.

Pinpoint Errors in a Process. A *where* query for a patient would be useful if we need to pinpoint where in the process a possible risk could occur as a result of performing a surgery on this patient. For example, a *where–provenance* query could be used to identify at which phase in the flow any medication administered to the patient had a negative interaction with the ones the patient is already taking. By using where queries, we could compare the information in an earlier version of the record (which is generated before surgery) with that in a later version of the record (which incorporates the recording of events during the surgery).

Identifying Private Information in Query Logs. There are pieces of information that can also be used in identifying private information. Queries for phone numbers, addresses, and names of individuals are all useful in narrowing down the population, and thus increases the chance of a successful attack. From the query logs, it is possible to generate the distribution of queries for a user, the query timing, and also the content of the queries. Furthermore, it is possible to cluster users and to some extent augment the query responses with the user behavior. Finally, we can also correlate queries (e.g., those who query for X also query for Y).

Use Case: Who Said That? The scenario is based on a financial architecture being done for a government agency. This is a large architecture involving information, services, and processes. Most of the stakeholders are nontechnical persons; many are accountants. As with any such architecture, it is based on a successive set of inputs and meetings with stakeholders—not all at the same time. While this architecture was not being done with SemWeb tooling (it was UML), the same situation arises despite the formalism used. Near the end of the project, one of the stakeholders was reviewing an information model for orders. This was not the first time this stakeholder had seen this part of the model, but they had not reviewed it in some time. The stakeholder pointed to a property on part of the model dealing with orders and asked, "Where did that come from? Who told you to put it in?" Certainly a reasonable question, but one we could not answer without a long dig through manual notes. There was nothing in the model to say where that property came from, when it was added, or under what authority. In addition, the stakeholder noted that something they thought was in the model had been removed and wanted to know where it had gone. Again, the tooling could not help. Conclusion: The source (both the person entering the data and who told them to put it there), the situation (such as a meeting), and the time of each intervention in the model need to be tracked. This should be part of the core knowledge management infrastructure and leads directly to the trustworthiness of the knowledge base as it evolves over time.

Use Case: Cheating Dictator. It seems that certain intelligence activities look at things like the college transcripts of interesting people and use these to draw conclusions about their capability and character. The story (and it may just be a story) is that Saddam Hussein attended a college in Australia decades ago. The transcripts for that college were obtained and made part of his personal profile. This profile influenced important political and military activities. It became apparent that for propaganda purposes, these transcripts had been modified. Analysts wanted to know what inferences had been made by human and automated means, what information was inferred, and how that could have changed Saddam's profile and potential actions. There was no way to trace this information path, making many of the opinions questionable. This is, of course, only one small example in the world where information may be intentionally falsified or obscured, and where the resulting conclusions are critically important. The source and downstream impact of information is critical, particularly when sources and information quality are reevaluated. Conclusion: The track of inferences may span decades, and this track may be of critical strategic value. In addition, inference is a combination of human and automated activities that affect downstream conclusions.

In this use case, we show that by annotating the entities in our generated workflow with actual attributes taken from the web, we can verify qualifications of physicians and also point the querying user to appropriate URLs. These URLs could be part of the annotations about entities in our provenance graph, but they mainly serve to point to actual sources that verify the credentials of physicians.

Other uses cases include the following:

Aerospace engineering: Maintain a historical record of design processes, up to 99 years.
Organ transplant management: Tracking of previous decisions, crucial to maximize the efficiency in matching and recovery rate of patients.

Below are some examples that illustrate policies relevant to the health-care domain:

Example 22.7

Protecting the name of the physician. In this case, any query that is issued should generate a response that does not divulge the name of the physician.

Example 22.8

For each patient, we generate workflows that capture the steps of various procedures generally performed in a hospital. In particular, we describe surgery, general check-ups, postcare operations, etc.

22.2.5   PROCESSING RULES

The inference rules can be encoded and processed in more than one format. These include encoding the rules using SPARQL queries, encoding the rules using description logic (DL), and, finally, the most expressive rules can be encoded as SWRL rules. There are differences in these approaches. A particular choice depends on the size of the knowledge base, the expressiveness of the rules, and decidability. A query-processing engine does not handle inference rules but is still powerful. For example, we can query for entailments in an RDF graph encoding of provenance. These queries can also be used to discover paths in a provenance graph (i.e., using regular expression path queries). The results of these queries can be combined to provide answers to complex inference problems. Also, where scalability is a factor, the best option is to query for the pieces of information and combine the relevant parts in a smaller knowledge base. On the other hand, there are cases where it may not be feasible to enumerate all the possible queries that will answer a particular inference problem. Therefore, we may need automated reasoners enriched with enough expressive power to do the inference for us. These reasoners may also produce new deductions that were previously unseen by a query engine alone. However, with this power comes a price: decidability.

Rules are normally inherently more complex than the logic in the situation without rules. For example, in an RDF query engine, only the simple principles of entailment on graphs are necessary. RuleML is an important effort to define rules that are usable for the World Wide Web. The inference web is a recent realization that defines a system for handling different inferencing engines on the semantic web (McGuinness et al., 2003).

22.3 IMPLEMENTATION OF THE INFERENCE CONTROLLER

22.3.1 ARCHITECTURE

Figure 22.2 presents the implementation of an inference controller for provenance. This inference controller is built using a modular approach; therefore, it is very flexible in that most of the modules can be extended or replaced by another application module. For example, an application user may substitute the policy parser module that handles the parsing of the high-level policies to a low-level policy object. This substitution would allow the application user to continue using his or her business policies independent of our software implementation of the provenance inference controller. Essentially, we have followed a *plug-and-play* approach for implementing the inference controller. We have used open source products as much as possible in our implementation.

The products we have used in our implementation include Jena and Pellet. Our policies and data are represented in RDF. Jena is used to manage the RDF data. Our reasoner is based on Pellet. That is, our inference controller reasons about the policies and the data utilizing Pellet. We built additional inference strategies utilizing Pellet. When a user poses a query in SPARQL, the inference controller will examine the policies, rewrite the query on the basis of the policies, query the Jena RDF store, and retrieve the data that the user is authorized to see. In the next several sections, we will give examples of how our inference controller functions based on a health-care application.

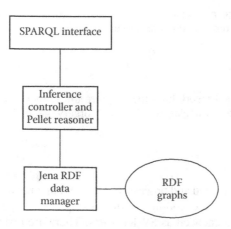

FIGURE 22.2 Implementation architecture.

22.3.2   PROVENANCE IN A HEALTH-CARE DOMAIN

The health-care domain sees provenance as a critical component of its operations. The provenance can be used to facilitate the communication and coordination between organizations and among members of a medical team. It can be used to provide an integrated view of the execution of treatment processes, to analyze the performance of distributed health-care services, and to carry out audits of a system to assess that, for a given patient, the proper decisions were made and the proper procedures were followed (Kifor et al., 2006).

We describe a medical domain with respect to sources available online, such as http://www .webmd.com/. Our medical domain is made up of patients, physicians, nurses, technicians, equipment, medical procedures, etc. We focus on one example of the medical domain, a fictitious hospital. This is a toy example of a hospital that carries out procedures described at credible websites such as http://www.nlm.nih.gov/ and http://www.mghp.com/services/procedure/. These procedures include heart surgery procedures, hip replacement procedures, and others. Since the procedures are described by actual documents on the web, our generated workflow structures typically follow a set of guidelines that are also known to the user. However, the workflows generated by our system may not reflect exactly what goes on in a real hospital. We take into consideration that real hospitals follow guidelines related to a patient's privacy; therefore, our fictitious hospital generates workflows so that the entities in the provenance graph are known only internally. This ensures that the content of a record (i.e., an artifact), the agent who generated a version of a record, the time when the record was updated, and the workflow processes are only revealed to a user via queries. Furthermore, the laws governing the release of the provenance (i.e., the contents of the generated workflow) are enforced by policies that are implemented by translating them into a suitable format for use internally by our system.

Populating the Provenance Knowledge Base. The provenance knowledge base is updated using a set of generators. There are background generators that are responsible for extracting background information that is normally available online. There is also a workflow generator that produces the actual provenance. The workflow generator produces synthetic provenance data that is not available online. It is this provenance data that has subsets that we must protect. We populate the provenance store by extracting information related to a health-care domain. The health-care domain is suitable in two ways. First, this domain actually records provenance and, second, data about this domain is partially available online (Kifor et al., 2006).

Generating and Populating the Knowledge Base. We create a set of seeds that consist of a first name, a last name, and a state and city. Each seed is used to create a query that is issued against the http://www.yellowpages.com/ or the http://www.whitepages.com/ website. These websites are useful for locating businesses and individuals via search terms. To extract information from these websites, we employ the services of a web crawler. A web crawler is a computer program that browses the World Wide Web in a methodical, automated manner or in an orderly fashion. Web crawlers are sometimes referred to as automatic indexers, bots, ants, harvesters, web spiders, web robots, or web scutters. These crawlers are computer programs that follow the link structure of the World Wide Web and perform some tasks on the web pages they visit.

After the pages matching our initial query seed are crawled, we store the results in an appropriate format in a text file. Because this process is expensive, we build all our web crawl routines offline, and load the text file contents into memory during the test cycles of our experimental phase. The first crawl gathers our assumed lists of patients. We use the zip codes of the patients to create queries for hospitals, doctors, and their specialties. The results of these searches are also stored in text files, which have predetermined formats. These predetermined formatted text files allow us to build object classes with properties for entities such as persons, hospitals, doctors, and nurses.

Generating Workflows. For each patient in our toy knowledge base, we initiate workflows that update the records for the patient. The recorded provenance is the only confidential data we assume in our system. The intent is to give the querying user an opportunity to guess the patient's disease, medications, or tests associated with the record. Provenance data is more interesting than traditional databases, because the controller not only has to anticipate inferences involving the users' prior knowledge, but also the inferences associated with the causal relationships among the provenance data objects.

Properties of the Workflow. We observe a few properties of the workflows we generated:

- Our provenance workflows are generated using the OPM toolbox (http://openprovenance .org/). This toolbox captures the skeleton of a workflow generated by using the predicates in V_G^P, where

$$V_G^P = \left\{ \text{WasControlledBy, Used, WasDerivedFrom, WasGeneratedBy, WasTriggeredBy} \right\}$$

That is, the initial workflows we generate are typically not annotated with RDF triples that are related to the entities in our workflow; for example, triples that make assertion about an agent's name, address, or age. Therefore, we avoid clutter, which makes it easier to visualize the medical procedures.

- Each entity in our workflow graph, G, can be annotated by RDF triples, which make assertions about the entities. Our workflow is typically stored in its full form. That is, we add annotations to each workflow by transforming it into one that has relevant background information corresponding to the entities in the workflow.

- Each entity in G has attributes that were derived from either the yellow pages (http://www .yellowpages.com) or the white pages (http://www.whitepages.com/) website. These attributes are the ones that are a part of the user background knowledge. We also add other fictitious attributes to the entities in our provenance graph. These fictitious attributes allow us to scale the size and complexity of a provenance graph so that we will have some experimental data about the scalability of our system.

- The workflow graph G contains the private information; that is, the provenance of the activities performed on a patient's record. This is the information our inference controller is protecting. The primary methods we employ for protecting this information are provided by the reasoning services available in semantic web reasoners and policies that operate over G.

22.3.3 POLICY MANAGEMENT

We discussed several aspects of policy management in the design. We will repeat some of the information in this section.

Policy Screen. A policy screen provides the user with options to load and execute policies against the provenance graph database. The user has the option of executing any policy type, for example, the default ones (access control, redaction, DL rules, or policies encoded as SWRL rules) or another policy type. The default policies are provided with a set of parsers that translate them to an internal policy representation. New policy types are compatible as long as a suitable parser is provided to translate each policy type to an internal representation. The internal representation can be any technology that operates over an RDF graph, for example, SPARQL query, DL rule, or SRWL rule. The policy screen has two panels (Figure 22.3). The left panel displays a list of policies loaded but not in effect, while the right panel displays the list of loaded policies that are in effect.

Parsing Process. A high-level policy has to be translated to a suitable format and representation in order to be processed by a provenance inference controller. This often involves the parsing of a high-level policy to a low-level representation. Our design makes use of an extensible language for expressing policies. This language has been used successfully to write access control policies (Moses et al., 2005; Ni et al., 2009). Our policies are written as XML documents that reside on disk

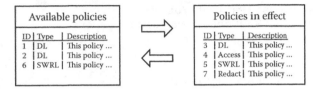

FIGURE 22.3   Policy screen.

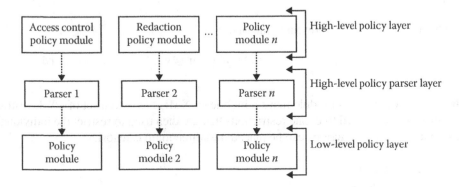

FIGURE 22.4   Parsing process.

until they are requested (Bray et al., 2000). XML is also equipped with features for writing rules (Grosof and Poon, 2003; Governatori, 2005; Horrocks et al., 2004). In addition, RDF and OWL can be represented in an XML syntax (Bechhofer et al., 2004; Horrocks et al., 2004). Our choice of an XML language allows us to take as input any high-level policy specification and an associated parser that maps it to a low-level policy format. The high-level application user also benefits from our use of an XML language, since XML is an open standard that is widely used and many data exchange formats are based on XML. For the rest of this book, we will refer to the policies as though they are in their XML standard form.

Figure 22.4 provides us with an overview of a policy parsing process. When an XML policy file is loaded, each policy in the policy file is parsed using a compatible parser. The parser is responsible for ensuring that the policies are well formed. The default policies (i.e., access control, redaction, and inference rules) are written in an XML file and the parser evaluates the XML file against an XML schema file. The policies in a successfully parsed XML file are then translated to a low-level representation.

High-Level Policy Translation. In this section, we will discuss how a correctly parsed high-level policy is translated to an internal low-level policy. We will first discuss two inference assemblers, the SWRL rule assembler and the DL rule assembler. Then, we will discuss two policy assemblers that translate the assess control and redaction high-level policies, respectively.

SWRL Rule Assembler. This module maps a high-level XML file onto a set of SWRL rules. A SWRL rule has a head and a body. The body is used to encode a condition that must be satisfied before the information encoded in the head is applied to the provenance knowledge base.

SWRL policy translation: The following is a policy that states that if a doctor has (or is attending to) a patient, then that doctor can also read the patient's record.

```
<policies>
<policy ID="1">
<description>...some description...</description>
<body>
<atom>?x rdf:type provac:Doctor</atom>
```

```
<atom>?y rdf:type provac:Patient</atom>
<atom>?y provac:patientHasDoctor ?x</atom>
<atom>?y provac:hasRecord ?r</atom>
</body>
<head>
<atom>?x provac:canReadRecord ?r</atom>
</head>
</policy>
</policies>
```

This policy could be represented internally as

```
Doctor(?x) ∧ Patient(?y) ∧ patientHasDoctor(?y, ?x) ∧ hasRecord(?r) →
canReadRecord(?x, ?r)
```

DL Rule Assembler. This module maps a high-level XML file onto a set of OWL restrictions. The OWL properties are used to create restrictions that are then used to restrict the individuals that belong to a class. These restrictions can be placed into three main categories:

1. Quantifier restrictions
2. Cardinality restrictions
3. hasValue restrictions

Quantifier restrictions: Quantifier restrictions consist of three parts:
  1. A quantifier, which is either the existential quantifier (∃) or the universal quantifier (∀)
  2. A property along which the restriction acts
  3. A filler that is a class description

For a given individual, the quantifier effectively puts constraints on the relationships that the individual participates in. It does this by either specifying that at least one kind of relationship must exist, or by specifying the only kinds of relationships that can exist (if they exist). An example of an existential quantifier can be used to define a physician as someone with a medical degree:

$$\text{Physician} \subseteq \exists \text{has.MedicalDegree}.$$

Universal restriction states that if a relationship exists for the property, then it must be to individuals that are members of a specific class. An example of a universal quantifier can be used to define a happy physician as one whose patients all have insurance:

$$\text{HappyPhysician} \subseteq \forall \text{hasPatients}.(\exists \text{hasCoverage.Insurer}).$$

Cardinality restrictions: OWL cardinality restrictions describe the class of individuals that have at least (≤), at most ≤, or exactly a specified number of relationships with other individuals or data type values. Let P be a property, then
  1. A minimum cardinality restriction specifies the minimum number of P relationships that an individual must participate in.
  2. A maximum cardinality restriction specifies the maximum number of P relationships that an individual can participate in.
  3. A cardinality restriction specifies the exact number of P relationships that an individual must participate in.

hasValue restriction: A hasValue restriction describes the set of individuals that have at least one relationship along a specified property to a specific individual. The hasValue restriction is denoted by the symbol $\in$. An example of a hasValue restriction is hasCountryOfOrigin $\in$ Italy (where Italy is an individual). This describes the set of individuals (the anonymous class of individuals) that has at least one relationship along the hasCountryOfOrigin property to the specific individual Italy.

Supporting restrictions: We currently support the following OWL restrictions:

1. SomeValuesFromRestriction. These are existential restrictions that describe the set of individuals that have at least one specific kind of relationship to individuals that are members of a specific class.
2. AllValuesFromRestriction. These are universal restrictions that constrain the filler for a given property to a specific class.
3. MinCardinalityRestriction. These are cardinality restrictions that specify the minimum number of relationships that an individual must participate in for a given property. The symbol for a minimum cardinality restriction is *greater than or equal to* ($\geq$).
4. MaxCardinalityRestriction. These are cardinality restrictions that specify the maximum number of relationships that an individual can participate in for a given property. The symbol for maximum cardinality restrictions is *less than or equal to* ($\leq$).
5. DataRange. This is a built-in property that links a property (or some instance of the class rdf:Property) to either a class description or a data range. An rdfs:range axiom asserts that the values of this property must belong to the class extension of the class description or to data values in the specified data range.
6. Domain. This is a built-in property that links a property (or some instance of the class rdf:Property) to a class description. An rdfs:domain axiom asserts that the subjects of such property statements must belong to the class extension of the indicated class description.

DL Policy Translation. The following is a policy that states that any process that is controlled by a surgeon is a sensitive process.

```
<policies>
<policy ID="1">
<description>...some description....</description>
<rule>
<restriction>AllValuesFromRestriction</restriction>
<property>opm:WasControlledBy</property>
<class>provac:Surgeon</class>
<label>provac:SensitiveProcess</label>
</rule>
</policy>
</policies>
```

This policy is converted internally as

$$\forall \text{WascontrolledBy.Surgeon} \subseteq \text{SensitiveProcess}.$$

Access Control Policy Assembler. This module maps a high-level access control XML policy file to a low-level access control policy.

Access control policy translation: The following is a policy that states that any user has permission to access Doc_2 if it was generated by a process that was controlled by a surgeon.

```
<policies>
<policy ID="1">
<description>description</description>
<target>
<subject>anyuser</subject>
<record>provac:Doc_2</record>
<restriction>Doc.WasGeneratedBy = = opm:Process</restriction>
<restriction>process.WasControlledBy = = provac:Surgeon</restriction>
</target>
<effect>NecessaryPermit</effect>
</policy>
</policies>
```

This policy could be translated to a query that retrieves the part of a provenance graph that this policy is allowing a user to view. A corresponding SPARQL query would then be

```
Select ?x
{
 med:Doc1_2 gleen:OnPath("([opm:WasGeneratedBy]/
        [opm:WasControlledBy])" ?x
        ?x rdf:type provac:Surgeon).
}
```

Redaction Policy Assembler. This module maps a high-level XML redaction policy file to a low-level redaction policy.

Redaction policy translation: The following is a policy that states that if there is a path that starts at Doc_4 and Doc_4 was derived from an artifact that was generated by a process that was controlled by a physician, then we should redact this path from the provenance subgraph containing the path.

```
</policies>
<policy ID="1">
<description>description</description>
<lhs>
<chain>
<start> provac:Doc_4</start>
<path>
        [opm:WasDerivedFrom]+ artifact AND artifact
[opm:WasGeneratedBy] process AND
        process [opm:WasControlledBy] physician
</path>
</lhs>
<rhs>_:A1</rhs>
<condition>
<application>null</application>
<attribute>null</attribute>
</condition>
<embedding>
<pre>null</pre>
<post>(provac:HeartSurgery_1,opm:Used, _:A1)</post>
</embedding>
</policy>
</policies>
```

This policy would evaluate over a provenance graph replacing any path that starts with a node labeled Doc_4 and connected to a process via a WasGeneratedBy link followed by a WasControlledBy link, which has an end node labeled as physician (or is of type physician). Each such path would be replaced by a blank label _:A1, and :_A1 would be joined to the original provenance graph to some node labeled provac:HearthSurgery_1 using a link with the label opm:Used.

22.3.4 EXPLANATION SERVICE LAYER

A good feature to have is one where the reasoner derives new knowledge and then explains how it derived that new knowledge. The Pellet reasoner can explain its inferences by providing the minimal set of facts or other knowledge necessary to justify the inference. For any inference that Pellet computes, we exploit a Pellet inference service that will explain why that inference holds. The explanation itself is a set of OWL axioms that, taken together, justify or support the inference in question. There may be many (even infinitely many) explanations for an inference; Pellet heuristically attempts to provide a good explanation.

Our provenance inference controller (discussed in detail in Thuraisingham et al., 2014) can then provide information about the classification of the knowledge base. For example, we may be interested in why a set of RDF triples was classified as sensitive, or why a concept is considered sensitive. The answers to these questions are left to the explanation service layer. This layer is built on top of Pellet explanation service and displays the set of axioms used to derive the concepts that are subsumed by another class.

The explanation service layer users pellet service to provide justifications (also warrants) for each piece of the provenance that is sensitive (Figure 22.5). The explanation service layer is useful for providing feedback to the application designer. The explanations are displayed using the low-level descriptions and may reveal details of how the internal classification works. This may be a bad feature of the system, since the application user may not understand DL or OWL. Nevertheless, this service provides a desired feature, whereby the application designer can view how his or her policies are interpreted by the low-level inference services. For example, since a high-level DL rule may be applied differently from what the author intended, the policy designer now has an opportunity to tweak the high-level policies for the desired outcome.

22.4 GENERATORS

We now explain the process whereby the knowledge is added to a provenance store. We build a set of generators. There is a set of background generators that are responsible for extracting background information that is normally available online. There is also a set of miscellaneous generators that build synthetic data about diseases, medication, tests, and treatments. The miscellaneous generator uses online sources to guide it in associating the diseases with related tests, treatment, and diseases; thus, there is additional background information produced by these miscellaneous generators. Finally, we will discuss the workflow generator that produces the actual provenance. The workflow

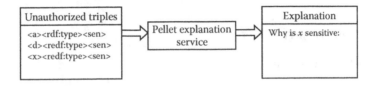

FIGURE 22.5 Explanation service layer.

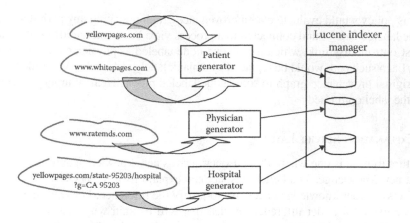

FIGURE 22.6 Background generator.

generator produces synthetic provenance data that is not available online. It is this provenance data that has subsets that we must hide.

Selecting Background Information. We use real information that actually exists on current web pages so that we can demonstrate the effectiveness of the inference controller with respect to a set of prior knowledge of the querying agent. We identify a city and state in the United States. For this city, we target a set of zip codes. The information is downloaded from freely available websites such as yellow pages and white pages. We crawl these websites and extract the name, address, telephone numbers, age, sex, and relatives of various individuals, by setting a seed for a list of popular first and last names. This would allow us to capture similar attribute values for each individual patient in our toy hospital. For the hospitals, we select only those within the zip codes of the patients. Each hospital has a name, an address, and telephone numbers. Because many hospitals do not release the names of their staff, we perform searches for doctors and their specialty within the same zip codes. This is normal, since most specialists are affiliated with a particular hospital close to their practice. Some insurance companies do provide a list of the doctors and their affiliation on their websites, but many of these websites require a login ID, or different verification code each time it is accessed. Because of these obstacles, we make do with a less accurate picture of the actual hospital. Also, since our system is user driven, automation and efficiency become a greater priority. This does not preclude a client from populating the knowledge base with their own data. Generating data this way makes the system more realistic than if we had used complete synthetic data. A querying user can combine the responses from the system with accessible background information to draw inferences. The querying user could then issue new queries to verify their guesses about the data in the knowledge base.

Background Generator Module. Figure 22.6 shows the different background generators. Each generator is built to target specific websites (or pages) that contain some information of interest. For example, www.ratemd.com provides structured information about doctors at a specific zip code.

Patient generator: The patient generator extracts the attributes of a person from a set of web pages. Algorithm 22.1 details the job of the patient generator.

Algorithm 22.1: findPersons()

   1: baseUri ← yellowpages.com;
   2: uri ← baseUri + name + zip;
   3: Link[] ← Spider(uri);
   4: For all $r \in$ RS do
   5: Contents ← Extract(Link[i]);

6: Person ← Parse(Contents);
7: AddToDatabase(Person);
8: End for

```
http://www.yellowpages.com/findaperson
?fap_terms%5Bfirst%5D="fname"
&fap_terms%5Blast%5D="Lname"
&fap_terms%5Bstate%5D="State"
&page=1"
```

Figure 22.7 shows the result when fname=John, lname=Smith, and State=CA. We then extract the address and telephone number from the result page. Figure 22.8 shows the result of executing Algorithm 22.1 when the base uri is www.whitepages.com and the parameters are fname=John, lname=Smith, and State=CA. We then extract the address and age from the result page. Figure 22.9 shows a list of attributes that we collect for each patient in our provenance knowledge base.

Physician generator: The physician generator extracts information as attribute values for a doctor. We modify the line 1 of Algorithm 22.1 by replacing the value of the base URI to base ratemd.com. Figures 22.10 through 22.12 display the user interface for searching a doctor and the results, respectively.

Hospital generator: We also generate hospital information from the yellowpages.com website. Figure 22.13 shows the results returned from searching for a hospital. Figure 22.14 shows a list of attributes we extracted for each physician in our provenance knowledge base.

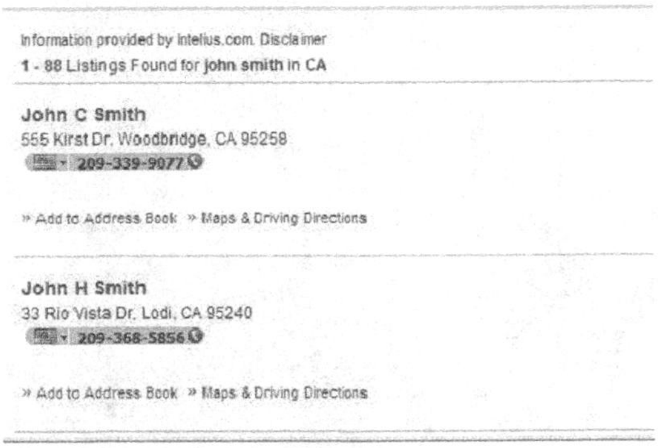

FIGURE 22.7   Partial page—yellowpages.com.

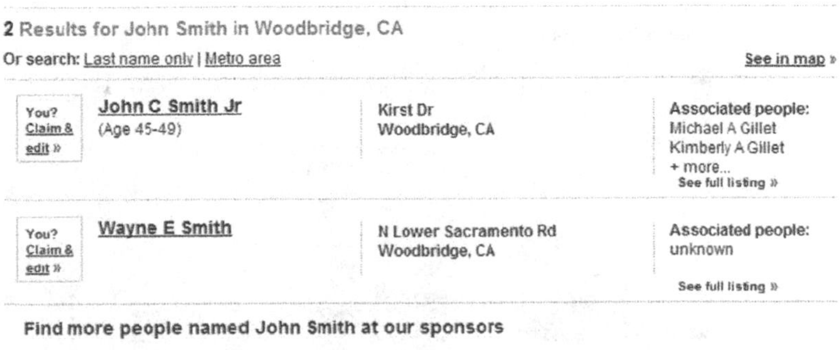

FIGURE 22.8   Partial page—whitepages.com.

```
<id> 1 </id>
<firstname> John </firstname>
<lastname> Smith </lastname>
<address> 555 Kirst Dr </address>
<city> Woodbrige </city>
<state> CA </state>
<zip> 95258 </zip>
<telephone> 209-339-9077 </telephone>
<age> 49 </age>
<sex> ? <sex>
```

FIGURE 22.9   Patient attributes.

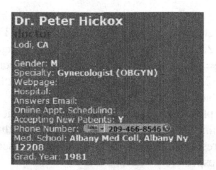

FIGURE 22.10   Single-result page (obtained from ratemd.com).

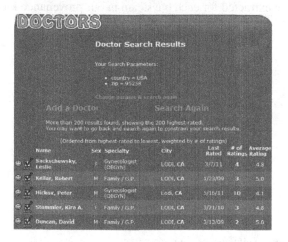

FIGURE 22.11   Multiresult page—ratemd.com.

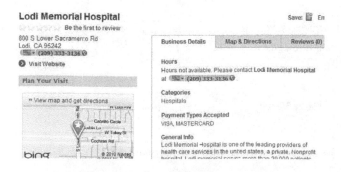

FIGURE 22.12   Partial page (hospital)—yellowpages.com.

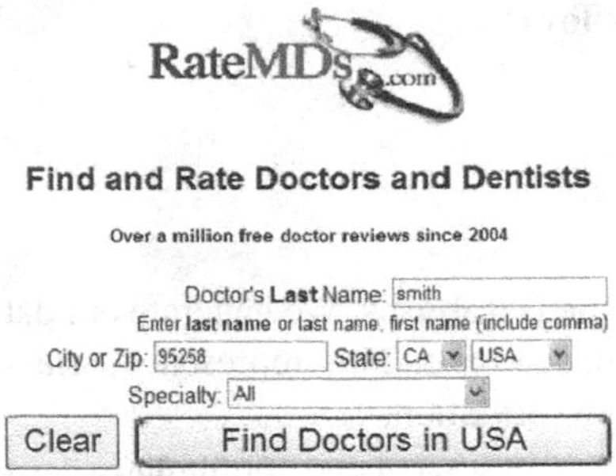

FIGURE 22.13 Partial page—ratemd.com.

```
<id> 3 </id>
<firstname> Peter </firstname>
<lastname> Hickox </lastname>
<address></address>
<city> Lodi </city>
<state> CA </state>
<zip></zip>
<telephone> 20

66-8546 </telephone>
<speciality>Gynecologist </speciality>
<age></age>
<sex> Male <sex>
<school> Albany Med Coll, Albany NY 12208
<school>
<sex> Male <sex>
```

FIGURE 22.14 Physician attributes.

Miscellaneous generators: This module uses www.webMD.com to determine the relationships between a disease, a medication, a test, and a treatment. Therefore, this allows us to add semantic association among these entities to our knowledge base. Since the relationships are background information that is also available to any user, we build rules that take these semantic relationships into consideration when disclosing provenance information.

Workflow generator: We build a set of standard workflows, which are taken from the procedures described at http://www.mghp.com/services/procedure/. Since these procedures are freely available, we build rules to protect some sensitive components in the generated workflows. Furthermore, the relationships among the entities in these workflows can be explicit or implicit. Therefore, our inference controller utilizes a mixture of policies and inference rules to protect the information in these workflows.

Annotating the Workflow. We annotate our workflow using the data produced by the background generator. Therefore, the associations between the attributes of a patient are the ones gathered from www.yellowpages.com and www.whitepages.com. Similarly, the hospital and physician attributes are, in fact, the ones gathered from www.yellowpages.com and www.ratemd.com.

Generating Workflows. As stated earlier, for each patient in our toy hospital example, we initiate workflows that update the record for the patient. The recorded provenance is the only confidential data we assume in our system. The intent is to give the querying user an opportunity to guess the patient's disease, medications, or tests associated with the record. Provenance poses more challenges than does traditional data. The controller not only anticipates inferences involving a user's prior knowledge but also considers the inferences associated with the causal relationships among the data items as well as the provenance entities (Algorithm 22.2).

Algorithm 22.2: generateworkflow()

> patient ← getPatient();
> graph ← generateOpmGraph();
> annotateGraph(graph);

Incomplete Information in the Databases. We generate our data from various web pages, each contributing a part to the knowledge base. This represents a classic case of our knowledge base containing partial or incomplete information.

An incomplete database is defined by a set of constraints and a partial database instance. Answering conjunctive queries over incomplete databases is an important computational task that lies at the core of many problems, such as information integration, data exchange, and data warehousing. A common example of partial information over a relational database is a view. A view can be defined so as to hide important data in the underlying database and thus restrict access to a user. This is usually done to satisfy some constraints; for example, employees in the accounts department can view the accounting records but not the human resources records. Given a query and an incomplete database, the task is to compute the set of certain answers. The certain answers are tuples that satisfy the query in every database instance that conforms to the partial instances and satisfies the constraints. Answering queries under general constraints is undecidable. Therefore, the expressivity of the constraint language considered is typically restricted to achieve decidability. An analogy to incomplete information in databases is an OWL ontology. In an OWL ontology, the TBox can be seen as a conceptual schema containing the set of constraints, and the ABox as some partial instances of the schema.

An incomplete database has an important property that an inference controller can use when answering queries over the RDF database. When a query returns a negative response, the user must decide whether the query was attempting to access confidential information or whether the query was not entailed in the RDF database.

22.5 USE CASE: MEDICAL EXAMPLE

In this section, we provide examples of provenance queries. These queries can be used to identify resources for a policy or identify the answer for a user query.

The provenance graph in Figure 22.15 shows a workflow that updates a fictitious record for a patient who went though three medical stages at a hospital. In the first phase, the physician performed

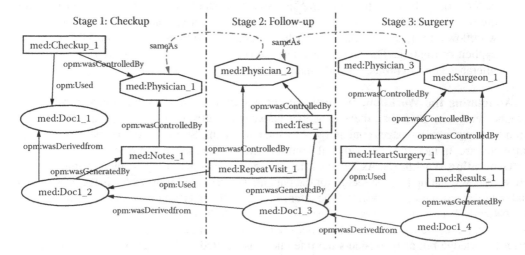

FIGURE 22.15 Provenance graph.

a checkup on the patient. At checkup, the physician consulted the history in the patient's record, med:Doc1_1, and performed the task of recording notes about the patient. At the end of the checkup, the physician then updated the patient's record, which resulted in a newer version, med:Doc1_2. In the second phase, the patient returned for a follow-up visit at the physician's request. During this visit, the physician consulted the patient's record for a review of the patient's history and then performed a series of tests on the patient. At the end of this visit, the physician then updated the patient's record, which resulted in a newer version, med:Doc1_3. In the third phase, the patient returned to undergo heart surgery. This was ordered by the patient's physician and carried out by a resident surgeon. Before the surgeon started the surgery operation, a careful review of the patient's record was performed by both the patient's physician and the surgeon. During the surgery process, the surgeon performed the task of recording the results at each stage of the heart surgery process. At the end of the surgery, the patient's record was updated by the surgeon, which resulted in a newer version, med:Doc1_4.

We assume that a hospital has a standard set of procedures that govern every health-care service that the hospital provides. Therefore, each patient who needs to use a health-care service will need to go through this set of procedures. We use a fixed set of notations in Figure 22.15 to represent an entity in the provenance graph, for example

```
<med:Checkup_n_1>.
```

The n denotes a particular patient who is undergoing a procedure at the hospital. Therefore, $n = 1$ identifies a patient with ID = 1, $n = 2$ identifies a patient with ID = 2, and so on. A larger number in the suffix of each process, agent, and artifact signifies that the particular provenance entity is used at a later stage in a medical procedure. In practice, n would be instantiated with an actual patient ID; this leads to the following set of RDF triples for a patient with ID = 1 at stage 1:

```
<med:Checkup_1_1><opm:WasControlledBy><med:Physician_1_1>
<med:Checkup_1_1><opm:Used><med:Doc_1_1>
<med:Doc_1_2><opm:WasDerivedFrom><med:Doc_1_1>
<med:Doc_1_2><opm:WasGeneratedBy><med:Notes_1_1>
<med:Notes_1_1><opm:WasControlledBy><med:Physician_1_1>
```

The sameAs annotations on the light-shaded arrows are meant to illustrate that the reference to physician is meant to be the same person in all the three phases.

This is not a complete picture of the provenance graph; it would be further annotated with RDF triples to indicate, for example, location, time, and other contextual information. Each entity in the graph would have a unique set of RDF annotations based on its type. Table 22.1 shows a set of compatible annotations for each type of provenance entity. A usage of these annotations in RDF representation for a physician associated with a patient with ID = 1 would be

```
<med:Physician_1_1><med:Name> "John Smith"
<med:Physician_1_1><med:Sex> "M"
<med:Physician_1_1><med:Age> "35"
<med:Physician_1_1><med:Zip> "76543"
```

TABLE 22.1

RDF Annotations

Entity	RDF Annotation
Process	Performed on
Agent	Name, sex, age, and zip code
Artifact	Updated on

Semantic Associations in the Workflow. We identified various semantic associations, such as, if X is a heart surgeon who updates patient Y's record, then patient Y's procedures and medications are related to heart surgery. This would allow the querying user to determine the disease of Y after querying for Y, X, and Y and X on the same path in the provenance for Y's record.

22.6 IMPLEMENTING CONSTRAINTS

Constraints are generally rules, but may also have additional conditions. The conditions may specify circumstances for applying the rules (e.g., some temporal or location criteria).

One of our approaches is to use regular expressions to write our constraints. Therefore, we could specify the LHS of a rule by using regular expressions so that the constraint is enforced whenever a pattern exists in a provenance graph. We have examined the following approaches to constraint processing. We will discuss the query modification process.

- DL concepts
- Query implementation
- SWRL rules
- Graph grammar/graph rewriting

Query Modification for Enforcing Constraints. We propose two approaches for modifying the graph patterns in a SPARQL query. These approaches use SPARQL filters and property functions. To determine the type of triple with respect to a security type (or label), the inference engine would use the domain ontology to determine the concept of each data item found in the subject or object of a triple or the classification of the property found in the TBox. This approach, however, fails when a triple pattern contains only variables and literals. We assume that either the subject, object, or predicate is a URI in any triple in the graph pattern. Special provisions could be made to determine the security type for kinds of literals occurring in the object of a triple; for example, identifying a nine-digit SSN or a sixteen-digit credit card number.

Query Filter. Graph pattern matching produces a solution sequence, where each solution has a set of bindings of variables to RDF terms. SPARQL FILTERs restrict solutions to those for which the filter expression evaluates to TRUE. The SPARQL specification (Prud'hommeaux and Seaborne, 2006) provides different techniques for modifying a graph pattern.

- SPARQL FILTERs can restrict the values of strings with regex.

```
PREFIX dc: <http://purl.org/dc/elements/1.1/>
SELECT ?title
WHERE  { ?x dc:title ?title
     FILTER regex(?title, "^SPARQL")
     }
```

- SPARQL FILTERs can restrict arithmetic expressions.

```
PREFIX dc: <http://purl.org/dc/elements/1.1/>
PREFIX ns: <http://example.org/ns#>
SELECT ?title ?price
WHERE  { ?x ns:price ?price.
     FILTER (?price < 30.5)
     ?x dc:title ?title.}
```

- Constraints in optional pattern matching, for example

```
PREFIX dc: <http://purl.org/dc/elements/1.1/>
PREFIX ns: <http://example.org/ns#>
SELECT ?title ?price
WHERE  { ?x dc:title ?title .
    OPTIONAL { ?x ns:price ?price . FILTER (?price < 30) }
  }
```

22.7 SUMMARY AND DIRECTIONS

In this chapter, we described the implementation of an inference controller for data provenance. The inference controller is built using a modular approach; therefore, it is very flexible in that most of the modules can be extended or replaced by another application module. For example, an application user may substitute the policy parser module that handles the parsing of the high-level policies to a low-level policy object. This substitution would allow the application user to continue using his or her business policies independent of our software implementation of the provenance inference controller. Essentially, we have followed a *plug-and-play* approach for implementing the inference controller. We have used open source products as much as possible in our implementation. The techniques we have implemented for inference control for provenance data can be applied for social media data represented using semantic web technologies.

This implementation is the first of its kind with respect to next-generation inference controllers. We have migrated from the relational database approach in the 1980s and 1990s to a semantic web-based approach. The reasoning capabilities of the semantic web technologies make this approach more powerful. Our next step is to adapt this inference controller for social graphs represented in RDF. Some directions were discussed in Chapter 21. We are also investigating more powerful reasoning strategies using machine learning techniques. Furthermore, we need to take into consideration the risks of unauthorized disclosure of provenance data. In addition, we can model the inference strategies as games where the players are the inference controller and the user of the system who could also be an adversary. That is, a game is played between the two parties, and each party's goal is to win the game. Essentially, the inference controller would try and prevent any unauthorized information from getting into the hands of the adversary while the adversary will attempt to extract as much information as possible from the system.

REFERENCES

Bechhofer, S., Van Harmelen, F., Hendler, J., Horrocks, I., McGuinness, D., Patel-Schneider, P., Stein, L., Patel-Schneider, P.F., and Stein, L.A. OWL web ontology language reference. *W3C Recommendation* 10, 2004.

Braun, U., Shinnar, A., and Seltzer, M. Securing provenance. In: *Proceedings of the 3rd Conference on Hot Topics in Security*, USENIX Association, 2008.

Bray, T., Paoli, J., Sperberg-McQueen, C., Maler, E., and Yergeau, F. Extensible markup language (XML) 1.0. *W3C Recommendation* 6, 2000.

Chang, L.W. and Moskowitz, I.S. Parsimonious downgrading and decision trees applied to the inference problem. In: *Proceedings of the 1998 Workshop on New Security Paradigms*, 1988.

Governatori, G. Representing business contracts in RuleML. *International Journal of Cooperative Information Systems* 14, 2005.

Grosof, B. and Poon, T. SweetDeal: Representing agent contracts with exceptions using XML rules, ontologies, and process descriptions. In: *Proceedings of the 12th International Conference on World Wide Web*, 2003.

Horrocks, I., Patel-Schneider, P., Boley, H., Tabet, S., Grosof, B., and Dean, M. SWRL: A semantic web rule language combining OWL and RuleML. *W3C Member Submission* 21, 2004.

Kifor, T., Varga, L.Z., Vazquez-Salceda, J., Alvarez, S., Willmott, S., Miles, S., and Moreau, L. Provenance in agent-mediated healthcare systems. *IEEE Intelligent Systems* 21(6), 2006.

McGuinness, D.L. and Da Silva, P.P. Inference web: Portable and shareable explanations for question answering. In: *Proceedings of the American Association for Artificial Intelligence Spring Symposium Workshop on New Directions for Question Answering*. Stanford University, Stanford, CA, 2003.

Moses, T. Editor. *Extensible Access Control Markup Language (XACML) version 2.0*. Oasis Standard, 2005.

Ni, Q., Xu, S., Bertino, E., Sandhu, R., and Han, W. An access control language for a general provenance model. In: *Secure Data Management, LCNS* 5766, pp. 68–88, Springer Verlag, Berlin, 2009.

Prud'hommeaux, E. and Seaborne, A. SPARQL query language for RDF. *W3C Working Draft*, vol. 20, 2006.

Reiter, R. On closed world databases. In: Gallaire, H. and Minker, J., editors, *Logic and Databases*. Plenum Press, New York, 1977.

Thuraisingham, B., Cadenhead, T., Kantarcioglu, M., and Khadilkar, V. *Secure Data Provenance and Inference Control with Semantic Web Technologies*. CRC Press, Boca Raton, FL, 2014.

Thuraisingham, B., Ford, W., Collins, M., and O'Keeffe, J. Design and implementation of a database inference controller. *Data & Knowledge Engineering* 11(3), 1993.

CONCLUSION TO SECTION V

Section V, which described experiential access and inference control for social networks, consisted of four chapters: Chapters 19 through 22.

In Chapter 19, we proposed an extensible fine-grained online social network access control model based on semantic web tools. In addition, we discussed authorization, administration, and filtering policies that are modeled using Web Ontology Language (OWL) and Semantic Web Rule Language (SWRL). The architecture of a framework in support of this model was also presented. In Chapter 20, we described the implementation of an extensible fine-grained online social network access control model based on semantic web tools. In particular, we discussed the implementation of the authorization, administration, and filtering policies that are modeled using OWL and SWRL. That is, we discussed the implementation of a version of the framework described in Chapter 19, and presented experimental results for the length of time access control can be evaluated using this scheme. In Chapter 21, we first described the design of an inference controller that operates over a semantic web-based provenance graph and protects important provenance information from unauthorized users. Since our social networks discussed in Chapters 19 and 20 are also represented by semantic web technologies, the techniques we have developed are applicable to such social media data. We used RDF as our data model as it supports the interoperability of multiple databases having disparate data schemas. In addition, we expressed policies and rules in terms of semantic web rules and constraints, and we classified data items and relationships between them using semantic web software tools. In Chapter 22, we described the implementation of an inference controller for data provenance discussed in Chapter 21. The inference controller is built using a modular approach; therefore, it is very flexible in that most of the modules can be extended or replaced by another application module.

Section VI

Social Media Integration and Analytics Systems

INTRODUCTION TO SECTION VI

Now that we have provided our fundamental work on social media analytics and security, we are now ready to discuss some of the experimental systems we have developed. In particular, we will discuss our systems that are represented using semantic web technologies and explain how reasoning is carried out in such social media systems.

Section VI consists of four chapters: Chapters 23 through 26. Chapter 23 will provide some basics on the use of semantic web technologies for representing and reasoning about social networks. We will first discuss aspects of entity representation and integration with semantic web. Next, we will discuss heuristic reasoning for Resource Description Framework (RDF) graphs. Third, we will discuss the analysis of RDF graphs that represent social networks. Finally, we will discuss ways of managing very large RDF graphs. In Chapter 24, we will first describe aspects of social network integration and explain the use of semantic web technologies for this purpose. We will then discuss three separate experimental cloud-based semantic web data management systems for social network integration. In Chapter 25, we will present a Hadoop-based framework capable of handling enormous amounts of RDF data that can be used to represent social networks. We will describe a schema to store RDF data, an algorithm to determine a query-processing plan, whose worst case is bounded, to answer a SPARQL query and a simplified cost model to be used by the algorithm. Chapter 26 will describe the design of SNODSOC (stream-based novel class detection for social network analysis). SNODSOC will be a great asset to analysts who have to deal with billions of blogs and messages. For example, by analyzing the behavioral history of a particular group of individuals, analysts will be able to predict behavioral changes in the near future and take necessary measures.

23 Social Graph Extraction, Integration, and Analysis

23.1 INTRODUCTION

As mentioned in Chapter 7, one of the major tasks in social network analysis is to represent the network. Typically, social networks are represented using graphs. One needs to come up with a way to electronically represent these graphs. Another task is to build the network. For example, in social networks such as Facebook, one can build a graph where the nodes are the people in the network and the links are the relationships between the people (e.g., friendships). In many situations, we may need to build a network from vast amounts of data, both structured and unstructured. The data could emanate from various databases as well as e-mails, blogs, and web pages. Therefore, we need to use various analytics techniques to extract the nuggets from the various data sources and then build the network. Once the network is developed, we can carry out analysis to extract information such as communities of interest and those who are leaders of the network. Recently, semantic web technologies are being applied to represent the graph structures presenting social networks (Mika, 2007). One of the prominent ontologies that have been developed based on Resource Description Framework (RDF) is FOAF (friend of a friend), which has been used to build a very large social network. We need techniques to extract graph structures from multimodal data, integrate the graph structures, and mine or analyze the structures and extract patterns.

Our initial research on RDF graph extraction, integration, and analysis for social network applications was carried out for the Intelligence Advanced Research Projects Agency under the KDD (Knowledge Discovery and Dissemination) program, between 2008 and 2010. In particular, we developed a layered architecture that included entity extraction and integration, ontology-based heuristics reasoning, RDF representation and analysis, and managing large RDF graphs. In this chapter, we will describe the design of each of the layers. Some of the layers have been implemented in some of the experimental systems we have discussed in this book.

The organization of this chapter is as follows. In Section 23.2, we will discuss entity extraction and integration. Ontology-based heuristic reasoning is discussed in Section 23.3. RDF graph extraction and analysis is discussed in Section 23.4. Managing large RDF graphs is discussed in Section 23.5. The chapter is summarized in Section 23.6. Figure 23.1 illustrates the contents of this chapter.

23.2 ENTITY EXTRACTION AND INTEGRATION

23.2.1 OVERVIEW

Entity extraction is a long-standing research problem in the natural language processing (NLP) community. Work on this problem was stimulated initially by the Defense Advanced Research Projects Agency (DARPA)-sponsored Message Understanding Conferences (MUCs) in the mid-1990s and recently by the National Institute of Standards and Technology (NIST)-sponsored Automatic Content Extraction (ACE) evaluations. Relation extraction was introduced as a major information extraction task in ACE and therefore was less studied than entity extraction. The most successful approach to entity and relation extraction to date has arguably been supervised machine learning approaches. In these approaches, both entity extraction and relation extraction are recast as classification tasks, where documents annotated with the entities and relations of interest are used in combination with a rich set of linguistic features to train a classifier via an off-the-shelf learning algorithm.

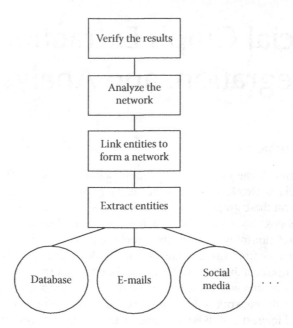

FIGURE 23.1 Social graph extraction, integration, and analysis.

Besides offering robust performance, there are three major reasons why a machine learning approach to entity and relation extraction is more appealing than an ontology-based approach. First, a learning-based extraction system does not have to depend on any ontology, since the linguistic knowledge required for extraction is learned directly from annotated data. Second, a learning-based approach is very flexible: if any user-defined, variable ontology is made available to the extraction system, the information acquired from the ontology can be easily incorporated into the system as linguistic features or constraints to improve system performance. Finally, classifiers trained via advanced machine learning algorithms (e.g., logical regression, maximum entropy) typically perform probabilistic classifications, which can serve as confidence values that would be helpful for downstream text-processing components.

Motivated by the successes of prior work, we have developed machine learning approaches to entity and relation extraction. In particular, we have developed two types of extensions to existing machine learning approaches. Figure 23.2 illustrates our approach.

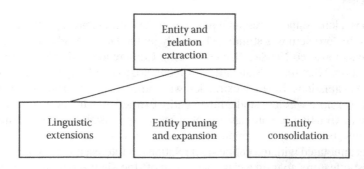

FIGURE 23.2 Entity and relation extraction.

23.2.2 MACHINE LEARNING APPROACHES

Linguistic Extensions. These extensions are concerned with incorporating additional linguistic knowledge sources into the existing machine learning framework for entity and relation extraction. While a wide variety of linguistic features have been investigated for these two tasks, we believe that there are at least two underinvestigated knowledge sources that can be exploited to improve system performance. First, we plan to examine how the information derived from the fixed ontology (and possibly a domain-specific ontology, if one is available) can be profitably integrated with the learned classifiers for making classification decisions. One possibility is to represent such information as features for training classifiers; another possibility is to classify an entity or relation directly using the available ontologies, and resort to the learned classifiers only if the desired information is absent from the ontologies. We plan to experiment with both approaches. Another, perhaps more important, knowledge source that we have explored is Wikipedia. Wikipedia can potentially provide up-to-date information. Also, a large number of Wikipedia pages are devoted to domain-specific topics; hence, exploiting Wikipedia knowledge can potentially make an extraction system more adaptive to different domains. The NLP community has only recently begun to investigate the use of Wikipedia for entity extraction, deriving information only from the title or the first sentence of a Wikipedia page using simple pattern-matching techniques (e.g., Cucerzan, 2007; Kazama and Torisawa, 2007; Watanabe et al., 2007). We have investigated ways of exploiting information extracted from other sections of a Wikipedia page not only for entity extraction but also for relation extraction.

Extralinguistic Extensions. While supervised machine learning approaches reduce a system's reliance on an ontology, the performance of a learning-based system depends heavily on the availability of a large amount of annotated data, which can be expensive to obtain. Consequently, we have developed three extralinguistic extensions that aim to improve the robustness of an extraction system in the face of limited annotated data.

a. *Combining knowledge-based and learning-based approaches to entity extraction and relation extraction*: Given the ambiguity inherent in natural languages and the variance that exists among different domains, we believe that a few simple heuristics, if carefully designed, can sometimes boost system performance substantially. Hence, rather than spending a large amount of time on handcrafting heuristics for each domain of interest, we investigate the benefits of combining a small set of heuristics with a learned classifier for entity and relation extraction.

b. *Incorporating domain adaptation techniques*: When moving to a new domain, we need to annotate a new set of training documents from that domain for classifier acquisition. The question, then, is this: is it possible to leverage training data from existing domains? To address this question, a number of domain adaptation techniques have been proposed (e.g., Jiang and Zhai, 2006, 2007). By exploiting data from existing domains, we hypothesize that these techniques could alleviate the problem of training data scarcity, and that the resulting classifiers would be more resistant to overfitting (because they are trained on data collected from different domains). We plan to incorporate domain adaptation techniques into our machine learning approach and empirically evaluate their benefits.

c. *Automatically generating additional training data*: Perhaps the most straightforward way to address the data scarcity problem is to annotate more data. However, instead of manually annotating additional data, we have designed a *bootstrapping* algorithm for automatically augmenting the existing training data for a particular entity type (e.g., PERSON) or relation type (e.g., PARENT-OF). The algorithm takes as input a set of unannotated texts, which are to be labeled with the entities or relations of interest. In addition, the algorithm requires as input a seed set that consists of a small number of examples of the entity or relation type to be extracted. This seed set can be easily created by extracting the entities

or relations of interest from existing annotated data. The algorithm then iterates over the following steps:
1. Learn patterns for extracting the seed entities or relations from the unannotated texts.
2. Optionally request a human to examine and discard the bad extraction patterns.
3. Apply the learned extraction patterns to extract new entities or relations from the texts.
4. Optionally request a human to examine and discard bad entities or relations.
5. Add the extracted entities or relations to the seed set.

Hence, the seed set is augmented with new entities or relations in each iteration of the bootstrapping algorithm. We can terminate this algorithm when we have a reasonably large number of entities or relations in the seed set. The remaining question is how to automatically acquire the extraction patterns in each bootstrapping iteration. While various methods for the automatic acquisition of extraction patterns exist, the AutoSlog system (Riloff, 1993) is arguably one of the most successful for extracting patterns from natural language texts. However, AutoSlog has mostly been applied to entity extraction. We have extended it to extracting relations.

Entity Integration. Once entities and relations are extracted from free text, we face the problem of integrating them for creating a combined semantic representation. During entity extraction, some extracted entities may be erroneous or irrelevant and some extracted ones are relevant. Hence, we need to discard irrelevant entities and keep relevant ones. Next, we need to consolidate entities that will come from multiple documents. It is possible that an entity may have multiple references in various documents that refer to the same entity in real life. We have examined the following two relevant challenges: (i) removing irrelevant entities in a document generated by information extraction techniques and (ii) consolidating the extracted entities among documents so that we can establish a *same as* relationship between entities that are indeed the same entity.

Entity Pruning and Expansion. With regard to the first challenge, the current state of the art, including our work, may produce many irrelevant entities or relations when mining textual documents. We have formulated an approach that augments a classical model (e.g., correlation model) (Mori et al., 1999) with the generic or domain-specific knowledge bases (e.g., WordNet). Our approach will strive to prune irrelevant entities by using publicly available knowledge bases. To identify irrelevant entities, we have examined various semantic similarity measures between entities and finally fuse the outcomes of these measures together to make a final decision using Dempster–Shafer evidence combination or linear combination. In our previous work on image annotation, we implemented various models to link visual regions or tokens with keywords based on WordNet, and evaluated the performance using precision and recall with a benchmark data set (Jin et al., 2005). Our results show that by augmenting a knowledge-based model with a classical model, we can improve annotation accuracy by removing irrelevant keywords. Here, we employ two steps, namely, pruning and expansion, to improve annotation accuracy. In the pruning step, we make use of fuzzy pruning to exclude irrelevant keywords, thus improving precision. In the expansion step, we use the association rule mining (ARM) algorithm to find missing relevant keywords by exploiting the training set.

Recall that removing irrelevant keywords in the image annotation process improves precision, and adding relevant keywords improves precision and recall. Hence, we have applied similar techniques for removing irrelevant extracted entities and adding relevant entities that may be missed during the extraction phase. In addition, since there may exist uncertainty in the entity extraction domain (i.e., irrelevant entities may be extracted with high confidence value), we can reformulate the removal of erroneous entities from entity extraction problem into a graph-partitioning problem, which is a weighted max-cut problem. For this, first, we have considered each extracted entity in a document as a vertex and the semantic distance between extracted entities as edges of a complete graph G. Next, we have used an efficient approximation algorithm for dividing a set of nodes in metric space into two parts (erroneous entity group and correct entity group) for maximizing the sum of distances between nodes belonging to each group.

Entity Consolidation. With regard to consolidating the extracted entities among documents, a name-reconciliation algorithm (Dong et al., 2005) will be utilized. A semantic similarity measure will be exploited between entities by gleaning context associated with entities. Here, similarity between two references will be defined as a combination of literal properties and resource properties in RDF. For example, two-person entities in the DBLP publication database will be the same when various attributes and relationships such as their names, affiliations, and the number of common coauthor relationships are similar to each other (Meza et al., 2006). However, various attributes and relationships will not carry the same weight during similarity calculation. Some attributes and relationships will carry more weight than others. Since these weight values will be adaptive in nature and vary with time, we would like to exploit some learning algorithm to learn the weight and calculate similarity accordingly.

23.3 ONTOLOGY-BASED HEURISTIC REASONING

23.3.1 RULE-BASED APPROACH TO JUST-IN-TIME RETRIEVAL

One of the major issues involved in just-in-time document retrieval is, in which order should the partially retrieved results be presented? We have investigated two approaches: a rule-based approach and a data mining approach based on user profiles. These two approaches will compute an incremental result set in such a way that the most relevant results will come first and the least relevant will come last. Since any newly computed partial result set will be augmented with previously computed partial result sets in a continuous manner, users will be satisfied by getting relevant results quickly without a significant delay. Figure 23.3 illustrates our approach.

During materialization, the ontology reasoner takes a Uniform Resource Identifier (URI) as input, and outputs the retrieved documents as results. In the rule-based approach, we rely on a set of handcrafted heuristics for determining the order in which we present the partial set of retrieved documents to the client. For instance, we can order the retrieved results based on

1. Vocabulary-based materialization (i.e., URI to vocabulary-based model)
2. Same-as Web Ontology Language (OWL) ontology
3. OWL-based inheritance
4. Reification
5. Other OWL statements

We have experimented with different sets of heuristics for ordering the retrieved results and evaluated this rule-based approach on the basis of user satisfaction. However, since these ordering rules are manually designed, one potential problem with this rule-based approach is that over time,

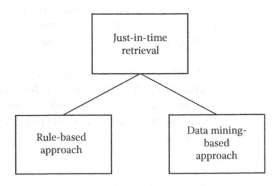

FIGURE 23.3   Just-in-time retrieval.

users may not be happy with the ordering of results. In other words, the ordering of results needs to be made more adaptive to individual users. For this, we need a mining technique to find the best rule ordering based on users' feedback.

23.3.2 DATA MINING APPROACHES BASED ON USER PROFILES TO JUST-IN-TIME RETRIEVAL

A user profile is a user's history of navigation within a period of time. User sessions will be extracted from the logs of the web servers that contain sequences of URIs users have visited, together with the types of relations involved in expansion. A user session is typically represented using an n-gram. In the context of a user session, an n-gram is composed of a tuple of the form $<X_1, X_2,..., X_n>$ that depicts a sequence of URI clicks by a user who surfs documents. However, in our work, we have considered a sequence that represents a set of relations (e.g., same-as, re-apply) involved in the expansion phase (e.g., X_2 = same-as). Using these profiles, we have investigated two types of data mining techniques that aim to customize the order of retrieval results to individual users, as described below.

Histogram-Based Ordering of Retrieved Results. In the histogram-based approach, the presentation order of the retrieved documents for a particular user will be a function of the frequency of relations associated with different documents retrieved previously for this user. In other words, documents associated with the most frequent relations will be expanded first, and documents associated with the least frequent relations will be expanded last. More specifically, given a log file represented as an n-gram (within a particular amount of time), we have (i) constructed a histogram based on the frequency of each relation, (ii) sorted the relations in descending order, and (iii) expanded the documents according to this order. Over time, a user's navigation pattern may change. As a result, we run this technique periodically, assigning more weight to the most recent expanded relations.

Sequence-Based Ordering of Retrieved Results Using ARM. It is conceivable that there are circumstances in which the above histogram-based approach may not be as adaptive to a user's preference as we want. For example, if certain recurring patterns can be found in a user profile (e.g., relation A often precedes relation B), then an approach that expands documents with relation A before relation B may correspond more closely with the user who owns this profile. To model recurring patterns in a user profile, we have exploited a Markov model (Pitkow and Pirolli, 1999) and ARM (Agrawal et al., 1993, 1999) to find the most frequently expanded sequence or longest repeating subsequences.

In our case, a *pattern* is simply a subsequence in the n-gram that represents a user profile and can be extracted using a sliding window. More specifically, we apply a sliding window at n-gram sessions to make instances the same length. For example, if we apply a sliding window of size 3 on the n-gram $<X_{10}, X_{21}, X_4, X_{12}, X_{11}>$, we have the following 3-gram sessions: $<X_{10}, X_{21}, X_4>$, $<X_{21}, X_4, X_{12}>$, and $<X_4, X_{12}, X_{11}>$.

In Markov modeling, we want to predict the next action based on the result of previous actions. Here, the next action corresponds to predicting the next relation to be expanded and the previous actions correspond to the previous relations that have already been visited. In our web prediction work (Awad et al., 2008), the kth-order Markov model predicts the probability that a user will visit the kth page provided that the user has visited $k - 1$ pages. More specifically,

$$\Pr(P_k \mid P_{k-1},...P_{k-n}) =$$

$$\Pr(S_k = P_k \mid S_{k-1} = P_{k-1},....,S_{k-n} = P_{k-n})$$

where P_i is a web page and S_i is the corresponding state in the Markov model. Notice that a Markov model cannot make predictions for sessions that do not occur in the training set since such sessions will be assigned a zero probability by the model. To address this problem, we employ an all-kth-order Markov model (Pitkow and Pirolli, 1999). The idea here is that for a given session x of length k, the kth-order Markov model is first used for prediction. If the kth-order Markov model cannot predict for x (because it assigns zero probability to the sequence under consideration), then the $(k-1)$th order Markov model is used for prediction using a new session x' of length $k-1$, where x' is computed by ignoring the first page ID in x. This process repeats until a prediction is obtained. Thus, unlike the basic Markov model, the all-kth-order Markov model can predict when a n-gram sequence does not exist in the training data, and it fails only when all orders of basic Markov models fail to predict. Using this Markov model enables us to find the longest repeating subsequences with maximum probability that appear in the log.

To find the *most frequently expanded sequence*, we employ related work on addressing the sequential pattern mining problem, which is based on ARM (Cooley et al., 1999). For instance, Srikant and Agrawal (1996) proposed the AprioriSome and AprioriAll algorithms to solve the sequential pattern mining problem. The sequential pattern mining problem is defined as follows. Given a database D of customer sequences, find the maximal sequences among all sequences in the database that satisfy a prespecified minimum support, where the sequence of a customer is of the form < itemset(T_1), itemset(T_2), ..., itemset(T_N) >, where an *itemset* is a nonempty set of items.

Once we identify the most frequently expanded sequence or the longest repeating subsequences using the above methods from the log, the ontology reasoner will expand relations based on the sequence. Recall that each value of the sequence represents a relation.

23.4 GRAPH ANALYSIS

23.4.1 EXTRACT RDF GRAPHS FROM MULTIMODAL DATA

We have designed and developed tools and techniques to analyze and mine RDF graphs extracted from multimodal data to determine patterns and trends. These tools are discussed in several of the remaining chapters of Section VI. Our technical approach mainly consists of extracting RDF graphs from multimodal data sources, integrating the graphs, and analyzing the graphs. These steps are illustrated in Figure 23.4.

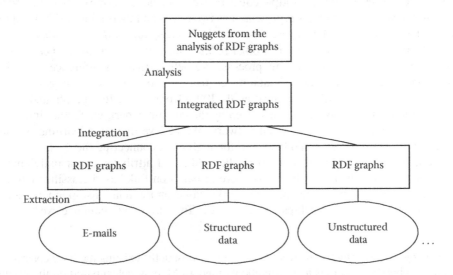

FIGURE 23.4   RDF graph extraction, reduction, integration, and analysis.

The data to be analyzed and integrated come from multiple sources such as e-mails, web logs, publications, and articles. For example, the web page of a professor will have pointers to his or her publications; some personal data such as family pictures and notes; media reports and news releases about him or her; and web blogs that describe his or her views on policies, politics, and technical topics. The extraction of RDF graphs from multimodal data will involve named-entity recognitions and domain-specific recognition tasks. We have developed tools that perform pattern-based annotation of the unstructured text using open source NLP tools. The role of pattern-based annotation is to find patterns for a defined initial set of entities in the corpus (Khalifa, 2007). When new entities are discovered along with new patterns, the procedure continues until there are no new patterns. E-mail is an example of an entity that fits well with this approach. We can also specify rules for finding specific entities in the text. The other approach used is the machine-based annotation, which uses two methods: probability and induction. Probability-based tools use statistical models to extract entities, whereas the induction approach relies on linguistic analysis through wrapper induction (University of Washington, 2007). These tools for extraction will be semiautomatic in nature, requiring minimum human intervention. Using these tools, we generate annotated RDF data from these heterogeneous resources.

23.4.2 Social Network Analysis Techniques

We have developed novel techniques for extracting patterns. However, before we apply data mining techniques, we reduce the complexity of the graphs. That is, the graphs have to be reduced so that they are more manageable. There have been discussions on whether to reduce the RDF graphs and then integrate them, or whether to integrate them first and then reduce them. In our research, we have used principal component analysis to reduce the data dimensions and then apply various data mining techniques.

After graph reduction, our focus has been on clustering techniques to group individuals based on their behavior patterns or some other criteria. We have applied various clustering techniques such as hierarchical clustering for clustering images, as well as for applications in security applications. We have augmented these techniques with novel techniques that we have developed called DGSOT. DGSOT essentially provides the capability to enhance performance when developing clusters (Awad et al., 2008). We have examined these techniques for the network of graph structures that result from graph integration.

Once the social network graphs are integrated, our second focus has been on developing analysis techniques that could leverage the multiple edges between the nodes. For example, in a social network, we could have two individuals represented as two nodes and their relationship is represented with multiple labeled edges such as *works-in-the-same-building* and *calls-each-others-cell-phone*. With such information, we may infer some other relationships such as *friends* and *colleagues*. The obvious question is, can we automate this process? We believe that this inference of further relationships among different individuals is automated using various data mining techniques. First, we learn various association rules (Agrawal et al., 1994) from an existing graph, and using these learned association rules or any other rules given by the domain expert, we further infer new relationships between individuals in the social network. We believe that such learning of additional relationships among individuals could be useful for analysts in connecting the dots.

In addition, we have developed tools to predict additional attributes about individuals in the social network. Recently, there has been extensive research on link-based classification (e.g., Sen and Getoor, 2007) to label nodes in social networks based on the relationship among nodes. The goal is to consider multiple relationships between nodes. To address this challenge, we have explored the following directions:

a. *Developing closeness metric between nodes*: Since most of the existing methods consider conditional probabilistic models (e.g., conditional random Markov fields) based on the neighborhood of the node (Sen and Getoor, 2007), on the basis of the links between nodes we can define various closeness metrics to form the neighborhood sets. For example, if we know that two individuals have multiple relationships such as *friend* and *colleague*, we may consider these two nodes to be *closer* to each other. These closeness metrics could be used to assign prior weights to nodes in conditional probability calculations. We explore the various closeness metrics and test the effect of prior probability assignments based on such closeness metrics.

b. *Developing classifier ensembles*: In the previous direction, we have reduced various links between nodes to one closeness metric and use this metric to set prior weight assignments in graphical random models. Instead, in this case, we have designed various classifiers based on each link and combined these various classifiers to create classifier ensembles. For example, we can create one classifier to label individuals as potential terrorists or not based on the *friend* relationship and create another classifier based on the *colleague* relationship, and then combine those two classifiers to create a classifier ensemble based on their performance on test data.

23.5 MANAGING AND QUERYING LARGE RDF GRAPHS

23.5.1 OUR APPROACH

While the previous three sections discussed entity extraction, heuristic reasoning, and graph analysis, we need an efficient way to manage the large graphs presented in RDF. Therefore, in this section, we will discuss our approach to managing and querying large graphs. In particular, we have designed tools and techniques to store and manage the complex and large RDF graph structures. We have also designed storage schemes as well as query optimization techniques, and transactions management techniques for these graphs structures. Figure 23.5 illustrates our approach.

First, we need an appropriate data model to represent these graphs. On the basis of the current trends and our expertise, we have designed a model based on RDF graphs. RDF is a semantic web language and has the efficient syntax of XML (eXtensible Markup Language), and incorporates semantics so that relationships and connections can be specified. RDF data sets are composed of RDF statements where each statement is in the form of <Subject, Predicate, Object>. RDF could be used for any data, irrespective of the application. Especially, using these RDF statements, complex RDF graphs that can capture relationships among different entities could be created and such RDF graphs could be processed, queried, and mined. For example, RDF graphs could be generated to capture possible relationships among different terrorist operatives.

One obvious challenge is to process large RDF data with billions of nodes and statements. Current existing solutions (e.g., Jena; Carroll et al., 2004) try to build the RDF graph model in

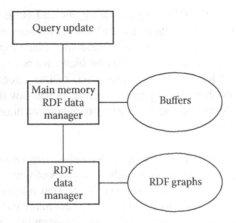

FIGURE 23.5 Managing and querying large RDF graphs.

memory using the RDF triples that are stored in some persistent storage. Clearly, building the RDF graph model in memory is not a viable option for large RDF data sets. In addition, currently, there is little work on developing storage, query, transaction, and version mechanisms for RDF. While query languages such as RQL and SPARQL have been developed, these languages lack the full query power of SQL. Furthermore, the notion of transactions in RDF data stores is not well understood. It is only recently that transactions and version management for XML documents are being investigated (Thuraisingham, 2002).

Although various approaches have been suggested to store and manage RDF graphs (Alexaki et al., 2001; Angles et al., 2005; Beckett, 2002; Bönström et al., 2003; Janik and Kochut, 2005; Wu and Li, 2007), either these approaches do not scale well to large RDF graphs or they require totally new data storage mechanisms (Bönström et al., 2003; Wu and Li, 2007). In our project, instead of reinventing the wheel, we have leveraged the existing database and semantic web technologies, to manage large RDF graphs. Currently, there are software tools like Jena (Carroll et al., 2004) that allow users to query RDF graphs and infer additional relations using various reasoning tools (e.g., OWL Description Logic-based reasoning). Unfortunately, existing RDF analysis tools do not scale well to very large RDF graphs. On the other hand, current relational database systems provide support for querying and storing very large amounts of RDF triples, but they do not provide effective tools for reasoning and analyzing RDF graphs.

Although there have been some simple buffer management (e.g., Deligiannidis et al., 2007) solutions to provide paging support for in-memory RDF graphs, these solutions do not consider the querying and reasoning done on the RDF graphs. Therefore, new approaches that are querying aware and reasoning aware are needed to manage large RDF graphs.

To address those challenges, we have designed an RDF graph manager that sits between RDF toolkits such as Jena and a relational database system. The main functionality of our RDF graph manager will be to issue necessary queries to the relational database system to retrieve the required RDF nodes and keep only the graph nodes that are needed by the graph analysis toolkit.

Our solution is implemented on top of the existing open source RDF toolkit Jena, and is composed of two main parts. First, we designed a smart buffer manager that considers the requirements of RQL and SPARQL queries and the possible reasoning that could be done on the large RDF graphs. In addition, we have redesigned a prefetching component that can try to retrieve the potentially needed RDF triples in advance. Finally, we explored how to use the transaction support provided by the relational database management systems to handle transactions on large RDF graphs. In the rest of this section, we discuss each major component of our solution.

23.5.2 Large RDF Graph Buffer Manager

Usually, tools like Jena retrieve the RDF triples one by one and build the RDF graph in memory. Even though simple paging ideas (Deligiannidis et al., 2007) are suggested to deal with large RDF graphs, to the best of our knowledge, they do not consider the effect of query processing and reasoning done on the large RDF graphs. To address this problem, we have profiled the access/traversal patterns of various queries on RDF graphs. On the basis of these access patterns, we would like to leverage some known facts about large graphs, such as power law distribution of node degrees (Faloutsos et al., 1999), to develop effective buffer management heuristics. Initially, we plan to explore the following heuristics:

a. *Giving more priority in buffering to high in-degree/out-degree nodes*: It is known that in many large social graphs, there are few high in-degree/out-degree nodes (Faloutsos et al., 1999). For example, in a graph that represents the citation relationship among various scientific papers, we may find few papers that are cited by many papers (i.e., nodes with high in-degree). In buffer management, such nodes may be given priority over other nodes since any traversal of the graph will more likely go through those high in-degree/out-degree nodes.

b. *Giving more priority in buffering to nodes that are connected with some special predicates*: In some cases, ontology-based reasoning could be used with RDF graphs to infer additional statements. For example, it may be known that two terrorist organizations with different names are actually the same. Using this fact, if we know that a terrorist is a member of one organization, we may conclude that the same terrorist is also a member of another terrorist organization (actually, Jena allows more powerful reasoning using OWL ontology; Carroll et al., 2004). During the reasoning, the reasoning engine may want to access the edges that represent some special relationships (e.g., edges that represent the *member of* relationship). In such cases, we may give priority in buffering to nodes that are linked with such special edges. In addition to the above heuristics, we explore other graph buffer management heuristics that may increase the performance of certain tasks.

RDF Triples Retrieval Manager. In some cases, we may want to prefetch some of the RDF triples even before they are asked by the RDF toolkit to improve the performance. For example, during the processing of the RDF graph, we may want to retrieve the RDF triples that may be accessed in the near future by issuing SQL queries to relational database. While the RDF toolkit is doing some processing in memory, we may start the retrieval of the related RDF triples. Such prefetching may overlap the disk I/O with graph processing to improve the performance.

In addition, we explore the effect of various indexing techniques that can be used on RDF triple retrieval in relational databases. Especially, we would like to see what kind of indexes could help with RDF triple retrieval needed for reasoning on RDF graphs.

Supporting Transactions on RDF Graphs. During the querying and the processing of the large RDF graphs, we may need to modify the underlying RDF graph. In addition, we may want to store some of the inferred statements on the persistent storage. At the same time, multiple users may want to access and modify the same underlying RDF graph. To enable concurrent access to large RDF graphs, we may want to provide transaction support. We believe that this could be easily achieved by leveraging the transaction support available in relational database management systems. Specifically, each modification on the original RDF graph could be translated into an equivalent set of SQL queries on the stored RDF triples. Later on, each set of such queries could be executed as a transaction on the database.

23.6 SUMMARY AND DIRECTIONS

This chapter has provided some basics on the use of semantic web technologies for representing and reasoning about social networks. We first discussed aspects of entity representation and integration with semantic web. Next, we discussed heuristic reasoning for RDF graphs. Third, we discussed the analysis of RDF graphs that represent social networks. Finally, we discussed ways of managing very large RDF graphs.

Several of the experimental systems we have designed or developed are based on semantic web technologies. For example, in Chapter 24, we discuss three semantic web-based systems for social network integration, and in Chapter 25 we describe a semantic web-based query-processing system. Chapters 23, 24, 25, 27, 28, 32, and 33 discuss various social network systems that are based on semantic web.

REFERENCES

Agrawal, R., Imielinski, T., and Swami A. Mining association rules between sets of items in large databases. In: *Proc. of the ACM SIGMOD Conference on Management of Data*, May 1993, Washington, DC, 1993.

Agrawal, R. and Srikant, R. Fast algorithms for mining association rules. In: *Proc. of the 20th International Conference on Very Large Databases*, September 1994, Santiago, Chile, 1994.

Agrawal, R., Aggarawal, C., and Prasad, V. A tree projection algorithm for generation of frequent itemsets. In: *Proc. of the High Performance Data Mining Workshop*, Puerto Rico, 1999.

Alexaki, S., Christophides, V., Karvounarakis, G., Plexousakis, D., and Tolle, K. The ICS-FORTH RDFSuite: Managing voluminous RDF description bases. In: *SemWeb*, 2001.

Angles, R. and Gutierrez, C. Querying RDF data from a graph database perspective. In: *ESWC2005*, May 2005, Heraklion, Greece, 2005.

Awad, M., Khan, L., and Thuraisingham, B.M. Predicting WWW surfing using multiple evidence combination. *The VLDB Journal* 17: 401–417, 2008.

Beckett, D. The design and implementation of the Redland RDF application framework. *Computer Networks* 39(5): 577–588, 2002.

Bönström, V., Hinze, A., and Schweppe, H. Storing RDF as a graph. In: *Proceedings of the First Conference on Latin American Web Congress*, November 10–12, 2003, p. 27, 2003.

Carroll, J.J., Dickinson, I., Dollin, C., Reynolds, D., Seaborne, A., and Wilkinson, K. Jena: Implementing the semantic web recommendations. In: *13th World Wide Web Conference*, WWW, 2004.

Cooley, R., Mobasher, B., and Srivastava, J. Data preparation for mining World Wide Web browsing patterns. *Journal of Knowledge and Information Systems* (1): 1, 1999.

Cucerzan, S. Large-scale named entity disambiguation based on Wikipedia data. In: *Proceedings of EMNLP-CoNLL*, pp. 708–716. Prague, Czech Republic, 2007.

Deligiannidis, L., Kochut, K.J., and Sheth, A.P. RDF data exploration and visualization. In: *ACM CIMS 2007, First Workshop on CyberInfrastructure: Information Management in eScience (CIMS)*, November 9, 2007. Lisboa, Portugal, 2007.

Dong, L., Halvey, A., and Madhavan, J. Reference reconciliation in complex information spaces. In: *ACM SIGMOD Conference*, Baltimore, 2005.

Faloutsos, M., Faloutsos, P., and Faloutsos, C. On power–law relationships of the Internet topology. In: *ACM SIGCOMM '99*, pp. 251–262. Cambridge, MA, 1999.

Janik, M. and Kochut, K. BRAHMS: A WorkBench RDF store and high performance memory system for semantic association discovery. In: *ISWC2005*, pp. 431–445. Galway, Ireland, 2005.

Jiang, J. and Zhai, C. Exploiting domain structure for named entity recognition. In: *Proceedings of HLT-NAACL*, pp. 74–81. New York, 2006.

Jiang, J. and Zhai, C. Instance weighting for domain adaptation in NLP. In: *Proceedings of the ACL*, pp. 264–271. Prague, Czech Republic, 2007.

Jin, Y., Khan, L., Wang, L., Awad, M. Image annotations by combining multiple evidence & WordNet. *ACM Multimedia* 706–715, 2005.

Kazama, J. and Torisawa, K. Exploiting Wikipedia as external knowledge for named entity recognition. In: *Proceedings of EMNLP-CoNLL*, pp. 698–707. Prague, Czech Republic, 2007.

Khalifa, H.S. Automatic document-level semantic metadata annotation using folksonomies and domain ontologies, Thesis, University of Southampton, 2007.

Meza, B.A., Nagarajan, M., Ramakrishnan, C., Ding, L., Kolari, P., Sheth, A.P., Arpinar, I.B., Joshi, A., and Finin, T. Semantic analytics on social networks: Experiences in addressing the problem of conflict of interest detection. In: *WWW 2006*, pp. 407–416, 2006.

Mika, P. *Social Networks and the Semantic Web*. Springer, New York, 2007.

Mori, Y., Takahashi, H., and Oka, R. Image-to-word transformation based on dividing and vector quantizing images with words. In: *MISRM'99 First International Workshop on Multimedia Intelligent Storage and Retrieval Management*, 1999.

Pitkow, J. and Pirolli, P. Mining longest repeating subsequences to predict World Wide Web surfing. In: *Proc. of 2nd USENIX Symposium on Internet Technologies and Systems (USITS'99)*, October 1999, Boulder, CO, 1999.

Riloff, E. Automatically constructing a dictionary for information extraction tasks. In: *Proc. of the Eleventh National Conference on Artificial Intelligence*, pp. 811–816, 1993.

Sen, P. and Getoor, L. Link-based classification, University of Maryland Technical Report CS-TR-4858, February 2007.

Srikant, R. and Agrawal, R. Mining sequential patterns: Generalization and performance. In: *Proceedings of the 5th Int. Conference Extending Database Technology (EDBT)*, vol. 1057, pp. 3–17. Avignon, France, 1996.

Thuraisingham, B. *XML, Databases and the Semantic Web*. CRC Press, Boca Raton, FL, 2002.

University of Washington. *Research on Wrapper Induction for Information Extraction*, http://www.cs .washington.edu/homes/weld/wrappers.html. Accessed on December 1, 2007.

Watanabe, Y., Asahara, M., and Matsumoto Y. A graph-based approach to named entity categorization in Wikipedia using conditional random fields. In: *Proceedings of EMNLP-CoNLL*, pp. 649–657. Prague, Czech Republic, 2007.

Wu, G. and Li, J. Managing large scale native RDF semantic repository from the graph model perspective. In: *Proceedings of ACM SIGMOD2007 Ph.D. Workshop on Innovative Database Research* (IDAR2007), Beijing, China, 2007.

24 Semantic Web-Based Social Network Integration

24.1 INTRODUCTION

Different organizations may have their own databases. These databases may be heterogeneous in nature. For example, one database may be based on a relational model, while another may be based on an object model; yet, a third database may be based on a semistructured data model such as XML. Various tools and techniques have been developed to integrate these heterogeneous databases. Today, we have migrated from heterogeneous databases to heterogeneous information systems, including social network systems. These systems may handle heterogeneous data types. Furthermore, social media systems, represented using semantic web technologies, may have to be merged to provide a uniform view of the disparate networks. For example, two social network companies may merge, and therefore the models and links have to be integrated to form a uniform view of the networks. Several technologies are needed for the integration of information and networks.

In this chapter, we describe three experimental cloud-based information integration systems that utilize semantic web technologies. These systems can be used to integrate information in social networks. The first system, called Jena–HBase, is a storage system for Resource Description Framework (RDF) triples. The second system, called StormRider, uses the Storm framework for hosting social networks in the cloud. StormRider also uses Jena–HBase in its implementation. The third system is an ontology-driven query-processing system that utilizes the MapReduce framework. We describe the motivation behind the three systems.

First, the lack of scalability is one of the most significant problems faced by single-machine RDF data stores. The advent of cloud computing has paved the way for a distributed ecosystem of RDF triple stores that can potentially allow up to a planet-scale storage along with distributed query-processing capabilities. Toward this end, we present Jena–HBase, an HBase-backed triple store that can be used with the Jena framework. Jena–HBase provides end users with a scalable storage and querying solution that supports all features from the RDF specification.

Second, the focus of online social media providers today has shifted from *content generation* toward finding effective methodologies for *content storage*, *retrieval*, and *analysis* in the presence of evolving networks. Toward this end, we present StormRider, a framework that uses existing cloud computing and semantic web technologies to provide application programmers with automated support for these tasks, thereby allowing a richer assortment of use cases to be implemented on the underlying evolving social networks.

Third, in view of the need for a highly distributed and federated architecture, a robust query expansion has great impact on the performance of information retrieval. We determine ontology-driven query expansion terms using different weighting techniques. For this, we consider each individual ontology and user query keywords to determine the Basic Expansion Terms (BET) using a number of semantic measures, including Betweenness Measure (BM) and Semantic Similarity Measure (SSM). We develop a MapReduce distributed algorithm for calculating all the shortest paths in ontology graph. A MapReduce algorithm will considerably improve the efficiency of BET calculation for large ontologies.

The organization of this chapter is as follows. Aspects of information integration are discussed in Section 24.2. We discuss Jena–HBase in Section 24.3. StormRider is discussed in Section 24.4. The ontology-driven query-processing tool implemented with MapReduce is discussed in Section 24.5. The chapter is concluded in Section 24.6. The contents of this chapter are illustrated in Figure 24.1.

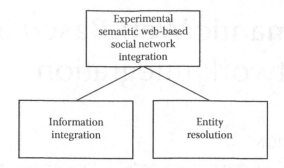

FIGURE 24.1 Experimental semantic web-based social network integration.

24.2 INFORMATION INTEGRATION IN SOCIAL NETWORKS

Consider, for example, the integration of two social networks. Each network is presented as a graph and has its own databases and schema/metadata. Metadata may include information about the types of data in the database and ontologies to handle semantic heterogeneity. In addition, the metadata may also include the structure of the networks. When integrating the networks, the information, the various policies, and the schema have to be integrated to provide a uniform view.

There are several challenges in integrating information especially in a heterogeneous environment. One is schema heterogeneity where system A is based on a one model and system B is based on another model. That is, when two systems are based on different models, we need to resolve the conflicts. One option is to have a common data model. This means that the constructs of both systems have to be transformed into the constructs of the common data model. Semantic heterogeneity occurs when an entity is interpreted differently at different sites or different entities are interpreted to be the same object. Semantic heterogeneity is one of the major challenges for data integration as well as information interoperability. In addition, semantic heterogeneity has to be handled when multiple networks are integrated. For example, John may be presented as John S in one network and John Smithy in the other. Therefore, when integrating the two networks, algorithms are needed that will uniquely identify John based on, say, his address, the colleges he attended, and other information he has posted on his social network pages. Semantic web technologies including ontology matching are being used for handling semantic heterogeneity and entity resolution in heterogeneous databases and social networks.

When two social networks have to be integrated due to, say, merging of two social networking companies, one major challenge is entity resolution and identification. That is, the networks have to be integrated on individuals common to both networks. However, the individuals may be represented differently in the two networks. Therefore, the first step is to uniquely identify the individuals. Second, the links may be named differently. Therefore, the next step is to uniquely identify the links and then merge the networks on the common entities and links. Figure 24.2 illustrates entity resolution in social network integration.

We have developed three experimental semantic web systems for social network integration. The first system is called Jena–HBase. It integrated the Jena RDF data management system with the HBase storage system to efficiently store RDF triples. Since our social networks are represented in RDF, such an approach enables us to efficiently store the social graphs. In the second system, we developed a framework called StormRider that uses a combination of cloud-based and semantic web-based tools to allow for the storage, retrieval, and analysis of evolving social networks. Finally, in the third system, we developed an ontology-driven query-processing approach. Specifically, we developed novel weighting mechanisms for ontology-driven query expansion called BET and New Expansion Terms (NET). For each user query, BET is calculated in each ontology based on some metrics, namely semantic similarity, density, and betweenness. NET is determined by aligning

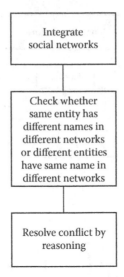

FIGURE 24.2   Entity resolution in social network integration.

ontologies to find robust expansion terms between different ontologies. BET metrics are defined using the shortest-path calculation in ontology graphs. The problem of finding the number of shortest paths that go through every entity in an ontology graph is not practical, especially for large ontologies. Therefore, we have utilized the MapReduce framework for the BET calculation in each ontology. Such an approach would aid in ontology-driven query expansion in social networks.

24.3   JENA–HBASE: A DISTRIBUTED, SCALABLE, AND EFFICIENT RDF TRIPLE STORE

The simplest way to store RDF triples comprises a relation/table of three columns, one each for *subjects*, *predicates*, and *objects*. However, this approach suffers from the lack of scalability and abridged query performance, as the single table becomes long and narrow when the number of RDF triples increases (Erétéo et al., 2009). The approach is not scalable since the table is usually located in a single machine. The cloud computing paradigm has made it possible to harness the processing power of multiple machines in parallel. Tools such as Hadoop and HBase provide advantages such as fault tolerance and optimizations for real-time queries. In this section, we present Jena–HBase, an HBase-backed triple store that can be used with the Jena framework along with a preliminary experimental evaluation of our prototype.

Our work focuses on the creation of a distributed RDF storage framework, thereby mitigating the scalability issue that exists with single-machine systems. The motivation to opt for Jena is its widespread acceptance, and its built-in support for manipulating RDF data as well as developing ontologies. Furthermore, HBase was selected for the storage layer for two reasons: (i) HBase is a column-oriented store and, in general, a column-oriented store performs better than row-oriented stores. (ii) Hadoop comprises the Hadoop Distributed File System (HDFS), a distributed file system that stores data, and MapReduce, a framework for processing data stored in HDFS. HBase uses HDFS for data storage but does not require MapReduce for accessing data. Thus, Jena–HBase does not require the implementation of a MapReduce-based query engine for executing queries on RDF triples. In contrast, existing systems that use a MapReduce-based query engine for processing RDF data are optimized for query performance; however, they are currently unable to support all features from the RDF specification. Our motivation with Jena–HBase is to provide end users with a cloud-based RDF storage and querying API that supports all features from the RDF specification.

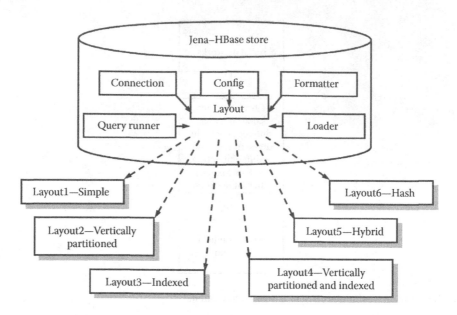

FIGURE 24.3   Jena–HBase architecture.

Jena–HBase provides the following: (i) a variety of custom-built RDF data storage layouts for HBase that provides a trade-off in terms of query performance/storage; (ii) support for reification, inference, and SPARQL processing through the implementation of appropriate Jena interfaces. Figure 24.3 presents an overview of the architecture employed by Jena–HBase. Jena–HBase uses the concept of a store to provide data manipulation capabilities on underlying HBase tables. A store represents a single RDF data set and can be composed of several RDF graphs, each with its own storage layout. A layout uses several HBase tables with different schemas to store RDF triples; each layout provides a trade-off in terms of query performance/storage. All operations on an RDF graph are implicitly converted into operations on the underlying layout. These operations include (i) formatting a layout, that is, deleting all triples while preserving tables (Formatter block); (ii) loading–unloading triples into a layout (Loader block); and (iii) querying a layout for triples that match a given *S, P, O* pattern (Query Runner block). (iv) Additional operations include the following: (a) maintaining an HBase connection (Connection block); (b) maintaining configuration information for each RDF graph (Config block).

We have performed benchmark experiments using SP^{2}Bench (noninference queries) (Potamias et al., 2009) and LUBM (inference queries) (Brandes, 2001) to determine the best layout currently available in Jena–HBase, as well as to compare the performance of the best layout with Jena TDB. We have compared Jena–HBase only with Jena TDB and not with other Hadoop-based systems for the following reasons: (i) Jena TDB gives the best query performance of all available Jena storage subsystems; (ii) the available Hadoop-based systems do not implement all features from the RDF specification. As part of the procedure to determine the best layout, we ran both benchmarks over several graph sizes and our results are given in our previous works (Khadilkar et al., 2012). Since LUBM contains inference queries, we used Pellet reasoner (v2.3.0) to perform inferencing.

24.4   StormRider: HARNESSING STORM FOR SOCIAL NETWORKS

The rise of social media applications has turned the once privileged realm of web authoring and publishing into a commonplace activity. This has led to an explosion in the amount of user-generated content online. The main concern for social media providers is no longer *content generation* but finding effective methodologies for *content storage*, *retrieval*, and *analysis*. There has been a significant amount of research (see, e.g., Erétéo et al., 2009) that addresses this issue. However, existing work views a network as a series of snapshots, where a snapshot represents the state of a network in a given time period. Therefore, different network operations need to be individually performed over each snapshot. In reality, online social networks are continuously evolving entities and, therefore, network operations should be automatically performed as they evolve. Moreover, viewing the problem from this perspective allows us to create a solution that supports advanced, real-world use cases such as the following: (i) tracking the neighborhood of a given node (this use case is relevant in law enforcement, e.g., to track the activities of potential criminals/terrorists), and (ii) being able to store and access prior snapshots of a network for auditing and verification tasks. Such a use case is relevant in health care, for example, in tracing the medical history of a patient.

In this section, we present StormRider, a framework that uses a combination of cloud-based and semantic web-based tools to allow for the storage, retrieval, and analysis of evolving social networks. In addition, users can perform these operations on networks of their choice by creating custom-built implementations of the interfaces provided in StormRider. The StormRider framework makes use of the following existing tools as basic building blocks: (i) The Storm framework allows StormRider to automatically store, query, and analyze data as the underlying network evolves over time. Storm was selected because it is a real-time computation system that guarantees message processing and is scalable, robust, and fault tolerant. (ii) The Jena–HBase framework (Khadilkar et al., 2012b) allows the storage of network data in an RDF representation as well as to query the data using SPARQL. (iii) Apache HBase was used to construct materialized views that store metadata related to nodes in the network. These views allow faster analytics to be performed on the network.

StormRider provides the following novel contributions: (i) the Jena–HBase framework facilitates the use several semantic web features with social networks, such as application of reasoning algorithms, reification, etc.; (ii) the ability to store, query, and analyze evolving networks through the use of novel algorithms (e.g., approximation algorithms for centrality estimation) implemented in Storm; and (iii) application programmers are provided with simple interfaces through which they can interact with social networks of their choice.

Figure 24.4 presents an architectural overview of StormRider. User applications interact with an abstract social network model (Model-SN) that translates high-level user-defined network operations (viz. store, query, and analyze) into low-level operations on the underlying network

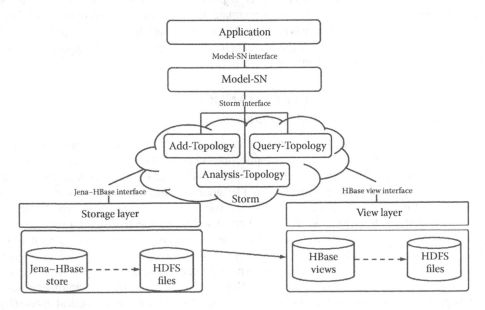

FIGURE 24.4   StormRider architecture.

representations used by StormRider. The low-level operations are implemented as Storm topologies and are designed to support evolving social networks. A Storm topology represents a graph of computation, where nodes contain the logic of the computation while links between nodes denote how data is passed from one node to another. Storm internally interfaces with the storage layer (Jena–HBase), through the Jena–HBase interface, and the view layer (HBase tables used as materialized views), through the HBase View interface, to execute topologies on the underlying networks.

The storage layer, composed of Jena–HBase, is used to store networks in an RDF representation in a cloud-based framework. The storage of networks in RDF when combined with topologies defined in Storm allows us to support realistic use cases through the use of concepts such as property–path queries and reification. For additional details about Jena–HBase, an interested reader is referred to our detailed technical report (Khadilkar et al., 2012a). The view layer is used to store metadata about nodes that make up a network. The metadata is mainly used to facilitate a speed-up in performance during the analysis of a network.

Additional details of the architecture along with a detailed description of sample Add-, Query- and Analyze-Topologies for the Twitter network are given in our previous work (Khadilkar et al., 2012c). Note that these topologies are only provided as examples with the StormRider framework. Consequently, an application programmer needs to define custom topologies based on their requirements to interact with networks they want to examine.

The sample topologies in StormRider have been implemented for Twitter. The Add-Topology is used to add data to the storage layer as well as to update node-related information in the view layer. The Analyze-Topology is then used to compute degree, closeness, and betweenness centrality using the metadata from the view layer. Some of these metrics require shortest-path computations, which we perform using the landmark-based approximation technique (Potamias et al., 2009). As a part of our experimental evaluation, we evaluated the effectiveness of this method versus the exact method given in Brandes (2001) for computing closeness and betweenness centrality on a maximum of 500,000 Twitter users. The number of nodes in the landmarks set was set as follows: (total no. of users)/100, where the factor 100 was randomly selected, while the elements in the landmarks set were selected as the top-k nodes with the highest degree. Finally, each experiment was conducted along the following dimensions: (i) *Approximation Error*: This metric measures the accuracy of StormRider in computing the centrality value versus the exact method and is computed as $|\hat{l} - l|$, where l is the actual centrality value and $\hat{l}$ is the approximation. (ii) *Execution Time*: This metric measures the time required to perform the approximate and exact calculations of the centrality values. The time for the approximate case is computed as a sum of both the time required to update the views and the time required to perform the actual centrality computation. Our experimental results are given in our previous works (Khadilkar et al., 2012c,d).

24.5 ONTOLOGY-DRIVEN QUERY EXPANSION USING MapReduce FRAMEWORK

Distributed and parallel computing continues to solve efficiency problems for many web applications in a federated architecture. Since data applications use distributed data sources in such architecture, it is required to enrich the original user query and cover the gap between the user query and required information by query expansion. The goal of many researchers is to discriminate between different expansion terms and improve the robustness of query expansion. In our previous work (Alipanah et al., 2010a), we developed novel weighting mechanisms for ontology-driven query expansions called BET and NET. For each user query, BET is calculated in each ontology based on some metrics, namely semantic similarity, density, and betweenness. NET is determined by aligning ontologies to find robust expansion terms between different ontologies. BET metrics are defined using the shortest-path calculation in ontology graphs. The problem of finding the number of shortest paths that goes through every entity in the ontology graph is not practical especially for large ontologies. Therefore, in this section, we concentrate on the MapReduce algorithm for BET

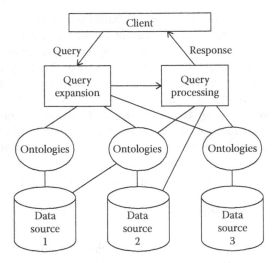

FIGURE 24.5   Architecture for query expansion.

calculation in each ontology. More details are given in Alipanah (2012) and Alipanah et al. (2010a,b, 2011a,b, 2012). Our architecture for query expansion is illustrated in Figure 24.5.

BET Calculation Using MapReduce Distributed Computing. In our BET calculation (Erétéo et al., 2009), we use BM and centrality, density measure (DM), and SSM metrics. For this, first we determine central entity (CE) using BM in each ontology. Next, we use central entity and calculate SSM for each of expansion terms in BET. In both BM and SSM metrics, we need to determine the shortest paths between different entities of each ontology several times as follows.

BM and CE: betweenness (BM) assigns the number of shortest paths that pass through each node in the ontology graph when calculating expansion terms. The node that occurs in many shortest paths for expanding user terms is considered as the central keyword in each ontology (Erétéo et al., 2009). Let e_i, $e_j \in O_k$. BM(e) is the betweenness measure of entity e.

$$\text{BM}(e) = \sum_{e_i \neq e_j \neq e} \left(\frac{\text{shortestpath}(e_i, e_j) \text{passing} e}{\text{shortestpath}(e_i, e_j)} \right) \tag{24.1}$$

BM dtetermines the central keyword that is used in SSM for finding BET. The central keyword has the highest BM value.

SSM: SSM uses an ontology graph as a semantic presentation of a domain to determine weights for all expansion terms in every ontology. Entities that are closer to the central node have more weight. SSM is calculated using the shortest-path measure. The more relationships entities have in common, the closer they will be in the ontology (Erétéo et al., 2009). If any entity is positioned relatively far from the central node, then it has smaller weight. Therefore, we use the shortest-path measure as the weight for the ontology vocabulary.

Let entities e_j, $c \in O_i$ and there is a path between c (central) and e_j.

$$\text{SSM}(c, e_j) = \left\{ \begin{array}{cc} \dfrac{1}{\text{length}(\text{minpath}(c, e_j))} & c \neq e_j \\ 1 & c = e_j \end{array} \right\} \tag{24.2}$$

BET in this method is all entities in the shortest path from central keyword to e_j. The shortest paths in BM and SSM calculations are determined by breadth-first search (BFS). Given a branching factor b and graph depth d in ontology graph, the asymptotic space and time complexity is the number of nodes at the deepest level, $O(b^d)$, that is exponential. For large ontologies, the shortest-path calculation is not practical. Therefore, in the next section, we explain about the MapReduce distributed algorithm that optimizes our federated query expansion.

Shortest-Path Calculation Using Iterative MapReduce Algorithm. The MapReduce programming model is a powerful interface for automatic parallelization and distribution of large-scale computations. In this model, the map and reduce functions are defined as follows:

$$\text{Map}(\text{in}_{\text{key}}, \text{in}_{\text{value}}) \rightarrow \text{Out}_{\text{key}}, \text{intermediate}_{\text{value}} \text{list}$$

$$\text{Reduce}(\text{out}_{\text{key}}, \text{intermediate}_{\text{value}} \text{ list}) \rightarrow \text{out}_{\text{value}} \text{list} \tag{24.3}$$

The data from data sources are fed into the map function as a pair of in_{key}, in_{value}. The map function produces one or more intermediate values along with the $\text{output}_{\text{key}}$ from input. After the map phase, all intermediate values for any given out_{key} are combined together into a list. Reduce function combines $\text{intermediate}_{\text{value}}$ into one or more final values for that same output out_{key}. In our BET calculation, we are using the ontology graph illustrated in Figure 24.6 as the input for the system. The ontology graph needs a transformation from graph to adjacency list to be used by map function. Step 1 explains the transformation and in_{key}, in_{value} for the map function.

Step 1: Given an ontology O_1, the algorithm constructs adjacency matrix for each entity $e_i \in O_1$. Each e_i is considered as in_{key}. For each entity e_i, we determine first neighbors of e_i and store them as a comma-delimited NeighborsList (NL) that are connected to this entity. We also specify Distance-From-Source (DFS), Path-From-Source (PFS), and color for each entity. There are three possible EntityColors (EC) for each entity. Source entities are determined using Gray color, while visited entities are defined by Black, and not visited entities are defined by White color. We use DFS = 0 for the source entity and DFS = Int.Maxval for other entities, because we are using BFS for source entity. Also, for the source entity PFS = in_{key} of the source, while PFS is empty for other entities. The concatenation of NL,

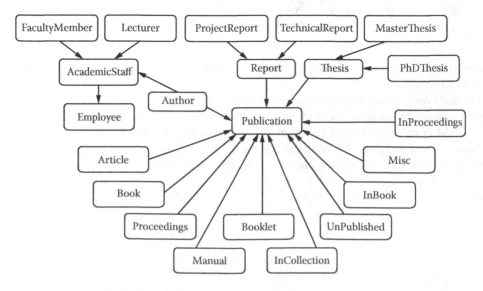

FIGURE 24.6 Karlsruhe bibliography ontology.

DFS, PFS, and EC is considered as in_{value} for the map function. Considering the ontology graph in Figure 24.6, suppose that MasterThesis is the source entity in the graph; thus, some sample keys and values are

Masterthesis, "Thesis |0|Masterthesis|Gray"

Author, "Publication, AcademicStaff|Int.Maxval| – |White"

Report, "Publication|Int.Maxval| – |White"

Thesis, "Publication|Int.Maxval| – |White"

Step 2: In this step, mappers produce $intermediate_{value}$ for each source entity in_{key}. For each source entity S_i in the ontology graph with the Gray color, the mappers first change its color to Black. Then, it creates some new nodes based on the number of neighbors with DFS = DFS + 1, PFS = $in_{key} \bigcup in_{keynewword}$, and Color = Gray. Since the mappers do not have the information about the next neighbors for new nodes, it considers the next neighbors as NULL. Also, it assumes PFS = "–" for non-Gray nodes. Back to our example, below is the result after the first iteration:

Masterthesis, "Thesis |0|Masterthesis|Black"

Thesis, "Null |1|Masterthesis – Thesis|Gray"

Author, "Publication, AcademicStaff|Int.Maxval| – |White"

Report, "Publication|Int.Maxval| – |White"

Thesis, "Publication|Int.Maxval| – |White"

Step 3: In this step, the reducer uses one out_{key} and the list of all $intermediate_{value}$ to calculate the final out_{value}. Each reducer takes all $intermediate_{value}$ of each key and constructs a new node using the "Not – Null" list of edges, the minimum DFS, "Not – Null" value for PFS, and the darkest color. That is, for the above example

Thesis, "Publication |1|Masterthesis – Thesis|Gray"

After reducing the $intermediate_{value}$ in step 3, the algorithm continues for the next iteration to explode new Gray nodes in step 2. This iteration continues until it expands all possible paths for each source examined and all nodes change to black color.

Betweenness and Centrality Measures Using MapReduce Computation. In BET calculation, first for each $q_i \in query_{keywords}$, we calculate the BM measure. Second, we determine the central $query_{keyword}$ (i.e., q_c) among all $query_{keywords}$. As discussed in the previous section, in each iteration, the $intermediate_{value}$ is updated and the PFS is determined. For betweenness of each q_i, we find the number of times q_i appears in the shortest paths between entities of ontology in the last iteration of the MapReduce step. After determining the BM(q_i), we specify the q_i with the maximum value of betweenness as the central keyword.

SSMs Using MapReduce Algorithm (Algorithm 24.1). We use the central entity from the previous section and calculate SSM for all the BET. For SSM calculation, we use the result of the MapReduce shortest path (MRSP) algorithm as explained in Algorithm 24.1. In lines 2 and 3, the algorithm uses MRSP and SSM using MRSP and returns SSM for each entity $\in$ BET.

Algorithm 24.1: SSM Using Map/Reduce Computation

Require: BET $B = \{b_1, b_2, \ldots, b_n\}$, central entity (CE), ontology O

Ensure: SSM for each b_i

1: **for** all $b_i \in B$ do

2:      MRSP = MapReduce shortest path result (b_i)

3:      $SSM(b_i) = \dfrac{1}{\text{lengthofMRSP}}$

4: **end for**

5: Return SSM(b_i)

24.6 SUMMARY AND DIRECTIONS

In this chapter, we have first described aspects of social network integration and explained the use of semantic web technologies for this purpose. We then discussed three separate experimental cloud-based semantic web data management systems for social network integration. The first system integrated a distributed RDF storage framework with existing cloud computing tools resulting in a scalable data-processing solution. Our solution maintains a reasonable query execution time overhead when compared with a single-machine RDF storage framework (viz. Jena TDB). Next, we presented StormRider, a framework that uses a novel combination of existing cloud computing and semantic web technologies to allow for the storage, retrieval, and analysis of evolving online social networks, thus enabling the support for several new, realistic use cases. Finally, we discussed an ontology-driven query expansion system in the cloud.

There are many areas for further research. First, we need to conduct extensive experiments with our systems to see if they scale. Next, we need to develop more robust algorithms that operate on the cloud. Finally, we need to test our system with some real-world social network example systems.

REFERENCES

Alipanah, N. Federated query processing using ontology structure and ranking in a service oriented environment, PhD Thesis, The University of Texas at Dallas, Richardson, TX, 2012.

Alipanah, N., Srivastava, P., Parveen, P., and Thuraisingham, B.M. Ranking ontologies using verified entities to facilitate federated queries. In: *Proceedings of Web Intelligence Conference*, Toronto, Canada, pp. 332–337, 2010a.

Alipanah, N., Parveen, P., Khan, L., and Thuraisingham, B. Ontology-driven query expansion methods to facilitate federated queries. In: *Proceedings of 2010 IEEE International Conference on Service Oriented Computing and Applications (SOCA10)*, Perth, Australia, 2010b.

Alipanah, N., Khan, L., and Thuraisingham, B. Ontology-driven query expansion methods to facilitate federated queries, Technical Report, UTDCS-30-11, The University of Texas at Dallas, Richardson, TX, 2011a.

Alipanah, N., Parveen, P., Khan, and Thuraisingham, B.M. Ontology-driven query expansion using map/reduce framework to facilitate federated queries. In: *Proceedings of International Conference on Web Services (ICWS)*, Washington, DC, pp. 712–713, 2011b.

Alipanah, N., Khan, L., and Thuraisingham, B.M. Optimized ontology-driven query expansion using map–reduce framework to facilitate federated queries. *International Journal of Computer Systems Science and Engineering* 27(2), 2012.

Brandes, U. A faster algorithm for betweenness centrality. *Journal of Mathematical Sociology* 25(2): 163–177, 2001.

Erétéo, G., Buffa, M., Gandon, F., and Corby, O. Analysis of a real online social network using semantic web frameworks. In: *Proceedings of International Semantic Web Conference (ISWC)*, Chantilly, VA, pp. 180–195, 2009.

Khadilkar, V., Kantarcioglu, M., Castagna, P., and Thuraisingham, B. Jena–HBase: A distributed, scalable and efficient RDF triple store. Technical report. 2012a.

Khadilkar, V., Kantarcioglu, M., Thuraisingham, B.M., and Castagna, P. Jena–HBase: A distributed, scalable and efficient RDF triple store. In: *Proceedings of International Semantic Web Conference (Posters & Demos)*, Boston, 2012b.

Khadilkar, V., Kantarcioglu, M., and Thuraisingham, B. StormRider: Harnessing "Storm" for social networks. Technical report. 2012c.

Khadilkar, V., Kantarcioglu, M., and Thuraisingham, B.M. StormRider: Harnessing "Storm" for social networks. In *Proceedings of World Wide Web (WWW) Conference (Companion Volume)*, Lyon, France, pp. 543–544, 2012d.

Potamias, M., Bonchi, F., Castillo, C., and Gionis, A. Fast shortest path distance estimation in large networks. In *Proceedings of Conference on Information and Knowledge Management (CIKM)*, Hong Kong, China, pp. 867–876, 2009.

25 Experimental Cloud Query Processing System for Social Networks

25.1 INTRODUCTION

As stated in the earlier chapters, cloud computing is an emerging paradigm in the information technology and data processing communities. Enterprises utilize cloud computing services to outsource data maintenance, which can result in significant financial benefits. Businesses store and access data at remote locations in the *cloud*. As the popularity of cloud computing grows, the service providers face ever-increasing challenges. They have to maintain huge quantities of heterogeneous data while providing efficient information retrieval. Thus, the key emphasis for cloud computing solutions is scalability and query efficiency. Semantic web technologies are being developed to present data in a standardized way such that such data can be retrieved and understood by both humans and machines. Historically, web pages are published in plain Hypertext Markup Language (HTML) files, which are not suitable for reasoning. Instead, the machine treats these HTML files as a bag of keywords. Researchers are developing semantic web technologies that have been standardized to address such inadequacies. The most prominent standards are the Resource Description Framework (RDF) (World Wide Web Consortium, 2014a) and SPARQL Protocol and RDF Query Language (SPARQL) (World Wide Web Consortium, 2014b). RDF is the standard for storing and representing data, and SPARQL is a query language to retrieve data from an RDF store. RDF is being used extensively to represent social networks, as we have discussed in Chapter 21. Cloud computing systems can utilize the power of these semantic web technologies to represent and manage social networks so that the users of these networks have the capability to efficiently store and retrieve data for data-intensive applications.

Semantic web technologies could be especially useful for maintaining data in the cloud. Semantic web-based social networks provide the ability to specify and query heterogeneous data in a standardized manner. Moreover, via the Web Ontology Language (OWL) ontologies, different schemas, classes, data types, and relationships can be specified without sacrificing the standard RDF/SPARQL interface. Conversely, cloud computing solutions could be of great benefit to the semantic web-based social networking community. Semantic web data sets are growing exponentially. In the web domain, scalability is paramount. Yet, high-speed response time is also vital in the web community. We believe that the cloud computing paradigm offers a solution that can achieve both of these goals.

Existing commercial tools and technologies do not scale well in cloud computing settings. Researchers have started to focus on these problems recently. They are proposing systems built from scratch. Wang et al. (2010) proposed an indexing scheme for a new distributed database (epiC, http://www.comp.nus.edu.sg/~epic/) that can be used as a cloud system. When it comes to semantic web data such as RDF, we are faced with similar challenges. With storage becoming cheaper and the need to store and retrieve large amounts of data increasing, developing systems to handle billions of RDF triples requiring terabytes of disk space is no longer a distant prospect. Researchers are already working on billions of triples (Newman et al., 2008; Rohloff et al., 2007). Competitions are being organized to encourage researchers to build efficient repositories (Semantic Web Challenge, http://challenge.semanticweb.org). At present, there are just a few frameworks (e.g.,

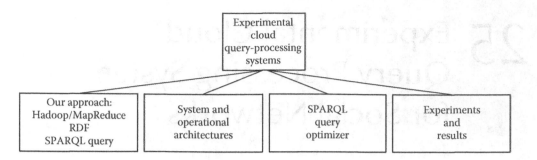

FIGURE 25.1   Experimental cloud query processing systems.

RDF-3X [Newman et al., 2008], Jena [Carroll et al., 2004], Sesame [rdf4j.org/], and BigOWLIM [Kiryakov et al., 2005]) for semantic web technologies, and these frameworks have limitations for large RDF graphs. Therefore, storing a large number of RDF triples and efficiently querying them is a challenging and important problem.

In this chapter, we discuss a query-processing system that functions in the cloud and manages a large number of RDF triples. These RDF triples can be used to represent social networks as discussed in Chapter 21. The organization of this chapter is as follows. Our approach is discussed in Section 25.2. In Section 25.3, we discuss related work. In Section 25.4, we discuss our system architecture. In Section 25.5, we discuss how we answer an SPARQL query. In Section 25.6, we present the results of our experiments. Finally, in Section 25.7, we draw some conclusions and discuss areas we have identified for improvement in the future. The contents of this chapter are illustrated in Figure 25.1. A more detailed discussion of the concepts, architectures, and experiments are provided in Husain et al. (2011) and Husain (2011). Since semantic web technologies can be used to model social networks, our query-processing system can be utilized to query social networks.

25.2   OUR APPROACH

A distributed system can be built to overcome the scalability and performance problems of current semantic web frameworks. Databases are being distributed to provide such scalable solutions. However, to date, there is no distributed repository for storing and managing RDF data. Researchers have only recently begun to explore the problems and technical solutions that must be addressed in order to build such a distributed system. One promising line of investigation involves making use of readily available distributed database systems or relational databases. Such database systems can use relational schema for the storage of RDF data. SPARQL queries can be answered by converting them to SQL first (Chebotko et al., 2007; Chong et al., 2005; Cyganiak, 2005). Optimal relational schemas are being probed for this purpose (Abadi et al., 2007). The main disadvantage with such systems is that they are optimized for relational data. They may not perform well for RDF data, especially because RDF data are sets of triples (World Wide Web Consortium, 2001) (an ordered tuple of three components called subject, predicate, and object, respectively) that form large directed graphs. In a SPARQL query, any number of triple patterns (TPs) (World Wide Web Consortium, 2008b) can join on a single variable (World Wide Web Consortium, 2008a), which makes a relational database query plan complex. Performance and scalability will remain a challenging issue because these systems are optimized for relational data schemata and transactional database usage.

Yet another approach is to build a distributed system for RDF from scratch. Here, there will be an opportunity to design and optimize a system with specific application to RDF data. In this approach, the researchers would be reinventing the wheel. Instead of starting with a blank slate, we built a solution with a generic distributed storage system that utilizes a cloud computing platform. We then tailored the system and schema specifically to meet the needs of semantic web data. Finally, we built a semantic web repository using such a storage facility.

Hadoop (http://hadoop.apache.org) is a distributed file system where files can be saved with replication. It is an ideal candidate for building a storage system. Hadoop features high fault tolerance and great reliability. In addition, it also contains an implementation of the MapReduce (Dean and Ghemawat, 2004) programming model, a functional programming model that is suitable for the parallel processing of large amounts of data. Through partitioning data into a number of independent chunks, MapReduce processes run against these chunks, making parallelization simpler. Moreover, the MapReduce programming model facilitates and simplifies the task of joining multiple TPs.

In this chapter, we will describe a schema to store RDF data in Hadoop, and we will detail a solution to process queries against these data. In the preprocessing stage, we process RDF data and populate files in the distributed file system. This process includes partitioning and organizing the data files and executing dictionary encoding. We will then detail a query engine for information retrieval. We will specify exactly how SPARQL queries will be satisfied using MapReduce programming. Specifically, we must determine the Hadoop *jobs* that will be executed to solve the query. We will present a greedy algorithm that produces a query plan with the minimal number of Hadoop jobs. This is an approximation algorithm using heuristics, but we will prove that the worst case has a reasonable upper bound. Finally, we will utilize two standard benchmark data sets to run experiments. We will present results for the data set ranging from 0.1 to more than 6.6 billion triples. We will show that our solution is exceptionally scalable. We will show that our solution outperforms leading state-of-the-art semantic web repositories, using standard benchmark queries on very large data sets.

Our contributions are listed as follows and illustrated in Figure 25.2. More details are given in Husain et al. (2011).

1. We designed a storage scheme to store RDF data in Hadoop Distributed File System (HDFS) (http://hadoop.apache.org/).
2. We developed an algorithm that is guaranteed to provide a query plan whose cost is bounded by the log of the total number of variables in the given SPARQL query. It uses summary statistics for estimating join selectivity to break ties.
3. We built a framework that is highly scalable and fault tolerant and supports data-intensive query processing.
4. We demonstrated that our approach performs better than Jena for all queries, and BigOWLIM and RDF-3X for complex queries having large result sets.

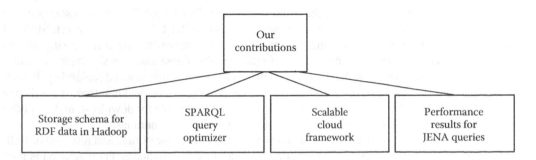

FIGURE 25.2 Our contributions.

25.3 RELATED WORK

MapReduce, though a programming paradigm, is rapidly being adopted by researchers. This technology is becoming increasingly popular in the community that handles large amounts of data. It is the most promising technology for solving the performance issues researchers are facing in cloud computing. Abadi (2009) discusses how MapReduce can satisfy most of the requirements to build an ideal cloud database management system (DBMS). Researchers and enterprises are using MapReduce technology for web indexing, searches, and data mining. In this section, we will first investigate research related to MapReduce. Next, we will discuss works related to the semantic web.

Google uses MapReduce for web indexing, data storage, and social networking (Chang et al., 2006). Yahoo! uses MapReduce extensively in its data analysis tasks (Olston et al., 2008). IBM has successfully experimented with a scale-up scale-out search framework using MapReduce technology (Moreira et al., 2007). Sismanis et al. (2010) have reported on how they integrated Hadoop and System R. Teradata did similar work by integrating Hadoop with a parallel DBMS (Xu et al., 2010).

Researchers have used MapReduce to scale up classifiers for mining petabytes of data (Moretti et al., 2008). They have worked on data distribution and partitioning for data mining, and have applied three data mining algorithms to test the performance. Data mining algorithms are being rewritten in different forms to take advantage of MapReduce technology. Chu et al. (2006) rewrote well-known machine learning algorithms to take advantage of multicore machines by leveraging the MapReduce programming paradigm. Another area where this technology is successfully being used is simulation (McNabb et al., 2007). Abouzeid et al. (2009) reported an interesting idea of combining MapReduce with existing relational database techniques. These works differ from our research in that we use MapReduce for semantic web technologies. Our focus is on developing a scalable solution for storing RDF data and retrieving them by using SPARQL queries.

In the semantic web arena, there has not been much work done with MapReduce technology. We have found two related projects: the BioMANTA (http://www.itee.uq.edu.au/eresearch/projects /biomanta) project and Scalable, High-Performance, Robust and Distributed (SHARD) (Zeyliger, 2010). BioMANTA proposes extensions to RDF molecules (Ding et al., 2005) and implements a MapReduce-based molecule store (Newman et al., 2008). They use MapReduce to answer the queries. They have queried a maximum of 4 million triples. Our work differs in the following ways: First, we have queried 1 billion triples. Second, we have devised a storage schema that is tailored to improve query execution performance for RDF data. We store RDF triples in files based on the predicate of the triple and the type of the object. Finally, we also have an algorithm to determine a query-processing plan whose cost is bounded by the log of the total number of variables in the given SPARQL query. By using this, we can determine the input files of a job and the order in which they should be run. To the best of our knowledge, we are the first to come up with a storage schema for RDF data using flat files in HDFS, and a MapReduce job determination algorithm to answer an SPARQL query.

SHARD is an RDF triple store using the Hadoop Cloudera distribution. This project shows initial results demonstrating Hadoop's ability to improve scalability for RDF data sets. However, SHARD stores its data only in a triple store schema. It currently does no query planning or reordering, and its query processor will not minimize the number of Hadoop jobs. There has been significant research into semantic web repositories, with particular emphasis on query efficiency and scalability. In fact, there are too many such repositories to fairly evaluate and discuss each. Therefore, we will pay attention to semantic web repositories that are open source or available for download, and that have received favorable recognition in the semantic web and database communities.

Abadi et al. (2007, 2009) reported a vertically partitioned DBMS for storage and retrieval of RDF data. Their solution is a schema with a two-column table for each predicate. Their schema is then implemented on top of a column-store relational database such as CStore (Stonebraker et al., 2005) or MonetDB (Boncz et al., 2006). They observed performance improvement with their scheme over traditional relational database schemes. We have leveraged this technology in our predicate-based partitioning within the MapReduce framework. However, in the vertical partitioning research, only small databases (<100 million) were used. Several papers (McGlothlin and Khan, 2009; Sidirourgos et al., 2008; Weiss et al., 2008) have shown that the performance of vertical partitioning is drastically reduced as the data set size is increased.

Jena (Carroll et al., 2004) is open source framework for semantic web data. True to its framework design, it allows integration of multiple solutions for persistence. It also supports inference through the development of reasoners. However, Jena is limited to a triple store schema. In other words, all data are stored in a single three-column table. Jena has very poor query performance for large data sets. Furthermore, any change to the data set requires complete recalculation of the inferred triples.

BigOWLIM (Kiryakov et al., 2005) is among the fastest and most scalable semantic web frameworks available. However, it is not as scalable as our framework and requires very high-end and costly machines. It requires expensive hardware (a lot of main memory) to load large data sets, and it has a long loading time. As our experiments show, it does not perform well when there is no bound object in a query. However, the performance of our framework is not affected in such a case.

RDF-3X (Neumann and Weikum, 2008) is considered the fastest existing semantic web repository. In other words, it has the fastest query times. RDF-3X uses histograms, summary statistics, and query optimization to enable high-performance semantic web queries. As a result, RDF-3X is generally able to outperform any other solution for queries with bound objects and aggregate queries. However, the performance of RDF-3X degrades exponentially for unbound queries, and queries with even simple joins if the selectivity factor is low. This becomes increasingly relevant for inference queries, which generally require unions of subqueries with unbound objects. Our experiments show that RDF-3X is not only slower for such queries, but it also often aborts and cannot complete the query. For example, consider the simple query *Select all students*. This query in LUBM requires us to select all graduate students, select all undergraduate students, and union the results together. However, there are a very large number of results in this union. While both subqueries complete easily, the union will abort in RDF-3X for LUBM (30,000) with 3.3 billion triples.

The RDF Knowledge Base (RDFKB) (McGlothlin and Khan, 2010) is a semantic web repository using a relational database schema built on bit vectors. RDFKB achieves better query performance than RDF-3X or vertical partitioning. However, RDFKB aims to provide knowledge base functions such as inference forward chaining, uncertainty reasoning, and ontology alignment. RDFKB prioritizes these goals ahead of scalability. RDFKB is not able to load LUBM (30,000) with 3 billion triples, so it cannot compete with our solution for scalability.

Hexastore (Weiss et al., 2008) and BitMat (Atre et al., 2008) are main memory data structures optimized for RDF indexing. These solutions may achieve exceptional performance on hot runs; however, they are not optimized for cold runs from persistent storage. Furthermore, their scalability is directly associated with the quantity of main memory RAM available. These products are not available for testing and evaluation.

In our previous work (Husain et al., 2009, 2010), we proposed a greedy and an exhaustive search algorithm to generate a query-processing plan. However, the exhaustive search algorithm was expensive and the greedy one was not bounded and its theoretical complexity was not defined. In this chapter, we present a new greedy algorithm with an upper bound. Also, we observed scenarios in which our old greedy algorithm failed to generate the optimal plan. The new algorithm is able to obtain the optimal plan in each of these cases. The join executer component runs the jobs using the MapReduce framework. It then relays the query answer from Hadoop to the user.

25.4 ARCHITECTURE

Our system architecture is illustrated in Figure 25.3. It essentially consists of a SPARQL query optimizer and an RDF data manager implemented in the cloud. The operational architecture is

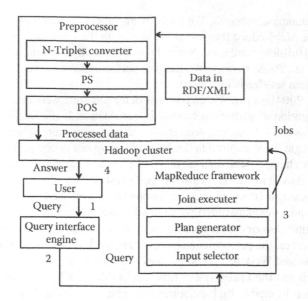

FIGURE 25.3 System architecture.

illustrated in Figure 25.4. It consists of two components. The upper part of Figure 25.4 depicts the data-preprocessing component and the lower part shows the query-answering component. We have three subcomponents for data generation and preprocessing. We convert RDF/XML (World Wide Web Consortium, 2014c) to N-Triples (World Wide Web Consortium, 2001) serialization format using our N-Triples Converter component. The Predicate Split (PS) component takes the N-Triples data and splits it into predicate files. The predicate files are then fed into the Predicate Object Split (POS) component, which splits the predicate files into smaller files based on the type of objects. These steps are described below.

> **Data Generation and Storage.** For our experiments, we use the LUBM (Guo et al., 2005) data set. It is a benchmark data set designed to enable researchers to evaluate the performance of a semantic web repository (Guo et al., 2004). The LUBM data generator

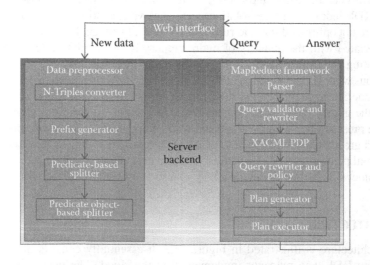

FIGURE 25.4 Operational architecture.

generates data in RDF/XML serialization format. This format is not suitable for our purpose because we store data in HDFS as flat files, and so to retrieve even a single triple, we would need to parse the entire file. Therefore, we convert the data to N-Triples to store the data, because with that format, we have a complete RDF triple (subject, predicate, and object) in one line of a file, which is very convenient to use with MapReduce jobs. The processing steps to go through to get the data into our intended format are described in the following sections.

File Organization. We do not store the data in a single file because in a Hadoop and MapReduce framework, a file is the smallest unit of input to a MapReduce job and, in the absence of caching, a file is always read from the disk. If we have all the data in one file, the whole file will be input to jobs for each query. Instead, we divide the data into multiple smaller files. The splitting is done in two steps, which we will discuss in the following sections.

Predicate Split. In the first step, we divide the data according to the predicates. This division immediately enables us to cut down the search space for any SPARQL query that does not have a variable predicate. For such a query, we can just pick a file for each predicate and run the query on those files only. For simplicity, we name the files with predicates; for example, all the triples containing a predicate p1:pred go into a file named p1-pred. However, when we have a variable predicate in a TP (World Wide Web Consortium, 2008b) and if we cannot determine the type of the object, we have to consider all files. If we can determine the type of the object, then we consider all files having that type of object. We discuss this further in Section 25.5. In real-world RDF data sets, the number of distinct predicates is, in general, not a large number (Stocker et al., 2008). However, there are data sets having many predicates. Our system performance does not vary in such a case because we just select files related to the predicates specified in a SPARQL query.

Split Using Explicit-Type Information of Object. In the next step, we work with the explicit-type information in the rdf_type file. The predicate rdf:type is used in RDF to denote that a resource is an instance of a class. The rdf_type file is first divided into as many files as the number of distinct objects the rdf:type predicate has. For example, if in the ontology, the leaves of the class hierarchy are $c_1, c_2, ..., c_n$, then we will create files for each of these leaves and the file names will be like type_c_1, type_c_2, ..., type_c_n. Please note that it is no longer necessary to store the object values $c_1, c_2, ..., c_n$ within the file as they can easily be retrieved from the file name. This further reduces the amount of space needed to store the data. We generate such a file for each distinct object value of the predicate rdf:type.

Split Using Implicit-Type Information of Object. We divide the remaining predicate files according to the type of the objects. Not all the objects are Uniform Resource Identifiers (URIs); some are literals. The literals remain in the file named by the predicate; no further processing is required for them. The type information of a URI object is not mentioned in these files but they can be retrieved from the type_*files. The URI objects move into their respective file named as predicate_type. For example, if a triple has the predicate p and the type of the URI object is ci, then the subject and object appear in one line in the file p_ci. To do this split, we need to join a predicate file with the type_*files to retrieve the type information.

Our MapReduce framework, described in Section 25.5, has three subcomponents in it. It takes the SPARQL query from the user and passes it to the input and plan generator. This component selects the input files by using our algorithm described in Section 25.5, decides how many MapReduce jobs are needed, and passes the information to the Join Executer component that runs the jobs using MapReduce framework. It then relays the query answer from Hadoop to the user.

25.5 MapReduce FRAMEWORK

25.5.1 OVERVIEW

The MapReduce framework is at the heart of our cloud computing efforts. We will discuss MapReduce in various chapters of this book as it relates to the contents of that chapter. In this section, we discuss how we answer SPARQL queries in our MapReduce framework component.

Section 25.5.2 discusses our algorithm to select input files for answering the query. Section 25.5.3 describes the cost estimation needed to generate a plan to answer a SPARQL query. It introduces a few terms that we use in the following discussions. We also describe the ideal model we should follow to estimate the cost of a plan, and introduce the heuristics-based model we use in practice. Section 25.5.4 presents our heuristics-based greedy algorithm to generate a query plan that uses the cost model introduced in Section 25.5.3. We face tie situations in order to generate a plan in some cases. In Section 25.5.5, we discuss how we handle these special cases. Section 25.5.6 shows how we implement a join in a Hadoop MapReduce job by working through an example query.

25.5.2 INPUT FILES SELECTION

Before determining the jobs, we select the files that need to be input to the jobs. We have some query-rewriting capability that we apply at this step of query processing. We take the query submitted by the user and iterate over the TPs. We may encounter the following cases:

1. In a TP, if the predicate is variable, we select all the files as input to the jobs and terminate the iteration.
2. If the predicate is rdf:type and the object is concrete, we select the type file having that particular type. For example, for LUBM Query 9 (Listing 1), we could select file type_Student as part of the input set. However, this brings up an interesting scenario. In our data set, there is actually no file named type_Student because the Student class is not a leaf in the ontology tree. In this case, we consult the LUBM ontology (http://www.lehigh .edu/~zhp2/2004/0401/univ-bench.owl) to determine the correct set of input files. We add the files type_GraduateStudent, type_UndergraduateStudent, and type_ResearchAssistant, as GraduateStudent, UndergraduateStudent, and ResearchAssistant are the leaves of the subtree rooted at node Student.
3. If the predicate is rdf:type and the object is variable, then if the type of the variable is defined by another TP, we select the type file having that particular type. Otherwise, we select all type files.
4. If the predicate is not rdf:type and the object is variable, then we need to determine if the type of the object is specified by another TP in the query. In this case, we can rewrite the query and eliminate some joins. For example, in LUBM Query 9 (Listing 1), the type of Y is specified as Faculty and Z as Course, and these variables are used as objects in the last three TPs. If we choose files advisor_ Lecturer, advisor_PostDoc, advisor_FullProfessor, advisor_AssociateProfessor, advisor_AssistantProfessor, and advisor_ VisitingProfessor as part of the input set, then the TP in line 2 becomes unnecessary. Similarly, TP in line 3 becomes unnecessary if files takesCourse_Course and takesCourse_GraduateCourse are chosen. Hence, we get the rewritten query shown in Listing 2. However, if the type of the object is not specified, then we select all files for that predicate.
5. If the predicate is not rdf:type and the object is concrete, then we select all files for that predicate.

```
Listing 1. LUBM Query 9
SELECT ?X ?Y ?Z WHERE {
?X rdf:type ub:Student
```

```
?Y rdf:type ub:Faculty
?Z rdf:type ub:Course
?X ub:advisor ?Y
?Y ub:teacherOf ?Z
?X ub:takesCourse ?Z}
```

Listing 2. Rewritten LUBM Query 9
```
SELECT ?X ?Y ?Z WHERE {
?X rdf:type ub:Student
?X ub:advisor ?Y.
?Y ub:teacherOf ?Z.
?X ub:takesCourse ?Z}
```

25.5.3 Cost Estimation for Query Processing

We run Hadoop jobs to answer an SPARQL query. In this section, we discuss how we estimate the cost of a job. However, before doing that, we introduce some definitions that we will use later.

Definition 25.1

Triple pattern (TP): A TP is an ordered set of subject, predicate, and object that appears in an SPARQL query WHERE clause. The subject, predicate, and object can be either a variable (unbounded) or a concrete value (bounded).

Definition 25.2

Triple pattern join (TPJ): A TPJ is a join between two TPs on a variable.

Definition 25.3

MapReduceJoin (MRJ): An MRJ is a join between two or more TPs on a variable.

Definition 25.4

Job (JB): A JB is a Hadoop job where one or more MRJs are done. JB has a set of input files and a set of output files.

Definition 25.5

Conflicting MapReduceJoins (CMRJ): CMRJ is a pair of MRJs on different variables sharing a TP.

Definition 25.6

Nonconflicting MapReduceJoins (NCMRJ): NCMRJ is a pair of MRJs either not sharing any TP or sharing a TP and the MRJs are on same variable.

An example will illustrate these terms better. In Listing 3, we show LUBM Query 12. Lines 2, 3, 4, and 5 each have a TP. The join between TPs in lines 2 and 4 on variable ?X is an MRJ. If we do two MRJs, one between TPs in lines 2 and 4 on variable ?X and the other between TPs in lines 4 and 5 on variable ?Y, there will be a CMRJ as TP in line 4 (?X ub:worksFor ?Y) takes part in two MRJs on two different variables ?X and ?Y. This type of join is called CMRJ because in a Hadoop job, more than one variable of a TP cannot be a key at the same time and MRJs are performed on keys. An NCMRJ shown would be one MRJ between TPs in lines 2 and 4 on variable ?X, and another MRJ between TPs in lines 3 and 5 on variable ?Y. These two MRJs can make up a JB.

Listing 3. LUBM Query 12
```
SELECT ?X WHERE {
?X rdf:type ub:Chair
?Y rdf:type ub:Department
?X ub:worksFor ?Y
?Y ub:subOrganizationOf http://www.U0.edu}
```

Ideal Model. To answer a SPARQL query, we may need more than one job. Therefore, in an ideal scenario, the cost estimation for processing a query requires individual cost estimation of each job that is needed to answer that query. A job contains three main tasks: reading, sorting, and writing. We estimate the cost of a job based on these three tasks. For each task, a unit cost is assigned to each TP it deals with. In the current model, we assume that costs for reading and writing are the same.

$$\text{Cost} = \left(\sum_{i=1}^{n-1} \text{MI}_i + \text{MO}_i + \text{RI}_i + \text{RO}_i \right) + \text{MI}_n + \text{MO}_n + \text{RI}_n \tag{25.1}$$

$$= \left(\sum_{i=1}^{n-1} \text{Job}_i \right) + \text{MI}_n + \text{MO}_n + \text{RI}_n \tag{25.2}$$

$$\text{Job}_i = + \text{MI}_i + \text{MO}_i + \text{RO}_i + \text{RI}_i \ (\text{if } i < n) \tag{25.3}$$

where
  MI_i = Map Input phase for job i
  MO_i = Map Output phase for job i
  RI_i = Reduce Input phase for job i
  RO_i = Reduce Output phase for job i

Equation 25.1 is the total cost of processing a query. It is the summation of the individual costs of each job and only the map phase of the final job. We do not consider the cost of the reduce output of the final job because it would be the same for any query plan as this output is the final result that is fixed for a query and a given data set. A job essentially performs a MapReduce task on the file data. Equation 25.2 shows the division of the MapReduce task into subtasks. Hence, to estimate the cost of each job, we will combine the estimated cost of each subtask.

Map Input (MI) phase: This phase reads the TPs from the selected input files stored in the HDFS. Therefore, we can estimate the cost for the MI phase to be equal to the total number of triples in each of the selected files.

Map Output (MO) phase: The estimation of the MO phase depends on the type of query being processed. If the query has no bound variable (e.g., [?X ub:worksFor ?Y]), then the output of the map phase is equal to the input. All of the TPs are transformed into key–value pairs and given as output. Therefore, for such a query, the MO cost will be the same as the MI cost. However, if the query involves a bound variable, (e.g., [?Y ub:subOrganizationOf <http://www.U0.edu>]), then, before making the key–value pairs, a bound component selectivity estimation can be applied. The resulting estimate for the TPs will account for the cost of the Map Output phase. The selected triples are written to a local disk.

Reduce Input (RI) phase: In this phase, the triples from the Map Output phase are read via HTTP and then sorted based on their key values. After sorting, the triples with identical keys are grouped together. Therefore, the cost estimation for the RI phase is equal to the MO phase. The number of key–value pairs that are sorted in RI is equal to the number of key–value pairs generated in the MO phase.

Reduce Output (RO) phase: The RO phase deals with performing the joins. Therefore, it is in this phase we can use the join TP selectivity summary statistics to estimate the size of its output. Below, we talk in detail about the join TP selectivity summary statistics needed for our framework.

In practice, the above discussion is applicable for the first job only. For the subsequent jobs, we lack both the precise knowledge and estimate of the number of TPs selected after applying the join in the first job. Therefore, for these jobs, we can take the size of the RO phase of the first job as an upper bound on the different phases of the subsequent jobs.

Equation 25.3 shows a very important postulation. It illustrates the total cost of an intermediate job, when $i < n$, and includes the cost of the RO phase in calculating the total cost of the job.

Heuristic Model. In this section, we show that the ideal model is not practical or cost-effective. There are several issues that make the ideal model less attractive in practice. First, the ideal model considers simple abstract costs, namely, the number of triples read and written by the different phases ignoring the actual cost of copying, sorting, etc., these triples, and the overhead for running jobs in Hadoop. But accurately incorporating those costs in the model is a difficult task. Even making a reasonably good estimation may be nontrivial. Second, to estimate intermediate join outputs, we need to maintain comprehensive summary statistics. In a MapReduce job in Hadoop, all the joins on a variable are joined together. For example, in the rewritten LUBM Query 9 (Listing 2), there are three joins on variable X. When a job is run to do the join on X, all the joins on X between TPs 1, 2, and 4 are done. If there were more than three joins on X, all will still be handled in one job. This shows that in order to gather summary statistics to estimate join selectivity, we face an exponential number of join cases. For example, between TPs having p_1, p_2, and p_3, there may be multiple types of joins because in each TP, a variable can occur either as a subject or an object. In the case of the rewritten Query 9, it is a subject–subject–subject join between 1, 2, and 4. There can be more types of join between these three, for example, subject–object–subject, object–subject–object, etc. That means that between P predicates, there can be 2^P types of joins on a single variable (ignoring the possibility that a variable may appear both as a subject and object in a TP). If there are P predicates in the data set, a total number of cases for which we need to collect summary statistics can be calculated by the formula

$$2^2 \times C_2^P + 2^3 \times C_3^P + \ldots + 2^P \times C_P^P$$

In the LUBM data set, there are 17 predicates. So, in total, there are 129,140,128 cases, which is a large number. Gathering summary statistics for such a large number of cases would be very time and space consuming. Hence, we took an alternate approach.

We observed that there is significant overhead for running a job in Hadoop. Therefore, if we minimize the number of jobs to answer a query, we get the fastest plan. The overhead is incurred by several disk I/O and network transfers that are integral part of any Hadoop job. When a job is submitted to a Hadoop cluster, at least the following set of actions takes place:

1. The executable file is transferred from the client machine to Hadoop JobTracker (http://wiki.apache.org/hadoop/JobTracker).
2. The JobTracker decides which TaskTrackers (http://wiki.apache.org/hadoop/TaskTracker) will execute the job.

3. The executable file is distributed to the TaskTrackers over the network.
4. Map processes start by reading data from HDFS.
5. Map outputs are written to discs.
6. Map outputs are read from discs, shuffled (transferred over the network to TaskTrackers, which would run Reduce processes), sorted, and written to discs.
7. Reduce processes start by reading the input from the discs.
8. Reduce outputs are written to discs.

These disk operations and network transfers are expensive operations even for a small amount of data. For example, in our experiments, we observed that the overhead incurred by one job is almost equivalent to reading a billion triples. The reason is that in every job, the output of the map process is always sorted before feeding the reduce processes. This sorting is unavoidable even if it is not needed by the user. Therefore, it would be less costly to process several hundred million more triples in n jobs, rather than processing several hundred million less triples in $n + 1$ jobs.

To further investigate, we did an experiment where we used the query shown in Listing 4. Here, the join selectivity between TPs 2 and 3 on ?Z is the highest. Hence, a query plan generation algorithm that uses selectivity factors to pick joins would select this join for the first job. As the other TPs 1 and 4 share variables with either TP 2 or 3, they cannot take part in any other join; moreover, they do not share any variables so the only possible join that can be executed in this job is the join between TPs 2 and 3 on ?X. Once this join is done, the two joins left are between TP 1 and the join output of first job on variable ?X and between TP 4 and the join output of first job on variable ?Y. We found that the selectivity of the first join is greater than the latter one. Hence, the second job will do this join and TP 4 will again not participate. In the third and last job, the join output of the second job will be joined with TP 4 on ?Y. This is the plan generated using join selectivity estimation. But the minimum job plan is a two-job plan where the first job joins TPs 1 and 2 on ?X and TPs 3 and 4 on ?Y. The second and final job joins the two join outputs of the first job on ?Z. The query runtimes we found are given in Husain et al. (2011).

Listing 4. Experiment Query
```
?S1 ub:advisor ?X
?X ub:headOf ?Z
?Z ub:subOrganizationOf ?Y
?S2 ub:mastersDegreeFrom ?Y
```

For each data set, we found that the two-job plan is faster than the three-job plan even though the three-job plan produced less intermediate data because of the join selectivity order. We can explain this by an observation we made in another small experiment. We generated files of sizes 5 and 10 MB containing random integers. We put the files in HDFS. For each file, we first read the file by using a program and recorded the time needed to do it. While reading, our program reads from one of the three available replica of the file. Then, we ran a MapReduce job that rewrites the file with the numbers sorted. We utilized MapReduce sorting to have the sorted output. Also note than when it writes the file, it writes three replications of it. We found that the MapReduce job, which does reading, sorting, and writing, takes 24.47 times longer to finish for 5 MB. For 10 MB, it is 42.79 times. This clearly shows how the write and data transfer operations of a MapReduce job are more expensive than a simple read from only one replica. Because of the number of jobs, the three-job plan is doing much more disk read and write operations as well as network data transfers, and as a result is slower than the two-job plan even if it is reading less input data.

For these reasons, we do not pursue the ideal model. We follow the practical model, which is to generate a query plan having minimum possible jobs. However, while generating a minimum job plan, whenever we need to choose a join to be considered in a job among more than one joins, instead of choosing randomly, we use the summary join statistics. This is described in Section 25.5.6. More details of our experimental results with the charts are provided in Husain et al. (2011).

25.5.4   Query Plan Generation

In this section, first we define the query plan generation problem, and show that generating the best (i.e., least cost) query plan for the ideal model as well as for the practical model is computationally expensive. Then, we will present a heuristic and a greedy approach to generate an approximate solution to generate the best plan.

We will use the following query as a running example in this section:

Listing 5. Running Example
```
SELECT ?V,?X,?Y,?Z WHERE{
?X rdf:type ub:GraduateStudent
?Y rdf:type ub:University
?Z ?V ub:Department
?X ub:memberOf ?Z
?X ub:undergraduateDegreeFrom ?Y}
```

To simplify the notations, we will only refer to the TPs by the variable in that pattern. For example, the first TP (?X rdf:type ub:GraduateStudent) will be represented simply as X. Also, in the simplified version, the whole query would be represented as follows: {X,Y,Z,XZ,XY}.

We will use the notation join (XY,X) to denote a join operation between the two TPs XY and X on the common variable X.

Definition 25.7

Minimum cost plan generation problem (Bestplan problem): For a given query, the Bestplan problem is to generate a job plan so that the total cost of the jobs is minimized. Note that Bestplan considers the more general case where each job has some cost associated with it (i.e., the ideal model).

Example 25.1

Given the query in our running example, two possible job plans are as follows:

Plan 1. job_1 = {X, XY, XZ}
Resultant TPs = {YZ, YZ}, job_2 = {Y, YZ}
Resultant TPs = {Z, Z}, job_3 = {Z, Z}, total cost = cost(job_1) + cost(job_2)

Plan 2. job_1 = {XZ, Z} and joint(XY, Y)
Resultant TPs = {X, X, X}, job_2 = join(X, X, X)
Total cost = cost(job_1) + cost (job_2)

The Bestplan problem is to find the least-cost job plan among all possible job plans.

Definition 25.8

Joining variable: A variable that is common in two or more TPs. For example, in the running example query, X, Y, and Z are joining variables, but V is not.

Definition 25.9

Complete elimination: A join operation that eliminates a joining variable. For example, in the example query, Y can be completely eliminated if we join (XY,Y).

Definition 25.10

Partial elimination: A join operation that partially eliminates a joining variable. For example, in the example query, if we perform join (XY,Y) and join (X,ZX) in the same job, the resultant TPs would be {X,Z,X}. Therefore, Y will be completely eliminated, but X will be partially eliminated. So, the join (X,ZX) performs a partial elimination.

Definition 25.11

E-count(v): E-count(v) is the number of joining variables in the resultant TP after a complete elimination of variable v. In the running example, join (X,XY,XZ) completely eliminates X, and the resultant TP (YZ) has two joining variables Y and Z. So, E-count(X) = 2. Similarly, E-count(Y) = 1 and E-count(Z) = 1.   ∎

Computational Complexity of Bestplan. It can be shown that generating the least-cost query plan is computationally expensive, since the search space is exponentially large. First, we formulate the problem, and then show its complexity.

Problem Formulation. We formulate Bestplan as a search problem. Let $G = (V, E)$ be a weighted directed graph, where each vertex $v_i \in V$ represents a state of the TPs, and each edge $e_i \in \left(v_{i_1}, v_{i_2} \right) \in E$ represents a job that makes a transition from state v_{i_1} to state v_{i_2}. v_0 is the initial state, where no joins have been performed, that is, the given query. Also, v_{goal} is the goal state, which represents a state of the TP where all joins have been performed. The problem is to find the shortest weighted path from v_0 to v_{goal}.

For example, in our running example query, the initial state v_0 = {X, Y, Z, XY, XZ} and the goal state $v_{goal} = \varnothing$, that is, no more TPs left. Suppose the first job (job$_1$) performs join(X, XY, XZ). Then, the resultant TPs (new state) would be v_1 = {Y, Z, YZ}, and job$_1$ would be represented by the edge (v_0, v_1). The weight of edge (v_0, v_1) is the cost of job$_1$ = cost(job$_1$), where cost is the given cost function.

Search Space Size. Given a graph $G = (V, E)$, Dijkstra's shortest-path algorithm can find the shortest path from a source to all other nodes in $O(|V|\log|V| + |E|)$ time. However, for Bestplan, it can be shown that in the worst case, $|V| \geq 2^K$, where K is the total number of joining variables in the given query. Therefore, the number of vertices in the graph is exponential, leading to an exponential search problem. In Husain et al. (2011), we have shown that the worst-case complexity of the Bestplan problem is exponential in K, the number of joining variables in the given query.

Relaxed Bestplan Problem and Approximate Solution. In the Relaxed Bestplan problem, we assume uniform cost for all jobs. Although this relaxation does not reduce the search space, the problem is reduced to finding a job plan having the minimum number of jobs. Note that this is the problem for the practical version of the model.

Definition 25.12

Relaxed Bestplan problem: The Relaxed Bestplan problem is to find the job plan that has the minimum number of jobs.

Next, we show that if joins are reasonably chosen, and no eligible join operation is left undone in a job, then we may set an upper bound on the maximum number of jobs required for any given query. However, it is still computationally expensive to generate all possible job plans. Therefore, we resort to a greedy algorithm (Algorithm 25.1) that finds an approximate solution to the Relaxed Bestplan problem but is guaranteed to find a job plan within the upper bound.

Algorithm 25.1: Relaxed-Bestplan (Query Q)

1:   $Q \leftarrow$ Remove nonjoining variables(Q)
2: **while** $Q \neq$ Empty **do**
3:       $J \leftarrow 1$ // Total number of jobs
4:       $U = \{u_1,\ldots,u_K\} \leftarrow$ all variables sorted in nondecreasing order of their E-counts
5:       $\text{job}_J \leftarrow$ Empty//list of join operations in the//current job
6:       tmp $\leftarrow$ Empty//temporarily stores resultant//triple patterns
7:       **for** $i = 1$ to K **do**
8:         **if** Can-Eliminate(Q, u_i) = true **then**//complete or partial elimination possible
9:            tmp $\leftarrow$ tmp $\cup$ Join-result(TP(Q, u_i))
10:           $Q \leftarrow Q - \text{TP}(Q, u_i)$
11:           $\text{job}_J \leftarrow \text{job}_J \cup \text{join}(\text{TP}(Q, u_i))$
12:       **end if**
13:       **end for**
14:       $Q \leftarrow Q \cup \text{tmp}$
15:       $J \leftarrow J + 1$
16: **end while**
17: Return $\{\text{job}_1,\ldots,\text{job}_{J-1}\}$

Definition 25.13

Early elimination heuristic: The early elimination heuristic makes as many complete eliminations as possible in each job. This heuristic leaves the fewest number of variables for join in the next job. To apply the heuristic, we must first choose the variable in each job with the least E-count. This heuristic is applied in Algorithm 25.1.

Description of Algorithm 25.1

The algorithm starts by removing all the nonjoining variables from the query Q. In our running example, $Q = \{X, Y, VZ, XY, XZ\}$, and removing the nonjoining variable V makes $Q = \{X, Y, Z, XY, XZ\}$. In the while loop, the job plan is generated, starting from Job_1. In line 4, we sort the variables according to their E-count. The sorted variables are $U = \{Y, Z, X\}$, since Y, and Z have E-count = 1, and X has E-count = 2. For each job, the list of join operations is stored in the variable job_J, where J is the ID of the current job. Also, a temporary variable tmp is used to store the resultant triples of the joins to be performed in the current job (line 6). In the for loop, each variable is checked to see if the variable can be completely or partially eliminated (line 8). If yes, we store the join result in the temporary variable (line 9), update Q (line 10), and add this join to the current job (line 11). In our running example, this results in the following operations: Iteration 1 of the for loop: $u_1 = (Y)$ can be completely eliminated. Here, TP(Q, Y); the TPs in Q containing iteration 3 of the for loop: $u_3 = (X)$ cannot be completely or partially eliminated, since there is no other TP left to join with it. Therefore, when the for loop terminates, we have $\text{job}_1 = \{\text{join}(Y, XY), \text{join}(Z, XZ)\}$, and $Q = \{X, X, X\}$. In the second iteration of the while loop, we will have $\{\text{job}_2 = \{X, X, X\}$. Since after this join, Q becomes empty, the while loop is exited. Finally, $\{\text{job}_1, \text{job}_2\}$ are returned from the algorithm.

    In Husain et al. (2011), we have proved that for any given query Q, containing K joining variables and N TPs, the algorithm Relaxed-Bestplan(Q) generates a job plan containing at most J jobs, where

$$J = \begin{cases} 0 & N = 0 \\ 1 & N = 1 \text{ or } K = 1 \\ \min\left(\lceil 1.71 \log_2 N \rceil, K\right) & N, K > 1 \end{cases} \tag{25.4}$$

25.5.5 BREAKING TIES BY SUMMARY STATISTICS

We frequently face situations where we need to choose a join for multiple join options. These choices can occur when both query plans (i.e., join orderings) require the minimum number of jobs. For example, the query shown in Listing 6 poses such a situation.

Listing 6. Query Having a Tie Situation
```
?X rdf:type ub:FullProfessor
?X ub:advisorOf ?Y
?Y rdf:type ub:ResearchAssistant
```

The second TP in the query makes it impossible to answer and solve the query with only one job. There are only two possible plans: we can join the first two TPs on X first and then join its output with the last TP on Y, or we can join the last two patterns first on Y and then join its output with the first pattern on X. In such a situation, instead of randomly choosing a join variable for the first job, we use join summary statistics for a pair of predicates. We select the join for the first job, which is more selective to break the tie. The join summary statistics we use are described in Stocker et al. (2008).

25.5.6 MAPREDUCE JOIN EXECUTION

In this section, we discuss how we implement the joins needed to answer SPARQL queries using the MapReduce framework of Hadoop. Algorithm 25.1 determines the number of jobs required to answer a query. It returns an ordered set of jobs. Each job has associated input information. The Job Handler component of our MapReduce framework runs the jobs in the sequence they appear in the ordered set. The output file of one job is the input of the next. The output file of the last job has the answer to the query.

Listing 7. LUBM Query 2
```
SELECT ?X, ?Y, ?Z WHERE {
?X rdf:type ub:GraduateStudent
?Y rdf:type ub:University
?Z rdf:type ub:Department
?X ub:memberOf ?Z
?Z ub:subOrganizationOf ?Y
?X ub:undergraduateDegreeFrom ?Y}
```

Listing 7 shows LUBM Query 2, which we will use to illustrate the way we do a join using map and reduce methods. The query has six TPs and nine joins between them on the variable X, Y, and Z.

Our input selection algorithm selects files type_GraduateStudent, type_ University, type_ Department, all files having the prefix memberOf, all files having the prefix subOrganizationOf, and all files having the prefix underGraduateDegreeFrom as the input to the jobs needed to answer the query.

The query plan has two jobs. In job_1, TPs of lines 2, 5, and 7 are joined on X and TPs of lines 3 and 6 are joined on Y. In job_2, TPs of line 4 is joined with the outputs of the previous two joins on Z and also the join outputs of job_1 are joined on Y.

The input files of job_1 are type_GraduateStudent, type_University, all files having the prefix memberOf, all files having the prefix subOrganizationOf, and all files having the prefix under-GraduateDegreeFrom. In the map phase, we first tokenize the input value, which is actually a line of the input file. Then, we check the input file name and, if input is from type_GraduateStudent, we output a key–value pair having the subject URI prefixed with X# as the key and a flag string GS# as the value. The value serves as a flag to indicate that the key is of type GraduateStudent. The subject

URI is the first token returned by the tokenizer. Similarly, for input from file type_University, we output a key–value pair having the subject URI prefixed with Y# as the key and a flag string U# as the value. If the input from any file has the prefix memberOf, we retrieve the subject and object from the input line by the tokenizer and output a key–value pair having the subject URI prefixed with X# as the key and the object value prefixed with MO# as the value. For input from files having the prefix subOrganizationOf, we output key–value pairs making the object prefixed with Y# as the key and the subject prefixed with SO# as the value. For input from files having the prefix underGraduate DegreeFrom, we output key–value pairs making the subject URI prefixed with X# as the key and the object value prefixed with UDF# as the value. Hence, we make either the subject or the object a map output key based on which we are joining. This is the reason why the object is made the key for the triples from files having the prefix subOrganizationOf: the joining variable Y is an object in the TP in line 6. For all other inputs, the subject is made the key because the joining variables X and Y are subjects in the TPs in lines 2, 3, 5, and 7.

In the reduce phase, Hadoop groups all the values for a single key, and for each key provides the key and an iterator to the values collection. Looking at the prefix, we can immediately tell if it is a value for X or Y because of the prefixes we used. In either case, we output a key–value pair using the same key and concatenating all the values to make a string value. So after this reduce phase, join on X is complete and on Y is partially complete.

The input files of job_2 are type_Department file and the output file of job_1, job1.out. Like the map phase of job_1, in the map phase of job_2, we also tokenize the input value, which is actually a line of the input file. Then, we check the input file name and if input is from type_Department, we output a key–value pair having the subject URI prefixed with Z# as the key and a flag string D# as the value. If the input is from job1.out, we find the value having the prefix Z#. We make this value the output key and concatenate the rest of the values to make a string and make it the output value. Basically, we make the Z# values the keys to join on Z.

In the reduce phase, we know that the key is the value for Z. The values collection has two types of strings. One has X values, which are URIs for graduate students and also Y values from which they received their undergraduate degree. The Z value, that is, the key, may or may not be a sub OrganizationOf the Y value. The other types of strings have only Y values, which are universities and of which the Z value is a suborganization. We iterate over the values collection and then join the two types of tuples on Y values. From the join output, we find the result tuples which have values for X, Y, and Z.

25.6   RESULTS

25.6.1   Experimental Setup

In this section, we first present the benchmark data sets with which we experimented. Next, we present the alternative repositories we evaluated for comparison. Then, we detail our experimental setup. Finally, we present our evaluation results.

Data Sets. In our experiments with SPARQL query processing, we used two synthetic data sets: LUBM (Guo et al., 2005) and SP2B (Schmidt et al., 2009). The LUBM data set generates data about universities by using an ontology (http://www.lehigh.edu/~zhp2/2004/0401/univ-bench.owl). It has 14 standard queries. Some of the queries require inference to answer. The LUBM data set is very good for both inference and scalability testing. For all LUBM data sets, we used the default seed. The SP2B data set is good for scalability testing with complex queries and data access patterns. It has 16 queries, most of which have complex structures.

Baseline Frameworks. We compared our framework with RDF-3X (Neumann and Weikum, 2008), Jena (http://jena.sourceforge.net), and BigOWLIM (https://confluence.ontotext.com/display /OWLIMv35/BigOWLIM+Fact+Sheet). RDF-3X is considered the fastest semantic web framework with persistent storage. Jena is an open source framework for semantic web data. It has several models that can be used to store and retrieve RDF data. We chose Jena's In-Memory and SDB models to compare our framework with. As the name suggests, the in-memory model stores the data in main memory and does not retain data. The SDB model is a persistent model and can use many off-the-shelf DBMSs. We used MySQL database as SDB's back-end in our experiments. BigOWLIM is a proprietary framework that is the state-of-the-art significantly fast framework for semantic web data. It can act both as persistent and nonpersistent storage. All of these frameworks run in a single machine setup.

Hardware. We have a 10-node Hadoop cluster that we use for our framework. Each of the nodes has the following configuration: Pentium IV 2.80 GHz processor, 4 GB main memory, and 640 GB disk space. We ran the Jena, RDF-3X, and BigOWLIM frameworks on a powerful single machine having 2.80 GHz quad core processor, 8 GB main memory, and 1 TB disk space.

Software. We used Hadoop 0.20.1 for our framework. We compared our framework with Jena-2.5.7, which uses MySQL 14.12 for its SDB model. We used BigOWLIM version 3.2.6. For RDF-3X, we used version 0.3.5 of the source code.

25.6.2 EVALUATION

We present a performance comparison between our framework, RDF-3X, Jena In-Memory and SDB models, and BigOWLIM. More details are found in Husain et al. (2011). We used three LUBM data sets: 10,000, 20,000, and 30,000, which have more than 1.1, 2.2, and 3.3 billion triples, respectively. The initial population time for RDF-3X took 655, 1756, and 3353 minutes to load the data sets, respectively. This shows that the RDF-3X load time is increasing exponentially. LUBM (30,000) has three times as many triples as LUBM (10,000); yet, it requires more than five times as long to load.

For evaluation purposes, we chose LUBM Queries 1, 2, 4, 9, 12, and 13 to be reported in this work. These queries provide a good mixture and include simple and complex structures, inference, and multiple types of joins. They are representatives of other queries of the benchmark, and so reporting only these covers all types of variations found in the queries we left out and also saves space. Query 1 is a simple selective query. RDF-3X is much faster than HadoopRDF for this query. RDF-3X utilizes six indexes (Neumann and Weikum, 2008), and those six indexes actually make up the data set. The indexes provide RDF-3X a very fast way to look up triples, similar to a hash table. Hence, a highly selective query is efficiently answered by RDF-3X. Query 2 is a query with complex structures, low selectivity, and no bound objects. The result set is quite large. For this query, HadoopRDF outperforms RDF-3X for all three data set sizes. RDF-3X fails to answer the query at all when the data set size is 3.3 billion triples. RDF-3X returns memory segmentation fault error messages and does not produce any query results. Query 4 is also a highly selective query; that is, the result set size is small because of a bound object in the second TP, but it needs inferencing to answer it. The first TP uses the class Person, which is a superclass of many classes. No resource in the LUBM data set is of type Person; rather, there are many resources that are its subtypes. RDF-3X does not support inferencing, so we had to convert the query to an equivalent query having some union operations. RDF-3X outperforms HadoopRDF for this query. Query 9 is similar in structure to Query 2, but it requires significant inferencing. The first three TPs of this query use classes that are not explicitly instantiated in the data set. However, the data set includes many instances of the corresponding subclasses. This is also the query that requires the largest data set join and returns the largest result set out of the queries we evaluated. RDF-3X is faster than HadoopRDF for the 1.1 billion triples data set, but it fails to answer the query at all for the other two data sets. Query 12 is similar to Query 4 because it is both selective and has inferencing in one TP. RDF-3X beats HadoopRDF for this query. Query 13 has only two TPs. Both of them involve inferencing. There is a bound subject in the second TP. It returns the second largest result set. HadoopRDF beats RDF-3X for this query for all data sets. The performance of RDF-3X is slow because the first TP has very low selectivity and requires low selectivity joins to perform inference via backward chaining.

These results lead us to some simple conclusions. RDF-3X achieves the best performance for queries with high selectivity and bound objects. However, HadoopRDF outperforms RDF-3X for queries with unbound objects, low selectivity, or large data set joins. RDF-3X cannot execute the two queries with unbound objects (Queries 2 and 9) for a 3.3 billion triples data set. This demonstrates that HadoopRDF is more scalable and handles low selectivity queries more efficiently than does RDF-3X.

We also compared our implementation with the Jena In-Memory, SDB, and BigOWLIM models. Because of space and time limitations, we performed these tests only for LUBM Queries 2 and 9 from the LUBM data set. We chose these queries because they have complex structures and require inference. It is to be noted that BigOWLIM needed 7 GB of Java heap space to successfully load the billion triples data set. We ran BigOWLIM only for the largest three data sets as we are interested in its performance with large data sets. For each set, we obtained the results for the Jena In-Memory model, Jena SDB model, our Hadoop implementation, and BigOWLIM. At times, the query could not complete or it ran out of memory. In most cases, our approach was the fastest. For Query 2, the Jena In-Memory and SDB models were faster than our approach, giving results in 3.9 and 0.4 seconds, respectively. However, as the size of the data set grew, the Jena In-Memory model ran out of memory space. Our implementation was much faster than the Jena SDB model for large data sets. For example, for 110 million triples, our approach took 143.5 seconds as compared with about 5000 seconds for the Jena SDB model. We found that the Jena SDB model could not finish answering Query 9. The Jena In-Memory model worked well for small data sets but became slower than our implementation as the data set size grew, and eventually ran out of memory.

For Query 2, BigOWLIM was slower than our implementation for the 110 and 550 million data sets. For the 550 million data set, it took 22693.4 seconds, which is abruptly high compared with its other timings. For the billion triple data set, BigOWLIM was faster. It should be noted that our framework does not have any indexing or triple cache whereas BigOWLIM exploits indexing, which it loads into the main memory when it starts. It may also prefetch triples into the main memory. For Query 9, our implementation was faster than BigOWLIM in all experiments.

It should also be noted that our RDF-3X and HadoopRDF queries were tested using cold runs. What we mean by this is that the main memory and file system cache were cleared before execution. However, for BigOWLIM, we were forced to execute hot runs. This is because it takes a significant amount of time to load a database into BigOWLIM. Therefore, we will always easily outperform BigOWLIM for cold runs. Thus, we actually tested BigOWLIM for hot runs against HadoopRDF for cold runs. This gives a tremendous advantage to BigOWLIM; yet, for large data sets, HadoopRDF still produced much better results. This shows that HadoopRDF is much more scalable than BigOWLIM, and provides more efficient queries for large data sets.

The final test we have performed is an in-depth scalability test. For this, we repeated the same queries for eight different data set sizes, all the way up to 6.6 billion.

In our experiments, we found that Query 1 is simple and requires only one join; thus, it took the least amount of time among all the queries. Query 2 is one of the two queries having the greatest number of TPs. Even though it has three times more TPs, it did not take thrice the Query 1 answering time because of our storage schema. Query 4 has one less TP than Query 2, but it requires inferencing. As we determined inferred relations on the fly, queries requiring inference take longer times in our framework. Queries 9 and 12 also require inferencing. Details are given in Husain et al. (2011).

As the size of the data set grows, the increase in time to answer a query does not grow proportionately. The increase in time is always less. For example, there are 10 times as many triples in the data set of 10,000 universities than in 1,000 universities; however, for Query 1, the time only increases by 3.76 times and for Query 9 by 7.49 times. The latter is the highest increase in time, yet it is still less than the increase in the size of the data sets. Owing to space limitations, we do not report query runtimes with PS schema here. We found that PS schema is much slower than POS schema.

25.7   SUMMARY AND DIRECTIONS

We have presented a framework capable of handling enormous amounts of RDF data that can be used to represent social networks. Since our framework is based on Hadoop, which is a distributed and highly fault-tolerant system, it inherits these two properties automatically. The framework is highly scalable. To increase the capacity of our system, all that needs to be done is to add new nodes to the Hadoop cluster. We have proposed a schema to store RDF data, an algorithm to determine a query-processing plan, whose worst case is bounded, to answer a SPARQL query and a simplified cost model to be used by the algorithm. Our experiments demonstrate that our system is highly scalable. If we increase the data volume, the delay introduced to answer a query does not increase proportionally. The results indicate that for very large data sets (more than 1 billion triples), HadoopRDF is preferable and more efficient if the query includes low-selectivity joins or significant inference. Other solutions may be more efficient if the query includes bound objects that produce high selectivity.

In the future, we would like to extend the work in multiple directions. First, we will investigate a more sophisticated query model. We will cache statistics for the most frequent queries and use dynamic programming to exploit the statistics. Second, we will evaluate the impact of the number of reducers, the only parameter of a Hadoop job specifiable by user, on the query runtimes. Third, we will investigate indexing opportunities and further usage of binary formats. Fourth, we will handle more complex SPARQL patterns, for example, queries having OPTIONAL blocks. Finally, we will demonstrate our system with realistic social networking applications.

REFERENCES

Abadi, D.J. Data management in the cloud: Limitations and opportunities. *IEEE Data Engineering Bulletin* 32(1): 3–12, 2009.

Abadi, D.J., Marcus, A., Madden, S.R., and Hollenbach, K. Scalable semantic web data management using vertical partitioning. In: *Proc. 33rd Int'l Conf. Very Large Data Bases*, Vienna, Austria, 2007.

Abadi, D.J., Marcus, A., Madden, S.R., and Hollenbach, K. SW-Store: A vertically partitioned DBMS for semantic web data management. *VLDB Journal* 18(2): 385–406, 2009.

Abouzeid, A., Bajda-Pawlikowski, K., Abadi, D.J., Silberschatz, A., and Rasin, A. HadoopDB: An architectural hybrid of MapReduce and DBMS technologies for analytical workloads, In: *Proc. VLDB Endowment*, vol. 2, pp. 922–933, 2009.

Atre, M., Srinivasan, J., and Hendler, J.A. BitMat: A main-memory bit matrix of RDF triples for conjunctive triple pattern queries. In: *Proc. Int'l Semantic Web Conf.*, Karlsruhe, Germany, 2008.

Boncz, P., Grust, T., van Keulen, M., Manegold, S., Rittinger, J., and Teubner, J. MonetDB/XQuery: A fast XQuery processor powered by a relational engine. In: *Proc. ACM SIGMOD Int'l Conf. on Management of Data*, pp. 479–490, Chicago, 2006.

Carroll, J.J., Dickinson, I., Dollin, C., Reynolds, D., Seaborne, A., and Wilkinson, K. Jena: Implementing the semantic web recommendations. In: *Proc. 13th Int'l World Wide Web Conf. Alternate Track Papers and Posters*, pp. 74–83, New York, 2004.

Chang, F., Dean, J., Ghemawat, S., Hsieh, W.C., Wallach, D.A., Burrows, M., Chandra, T., Fikes, A., and Gruber, R.E. Bigtable: A distributed storage system for structured data. In: *Proc. Seventh USENIX Symp. Operating System Design and Implementation*, November 2006, pp. 205–218, Seattle, WA, 2006.

Chebotko, A., Lu, S., and Fotouhi, F. Semantics preserving SPARQL-to-SQL translation. Technical Report TR-DB-112007-CLF, 2007.

Chong, E.I., Das, S., Eadon, G., and Srinivasan, J. An efficient SQL-based RDF querying scheme. In: *Proc. Int'l Conf. Very Large Data Bases (VLDB '05)*, Trondheim, Norway, pp. 1216–1227, 2005.

Chu, C.T., Kim, S.K., Lin, Y.A., Yu, Y., Bradski, G., Ng, A.Y., and Olukotun, K. Map–reduce for machine learning on multicore. In: *Proc. Neural Information Processing Systems (NIPS)*, Vancouver, BC, Canada, 2006.

Cyganiak, R. A relational algebra for SPARQL. Technical Report HPL-2005-170, 2005.

Dean, J. and Ghemawat, S. MapReduce: Simplified data processing on large clusters. In: *Proc. Sixth Conf. Symp. Operating Systems Design and Implementation*, San Francisco, pp. 137–150, 2004.

Ding, L., Finin, T., Peng, Y., da Silva, P.P., and Mcguinness, D.L. Tracking RDF graph provenance using RDF molecules. In: *Proc. Fourth Int'l Semantic Web Conf.*, Galway, Ireland, 2005.

Guo, Y., Pan, Z., and Heflin, J. An evaluation of knowledge base systems for large OWL datasets. In: *Proc. Int'l Semantic Web Conf.*, Hiroshima, Japan, 2004.

Guo, Y., Pan, Z., and Heflin, J. LUBM: A benchmark for OWL knowledge base systems. In: *Web Semantics: Science, Services and Agents on the World Wide Web*, vol. 3, pp. 158–182, 2005.

Husain, M.F. Data intensive query processing for semantic web data using Hadoop and MapReduce, PhD Thesis, The University of Texas at Dallas, May 2011.

Husain, M.F., Doshi, P., Khan, L., and Thuraisingham, B. Storage and retrieval of large RDF graph using Hadoop and MapReduce. In: *Proc. First Int'l Conference on Cloud Computing*, Beijing, China. 2009.

Husain, M.F., Khan, L., Kantarcioglu, M., and Thuraisingham, B. Data intensive query processing for large RDF graphs using cloud computing tools. In: *Proc. IEEE Int'l Conf. Cloud Computing*, July 2010, Miami, FL, pp. 1–10, 2010.

Husain, M.F., McGlothlin, J.P., Masud, M.M., Khan, L.R., and Thuraisingham, B.M. Heuristics-based query processing for large RDF graphs using cloud computing. *IEEE Transactions on Knowledge and Data Engineering* 23(9): 1312–1327, 2011.

Kiryakov, A., Ognyanov, D., and Manov, D. OWLIM: A pragmatic semantic repository for OWL. In: *Proc. Int'l Workshop Scalable Semantic Web Knowledge Base Systems (SSWS)*, New York, 2005.

McGlothlin, J.P. and Khan, L.R. RDFKB: Efficient support for RDF inference queries and knowledge management. In: *Proc. Int'l Database Engineering and Applications Symposium* (IDEAS), Cetraro, Italy, 2009.

McGlothlin, J.P. and Khan, L.R. Materializing and persisting inferred and uncertain knowledge in RDF datasets. In: *Proc. AAAI Conf. Artificial Intelligence*, Atlanta, GA, 2010.

McNabb, A.W., Monson, C.K., and Seppi, K.D. MRPSO: MapReduce particle swarm optimization. In: *Proc. Annual Conference on Genetic and Evolutionary Computation (GECCO)*, London, 2007.

Moreira, J.E., Michael, M.M., Da Silva, D., Shiloach, D., Dube, P., and Zhang, L. Scalability of the Nutch search engine. In: *Proc. 21st Annual Int'l Conference on Supercomputing (ICS '07)*, June 2007, Rotterdam, The Netherlands, pp. 3–12, 2007.

Moretti, C., Steinhaeuser, K., Thain, D., and Chawla, N. Scaling up classifiers to cloud computers. In: *Proc. IEEE Int'l Conference. Data Mining (ICDM '08)*, Pisa, Italy, 2008.

Neumann, T. and Weikum, G. RDF-3X: A RISC-style engine for RDF. In: *Proc. VLDB Endowment*, vol. 1, no. 1, pp. 647–659, 2008.

Newman, A., Hunter, J., Li, Y.F., Bouton, C., and Davis, M. A scale-out RDF molecule store for distributed processing of biomedical data. In: *Proc. Semantic Web for Health Care and Life Sciences Workshop*, Karlsruhe, Germany, 2008.

Olston, C., Reed, B., Srivastava, U., Kumar, R., and Tomkins, A. Pig Latin: A not-so-foreign language for data processing. In: *Proc. ACM SIGMOD Int'l Conf. Management of Data*, Vancouver, BC, Canada, 2008.

Rohloff, K., Dean, M., Emmons, I., Ryder, D., and Sumner, J. An evaluation of triple-store technologies for large data stores. In: *Proc. OTM Confederated Int'l Conf. on the Move to Meaningful Internet Systems*, Vilamoura, Portugal, 2007.

Schmidt, M., Hornung, T., Lausen, G., and Pinkel, C. SP2Bench: A SPARQL performance benchmark. In: *Proc. 25th Int'l Conference on Data Engineering (ICDE '09)*, Shanghai, China, 2009.

Sidirourgos, L., Goncalves, R., Kersten, M., Nes, N., and Manegold, S. Column-store support for RDF data management: Not all swans are white. In: *Proc. VLDB Endowment*, August 2008, vol. 1, no. 2, pp. 1553–1563, 2008.

Sismanis, Y., Das, S., Gemulla, R., Haas, P., Beyer, K., and McPherson, J. Ricardo: Integrating R and Hadoop. In: *Proc. ACM SIGMOD Int'l Conf. Management of Data (SIGMOD)*, Indianapolis, IN, 2010.

Stocker, M., Seaborne, A., Bernstein, A., Kiefer, C., and Reynolds, D. SPARQL basic graph pattern optimization using selectivity estimation. In: *WWW '08: Proc. 17th Int'l Conf. World Wide Web*, Beijing, China, 2008.

Stonebraker, M., Abadi, D.J., Batkin, A., Chen, X., Cherniack, M., Ferreira, M., Lau, E., Lin, A., Madden, S., O'Neil, E. et al. C-Store: A column-oriented DBMS. In: *VLDB '05: Proc. 31st Int'l Conf. Very Large Data Bases*, Trondheim, Norway, pp. 553–564, 2005.

Wang, J., Wu, S., Gao, H., Li, J., and Ooi, B.C. Indexing multi-dimensional data in a cloud system. In: *Proc. ACM SIGMOD Int'l Conf. Management of Data (SIGMOD)*, Indianapolis, IN, 2010.

Weiss, C., Karras, P., and Bernstein, A. Hexastore: Sextuple indexing for semantic web data management. In: *Proc. VLDB Endowment*, vol. 1, no. 1, pp. 1008–1019, 2008.

World Wide Web Consortium. N-triples: W3C RDF core WG internal working draft. Available at http://www .w3.org/2001/sw/RDFCore/ntriples, 2001.

World Wide Web Consortium. Query variables. SPARQL query language for RDF: W3C recommendation. Available at http://www.w3.org/TR/rdf-sparql-query/#defn_QueryVariable, 2008a.

World Wide Web Consortium. Triple patterns. SPARQL query language for RDF: W3C recommendation. Available at http://www.w3.org/TR/rdf-sparql-query/#defn_TriplePattern, 2008b.

World Wide Web Consortium. Latest "RDF concepts and abstract syntax" versions. Available at http://www.w3.org/TR/rdf-concepts/#dfn-rdf-triple, 2014a.

World Wide Web Consortium. Latest "RDF primer" versions. Available at http://www.w3.org/TR/rdf-primer, 2014b.

World Wide Web Consortium. RDF 1.1 XML syntax: W3C recommendation. Available at http://www.w3.org/TR/rdf-syntax-grammar, 2014c.

Xu, Y., Kostamaa, P., and Gao, L. Integrating Hadoop and parallel DBMs. In: *Proc. ACM SIGMOD Int'l Conf. Management of Data (SIGMOD)*, Indianapolis, IN, 2010.

Zeyliger, P. How Raytheon BBN technologies researchers are using Hadoop to build a scalable, distributed triple store. Available at http://www.cloudera.com/blog/2010/03/how-raytheon-researchers-are-using-hadoop-to-build-a-scalable-distributed-triple-store, 2010.

26 Social Networking in the Cloud

26.1 INTRODUCTION

This chapter describes a system called SNODSOC (stream-based novel class detection for social network analysis) to detect evolving patterns and trends in social blogs, and shows how it may be hosted on a cloud. We also discuss security issues for cloud-based social network analysis. SNODSOC extends our powerful data mining system called SNOD (stream-based novel class detection) for detecting classes of blogs. We also describe SNODSOC++, which is an extended version of SNODSOC for detecting multiple novel classes. We have used many of the technologies discussed in the previous chapters in developing SNODSOC and SNODSOC++.

Social media such as Facebook, Twitter, and YouTube have become the most popular way for groups to communicate and share information with each other. Social media communication differs from traditional data communication in many ways. For example, with social media communication, it is possible to exchange numerous messages in a very short space of time. Furthermore, the communication messages (e.g., blogs and tweets) are often abbreviated and difficult to follow. To understand the motives, sentiments, and behavior of the various social media groups, some of them malicious, tools are needed to make sense out of the social network communication messages often represented as graphs. To address this need, we have designed a semantic framework for analyzing stream-based social media communication data.

We have developed a powerful machine learning system/tool called SNOD. SNOD is a unique data stream classification technique that can classify and detect novel classes in data streams. SNOD has been successfully applied on the Aviation Safety Reporting System (ASRS) data set of the National Aeronautics and Space Administration (NASA). SNOD has many potential applications, such as analyzing social networks, detecting credit card fraud, detecting blogs and tweets, and classifying text streams. We have utilized SNOD to develop a sophisticated social network analysis system called SNODSOC. Mining blogs and Twitter messages can be modeled as a data stream classification problem. SNODSOC will analyze social network data such as blogs and Twitter messages. We demonstrate the scalability of our system utilizing the cloud computing framework we have developed. In addition to SNODSOC, we have also developed tools for location extraction (LOCEXT), concept/entity extraction (ENTEXT), and ontology construction (ONTCON). These tools are being integrated to develop a semantic framework for analyzing social media communication data. The integrated system is called SNODSOC++. Figure 26.1 illustrates our framework.

This chapter is organized as follows. Section 26.2 discusses the foundational technologies that we have used to develop scalable solutions for SNODSOC, LOCEXT, ENTEXT, and ONTCON. These include SNOD as well as our preliminary tools for location extraction, entity extraction, ontology construction, and cloud query processing. SNODSOC will be detailed in Section 26.3. SNODSOC++ will be discussed in Section 26.4. Cloud-based social network analysis is discussed in Section 26.5. StormRider, which facilitates implementing social networks in the cloud, is discussed in Section 26.6. Related work is discussed in Section 26.7. The chapter is concluded in Section 26.8. Figure 26.2 illustrates the contents of this chapter.

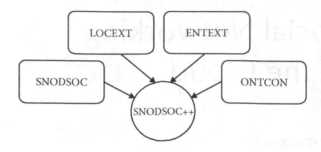

FIGURE 26.1 Framework.

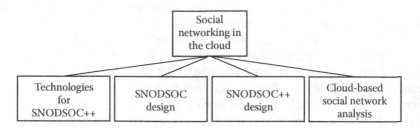

FIGURE 26.2 Social networking on the cloud.

26.2 FOUNDATIONAL TECHNOLOGIES FOR SNODSOC++

In this section, we describe the several tools we have developed that form the basis for the components illustrated in Figure 26.1. These components are discussed in Section 26.3.

26.2.1 SNOD

SNOD uses our data stream learning algorithms to detect novel classes (Masud et al., 2010, 2011a,b, 2012). Three of the major challenges in data stream classification are infinite stream length, concept drift, and concept evolution. SNOD addresses the infinite stream length and concept drift problems by applying a hybrid batch-incremental process, which is carried out as follows. The data stream is divided into equal-sized chunks, and a classification model is trained from each chunk.

An ensemble of L such models is used to classify the unlabeled data. When a new model is trained from a data chunk, it replaces one of the existing models in the ensemble. In this way, the ensemble is kept current. The infinite stream length problem is addressed by maintaining a fixed-sized ensemble, and the concept drift is addressed by keeping the ensemble current. SNOD solves the concept evolution problem by automatically detecting novel classes in the data stream. To detect a novel class, it first builds a decision boundary around the training data. During classification of unlabeled data, it first identifies the test data points that are outside the decision boundary. Such data points are called *filtered outliers* (*F-outliers*); they represent data points that are well separated from the training data. If a sufficient number of F-outliers are found that show strong cohesion among themselves (i.e., they are close together), the F-outliers are classified as novel class instances.

Figure 26.3 summarizes the SNOD algorithm proposed by Masud et al. (2011a). A classification model is trained from the last labeled data chunk. This model is used to update the existing ensemble. The latest data point in the stream is tested by the ensemble. If it is found to be an outlier, it is temporarily stored in a buffer. Otherwise, it is classified immediately using the current ensemble. The temporary buffer is processed periodically to detect whether the instances in the buffer belong to a novel class.

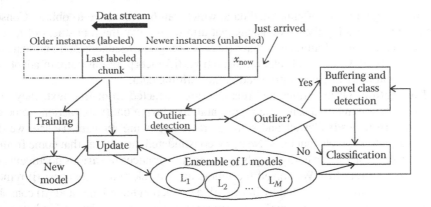

FIGURE 26.3   SNOD algorithm.

26.2.2   Location Extraction

We will discuss some of our prior work on location extraction and social network analysis. Our first related work, MapIt (Abrol et al., 2009), uses an efficient algorithm and heuristics to identify and disambiguate the correct location from the unstructured text present in Craigslist advertisements. The major challenge associated with geo-parsing (determining geographic coordinates of textual words and phrases that occur in unstructured content) is the resolution of ambiguity. There are two types of ambiguities that exist: geo/non-geo and geo/geo ambiguities. Geo/non-geo ambiguity is the case of a place name having another, nongeographic meaning; for example, Paris might be the capital of France or might refer to the socialite Paris Hilton. Geo/geo ambiguity arises from two places having the same name but different geographic locations; for example, Paris is the capital of France and is also a city in Texas. Smith and Crane (2001) reported that 92% of all names occurring in their corpus are ambiguous. MapIt resolves ambiguity by using a nine-point heuristic algorithm that goes beyond the previous work to identify the location up to the street level with 85% accuracy. We have developed a fully functional prototype and tested it on a real data set collected from the Craigslist website.

In our second related work (Chandra and Khan, 2011), we use a probabilistic framework to estimate the city-level Twitter user location for each user. The probabilities are based on the contents of the tweet messages with the aid of reply-tweet messages generated from the interaction between different users in the Twitter social network. The use of reply-tweet messages provides better association of words with the user location, thus reducing the noise in the spatial distribution of terms. We also provide the top k list of the most probable cities for each user. We found that our estimation of the user location is within 100 miles of the actual user location 22% of the time, as compared with the previous work, which had an accuracy of about 10%, using a similar probabilistic framework.

26.2.3   Entity/Concept Extraction and Integration

We have developed a machine learning approach for entity and relation extraction. In particular, we investigated two types of extensions to existing machine learning approaches.

Linguistic Extensions. These extensions are concerned with incorporating additional linguistic knowledge sources into the existing machine learning framework for entity and relation extraction. First, we examined how the information is derived from the fixed ontology (and can be profitably integrated with the learned classifiers for making classification decisions). We represented such information as features for training classifiers; we also classified an entity or relation directly using the available ontologies, and resorted to the learned classifiers only if the desired information is absent from the ontologies.

Extralinguistic Extensions. While supervised machine learning approaches reduce a system's reliance on an ontology, the performance of a learning-based system depends heavily on the availability of a large amount of annotated data, which can be expensive to obtain. Consequently, we developed three extralinguistic extensions that aim to improve the robustness of an extraction system in the face of limited annotated data: (i) combining knowledge-based and learning-based approaches to entity extraction and relation extraction, (ii) incorporating domain adaptation techniques, and (iii) automatically generating additional training data.

Entity Integration. Once entities and relations are extracted from free text, they have to be integrated to create a combined semantic representation. During entity extraction, some extracted entities may be erroneous/irrelevant and some extracted ones are relevant. Hence, we discarded irrelevant entities and kept relevant ones. Next, we consolidated the entities that come from multiple documents. It is possible that an entity may have multiple references in various documents that refer to the same entity in real life. We solved the following two relevant challenges: (i) remove irrelevant entities in a document generated by information extraction techniques and (ii) consolidate the extracted entities among documents so that we can establish a *same as* relationship between entities that are indeed the same entity.

26.2.4 ONTOLOGY CONSTRUCTION

We proposed a potentially powerful and novel approach for the automatic construction of domain-dependent ontologies (Khan and Luo, 2002). The crux of our innovation is the development of a hierarchy, and the concept selection from generic ontology for each node in the hierarchy. For developing a hierarchy, we have modified the existing self-organizing tree algorithm (SOTA) that constructs a hierarchy from top to bottom. Next, we need to assign a concept for each node in the hierarchy. For this, we deploy two types of strategy and adopt a bottom-up concept assignment mechanism. First, for each cluster consisting of a set of documents, we assign a topic based on a modified Rocchio algorithm for topic tracking. However, if multiple concepts are candidates for a topic, we propose an intelligent method for arbitration. Next, to assign a concept to an interior node in the hierarchy, we use WordNet, a linguist ontology. Descendent concepts of the internal node will also be identified in WordNet. From these identified concepts and their hypernyms, we can identify a more generic concept that can be assigned as a concept for the interior node (Alipanah et al., 2010; McGlothlin and Khan, 2010).

26.2.5 CLOUD QUERY PROCESSING

As discussed in Chapter 23, we have developed a SPARQL query processing system on the cloud. Essentially, we have developed a framework to query RDF data stored over Hadoop. We used the Pellet reasoner to reason at various stages. We carried out real-time query reasoning using the Pellet libraries coupled with Hadoop's MapReduce functionalities. Our RDF query processing is composed of two main steps: (i) preprocessing and (ii) query optimization and execution (Figure 26.4).

Preprocessing. To execute a SPARQL query on RDF data, we carried out data preprocessing steps and stored the preprocessed data into HDFS. A separate MapReduce task was written to perform the conversion of RDF/XML data into N-Triples as well as for prefix generation. Our storage strategy is based on predicate splits (Husain et al., 2011).

Query Execution and Optimization. We have developed a SPARQL query execution and optimization module for Hadoop. As our storage strategy is based on predicate splits, first, we examine the predicates present in the query. Second, we examine a subset of the input files that are matched with predicates. Third, SPARQL queries generally have many joins in them, and all of these joins may not be possible to perform in a single map–reduce job. Therefore, we have developed an algorithm that decides the number of jobs required for each kind of query. As part of optimization, we applied a greedy strategy and cost-based optimization to reduce query-processing time (Husain et al., 2011).

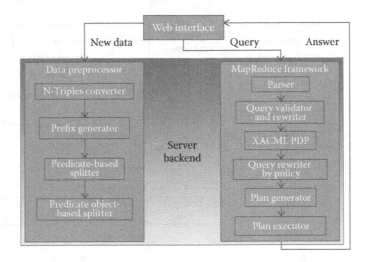

FIGURE 26.4   Cloud query processing.

26.3   DESIGN OF SNODSOC

26.3.1   OVERVIEW OF THE MODULES

Internet social media services, such as microblogging and social networking, which are offered by platforms such as Twitter, have seen phenomenal growth in their user bases. This microblogging phenomenon has been discussed as early as the mid-2000s, noting that users use the service to talk about their daily activities and to seek or share information. This growth has spurred interest in using the data provided by these platforms for extracting various types of information. We have designed the following tools for social network analysis (as illustrated in Figure 26.1):

1. Trend analysis including stream-based novel class detection for social networks (SNODSOC)
2. Geographic location extraction of the users from the blogs and tweets (LOCEXT)
3. Message categorization and entity extraction (ENTEXT)
4. Ontology construction (ONTCON)

These tools will form the framework for SNODSOC++ that will carry out sophisticated social network analysis. In particular, we developed a set of techniques that will facilitate (i) emerging trend analysis, (ii) geographic location extraction, (iii) message categorization and entity extraction, and (iv) ontology construction. The mentioned extraction process will be time consuming. Hence, we are exploiting a cloud computing solution to speed up the extraction process. The extracted knowledge can be used to provide users with personalized services, such as local news, local advertisements, application sharing, etc. With more than 200 million accounts on Twitter in diverse geographical locations, the short messages, or tweets, form a huge data set that can be analyzed to extract such geographic information.

26.3.2   SNODSOC AND TREND ANALYSIS

Twitter has emerged as not only a major form of social networking but also as a new and growing form of communication. Twitter continues to increase both in the number of users and in the number of tweets. Tweets quickly reflect breaking news stories. Often, the first source of news about a natural disaster, a crime, or a political event is tweets. Twitter also serves as the communications

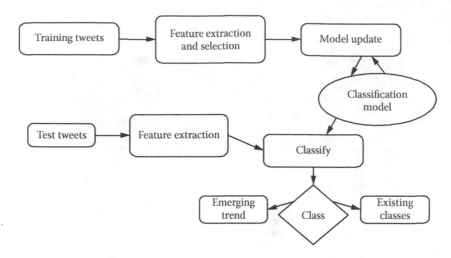

FIGURE 26.5 Classification model.

mechanism for groups and community organizations. Twitter has had significant impact on political events and protest groups.

Twitter communications were credited for their significant influence on the toppling of political regimes in Egypt and Libya. Twitter can provide a way for individuals to communicate without depending on traditional media outlets. This new paradigm of communication via Twitter services provides new challenges for stream data mining. Tweets flow in a continuous stream. Our goal is to decipher and monitor the topics in these tweets, as well as detect when trends emerge. This includes general changes in topics such as sports or fashion, and it includes new, quickly emerging trends such as deaths or catastrophes. It is a challenging problem to correctly associate tweet messages to trends and topics. This challenge is best addressed with a streaming model owing to the continuous and large volume of incoming messages.

At the heart of our system is the classification model of SNOD (Figure 26.5). To build this model, we can use the *K*-nearest neighbor (K-NN) approach or multilabel text classification. This model will be incrementally updated with feature data obtained from new Twitter messages. When a new message (i.e., tweet) is chosen as a training example, it will be analyzed and its features will be recorded. This recorded data will be stored in a temporal database that will hold the data for a batch of *N* messages at a time. When a batch of data has been processed, it will be discarded and a new batch will be stored. Each batch of data will undergo a feature extraction and selection phase. The selected features will be used to compute feature vectors (one vector per message). These vectors will be used to update the existing classification model using an incremental learning technique. When an unknown executable appears in the system, at first its runtime and network behavior will be monitored and recorded. This data will then undergo a similar feature extraction phase; however, no feature selection will be needed here because the same features selected in the training/update phase will be used to build the feature vector. This feature vector will be classified using the classification model. On the basis of the class label, appropriate measures will be taken.

26.3.3 NOVEL CLASS DETECTION

The feature extraction and categorization process discussed above generates feature vectors for fixed-sized training data. To cope with the ever-growing volume of tweets, we must extend this to a data stream framework. Our data stream classifier (Masud et al., 2010, 2011a,b, 2012) can handle massive volumes of training and test data, as well as concept drift, novel classes, and feature evolution in the stream. Recall that we assume that the data stream is divided into equal-sized chunks.

The heart of this system is an ensemble L of M classifiers $\{L_1, ..., L_M\}$. When a new unlabeled executable (test instance) arrives, the ensemble is used to classify the instance. If the test instance is identified as outlier, it is temporarily stored in a buffer *buf* for further inspection. Otherwise, if it is not outlier, then it is classified as either *benign* or *malicious*. The buffer is periodically checked to see if a novel class has appeared. If a novel class is detected, the instances belonging to the novel class are identified and tagged accordingly. As soon as a new labeled data chunk arrives, it is used to train a classifier L'. Then, the existing ensemble is updated by choosing the best M classifiers from the $M + 1$ classifiers $L \cup \{L'\}$ based on their accuracies on the latest labeled data chunk D_n (see Algorithm 26.1).

The central concept of our novel class detection technique is that the data points belonging to a common class should be closer to each other (cohesion) and should be far apart from the data points belonging to other classes (separation). When the *buf* is examined for novel classes, we look for strong cohesion among the outliers in *buf*, and large separation between the outliers and training data. If such strong cohesion and separation is found, we declare a novel class. When the true labels of the novel class instances are revealed by human experts, these instances are used as training data, and a new model is trained. Finally, the existing ensemble is updated with that model. Therefore, the ensemble of models is continuously enriched with new classes. Algorithm 26.1 summarizes the technique.

Creating Decision Boundary during Training. The training data are clustered using K means, and the summary of each cluster is saved as a *pseudopoint*. Then, the raw training data are discarded. These pseudopoints form a decision boundary for the training data.

Storing the Cluster Summary Information. For each cluster, we store the following summary information in a pseudopoint data structure: (i) weight w, the total number of points in the cluster; (ii) centroid μ; (iii) radius r, the distance between the centroid and the farthest data point in the cluster; and (iv) mean distance μd, the mean distance from each point to the cluster centroid. Thus, notation $w(h)$ denotes the weight value of a pseudopoint h, etc. After computing the cluster summaries, the raw data are discarded and only the pseudopoints are stored in memory. Any pseudopoint having too few (less than three) instances is considered as noise and is also discarded. Thus, the memory requirement for storing the training data becomes constant, that is, $O(K)$.

Algorithm 26.1: Our Approach

> **Input:** L: Current ensemble of best M classifiers
> x: An unknown instance to be classified
> **Output:** Class label of x or detection of novel class
> 1. *outlier* ← detectOutlier(x, L)
> 2. **if** (*outlier = false*) **then**
> 3.   classify (x, L) //classify as benign or malicious
> 4. **else** *buf* $\Leftarrow x$ //save in outlier buffer
> 5: **if** time to check *buf* **then**
> *found* ← *DetectNovelClass(buf, L)*
> 6: **if** *found* **then** { Y ← Novel_instances(D_n); }   //tag novel instances
> //if a new labeled chunk D_n is ready for training
> 7: L' ← *Train-new-model(D_n)*
> 8: L ← *Update(L, L', D_n)*

26.3.4 OUTLIER DETECTION AND FILTERING

Each pseudopoint h corresponds to a hypersphere in the feature space having center $\mu(h)$ and radius $R(h)$. The portion of the feature space covered by a pseudopoint h is the pseudopoint's region $RE(h)$.

The union of the regions of all pseudopoints in classifier L_i is the decision boundary for the training data of L_i. The decision boundary for the ensemble of classifiers L is the union of the decision boundaries of all classifiers in the ensemble. The decision boundary plays an important role in novel class detection. It defines the physical boundary of existing class instances.

Each test instance is first tested to see if it is outside the decision boundary of the existing class instances. To compute this, we find the nearest pseudopoint from the test instance in each classifier. If the test instance is outside the radius of each of the pseudopoints in all the classifiers, it is considered as an outlier. We refer to any test instance outside the decision boundary as an F-outlier.

Novel Class Detection. We perform several computations on the F-outliers to detect the arrival of a new class. For every F-outlier x, we define its λ_c-neighborhood $\lambda_0(x)$ to be the set of N-nearest neighbors of x belonging to class c. Here, N is a user-defined parameter. For example, neighborhood $\lambda_+(x)$ is the set of N instances of class c_+ nearest x. Similarly, $\lambda_0(x)$ refers to the set of N F-outliers nearest x.

Using this neighborhood information, we compute the N-neighborhood silhouette coefficient (N-NSC) metric as follows: Let $a(x)$ be the average distance from an F-outlier x to the instances in $\lambda_0(x)$, and let $b_c(x)$ be the average distance from x to the instances in $\lambda_c(x)$ (where c is an existing class). Let $b_{\min}(x)$ be the minimum $b_c(x)$ for all classes c. Then, metric N-NSC(x) is given by

$$N\text{-NSC}(x) = \frac{b_{\min}(x) - a(x)}{\max(b_{\min}(x), a(x))}$$

According to this definition, the value of N-NSC is between -1 and $+1$. It is actually a unified measure of cohesion and separation. A negative value indicates that x is closer to the other classes (less separation) and farther away from its own class (less cohesion). We declare a *new class* if for all the classifiers L_i, there are at least N' ($>N$) F-outliers whose N-NSC is positive.

It should be noted that the larger the value of N, the greater the confidence with which we can decide whether a novel class has arrived. However, if N is too large, then we may also fail to detect a new class if the total number of instances belonging to the novel class in the corresponding data chunk is $\leq N$. Therefore, it will be important to determine an optimal value of N through experimental testing on realistic data sets.

Novel Class Detection with Feature Evolution. The feature space that represents a data point in the stream may change over time; we call these phenomena *feature evolution* (Goyal et al., 2009; Lin et al., 2011). For example, consider a text stream where each data point is a tweet message, and each word is a feature. Since it is impossible to know which words will appear in the future, the complete feature space is unknown. Besides, it is customary to use only a subset of the words as the feature set because most of the words are likely to be redundant for classification. Therefore, at any given time, the feature space is defined by the useful words (i.e., features) selected using some selection criteria. Since in the future, new words may become useful and old useful words may become redundant, the feature space changes dynamically. To cope with feature evolution, the classification model should be able to correctly classify a data point having a different feature space than the feature space of the model. The following example demonstrates the feature evolution in two continuous data chunks. In the ith chunk, the key feature set is {runway, climb}, and in the $(i + 1)$st chunk, the key feature set is {runway, clear, ramp}. Apparently, the key feature set in two different chunks is different, while the new key features come with the novel class emerged in the $(i + 1)$st chunk. If we use the feature set of the ith chunk to test the instances of the $(i + 1)$st chunk, we might not be able to detect the novel class.

Most of the existing data stream classification techniques assume that the feature space of the data points in the stream is static. As seen in the above example, this assumption may be impractical for some data streams, such as text stream. Our technique will consider the dynamic nature of the feature space and provides an elegant solution for classification and novel class detection when the feature space is dynamic. If the feature space is dynamic, then we would have different feature sets in different data chunks. As a result, each model in the ensemble would be trained on different feature sets. Besides, the feature space of the test instances would also be different from the feature space of the models. When we need to classify an instance, we need to come up with a homogeneous feature space for the model and the test instances. There are three possible alternatives.

i. Lossy fixed conversion (or *lossy-F* conversion in short): here, we use the same feature set for the entire stream, which had been selected for the first data chunk (or first *n* data chunks). This will make the feature set fixed, and therefore all the instances in the stream, whether training or testing, will be mapped to this feature set. We call this a lossy conversion because future models and instances may lose important features because of this conversion.

ii. Lossy local conversion (or *lossy-L* conversion in short): in this case, each training chunk, as well as the model built from the chunk, will have its own feature set selected using the feature extraction and selection technique. When a test instance is to be classified using a model M_i, the model will use its own feature set as the feature set of the test instance. This conversion is also lossy because the test instance might lose important features as a result of this conversion.

iii. Lossless homogenizing conversion (or *lossless* conversion in short): here, each model has its own selected set of features. When a test instance x is to be classified using a model M_i, both the model and the instance will convert their feature sets to the union of their feature sets. We call this conversion *lossless homogenizing* since both the model and the test instance preserve their dimensions (i.e., features), and the converted feature space becomes homogeneous for both the model and the test instance. Therefore, no useful features are lost as a result of the conversion.

Since an instance may not have a fixed predetermined feature vector and due to text, we end up with variable-length, high-dimensional features. Therefore, we apply feature selection to select the best features for each chunk and apply the above-mentioned techniques to make homogeneous feature space. To tackle sparsity, we are examining the following option. To track topics/trends in a continuous stream having short messages, we are examining a hybrid model based on the combination of a foreground model and a background model. The foreground model will capture *what's happening right now* based on the ensemble-based technique as described above and a background model will combat data sparsity (Lin et al., 2011).

26.3.5 CONTENT-DRIVEN LOCATION EXTRACTION

Twitter allows its users to specify their geographical location as user information (metadata). This location information is manually entered by the user or updated with a GPS (Global Positioning System)-enabled device. The feature to update the user location with a GPS-enabled device has not been adopted by a significant number of users (Cheng et al., 2010). Hence, this geographic location data for most users may be missing or incorrect. There are several drawbacks to relying on a user's manual update of location:

1. Users may have incorrect geographic location data. For example, a Twitter user may enter his or her location as *Krypton*. This may not be the name of a real geographic location.
2. Users may not always have a city-level location. Users can input location names vaguely, such as the name of a state (e.g., Arizona) or the name of a country (e.g., US). These location names cannot be directly used in determining the city-level location of the user.
3. Users may have multiple locations. If a user travels to different locations, he or she might mention more than one location in the metadata of his or her Twitter page. This makes it very difficult to determine the user's current, singular city-level geographic location.

4. Users may have incomplete location data. A user may have specified an ambiguous name that may refer to different locations. For example, if a user specifies a location such as *Washington*, this name can be related to a state name or a city name (Washington, DC). These types of ambiguous names make it difficult to determine the exact user location.

Therefore, the reliability of such data for determining a city-level geographic location of a user is low. To overcome this problem of sparsely available geo-location information of users, we evaluate the Twitter user's city-level geographic location based purely on his or her tweet content, along with the content of the related reply-tweet messages. We use a probabilistic framework that considers a distribution of terms used in the tweet messages of a certain conversation containing reply-tweet messages, initiated by the user. Our tool is built on our foundational work discussed in Section 26.2.

Motivation. On Twitter, users can post microblogs known as tweets, which can be read by other users. Along with this microblogging service, Twitter also provides a social networking service where a user (*follower*) can *follow* another user (*followee*). Each edge of the social network is formed by this *follow* relationship. As a *follower*, a user receives all the tweets posted by the *followee*, and in turn can reply to these tweets with a reply-tweet. This reply-tweet is received by the *followee* from the *follower*. This forms the basis of a conversation between two different users. Huberman and Wu (2009) analyzed more than 300 thousand users and found that reply-tweets and directed tweets constitute about 26.4% of all posts on Twitter. This shows that the reply-tweet feature is used widely among Twitter users. (Figure 26.6 illustrates an example tweet.)

Our intuition is that a conversation between users can be related to a set of topics such as weather, sports, etc., including certain location-specific topics such as an event related to a city or a reference to a specific place or an entity in a city. We assume that this set of topics remains constant during a conversation. When a user posts a tweet message, it can be seen as the start of a conversation. This conversation can continue when another user posts a reply-tweet to the original tweet. Without detailing the topic of the reply-tweet, it can be assumed that the topic is the same as the original tweet message. Under this assumption, any content of the reply-tweet can be related back to the topic of the original tweet message. For example, consider the tweet messages exchanged by two users in Figure 26.6. A user posts a tweet message, and another user replies back with a reply-tweet message. Note that the topic of conversation remains the same during the conversation. Thus, by combining the above assumption, with the use of tweet content that may have location-specific data, we should obtain a better result than if we considered tweets in isolation, or if we just relied on user-specified location.

Challenges: Proposed Approach. The use of pure tweet content for estimating the Twitter user location, along with the above-mentioned intuition, presents some challenges. These challenges are based on the semantic complexities of the natural language used in tweets. Some users may use non-standard vocabulary in their tweets. Users from a city may refer to the same location-specific entity

FIGURE 26.6 Example tweet.

with different names. For example, a user from Los Angeles can refer to the name of the city as LA, L.A., or City of Los Angeles, etc. Users may also refer to different locations with the same name. For example, a user from New York can refer to 6th Street as a street name in New York, whereas a user from Austin may refer to the street with the same name in Austin. These examples can dilute the spatial distribution of the terms.

The tweets do not always contain location-specific terms. They may contain many general words from a natural language, as users tweet about general topics. Hence, the content of the tweets are considered noisy.

A tweet can have terms referencing to multiple locations. This reduces the ability to estimate a specific location of the user. When considering a conversation, the topic of a conversation may not remain the same throughout the conversation, as assumed. A change of topic in a reply-tweet may result in multiple location-specific terms or dilution of the spatial distribution of terms. Taking note of these challenges, we propose two approaches to extract city-level home location of a user from his messages or blog.

In the first approach, we use a probabilistic distribution framework to estimate the city-level Twitter user location for each user. The probabilities are based on the contents of the tweet messages with the aid of reply-tweet messages generated from the interaction between different users in the Twitter social network. The use of reply-tweet messages provides better association of words with the user location, thus reducing the noise in the spatial distribution of terms. We also provide the top k list of the most probable cities for each user.

As noted earlier, extracting geographic location-specific information from the tweet content alone is challenging. With the social interaction model, we use the content of the tweets in any interaction between users to determine the probability distribution of terms used during the conversation. In the second approach, we examine a user-centric location-mining approach that looks to identify a single city-level home location of a particular user from his messages. Unlike the first approach, which is specific to messages originating from social interactions, this approach is a more general approach that works for all social media, including Twitter, blogs, etc.

Social Interactions—Probability Distribution Model (PDM). In this probability distribution technique, each user can be assumed to belong to a particular city. Hence, the tweets of the user can be assumed to be related to a particular city, specifically the geographical location of the user who posted the tweet; that is, the terms occurring in the user's tweet can be assigned as terms related to the user's city. This forms the basic distribution of terms for the set of cities considered in the complete data set. The probability distribution of term t over the entire data set, for each city c, is given as

$$p(t|c) = |\{t|t \in \text{terms} \land t \text{ occurs in city } c\}|/|t|$$

A probability distribution matrix of size $n \times m$ is formed, where n is the size of the term list (i.e., size of the dictionary) and m is the total number of cities in the data set that is considered for evaluation.

Reply-Based Probability Distribution Model (RBPDM). In the basic probability distribution calculation of PDM, the terms used by a user in his or her tweet are assigned to a city to which the user belongs. It does not consider the relation between different tweet messages.

Twitter offers a feature to tag another user in a tweet called a *reply tag*. This tag directs the message to the user who is addressed in the tweet. With this in mind, a tweet message can be classified into three different types:

1. The first type of tweet message is a general message that a user typically posts on Twitter. These tweet messages do not contain any reply tag. The terms used in this type of tweet message can be used to form a direct relation with that of the user's city in evaluating the spatial distribution of terms.

2. The second kind of tweet message is one that contains the reply tag addressing a user. This type of message is called a *reply-tweet*. This message is used generally to reply to a certain tweet posted by another user. The reply-tweet message will be directed to the user who is being replied to, that is, the user who had posted the original tweet message. This tweet will generally contain the reply tag at the beginning of the tweet message.

3. The third type of tweet message is one that has a reply tag but may not be a reply-tweet. It may be a tweet message that may be directed to a user but need not be a reply to a tweet from that user. This message generally may contain the reply tag in between the tweet words. It can also be a retweet where users repost the tweet message of a user so that his or her followers can receive the tweet message.

The relationship between two tweet messages occurs when the reply tag in a tweet is taken into consideration. The reply-tweet will have a direct relationship with the original tweet that generated the reply-tweet message from a user. The PDM distribution ignores all relationships between tweet messages. The relationship between two tweet messages occurs when the reply tag in a tweet is taken into consideration. The reply-tweet will have a direct relationship with the original tweet that generated the reply-tweet message from a user. Here, we consider this relationship between different tweet messages while calculating the probability distribution of terms from the data set. This relationship forms the basis of a conversation between different users; that is, a tweet message and its reply messages can be considered as a dialogue between the users. Hence, with the application of the assumption that the topic of a conversation is to remain constant in the reply-tweet messages, the terms used in the conversation can be related to the topic of the conversation. The conversation may involve location-specific terms related to the topic. Instead of plainly assigning the terms used in a tweet to the user who posted the tweet, the terms occurring in the complete conversation can be assigned to the user who initiated the conversation since the initiator may initiate a conversation topic involving his or her geographic location. Thus, when a reply-tweet is encountered in the data set, we assign the terms involved in the tweet to the user to which the tweet is addressed rather than to the user who posted the reply-tweet message. With this assignment of terms to different users, we evaluate the probability distribution that does not ignore recognizing the different types of tweet messages and the relationship between them. Hence, the social structure of the network is considered while estimating the geographic location of a user in the Twitter social network.

Term Distribution Estimator. Using the distribution of terms across the cities considered in the data set, the probability of a city c given a term t can be calculated on the basis of maximum likelihood estimation.

$$p(c|t) = \max_{\forall c \in \text{cities}} p(t|c)$$

The probability estimate of the user u being located in city c is the total probability of the terms extracted from the user tweet for the city c; that is

$$p(c|u) = \Sigma_{(w \in \text{terms})} p(c|w) * p(w)$$

Using this equation, the probability estimation matrix is obtained as mentioned previously, which has size $p \times q$, where p is the size of the user list being considered and q is the size of the city list being considered in the data set. The city-level geographic location estimation can be obtained by considering the city with the highest probability for that user. A list of top k estimated cities can also be obtained by sorting the probability estimation matrix for each user and listing the top k most probable cities from it.

Using Gazetteer and Natural Language Processing. Before running the actual algorithm (see Algorithm 26.2), we perform preprocessing of data, which involves first using an external dictionary

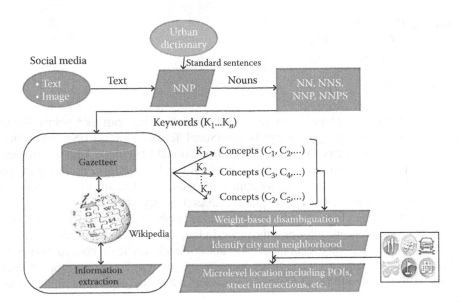

FIGURE 26.7   Using gazetteer and natural language processing approach.

such as the urban dictionary in order to understand slang words and replace them with appropriate phrases to obtain grammatically correct sentences. After which, we remove all those words from the messages that are not references to geographic locations (Figure 26.7). For this, we use the Part of Speech (POS) tagger for English. The POS tagger identifies all the proper nouns from the text and terms them as keywords $\{K_1, K_2, ..., K_n\}$. In the next step, the TIGER (Topologically Integrated Geographic Encoding and Referencing system) data set is searched for identifying the city names from among them. The TIGER data set is an open source gazetteer consisting of topological records and shape files with coordinates for cities, counties, zip codes, street segments, etc., for the entire United States.

We search the TIGER gazetteer for the concepts $\{C_1, C_2, ..., C_n\}$ pertaining to each keyword. Now our goal for each keyword would be to pick out the right concept among the list; in other words, to disambiguate the location. For this, we use a weight-based disambiguation method. We assign the weight to each concept based on the occurrence of its terms in the text (phase 1). Specific concepts are assigned a greater weight as compared with the more general ones. We check for correlation between concepts, in which one concept subsumes the other (phase 2). In that case, the more specific concept gets the boosting from the more general concept. If a more specific concept C_i is part of another C_j, then the weight of C_j is added to that of C_i.

Algorithm 26.2: Location Identification (User_Messages)

    Input: UM: *all messages of user*
    Output: Vector (C, S): concepts and score vector
    1: for each keyword, K_i //phase 1
    2:     for each $C_j \in K_i$ //C_j – city concept
    3:         for each $T_f \in C_j$
    4:            type = Type (T_f)
    5:                If (T_f occurs in UM) then $S_{Cj} = S_{Cj} + S_{type}$
    6: for each K_i //phase 2
    7:     for each $C_j \in K_i$

8:     for $T_f \in C_j$, $T_s \in C_L$
9:        If ($T_f = T_s$) and ($C_j \neq C_L$) then
10:               type = Type (T_f)
11:                   $S_{Sj} = S_{Cj} + S_{type}$
12: return (C, S)

For example, city carries 15 points, state 10, and a country name carries 5 points. For the keyword *Dallas*, consider the concept of {City} Dallas/{State} Texas/{Country} USA. The concept gets 15 points because Dallas is a city name, and it gets an additional 10 points if Texas is also mentioned in the text. In phase 2, we consider the relation between two keywords. Considering the previous example, if {Dallas, Texas} are the keywords appearing in the text, then among the various concepts listed for *Dallas* would be {City} Dallas/{State} Texas/{Country} USA and one of the concepts for *Texas* would be {State} Texas/{Country} USA. Now, in phase 2, we check for such correlated concepts, in which one concept subsumes the other. In that case, the more specific concept gets the boosting from the more general concept. Here, the above-mentioned Texas concept boosts the more specific Dallas concept. After the two phases are complete, we reorder the concepts in descending order of their weights. Next, each concept is assigned a probability depending on their individual weights.

Once the city-level location has been identified, the algorithm will next focus on identifying microlevel locations that may be mentioned in the text (blogs, tweets, etc.). For this, we would use geospatial proximity and a context-based disambiguation algorithm that uses a rich Point of Interest (POI) database (the Foursquare Venue data set is an example) to identify potential microlevel places like coffee shops, schools, restaurants, places of worship, and others. The algorithm would return a list of places that match that particular keyword and are located in the city determined by us previously. Now, our goal for each keyword would be to pick out the right concept among the list; in other words, identify the correct POI the user is referring to. For this, we use a two-phase disambiguation process. The first phase consists of context-based scoring. Each POI entry in the gazetteer is associated with tags, and by using the WordNet semantic similarity measure, we compute the similarity between the message and the POI entry. This serves the purpose of disambiguating the correct POI based on the type of place the user might be referring to. After which, in phase 2, we simply boost the scores based on the proximity of each POI candidate to previously determined POIs for that particular user. Thus, if for a user, there are multiple Starbucks coffee shops returned in the Los Angeles area, the algorithm would choose the Starbucks closer to his comfort zone (probably his home or office).

26.3.6 Categorization

A major objective of our project is to extract entities from tweets and categorize the messages. Then, we provide *semantic* representation of the knowledge buried in the tweets. This would enable an analyst to interact more directly with the hidden knowledge. We build on the foundational work discussed in Section 26.2.3 for categorization.

Entity Extraction. Entities are basic elements in knowledge representation. We have developed techniques to recognize several important entities in the messages, including event, location, people, organization, and so on. Entity extraction has been extensively studied in the literature. The most effective methods tend to cast the problem as a classification problem and apply supervised learning methods. We adopt the same strategy and leverage the many tools that are publicly available to perform this task (e.g., feature extraction and logistic regression; Ahmed et al., 2010a).

While some existing algorithms and tools are available for us to use, a major challenge we have to solve is to create labeled data for training. Labeling data is, in general, an expensive process. We propose to study two strategies for solving this problem: (i) we adopt a bootstrapping approach, in which we would first rely on linguistic rules to recognize easy-to-recognize instances of a given type of entity and then use the rule-based recognizer to generate training data for supervised learning, and (ii) we apply domain adaptation techniques based on some existing work to leverage training data that already exists in other related domain (e.g., news domain); these techniques can effectively avoid overfitting when we reuse some existing training data. Since the extracted entities are meant to be used for data mining, we expect that we can tolerate some errors in entity recognition. In case we need to further improve accuracy, we explore possibilities to manually label some examples. The strategies discussed above can help generate the most promising positive examples for labeling. In general, active learning can be applied to selecting examples for users to judge.

Multilabel Text Classification. Classification of social communication data and related messages plays an important role in such data analysis. To find a classification technique that is well suited for social media data, we first need to find out how such data is different from its nontext counterpart. First of all, messages in such data sets are usually written nonformally. These include very high and sparse dimensionality, as the dimension or feature space consists of all the distinct words appearing in the vocabulary of the corresponding natural language.

The second difference that we consider is its increasing tendency to associate with multiple classes for classification. Text data sets can be binary, multiclass, or multilabel in nature. For the binary and multiclass categories, only a single class label can be associated with a document and the class label association is mutually exclusive. However, in case of multilabel data, more than one class label can be associated with a message at the same time.

In multilabeled data classification, class labels can co-occur and the frequency with which different class labels co-occur indicates that the class labels are not independent of each other. Also, not all class label combinations occur in the data set. Hence, making an assumption that class labels are independent is inherently incorrect during the classification process. For example, in the NASA ASRS data set, we consider a total of 21 classes. There are class label combinations that can never occur together. For instance, given the label for two attributes *Aircraft equipment problem: critical* and *Less severe and conflict: less severe* and *critical*, we know that the labels *Aircraft equipment problem: critical* and *Conflict: less severe* can never occur together, which is apparent from their names. However, *Aircraft equipment problem: critical* and *Conflict: critical* classes can co-occur. During classification, considering the probability of such varying co-occurrence can, to some extent, allows us to generate clusters where such class label pairs do not co-occur.

To categorize tweets, we exploit text classification. For this, we use the SISC (semi-supervised impurity-based subspace clustering) algorithm (Ahmed et al., 2009, 2010a,b), which uses subspace clustering, in conjunction with the K-NN approach along with a semisupervised learning approach, under small or limited amount of labeled training data sets. To correctly interpret the multilabel property of such data, fuzzy clustering can perform this interpretation in a more meaningful way. In fact, the notion of fuzzy subspace clustering matches that of text data, that is, having high and sparse dimensionality and multilabel property. Subspace clustering allows us to find clusters in a weighted hyperspace (Frigui and Nasraoui, 2004) and can aid us in finding documents that form clusters in only a subset of dimensions. SISC (Ahmed et al., 2009) is one such algorithm that we use in our experiments.

26.3.7 Ontology Construction

Ontology is a collection of concepts and their interrelationships that can collectively provide an abstract view of an application domain (Khan and Luo, 2002). There are two distinct problem/tasks for an ontology-based model: one is the extraction of semantic concepts from the keywords, and the other is the actual construction of the ontology. With regard to the first problem, the key issue is to identify appropriate concepts that describe and identify messages (as described before). In this way, it is important to make sure that irrelevant concepts will not be associated and matched, and that relevant concepts will not be discarded. With regard to the second problem, we would like to construct ontology automatically. Here, we address these two problems together by proposing a new method for the automatic construction of ontology.

We build on the foundational work discussed in Section 26.2.4 for ontology construction. Our method constructs ontology automatically in bottom-up fashion. For this, we first construct a hierarchy using some clustering algorithms. Recall that if documents are similar to each other in content, they will be associated with the same concept in ontology. Next, we need to assign a concept for each node in the hierarchy. As stated earlier, for this, we deploy two types of strategy and adopt a bottom-up concept assignment mechanism. First, for each cluster consisting of a set of documents, we assign a topic based on a modified Rocchio algorithm for topic tracking. However, if multiple concepts are candidates for a topic, we propose an intelligent method for arbitration. Next, to assign a concept to an interior node in the hierarchy, we use WordNet, a linguist ontology. Descendent concepts of the internal node will also be identified in WordNet. From these identified concepts and their hypernyms, we can identify a more generic concept that can be assigned as a concept for the interior node.

With regard to the hierarchy construction, we construct ontology automatically. For this, we rely on a SOTA that constructs a hierarchy from top to bottom. We modify the original algorithm, and propose an efficient algorithm that constructs hierarchy with better accuracy as compared with hierarchical agglomerative clustering algorithm (Luo et al., 2004). To illustrate the effectiveness of the method of automatic ontology construction, we have explored our ontology construction in the text documents. The Reuters21578 text document corpus has been used. We have observed that our modified SOTA outperforms agglomerative clustering in terms of accuracy. The main contributions of this work will be as follows:

1. We propose a new mechanism that can be used to generate ontology automatically to make our approach scalable. For this, we modify the existing SOTA that constructs a hierarchy from top to bottom.
2. Furthermore, to find an appropriate concept for each node in the hierarchy, we developed an automatic concept selection algorithm from WordNet, linguistic ontology.

Figure 26.8 illustrates an example of ontology construction.

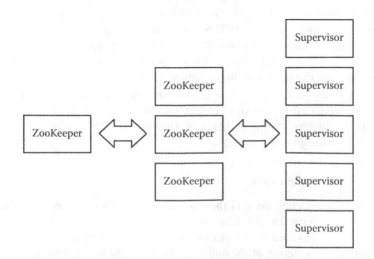

FIGURE 26.8   Ontology construction.

26.4   TOWARD SNODSOC++

We are examining the integration of the multiple tools to develop SNODSOC++. Note that SNODSOC is based on SNOD and has several limitations. First, SNOD does not consider the *feature evolution* problem, to be explained shortly, which occurs because of the dynamic nature of the stream. Second, if more than one novel class appears in the stream, SNOD cannot detect them. Third, SNOD does not address the problem of high-dimensional feature spaces, which may lead to higher training and classification error. Finally, SNOD does not apply any optimizations for feature extraction and classification. Therefore, we are developing a practical and robust blogs and tweets detection tool, which we call SNODSOC. To develop SNODSOC++ from SNODSOC, we first need to extend SNOD TO SNOD++. That is, we propose to enhance SNOD into SNOD++ that is more practical and robust than SNOD. In addition to addressing the infinite length, concept drift, and concept evolution problems, SNOD++ addresses feature evolution and multiple novel classes, as well as applies subspace clustering and other optimizations, all of which improve the robustness, power, and accuracy of the algorithm. All of the tools we have developed (e.g., LOCEXT, ONTCON, and ENTEXT) are being integrated with SNODSOC in the development of SNODSOC++. SNODSOC++ will essentially combine SNODSOC with the semantic knowledge extracted from the tweets and blogs.

Benefits of SNODSOC++. SNODSOC++ will be useful in social network analysis applications, including detecting reactively adaptive blogs and tweets. SNODSOC++ will be capable of handling massive volumes of training data, and will also be able to cope with concept drift in the data. These attributes make it more practical and robust than blog and tweet detectors that are trained with static data. Furthermore, it can be used in detecting one or more novel classes of blogs and tweets. Also, recall that existing blog and tweet detection techniques may fail to detect completely new patterns, but SNODSOC++ should be able to detect such novel classes and raise an alarm. The blogs would be later analyzed and characterized by human experts. In particular, SNODSOC++ will be more robust and useful than SNODSOC because SNODSOC++ will be capable of detecting multiple novel blogs and tweets in the stream, and will also exhibit a much higher classification accuracy and a faster training time because of its robustness to higher feature dimensions and application of distributed feature extraction and selection.

26.5   CLOUD-BASED SOCIAL NETWORK ANALYSIS

As we have discussed in earlier chapters, cloud computing is growing in popularity as a design model for enabling extreme scalability for data intensive applications. In the cloud computing paradigm, data storage and retrieval operations are performed in parallel over clusters of commodity hardware. Cloud computing solutions have been used in production at major industry leaders such as Google, Amazon, and Facebook. Our goal is to integrate multiple social networks and analyze the data in the cloud, as illustrated in Figure 26.9.

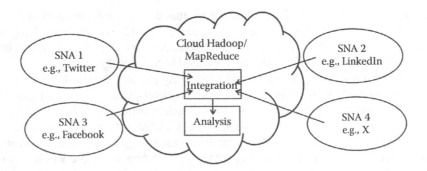

FIGURE 26.9   Cloud-based social network analysis.

To develop a scalable SNODSOC++, we are using Twitter Storm, which is the distributed, fault-tolerant, real-time computation system at GitHub under Eclipse Public License 1.0. Storm is the real-time processing system developed by BackType, which is now under the Twitter umbrella. It can be thought to be the Hadoop of real time; it does for real-time processing what Hadoop does for batch processing.

Stream Processing. Storm can be used to process a stream of new data and update databases in real time. Unlike the standard approach of doing stream processing with a network of queues and workers, Storm is fault tolerant and scalable. A Storm cluster is superficially similar to a Hadoop cluster. Whereas on Hadoop, you run *MapReduce jobs*, on Storm you run *topologies*. *Jobs* and *topologies* themselves are very different; one key difference is that a MapReduce job eventually finishes, whereas a topology processes messages forever (or until you kill it). There are two kinds of nodes on a Storm cluster: the master node and the worker nodes. The master node runs a daemon called *Nimbus* that is similar to Hadoop's JobTracker. Nimbus is responsible for distributing codes around the cluster, assigning tasks to machines, and monitoring for failures.

Each worker node runs a daemon called the Supervisor. The Supervisor listens for work assigned to its machine, and starts and stops worker processes as necessary on the basis of what Nimbus has assigned to it. Each worker process executes a subset of a topology; a running topology consists of many worker processes spread across many machines. All coordination between Nimbus and the Supervisors is done through a ZooKeeper cluster. Additionally, the Nimbus and Supervisor daemons are fail fast and stateless; all state is kept in ZooKeeper or on local disk. This means you can kill −9 Nimbus or the Supervisors, and they will start back up as if nothing happened. This design leads to Storm clusters being incredibly stable. We have had topologies running for months without requiring any maintenance.

Twitter Storm for SNODSOC. A data loading module will add Twitter user data into a cloud-based semantic web database. For this part, a vocabulary of terms that Twitter uses will be created. This vocabulary is the simplest way of moving into the semantic web world; a vocabulary is the least expressive of all semantic web languages, but is the most efficient in terms of processing. The idea is to build such vocabularies for all other data sources we wish to use, such as Google Plus, LinkedIn, etc., and then perform a certain amount of automated integration of data based on these vocabularies. To perform complex reasoning over the data, which is our eventual goal, we later refine these vocabularies into more complicated ontologies that are far more expressive but require a longer processing effort. Twitter Storm would provide a framework for near real-time processing of tweets and other social media messages for entity extraction, location mining, and, more important, novel class detection. Our SPARQL query processor discussed in Chapter 25 is being examined for querying the semantic web database. We will discuss another experimental social network cloud system called StormRider, which is part of our ongoing work, in the next section.

26.6 StormRider: HARNESSING STORM FOR SOCIAL NETWORKS

In this section, we present StormRider, a framework that uses a combination of cloud-based and semantic web-based tools to allow for the storage, retrieval, and analysis of evolving social networks. In addition, users can perform these operations on networks of their choice by creating custom-built implementations of the interfaces provided in StormRider.

The StormRider framework makes use of the following existing tools as basic building blocks: (i) The Storm framework allows StormRider to automatically store, query, and analyze data as the underlying network evolves over time. Storm was selected because it is a real-time computation system that guarantees message processing and is scalable, robust, and fault tolerant. (ii) The Jena–HBase framework (Khadilkar et al., 2012a) allows the storage of network data in an RDF representation, as well as to query the data using SPARQL. (iii) Apache HBase was used to construct materialized views that store metadata related to nodes in the network. These views allow faster analytics to be performed on the network.

StormRider provides the following novel contributions: (i) The Jena–HBase framework facilitates the use of several semantic web features with social networks, such as application of reasoning algorithms, reification, etc. (ii) It allows the ability to store, query, and analyze evolving networks through the use of novel algorithms (e.g., approximation algorithms for centrality estimation) implemented in Storm. (iii) Application programmers are provided with simple interfaces through which they can interact with social networks of their choice.

26.7 SUMMARY AND DIRECTIONS

This chapter has described the design of SNODSOC. SNODSOC will be a great asset to the analysts who have to deal with billions of blogs and messages. For example, by analyzing the behavioral history of a particular group of individuals, analysts will be able to predict behavioral changes in the near future and take necessary measures. This line of research will stimulate a new branch of social network analysis technology and inspire a new field of study. We have also discussed how cloud computing may be used to implement SNODSOC. Finally, security issues for cloud-based social networks were discussed.

New blogs swarm the cyberspace every day. Analyzing such blogs and updating the existing classification models is a daunting task. Most existing behavior-profiling techniques are manual, which require days to analyze a single blog sample and extract its behavioral profile. Even existing automated techniques have been tested only on a small sample of training data. By integrating our approach with a cloud computing framework, we overcome this barrier and will provide a highly scalable behavior modeling tool, thereby achieving higher accuracy in detecting new patterns. Furthermore, no existing profiling (manual or automated) technique addresses the evolving characteristics of blogs and messages. Therefore, our product will have a tremendous advantage over other behavior-based products by quickly responding to the dynamic environment.

While SNODSOC is a considerable improvement over currently available social network analysis tools, the underlying SNOD technology has some limitations. For example, SNOD lacks the ability to detect multiple novel classes emerging simultaneously. Since blogs and messages could have multiple concurrent evolutions, we need a system that can detect multiple novel classes. Therefore, we are extending SNOD to achieve a more powerful detection strategy (SNOD++) that addresses these limitations. Our goal is to develop a fully functional and robust blog analysis system called SNODSOC++. SNODSOC++ will be a breakthrough technology for social network analysis because it can handle dynamic data, changing patterns, and dynamic emergence of novel classes. We utilize our cloud computing framework to develop SNODSOC++. Our tool will provide a high degree of accuracy, be scalable, and operate in real time. SNODSOC++ will also integrate the tools LOCEXT, ENTEXT, and ONTCON so that highly accurate and evolving patterns and trends can be detected with the semantic knowledge extracted. Finally, using our cloud computing framework, we can develop scalable solutions for mining social network data.

REFERENCES

Abrol, S., Khan, L., and Al-Khateeb, T.M. MapIt: Smarter searches using location driven knowledge discovery and mining. In: *1st SIGSPATIAL ACM GIS 2009 International Workshop on Querying and Mining Uncertain Spatio-Temporal Data (QUeST)*, November 2009, Seattle, WA, 2009.

Ahmed, M.S. and Khan, L. SISC: A text classification approach using semisupervised subspace clustering. In: *ICDM Workshops*, Miami, FL, pp. 1–6, 2009.

Ahmed, M.S., Khan, L., and Rajeswari, M. Using correlation based subspace clustering for multi-label text data classification. In: *ICTAI (2)*, pp. 296–303, Arras, France, 2010a.

Ahmed, M.S., Khan, L., Oza, N.C., and Rajeswari, M. Multi-label ASRS dataset classification using semisupervised subspace clustering. In: *Proceedings of Conference on Intelligent Data Understanding (CIDU)*, Mountain View, CA, pp. 285–299, 2010b.

Alipanah, N., Parveen, P., Menezes, S., Khan, L., Seida, S., and Thuraisingham, B.M. Ontology-driven query expansion methods to facilitate federated queries. In: *Proc. of International Conference on Service-Oriented Computing and Applications (SOCA)*, Perth, Australia, 2010.

Backstrom, L., Kleinberg, J., Kumar, R., and Novak, J. Spatial variation in search engine queries. In: *Proceedings of World Wide Web Conference (WWW)*, Beijing, China, 2008.

Brandes, U. A faster algorithm for betweenness centrality. *Journal of Mathematical Sociology* 25(2): 163–177, 2001.

Chandra, S. and Khan, L. Estimating Twitter user location using social interactions—A content based approach. In: *The Third IEEE International Conference on Social Computing*, October 9–11, 2011, MIT, Boston, 2011.

Cheng, Z., Caverlee, J., and Lee, K. You are where you tweet: A content-based approach to geo-locating Twitter users. In: *Proceeding of the 19th ACM Conference on Information and Knowledge Management (CIKM)*, Toronto, Canada, October 2010.

Erétéo, G., Buffa, M., Gandon, F., and Corby, O. Analysis of a real online social network using semantic web frameworks. In: *Proc. of International Semantic Web Conference (ISWC)*, Chantilly, VA, pp. 180–195, 2009.

Frigui, H. and Nasraoui, O. Unsupervised learning of prototypes and attribute weights. *Pattern Recognition* 37(3): 567–581, 2004.

Goyal, A., Daum, H., and Venkatasubramanian, S. Streaming for large scale NLP: Language modeling. In: *Proceedings of Human Language Technologies. The 2009 Annual Conference of the North American Chapter of the Association for Computational Linguistics*, Boulder, CO, pp. 512–520, 2009.

Huberman, B. and Wu, D.R.F. Social networks that matter: Twitter under the microscope. *First Monday* 14, 2009.

Husain, M.F., McGlothlin, J.P., Masud, M.M., Khan, L.R., and Thuraisingham, B.M. Heuristics-based query processing for large RDF graphs using cloud computing. *IEEE Transactions on Knowledge and Data Engineering* 23(9): 1312–1327, 2011.

Katakis, I., Tsoumakas, G., and Vlahavas, I. Dynamic feature space and incremental feature selection for the classification of textual data streams. In: *Proceedings of European Conference on Machine Learning and Principles and Practice of Knowledge Discovery (ECML PKDD)*, Berlin, Germany, pp. 102–116, 2006.

Khadilkar, V., Kantarcioglu, M., Castagna, P., and Thuraisingham, B. Jena–HBase: A distributed, scalable and efficient RDF triple store. Technical Report, 2012a.

Khadilkar, V., Kantarcioglu, M., and Thuraisingham, B. StormRider: Harnessing "Storm" for social networks. The University of Texas at Dallas Technical Report, 2012b.

Khadilkar, V., Kantarcioglu, M., Thuraisingham, B.M. StormRider: Harnessing "Storm" for social networks. In: *Proceedings of World Wide Web Conference (WWW)*, Lyon, France, pp. 543–544, 2012c.

Khan, L. and Luo, F. Ontology construction for information selection. In: *Proceedings of Intl. Conference on Tools with Artificial Intelligence (ICTAI 2002)*, Washington, DC, p. 122, 2002.

Lin, J., Snow, R., and Morgan, W. Smoothing techniques for adaptive online language models: Topic tracking in tweet streams. In: *Proc. of ACM SIGKDD Conference on Knowledge Discovery and Data Mining*, August 2011, San Diego, CA, 2011.

Luo, F., Khan, L., Bastani, F.B., Yen, I.-L., and Zhou, J. A dynamically growing self-organizing tree (DGSOT) for hierarchical clustering gene expression profiles. *Bioinformatics* 20(16): 2605–2617, 2004.

Markou, M. and Singh, S. Novelty detection: A review. Part 1: Statistical approaches, Part 2: Neural network based approaches. *Signal Processing* 83: 2481–2497, 2499–2521, 2003.

Masud, M.M., Chen, Q., Khan, L., Aggarwal, C.C., Gao, J., Han, J., and Thuraisingham, B.M. Addressing concept-evolution in concept-drifting data streams. In: *Proc. of International Conference on Data Mining (ICDM)*, Sydney, Australia, pp. 929–934, 2010.

Masud, M.M., Al-Khateeb, T.M., Khan, L., Aggarwal, C.C., Gao, J., Han, J., and Thuraisingham, B.M. Detecting recurring and novel classes in concept-drifting data streams. In: *Proc. of International Conference3 on Data Mining (ICDM)*, Vancouver, BC, Canada, 2011a.

Masud, M.M., Gao, J., Khan, L., Han, J., and Thuraisingham, B.M. Classification and novel class detection in concept-drifting data streams under time constraints. *IEEE Transactions on Knowledge and Data Engineering* 23(1): 859–874, 2011b.

Masud, M.M., Gao, J., Khan, L., Han, J., Hamlen, K.W., and Oza, N.C. Facing the reality of data stream classification: Coping with scarcity of labeled data. *International Journal of Knowledge and Information Systems* 33(1): 213–244, 2012.

McGlothlin, J.P. and Khan, L.R. Materializing and persisting inferred and uncertain knowledge in RDF datasets. In: *Proceedings of the AAAI Conference on Artificial Intelligence*, Atlanta, GA, 2010.

Potamias, M., Bonchi, F., Castillo, C., and Gionis, A. Fast shortest path distance estimation in large networks. In: *Proc. of Conference on Information and Knowledge Management (CIKM)*, Hong Kong, China, pp. 867–876, 2009.

Smith, D.A. and Crane, G. Disambiguating geographic names in a historical digital library. In: *5th European Conference on Research and Advanced Technology for Digital Libraries (ECDL 2001), Lecture Notes in Computer Science*, September 2001, Darmstadt, Germany, pp. 127–136, 2001.

Spinosa, E.J., de Leon, A.P., de Carvalho, F., and Gama, J. Cluster-based novel concept detection in data streams applied to intrusion detection in computer networks. In: *Proc. ACM Symposium on Applied Computing (ACM SAC)*, New York, pp. 976–980, 2008.

Wenerstrom, B. and Giraud-Carrier, C. Temporal data mining in dynamic feature spaces. In: *Proceedings of the International Conference on Data Mining, (ICDM)*, Hong Kong, China, pp. 1141–1145, 2006.

CONCLUSION TO SECTION VI

While Sections IV and V discussed our fundamental techniques and solutions for analyzing and securing social media, in this section we have discussed the experimental social media analytics systems. In many of the systems we have developed, we assume that semantic web technologies are used to represent and reason about the social media systems.

Chapter 23 provided some basics on the use of semantic web technologies for representing and reasoning about social networks. We first discussed aspects of entity representation and integration with the semantic web. Next, we discussed heuristic reasoning for Resource Description Framework (RDF) graphs. Third, we discussed the analysis of RDF graphs that represent social networks. Finally, we discussed ways of managing very large RDF graphs. In Chapter 24, we first described aspects of social network integration and explained the use of semantic web technologies for this purpose. We then discussed three separate experimental cloud-based semantic web data management systems for social network integration. In Chapter 25, we presented a Hadoop-based framework capable of handling enormous amounts of RDF data that can be used to represent social networks. We described a schema to store RDF data, an algorithm to determine a query-processing plan whose worst case is bounded, to answer a SPARQL query, and a simplified cost model to be used by the algorithm. Chapter 26 described the design of SNODSOC (stream-based novel class detection for social network analysis). SNODSOC will be a great asset to analysts who have to deal with billions of blogs and messages. For example, by analyzing the behavioral history of a particular group of individuals, analysts will be able to predict behavioral changes in the near future and take necessary measures.

Section VII

Social Media Application Systems

INTRODUCTION TO SECTION VII

While Section VI discussed our prototypes on social media systems, in Section VII we will discuss the use of social media systems for various applications. In particular, we will discuss the use of social media for insider threat detection, bioterrorism applications, and detection of suspicious activities.

Section VII consists of four chapters: Chapters 27 through 30. Chapter 27 will discuss our approach to insider threat detection. We represent the insiders and their communication as Resource Description Framework (RDF) graphs, and then query and mine the graphs to extract the nuggets. Chapter 28 will describe the challenges for developing a system for stability and reconstruction operations (SARO). In particular, we will discuss the design of a temporal geospatial mobile social semantic web that can be utilized by military personnel, decision makers, and local/government personnel to reconstruct after a major combat operation. In Chapter 29, we will discuss our approach to enhancing the susceptible, infected, and recovered (SIR) model through epidemiology approximation. Our model is based on social interactions. We have created a hybridized model that balances the simplicity of the original with an approximation of what more complex agent–based models already offer, with an emphasis on the exploration of large search spaces. In Chapter 30, we will describe the design of InXite. InXite will be a great asset to the analysts who have to deal with massive amounts of data streams in the form of billions of blogs and messages, among others. For example, by analyzing the behavioral history of a particular group of individuals as well as details of concepts such as events, analysts will be able to predict behavioral changes in the near future and take necessary measures.

Section VII

Social Media Application Systems

INTRODUCTION TO SECTION VII

27 Graph Mining for Insider Threat Detection

27.1 INTRODUCTION

Effective detection of insider threats from social media data requires monitoring mechanisms that are far more fine grained than for external threat detection. These monitors must be efficiently and reliably deployable in the software environments for actions endemic to malicious insider missions to be caught in a timely manner. Such environments typically include user-level applications, such as word processors, e-mail clients, and web browsers for which reliable monitoring of internal events by conventional means is difficult.

To monitor the activities of the insiders, tools are needed to capture the communications and relationships between them, store the captured relationships, query the stored relationships, and ultimately analyze the relationships so that patterns can be extracted that would give the analyst better insights into the potential threats. Over time, the number of communications and relationships between the insiders could be in the billions. The entities, including the insiders and their communications, can be represented as social graphs. Therefore, we need graph mining tools to analyze these graphs and extract the patterns. We need tools to capture the billions of relationships between the insiders and subsequently store, query, and analyze this information to detect malicious insiders.

In this chapter, we will discuss how graph mining technologies may be applied for insider threat detection. First, we will discuss how semantic web technologies may be used to represent the communication between insiders. Next, we will discuss our approach to insider threat detection. Finally, we will provide an overview of our framework for insider threat detection that also incorporates some other techniques.

The organization of this chapter is as follows. In Section 27.2, we will discuss the challenges, related work, and our approach to this problem. Our approach will be discussed in detail in Section 27.3. Our framework will be discussed in Section 27.4. The chapter is concluded in Section 27.5. Figure 27.1 illustrates the contents of this chapter.

27.2 CHALLENGES, RELATED WORK, AND OUR APPROACH

The insiders and the relationships between them will be presented as nodes and links in a graph. Therefore, the challenge is to represent the information in graphs, develop efficient storage strategies, develop query-processing techniques for the graphs, and subsequently develop data mining and analysis techniques to extract information from the graphs. In particular, there are three major challenges:

1. Storing these large graphs in an expressive and unified manner in a secondary storage
2. Devising scalable solutions for querying the large graphs to find relevant data
3. Identifying relevant features for the complex graphs and subsequently detecting insider threats in a dynamic environment that changes over time

The motivation behind our approach is to address the three challenges we have mentioned above. (i) We are developing solutions based on cloud computing to characterize graphs containing up to billions of nodes and edges between nodes representing activities (e.g., credit card transactions), e-mail, or text messages. Since the graphs will be massive, we will develop technologies for efficient and persistent storage. (ii) To facilitate novel anomaly detection, we require an efficient interface

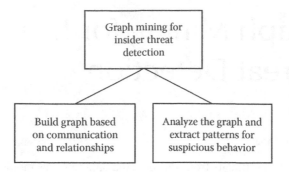

FIGURE 27.1 Graph mining for insider threat detection.

to fetch relevant data in a timely manner from this persistent storage. Therefore, we will develop efficient query techniques on the stored graphs. (iii) The fetched relevant data can then be used for further analysis to detect anomalies. To do this, first we have to identify relevant features from the complex graphs and subsequently develop techniques for mining large graphs to extract the nuggets.

Insider threat detection is a difficult problem (Maybury et al., 2005). The problem becomes increasingly complex with more data originating from heterogeneous sources and sensors. Some recent research has focused on anomaly-based insider threat detection from graphs (Eberle and Holder, 2009). This method is based on the minimum description length principle. The solution proposed by Eberle and Holder (2009) has some limitations. First, with their approach, scalability is an issue. In other words, they have not discussed any issue related to large graphs. Second, the heterogeneity issue has not been addressed. Finally, it is unclear how their algorithm will deal with a dynamic environment that changes over time.

There are also several graph mining techniques that have been developed especially for social network analysis (Carminati et al., 2009; Cook and Holder, 2006; Tong, 2009; Thuraisingham et al., 2009). The scalability of these techniques is still an issue. Some work from the mathematics research community has applied linear programming techniques for graph analysis (Berry et al., 2007). Whether these techniques will work in real-world settings is not clear.

For a solution to be viable, it must be highly scalable and support multiple heterogeneous data sources. Current state-of-the art solutions do not scale well and preserve accuracy. By leveraging Hadoop technology, our solution will be highly scalable. Furthermore, by utilizing the flexible semantic web Resource Description Framework (RDF) data model, we are able to easily integrate and align heterogeneous data. Thus, our approach will create a scalable solution in a dynamic environment. No existing threat detection tools offer this level of scalability and interoperability. We will combine these technologies with novel data mining techniques to create a complete insider threat detection solution.

We have exploited the cloud computing framework based on Hadoop/MapReduce technologies. The insiders and their relationships are represented by nodes and links in the form of graphs. In particular, in our approach, the billions of nodes and links will be presented as RDF graphs. By exploiting RDF representation, we will address heterogeneity. We will develop mechanisms to efficiently store the RDF graphs, query the graphs using SPARQL technologies, and mine the graphs to extract patterns within the cloud computing framework. We will also describe our plans to commercialize the technologies developed under this project.

27.3 GRAPH MINING FOR INSIDER THREAT DETECTION

27.3.1 OUR SOLUTION ARCHITECTURE

Figure 27.2 shows the architectural view of our solution. Our solution will pull data from multiple sources and then extract and select features. After feature reduction, the data will be stored in our

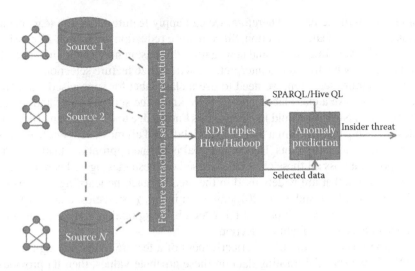

FIGURE 27.2 Solution architecture.

hardtop repository. Data will be stored in the RDF format, so a format conversion may be required if the data is in any other format. RDF is the data format for the semantic web and is very able to represent graph data. The Anomaly Prediction component will submit SPARQL Protocol and RDF Query Language (SPARQL) to the repository to select data. It will then output any detected insider threats. SPARQL is the query language for RDF data. It is similar to SQL in syntax. The details of each of the components are given in the following sections. By choosing RDF representation for graphs over relational data models, we will address the heterogeneity issue effectively (semistructured data model). For querying, we will exploit the standard query language, SPARQL, instead of starting from scratch. Furthermore, in our proposed framework, inference will be provided.

We are assuming that the large graphs already exist. To facilitate persistent storage and efficient retrieval of this data, we use a distributed framework based on the cloud computing framework Hadoop (http://hadoop.apache.org/). By leveraging the Hadoop technology, our framework is readily fault tolerant and scalable. To support large amounts of data, we can simply add more nodes to the Hadoop cluster. All the nodes of a cluster are commodity class machines; there is no need to buy expensive server machines. To handle large complex graphs, we will exploit the Hadoop distributed file system (HDFS) and MapReduce framework. The former is the storage layer that stores data in multiple nodes with replication. The latter is the execution layer where MapReduce jobs can be run. We use HDFS to store RDF data and the MapReduce framework to answer queries.

27.3.2 FEATURE EXTRACTION AND COMPACT REPRESENTATION

In traditional graph analysis, an edge represents a simple number that represents strength. However, we may face additional challenges in representing link values because of the unstructured nature of the content of text and e-mail messages. One possible approach is to keep the whole content as a part of link values, which we call explicit content (EC). EC will not scale well, even for a moderate-size graph. This is because content representing a link between two nodes will require large main memory space to process the graph in the memory. We propose a vector representation of the content (VRC) for each message. In RDF triple representation, this will simply be represented as a unique predicate. We will keep track of the feature vector along with physical location or URL of the original raw message in a dictionary encoded table.

VRC. During the preprocessing step for each message, we will extract keywords and phrases (n-grams) as features. Then, if we want to generate vectors for these features, the dimensionality of these vectors will be very high. Here, we will observe the curse of dimensionality (i.e., sparseness and processing time will increase). Therefore, we can apply feature reduction (e.g., principal component analysis) as well as feature selection. Since feature reduction maps high-dimensional feature spaces to a space of fewer dimensions, and new feature dimension may be the linear combination of old dimensions that may be difficult to interpret, we will utilize feature selection.

With regard to feature selection, we need to use a class label for supervised data. Here, for the message, we may not have a class label; however, we know the source/sender and the destination/ recipient of a message. Now, we would like to use this knowledge to construct an artificial label. The sender and destination pair will form a unique class label, and all messages sent from this sender to the recipient will serve as data points. Hence, our goal is to find appropriate features that will have discriminating power across all these class labels based on these messages. There are several methods for feature selection that are widely used in the area of machine learning, such as information gain (IG) (Mitchell, 1997; Masud et al., 2010a,b), Gini index, χ^2 statistics, and subspace clustering (Ahmed et al., 2009). Here, we will present IG, which is very popular, and for the text domain, we can use subspace clustering for feature selection.

IG can be defined as a measure of the effectiveness of a feature in classifying the training data (Mitchell, 1997). If we split the training data on these attribute values, then IG provides the measurement of the expected reduction in entropy after the split. The more an attribute can reduce entropy in the training data, the better the attribute in classifying the data. The IG of an attribute A on a collection of examples S is given by

$$\mathrm{Gain}(S, A) \equiv \mathrm{Entropy}(S) - \sum_{V \in \mathrm{values}(A)} \frac{|S_v|}{|S|} \mathrm{Entropy}(S_v) \tag{27.1}$$

where values(A) is the set of all possible values for attribute A, and S_v is the subset of S for which attribute A has value v. The entropy of S is computed using the following equation:

$$\mathrm{Entropy}(S) = -\sum_{i=1}^{n} p_i(S) \log_2 p_i(S) \tag{27.2}$$

where $p_i(S)$ is the prior probability of class i in the set S.

Subspace Clustering. Subspace clustering can be used for feature selection. Subspace clustering is appropriate when the clusters corresponding to a data set form a subset of the original dimensions. On the basis of how these subsets are formed, a subspace clustering algorithm can be referred to as soft or hard subspace clustering. In the case of soft subspace clustering, the features are assigned weights according to the contribution each feature/dimension plays during the clustering process for each cluster. In the case of hard subspace clustering, however, a specific subset of features is selected for each cluster, and the rest of the features are discarded for that cluster. Therefore, subspace clustering can be utilized for selecting which features are important (and discarding some features if their weights are very small for all clusters). One such soft subspace clustering approach is SISC (semisupervised impurity-based subspace clustering) (Ahmed et al., 2009). The following objective function is used in that subspace clustering algorithm. An E–M formulation is used for the clustering. In every iteration, the feature weights are updated for each cluster, and by selecting the features that have higher weights in each cluster, we can select a set of important features for the corresponding data set.

$$F(W, Z, \Lambda) = \sum_{l=1}^{k} \sum_{j=1}^{n} \sum_{i=1}^{m} w_{lj}^{f} \lambda_{li}^{q} D_{lij} * (1 + \mathrm{Imp}_l) + \gamma \sum_{l=1}^{k} \sum_{i=1}^{m} \lambda_{li}^{q} \chi_{li}^{2}$$

where

$$D_{lij} = (z_{li} - x_{ji})^2$$

subject to

$$\sum_{l=1}^{k} w_{lj} = 1, 1 \le j \le n, 1 \le l \le k, 0 \le w_{lj} \le 1$$

$$\sum_{i=1}^{m} \lambda_{li} = 1, 1 \le i \le m, 1 \le l \le k, 0 \le \lambda_{li} \le 1$$

In this objective function, W, Z, and Λ represent the cluster membership, cluster centroid, and dimension weight matrices, respectively. Also, the parameter f controls the fuzziness of the membership of each data point, q further modifies the weight of each dimension of each cluster (λ_{li}), and γ controls the strength of the incentive given to the χ^2 component and dimension weights. It is also assumed that there are n documents in the training data set, m features for each of the data points, and k subspace clusters are generated during the clustering process. Imp_l indicates the cluster impurity, whereas χ^2 indicates the *chi-square statistic*. Details about these notations and how the clustering is done can be found in our prior work, funded by the National Aeronautics and Space Administration (Ahmed et al., 2009). It should be noted that feature selection using subspace clustering can be considered as an unsupervised approach toward feature selection as no label information is required during an unsupervised clustering process.

Once we select features, a message between two nodes will be represented as a vector using these features. Each vector's individual value can be binary or weighted. Hence, this will be a compact representation of the original message and it can be loaded into the main memory along with a graph structure. In addition, the location or URL of the original message will be kept in the main memory data structure. If needed, we will fetch the message. Over time, the feature vector may be changed due to dynamic nature content (Masud et al., 2010a), and hence the feature set may evolve. On the basis of our prior work for evolving streams with dynamic feature sets (Masud et al., 2010b), we will investigate alternative options.

27.3.3 RDF Repository Architecture

RDF is the data format for semantic web. However, it can be used to represent any linked data in the world. RDF data is actually a collection of triples. Triples consist of three parts: subject, predicate, and object. In RDF, almost everything is a resource, and hence the name of the format. Subject and predicate are always resources. Objects may be either a resource or a literal. Here, RDF data can be viewed as a directed graph where predicates are edges that flow from subjects to objects. Therefore, in our proposed research to model any graph, we will exploit the RDF triple format. Here, an edge from the source node to the destination node in graph data set will be represented as the predicate, subject, and object of an RDF triple, respectively. To reduce the storage size of RDF triples, we will exploit dictionary encoding; that is, replace each unique string with a unique number and store the RDF data in binary format. Hence, RDF triples will have a subject, predicate, and object in an encoded form. We will maintain a separate table/file for keeping track of dictionary encoding information. To address the dynamic nature of the data, we will extend RDF triple to quad by adding a time stamp along with subject, predicate, and object representing information in the network.

Figure 27.3 shows our repository architecture, which consists of two components. The upper part of the figure depicts the data preprocessing component, and the lower part shows the component that

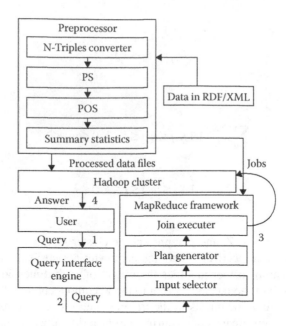

FIGURE 27.3 RDF repository architecture.

answers a query. We have three subcomponents for data generation and preprocessing. If the data is not in N-Triples, we will convert it to N-Triples serialization format using the N-Triple converter component. The PS component takes the N-Triples data and splits them into predicate files. The predicate-based files then will be fed into the Predicate Object Split (POS) component, which would split the predicate files into smaller files based on the type of objects.

Our MapReduce framework has three subcomponents. It takes the SPARQL query from the user and passes it to the input selector and plan generator. This component will select the input files and decide how many MapReduce jobs are needed and pass the information to the join executer component, which runs the jobs using MapReduce framework. It will then relay the query answer from Hadoop to the user.

27.3.4 DATA STORAGE

We will store the data in N-Triples format because in this format, we have a complete RDF triple (subject, predicate, and object) in one line of a file, which is very convenient to use with MapReduce jobs. We carry out dictionary encoding of the data for increased efficiency. Dictionary encoding means replacing text strings with a unique binary number. This not only reduces the disk space required for storage, but also query answering will be fast because handling the primitive data type is much faster than string matching. The processing steps to place the data in our intended format are described below.

File Organization. We will not store the data in a single file because in Hadoop and the MapReduce framework, a file is the smallest unit of input to a MapReduce job and, in the absence of caching, a file is always read from the disk. If we have all the data in one file, the whole file will be input to jobs for each query. Instead, we divide the data into multiple smaller files. The splitting will be done in two steps, which we will discuss in the following sections.

Predicate Split (PS). In the first step, we will divide the data according to the predicates. In real-world RDF data sets, the number of distinct predicates is no more than 100. This division will immediately enable us to cut down the search space for any SPARQL query that does not have a variable predicate. For such a query, we can just pick a file for each predicate and run the query on those files only. For simplicity, we will name the files with predicates; for example, all the triples containing a predicate *p1:pred* go into a file named *p1-pred*. However, if we have a variable predicate in a triple pattern and we cannot determine the type of the object, we have to consider all files. If we can determine the type of the object, then we will consider all files having that type of object.

Predicate Object Split (POS). In the next step, we will work with the explicit type information in the *rdf_type* file. The file will be first divided into as many files as the number of distinct objects the *rdf:type* predicate has. The object values will no longer need to be stored inside the file as they can easily be retrieved from the file name. This will further reduce the amount of space needed to store the data.

Then, we will divide the remaining predicate files according to the type of the objects. Not all the objects are Uniform Resource Identifiers (URIs); some are literals. The literals will remain in the file named by the predicate; no further processing is required for them. The type information of a URI object is not mentioned in these files, but they can be retrieved from the *rdf-type_** files. The URI objects will move into their respective file named as *predicate_type*.

27.3.5 ANSWERING QUERIES USING HADOOP MAPREDUCE

For querying, we can utilize HIVE, an SQL-like query language, and SPARQL, the query language for RDF data. When a query is submitted in HiveQL, Hive, which runs on top of the Hadoop installation, can answer that query based on our schema presented above. When a SPARQL query is submitted to retrieve relevant data from the graph, we will first generate a query plan having the minimum number of Hadoop jobs possible.

Next, we will run the jobs and answer the query. Finally, we will convert the numbers used to encode the strings back to the strings when we present the query results to the user. We will focus on minimizing the number of jobs because, in our observation, we have found that setting up Hadoop jobs is very costly and the dominant factor (time-wise) in query answering. The search space for finding the minimum number of jobs is exponential, so we will try to find a greedy-based solution or, generally speaking, an approximation solution. Our proposed approach will be capable of handling queries involving inference. We can infer on the fly and, if needed, we can materialize the inferred data.

27.3.6 GRAPH MINING APPLICATIONS

To detect anomaly/insider threat, we are examining machine learning, and propose domain knowledge-guided techniques. Our goal is to create a comparison baseline to assess the effectiveness of chaotic attractors. As a part of this task, rather than modeling normal behavior and detecting changes as anomaly, we will apply a holistic approach based on a semisupervised model. In particular, first, in our machine learning technique, we will apply a sequence of activities or dimensions as features. Second, domain knowledge (e.g., adversarial behavior) will be a part of semisupervised learning and will be used for identifying correct features. Finally, our techniques will be able to identify an entirely brand new anomaly. Over time, activities/dimensions may change or deviate. Hence, our classification model needs to be adaptive and identify new types or brand new anomalies. We will develop adaptive and novel class detection techniques so that our insider threat detection can cope with changes and identify or isolate new anomalies from existing ones.

We will apply a classification technique to detect insider threat/anomaly. Each distinct insider mission will be treated as class and dimension, and/or activities will be treated as features. Since classification is a supervised task, we require a training set. Given a training set, feature extraction will be a challenge. We will apply n-gram analysis to extract features or generate a number of sequences based on temporal property. Once a new test case comes, first, we test it against our classification model. For the classification model, we can apply support vector machine, K nearest neighbor, and the Markovian model.

From a machine learning perspective, it is customary to classify behavior as either anomalous or benign. However, the behavior of a malevolent insider (i.e., insider threat) may not be immediately identified as malicious, and it should also have subtle differences from benign behavior. A traditional machine learning-based classification model is likely to classify the behavior of a malevolent insider as benign. It will be interesting to see whether a machine learning-based novel class detection technique (Masud et al., 2010a) can detect the insider threat as a novel class, and therefore trigger a warning.

The novel class detection technique will be applied on the massive amounts of data that are being generated from user activities. Since this data has temporal properties and is produced continuously, it is usually referred to as data streams. The novel class detection model will be updated incrementally with the incoming data. This will allow us to keep the memory requirement within a constant limit, since the raw data will be discarded; however, the characteristic/pattern of the behaviors will be summarized in the model. Besides, this incremental learning will also reduce the training time, since the model need not be built from scratch with the new incoming data. Therefore, this incremental learning technique will be useful in achieving scalability.

We will examine the techniques that we have developed as well as other relevant techniques to modeling and anomaly detection. In particular, we are developing

- Tools that will analyze and model benign and anomalous mission
- Techniques to identify right dimensions and activities and apply pruning to discard irrelevant dimensions
- Techniques to cope with changes and novel class/anomaly detection

In a typical data stream classification task, it is assumed that the total number of classes is fixed. This assumption may not be valid in insider threat detection cases where new classes may evolve. Traditional data stream classification techniques are not capable of recognizing novel class instances until the appearance of the novel class is manually identified, and labeled instances of that class are presented to the learning algorithm for training. The problem becomes more challenging in the presence of concept drift, when the underlying data distribution changes over time. We have proposed a novel and efficient technique that can automatically detect the emergence of a novel class (i.e., brand-new anomaly) by quantifying cohesion among unlabeled test instances, and separating the test instances from training instances. Our goal is to use the available data and build this model.

One interesting aspect of this model is that it should capture the dynamic nature of dimensions of the mission, as well as filter out the noisy behaviors. The dimensions (both benign and anomalous) have a dynamic nature because they tend to change over time, which we denote as concept drift. A major challenge of the novel class detection is to differentiate the novel class from concept drift and noisy data. We are exploring this challenge in our current work.

27.4 COMPREHENSIVE FRAMEWORK

As we have stated earlier in Section 27.2, insider threat detection is an extremely challenging problem. In the previous section, we discussed our approach to handling this problem. Insider threat occurs not only at the application level, but it also occurs at all levels, including the operating system, database system, and the application. Furthermore, because the insider will be continually changing patterns, it will be impossible to detect all types of malicious behavior using a purely static

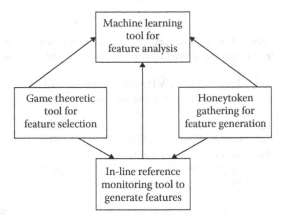

FIGURE 27.4   Framework for insider threat detection.

algorithm; a dynamic learning approach is required. Essentially, we need a comprehensive solution to the insider threat problem. However, to provide a more comprehensive solution, we need a more comprehensive framework. Therefore, we are proposing a framework for insider threat detection. Our framework will implement a number of interrelated solutions to detect malicious insiders. Figure 27.4 illustrates such a framework. We propose four approaches to this problem. At the heart of our framework is the module that implements in-line reference monitor-based techniques for feature collection. This feature collection process will be aided by two modules: one uses a game theory approach and the other uses the natural language-based approach to determine which features could be collected. The fourth module implements machine learning techniques to analyze the collected features. In summary, the relationship between the four approaches can be characterized as follows:

- In-line reference monitors (IRMs) perform covert, fine-grained feature collection.
- Game theoretic techniques will identify which features should be collected by the IRMs.
- Natural language processing techniques in general and honey token generation in particular will take an active approach to introduce additional useful features (i.e., honey token accesses) that can be collected.
- Machine learning techniques will use the collected features to infer and classify the objectives of malicious insiders.

Details of our framework are provided in Hamlen et al. (2011). We assume that the in-line reference monitor tool, game theoretic tool, and honey token generation tool will select and refine the features we need. Our data mining tools will analyze the features and determine whether there is a potential for insider threat.

27.5   SUMMARY AND DIRECTIONS

In this chapter, we have discussed our approach to insider threat detection. We represent the insiders and their communication as RDF graphs, and then query and mine the graphs to extract the nuggets. We also provided a comprehensive framework for insider threat detection.

The insider threat problem is a challenging one. Research is only beginning. The problem is that the insider may change his or her patterns and behaviors. Therefore, we need tools that can be adaptive. For example, our stream mining tools may be used for detecting such threats. We also need real-time graph mining solutions so that malicious insiders can be detected before they cause serious damage.

REFERENCES

Ahmed, M.S. and Khan, L. SISC: A text classification approach using semisupervised subspace clustering. In: *DDDM '09: The 3rd International Workshop on Domain Driven Data Mining*, December 6, 2009, Miami, 2009.

Berry, M.W., Browne, M., Langville, A., Pauca, V.P., and Plemmons, R.J. Algorithms and applications for approximate nonnegative matrix factorization. *Computational Statistics & Data Analysis* 52(1): 155–173, 2007.

Carminati, B., Ferrari, E., Heatherly, R., Kantarcioglu, M., and Thuraisingham, B. A semantic web based framework for social network access control. *SACMAT* 177–186, 2009.

Cook, D. and Holder, L. *Mining Graph Data*. Wiley Interscience, New York, 2006.

Eberle, W. and Holder, L. Applying graph-based anomaly detection approaches to the discovery of insider threats. In: *IEEE International Conference on Intelligence and Security Informatics (ISI)*, Dallas, June 2009, pp. 206–208, 2009.

Hamlen, K., Khan, L., Kantarcioglu, M., Ng, V., and Thuraisingham, B. Insider threat detection, UTD Report, April 2011.

Masud, M., Gao, J., Khan, L., Han, J., and Thuraisingham, B. Classification and novel class detection in concept-drifting data streams under time constraints. In: *IEEE Transactions on Knowledge & Data Engineering (TKDE)*, April 2010, IEEE Computer Society, 2010a.

Masud, M., Chen, Q., Gao, J., Khan, L., Han, J., and Thuraisingham, B. Classification and novel class detection of data streams in a dynamic feature space. In: *Proc. of European Conference on Machine Learning and Knowledge Discovery in Databases, ECML PKDD 2010*, Barcelona, Spain, September 20–24, 2010, pp. 337–352. Springer, Berlin, 2010b.

Maybury, M., Chase, P., Cheikes, B., Brackney, D., Matzner, S., Hetherington, T., Wood, B. et al. Analysis and detection of malicious insiders. In: *2005 International Conference on Intelligence Analysis*, McLean, VA, 2005.

Mitchell, T., *Machine Learning*. McGraw Hill, New York, 1997.

Thuraisingham, B., Kantarcioglu, M., and Khan, L. Building a geosocial semantic web for military stabilization and reconstruction operations. *PAISI* 2009: 1.

Tong, H. Fast algorithms for querying and mining large graphs. *CMU Report*, ML-09-112, September 2009.

28 Temporal Geosocial Mobile Semantic Web

28.1 INTRODUCTION

The integration of geospatial technology, semantic web, mobile systems, and social media are important for many applications ranging from crisis management, prevention of the spread of infectious diseases, fighting the global war on terror, and military stabilization and reconstruction operations (SARO). For these applications, it is important to form partnerships between the various communities (e.g., government, local, or foreign), form a social network, identify locations of interest, check weather-related data, and ensure that the operations are carried out in a timely manner. Essentially, we need to build an integrated system that includes geospatial, semantic web, mobile, and social media technologies. In this chapter, we will discuss the design of such an integrated system for military SARO.

The United States and its allied forces have had tremendous success in combat operations. This includes combat in Germany, Japan, and, more recently, in Iraq and Afghanistan. However, not all SARO have been as successful. Recently, several studies have been carried out on SARO by the National Defense University (NDU) as well as for the Army Science and Technology. One of the major conclusions is that we need to plan for SARO while we are planning for combat. That is, we cannot start planning for SARO after the enemy regime has fallen. In addition, the studies have shown that security, power, and jobs are key ingredients for success during SARO. It is important to give positions to some of the power players from the fallen regime provided they are trustworthy. It is critical that investments are made to stimulate the local economies. The studies have also analyzed the various technologies that are needed for successfully carrying out SARO, which includes sensors, robotics, and information management. In this chapter, we will focus on the information management component for SARO. As stated in the work by the Naval Postgraduate School (NPS), we need to determine the social, political, and economic relationships between the local communities as well as determine who the important people are. This work has also identified the who, when, what, where, and why (5Ws) and the how (1H).

To address the key technical challenges for SARO, we have defined a life cycle for SARO (SAROL), and are subsequently developing a temporal geosocial mobile service-oriented architecture system (TGSM-SOA) that utilizes temporal geosocial mobile semantic web (TGSM-SW) technologies for managing this life cycle. We are developing techniques for representing temporal geosocial information and relationships, integrating such information and relationships, querying such information and relationships, and finally reasoning about such information and relationships so that the commander can answer questions related to the 5Ws and 1H. To our knowledge, this is the first attempt to develop TGSM-SW technologies and life cycle management for SARO. Our system can be adapted for other applications, including crisis management, prevention of the spread of infectious diseases, and fighting the global war on terror.

According to a Government Accountability Office (GAO) Report published in October 2007 (GAO, 2007), "DoD has taken several positive steps to improve its ability to conduct stability operations but faces challenges in developing capabilities and measures of effectiveness, integrating the contributions of non-DoD agencies into military contingency plans, and incorporating lessons learned from past operations into future plans. These challenges, if not addressed, may hinder DoD's ability to fully coordinate and integrate stabilization and reconstruction activities with other agencies or to develop the full range of capabilities those operations may require." Around the same

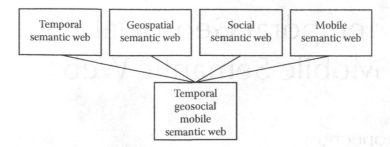

FIGURE 28.1 Temporal geosocial mobile semantic web.

time, the Center for Technology and National Security Policy at NDU (Binnendjik and Johnson, 2004) and the NPS (Guttieri, 2007a) identified some key technologies crucial for the military stabilization and reconstruction processes in Iraq and Afghanistan. These technologies include those in electronics, sensors, and medical as well as in information management.

The NPS has identified three types of reconstruction efforts. One of these efforts they classify as the *easy* activities, including building bridges and schools (Guttieri, 2007a). The second, which they identify as *sensitive*, is to develop policies for governance. The third, which they identify as *hard*, is to understand the cultures of people and to engage warlords in negotiation as well as to get their buy-in so as to sustain long-term security. In addition, the military needs to obtain information about the location of the fiefdoms of the warlords, the security breaches (e.g., improvised explosive devices) at the various locations, and associations between different groups.

We are addressing the difficult challenges of military stabilization by developing innovative information management technologies. In particular, we are designing and developing a temporal geosocial semantic web that will integrate heterogeneous information sources, identify the relationships between the different groups of people that evolve over time and location, and facilitate sharing of the different types of information to support SARO. Our goal is to get the right information to the decision maker so that he or she can make decisions in the midst of uncertain and unanticipated situations.

The organization of this chapter is as follows. Some of the unique challenges will be discussed in Section 28.2. The supporting technologies we are utilizing are discussed in Section 28.3. Our approach to designing and developing the system for SARO is discussed in Section 28.4. The chapter is concluded in Section 28.5. Figure 28.1 presents the concepts used in this chapter. It should be noted that much of our work has been focusing on developing a temporal geosocial semantic web (TGS-SW). We are examining the issues on incorporating the mobile aspects to TGS-SW to develop a TGSM-SW.

28.2 CHALLENGES FOR A SUCCESSFUL SARO

28.2.1 INGREDIENTS FOR A SUCCESSFUL SARO

Recently, several studies on SARO are emerging. Notable among them is the study carried out by the NDU (Binnendjik and Johnson, 2004). In this study, the authors give examples of several successful and failed SAROs. The authors state that the Iraq war was hugely successful in that the United States and the allied forces were able to defeat the enemy in record time. However, the United States and the allied forces were not prepared for SARO and, subsequently, nation building. For SARO to be successful, its planning should be carried out concurrently with the planning of the war. This means as soon as the war ends, plans are already in place to carry out SARO. Sometimes, the latter part of the war may be carried out in conjunction with SARO.

The authors have discussed the various SAROs that the United States has engaged in, including in Germany, Japan, Somalia, and the Balkans, and describe the successes of SAROs like in Germany and

Japan and the failure of SARO in Somalia. The authors also discuss why Field Marshall Montgomery's mission for regime change in Egypt in 1956 failed. This was because then Prime Minister Anthony Eden did not plan for what happens after the regime change. As a result, the operation was a failure. However, overthrowing communism in Malaya in the 1950s was a huge success by Field Marshall Sir Gerald Templer because he achieved the buy-in of the locals—the Malayans, Chinese, and Indians. He also gave them the impression that Britain was not intending to stay long in Malaya. As a result, the locals gave him the support and together they were able to overthrow communism.

On the basis of the above examples, the authors state that four concurrent tasks have to be carried out in parallel. (i) *Security:* Ensure that those who attempt to destroy the emergence of a new society are suppressed. This will include identifying those that are troublemakers or terrorists, and destroy their capabilities. (ii) *Law and order:* Military and police skills are combined to ensure that there are no malicious efforts to disturb the peace. (iii) *Repair infrastructure:* Utilize the expertise of engineers and geographers both from allied countries and local people, and build the infrastructure. (iv) *Establish an interim government effectively:* Understand the cultures of the local people, their religious beliefs, and their political connections, and establish a government.

The authors also state that there are key elements to success: (i) security, (ii) power, and (iii) jobs. We have already explained the importance of security. Power has to be given to key people. For example, those who were in powerful positions within the fallen regime may make alliances with the terrorists. Therefore, such people have to be carefully studied and given power if appropriate. Usually after a regime change, people are left homeless and without jobs. Therefore, it is important to give incentives for foreign nations to invest in the local country and create jobs. This means forming partnerships with the locals as well as with foreign investors.

To end this section, we will take a quote from General Anthony Zinny, USMC (Ret). former Commander, US Central Command, "What I need to understand is how these societies function. What makes them tick? Who makes the decisions? What is it about their society that is so remarkably different in their values and the way they think in my western white man mentality." Essentially, he states what is crucial is getting cultural intelligence. In fact, our work proposes solutions to precisely capture the cultural and political relationships and information about the locals, model these relationships, and exploit these relationships for SARO.

28.2.2 Unique Technology Challenges for SARO

A technology analysis study carried out by the Army Science and Technology states that many of the technologies for SARO are the same as those for combat operations (Chait et al., 2006). However, the study also states that there are several unique challenges for SARO and elaborates as follows:

> The nature of S&R operations also demands a wider focus for ISR (intelligence surveillance and reconnaissance). In addition to a continuing need for enemy information (e.g., early detection of an insurgency), S&R operations require a broad range of essential information that is not emphasized in combat operations. A broader, more specific set of information needs must be specified in the Commander's Critical Information Requirements (CCIR) portfolio. CCIR about areas to be stabilized include the nature of pre-conflict policing and crime, influential social networks, religious groups, and political affiliations, financial and economic systems as well as key institutions and how they work are other critical elements of information. Mapping these systems for specific urban areas will be tedious though much data is already resident in disparate databases. The challenges involved in computational modeling for culturally infused social networks for SARO is given in Santos (2007).

28.3 SUPPORTING TECHNOLOGIES FOR SARO

We are integrating several of our existing technologies and building new technologies for SARO. We will describe the supporting (i.e., existing) technologies we are using in this section, and the new technologies in the next.

28.3.1   GEOSPATIAL SEMANTIC WEB, POLICE BLOTTER, AND KNOWLEDGE DISCOVERY

We have developed a geospatial semantic web and information integration and mining tools and techniques. In particular, we have developed (i) techniques for matching or aligning ontologies, (ii) police blotter prototype demonstrated at GEOspatial INTelligence (GEOINT), and (iii) the Geospatial Resource Description Framework (GRDF) and Geospatial Ontologies for Emergency Response.

Matching or Aligning Ontologies. In open and evolving systems various parties continue to adopt differing ontologies (Khan et al., 2004), with the result that instead of reducing heterogeneity, the problem becomes compounded. Matching, or aligning ontologies, is a key interoperability enabler for the semantic web. In this case, ontologies are taken as input and correspondences between the semantically related entities of these ontologies are determined as output, as well as any transformations required for alignment. It is helpful to have ontologies that we need to match to refer to the same upper ontology or to conform to the same reference ontology (Ehrig et al., 2005; Noy and Musen, 2003). A significant amount of work has already been done from the database perspective (Doan and Halevy, 2005; Madhavan et al., 2005; Rahm and Bernstein, 2001) and from the machine learning perspective (Doan et al., 2004; Kalfoglou and Schorlemmer, 2003; Rahm and Bernstein, 2001; Stumme and Maedche, 2001). Our approach falls into the latter perspective. However, it focuses not only on traditional data (i.e., text), but also goes beyond text (i.e., geospatial data). The complex nature of this geospatial data poses further challenges and additional clues in matching process. Given a set of data sources, S_1, S_2, ..., each of which is represented by data model ontologies O_1, O_2, ..., the goal is to find similar concepts between two ontologies (namely, O_1 and O_2) by examining their respective structural properties and instances, if available. For the purposes of this problem, O_1 and O_2 may belong to different domains drawn from any existing knowledge domain. Additionally, these ontologies may vary in breadth, depth, and through the types of relationships between their constituent concepts.

The challenges involved in the alignment of these ontologies, assuming that they have already been constructed, include the proper assignment of instances to concepts in their identifying ontology. Quantifying the similarity between a concept from the ontology, O_1 (called concept A) and a concept from the O_2 ontology (called concept B) involves computing measures taking into account three separate types of concept similarity: *name similarity, relationship similarity,* and *content similarity.* Matching is accomplished through determining the weighted similarity between the name similarity and content similarity along with their associated instances. The *name similarity* between A and B will exploit name match with the help of WordNet, and the Jaro–Winkler string metric. The *relationship similarity* between A and B takes into account the number of equivalent spatial relationships, along with their sibling similarity and parent similarity.

Content similarity: We describe two algorithms we have developed for content similarity. The first is an extension of the ideas presented in Dai et al. (2008) regarding the use of *n*-grams extracted from the values of the compared attributes. Despite the utility of this algorithm, there are situations when this approach produces deceptive results. To resolve these difficulties, we will present a second instance-matching algorithm, called *K*-means with normalized Google distance (KM-NGD), which determines the semantic similarity between the values of the compared attributes by leveraging *K*-medoid clustering and a measure known as the normalized Google distance (NGD).

Content similarity using n-grams: Instance matching between two concepts involves measuring the similarity between the instance values across all pairs of compared attributes. This is accomplished by extracting instance values from the compared attributes, subsequently extracting a characteristic set of *n*-grams from these instances, and finally comparing the respective *n*-grams for each attribute. In the following, we will use the term *value type* to refer to a unique value of an attribute involved in the comparison. We extract distinct

2-grams from the instances and consider each unique 2-gram extracted as a value type. As an example, for the string *Locust Grove Dr.* that might appear under an attribute named Street for a given concept, some *n*-grams that would be extracted are *Lo*, *oc*, *cu*, *st*, *t*, *ov*, *Dr*, and *r*.

The *n*-gram similarity is based on a comparison between the concepts of entropy and conditional entropy known as entropy-based distribution (EBD):

$$\text{EBD} = \frac{H(C|T)}{H(C)} \tag{28.1}$$

In Equation 28.1, C and T are random variables, where C indicates the union of the attribute types C_1 and C_2 involved in the comparison (C indicates *column*, which we will use synonymously with the term *attribute*) and T indicates the value type, which in this case is a distinct *n*-gram. EBD is a normalized value with a range from 0 to 1. Our experiments involve one-to-one comparisons between attributes of compared concepts, so the value of C would simply be $C_1 \cup C_2$. $H(C)$ represents the entropy of a group of value types for a particular column (or attribute) while $H(C|T)$ indicates the conditional entropy of a group of identical value types.

Intuitively, an attribute contains high entropy if it is impure; that is, the ratios of value types making up the attribute values are similar to one another. On the other hand, low entropy in an attribute exists when one value type exists at a much higher ratio than any other type. Conditional entropy is similar to entropy in the sense that ratios of value types are being compared. However, the difference is that we are computing the ratio between identical value types extracted from different attributes. Figure 28.2 provides examples to help visualize the concept. In both examples, crosses indicate value types originating from C_1, while squares indicate value types originating from C_2. The collection of a given value type is represented as a cluster (larger circle). In Figure 28.2a, the total number of crosses is 10 and the total number of squares is 11, which implies that entropy is very high. The conditional entropy is also high, since the ratios of crosses to squares within two of the clusters are equal within one and nearly equal within the other. Thus, the ratio of conditional entropy to entropy will be very close to 1, since the ratio of crosses to squares is nearly the same from an overall value type perspective and from an individual value type perspective. Figure 28.2b portrays a different situation: while the entropy is 1.0, the ratio of crosses to squares within each individual cluster varies considerably. One cluster features all crosses and no squares, while another cluster features a 3:1 ratio of squares to

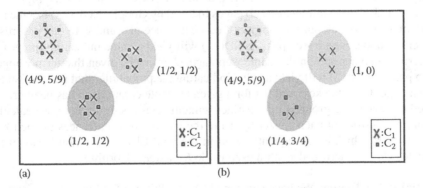

(a)   (b)

FIGURE 28.2 Distribution of different value types when EDB is high (a) and low (b). $H(C)$ is similar to $H(C|T)$ but dissimilar in (b).

crosses. The EBD value for this example consequently will be lower than the EBD for the first example because $H(C|T)$ will be a lower value.

Problems of the n-gram approach for instance matching: Despite the utility of the aforementioned method, it is susceptible to misleading results. For example, if an attribute named *City* associated with a concept from O_1 is compared against an attribute named *ctyName* associated with a concept from O_2, the attribute values for both concepts might consist of city names from different parts of the world. City might contain the names of North American cities, all of which use English and other Western languages as their basis language, while ctyName might describe East Asian cities, all of which use languages that are fundamentally different from English or any Western language.

According to human intuition, it is obvious that the comparison occurs between two semantically similar attributes. However, because of the tendency for languages to emphasize certain sounds and letters over others, the extracted sets of 2-grams from each attribute would very likely be quite different from one another. For example, some values of City might be *Dallas, Houston*, and *Halifax*, while values of ctyName might be *Shanghai, Beijing*, and *Tokyo*. On the basis of these values alone, there is virtually no overlap of *n*-grams. Because most of the 2-grams belong specifically to one attribute or the other, the calculated EBD value would be low. This would most likely be a problem every time global data needed to be compared for similarity.

Using clustering and semantic distance for content similarity: To overcome the problems of the *n*-gram, we have developed a method that is free from the syntactic requirements of *n*-grams and uses the keywords in the data in order to extract relevant semantic differences between compared attributes. This method, known as KM-NGD, extracts distinct keywords from the compared attributes and places them into distinct semantic clusters via the *K*-medoid algorithm, where the distance metric between each pair of distinct data points in a given cluster (a data point is represented as an occurrence of one of the distinct keywords) is known as the NGD. The EBD is then calculated by comparing the words contained in each cluster, where a cluster is considered a distinct value type.

Normalized Google distance: Before describing the process in detail, NGD must be formally defined:

$$\text{NGD}(x, y) = \frac{\max\{\log f(x), \log f(y)\} - \log f(x, y)}{\log M - \min\{\log f(x), \log f(y)\}} \tag{28.2}$$

In Equation 28.2, $f(x)$ is the number of Google hits for search term x, $f(y)$ is the number of Google hits for search term y, $f(x,y)$ is the number of Google hits for the tuple of search terms xy, and M is the number of web pages indexed by Google. $\text{NGD}(x,y)$ is a measure for the symmetric conditional probability of co-occurrence of x and y. In other words, given that term x appears on a web page, $\text{NGD}(x,y)$ will yield a value indicating the probability that term y also appears on that same web page. Conversely, given that term y appears on a web page, $\text{NGD}(x,y)$ will yield a value indicating the probability that term x also appears on that page. Once the keyword list for a given attribute comparison has been created, all related keywords are grouped into distinct semantic clusters. From here, we calculate the conditional entropy of each cluster by using the number of occurrences of each keyword in the cluster, which is subsequently used in the final EBD calculation between the two attributes. The clustering algorithm used is the *K*-medoid algorithm.

Geospatial Police Blotter. We have developed (i) a toolkit that facilitates integration of various police blotters into a unified representation and (ii) a semantic search with various levels of abstraction along with spatial and temporal view. Software has been developed for integration of various police blotters along with semantic search capability. We are particularly interested in police blotter crime analysis. Police blotter is the daily written record of events (as arrests) in a police station that is released by every police station periodically. These records are available publicly on the web, which provides us a wealth of information for analyzing crime patterns across multiple jurisdictions. The blotters may come in different data formats like structured, semistructured (HTML), and unstructured (NL) text. In addition, many environmental criminology techniques assume that data are locally maintained and the data set is homogeneous as well as certain. This assumption is not realistic as data is often managed by different jurisdictions and, therefore, the analyst may have to spend an unusually large amount of time to link related events across different jurisdictions (e.g., the sniper shootings across Washington DC, Virginia, and Maryland in October 2002). There are major challenges that a police officer would face when he or she wants to analyze different police blotters to study a pattern (e.g., a spatial–temporal activity pattern) or trail of events. There is no way a police officer can pose a query where the query will be handled by considering more than one distributed police blotter on the fly. There is no cohesive tool for the police officer to view the blotters from different counties, interact and visualize the trail of crimes, and generate analysis reports. The blotters can currently be searched only by keyword through current tools and does not allow conceptual search, and fails to identify spatial–temporal patterns and connect various dots/pieces. Therefore, we need a tool that will integrate distributed multiple police blotters, extract semantic information from a police blotter, and provide a seamless framework for queries with multiple granularities.

We have developed a toolkit that

* Facilitates integration of various police blotters into a unified representation
* Is capable of semantic search with various levels of abstraction along with spatial and temporal view

With regard to integration, structured, semistructured, and unstructured data are mapped into relational tables and stored in Oracle 10g2. For information extraction from unstructured text, we used LingPipe (http://www.alias-i.com/lingpipe/). During the extraction and mapping process, we exploited a crime event ontology similar to National Incident-Based Reporting System (NIBRS) Group A and Group B offenses. During the extraction process, we extracted crime type, offender sex, and offender race (if available). This ontology is multilevel with depth 4.

We have facilitated basic and advanced query to perform semantic search (Figure 28.3). Basic query allows query by crime type from ontology along with date filter. Advanced query extends basic query facility by augmenting the address field (block, street, city). Ontology allows users to search at various levels of abstraction. Results are shown in two forms of view: spatial and temporal. Furthermore, in each view, results are shown either in individual crime form or aggregated (number of crimes) form. In temporal view, results are shown either in weekly, biweekly, monthly, quarterly, or yearly basis. Clicking on a crime location in spatial view will show the details of the crime along with the URL of the original source.

To identify correlation of various crimes that occurred in multiple jurisdictions, an SQL query is submitted to the database. After the fetching relevant tuples, subsequent correlation analysis is performed in main memory.

Correlation analysis is accomplished by calculating the pairwise similarity of these tuples and constructing a directed graph from the results. Nodes in the graph represent tuples, and edges represent similarity values between tuples. If similarity of two tuples falls below a certain threshold, we remove its corresponding edge from the graph. Finally, a set of paths in the graph demonstrate the correlation of crimes across multiple jurisdictions. By clicking on the path, all relevant tuples similar to each other are shown in a popup window (see Figure 28.4). For implementation, we have developed our application as an applet in portlet. To show address in map, we have exploited Yahoo's geocoder that converts latitude/longitude from street address. To display map, OpenMap

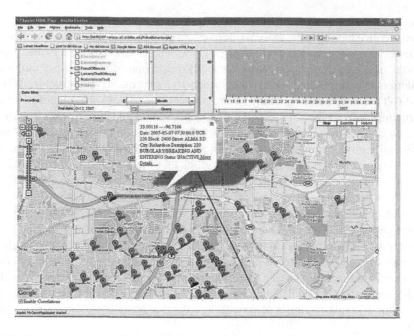

FIGURE 28.3 Basic and advanced query interface to perform semantic search using Google Maps API. Details of a crime are shown in a popup window.

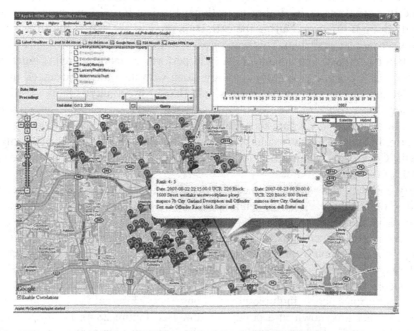

FIGURE 28.4 Demonstration of correlation of crimes across multiple jurisdictions using Google Maps API. By clicking on the straight line, all relevant crime records similar to each other are shown in popup windows.

and Google Map API both are used. We have used police blotter data sets from Dallas County in our demonstrations.

GRDF and Geospatial Ontologies for Emergency Response. We have developed a system called DAGIS, which utilizes GRDF (our version of geospatial RDF; Ashraful et al., 2011) and associated geospatial ontologies. DAGIS is a service-oriented architecture (SOA)-based system for geospatial data, and we use a SPARQL-like query language to query the data sources. Furthermore, we have also implemented access control for DAGIS. We are currently investigating how some of the temporal concepts we have developed for police blotter can be incorporated into GRDF and DAGIS (Subbiah, 2007). We have also presented this research to the Open Geospatial Consortium (OGC) (Thuraisingham, 2006). In addition to this effort, we have also developed a geospatial emergency response system to detect chemical spills using commercial products, such as ArcGIS (Chittumala et al., 2007). Our goal is to build on our extensive experience on geospatial technology as well as our systems DAGIS/GRDF, police blotter, ontology matching tools, and the geospatial emergency response system to develop a SARO prototype.

28.3.2 SOCIAL NETWORKING FOR FIGHTING AGAINST BIOTERRORISM

Our own model for analyzing various bioterrorism scenarios is a hybridization of social interactions on a household scale, situation intervention, and the simplicity of the susceptible, infected, and recovered (SIR) approach (Newman, 2003). The system arose out of a need for a deterministic model that can balance a desire for accuracy in representing a potential scenario with computational resources and time. Recent work has suggested that more detailed models of social networks have a diminished role over the results in the spread of an epidemic (Newman, 2003). We believe we can generalize complex interactions into a much more concise simulation without adversely affecting accuracy. The ultimate goal of our research is to integrate a model for biological warfare with a system that can evaluate multiple attacks with respect to passive and active defenses. As a result, we have created a simulation that serves as an approximation of the impact of a biological attack with speed in mind, allowing us to explore a large search space in a relatively shorter amount of time as compared with existing detailed models.

The base component of our model is the home unit. A home can range in size from a single individual to a large household. Within this unit, the probable states of the individuals are tracked via a single vector of susceptibility, infection, and recovery. Given a population distribution of a region and basic statistical data, we can easily create a series of family units that represents the basic social components from a rural community to a major metropolitan area. A single home unit with no interaction is essentially a basic representation of the SIR model. Interaction occurs within what we call social network theaters. A theater is essentially any gathering area at which two or more members of a home unit meet. The probability of interaction depends on the type of location and the social interaction possible at it. To capture this, separate infection rates are assignable to each theater. In the event of a life-threatening scenario such as a bioterrorist attack, we assume a civil authority will act at some point to prevent a full-scale epidemic. We model such an entity by providing means in our models to affect social theaters and the probabilities associated with state transitions. For simplicity at this point, we do not consider resource constraints, nor do we model how an event is detected. The recognition of an attack will be simulated using a variable delay. After this delay has passed, the infection is officially recognized.

The most basic form of prevention is by inoculating the population against an expected contagion. Several options exist at this level, ranging from key personnel to entire cities. Anyone inoculated is automatically considered recovered. Second, a quarantine strategy can be used to isolate the infected population from the susceptible population. This requires the explicit removal of individuals from home units to appropriate facilities, and can be simulated on a fractional basis representing probability of removal with varying levels of accuracy. Third, the infection and recovery rates can be altered, through such means as allocating more resources to medical personnel and educating the general public on means to avoid infection. Finally, a potentially controversial but interesting option is the isolation of communities by temporarily eliminating social gathering areas. For example, public schools could be closed, or martial law could be declared. The motivating factor is finding ways to force the population at risk to remain at home. Such methods could reduce the number of vectors over which an infection could spread.

On the basis of the above model, we simulated various bioterrorism scenarios. A powerful factor that we saw in several of our results in the epidemiology models was the small world phenomenon. The small world effect is when the average number of hops on even the largest of networks tends to be very small. In several cases, the infection spread to enough individuals within 4 days to pose a serious threat that could not be easily contained. The results from closing social theaters made this particularly clear, as many closures beyond the third day did little to slow the advance of many epidemics. However, not all intervention methods are available in every country. It is important to understand how local governmental powers, traditions, and ethics can affect the options available in a simulation. In some countries, a government may be able to force citizens to be vaccinated, while others may have no power at all and must rely on the desire for protection to motivate action. In other situations, closing any social theater may be an explicit power of the state, in contrast to governing entities that may have varying amounts of abilities to do the same but will not consider it due to a severe social backlash. The impact on society must be carefully considered beyond economical cost in any course of action, and there is rarely a clear choice. These answers are outside the scope of our work, and are better suited to political and philosophical viewpoints. However, our model helps governing bodies consider these efforts carefully in light of public safety and the expenditure of available resources. A major goal of our research is to provide a means to further our understanding of how to provide a higher level of security against malicious activities. This work is a culmination of years of research into the application of social sciences to computer science in the realm of modeling and simulation. With detailed demographic data and knowledge of an impending biological attack, this model provides the means to both anticipate the impact on a population and potentially prevent a serious epidemic. An emphasis on cost–benefit analysis of the results could potentially save both lives and resources that can be invested in further refining security for a vulnerable population.

28.3.3 ASSURED INFORMATION SHARING, INCENTIVES, AND RISKS

Our current research is focusing extensively on incentive-based information sharing, which is a major component of the SARO system. In particular, we are working on building mechanisms to give incentives to individuals/organizations for information sharing. Once such mechanisms are built, we can use concepts from the theory of contracts (Laffont and Martimort, 2001) to determine appropriate rewards such as ranking or, in the case of certain foreign partners, monetary benefits. Currently, we are exploring how to leverage secure distributed audit logs to rank individual organizations between trustworthy partners. To handle situations where it is not possible to carry out auditing, we are developing game theoretic strategies for extracting information from the partners. The impact of behavioral approaches to sharing is also currently considered. Finally, we are conducting studies based on economic theories and integrate relevant results into incentivized assured information sharing as well as collaboration.

Auditing System. One motivation for sharing information and behaving truthfully is the liability imposed on the responsible partners if the appropriate information is not shared when needed. For example, an agency may be more willing to share information if it is held liable. We are devising an auditing system that securely logs all the queries and responses exchanged between agencies. For example, agency B's query and the summary of the result given by agency A (e.g., number of documents, document IDs, and their hash values) could be digitally signed and stored by both agencies. Also, we may create logs for subscriber-based information services to ensure that correct and relevant information are pushed to intended users. Our mechanism needs to be distributed, secure, and efficient. Such an audit system could be used as a basis for creating information-sharing incentives. First, using such a distributed audit system, it may be possible to find out whether an agency is truthful or not by conducting an audit using the audit logs and the documents stored by the agency. Also, an agency may publish accurate statistics about each user's history using the audit system. For example, agency B could publish the number of queries it sent to agency A that resulted in positive responses, the quantity of documents that are transmitted, and how useful those documents were according to scoring metrics. The audit logs and aggregate statistics could be used to set proper incentives for information sharing. For example, agencies that are deemed to provide useful information could be rewarded. At the same time, agencies that do not provide useful information or withhold information could be punished. An issue in audit systems is to determine how the parties involved evaluate the signals produced by the audit. For example, in public auditing systems, simplicity and transparency are required for the audit to have necessary political support (Berg, 2006). Since the required transparency could be provided mainly among trusted partners, such an audit framework is suitable for trustworthy coalition partners. Currently, we are exploring the effect of various alternative parameter choices for our audit system on the Nash equilibrium (Osborne and Rubinstein, 1994) in our information-sharing game.

Other research challenges in incentivizing information sharing are also currently being explored. First, in some cases, owing to some legal restrictions or for security purposes, an agency may not be able to satisfactorily answer the required query. This implies that our audit mechanisms, rating systems, and incentive setup should consider the existing security policies. Second, we need to ensure that subjective statistics such as ratings should not be used for playing with the incentive system. That is, we need to ensure that partners do not have incentives to falsify rating information. For example, to get better rankings, agencies may try to collude and provide fake ratings. To detect such a situation and discourage collusion, we are working on various social analysis techniques. In addition, we will develop tools to analyze the underlying distributed audit logs securely by leveraging our previous work on accountable secure multiparty computation protocols (Jiang et al., 2007).

Behavioral Aspects of Assured Incentivized Information Sharing. A risk in modeling complex issues of information sharing in the real world to formal analysis is making unrealistic assumptions. By drawing on insights from psychology and related complementary decision sciences, we are considering a wider range of behavioral hypotheses. The system we are building seeks to integrate numerous sources of information and provides a variety of quantitative output to help monitor the system's performance, most important, sending negative alerts when the probability that information is being misused rises above preset thresholds. The quality of the system's overall performance will ultimately depend on how human beings eventually use it.

The field of behavioral economics emerged in recent decades, borrowing from psychology to build models with more empirical realism underlying fundamental assumptions about the way in which decision makers arrive at inferences and take actions. For example, Nobel Prize winner Kahneman's work focused primarily on describing how actual human behavior deviates from how it is typically described in economics textbooks. The emerging field of normative behavioral economics now focuses on how insights from psychology can be used to better design institutions (Berg, 2003). A case in point is the design of incentive mechanisms that motivate a network of users to properly share information. One way in which psychology can systematically change the shape of the utility function in an information-sharing context concerns relative outcomes, interpersonal comparisons, and status considerations in economic decision making. For example, is it irrational or uneconomical to prefer a payoff of 60 among a group where the average payoff is 40, over a payoff of 80 in a group context where the average among others is over 100? While nothing in economic theory ever ruled out these sorts of preferences, their inclusion in formal economic analysis was rather rare until recent years.

We are trying to augment the formal analysis of the incentivized information-sharing component of our work with a wider consideration of motivations, including interpersonal comparisons, as factors that systematically shape behavioral outcomes and, consequently, the performance of information-sharing systems. Another theme to emerge in behavioral economics is the importance of simplicity (Gigerenzer and Todd, 1999) and the paradox of too much choice. According to psychologists and evolutionary biologists, simplicity is often a benefit worth pursuing in its own right, paying in terms of improved prediction, faster decision times, and higher satisfaction of users. We are considering a wide range of information configurations that examine environments in which more information is helpful, and those in which less is more. With intense concern for the interface between real-world human decision makers and the systems, we will provide practical hints derived from theory to be deployed by the design team in the field.

28.4   OUR APPROACH TO BUILDING A SARO SYSTEM

Our approach is described in the following seven subsections. In particular, we will describe SAROL, and our approach to designing and developing SAROL through a temporal geosocial semantic web.

28.4.1   OVERVIEW

In one of our projects, we have developed what is called an assured information sharing life cycle (AISL). AISL focuses on policy enforcement as well as incentive-based information sharing. Semantic web technology is utilized as the glue. AISL's goal is to implement Department of Defense (DoD's) information-sharing strategy set forth by Hon. John Grimes (Grimes, 2007). However, AISL does not capture geospatial information or track social networks based on locations. (Note that the main focus of AISL is to enforce confidentiality for information sharing.)

Our design of the SARO system is influenced by our work for the MURI project with our partners. Our goal is to develop technologies that will capture not only information but also social/political relationships, map the individuals in the network to their locations, reason about the relationships and information, and determine how the nuggets can be used by the commander for stabilization and reconstruction. In doing so, the commander also has to determine potential conflicts, terrorist activities, and any operation that could hinder and suspend stabilization and reconstruction. To reason about the relationships as well as to map the individuals of a network to locations, we are utilizing the extensive research we have carried out both on social network models and geospatial semantic web and integration technologies. We need to develop scenarios based on use cases that are discussed in a study carried out for the Army Science and Technology (Chait et al., 2007) as well as by interviewing experts (e.g., Chait et al.). Furthermore, in her work, Dr. Karen Guttieri states that human terrain is a crucial aspect and we need hyperlinks to people, places, things, and events to answer questions such as, Which people are where? Where are their centers and boundaries? Who are their leaders? Who is who in the zoo? What are their issues and needs? What is the news and reporting? Essentially, the human domain associations build relationships between the who, what, where, when, and why (5Ws) (Guttieri, 2007b).

Our goal is to design what we call SAROL. SAROL will consist of multiple phases and will discover relationships and information, model and integrate the relationships and information, as well as exploit the relationships and information for decision support. The system that implements SAROL will utilize geosocial semantic web technologies, a novel semantic web that we will develop. The basic infrastructure that will glue together the various phases of SAROL will be based on the SOA paradigm. We will utilize the technologies that we have developed in social networking and geospatial semantic web to develop temporal geosocial semantic web technologies for SAROL.

It should be noted that in our initial design, we are focusing on the basic concepts for SAROL that will involve the development of TGSM-SW. This will include capturing the social relationships and mapping them to the geolocations. In our advanced design, we will include some advanced techniques such as knowledge discovery and risk-based trust management for the information and relationships.

28.4.2 Scenario for SARO

In the study carried out for the army, the authors have discussed the surveys they administered and elaborated on the use cases and scenarios they developed (Chait et al., 2007). For example, at a high level, a City Rebuild use case is the following: "A brigade moves into a section of a city and is totally responsible for all S&R operations in that area, which includes the reconstruction of an airfield in its area of responsibility." They further state that to move from A to B in a foreign country, the commander should consider various aspects including the following: "Augmenting its convoy security with local security forces (political and military considerations)" and "Avoid emphasizing a military presence near political or religious sites (political and social considerations)."

The authors then go on to explain how a general situation can then be elaborated for a particular situation, say, in Iraq. They also discuss the actions to be taken and provide the results of their analysis. This work is influencing our development of scenarios and use cases. The use case analysis will then guide us in the development of SAROL.

28.4.3 SAROL

SAROL consists of three major phases shown in Figure 28.5: (i) information and relationship discovery and acquisition, (ii) information and relationship modeling and integration, and (iii) information and relationship exploitation. During the discovery and acquisition phase, commanders and key people will discover the information and relationships based on those advertised as well as those obtained through inference. During the modeling and integration phase, the information and the relationship have to be modeled, additional information and relationships inferred, and the information and relationships integrated. During the exploitation phase, the commanders and those with authority will exploit the information, make decisions, and take effective actions.

SAROL is highly dynamic as relationships and information change over time and can rapidly react to situations. The above three phases are executed multiple times by several processes. For example, during a follow-on cycle, new relationships and information that is, say, political in nature could be discovered, modeled, integrated, and exploited. Figure 28.6 illustrates the various modules that will implement SAROL. The glue consists of the temporal geosocial service oriented architecture (TGS-SOA) that supports web services and utilizes TGS-SWs. The high-level web services include social networking, geospatial information management, incentive management, and federation management.

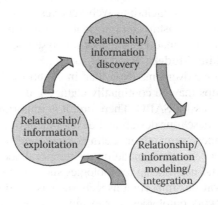

FIGURE 28.5   SAROL.

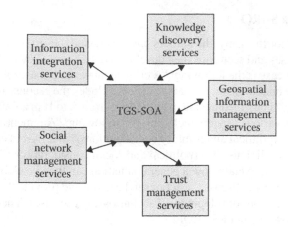

FIGURE 28.6 Web services for SOA.

28.4.4 TGS-SOA

Our architecture is based on services, and we will design and prototype a TGS-SOA for managing the SAROL. Our TGS-SOA will utilize TGS-SW technologies. Through this infrastructure, information and relationships will be made visible, accessible, and understandable to any authorized DoD commanders, allied forces, and external partners. As discussed by Karen Guttieri, it is important that the partners have a common operational picture, common information picture, and common relationship picture. On the basis of the use cases scenarios, we will capture the various relationships, extract additional relationships, and also locate the individuals in the various networks. This will involve designing the various services such as geospatial integration services and social network management services as illustrated in Figure 28.6. The glue that connects these services is based on the SOA paradigm. However, such an architecture should support temporal geosocial relationships. We call such an architecture a TGS-SOA.

It is important that our system captures the semantics of information and relationships. Therefore, we are developing semantic web technologies for representing, managing, and deducing temporal geosocial relationships. Our current work in geospatial information management and social networks is exploring the use of friend of a friend (FOAF), GRDF, and social network RDF (SNRDF). Therefore, we will incorporate the temporal element into these representations and subsequently develop appropriate representation schemes based on RDF and Web Ontology Language (OWL). We call such a semantic web the TGS-SW (Figure 28.7). We are using commercial tools and standards as much as possible in our work including Web Services Description Language (WSDL) and SPARQL. Capturing temporal relationship and information, for example, evolving spatial relationships and changes to geospatial information, is key for our systems.

Temporal Social Networking Models. Temporal social networks model, represent, and reason about social networks that evolve over time. Note that in countries like Iraq and Afghanistan, the social and political relationships may be continually changing due to security, power, and jobs—the three ingredients for a successful SARO. Therefore, it is important to capture the evolution of the relationships. In the first phase, our design and development of temporal social networks will focus on two major topics, namely, semantic modeling of temporal social networks and fundamental social network analysis. For semantic modeling of temporal social networks, we will extend the existing semantic web social networking technologies such as the FOAF ontology (http://www.foaf-project.org/) to include various important aspects such as relationship history that is not represented in current social network ontologies. For example, we will include features to model the strength and trust of relationships among individuals based on the frequency and the context of the relationship. In addition, we will include features to model relationship history (e.g., when the

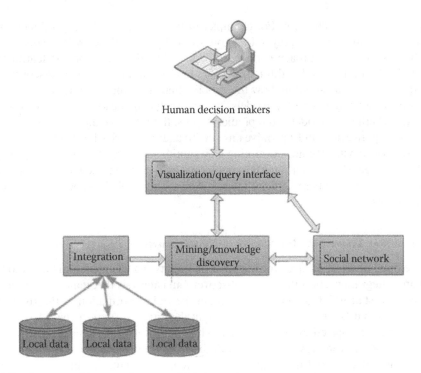

Human decision makers

FIGURE 28.7 System architecture for geosocial information management.

relationship has started and how the relationship has evolved over time) and the relationship roles (e.g., in the leader/follower relationship, there is one individual playing the role of the leader and one individual playing to role of the follower). In essence, by this modeling, we intend to create an advance version of social network such as Facebook specifically designed for SARO objectives. Note that there are XML-based languages for representing social network data (SNML) and temporal data (TML). However, we need a semantic language based on RDF and OWL for representing semantic relationships between the various individuals. We are exploring RDF for representing social relationships (SNRDF and extended FOAF). Representing temporal relationships (*when*) is an area that needs investigation for RDF and OWL-based social networks.

We are using social network analysis to identify important properties about the underlying network to address some of the who, what, when, where, and why (5Ws) and how (1H) queries. To address queries for determining who to communicate with, we plan to use various centrality measures, such as degree centrality and betweenness centrality (Newman, 2003), to measure the importance of a certain individuals in a given social network. On the basis of such measures that are developed for social network analysis, we can test which of the centrality measures could be more appropriate in finding influential individuals in social networks. Especially, we will test these measures on available social networks such as Facebook (it is possible to download information about individuals in your own network on Facebook). For example, if a centrality measure is a good indicator, than we may expect individuals with high centrality value to have more posts on their walls on Facebook or tagged in more pictures.

To answer the queries for determining what information is needed, we are examining the use of relational naïve Bayes models to predict which attributes of the individual are more reliable indicators for predicting their friendliness to the military. Since we do not have any open data on such military data, we are using Facebook data to predict attributes that are more important indicators for an individual's political affiliation to test our relational naïve Bayes models. To address queries for determining when to approach them, we are using various domain knowledge rules to first address when not to approach them. For example, in Iraq, it may not be a good idea to approach Muslim individuals during Friday prayer. Later on, we will try to build knowledge discovery models to predict the best times to approach certain individuals based on their profile features (i.e., their religion, social affiliation, etc.). In addition, we plan to use similar knowledge discovery models to answer the queries for understanding how those individuals may interact with the military personnel. To test our knowledge discovery models, we are analyzing various e-mail logs of our group members to see whether our model could predict the best times to send an e-mail to an individual to get the shortest response time and a positive answer. To address queries for determining why certain individuals' support is vital, we are examining community structure mining techniques, especially cluster analysis, to see which group a certain individual belongs to and how the homophily between individuals in the group affects the link structures. Again, Facebook data could be used to test some of these hypotheses.

28.4.5 TEMPORAL GEOSPATIAL INFORMATION MANAGEMENT

We have developed novel techniques for information quality management and validation, information search and integration, and information discovery and analysis that make "information a force multiplier through sharing." Our objective is to get the right information at the right time to the decision maker so that he or she can make the right decisions to support the SARO in the midst of uncertain and unanticipated events. Note that while our prior work focused mainly on information sharing of structured and text data, our work discussed in this chapter is focused on managing and sharing temporal geosocial information. The system architecture is illustrated in Figure 28.7. It shows how the various geospatial information management components are integrated with the social networking components.

Information Management and Search. Our system, like most other current data and information systems, collects and stored huge amounts of data and information. Such a system is usually distributed across multiple locations and is heterogeneous in data/storage structures and contents. It is crucial to organize data and information systematically and build infrastructures for efficient, intelligent, secure, and reliable access, while maintaining the benefits of autonomy and flexibility of distribution. Although such a system is building on top of database system and web information system technology, it is still necessary to investigate several crucial issues to ensure our system has high scalability, efficiency, fast or real-time response, and high quality and relevance of the answers in response to users' queries and requests, as well as high reliability and security. We are exploring ways to develop, test, and refine new methods for effective and reliable information management and search. In particular, the following issues are being explored: (i) data and information indexing, clustering, and organizing in a structured way to facilitate not only efficient but also trustable search and analysis; (ii) relevance analysis to ensure the return of highly relevant and ranked answers; and (iii) aggregation and summary over a time window. For example, a user may like to ask some information that may involve weapons and insurgents of a particular location over a particular time frame. Our design and prototype of the police blotter system is being leveraged for the SARO system.

Information Integration. We are examining *scalable* integration techniques for handling heterogeneous geosocial data utilizing our techniques on ontology matching and aligning. Moreover, to ensure that data/information from multiple heterogeneous sources can be integrated smoothly, we are exploring data/information conversion and transformation rules, and identifying redundancy and inconsistency. In our recent research on geospatial information integration, we have developed knowledge discovery methods that resolve semantic disparities among distinct ontologies by considering instance alignment techniques (Khan et al., 2007). Each ontological concept is associated with a set of instances, and using these, one concept from each ontology is compared for similarity. We examine the instance values of each concept and apply a widely popular matching strategy utilizing *n*-grams present in the data. However, this method often fails because it relies on shared syntactical data to determine semantic similarity. Our approach resolves these issues by leveraging *K*-medoid clustering and a semantic distance measure applied to distinct keywords gleaned from the instances, resulting in distinct semantic clusters. We claim that our algorithm outperforms *n*-gram matching over large classes of data. We have justified this with a series of experimental results that demonstrate the efficacy of our algorithm on highly variable data. We are exploiting not only instance matching but also name and structural matching in our project for geosocial data that evolves over time.

Information Analysis and Knowledge Discovery. The tools we have developed for information analysis and knowledge discovery are being exploited for the SARO system (Khan et al., 2007). Some of the challenges include applying information warehousing, mining and knowledge discovery to distributed information sources to extract summary/aggregate information, as well as the frequency, discrimination, and correlation measures, in multidimensional space for items and item sets. Note that the 5Ws and 1H (who, what, why, when, where, and how) are important for SARO. For example, "When to approach them" might be used where a need exists to meet with road construction crews in an area that has experienced sporadic ethnic violence mostly during specific times in the day. For example, "find all times in a given day along major roads in Baghdad less than 10 miles from Diyala Governorate where violent activity has not occurred in at least 2 years." We are extending our geospatial and social network analysis techniques to address such questions.

Our focus is on the following aspects: (i) scalable algorithms that can handle large volumes of geosocial information (information management and search) to facilitate who, where, and when issues; (ii) information integration analysis algorithms to address where and who issues; and (iii) knowledge discovery techniques that can address why and how issues.

28.4.6 TEMPORAL GEOSOCIAL SEMANTIC WEB

We are integrating our work on modeling and reasoning about geospatial information with social networking. First, we are utilizing concepts from Social Network Markup Language (SNML), Geospatial Markup Language (GML), and Temporal Markup Language (TML). However, to capture the semantics and make meaningful inferences, we need something beyond syntactic representation. As we have stated, we have developed GRDF (geospatial RDF) that basically integrates RDF and GML. One approach is to integrate SNRDF (social network RDF that we are examining) with GRDF and also incorporate the temporal element. Another option is to make extensions to FOAF to represent temporal geosocial information.

Next, we are integrating geosocial information across multiple sites so that the commanders and allied forces as well as partners in the local communities can form a common picture. We have developed tools for integrated social relationships as well as geospatial data using ontology matching and alignment. However, we are exploring ways of extending our tools to handle possibly heterogeneous geosocial data in databases across multiple sites.

We are also exploring appropriate query languages to query geosocial data. There are query languages such as SPARQL and RQL being developed for RDF databases. We have adapted SPARQL to query geospatial databases. We are also exploring query languages for social network data. Query languages for temporal databases have been developed. Therefore, our challenge in this subtask is to determine the constructs that are needed to extend languages like SPARQL to query geosocial data across multiple sites.

It is also crucial to reason about the information and relationships to extract useful nuggets. Here, we are developing ontologies for temporal geospatial information. We have developed ontologies and reasoning tools for geospatial data and social network relationships based on OWL and OWL-S. We are incorporating social relationships and temporal data and reason about the data to uncover

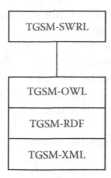

FIGURE 28.8 Temporal geosocial mobile semantic web.

new information. For example, if some event occurs at a particular time at a particular location for two consecutive days in a row and involves the same group of people, then it will likely occur on the third day at the same time and same location involving the same group of people. We can go on to explore why such an event has occurred. Perhaps this group of people belongs to a cult and has to carry out activities in such a manner. Therefore, we are developing reasoning tools for geosocial data and relationships.

28.4.7 INTEGRATION OF MOBILE TECHNOLOGIES

Our goal is to extend the TGS-SW to TGSM-SW by incorporating a mobile web. Today, there are billions of users of mobile technologies such as iPhone, Android, and iPad among others. These users will access the TGM-SW via their mobile devices. Therefore, the TGS-SW needs to provide support for such integration. We call such a TGS-SW as TGSM-SW.

Recently, there was been work on developing mobile semantic webs. In fact, a tutorial on such technologies was presented at a recent WWW conference (Tutorial on Mobile Semantic Web, 2014). Furthermore, XML and RDF are being adapted for mobile devices. We need to integrate such a mobile semantic web into TGS-SW to result in TGSM-SW. This is illustrated in Figure 28.8.

28.5 SUMMARY AND DIRECTIONS

This chapter has described the challenges for developing a system for SARO. In particular, we are designing a temporal geospatial social semantic web that can be utilized by military personnel, decision makers, and local/government personnel to reconstruct after a major combat operation. We essentially develop a life cycle for SARO. We will utilize the technologies we have developed including geospatial semantic web and social network system, as well as build new technologies to develop SAROL. We believe that this is the first attempt to build such a system for SARO.

There are several areas that need to be included in our research. One is security and privacy. We need to develop appropriate policies for SAROL. These policies may include confidentiality policies, privacy policies, and trust policies. Only certain geospatial as well as social relationships may be visible to certain parties. Furthermore, the privacy of the individuals involved has to be protected. Different parties may place different levels of trust on each other. We believe that building a TGSM-SW is a challenge. Furthermore, incorporating security will make it even more complex. Nevertheless, security has to be considered at the beginning of the design and not as an afterthought. Our future work will also include handling dynamic situations where some parties may be trustworthy at one time and may be less trustworthy at another time. We believe that the approach we have stated is just the beginning to building a successful system for SARO.

REFERENCES

Ashraful, A. et al. GRDF and secure GRDF. In: *IEEE ICDE Workshop on Secure Semantic Web*, Cancun Mexico, April 2008. Version also appeared in *Computer Standards and Interfaces Journal: Geospatial Resource Description Framework (GRDF) and Security Constructs* 33: 35–41, 2011.

Berg, N. Normative behavioral economics. *Journal of Socio-Economics* 32: 411–423, 2003.

Berg, N. A simple Bayesian procedure for sample size determination in an audit of property value appraisals. *Real Estate Economics* 34(1): 133–155, 2006.

Binnendjik, H. and Johnson, S. *Transformation for Stabilization and Reconstruction Operations*. Center for Technology and National Security Policy, NDU Press, Washington, DC, 2004.

Chait, R., Sciarretta, A., and Shorts, D. *Army Science and Technology Analysis for Stabilization and Reconstruction Operations*. Center for Technology and National Security Policy, NDU Press, Washington, DC, 2006.

Chait, R., Sciarretta, A., Lyons, J., Barry, C., Shorts, D., and Long, D. *A Further Look at Technologies and Capabilities for Stabilization and Reconstruction Operations*. Center for Technology and National Security Policy, NDU Press, Washington, DC, 2007.

Chittumala, P. et al. Emergency response system to handle chemical spills. *IEEE Internet Computing*, November 2007.

Dai, B.T., Koudas, N., Srivastava, D., Tung, A.K.H., and Venkatasubramanian, S. Validating multi-column schema matchings by type. In: *24th International Conference on Data Engineering (ICDE)*, pp. 120–129, 2008.

Doan, A.H., Madhavan, J., Domingos, P., and Halevy, A.Y. Ontology matching: A machine learning approach. *Handbook on Ontologies*, pp. 385–404, 2004.

Doan, A. and Halevy, A. Semantic integration research in the database community: A brief survey. *AI Magazine*, Special Issue on Semantic Integration, Spring 2005.

Ehrig, M., Staab, S., and Sure, Y. Bootstrapping ontology alignment methods with APFEL. In: Gil, Y., Motta, E., Benjamins, V.R., and Musen, M.A. In: *Proceedings of the 4th International Semantic Web Conference, ISWC 2005*, Galway, Ireland, November 6–10, 2005, vol. 3729 of LNCS, pp. 186–200. Springer, Berlin, 2005.

Gigerenzer, G. and Todd, P.M. *Simple Heuristics That Make Us Smart*. Oxford University Press, New York, 1999.

Government Accountability Office. GAO report. Stabilization and reconstruction actions needed to improve governmentwide planning and capabilities for Future Operations Statement of Joseph A. Christoff, Director International Affairs and Trade, and Janet A. St. Laurent, Director Defense Capabilities and Management, October 2007.

Grimes, J. DoD Information Sharing Strategy, 2007.

Guttieri, K. Integrated education and training workshop. Peacekeeping and Stability Operations Institute, Naval Postgraduate School, September 2007a.

Guttieri, K. Stability, security, transition reconstruction: Transformation for peace. Quarterly Meeting of Transformation Chairs, Naval Postgraduate School, February, 2007b.

Jiang, W., Clifton, C., and Kantarcioglu, M. Transforming semi-honest protocols to ensure accountability. *Data and Knowledge Engineering (DKE)* 65: 57–74, 2008.

Kalfoglou, Y. and Schorlemmer, M. IF-Map: An ontology mapping method based on information flow theory. *Journal on Data Semantics* 1(1): 98–127, 2003.

Khan, L., McLeod, D., and Hovy, E.H. Retrieval effectiveness of an ontology-based model for information selection. *VLDB Journal* 13(1): 71–85, 2004.

Khan, L. et al. Geospatial data mining for national security. In: *Proceedings Intelligence and Security Conference*, New Brunswick, NJ, May 2007.

Laffont, J. and Martimort, D. *The Theory of Incentives: The Principal-Agent Model*. Princeton University Press, Princeton, NJ, 2001.

Madhavan, J., Bernstein, P., Doan, A., and Halevy, A. Corpus-based schema matching. In: *Proceedings of the International Conference on Data Engineering (ICDE 2005)*, Tokyo, Japan, 2005.

Newman E.J. The structure and function of complex networks, arXiv. Available at http://arxiv.org/abs/cond-mat /0303516v1, 2003.

Noy, N.F. and Musen, M.A. The PROMPT suite: Interactive tools for ontology merging and mapping. *International Journal of Human–Computer Studies* 59(6): 983–1024, 2003.

Osborne, M. and Rubinstein, A. *A Course in Game Theory*. MIT Press, Cambridge, MA, 1994.

Rahm, E. and Bernstein, P.A. A survey of approaches to automatic schema matching. *The VLDB Journal* 10(4): 334–350, 2001.

Santos, E.E. Computational modeling: Culturally-infused social networks. In: *Office of Naval Research (ONR) Workshop on Social, Cultural, and Computational Science, and the DoD Workshop on New Mission Areas: Peace Operations, Security, Stabilization, and Reconstruction*, Arlington, VA, 2007.

Stumme, G. and Maedche, A. FCA-merge: Bottom-up merging of ontologies. In: *7th Intl. Conf. on Artificial Intelligence (IJCAI '01)*, pp. 225–230, Seattle, WA, 2001.

Subbiah, G. DAGIS system. MS Thesis, The University of Texas at Dallas, 2007.

Thuraisingham, B. Geospatial data management research at the University of Texas at Dallas, presented at OGC Meeting for University Members and OGC Interoperability Day, Tysons Corner, VA, October 2006.

Tutorial on Mobile Semantic Web, WWW Conference, Seoul, Korea, 2014.

29 Social Media and Bioterrorism

29.1 INTRODUCTION

The threat of bioterrorism has remained at the forefront of disaster preparation for countries such as the United States in the wake of the events of 2001 (Shadel et al., 2003). Unlike other threats such as direct physical attacks, a biological weapon can be effective far beyond the initial target; the very nature of a biological agent makes it possible for a relatively small attack to have far-reaching consequences on an entire population. To date, no known intentional attack has spread beyond the original initial target.

However, the lack of full-scale incidents of biological warfare in recent world history has created a difficult situation for those attempting to prepare for an epidemic. Several isolated incidents involving potential weapons, such as the SARS (severe acute respiratory syndrome) outbreak in Canada (Booth et al., 2003), provide glimpses into how a situation might unfold. Rigorous study of diseases and agents that could be used is undeniably helpful; however, the need for data remains. The only safe means by which this data can be provided is through the use of epidemiological simulations.

A variety of simulations have already been created to model the spread of contagious disease and infection. BioWar is an agent-based model based on a variety of factors that simulate a number of infectious diseases at the lowest level possible (Carley et al., 2006). People are represented individually in such a way that travel, human contact, and even physical location are all considered. EpiSimS is a product of research efforts at Los Alamos National Laboratory (Eubank et al., 2004) designed to model epidemics at a similar level of detail, with a greater focus on the demographic a person belongs to, their location, and activities. Some of this information is taken directly from a small public survey aimed at gathering information about an individual's daily routine, while the transportation data is derived from TransSims. Users of the model include Eubank (2005), whose work suggests that epidemics can be contained with simple vaccination policies targeted at major convergent components of the network.

Complexity is not without cost. Each level of detail adds both a need for more storage and computational resources on a system. EpiSimS requires high-performance computing resources to run a simulation within a reasonable amount of time (Bonnett, 2009). More important, if a model is designed to address a certain level of realism, the appropriate data must be available to take advantage of it. For example, a model that considers a large population's daily hygiene would be difficult to justify without an appropriate cross section of surveyed data of the region in question.

A far simpler approach for simulating epidemics is the SIR (susceptible, infected, and recovered) model. This compartmental mathematical approach is based on probabilistic transitions over the passage of time. It is considered one of the most widely used models in epidemiology (Moghadas, 2006). Individuals are modeled by assigning them to one of three states: susceptible, infected, and recovered. A susceptible individual is considered one who can be infected. They have no natural or artificial immunity to the contagion. An infected individual is considered stricken with a disease and contagious to those that are susceptible. Eventually, an infected person will no longer be contagious by transitioning to *recovered*, either by successfully overcoming the disease and acquiring immunity, or dying. The transitions are based on three factors: the probability of contact between susceptible and infected groups, the rate of infection, and the rate of recovery. Any considerations of intervention or exception must be captured through these rates.

Although popular, the SIR model falls short in several key areas. First, all participants are considered identical in terms of susceptibility. Someone who interacts with a variety of individuals on

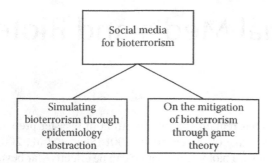

FIGURE 29.1   Social media and bioterrorism.

a daily basis is considered just as susceptible as someone who does not interact at all. Second, the area being simulated is completely homogeneous. There are no concepts in the model of locations, transportation, or variance in rates. Finally, the model requires a broad generalization of infection rates and the percentage of a population. Complex dynamic or dependent factors simply cannot be accounted for without collapsing them into a single dimension.

In this chapter, we discuss our approach to enhancing the SIR model through epidemiology approximation. Our model is based on social interactions. We have created a hybridized model that balances the simplicity of the original with an approximation of what more complex agent-based models already offer, with an emphasis on the exploration of large search spaces. Our experiments focus on more unconventional methods of intervention in the event of an epidemic, the results of which suggest that a much more basic approach can be taken beyond the thoroughly explored realm of inoculation strategies. We also briefly discuss the application of game theory to mitigate bioterrorism. Our approach is to create a Stackelberg game to evaluate all possibilities with respect to the investment of available resources and consider the resulting scenarios. The analysis of our experimental results yields the opportunity to place an upper bound on the worst-case scenario for a population center in the event of an attack, with consideration of defensive and offensive measures. The organization of this chapter is as follows. We discuss our model based on epidemiology approximation in Section 29.2. Applying game theory to mitigate a bioterrorism attack is discussed in Section 29.3. The chapter is concluded in Section 29.4. Figure 29.1 illustrates the concepts discussed in this chapter.

29.2   SIMULATING BIOTERRORISM THROUGH EPIDEMIOLOGY ABSTRACTION

29.2.1   OUR APPROACH

Several branches of research have already taken advantage of the foundations provided by the SIR model by altering it for a more realistic simulation. Moshe Kress of the Naval Operations Research Department (Kress, 2005) abstracted the equations and applied it to the spread of smallpox through an urban population of 6 million. A host of states were introduced to reflect infectious conditions associated with the life cycle of the disease. The social network was constructed across a population of several million, though the household size was fixed and the members of which could visit any gathering area with equal probability. The author asserts that this is a basic generalization founded upon the small-world property of most real-life networks. Satuma et al. (2004) considered the more complex functionality attached to state transitions in both continuous and discrete forms of the model while retaining all of the SIR model's most desirable qualities. The work of Stattenspiel and Dietz (1995) applies the original model to deal with mobility among geographical regions to describe a measles epidemic in Dominica.

Our own model is a hybridization of social interactions on a household scale, situation intervention, and the simplicity of the SIR approach, and is illustrated in Figure 29.2. The system arose out

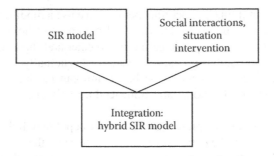

FIGURE 29.2 Hybrid SIR model.

of a need for a deterministic model that can balance a desire for accuracy in representing a potential scenario with computational resources and time. Recent work has suggested that more detailed models of social networks have a diminished role over the results in the spread of an epidemic (Fukś et al., 2006). We believe that we can generalize complex interactions into a much more concise simulation without adversely affecting accuracy. The ultimate goal of our research is to integrate a model for biological warfare with a system that can evaluate multiple attacks with respect to passive and active defenses. As a result, we have created a simulation that serves as an approximation of the impact of a biological attack with speed in mind, allowing us to explore a large search space in a relatively shorter amount of time as compared with existing detailed models.

The base component of the simulation is the home unit. A home can range in size from a single individual to a large household. Within this unit, the probable states of the individuals are tracked via a single vector of susceptibility, infection, and recovery. Given a population distribution of a region and basic statistical data, we can easily create a series of family units that represents the basic social components from a rural community to a major metropolitan area. A single home unit with no interaction is essentially a basic representation of the SIR model.

Interaction occurs within what we call social network theaters. A theater is essentially any gathering area at which two or more members of a home unit meet. The probability of interaction depends on the type of location and the social interaction possible at it. To capture this, separate infection rates are assignable to each theater.

In the event of a life-threatening scenario such as a bioterrorist attack, we assume a civil authority will act at some point to prevent a full-scale epidemic. We model such an entity by providing means in our models to affect social theaters and the probabilities associated with state transitions. For simplicity at this point, we will not consider resource constraints, nor will we model how an event is detected. The recognition of an attack will be simulated using a variable delay. After this delay has passed, the infection is officially recognized.

Several known types of options are available deal with an epidemic (Floyd et al., 2008; Shulgin et al., 1998; Stattenspiel and Herring, 2003). The most basic form of prevention is by inoculating the population against it. Several options exist at this level, ranging from key personnel to entire cities. Anyone inoculated is automatically considered recovered. Second, a quarantine strategy can be used to isolate the infected population from the susceptible population. This requires the explicit removal of individuals from home units to appropriate facilities, and can be simulated on a fractional basis (representing probability of removal) with varying levels of accuracy. Third, the infection and recovery rates can be altered, through such means as allocating more resources to medical personnel and educating the general public on means to avoid infection.

Finally, a potentially controversial but interesting option is the isolation of communities by temporarily eliminating social gathering areas. For example, public schools could be closed, or martial law could be declared. The motivating factor is finding ways to force the population at risk to remain at home. Such methods could reduce the number of vectors over which an infection could spread.

A day is represented by multiple distinct time periods. We use a modified form of the SIR model to represent the various contributions by the involved members of home units. We have broken down the contributions by both those participating in a theater and those at home during each segment. Individually, each home unit as previously mentioned is actually a self-contained SIR model representation. However, since members of the home unit can participate in social theaters, the calculations required to update the model are influenced directly and indirectly by the rest of the units in the simulation.

Our model includes functions to represent how many susceptible individuals have become infectious in a home unit due to social theaters. Every one of the theaters that an individual participates in must be considered. We also distinguish types of theaters across time. No participation means that the specified theater does not affect any result during a particular time. Next, we must also consider the individual infection rate for a theater. We assume that the infection rate starts out at some level of *normal*, uninhibited probability. However, at some point in time, there exists the possibility that a civil authority will step in and decrease this factor by bolstering public awareness, providing necessary information to hospitals to enhance treatment, etc. We represent this by adding a new function that can factor in both the custom rate and any modifiers we need, applying them at a predetermined time to represent detection and subsequent intervention. Our model also includes the probability that we will have a susceptible individual interact with an infected individual. We also determine the part of the household being affected. This is obtained by taking the susceptible population of the home unit and dividing it by the size of the home. Note that this does not entirely compartmentalize participants from each home unit and suggests that a single individual from the household is selected with equal probability to participate. We allow this to simplify the calculations necessary to avoid tracking each individual separately in a pure agent-based format. Finally, we consider whether or not the social theater is going to affect a household. We base this on three factors. The time of day determines which time segment the simulation is in and which theaters the home units are involved in. We also determine how many people, during the time segment, stayed home and participated in the home unit update model. Most of our calculations here are identical to those of the original SIR model. We calculate the probability that a susceptible person at home will become infected by those already carrying the contagion. However, we also must calculate the portion of the individual updated by considering the fraction not present. We thus determine the number of people not present, divide it by the total number of people in the home unit, and invert the percentage by subtracting it from 1. We also sum up this participation by type assigned to a given time period.

The calculations for recovery of infected individuals are much simpler. Regardless of theaters that they participate in, individuals recover at a uniform rate during the course of the simulation. We assume that it is possible for a civil authority to affect the base recovery rate. For example, a state can bolster the level of hospital care by bringing in doctors from other locations, providing emergency resources to the existing facilities. Other possibilities include direct emergency funding and simply making a medical examiner aware of what symptoms to look for. When no social theaters are considered in use, the simulation enters a *home* period. During this portion of the day, the members of the home units only interact internally. It is important to note the use of *fuzzy* states in the home units. The three population states are considered probabilities of the household's overall condition. For example, a susceptible size of 80% and an infection size of 20% mean that there is a one-in-five chance that a member of the household is sick. Note that a small attack can potentially infect the same size of a population as a larger attack when no intervention is present; there may simply be a smaller chance that each member of the population is infected. Note that within a unit, there is not necessarily a distinction in how many members are infected.

29.2.2 EXPERIMENTS

For our experiments, we wanted to have a variety of home units with a predictable set of sizes based on household statistics. Starting with a population of 10,000, we divided them into groups ranging from a single individual to a family of size 6. The biggest set was the three-person household. Exactly 5165 total households were generated from this pool of individuals and used consistently throughout all of our experiments.

The social theaters are generated by the population size that they will ultimately contain. The assignments themselves are divided on the basis of power law averages, used to generate random sizes. To keep these assignments consistent, we use a predetermined seed in an isolated random number generator for each distribution session. For work theaters, we have a maximum population of 5000 theaters randomly generated by power law from size 1 to 15^2. Education and recreation theaters are allocated 2000 people each, with maximum sizes of 900 and 25, respectively. These assignments give us 57 theaters for work, 144 theaters for recreation, and 3 theaters for education. We use this assignment throughout all of our experiments. Note that we can use specific assignments if needed for more accurate representations of populated theaters. We do not consider high-traffic transportation hubs such as airports; not all cities have them, and our simulated city comprised only 10,000 people. Adding in these locations in future work can be done by simply adding a large theater.

We divide the day into three 8-hour segments. The first segment represents participation in both the job market and education. Bioterrorist attacks would be most effective here because of a high transitory population. Those that have a job go to their workspace and interact with coworkers. The infection rate at a business is only 80% of the baseline, owing to the formal interaction and greater possible isolation during the time period. However, other household members may instead attend an educational institution. Here, the levels vary based on age groups, but the general proximity of people to each other is far greater due to enclosed classroom environments. To represent this, the infection rate is 10% greater than the baseline.

Next, in the second segment, we have recreational pursuits. Fewer people are involved while interaction is less formal. We assert that such groups would typically be much smaller than those found during the previous segment. The resulting infection rate is estimated at 90% of the baseline. Finally, we end with a simulation of the household, representing a normal sleep cycle and estimated home visitation pattern.

We explored several factors in our models across a spectrum of infection and recovery rates to determine some of the most effective ways of dealing with outbreaks of infectious disease. To consider this, we experimented with the shutting down of social network theaters with varying degrees of severity. In theory, if any given theater is no longer in play, we essentially remove its node and corresponding links from the social network. When this shutdown occurs is dependent on when the attack is either announced by the responsible party or the civil authorities are aware of the situation. Detection is outside of the scope of this research. To simplify this, we experiment with specific dates on which the shutdown occurs. In all of our experiments, we simulated a hypothetical contagion during the course of 40 days. We set our base infection rate to 60% and our recovery rate to 25%. Our goal is to represent a relatively aggressive infection that takes a minimum of several days to recover from. The initial infection is of a single person in the same household each time.

We first wanted to establish the relevancy of our work to the existing body of research in the SIR model. To establish this, we compared the original model to our own and attempted to find correlation between them. We found that the characteristics of the infection rate were virtually identical with some adjustments to reflect the average infection rate across different theaters. For example, a traditional model with an infection rate of 72.5% and a recovery rate of 33% acted similarly to our own model under our default setup. However, the matches were not perfect. Regardless of the total number of infections and the nature of the peak infection, the family is the most susceptible to the spread of a contagion, owing to both close physical proximity and deeper levels of interaction. The infection rate used during this period is the strict baseline rate established throughout the simulation.

At any point, if a person is not participating in one of the theaters in the first two segments, they are assumed to be at home. Those remaining in the home unit are calculated the same way as during the first segment, although the effects are reduced on the basis of the number of people present. This reflects parts of the population that either do not work or prefer to remain at home during the evening. When assigning parts of the population to social theaters, we enforce a few rules of assignment. We limit membership to one theater per individual per segment. Multiple members of a household can participate in the same theater, and one individual can participate in multiple theaters on different segments. However, we do not model those that hold multiple jobs. We also do not model those with jobs at night or other parts of the day; jobs and educational participation is limited to the second 8-hour segment. This difference was traced back to how our model requires a lead time for the infection to spread across the social network from the initial point of contact, versus the original model, which stated that the infection could potentially reach anyone in the city on day 1. The results showed that the impact of the epidemic can be substantially reduced through the closing down of social theaters even with a significant delay. Analysis shows that shutting down any kind of social theater yielded a net loss to the total number of individuals infected over time. Shutting down all public education buildings reduced the tally by a minimum of 8% as late as day 7 after the attack. When businesses were asked to close, the results showed a 19.5% reduction of infection totals under total cooperation.

In reality, however, there is no guarantee of cooperation when shutting down social gathering areas of any kind beyond public institutions. We next experimented with requests to shut down of varying efficiency, ranging from one out of every five organizations complying with the request to complete cooperation. Our results suggest that the degree of compliance is directly proportional to the effectiveness of the request. For example, a request to close all educational and work theaters on the third day has a 60% compliance rate. In this scenario, 4640 are infected; without any intervention, the normal result would have been 5367. This translates into a 13.5% improvement. However, at 100% compliance, only 3769 people would become sick, a more efficient 29.8% reduction.

Alteration of the recovery rates in our model unsurprisingly assisted in reducing the total number of infections. However, the effect was negligible below a particular threshold. When the recovery rate was increased by 10% and the infection rate was reduced by the same amount, the modification reduced the number of infected individuals to 4549, a 20% decrease for any time period between initial release and day 9. However, beyond that point, there is a dramatic increase in infection counts up to day 15, after which the total is identical to no intervention at all. This essentially translates into a 2-week window for any alterations to existing rates. Looking at these rates individually in our experiments, it is clear that prohibiting the spread of infection will benefit more than enhancing recovery.

For an overall analysis of the techniques we have considered, we ran a comprehensive battery of experiments across several days. If the epidemic can be detected early, the single most effective technique is closing work with 80% compliance in terms of the peak severity of the epidemic as well as a 15.1% reduction in the total number of infections. However, adjustment of the infection and recovery rates offered the greatest reduction in infections, reducing the total by 16.4%. Across a range of days on which these combinations of interventions occur, we find that the benefits are fairly consistent. However, as the delay between the introduction of the contagion and its detection increases, the differences among these options begin to shrink. Intervention on the third day can be up to a 48.6% decrease in the number of infections when using all of the methods available. However, beyond day 13, we found that the overall benefits were only a marginal variance among all combinations of options.

We analyzed a worse-case-scenario epidemic with the same infection rate but a recovery rate of only 5%, representing a contagion that was much more difficult to treat. Under these conditions, even a combination of 80% compliance in the closing of both work and school theaters, a 10% boost to recovery rates, and a 10% reduction of infection rates as early as day 3 reduced the total number of infections by only 7.5%. When dealing with these scenarios, even aggressive policies on civil intervention would make very little difference to the outcome.

29.3   ON THE MITIGATION OF BIOTERRORISM THROUGH GAME THEORY

In the wake of the frequently tragic aftermath of an act of terrorism, one of the first questions much of the afflicted population will ask is, *why*. Namely, it is puzzling for many as to what would motivate an individual or group to resort to acts of terrorism carried out on a civilian (Borum, 2004). This is clearly a difficult question to answer, one that is rife with considerations of ideologies, the value of human life, and what constitutes acceptable behavior amidst conflicting beliefs. Such an answer is vital to understanding and predicting biological attacks.

Securing a population against a bioterrorism event is clearly an important goal. However, there is frequently a schism between the need for protection and available resources. As precious as human life is in the eyes of many, the challenge of limited resources must be weighed with regard to both present and future challenges. The goal of our work is to answer a considerably difficult question that is naturally derived from these constraints: Is it possible to maximize the use of existing resources to minimize the impact of a biological attack in the *worst-case* scenario?

Assuming that the goal of a terrorist organization is to maximize casualties, and the goal of the local government of the targets is to minimize them, it becomes possible to realize the scenario as a perilous game between two opponents. Game theory is an approach to strategy and mathematics that is rooted in the assumption that two or more rational players wish to maximize their overall utility in light of their opponents' choices (Myerson, 1997). Through game theory, it becomes possible to effectively consider all options with regard to the costs and benefits involved.

The work of Banks and Anderson (2006) directly applies game theory to a simulated epidemic of smallpox within the United States due to bioterrorism. The uncertainty regarding perceived values by an opponent are considered and mitigated via Monte Carlo methods. This particular work is perhaps the closest one to our own, although our approach via Stackelberg games and the customized epidemic modeling provide an important distinction. We create a Stackelberg game to evaluate all possibilities with respect to the investment of available resources and consider the resulting scenarios. A Stackelberg game is one in which two players, a leader and a follower, attempt to maximize their own utility in light of disparate knowledge. The leader goes first, choosing a strategy first from available options. The second player, the follower, then picks his or her own strategy with perfect knowledge of what the leader has chosen. The leader, however, does not know any more than the strategies available to the follower, and as such, must attempt to make a decision that maximizes their own utility in light of what the follower wants.

Thus, the leader must choose the most profitable strategy while understanding that the follower will choose their own. The strategies available to either player are determined by our experiments via the choice function, which, given a particular parameter, generates the strategies available. The defender must choose from a set of strategies that contain the number of random inoculations, what type of intervention will be administered, and what type of closings will be performed when. The attacker's strategy set is composed of what to attack and how large of an attack to carry out. The utility function for the defender determines how the outcome of the simulated epidemic will be perceived. The simplest approach to this would be counting the number of casualties that result. However, the function can also be based on real-world data, providing an estimated currency-driven value on which to consider both the investment needed for the defensive choices made as well as the casualty count. An attacker's utility was difficult to determine, as our research did not uncover reliable statistics on the costs to a terrorist organization. We instead used the number of people infected during the attack.

Gauging the results of choices in a game remains one of the most crucial aspects of a realistic scenario. Since this area is subject to speculation and inherently involves philosophical debate on the topic, we will focus our concerns primarily on the financial impact of an attack amidst varying considerations of cost to both players. Ideally, we wish to find a defense strategy that provides a reasonable and theoretically guaranteed upper bound to the impact of an actual attack. This suggests that we should seek a dominant strategy within our game, which, in this instance, is simply a strategy choice made by the leader that minimizes the maximum damage done by the follower's moves (Osborne and Rubinstein, 1994). Since there are so many factors involved, it is possible that we may find several different equilibrium-spanning scenarios.

Details of our approach together with the experimental results are discussed in Layfield et al. (2008, 2009). We simulated cities, individuals, and theaters, as well as the spread of smallpox and inoculations. Throughout all experiments, it became clear that inoculations are a highly effective and relatively low-cost way of fighting a biological attack. However, an actual attack would likely run the risk of alarming more than just one city. Unless the governing body has the power to fix the cost of the vaccine, there is a high probability that a free market will continue to drive up prices as not only governing bodies attempt to protect the population but concerned individuals as well. Additionally, inoculation is done under the assumption that there is a warning far enough in advance either directly or through intelligence gathering that indicates which contagion will be used. Normally, a single vaccine may require months to prepare in order to deal with a *weaponized* or exotic strain, and it can take days for the benefits of a vaccination to fully develop in a patient (Center for Disease Control, 2007). Even then, there is no guarantee of effectiveness.

29.4 SUMMARY AND DIRECTIONS

With respect to simulating bioterrorism with epidemiology approximations, although the quarantine method could be considered controversial under certain political ideologies, our results demonstrate that they are potentially highly effective. In a democratic country such as the United States, the protection of civil liberties has often been at odds with the need for greater security. However, regardless of public opinion, these options should not be eliminated. In fact, in instances where inoculation is not a viable option, quarantine efforts may be the only way to ensure that the epidemic does not spread any farther.

However, as these studies also suggest, all of the methods will only be effective if used within a reasonable amount of time from the original infection. Once the infection has spread beyond a particular threshold, the effort taken to act may be wasted. We conclude then that there must be particular emphasis in the field of bioterrorism research to analyze and improve detection methods. Likewise, there must also be a rudimentary communication structure in place that brings any possibility of an epidemic to the attention of the appropriate civil authorities as quickly as possible.

We have several improvements planned already on the model itself. One goal is to further refine the transitions between segments by allowing for a finer-grained consideration of time. We want to capture a larger spectrum of activities through social theaters to enhance accuracy and provide more possible levels of detail within the model, including probabilistic choice of activities. Another improvement planned is to arrange the home units themselves as social network theaters, allowing us to model individuals independently. This potentially would allow us to approach the accuracy of an agent-based model population without significantly increasing complexity or resource requirements. The biggest obstacle we face in implementing these enhancements is the impact on performance.

The ultimate goal of our work is to use this model in conjunction with a cost–benefit analysis model to optimize defensive strategies. There are several possible attack vectors in a given location. Our data suggests that optimal attacks will differ based on strategies to mitigate the effects of a bioterrorist attack already in place. Thus, we believe that a model that provides a cost-effective use of computational resources to search a large space of possibilities will allow us to better understand a means of ensuring that any attack does not succeed.

REFERENCES

Banks, D. and Anderson, S. Game theory and risk analysis in the context of the smallpox threat. In: *Statistical Methods in Counterterrorism* (A. Wilson, G. Wilson and D. Olwell, eds), Springer, New York, pp. 9–22, 2006.

Bonnett, J. High performance computing: An agenda for the social sciences and the humanities in Canada. *Digital Studies* 1(2), 2009. Available at http://www.digitalstudies.org/ojs/index.php/digital_studies /article/view/168/211.

Booth, C., Matuka, L., Tomlinson, G., Rachlis, A.R., Rose, D.B., Dwosh, H.A., Walmsley, S.L. et al. Clinical features and short-term outcomes of 144 patients with SARS in the greater Toronto area. *Journal of the American Medical Association* 289(21), 2003.

Borum, R. *Psychology of Terrorism*. University of South Florida, Mental Health Law & Policy Faculty Publications, Tampa, FL, 2004.

Carley, K., Fridsma, D., Casman, E., Yahja, A., Altman, N., Chen, L., Kaminsky, B., and Nave, D. BioWar: Scalable agent-based model of bioattacks. *Transactions on Systems, Man and Cybernetics, Part A* 36(2): 252–265, 2006.

Centers for Disease Control. Smallpox fact sheet: Vaccine overview. Centers for Disease Control. [Online] February 7, 2007. Available at http://www.bt.cdc.gov/agent/smallpox/vaccination/facts.asp, 2007.

Eubank, S. Network based models of infectious disease spread. *Japan Journal of Infectious Diseases* 58(6): 9–13, 2005.

Eubank, S., Guclu, H., Kumar, V., Marathe, M., Srinivasan, A., Toroczkai, Z., and Wang, N. Modeling disease outbreaks in realistic urban social networks. *Nature* 429: 180–184, 2004.

Floyd, W., Kay, L., and Shapiro, M. Some elementary properties of social networks. *Bulletin of Mathematical Biology* 70(3): 713–727, 2008.

Fukś, H., Lawniczak, A., and Duchesne, R. Effects of population mixing on the spread of SIR epidemics. *European Physical Journal B* 50: 209–214, 2006.

Kress, M. The effect of social mixing controls on the spread of smallpox—A two-level model. *Health Care Management Science* 8: 277–289, 2005.

Layfield, R., Kantarcioglu, M., and Thuraisingham, B. Simulating bioterrorism through epidemiology approximation. In: *IEEE International Conference on Intelligence and Security Informatics, 2008 (ISI 2008)*, June 17–20, pp. 82–87, 2008.

Layfield, R., Kantarcioglu, M., and Thuraisingham, B. On the mitigation of bioterrorism through game theory. In: *IEEE International Conference on Intelligence and Security Informatics, 2009 (ISI 2009)*, June 8–11, pp. 1–6, 2009.

Moghadas, S. Gaining insights into human viral diseases through mathematics. *European Journal of Epidemiology* 21: 337–342, 2006.

Myerson, R.B. *Game Theory: Analysis of Conflict*. Harvard University Press, Cambridge, MA, 1997.

Osborne, M. and Rubinstein, A. *A Course in Game Theory*. MIT Press, Cambridge, MA, 1994.

Satuma, J., Willox, R., Ramani, A., Grammaticos, B., and Carstea, A. Extending the SIR epidemic model. *Physica A* 336: 369–375, 2004.

Shadel, B., Rebmann, T., Clements, B., Checn, J., and Evans, R. Infection control practitioners' perceptions and educational needs regarding bioterrorism: Results from a national needs assessment survey. *American Journal of Infection Control* 31: 29–134, 2003.

Shulgin, B., Stone, L., and Agur, Z. Pulse vaccination strategy in the SIR epidemic model. *Bulletin of Mathematical Biology* 60: 1123–1148, 1998.

Stattenspiel, L. and Dietz, K. A structured epidemic model incorporating geographic mobility among regions. *Mathematical Biosciences* 128: 71–91, 1995.

Stattenspiel, L. and Herring, D. Simulating the effect of quarantine on the spread of the 1918–19 flu in central Canada. *Bulletin of Mathematical Biology* 65: 1–26, 2003.

30 Stream Data Analytics for Multipurpose Social Media Applications

30.1 INTRODUCTION

This chapter describes a cloud-based system called InXite, also called InXite-Security (stream-based data analytics for threat detection and prediction), which is designed to detect evolving patterns and trends in streaming data. InXite comprises four major modules: InXite information engine, InXite profile generator, InXite psychosocial analyzer, and InXite threat evaluator and predictor, each of which is outlined in this chapter, We also describe the novel methods we have developed for stream data analytics that are at the heart of InXite.

InXite integrates information from a variety of online social media sites such as Twitter, Foursquare, Google+, and LinkedIn, and builds people profiles through correlation, aggregation, and analyses in order to identify persons of interest who pose a threat. Other applications include garnering user feedback on a company's products, providing inexpensive targeted advertising, and monitoring the spread of an epidemic, among others.

InXite is designed to detect evolving patterns and trends in streaming data, including e-mails, blogs, sensor data, and social media data such as tweets. InXite is designed on top of two powerful data mining systems, namely patented TweetHood (location extraction for tweets), with the explicit aim of detecting and predicting suspicious events and people and SNOD (stream-based novel class detection). We also designed a separate system, SNOD++, an extension of SNOD, for detecting multiple novel classes of threats for InXite. Our goal is to decipher and monitor topics in data streams as well as to detect when trends emerge. This includes general changes in topics such as sports or politics, and also includes new, quickly emerging trends such as hurricanes and bombings. The problem of correctly associating data streams (e.g., tweet messages) with trends and topics is a challenging one. The challenge is best addressed with a streaming model because of the continuous and large volume of incoming messages.

It should be noted that InXite is a general-purpose system that can be adapted for a variety of applications, including security, marketing, law enforcement, health care, emergency response, and finance. This chapter mainly focuses on the adaptation of InXite for security applications, which we call InXite-Security. Other adaptations of InXite are called InXite-Marketing, InXite-Law, InXite-Healthcare, InXite-Emergency, and InXite-Finance among others. That is, while InXite-Security is developed mainly for counterterrorism and intelligence applications, all of the features can be tailored for law enforcement applications with some effort. For convenience, we will use the term InXite to mean InXite-Security in this chapter.

The organization of this chapter is as follows. Our premise for InXite is discussed in Section 30.2. We will describe in detail the design of all the modules of InXite and the implementation in Section 30.3. A note on InXite-Marketing is discussed in Section 30.4. Related work is discussed in Section 30.5. The chapter is concluded in Section 30.6. Figure 30.1 describes the concepts discussed in this chapter.

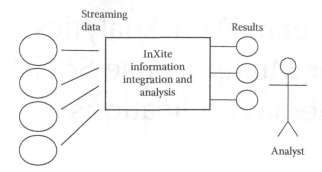

FIGURE 30.1   Stream data analytics for social media applications.

30.2 OUR PREMISE

Like a blunt instrument that destroys more than is intended, the National Security Agency's (NSA's) PRISM program dredges the communications landscape and gathers more information than should be necessary to ferret out terrorists and terrorist cells communicating inside the United States and worldwide. The NSA PRISM program is deemed necessary in order to prevent future terrorist acts against the United States. This top-down approach not only breaches the privacy of US citizens and upset and angered them but it has also drawn the ire of foreign governments who have been spied upon.

By contrast, InXite utilizes a bottom-up approach that uses specific keywords designed to reveal people around the world tweeting about a topic of particular interest. For instance, the keywords pair *Egypt* and *Muslim-brotherhood* would display a list of people in Egypt tweeting to others around the world using the keyword *Muslim-brotherhood*. In other words, InXite uses a targeted approach without needing to gather massive amounts of data.

Data streams are emanating from numerous data sources, including blogs and social media data. Such data could be structured, unstructured, semistructured, and real time/non-real time, static or dynamic data. It also includes relational and object data as well as semantic web data such as Resource Description Framework (RDF) graphs and multimedia data such as video, audio, and images. With modern technology, it is possible to exchange numerous messages in a very short space of time. Furthermore, communication messages (e.g., blogs and tweets) are often abbreviated and difficult to follow. To understand the motives, sentiments, and behavior of individuals and groups, where some of them could be malicious, tools are needed to make sense out of the massive amounts of streaming data often represented as graphs. To address this need, we have designed a framework called InXite for analyzing stream-based data.

We have utilized TweetHood and SNOD to develop a sophisticated data analytics system called InXite. InXite is a multipurpose system that can be applied to security, law enforcement, marketing, health-care, and financial applications, among others. We have designed and developed two InXite applications. One is InXite-Security and the other is InXite-Marketing. InXite-Security (which we will refer to as InXite for convenience since much of the InXite system initially focused on security applications) will detect and predict threats, including potential terrorists, harmful events, and the time and place of such events. The data sources for InXite include blogs, sensors, and social media data among others. InXite is a cloud-based application owing to the numerous advantages of clouds such as on-demand scalability, reliability, and performance improvements. InXite-Marketing utilizes the various modules of InXite and gives recommendations to businesses for selling products. The design of InXite uses TweetHood to obtain demographics information about individuals, and SNOD and SNOD++ for detecting novel classes of threats and sentiments.

30.3   MODULES OF InXite

30.3.1   OVERVIEW

Figure 30.2 illustrates the various modules of InXite, each of which is described in the ensuing subsections. InXite gets the data from various social media sites including streaming data from Twitter. The information is integrated by the information engine, which carries out various functions such as entity resolution and ontology alignment. Then the information analytics engine will analyze the integrated data using data mining techniques.

The results are then given to the analyst. The major modules of InXite are common to our applications, such as security, marketing, and law enforcement. Each application also has a small number of tailored components. InXite also follows a plug-and-play approach. That is, the analyst can plug his components if he or she has a preference for various tasks. In the ensuing sections, we will describe each of the modules in more detail.

30.3.2   INFORMATION ENGINE

The first step is to extract concepts and relationships form the vast amount of data streams and categorize the messages. Then, we provide *semantic* representation of the knowledge buried in the streams. This would enable an analyst to interact more directly with the hidden knowledge. The second step is to represent the concepts as ontologies, and subsequently integrate and align the ontologies. Once the multiple graphs extracted from the streams are integrated, then our analytics tools will analyze the graphs and subsequently predict threats.

The information engine module, illustrated in Figure 30.3, integrates the attributes of a user from multiple data streams including social networks (e.g., Twitter, LinkedIn, or Foursquare) and performs entity resolution, ontology alignment, conflict resolution, data provenance, and reasoning under uncertain and incomplete information. At the heart of the information engine is TweetHood, a novel, patent-pending method/algorithm to determine user attributes, including, but not limited to, location, age, age group, race, ethnicity, threat, languages spoken, religion, economic status, education level, gender, hobbies, or interests, based on the attribute values for the friends of the user (Motoyama et al., 2009).

While entity resolution algorithms have been around since the mid-1990s, InXite uses a combination of content-based similarity matching (Tung et al., 2006) and friends-based similarity

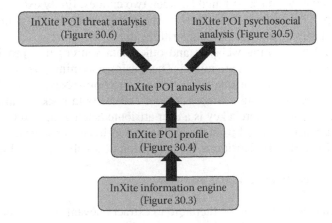

FIGURE 30.2   InXite modules.

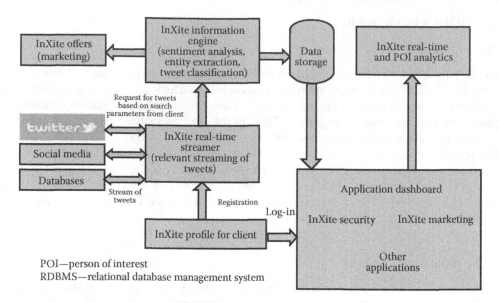

FIGURE 30.3   InXite information engine module.

matching (Motoyama and Varghese, 2009) algorithms. The information engine module consists of two major components:

1. Entity extraction—The process of extracting (mining) and/or, in certain cases, predicting user-specific attributes, which include demographic information (such as age and gender) and information about the user's social networks (such as friends, followers, and people he or she is following).
2. Information integration—The process of integrating or joining two or more user profiles from the same or different sources, such as social networks and blogs. This is done using the information obtained from the previous step.

In the following sections, we describe our methodology for implementing these two modules.

Entity Extraction. For data integration to take place properly, a certain number of content- and friend-based similarities must be found between two entities. Entity extraction is the first step toward that goal. Upon integrating all the known aspects of a user's profile, additional information is added through text mining and our novel algorithms like TweetHood.

All popular social networking websites and other data sources that provide data in either structured or semistructured format are mined. Then, using text mining techniques, various entities associated with the persons of interest for us are extracted. Next, in our iterative process, the structured data is parsed using a simple crawler and we obtain <key, value> pairs for each profile from the information, where a key is a user attribute (such as age and gender) and a value is the corresponding value obtained from the profile. After this is done, we use our content-based and friend-based (TweetHood) algorithms for prediction of attributes for which no values have been found.

The pseudocode for entity extraction is as follows:

1. Use text mining techniques in the literature to extract relevant information about the user from the multiple sources of data (including social networks, databases, etc.).
2. Organize the information into (key, value) pairs.
3. Use TweetHood to predict values that are unknown for any keys.

Information Integration. In this step, we integrate or join two or more profiles from different data sources that belong to the same individual based on matching of the attribute <key, value> pairs we obtained in the previous step. We pick one profile from data source A and try to find the closest match for it in data source B, by forming pairs and assigning them scores. This score is assigned based on the similarity of the two profiles, determined by the proximity of different user attributes in the two. If this score crosses a predetermined threshold and is also the highest for that chosen profile from data source A, we link the two indicating that the two profiles point to the same user.

Finding a partial verification of entities and friends can be a difficult process. The amount of information similarities needed to make a conclusive match is constantly changing. These decisions therefore need to also be made from constantly changing ontologies. InXite constructs ontologies for partial entity resolution dynamically by observing patterns in complete resolutions. We define an ontology for each data source, such as an online social network, blog, and others. These ontologies are then linked so that the system understands that an attribute key A, such as gender, from one data source points to the same thing as attribute B, such as sex, from another data source. This linkage of ontology structures constructed from different data sources is essential for the integration/disambiguation of two or more profiles.

The pseudocode for information integration is as follows:

1. Construct ontologies for the entities extracted using various ontology construction techniques in the literature.
2. Carry out entity resolutions by determining whether two entities are the assigning scores as to how similar the entities are.
3. Apply data mining techniques to observe patterns in the entity resolution process.
4. For those entities that cannot be completely resolve, use the patterns observed in step 3 and resolve the entities.
5. Link the various ontologies constructed using the results from the entity resolution process to form a linkage of ontologies that are essentially person of interest (i.e., user) profiles.

30.3.3 Person of Interest Analysis

Once the information engine integrates the multiple data sources, extracts entities, constructs ontologies, resolves conflicts, determines similarities, and links the ontologies, the next step is to analyze a person of interest (POI) based on various attributes and algorithms. In this section, we will discuss our techniques for such an analysis. Note that in Section 30.3.3, we will discuss our data mining techniques for threat prediction.

InXite POI Profile Generation and Analysis. The InXite POI profile generation and analysis modules are illustrated in Figure 30.4. A generated profile represents one or more aggregated entities from the extraction step. If two profiles are determined to belong to the same person at any point before or after profile generation, then the attributes and data of the two are merged into a single profile. This may happen because of ontology shifts during analysis or manual discovery by an analyst. Even though attribute prediction happens during the entity extraction and alignment steps, SNOD is continuously used in several modules to detect novel information nodes as long as information is added or discovered in the searching process. This means that profiles are constantly edited, updated, and merged after profile generation.

InXite POI Threat Analysis. The InXite POI threat analysis (module 3 in Figure 30.2) is a core InXite feature that combines several individual scores, some based on existing studies and some novel, to come up with a final score for evaluating the seriousness of a potential threat. Each of the individual scores and the final score has a range from 0 to 100, with 0 meaning a low threat and 100 meaning a high threat. Listed below are the seven major components of the threat evaluation module that contribute to the final threat evaluation score:

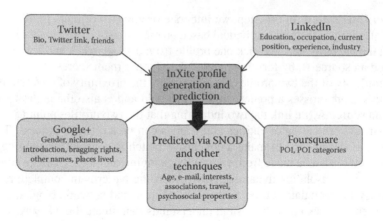

FIGURE 30.4 InXite person of interest profile generation and analysis.

i. *Demographics-based score computation*

InXite predicts and aggregates user-related attributes such as age, location, and religion. Using existing studies on terrorists such as the one by Marc Sageman (2004), InXite determines if the POI fits the profile of a terrorist or not.

Example: If (age between 22 and 35) AND (education = college) AND (ethnicity = Arab) → high score

ii. *Psychological score computation*

For calculating the psychological scores, we design algorithms that analyze the language used by the POI; in particular, we look at the adjectives and the nouns, to come up with five personality traits—sociability, evaluation, negativity, self-acceptance, fitting in, psychological stability, and maturity. On the basis of these scores, we derive a final psychological score (Shaver et al., 1992).

Example: Sociability AND Negativity AND Psychological Instability AND Fitting In → high score

iii. *Content-based score computation*

An important source of information about a user is the messages/posts that he or she puts on his or her page. To calculate the content-based threat score for a user, we define a rule-based system that looks for suspicious nouns and verbs, analyzes their relationship, and assigns a score based on that.

Example: I want to bomb the Pentagon → I/PRP want/VBP to/TO bomb/VB the/DT Pentagon/NN → high score

This metric is particularly useful for identifying mal-intent users who are expressive about their intents.

iv. *Background check score computation*

For individuals located in the United States, we run background checks using existing software/websites. The integration and prediction of user attributes helps in successful user disambiguation and allows us to do an advanced search of the database.

On the basis of the previous crimes committed by the individual, we assign a score that reflects the likelihood of him or her being a threat in the near future.

Example: If criminal and Type_of_Crime = Violent or Federal → high score

v. *Online reputation-based score computation*

InXite analyzes various online data sources such as newspapers, blogs, and social networking sites to analyze the sentiment about the user, and determines his or her involvement in political events like rallies, riots, scams, frauds, and robberies, among others. As in the case for other modules, the integration and prediction of other attributes allows for successful user disambiguation.

Example: If the user received an award from the president, it could lead to a low score. On the other hand, an individual who is an active participant in rallies (news article in *New York Times*) → high score

vi. *Social graph-based score computation*

The final module is based on our patent pending algorithm, TweetHood. We predict the threat level for all friends of the POI (based on the above-listed factors) and aggregate to obtain the score for the central POI.

Example: If Threat (friend1) = 0.9 AND Threat (friend2) = 0.1 AND Threat (friend3) = 0.8 AND Threat (friend4) = 0.7 AND Threat (friend5) = 0.5, then Threat (POI) = 0.6

Threat assessment: Once the profiles of a user have been constructed, we then examine the various attributes to determine whether the given user is a potential terrorist. For example, a user's attributes (e.g., age and location) as well as his or her behavioral, social, and psychological properties are extracted using our analytics algorithms. We then also apply existing algorithms (e.g., Mark Sageman's algorithms; Sageman, 2004, 2008) to enhance a user's psychological profile. These profiles will be used to determine whether the current user will carry out terrorist attacks, homicides, etc. For threat assessment, here are some results that we have obtained using existing algorithms as well as using our data analytics algorithms.

- Demographics: Up to 0.2 points are assigned to fitting into rages for the following categories: age, education, religion, politics, and hobbies. These are then added up for the final demographics score. The ranges for these categories are based on the research of Marc Sageman (2008).
- Psychology: Verb usage is categorized into traits. Four of these traits are found to be indicative of low psychological stability. These four traits are measured by percentage of total verb usage and added together to form the psychology score. The psychology submodule is based on techniques given in Markou and Singh (2003) and Shaver et al. (1992).
- NLP (Natural Language Processing): The weighted average of sentiment used between verbs and high-profile nouns (i.e., White House or Pentagon). Negative or threatening verb analyses have a weight of 1, while positive or benign verb analyses have a weight of 0.1. This allows strong statements such as a correlation of *bomb* and *Pentagon* to produce an overwhelmingly high score.
- Social structure: Standard mean average of friends' threat scores. A friend's threat score is the average of their other scores (demographics, psychology, NLP, social structure, background, and online reputation).
- Background checks: Represents a Department of Defense standard background check on the individual.
- Online reputation: If no previous association is found with this person or all associations are positive, the score will be 0. Any score higher than this directly represents the percentage of previous associations from mainstream media that are analyzed to have a negative sentiment.

Our design utilizes TweetHood and SNOD as well as existing algorithms to develop a comprehensive system for threat assessment/evaluation.

InXite Psychosocial Analysis. This module is illustrated in Figure 30.5. It consists of a variety of techniques including visualizing ontologies and generating word clouds. This module also uses two novel data analytics techniques that we have developed, namely microlevel location mining and sentiment mining. We begin the discussion with these two novel techniques, after which we discuss the remaining techniques.

Microlevel location mining refers to a method for determining specific or fine-grained locations that may be mentioned in communications between individuals or groups of individuals. In addition to locations, the technique can also be used to carry out fine-grained detection of other attributes

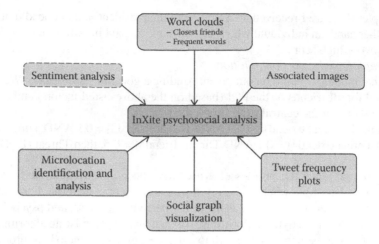

FIGURE 30.5   InXite psychosocial analysis and prediction.

such as hobbies, places traveled, and events. Our technique for microlevel location mining is unique and uses a crowd-sourced database, namely Foursquare. Furthermore, the technique uses the following tools/algorithms:

- WordNet is used for disambiguation of locations mentioned in communications between individuals/groups such as messages or tweets.
- TweetHood is used for identifying a city-level location, which, in turn, is used to narrow the search for microlevel locations within the identified city.

The work in Kinsella et al. (2011) aims to identify zip codes/locations based on the particular language used in tweets, and is thus a different approach toward location identification. We have considerably enhanced current efforts and have developed a novel technique for microlevel location mining.

The pseudocode for microlevel location mining is as follows:

1. Disambiguate locations mentioned in tweets using WorldNet.
2. Use Foursquare to find the general locations.
3. When locations are missing in the tweets, use TweetHood to find the locations as well as the city-level locations.
4. Use variations of TweetHood to mine further to pinpoint the exact location.

Other features: We have designed a number of features that would enhance psychosocial analysis, including the following:

Sentiment Mining: We have also designed sentiment mining techniques about a certain keyword/topic; for example, what does *John Smith* feel about *Tax Breaks* or what does *John Smith* feel about *Osama bin Laden*? Our methods use existing as well as our own algorithms (TweetHood, SNOD) for classifying user messages as positive, negative, or neutral, or whether it belongs to a novel class. We use emotion mining and also social behavioral mining to determine sentiments. In particular, we use the following two techniques:

- User demographics based—For example, if we know that 95% of all African Americans are pro-Obama, then our system will give a positive bias to a tweet from an African American about President Obama.
- Social factor-based (based on TweetHood)—If we know that 9 of 10 friends of a user are pro-Obama, then we will give a positive bias to tweets from that user.

Our training data set is a labeled data set—each tweet with its sentiment type positive or negative or neutral. We obtained the labeled training data set from sets of tweets that have emo-icons in them. On the basis of the emo-icon, we determined the label of the tweet and made the training data set. For each of the training data/tweet, we first remove the stopwords in it. Then, we remove all the words starting with @ or *http*. Then, we convert each token of the tweet to standard form means: we convert a token like *hungryyyyyy* to *hungry*. Then, from each tweet, we make the list of unigrams and bigrams for that tweet with its sentiment type. We saved the list of unigrams and bigrams in a HashSet and also convert the tweet as unigram and bigrams.

Now, for each token in the HashSet and for each tweet, we check whether the tweet contains the token or not. Then, we make the occurrence matrix based on their presence/absence. Thus, at this point, we have a data set of large numbers of dimensions. So to reduce the dimensionality, we leverage the entropy concept. We choose the best N attribute based on the higher information gain. Now, we have considerably good data and then we use WEKA for classifying purpose and we use the naïve Bayesian classifier and decision tree (J48) classifier.

The pseudocode for the sentiment mining algorithm is as follows:

Input: Set of training tweets T, Bag of stopword S, Set of testing tweets R, number of attribute N
Output: Labels of each of the tweet of R
For every tweet in T
    Remove all the stopwords in S
    Remove the words starting with @ or http and make each token as standard form
    Make the set G, of unigrams and bigrams and convert each tweet as a set of those and make the
        set W [W contains the unigrams and bigrams of each tweet]
For each token g in G
    For each token w in W
        If g matches w then encode it as 1 and fill up the occurrence matrix M
        Else encode it as 0 and fill up the occurrence matrix M
Choose the best N attribute from M based on the information gain and make new data set D
Use D as the training data set and build the classifier NB or J48
Use the trained classifier to classify the instances of test set R

Word clouds: Shows frequently used words. More frequent words are shown with a larger font.

Entity clouds: Shows frequently used entities. Entities of interest among the profile and their friends are shown in size by correlation to frequency of discussion.

Tweet frequency: Line graphs of tweets over time showing useful timing information. Lack of tweets are as important as writing tweets. Sleeper agents are known to cut contact and go silent before acting.

Social graph visualization: Visually shows the threat level of the most popular friends that are associated with a given user online.

Associated images: Brought to life in a slide show; all the images gathered from online sources for the given user profile.

30.3.4 INXITE THREAT DETECTION AND PREDICTION

InXite threat detection and prediction is module is depicted in Figure 30.2. While the threat evaluation and assessment techniques described in the previous section will determine whether a person is a threat or not based on some predetermined attributes, we have also designed data mining techniques to determine whether a person will commit future terrorist attacks. That is, threat prediction in InXite is carried out through a series of stages either meant to find suggested threatening behavior in a user or to eliminate individuals who are unlikely to be a current or become a future threat.

By leveraging both manually configured word analysis and automated data mining classifications, InXite is able to separate likely threats from a vast number of individuals.

A very broad list of users is created by first picking out those who use a list of specific nouns and verbs. This list is manually maintained and may include code words that are added after the discovery that they are being used. Persons who use enough of these words in a single statement are flagged and classified in the next stage. The number of statements or tweets that pass this stage contains a high number of false positives.

In the next stage, the flagged statements are tagged by part of speech similar to the content-based score in the threat evaluation section. Classifiers are trained on labeled and tagged data from statements manually confirmed by analysts or engineers to indicate imminent threats. Because many nonthreatening statements can contain threatening words like *kill*, the classifiers are useful in removing false positives from the statements passed in from the first phase.

Phrases like *killing time* or *people would kill for this opportunity* are eliminated in this way. This method of classification also serves to solidify seemingly innocent sentences that may be using code words. Even if the words of the sentence are replaced, the sentences' structure and placement remain the same, and compared similarly to sentences that explicitly state the obvious threatening language.

This automated method is effective because every word in a statement contributes an equal probability to the statement's classification as a threat or not. Given enough samples of threats and nonthreats, as each word is compared to its individual threat level and placement within the whole statement, the algorithm can determine where it belongs. When the algorithm decides that a statement is threatening, it is grouped with similar statements based on identified threatening words and grammatical structure. Using feedback from the analyst or user, these groups can be solidified or changed to reflect similar threatening statements.

Predicting threats based on data content first requires that the threatening or useful data be separated from the extremely large amount of benign or useless data. This can be accomplished with high accuracy through the union of linear discriminate analysis and bag of words filtering. This process has the benefit of breaking possibly threatening content into feature groups and dynamically detecting new threatening content categories. However, it also produces a large amount of false positives. We have multiple methods. One is based on a naïve Bayes classifier to help eliminate false positives. The classifier trains threats and benign content based on individual words and their part

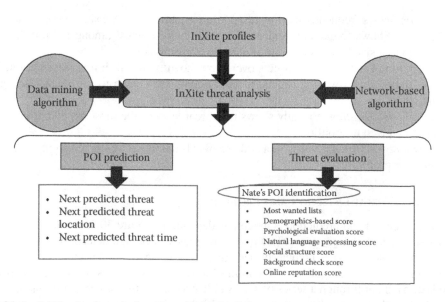

FIGURE 30.6   InXite threat analysis and prediction module.

of speech obtained from a tagger developed by Carnegie Mellon University specifically for Twitter language usage instead of published text documents. The other is based on our patent-pending technology SNOD. Our integrated algorithms provide much higher accuracy than the current approaches. Figure 30.6 illustrates details of the threat prediction module (module 5 of Figure 30.2).

The pseudocode for the threat detection algorithm is as follows:

1. Identifying threatening tweets
Input: Set of tweets T, Bag of words A, B, C
Output: Set of threatening tweets X
    For every tweet t in *T*,
        If t contains a word from set B then let n = location of this word
        If at least two words from (n − 3, n − 1) exist in set A, then
        If at least two words from (n + 1, n + 3) exist in set C
            Set X = X + t
//X now contains all preliminary identified threatening content and moves onto the classifier
2. Naïve Bayes classification (NB)
Input: Set of threatening tweets X; Set of training tweets P, N
//P is positively identified threats; N is originally empty until feedback loop initiated, are false positive nonthreats
Output: Revised threatening tweets X
    For every tweet p in P NB trained on positive threat
    For every tweet n in N NB trained on negative threat
    For every tweet x in X
        For every word w in x Part of speech is tagged
        For every set of three words from (w1, w3) to (wn − 2, wn)
        Classify probability of threat based of part of speech using NB
        NB classifies x as real threat or false positive
        If false positive
            Apply SNOD to see if it could be a novel positive class, If not
        X = X − x//classification is finished at this point and the feedback loop is initiated
3. Get feedback from analyst whether the tweet is threatening or not
    For every tweet x in X
        x is displayed to the analyst
        if x is confirmed as a threat   P = P + x
        If x is labeled as false positive by the analyst   N = N + x;   X = X − x

In the case of outliers, those statements that cannot be grouped with similar ones, novel class detection is used to determine their viability as an actual threat. In this regard, SNOD is a very useful tool.

30.3.5 APPLICATION OF SNOD

In addition to the traditional algorithms (Go et al., 2009; Pak and Paroubek, 2010), InXite also uses SNOD for predicting novel threats. In addition, we have designed a more powerful data mining technique called SNOD++, which is far superior to SNOD for threat prediction. Below we discuss SNOD++.

SNOD++. InXite is based on SNOD, which occurs because of the dynamic nature of the stream. Second, if more than one novel class appears in the stream, SNOD cannot detect them. Third, SNOD does not address the problem of high-dimensional feature spaces, which may lead to higher training and classification error. Finally, SNOD does not apply any optimizations for feature extraction and classification. Therefore, we have designed a practical and robust blogs and tweets detection tool using a powerful system called SNOD++. That is, we have enhanced SNOD into SNOD++, which is more practical and robust than SNOD. In addition to addressing the infinite length, concept drift, and concept evolution problems, SNOD++ addresses feature evolution and multiple novel classes, as well as applies subspace clustering and other optimizations, all of which improve the robustness, power, and accuracy of the algorithm.

Benefits of SNOD++. Systems based on SNOD++ can handle massive volumes of training data and will also be able to cope with concept drift in the data. These attributes make it more practical and robust than blogs and tweets detectors that are trained with static data. Furthermore, it can be used in detecting one or more novel classes of blogs and tweets. Also, recall that existing blogs and tweets detection techniques may fail to detect completely new patterns, but InXite++ should be able to detect such novel classes and raise an alarm. The blogs would be later analyzed and characterized by human experts. In particular, InXite++ will be more robust and useful than InXite because InXite++ will be capable of detecting multiple novel blogs and tweets in the stream, and will also exhibit much higher classification accuracy and a faster training time because of its robustness to higher feature dimensions and application of distributed feature extraction and selection.

30.3.6 EXPERT SYSTEMS SUPPORT

InXite provides basic support for expert systems to provide explanations for decisions and the ability to add additional modules as needed. Essentially, InXite integrates an expert system for analyzing and interpreting the results of the scores explained in previous paragraphs (e.g., reputation-based score, social graph-based score). This is meant to help the analyst to better interpret the information he or she is provided with. With the ability to customize and add additional modules, the inclusion of expert systems into In-Xite allows for near endless assistance and extensibility.

The pseudocode for the expert system is given below.

Input: Expert System E; Starting node n
Output: Result Graph R Explanation Graph Q Final Node N
While N = null
    Evaluate decision of n
        Q = Q + decision   R = R + n
        If decision leads to end point   N = destination node
        Else   n = destination node
    //N displays the final result of the expert system, while R displays the nodes that were evaluated in the process, and Q displays all of the logical steps used to reach N

30.3.7 CLOUD DESIGN OF INXITE

For InXite to function in real time and to handle massive numbers of tweets and data, we need a cloud to host all of the modules of InXite. In this section, we describe our cloud-based design for various InXite modules. The design uses two separate tools, namely Storm and HBase, for the development of the various InXite modules. A separate Storm topology is constructed for each of the InXite modules. Furthermore, HBase is used by all topologies for storage and retrieval of user profiles. We now present the design of the various topologies in the form of pseudocode-based algorithms.

InXite Information Engine in the Cloud
1. Identify a user of interest using a spout.
2. Perform the steps included in the entity extraction and information integration module for the user selected in step 1 in a custom bolt (this also includes the implementation of TweetHood in the cloud).

3. Store the identified attribute <key, value> pairs in HBase.
4. Perform the steps for information integration for the user selected in step 1 using the attribute <key, value> pairs obtained in step 2 in a separate custom bolt.
5. Update the results stored in HBase with the results of step 4.

InXite Profile Generation and Prediction
1. Identify a user of interest using a spout.
2. Use the attribute <key, value> pairs created by the information engine to build a user profile in a bolt, which is stored in an HBase schema.
3. Update the user profile by predicting values for other attributes using the attribute <key, value> pairs in a separate custom bolt.
4. Conduct a threat assessment of the identified user with the help of the various scores described earlier (demographics based, psychological, etc.) using a custom bolt.
5. Update the user profile with the results of threat assessment.

InXite Psychosocial Analysis and Prediction
1. Identify a user of interest using a spout.
2. Identify microlevel locations for the user and store them as a part of their profile using a custom bolt (this includes the implementation of TweetHood in the cloud).
3. Perform a sentiment analysis of the user's messages/posts/tweets using a custom bolt and store the results as a part of their profile.
4. Use a separate custom bolt to construct word/entity clouds, graph for tweet frequency, determine the threat score for the top friends of this user, and download images associated with this user.
5. Store all information obtained in step 4 as a part of the user's profile.

InXite Threat Detection and Prediction
1. Identify a user of interest using a spout.
2. Perform threat prediction for the identified user in a custom bolt using the classification algorithms described earlier.
3. Store the results of threat prediction as a part of the user's profile.

30.3.8 IMPLEMENTATION

All of the modules of InXite illustrated in Figure 30.2 have been implemented. These include entity extraction and information integration, profile generation and threat analysis, psychosocial analysis, and threat prediction. With respect to the cloud implementation, we have completed the implementation of TweetHood in the cloud as well as SNOD in the cloud. The remaining modules of InXite are yet to be implemented in the cloud.

Multiple demonstrations of InXite are available. These include canned demonstrations, real-time demonstrations (that requires access to numerous tweets), as well as TweetHood in the cloud. We have taken a plug-and-play approach (i.e., a component-based approach) to the development of InXite. This means that if a customer has a certain module of his or her own (e.g., sentiment mining) that he or she wishes to use, then he or she can replace our sentiment mining module with that of his or her choice. This feature is a great strength of InXite. Many of the products require an all-or-nothing approach. With InXite, you can select the modules you want to meet your needs. It should also be noted that while the design of InXite does not limit the data to tweets, the implementation handles only tweets. That is, the design of InXite can handle any data whether it is structured data in databases or unstructured data in the form of social graphs or tweets.

30.4   OTHER APPLICATIONS

As stated in Section 30.1, InXite is a multipurpose system. In addition to InXite-Security described in Section 30.3, we have also designed and developed other applications for InXite, including InXite-Marketing and InXite-Law. In this section, we discuss InXite-Marketing, which will provide advice to businesses as to who to target for a particular product based on the user's social graphs and tweets.

InXite-Marketing carries out entity extraction and information integration, and builds profiles of persons of interest. In this case, the POI is the user who is interested in a product, such as iPhone or a particular kind if pizza. We can develop word clouds as well as associated images for this user. We can also carry out sentiment mining and obtain results such as 'John prefers iOS to Android'. InXite-Marketing also finds locations from TweetHood and novel classes using SNOD.

However, there are some differences between the features between InXite-Security and InXite-Marketing. It does not make sense to determine whether a person is a threat or whether he will commit a crime for InXite-Marketing. Furthermore, it does not make sense to determine the psychosocial profile of a user. What is useful for InXite-Marketing is integrating with a *recommender* system. For example, we can analyze the user preferences and make recommendations.

As discussed in the sentiment analysis section, we can predict the sentiment of tweet for a person; however, it needs some further improvement like incorporating NLP techniques. Our system is easily workable for a particular person's tweet and a particular subject. For example, if we want to determine John Smith's sentiment about iPhone 5, we can go through all his tweets about the iPhone 5 and based on the sentiment of each tweet, we can determine the overall sentiment of John Smith about iPhone 5. So now, once we know the sentiment of John Smith about iPhone 5, say it is positive, we can recommend him some more *i-products* or products related to the iPhone 5, for example, headphone and charger. Here is another factor to consider that we call *peer effect*. The positive statements made by an individual's friends can be mined for individual products. Because the friends or associates of this individual talk positively about a product, especially one that the individual does not mention themselves, we can extrapolate these products for the recommender system. For example, if John Smith has 10 friends and all of them have a positive sentiment about Android phones, then it is a good idea to recommend some Android products to John Smith. Thus, we can consider it as a weighted vector of *personal sentiment* and *peer sentiment*. On the basis of the weighted factor, we can decide what product, and to what extent, we should recommend to him. These weights will be mostly influenced by the individual's personal sentiment, and the sentiment of his peers will help fill in the gaps and more greatly expand the recommendation options for this person.

The pseudocode for the recommender system is as follows:

Query: Find John's sentiment about product X
Analyze John's Tweets about X applying data mining techniques
    If Positive, then give additional recommendation related to product X
Analyze the Tweets of John's friends using weighted vectors
    If they are positive about X, then give recommendations to John about X

We have a demonstration system for InXite-Marketing (as well as InXite-Law) that has implemented all of the features that we have described above, including the recommender system. There are also additional features we have implemented. For example, on the basis of the interests of a user, we could predict the product he would be interested in the future, and this way a business can market this product first to this user and gain a competitive advantage.

30.5 RELATED WORK

In addition to TweetHood, SNOD, and the information integration techniques, other works that have influenced our approach include those of Goyal et al. (2009), Katakis et al. (2006), Lin et al. (2011), Markou and Singh (2003), Smith and Crane (2001), Spinosa et al. (2008), Frigui and Nasraoui (2004), Backstrom (2008), and Wenerstrom and Giraud-Carrier (2006), Dong et al. (2005), and Huberman and Wu (2009). In addition, much of our work has also been applied for the InXite system. These include the work discussed in Abrol et al. (2009), Ahmed and Khan (2009), Ahmed et al. (2010), Chandra and Khan (2011), Khan and Luo (2002), and Masud et al. (2010, 2011).

Many tools exist for entity extraction and location identification from web pages and other structured text. Although the details of some of these detection strategies are proprietary, it is well known that all of them use standard NLP or machine learning techniques that assume that the text is structured and consists of complete sentences with correct grammar. Our work, on the other hand, focuses on unstructured text consisting of slang and incomplete sentences, which is usually associated with social media. With regard to the cloud-based stream mining and novel class detection framework, to the best of our knowledge, there is no significant commercial competition for a cloud-centric trend detection tool. The current work on trend detection (TwitterMonitor and "Streaming Trend Detection in Twitter" by James Benhardus) is primitive and makes use of a keyword-based approach instead of choosing feature vectors. Additionally, since we have taken a modular approach to the creation of our tools, we can iteratively refine each component (novel class detection for trend analysis, entity extraction, scalability on cloud, and ontology construction) separately. All the frameworks and tools that we have used (or are using) for the development of InXite are open source and have been extensively used in our previous research, and hence our tools will be able to accommodate any changes to the platform.

30.6 SUMMARY AND DIRECTIONS

In this chapter, we have described the design of InXite. InXite will be a great asset to the analysts who have to deal with massive amounts of data streams in the form of billions of blogs and messages, among others. For example, by analyzing the behavioral history of a particular group of individuals as well as details of concepts such as events, analysts will be able to predict behavioral changes in the near future and take necessary measures. We have also discussed our use of cloud computing in the implementation of InXite.

New streams of data swarm the cyberspace every day. Analyzing such streams and updating the existing classification models is a daunting task. Most existing behavior-profiling techniques are manual, which require days to analyze a single blog sample and extract its behavioral profile. Even existing automated techniques have been tested only on a small sample of training data. By integrating our approach with a cloud computing framework, we have overcome this barrier and provided a highly scalable behavior modeling tool, thereby achieving higher accuracy in detecting new patterns. Furthermore, no existing profiling (manual or automated) technique addresses the evolving characteristics of data streams such as blogs and messages. Therefore, our product will have a tremendous advantage over other behavior-based products by quickly responding to the dynamic environment.

While InXite is a considerable improvement over currently available analysis tools, the underlying SNOD technology has some limitations. For example, SNOD lacks the ability to detect multiple novel classes emerging simultaneously. Since data streams such as blogs and messages could have multiple concurrent evolutions, we need a system that can detect multiple novel classes. Therefore, we have extended SNOD to achieve a more powerful detection strategy (SNOD++) that addresses these limitations. SNOD++ is utilized by InXite. We believe that InXite will be a novel product for streaming data analysis because it can handle dynamic data, changing patterns, and dynamic emergence of novel classes. We have utilized our cloud computing framework to develop InXite for scalable solutions for mining streaming data.

REFERENCES

Abrol, S., Khan, L., and Al-Khateeb, T.M. MapIt: Smarter searches using location driven knowledge discovery and mining. In: *1st SIGSPATIAL ACM GIS 2009 International Workshop on Querying and Mining Uncertain Spatio-Temporal Data (QUeST)*, November 2009, Seattle, WA, 2009.

Ahmed, M.S. and Khan, L. SISC: A text classification approach using semisupervised subspace clustering. In: *ICDM Workshops*, Miami, FL, pp. 1–6, 2009.

Ahmed, M.S., Khan, L., and Rajeswari, M. Using correlation based subspace clustering for multi-label text data classification. *ICTAI* (2): 296–303, 2010.

Backstrom, L., Kleinberg, J., Kumar, R., and Novak J. Spatial variation in search engine queries. In: *WWW, Beijing, China,*, 2008.

Chandra, S., Khan, L. Estimating Twitter user location using social interactions: A content based approach. In: *The Third IEEE International Conference on Social Computing*, October 9–11, 2011, MIT, Boston, 2011.

Dong, X., Halevy, A.Y., and Madhavan, J. Reference reconciliation in complex information spaces. In: *ALM SIGMOD Conference*, Baltimore, pp. 85–96, 2005.

Frigui, H. and Nasraoui, O. Unsupervised learning of prototypes and attribute weights. *Pattern Recognition* 37(3): 567–581, 2004.

Go, A., Bhayani, R., and Huang, L. Twitter sentiment classification using distant supervision. CS224N Project Report, Stanford 1–12, 2009.

Goyal, M.A., Daum, H., and Venkatasubramanian, S. Streaming for large scale NLP: Language modeling. In: *Human Language Technologies: The 2009 Annual Conference of the North American Chapter of the Association for Computational Linguistics*, Boulder, CO, 2009.

Huberman, B. and Wu, D.R.F. Social networks that matter: Twitter under the microscope. *First Monday* 14, 2009.

Katakis, I., Tsoumakas, G., and Vlahavas, I. Dynamic feature space and incremental feature selection for the classification of textual data streams. In: *ECML PKDD*, Berlin, Germany, pp. 102–116, 2006.

Khan, L. and Luo, F. Ontology construction for information selection. In: *ICTAI*, Washington, DC, 2002.

Kinsella, S., Murdock, V., and O'Hare, N. I'm eating a sandwich in Glasgow: Modeling locations with tweets. In: *Proceedings of the 3rd International Workshop on Search and Mining User-Generated Contents*, Glasgow, UK, pp. 61–68. ACM, 2011.

Lin, J., Snow, R., and Morgan, W. Smoothing techniques for adaptive online language models: Topic tracking in tweet streams. In: *Proc. of ACM SIGKDD Conference on Knowledge Discovery and Data Mining*, August 2011, San Diego, CA, 2011.

Markou, M. and Singh, S. Novelty detection: A review. Part 1: Statistical approaches, Part 2: Neural network based approaches. *Signal Processing* 83: 2481–2497, 2499–2521, 2003.

Masud, M.M., Chen, Q., Khan, L., Aggarwal, C.C., Gao, J., Han, J., and Thuraisingham, B.M. Addressing concept-evolution in concept-drifting data streams. In: *Proc. ICDM*, Sydney, Australia, 2010.

Masud, M.M., Gao, J., Khan, L., Han, J., and Thuraisingham, B.M. Classification and novel class detection in concept-drifting data streams under time constraints. *IEEE TKDE* 23(1), 2011.

Motoyama, M. and Varghese, G. I seek you: Searching and matching individuals in social networks. In: *ACM WIDM*, Hong Kong, 2009.

Pak, A. and Paroubek, P. Twitter as a corpus for sentiment analysis and opinion mining. In: *Proceedings of LREC*, Malta, vol. 2010. 2010.

Sageman, M. *Understanding Terror Networks*. University of Pennsylvania Press, Philadelphia, PA, 2004.

Sageman, M. *Leaderless Jihad: Terror Networks in the Twenty-First Century*. University of Pennsylvania Press, Philadelphia, PA, 2008.

Shaver, P.R. and Brennan, K.A. Attachment styles and the Big Five personality traits: Their connections with each other and with romantic relationship outcomes. *Personality and Social Psychology Bulletin* 18(5): 536–545, 1992.

Smith, D.A. and Crane, G. Disambiguating geographic names in a historical digital library. In: *5th European Conference on Research and Advanced Technology for Digital Libraries (ECDL01)*, Lecture Notes in Computer Science, Darmstadt, September 2001.

Spinosa, E.J., de Leon, A.P., de Carvalho, F., and Gama, J. Cluster-based novel concept detection in data streams applied to intrusion detection in computer networks. In: *Proc. ACM SAC*, Ceará, Brazil, pp. 976–980, 2008.

Tung, A., Zhang, R., Koudas, N., and Doi, B. Similarity search: A matching based approach. In: *Proc of VLDB* .06, Seoul, Korea, 2006.

Wenerstrom, B. and Giraud-Carrier, C. Temporal data mining in dynamic feature spaces. ICDM, Hong Kong, pp. 1141–1145, 2006.

CONCLUSION TO SECTION VII

In Section VII, we discussed the use of social media systems for various applications. In particular, we discussed the use of social media for insider threat detection, for bioterrorism applications, and for detecting suspicious activities.

Chapter 27 discussed our approach to insider threat detection. We represent the insiders and their communication as Resource Description Framework (RDF) graphs and then query and mine the graphs to extract the nuggets. Chapter 28 described the challenges for developing a system for SARO (stability and reconstruction operations). In particular, we discussed the design of a temporal geospatial mobile social semantic web that can be utilized by military personnel, decision makers, and local/government personnel to reconstruct after a major combat operation. In Chapter 29, we discussed our approach to enhancing the SIR (susceptible, infected, and recovered) model through epidemiology approximation. Our model is based on social interactions. We have created a hybridized model that balances the simplicity of the original with an approximation of what more complex agent-based models already offer, with an emphasis on the exploration of large search spaces. In Chapter 30, we have described the design of InXite. InXite will be a great asset to the analysts who have to deal with massive amounts of data streams in the form of billions of blogs and messages, among others. For example, by analyzing the behavioral history of a particular group of individuals as well as details of concepts such as events, analysts will be able to predict behavioral changes in the near future and take necessary measures.

Section VIII

Secure Social Media Systems

INTRODUCTION TO SECTION VIII

Much of the discussions in Sections VI and VII focused on the experimental social network systems and applications we have developed. Many of our systems utilize semantic web technologies for representation and reasoning. In Section VIII, we discuss experimental secure social media systems. In particular, we discuss multiple query-processing prototypes for social media systems. We also discuss privacy-preserving social media integration.

Section VIII consists of five chapters: Chapters 31 through 35. In Chapter 31, we will present a system that allows cooperating organizations to securely share large amounts of data. We ensure that the organizations have a large common storage area by using Hadoop. Furthermore, we use Hive to present users of our system with a structured view of the data and to also enable them to query the data with an SQL-like language. In Chapter 32, we will describe an access control system for Resource Description Framework (RDF) data that incorporates a token-based mechanism. In Chapter 33, we will describe our design and implementation of a cloud-based information sharing system called CAISS. CAISS utilizes several of the technologies we have developed as well as open source tools. We also describe the design of an ideal cloud-based assured information sharing system called CAISS++. In Chapter 34, we will discuss a generalized social network in which only insensitive and generalized information is shared. We will also discuss the integration of the generalized information and how it can satisfy a prescribed level of privacy leakage tolerance that is measured independently of the privacy-preserving techniques. In Chapter 35, we will discuss attacks on social networks and then describe a cloud-based malware detection data mining system that would be used to detect suspicious activity in Twitter data streams.

31 Secure Cloud Query Processing with Relational Data for Social Media

31.1 INTRODUCTION

The World Wide Web (WWW) is envisioned as a system of interlinked hypertext documents that are accessed using the Internet (http://en.wikipedia.org/wiki/World_Wide_Web). With the emergence of organizations that provide e-commerce such as Amazon and social network applications such as Facebook and Twitter on the WWW, the volume of data generated by them daily is massive (Axon, 2010). It was estimated that the amount of data that would be generated by individuals in the year 2009 would be more than that generated in the entire history of mankind through 2008 (Weigend, 2009). The large amount of data generated by one organization could be valuable to other organizations or researchers if it can be correlated with the data that they have. This is especially true for various governmental intelligence organizations. This has led to another trend of forming partnerships between business organizations and universities for research collaborations (Nokia Research Center–Open Innovation, http://networks.nokia.com/innovation/futureworks /openinnovationchallenge) and between business organizations for data sharing to create better applications (Salesforce, 2008).

The two main obstacles to this process of collaboration among organizations are arranging a large, common data storage area and providing secure access to the shared data. Organizations across the world invest a great deal of resources in minimizing storage costs, and with the introduction of cloud-based services, it is estimated that this cost would be reduced further (All, 2010). Additionally, organizations spend a large amount of their yearly budget on security; however, this is still not sufficient to prevent security breaches (Ponemon Institute, 2010; Sawyer, 2010). In this chapter, we present a web-based system (Hive Access Control) that aims to achieve the previously stated goals by combining cloud computing technologies with policy-based security mechanisms. This idea comes in part from the recommendations of the Cloud Security Alliance for Identity and Access Management (Kumaraswamy et al., 2010) and our previous work using XACML policies (Parikh, 2009). We have combined the Hadoop Distributed File System (HDFS) (Borthakur, 2010) with Hive (Apache Software Foundation, 2015) to provide a common storage area for participating organizations. Furthermore, we have used an XACML (Moses, 2005) policy-based security mechanism to provide fine-grained access controls over the shared data. Users of our system are divided into groups based on the kinds of queries that they can run such as SELECT and INSERT. Our system provides a secure log-in feature to users based on a salted hash technique. When a user logs into our system, based on the group that the user belongs to, he or she is provided with different options. We allow collaborating organizations to load data to the shared storage space in the form of relational tables and views. Users can also define fine-grained XACML access control policies on tables/views for groups of users. Users can then query the entire database based on the credentials that they have. We have provided some basic query-rewriting rules in our system that abstract users from the query language of Hive (HiveQL). This allows them to enter regular SQL queries in the web application that are translated into HiveQL using the basic rewriting rules. Our system also allows new users to register; however, only a

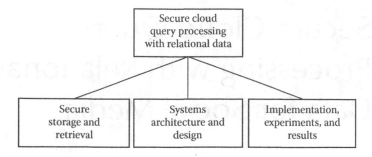

FIGURE 31.1 Secure cloud query processing with relational data.

designated special user *admin* can assign these users to the appropriate groups. Our contributions include the following:

- Mechanism to load and query shared data securely that is stored in HDFS using Hive
- Additional layer of security above HDFS and Hive using a XACML policy-based mechanism
- Basic query-rewriting rules that abstract a user from HiveQL and allow him or her to enter SQL queries
- Incorporation of the above mechanisms into a web-based system

This chapter is organized as follows: Section 31.2 presents the related work in the area of secure storage and retrieval of information in the cloud. In Section 31.3, we present our architecture for solving the problem of secure large-scale data sharing based on combining cloud computing technologies with XACML policy-based security mechanisms. Furthermore, in Section 31.4, we present the details of our implementation. Finally, Section 31.5 presents our conclusions and future work. Figure 31.1 illustrates the contents of this chapter.

31.2 RELATED WORK

We combine cloud computing technologies with security mechanisms so that cooperating organizations can share vast amounts of data securely. Since the birth of cloud computing technologies, there has been much interest generated among researchers, business organizations, and media outlets about security issues with these technologies (Mitchell, 2009; Talbot, 2009). This interest has resulted in large-scale research and development efforts from business organizations (AWS, 2009; Microsoft Corporation, n.d.; O'Malley et al., 2009). A part of the work related to security in the cloud has been focused on implementing security at the infrastructure level. O'Malley et al. (2009) present their vision for security in Hadoop. Their work presents a few security risks with Hadoop and outlines solutions to them. These solutions have been implemented in beta versions of Hadoop v0.20. This development effort is an important step toward securing cloud infrastructures but is only in its inception stage. The goal of our system is to add another layer of security above the security offered by Hadoop. Once the security offered by Hadoop becomes robust, it will only strengthen the effectiveness of our system.

Amazon Web Services (AWS) is a web services infrastructure platform in the cloud (http://aws.amazon.com/). AWS (2009) offers an overview of security aspects that are relevant to AWS such as physical security, network security, and AWS security. Our system is different from AWS in the sense that our cloud infrastructure is completely private versus AWS's infrastructure that is in the public domain. This distinguishing factor makes our infrastructure *trusted* over the AWS infrastructure where data must be stored in an encrypted format since AWS is in the public domain. In the future, we plan to extend our work to include both public and private clouds.

The Windows Azure platform is an Internet-scale cloud computing services platform. Marshall et al. (2010) provides an overview of the security challenges and recommended approaches to design and develop more secure applications for the Windows Azure platform. However, according to Brodkin (2010), the Windows Azure platform is suitable for building new applications, but it is not optimal for migrating existing applications. The main reason why we did not use the Windows Azure platform is that we wanted to port our existing application to an open source system instead of writing our code from scratch, as would be needed with Windows Azure. We also did not want to be tied to the Windows framework but rather allow our work to be used on any kind of system. We will be able to test our system on the Windows Azure platform once the platform supports the use of virtual machines to run existing applications (Brodkin, 2010).

31.3 SYSTEM ARCHITECTURE

In this section, we present our architecture that securely provides access to a large common storage space (the *cloud*), thus allowing cooperating organizations to share data reliably. We begin by giving an overview of the architecture followed by a discussion of each of its component layers.

Figure 31.2 shows the architecture of our system. Each rectangle in the figure represents a different component of our framework. The various line styles for arrows indicate the flow of control for a specific task that can be accomplished with this system. Next, we present each of the component layers in the architecture.

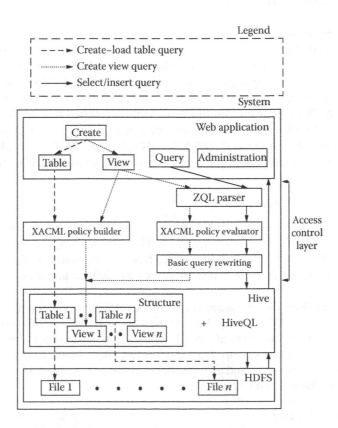

FIGURE 31.2 System architecture.

31.3.1 WEB APPLICATION LAYER

The web application layer is the only interface provided by our system to the user to access the cloud infrastructure. We provide different functions based on the permissions assigned to a user. The web application provides a log-in page that can be used by any user to log into the system. We use the Java simplified encryption (JASYPT) library's (http://www.jasypt.org/index.html) salted hash technique to store usernames and passwords in a file. Furthermore, that file is stored in a secure location that is not accessible to any user. The system currently supports three types of users:

- Users who can only query the existing tables/views
- Users who can create tables/views and define XACML policies on them in addition to querying all tables/views
- A special *admin* user who, in addition to the previous functions, can also assign new users to either of the above categories

31.3.2 ZQL PARSER LAYER

The ZQL parser (http://zql.sourceforge.net/) layer takes as input any query submitted by a user and either proceeds to the XACML policy evaluator if the query is successfully parsed or returns an error message to the user. The ZQL parser is an SQL parser written in Java that takes an SQL query as input and fills different Java vectors with different parts of the query (http://zql.sourceforge.net/). For example, consider the following query:

SELECT a.id, a.name FROM a WHERE a.id > 5

The ZQL parser parses the query and constructs different Java vectors for every part of the query (SELECT, FROM, and WHERE). In our system, the vector of attribute names in the SELECT clause for the query above is returned to the web application layer to be used in displaying the results returned by the query. The vector of table/view names in the FROM clause is passed to the XACML policy evaluator to ensure that the current user has permissions to access all tables/views specified in the query. If the evaluator determines that the current user has the required permissions, the query is processed further, else an error message is returned to the web application layer. The ZQL parser currently supports the SQL DELETE, INSERT, SELECT, and UPDATE statements. Our future work involves adding support for other keywords such as CREATE, DROP, etc.

31.3.3 XACML POLICY LAYER

The eXtensible Access Control Markup Language (XACML) is an XML-based language that is used to define access control policies on resources. The same language is also used to determine whether access is allowed for a particular resource based on the policy defined for that resource (http://zql.sourceforge.net/). Next, we explain how we have defined and used XACML policies in our framework.

XACML Policy Builder. In our framework, the tables and views defined by users are treated as resources for building XACML policies. Furthermore, we have defined role-based access control (Ferraiolo and Kuhn, 1992; Sandhu et al., 1996) policies on these resources based on the kinds of queries that are provided by our system. For every type of query supported by our framework, we define a mapping between this type and all users that are allowed to run that kind of query. A sample listing of such a mapping is given below:

INSERT admin user1 user2
SELECT admin user1 user3

In our system, for every table/view that a user wants to create, they are given the option of uploading their own predefined XACML policy or having the framework build a policy for them. If a user selects the latter option, they must also specify the kinds of queries (e.g., INSERT, SELECT, etc.) that will be allowed on the table/view. We then use Sun's XACML implementation (http://sunxacml.sourceforge.net/) to build a policy for that table/view with the groups specified by that particular user.

XACML Policy Evaluator. Our system uses Sun's XACML implementation (http://sunxacml.sourceforge.net/) to evaluate if the current user has access to all tables/views that are defined in any user query. If permission is granted for all tables/views, then the query is processed further, else an error message is returned to the user. The policy evaluator is used both during regular user query execution, as well as during view creation, since the only way to create a view in Hive is by specifying a SELECT query on the existing tables/views. The current user must have access to all tables/views specified in this SELECT query before the view can be created.

Basic Query-Rewriting Layer. This layer enables us to add another layer of abstraction between the user and HiveQL by allowing users to enter SQL queries that are rewritten according to HiveQL's syntax. In our current system, we provide two basic rewriting rules for user-specified SQL queries.

- HiveQL does not allow multiple tables in the FROM clause of a query, but rather expects this kind of query to be given as a sequence of JOIN statements. The user is abstracted from this fact by allowing him or her to enter a regular SQL query with multiple tables in the FROM clause that we transform to a sequence of JOIN statements in conformance with HiveQL's syntax. The following is an example:

  SELECT a.id, b.age FROM a, b; → SELECT a.id, b.age FROM a JOIN b

- HiveQL uses a modified version of SQL's INSERT–SELECT statement, INSERT OVERWRITE TABLE <tablename> SELECT rather than INSERT INTO <tablename> SELECT. Again, we abstract this from the user by allowing him or her to enter the traditional INSERT INTO <tablename> SELECT, which we then rewrite into HiveQL's INSERT OVERWRITE TABLE <tablename> SELECT. The following is an example:

  INSERT INTO a SELECT * FROM b; → INSERT OVERWRITE TABLE a
  SELECT * FROM b

As part of our future work, we plan to extend these basic rewriting rules with more complicated rules in a complete query-rewriting engine.

Hive Layer. Hive is a data warehouse infrastructure built on top of Hadoop (https://hive.apache.org). Hive provides the ability to structure the data in the underlying HDFS as well as to query this data. The arrows in Figure 31.2 between the tables in this layer and the files in the HDFS layer indicate that each table in Hive is stored as a file in the HDFS. These files contain the data that this table represents. There are no arrows between the views in this layer and the files in the HDFS layer since a view is only a logical concept in Hive that is created with a SELECT query. In our framework, Hive is used to structure the data that will be shared by collaborating organizations. Furthermore, we use Hive's SQL-like query language, HiveQL, to enable access to this data. The advantage of using Hive in our system is that users can query the data using a familiar SQL-like syntax.

HDFS Layer. The HDFS is a distributed file system that is designed to run on basic hardware (Borthakur, 2010). The HDFS layer in our framework stores the data files corresponding to tables that are created in Hive (Thusoo et al., 2009). Our security assumption is that these files can neither be accessed using Hadoop's (http://hadoop.apache.org/) web interface nor Hadoop's command line interface but only by using our system.

31.4 IMPLEMENTATION DETAILS AND RESULTS

In this section, we present the implementation of our system by providing performance graphs for the insert and query processes for tables with different sizes. Details of our experiments and performance graphs are given in Thuraisingham et al. (2010). We begin by giving a brief description of our implementation setup followed by the implementation details.

31.4.1 IMPLEMENTATION SETUP

Our implementation was carried out on a 19-node cluster with a mix of two different configurations for nodes. Furthermore, all the nodes are in the same rack. Of the 19 nodes, 11 nodes ran Ubuntu v10.04 Lucid Lynx, on an Intel Pentium 4, 3.2 GHz CPU with 4 GB SDRAM 400 MHz memory and a 40 GB Western Digital WDC WD400BB-75FJ SATA hard drive as the primary drive and a 250 GB Western Digital WD2500AAJB-0 SATA hard drive as the secondary drive. The other eight nodes ran Ubuntu v9.04 Jaunty Jackalope, on an Intel Pentium 4, 2.8 GHz CPU with 4 GB SDRAM 333 MHz memory and two 40 GB Western Digital WDC WD400BB-75FJ SATA hard drives. We used the Java version JRE v1.6.0_18 for our implementation. For the cloud infrastructure, we used Hadoop version v0.19.1, with a 1000 MB heap space and Hive version v0.5, with the default heap space. We also used Apache Tomcat v7.0.0 as the web server for our application with a 2 GB heap space. We also used default values for all parameters that are provided by Hadoop and Hive. We understand that we will have a performance gain when we set optimal values for these parameters. However, since this is preliminary work, we have chosen not to focus on these parameters, which will be done in the future.

31.4.2 EXPERIMENTAL DATA SETS

We have used two different data sets to test the performance of our system versus Hive. The first data set is the Freebase (http://www.freebase.com/) system, which is an open repository of structured data that has approximately 12 million topics or entities. An entity is a person, place, or thing with a unique identifier. We wanted to simulate an environment of cooperating organizations by using the people, business, film, sports, organization, and awards data sets from the Freebase system. We assume that each data set is loaded into our system by a different organization and, further, users can run various queries across these data sets on the basis of their permissions. The queries we have used to test our implementation were created by us based on the data sets of the Freebase system.

The second data set we have used to test our system is the well-known TPC-H benchmark (http://tpc.org/tpch/spec/tpch2.11.0.pdf). The TPC-H benchmark is a decision support benchmark that consists of a schema that is typical to any business organization. The benchmark contains eight tables and provides 22 queries with a high degree of complexity. We have used this benchmark to test the performance of our system versus Hive in performing complex queries. The TPC-H benchmark provides a tool for data generation (DBGEN) and a tool for query generation (QGEN). We have used DBGEN to generate data sets with varying scale factors (SFs) from 1 to 1000 as specified in the benchmark document. The reader should note that a scale factor of 1 is approximately 1 GB of data. Thus, we have tested our system with data sizes varying from 1 GB to 1000 GB. The smaller data sets (SF = 1, SF = 10, and SF = 30) are used to test the loading performance of our system versus Hive. On the other hand, the larger data sets (SF = 100, SF = 300, and SF = 1000) are used to run a few of the benchmark queries. We have used queries Q1, Q3, Q6, and Q13 of the TPC-H benchmark to test our system. These queries were randomly selected after applying the following criterion to the study by Jia (2009). The original query does not need to be divided into subqueries manually since our web application does not support this feature. We also think that the results obtained by running the queries selected above are indicative of the performance of all the other TPC-H benchmark queries that can be run on our system.

31.4.3   IMPLEMENTATION RESULTS

We have tested our web-based system for performance metrics such as data loading and querying times. Furthermore, we have compared these metrics with the Hive command line interface (CLI). All query times that are used in performance graphs and result tables in this subsection were averaged over three separate runs. We ran two sets of experiments, one using the Freebase system and the other using the TPC-H benchmark.

We have compared the time it takes to load and query the data for our application versus Hive for the Freebase data sets. The data loading time for our application is almost the same as Hive's time for small tables (0.1 and 0.3 million tuples). As the number of tuples increases to 0.5 million and then to 1.67 million tuples, our system gets slower than Hive at loading tuples. This is primarily because of the overhead associated with establishing a connection with the Hive database as well as the time associated with building an XACML policy for the table being loaded.

In addition, we have compared the running time for a simple *SELECT * FROM* query between our application and Hive. We have run the query on the same tables that were used for data loading, but we restricted our results by using the LIMIT clause to only the first 100 tuples. This was done to avoid the large time difference that would occur between our application and Hive's CLI since we have implemented a paging mechanism on the results, whereas Hive's CLI would display all results on the screen. Our application running time is slightly faster than the running time for the query on the Hive CLI. This difference is due to the time taken by the Hive CLI to display the results of the query on the screen. Both running times are fast because Hive does not need to run a MapReduce (http://hadoop.apache.org/docs/r.1.2.1/mapred_tutorial.html) job for this query, but simply needs to return the whole file for the corresponding table from the HDFS.

We have also run a number of other queries and compared the running times of these queries on our system versus Hive for the Freebase system. These queries test the performance of our system in creating and querying views/tables versus Hive. We have tested a variety of queries, including insert, create, select, aggregate, and join queries.

We have also compared the data loading time of our application versus Hive for the *Customer* and *Supplier* tables for SF = 1, 10, and 30 from the TPC-H benchmark. Our system currently allows users to upload data files that are at most 1 GB in size. The TPC-H benchmark's DBGEN tool generates files for the Customer and Supplier tables for SF = 1, 10, and 30 that are less than 1 GB in size. These are the reasons why we have selected the Customer and Supplier tables with SF = 1, 10, and 30 to compare the data loading performance of our system versus Hive. Our system performs similar to Hive at the smallest SF of 1, and as the SF increases our system gets slower than Hive for data loading. Again, this difference in execution performance is because of the overhead associated with the Hive database connection and XACML policy generation. The trend for both our system and Hive is linear as expected, since the size of these tables increases linearly with the SF.

Finally, we have compared the performance of four TPC-H benchmark queries on our system versus Hive. Our system performs as well as the Hive command line interface for the selected queries. On the basis of the query performance times for both our system and Hive, as the size of the tables increases, the time for benchmark query execution also increases as expected. In a production environment, such queries would not be performed at runtime on large data sets. We would rather run these queries offline and could store the results in Hive as views. We could then use a query-rewriting mechanism to return these results efficiently.

31.5   SUMMARY AND DIRECTIONS

In this chapter, we have presented a system that allows cooperating organizations to securely share large amounts of data. We have ensured that the organizations have a large common storage area by using Hadoop. Furthermore, we have used Hive to present users of our system with a structured view of the data and to also enable them to query the data with an SQL-like language. We have used a simple salted hash mechanism to authenticate users in the current version of our system. We plan to implement a more sophisticated technique for authentication in future versions of our system. In this chapter, we have used the ZQL parser to parse any SQL query that is input by the user. We plan to extend this parser with support for keywords such as DESCRIBE and JOIN, which are currently not supported in ZQL. We have abstracted the user from the use of Hive by implementing some basic query-rewriting rules. A part of our future work is to implement materialized views in Hive and extend the basic query-rewriting rules into a complete engine for Hive that takes into account all existing tables/materialized views and the XACML policies defined on them. We have provided fine-grained access control on the shared data using XACML policies. We have also incorporated role-based access control in our framework based on the kinds of queries that users will submit to our system. In the current version of our system, we only provide support for two types of keywords, INSERT and SELECT, as groups for XACML policies.

In the future, we plan to extend our system to include other keyword-based groups such as DELETE and UPDATE. We also plan to test the impact of using different values for parameters provided by Hadoop and Hive on query execution performance. Lastly, the current system is implemented in a private cloud that will be extended to include public clouds such as Amazon Web Services and Amazon Simple Storage Services in future versions.

REFERENCES

All, A. Cloud data storage: It'll still cost you, so give it some thought. Available at http://www.itbusinessedge .com/cm/blogs/all/cloud-data-storage-itll-still-cost-you-so-give-it-some-thought/?cs=38733, January 2010.

Amazon Web Services. Overview of security processes. Available at https://do.awsstatic.com/whitepapers /security/AWS_Security_Whitepaper.pdf, August 2015.

Apache Software Foundation. Apache Hive. Available at https://cwiki.apache.org/confluence/display/Hive /Home%3bjsessionid = 8946C5F66E7FBD0CE2466BAA5C699289, last modified October 2015.

Axon, S. Facebook will celebrate 500 million users next week. Available at http://mashable.com/2010/07/17 /facebook-500-million/, July 2010.

Borthakur, D. HDFS architecture. Available at http://hadoop.apache.org/docs/r1.2.1/hdfs_design.html, 2010.

Brodkin, J. Microsoft Windows Azure and Amazon EC2 on collision course. Available at http://www.networkworld .com/news/2010/062510-microsoft-azure-amazon-ec2.html, June 2010.

Ferraiolo, D.F. and Kuhn, D.R. Role-based access controls. In: *National Computer Security Conference*, Baltimore, pp. 554–563, 1992.

Jia, Y. Running the TPC-H benchmark on Hive, August 2009. Available at https://issues.apache.org/jira/secure /attachment/12416257/TPC-H_on_Hive 2009-08-11.pdf, 2009.

Kumaraswamy, S., Lakshminarayanan, S., Reiter, M., Stein, J., and Wilson, Y. *Domain 12: Guidance for Identity & Access Management V2.1*, April 2010.

Marshall, A., Howard, M., Bugher, G., and Harden, B. Security best practices for developing Windows Azure applications. Available at http://download.microsoft.com/download/7/8/a/78ab795a-8a5b-4860-9422 -fdeleee8f70c1/SecurityBestPracticesWindowsAzuresolutionsfeb2014.docx.

Mitchell, R.L. Cloud storage triggers security worries. Available at http://www.computerworld.com/s/article /340438/Confidence_in_the_Cloud. html, July 2009.

Moses, T. eXtensible Access Control Markup Language (XACML) version 2.0. Available at http://docs.oasis -open.org/xacml/3.0/xacml-3.0-core-spec-os.-en.html, January 2013.

O'Malley, O., Zhang, K., Radia, S., Marti, R., and Harrell, C. Hadoop security design. Available at http://bit .ly/75011o, October 2009.

Parikh, P. Secured information integration with a semantic web based framework. Master's thesis, The University of Texas at Dallas, December 2009.

Ponemon Institute. First annual cost of cyber crime security. Technical report, Ponemon Institute, July 2010.

Salesforce. Salesforce.com and Facebook create new opportunities for enterprise applications to serve Facebook's 120 million users. Available at http://www.salesforce.com/company/news-press/press-releases /2008/11/081103-4.jsp, November 2008.

Sandhu, R.S., Coyne, E.J., Feinstein, H.L., and Youman, C.E. Role-based access control models. *IEEE Computer* 29(2): 38–47, 1996.

Sawyer, J. Tech insight: How to cut security costs without a lot of pain. Available at http://www.darkreading .com/tech-insight-how-to-cut-security-costs-without-a-lot-of-pain/d/d-id/1134035226200159, July 2010.

Talbot, D. How secure is cloud computing? Available at http://www.technologyreview.com/computing/23951/, November 2009.

Thuraisingham, B.M., Khadilkar, V., Gupta, A., Kantarcioglu, M., and Khan, L. Secure data storage and retrieval in the cloud. *CollaborateCom* 1–8, 2010.

Thusoo, A., Sarma, J.S., Jain, N., Shao, Z., Chakka, P., Anthony, S., Liu, H., Wyckoff, P., and Murthy, R. Hive—A warehousing solution over a map-reduce framework. *PVLDB* 2(2): 1626–1629, 2009.

Weigend, A. The social data revolution(s). Available at http://blogs.hbr.org/now-new-next/2009/05/the-social -data-revolution.html, May 2009.

32 Secure Cloud Query Processing for Semantic Web-Based Social Media

32.1 INTRODUCTION

As we have discussed, the semantic web is becoming increasingly ubiquitous. More small and large businesses, such as Oracle, IBM, Adobe, Software AG, and many others, are actively using semantic web technologies, and broad application areas such as health-care and life sciences are considering its possibilities for data integration (W3C, 2009). Sir Tim Berners-Lee originally envisioned the semantic web as a machine-understandable web (Berners-Lee, 1998). The power of the semantic web lies in its codification of relationships among web resources (W3C, 2009). Because of this, semantic web technologies are being used to represent and analyze social media data. For example, Resource Description Framework (RDF) is being used to represent social networks, while Web Ontology Language (OWL) is being used to represent ontologies for understanding social networks. Furthermore, SPARQL is being used to query social networks, while Semantic Web Rule Language (SWRL) is being used to analyze social networks.

Semantic web, along with ontologies, is one of the most robust ways to represent knowledge as well as social media data. An ontology formally describes the concepts or classes in a domain, various properties of the classes, the relationships between classes, and restrictions. A knowledge base can be constructed by an ontology and its various class instances. An example of a knowledge base (ontology and its instance) is presented in Figure 32.1.

RDF is widely used for semantic web-based social media, owing to its expressive power, semantic interoperability, and reusability. Most RDF stores in current use, including Joseki (http://www.joseki.org), Kowari (http://kowari.sourceforge.net), 3store (Harris and Shadbolt, 2005), and Sesame (Broekstra et al., 2002) are not primarily concerned with security. Efforts have been made to incorporate security, especially in Jena (Jain and Farkas, 2006; Reddivari et al., 2005); however, one drawback of Jena is that it lacks scalability. Its execution times can become rather slow with larger data sets, making certain queries over large stores intractable (e.g., those with 10 million triples or more) (Husain et al., 2009, 2010). On the other hand, large RDF stores can be stored and retrieved from cloud computers owing to their scalability, parallel processing ability, cost-effectiveness, and availability. Hadoop (http://hadoop.apache.org/), one of the most widely used cloud computing environments, uses Google's MapReduce framework. MapReduce splits large jobs into smaller jobs, and combines the results of these jobs to produce the final output once the subjobs are complete. Prior work has demonstrated that large RDF graphs can be efficiently stored and queried in these clouds (Choi et al., 2009; Husain et al., 2009, 2010; Mika and Tummarello, 2008).

While storing and managing large RDF graphs has received some attention, access control for RDF stores in Hadoop has received very little attention. In Chapter 25, we discussed a cloud-based semantic web cloud query-processing system that utilizes Hadoop for distributed storage. In this chapter, we describe a system that implements access control for RDF data on Hadoop. In particular, our access control system is implemented on top of the query-processing systems discussed in Chapter 25. Specifically, we have designed and implemented a token-based access control system. System administrators grant access tokens for security-relevant data according to agents' needs and security levels. Conflicts that might arise due to the assignment of conflicting access tokens to the

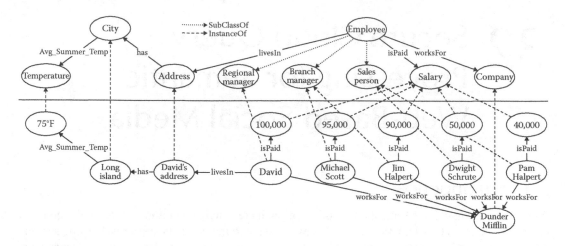

FIGURE 32.1   Knowledge base.

same agent are resolved using the time stamps of the access tokens. We use the Lehigh University Benchmark (LUBM) (Guo et al., 2005) test instances for experiments. A few sample scenarios have been generated and implemented in Hadoop.

We have made several contributions. First, we designed an architecture that scales well to extremely large data sets. Second, we addressed access control not only at the level of users but also at the level of subjects, objects, and predicates, making policies finer grained and more expressive than in past works. Third, a time stamp-based conflict detection and resolution algorithm was designed. Fourth, the architecture was implemented and tested on benchmark data in several alternative stages: query rewriting (preprocessing phase), embedded enforcement (MapReduce execution phase), and postprocessing enforcement (data display phase). Finally, the entire system is being implemented on Hadoop, an open source cloud computing environment. The work discussed in the chapter is especially beneficial for others considering access control for RDF data in Hadoop for social media data.

The organization of this chapter is as follows. In Section 32.2, we present related work and a brief overview of Hadoop and MapReduce. Section 32.3 introduces access tokens, access token tuples, conflicts, and our conflict resolution algorithm. We describe the architecture of our system in Section 32.4. In Section 32.5, we describe the impact of assigning access tokens to agents, including experiments and their running times. Finally, Section 32.6 concludes with a summary and suggestions for future work. Figure 32.2 illustrates the contents of this chapter.

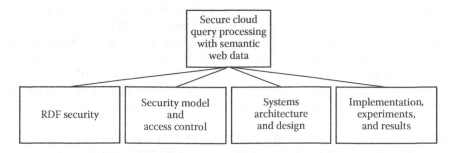

FIGURE 32.2   Secure cloud query processing with semantic web-based social media.

32.2   BACKGROUND

32.2.1   RELATED WORK

We begin by describing prior work on RDF security for single machines. We then summarize some of the cloud computing architectures that store RDF data. Finally, we provide a summary of our own prior work.

Although extensive research has been undertaken on storing, representing, and reasoning about RDF knowledge, research on security and access control issues for RDF stores is comparatively sparse (Reddivari et al., 2005). Reddivari et al. (2005) have implemented access control based on a set of policy rules. They address insertion/deletion actions of triples, models, and sets in RDF stores, as well as see and use actions. Jain and Farkas (2006) have described RDF protection objects as RDF patterns, and designed security requirements for them. They show that the security level of a subclass or subproperty should be at least as restricted as the supertype. The RDF triple-based access control model discussed in Kim et al. (2008) considers explicit and implicit authorization propagation.

Most of these works are implemented in Jena. However, Jena scales poorly in that it runs on single machines and is unable to handle large amounts of data (Husain et al., 2009, 2010). Husain et al. (2009, 2010) designed and implemented an architecture for storing and querying large RDF graphs. Mika and Tummarello (2008) stored RDF data in Hadoop. The SPIDER system (Choi et al., 2009) stores and processes large RDF data sets, but lacks an access control mechanism.

Our architecture supports access control for large data sets by including an access control layer in the architecture discussed in Husain et al. (2010). Instead of assigning access controls directly to users or agents, our method generates tokens for specific access levels and assigns these tokens to agents, considering the business needs and security levels of the agents. Although tokens have been used by others for access control to manage XML documents (Bouganim et al., 2004) and digital information (Holmquist et al., 1999), these have not been used for RDF stores. One of the advantages of using tokens is that they can be reused if the needs and security requirements for multiple agents are identical.

Hadoop and MapReduce. Next, we provide a brief overview of Hadoop (http://hadoop.apache .org/) and MapReduce. In Hadoop, the unit of computation is called a *job*. Users submit jobs to Hadoop's JobTracker component. Each job has two phases: map and reduce. The map phase takes as input a key–value pair and may output zero or more key–value pairs. In the reduce phase, the values for each key are grouped together into collections traversable by an iterator. These key–iterator pairs are then passed to the reduce method, which also outputs zero or more key–value pairs. When a job is submitted to the JobTracker, Hadoop attempts to position the map processes near the input data in the cluster. Each map and reduce process works independently without communicating. This lack of communication is advantageous for both speed and simplicity.

32.3   ACCESS CONTROL

32.3.1   MODEL

Definition 32.1

Access tokens (AT) permit access to security-relevant data. An agent in possession of an AT may view the data permitted by that AT. We denote ATs by positive integers.

Definition 32.2

Access token tuples (ATT) have the form <AccessToken, Element, ElementType, ElementName>, where Element can be Subject, Object, or Predicate, and ElementType can be described as URI,

DataType, Literal, Model, or BlankNode. Model is used to access subject models, and will be explained later in the section.

For example, in the ontology/knowledge base in Figure 32.1, David is a subject and <1, Subject, URI, David> is an ATT. Any agent having AT_1 may retrieve David's information over all files (subject to any other security restrictions governing access to URIs [Uniform Resource Identifiers], literals, etc., associated with David's objects). When describing ATTs, we leave the ElementName blank (_).

On the basis of the record organization, we support six access levels along with a few subtypes described below. Agents may be assigned one or more of the following access levels. Access levels with a common AT combine conjunctively, while those with different ATs combine disjunctively.

1. *Predicate data access*: If an object type is defined for one particular predicate in an access level, then an agent having that access level may read the whole predicate file (subject to any other policy restrictions). For example, <1, Predicate, isPaid, _> is an ATT that permits its possessor to read the entire predicate file isPaid.

2. *Predicate and subject data access*: Agents possessing a subject ATT may access data associated with a particular subject, where the subject can be either a URI or a DataType. Combining one of these subject ATTs with a predicate data access ATT having the same AT grants the agent access to a specific subject of a specific predicate. For example:
   a. Predicate and subject as URIs: Combining the ATTs <1, Predicate, isPaid> and <1, Subject, URI, MichaelScott> (drawn from the ontology in Figure 32.1) permits an agent with AT_1 to access a subject with URI MichaelScott of predicate isPaid.
   b. Predicate and subject as DataTypes: Similarly, Predicate and DataType ATTs can be combined to permit access to subjects of a specific data type over a specific predicate file.

   For brevity, we omit descriptions of the different subject and object variations of each of the remaining access levels.

3. *Predicate and object*: This access level permits a principal to extract the names of subjects satisfying a particular predicate and object. For example, with ATTs <1, Predicate, hasVitamins, _> and <1, Object, URI, E>, an agent possessing AT_1 may view the names of subjects (e.g., foods) that have vitamin E. More generally, if X_1 and X_2 are the set of triples generated by Predicate and Object triples (respectively) describing an AT, then agents possessing the AT may view set $X_1 \cap X_2$ of triples. An illustration of this example is displayed in Figure 32.3.

4. *Subject access*: With this access level, an agent may read the subject's information over all the files. This is one of the less restrictive access levels. The subject can be a DataType or BlankNode.

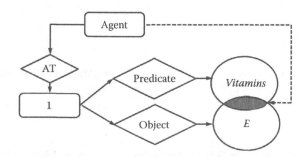

FIGURE 32.3 Conjunctive combination of ATTs with a common AT.

5. *Object access*: With this access level, an agent may read the object's subjects over all the files. Like the previous level, this is one of the less restrictive access levels. The object can be a URI, DataType, Literal, or BlankNode.

6. *Subject model level access*: Model level access permits an agent to read all necessary predicate files to obtain all objects of a given subject. Of these objects, the ones that are URIs are next treated as subjects to extract their respective predicates and objects. This process continues iteratively until all objects finally become literals or blank nodes. In this manner, agents possessing model-level access may generate models on a given subject.

The following example drawn from Figure 32.1 illustrates David lives in LongIsland. LongIsland is a subject with an Avg_Summer_Temp predicate having object 75°F. An agent with model level access of David reads the average summer temperature of Long Island.

32.3.2 Access Token Assignment

Definition 32.3

An *access token list* (AT list) is an array of one or more ATs granted to a given agent, along with a time stamp identifying the time at which each was granted. A separate AT list is maintained for each agent.

When a system administrator decides to add an AT to an agent's AT list, the AT and time stamp are first stored in a temporary variable. Before committing the change, the system must first detect potential conflicts in the new AT list.

Final Output of an Agent's ATs. Each AT permits access to a set of triples. We refer to this set as the AT's *result set*. The set of triples accessible by an agent is the union of the result sets of the ATs in the agent's AT list. Formally, if Y_1, Y_2, ..., Y_n are the result sets of ATs AT_1, AT_2, ..., AT_n (respectively) in an agent's AT list, then the agent may access the triples in set $Y_1 \cup Y_2 \cup$, ..., $\cup Y_n$.

Security Level Defaults. An administrator's AT assignment burden can be considerably simplified by conservatively choosing default security levels for data in the system. In our implementation, all items in the data store have default security levels. The personal information of individuals is kept private by denying access to any URI of data type Person by default. This prevents agents from making inferences about any individual to whom they have not been granted explicit permission. However, if an agent is granted explicit access to a particular type or property, the agent is also granted default access to the subtypes or subproperties of that type or property.

As an example, consider a predicate file Likes that lists elements that an individual likes. Assume further that Jim is a person who likes Flying, SemanticWeb, and Jenny, which are URIs of type Hobby, ResearchInterest, and Person, respectively, and 1 is an AT with ATTs <1, Subject, URI, Jim> and <1, Likes, Predicate, _>. By default, agent Ben, having only AT_1, cannot learn that Jenny is in Jim's Likes list since Jenny's data type is Person. However, if Ben also has AT_2 described by ATT <2, Object, URI, Jenny>, then Ben will be able to see Jenny in Jim's Likes list.

32.3.3 Conflicts

A conflict arises when the following three conditions occur: (i) an agent possesses two ATs, AT_1 and AT_2; (ii) the result set of AT_2 is a proper subset of AT_1; and (iii) the time stamp of AT_1 is earlier than the time stamp of AT_2. In this case, the latter, more specific AT supersedes the former, so AT_1 is discarded from the AT list to resolve the conflict. Such conflicts arise in two varieties, which we term *subset conflicts* and *subtype conflicts*.

A subset conflict occurs when AT_2 is a conjunction of ATTs that refines those of AT_1. For example, suppose AT_1 is defined by ATT <1, Subject, URI, Sam> and AT_2 is defined by ATTs <2, Subject, URI, Sam> and <2, Predicate, HasAccounts, _>. In this case, the result set of AT_2 is a subset of the result set of AT_1. A conflict will therefore occur if an agent possessing AT_1 is later assigned AT_2. When this occurs, AT_1 is discarded from the agent's AT list to resolve the conflict.

Subtype conflicts occur when the ATTs in AT_2 involve data types that are subtypes of those in AT_1. The data types can be those of subjects, objects, or both.

Conflict resolution is summarized by Algorithm 32.1. Here, Subset(AT_1, AT_2) is a function that returns true if the result set of AT_1 is a proper subset of the result set of AT_2, and SubjectSubType(AT_1, AT_2) returns true if the subject of AT_1 is a subtype of the subject of AT_2. Similarly, ObjectSubType(AT_1, AT_2) decides subtyping relations for objects instead of subjects.

Algorithm 32.1: Conflict Detection and Resolution

Input: AT newAT with time stamp TS_{newAT}
Result: Detect conflict and, if none exists, add
    (newAT, TS_{newAT}) to the agent's AT list
1   currentAT[]← the ATs and their time stamps;
2 if (!Subset(newAT, tempATTS) AND
   !Subset(tempATTS, newAT) AND
   !SubjectSubType(newAT, tempATTS)) AND
   !SubjectSubType(tempATTS, newAT) AND
   !ObjectSubType(newAT, tempATTS)) AND
   !ObjectSubType(tempATTS, newAT)) then
3   currentAT[$length_{currentAT}$].AT ← newAT;
4   currentAT[$length_{currentAT}$].TS ← TS newAT;
5 else
6   count ← 0;
7   **while** count < $length_{currentAT}$ **do**
8   AT tempATTS ← currentAT [count].AT
9   tempTS ← currentAT [count].TS;
10   /* the time stamp during the AT assignment */
11   **if** (Subset(newAT, tempATTS) AND ($TS_{newAT} \geq$ tempTS)) **then**
12   /* a conflict occurs */
13   currentAT [count].AT ← newAT;
14   currentAT [count].TS ← TS newAT;
15   **else if** ((Subset(tempATTS, newAT)) AND (tempTS < TS_{newAT})) **then**
16   currentAT [count].AT ← newAT;
17   currentAT [count].TS ← TS newAT;
18   **else if** ((SubjectSubType(newAT, tempATTS) OR
            ObjectSubType (newAT, tempATTS)) AND ($TS_{newAT} \geq$ tempTS) **then**
19   /* a conflict occurs */
20   currentAT [count].AT ← newAT;
21   currentAT [count].TS ← TS newAT;
22   **else if** ((SubjectSubType(tempATTS, newAT) OR ObjectSubType (tempATTS, newAT))
      AND (tempATTS < TS_{newAT})) **then**
23   currentAT [count].AT ← newAT;
24   currentAT [count].TS ← TS newAT;
25   end
26   count ← count + 1
27   end
28 end

32.4 SYSTEM ARCHITECTURE

32.4.1 OVERVIEW OF THE ARCHITECTURE

Our architecture consists of two components. The upper part of Figure 32.4 depicts the data preprocessing component, and the lower part shows the components responsible for answering queries.

Three subcomponents perform data generation and preprocessing. We convert RDF/XML (Beckett, 2004) to N-Triples serialization format (Grant and Beckett, 2004) using our N-Triple converter component. The Predicate Split (PS) component takes the N-Triples data and splits it into predicate files. These steps are described in this section. The output of the last component is then used to gather summary statistics, which are delivered to the Hadoop Distributed File System (HDFS).

The bottom part of the architecture shows the access control unit and the MapReduce framework. The access control unit takes part in different phases of query execution. When the user submits a query, the query is rewritten (if possible) to enforce one or more access control policies. The MapReduce framework has three subcomponents. It takes the rewritten SPARQL query from the query interface engine and passes it to the input selector and plan generator. This component selects the input files, decides how many jobs are needed, and passes the information to the job executer component, which submits corresponding jobs to Hadoop. The job executer component communicates with the access control unit to get the relevant policies to enforce, and runs jobs accordingly. It then relays the query answer from Hadoop to the user. To answer queries that require inferencing, we use the Pellet OWL reasoner. The policies are stored in the HDFS and loaded by the access control unit each time the framework loads.

32.4.2 DATA GENERATION AND STORAGE

We use the LUBM (Guo et al., 2005) data set for our experiments. This benchmark data set is widely used by researchers (Guo et al., 2005). The LUBM data generator generates data in RDF/XML serialization format. This format is not suitable for our purpose because we store data in HDFS as flat

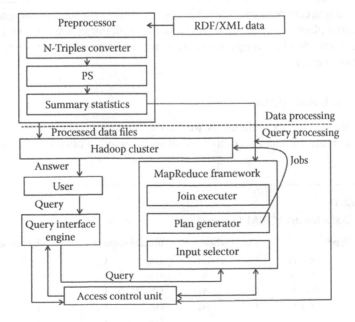

FIGURE 32.4 System architecture.

files. If the data is in RDF/XML format, then to retrieve even a single triple, we need to parse the entire file. Also, the RDF/XML format is not suitable as an input for a MapReduce job. Therefore, we store data as N-Triples, because with that format we have a complete RDF triple (subject, predicate, and object) in one file line, which is very convenient for MapReduce jobs. We therefore convert the data to N-Triple format, partitioning the data by predicate. This step is called PS. In real-world RDF data sets, the number of distinct predicates is no more than 10 or 20 (Stocker et al., 2008). This partitioning reduces the search space for any SPARQL query that does not contain a variable predicate (Prud'hommeaux and Seaborne, 2008). For such a query, we can just pick a file for each predicate and run the query on those files only. We name the files by predicate for simplicity; for example, all the triples containing predicate p1:pred are stored in a file named p1-pred. A more detailed description of this process is provided in Husain et al. (2010).

Example Data. Table 32.1 shows sample data for three predicates. The leftmost column shows the type file for student objects after the PS step. It lists only the subjects of the triples having rdf:type predicate and student object. The remaining columns show the advisor, takesCourse, and teacherOf predicate files after the PS step. Each row has a subject–object pair. In all cases, the predicate can be retrieved from the file name.

32.4.3 POLICY ENFORCEMENT

Our MapReduce framework enforces policies in two phases. Some policies can be enforced by simply rewriting a SPARQL query during the query-parsing phase. The remaining policies can be enforced in the query-answering phase in two ways. First, we can enforce the policies as we run MapReduce jobs to answer a query. Second, we can run the jobs for a query as if there is no policy to enforce, and then take the output and run a set of jobs to enforce the policies. These postprocessing jobs are called filter jobs. In both cases, we enforce predicate-level policies while we select the input files by the input selector. In the following sections, we discuss these approaches in detail.

Query Rewriting. Policies involving predicates can be enforced by rewriting a SPARQL query. This involves replacing predicate variables by the predicates to which a user has access. An example illustrates. Suppose a user's AT list consists of AT_1 described by ATT <1, Predicate, takesCourses> (i.e., the user may only access predicate file takesCourse). If the user submits the query on the left of Figure 32.5, we can replace predicate variable $?p$ with takesCourse. The rewritten query is shown on the right of the figure. After the query is rewritten, we can answer the query in two ways, detailed in the following two sections.

32.4.4 EMBEDDED ENFORCEMENT

In this approach, we enforce the policies as we answer a query by Hadoop jobs. We leverage the query language's join mechanism to do this kind of enforcement. Policies involving URIs, literals,

---

TABLE 32.1

Sample Data for an LUBM Query

Type		ub:advisor		ub:takesCourse		ub:teacherOf	
GS_1	Student	GS_2	A_2	GS_1	C_2	A_1	C_1
GS_2	Student	GS_1	A_1	GS_3	C_1	A_2	C_2
GS_3	Student	GS_3	A_3	GS_3	C_3	A_3	C_3
GS_4	Student	GS_4	A_4	GS_2	C_4	A_4	C_4
				GS_1	C_1	A_5	C_5
				GS_4	C_2		

SELECT ?o WHERE   SELECT ?o WHERE

{ A?p ?o }   ⇒   { A takesCourse ?o }

FIGURE 32.5   SPARQL query before and after rewriting.

etc., can be enforced in this way. For example, suppose access to data for some confidential courses is restricted to only a few students. If an unprivileged user wishes to list the courses a student has taken, we can join the file listing the confidential courses with the file takesCourse, and thereby enforce the desired policy within the Reduce phase of a Hadoop job. Suppose courses C_3 and C_4 are confidential courses. If an unprivileged user wishes to list the courses taken by GS_3, then we can answer the query by the map and reduce code shown in Algorithms 32.2 and 32.3.

Algorithm 32.2: Pseudo-Code for EEMAP

1: splits ← value.split ()
2: **if** Input file = sensitiveCourses **then**
3:   output (splits [0], "S")
4:   else if splits [0] = GS_3 then
5:   output (splits [1], "T")
6: **end if**

Algorithm 32.3: Pseudo-Code for EEREDUCE

1: count ← 0
2: iter ← values.iterator ()
3: **while** iter.hasNext () **do**
4:   count ++
5:   t ← iter.next ()
6: **end while**
7: **if** count = 1 AND t = "T" **then**
8:   output (key)
9: **end if**

Algorithm 32.2 shows the code of the map phase. It first splits each line into a key and a value. If the input is from a confidential course file, it outputs the course and a flag ("S" for *secret*) denoting a confidential course as the output whether the subject is GS_3 in line 4. If so, it outputs the course as the key and a flag ("T" for *takes*) indicating that the course is of student GS_3. The left half of Table 32.2 shows the output of Algorithm 32.2 on the example data.

TABLE 32.2

EEMap Output and EEReduce Input

EEMap Output		EEReduce Input	
Key	Value	Key	Values
C1	T	C1	T
C3	S	C3	S,T
C3	T	C4	S,T
C4	S		

Algorithm 32.3 shows the code of the reduce phase. It gets a course as the key and the flag strings as the value. The right half of Table 32.2 shows the input of Algorithm 32.2 on the example data. The code simply counts the number of student GS_3 (line 7), then it outputs the course (line 8). A confidential course that is taken by the student GS_3 has an additional flag, raising the count to 2, and preventing those courses from being reported. A confidential course not taken by the student will also have one flag, indicating that it is a confidential course. The check whether the flag is the one for the course taken by student GS_3 prevents such courses from being reported. These two checks together ensure that only nonconfidential courses taken by GS_3 are divulged in the output. Hence, only course C_1 appears in the output.

Postprocessing Enforcement. The second approach runs jobs as if there are no access controls, and then runs one or more additional jobs to filter the output in accordance with the policy. The advantage of this approach is that it is simple to implement; however, it may take longer to answer the query. We can use the previous example to illustrate this approach. We first run the job as if there is no restriction on courses. Then, we run one extra job to enforce the policy. The extra job takes two files as input: the output of the first job and the confidentialCourses file containing the URIs of confidential courses. In the map phase, we output the course as the key and, depending on the input file, a flag string. The map code is largely the same as Algorithm 32.2. The only difference is that we do not need to check the URI identifying the student, since the output of the first job will contain the courses taken by only that student. The code for the reduce phase remains the same. Hence, at the end of the second job, we obtain output that does not contain any confidential courses.

32.5   EXPERIMENTAL SETUP AND RESULTS

We ran our experiments in a Hadoop cluster of 10 nodes. Each node had a Pentium IV 2.80 GHz processor, 4 GB main memory, and 640 GB disk space. The operating system was Ubuntu Linux 9.04. We compared our embedded enforcement approach with our postprocessing enforcement approach. We used the LUBM100, LUBM500, LUBM1000, LUBM2000, LUBM6000, and LUBM9000 data sets for the experiments.

We experimented with these approaches using two scenarios: takesCourse and displayTeachers. In the takesCourse scenario, a list of confidential courses cannot be viewed by an unprivileged user for any student. A query was submitted to display the courses taken by one particular student. In the displayTeachers scenario, an unprivileged user may view information about the lecturers only. A query was submitted to display the URI of people who are employed in a particular department. Even though professors, assistant professors, associate professors, etc., are employed in that department, only URIs of Lecturers are returned because of the policy. The detailed results are given in Khaled et al. (2010). We observed that postprocessing enforcement always takes 20–80% more time than the embedded enforcement approach. This can be easily explained by the extra job needed in postprocessing. Hadoop takes roughly equal times to set up jobs regardless of the input and output data sizes of the jobs. The postprocessing enforcement approach runs more jobs than the embedded enforcement approach, yielding the observed overhead.

32.6   SUMMARY AND DIRECTIONS

Access controls for RDF data on single machines have been widely discussed in the literature; however, these systems scale poorly to large data sets. The amount of RDF data on the web is growing rapidly, so this is a serious limitation. One of the most efficient ways to handle this data is to store it in cloud computers. However, access control has not yet been adequately addressed for cloud-resident RDF data. Our implemented mechanism incorporates a token-based access control system where users of the system are granted tokens based on business needs and authorization levels. We are currently building a generic system that incorporates tokens and resolves policy conflicts. Our goal is to implement subject model level access that recursively extracts objects of subjects and treats these objects as subjects as long as these objects are URIs. This will allow agents possessing model level access to generate models on a given subject.

Our current work also examines secure query processing in hybrid clouds (Khadilkar et al., 2012; Oktay et al., 2012), and we will apply them for social media systems in the cloud. In the future, we will explore various types of access control models for social media query processing and evaluate them. This will give us a better idea of the most suitable access control models for cloud-based social media query processing.

REFERENCES

Beckett, D. RDF/XML syntax specification (revised). Technical report, W3C, February 2004.

Berners-Lee, T. Semantic web road map. Available at http://www.w3.org/DesignIssues/Semantic.html, 1998.

Bouganim, L., Ngoc, F.D., and Pucheral, P. Client-based access control management for XML documents. In: *Proc. 20émes Journées Bases de Données Avancées (BDA)*, Montpellier, France, October 2004, pp. 65–89, 2004.

Broekstra, J., Kampman, A., and van Harmelen, F. Sesame: A generic architecture for storing and querying RDF. In: *Proc. 1st International Semantic Web Conference (ISWC)*, June 2002, Sardinia, Italy, pp. 54–68, 2002.

Choi, H., Son, J., Cho, Y., Sung, M.K., and Chung, Y.D. SPIDER: A system for scalable, parallel/distributed evaluation of large-scale RDF data. In: *Proc. 18th ACM Conference on Information and Knowledge Management (CIKM)*, November 2009, Hong Kong, China, pp. 2087–2088, 2009.

Grant, J. and Beckett, D. RDF test cases. Technical report, W3C, February 2004.

Guo, Y., Pan, Z., and Heflin, J. LUBM: A benchmark for OWL knowledge base systems. *Journal of Web Semantics* 3(2–3): 158–182, 2005.

Harris, S. and Shadbolt, N. SPARQL query processing with conventional relational database systems. In: *Proc. Web Information Systems Engineering (WISE) International Workshop on Scalable Semantic Web Knowledge Base Systems (SSWS)*, November 2005, New York, pp. 235–244, 2005.

Holmquist, L.E., Redström, J., and Ljungstrand, P. Token-based access to digital information. In: *Proc. 1st International Symposium on Handheld and Ubiquitous Computing (HUC)*, September 1999, Karlsruhe, Germany, pp. 234–245, 1999.

Husain, M.F., Doshi, P., Khan, L., and Thuraisingham, B.M. Storage and retrieval of large RDF graph using Hadoop and MapReduce. In: *Proc. 1st International Conference on Cloud Computing (CloudCom)*, December 2009, pp. 680–686, Beijing, China, 2009.

Husain, M.F., Khan, L., Kantarcioglu, M., and Thuraisingham, B. Data intensive query processing for large RDF graphs using cloud computing tools. In Proc. IEEE 3rd International Conference on Cloud Computing (CLOUD), July 2010, Miami, FL, pp. 1–10, 2010.

Jain, A. and Farkas, C. Secure resource description framework: An access control model. In: *Proc. 11th ACM Symposium on Access Control Models and Technologies (SACMAT)*, Lake Tahoe, CA, June 2006, pp. 121–129, 2006.

Khadilkar, V., Oktay, K.Y., Kantarcioglu, M., and Mehrotra, S. Secure data processing over hybrid clouds. *IEEE Data Engineering Bulletin* 35(4): 46–54, 2012.

Khaled, A., Husain, M.F., Khan, L., Hamlen, K.W., and Thuraisingham, B.M. A token-based access control system for RDF data in the clouds. In: *IEEE CloudCom*, Indianapolis, IN, December 2010.

Kim, J., Jung, K., and Park, S. An introduction to authorization conflict problem in DRDF access control. In: *Proceedings of the 12th International Conference on Knowledge-Based Intelligent Information and Engineering Systems (KES)*, Zagreg, Croatia, September 2008, pp. 583–592, 2008.

Mika, P. and Tummarello, G. Web semantics in the clouds. *IEEE Intelligent Systems* 23(5): 82–87, 2008.

Oktay, K.Y., Khadilkar, V., Hore, B., Kantarcioglu, M., Mehrotra, S., and Thuraisingham, B.M. Risk-aware workload distribution in hybrid clouds. In: *IEEE Cloud*, Honolulu, HI, June 2012.

Prud'hommeaux, E. and Seaborne, A. SPARQL query language for RDF. Technical report, W3C, January 2008.

Reddivari, P., Finin, T., and Joshi, A. Policy based access control for an RDF store. In: *Proc. IJCAI Workshop on Semantic Web for Collaborative Knowledge Acquisition*, Hyderabud, India, January 2007.

Stocker, M., Seaborne, A., Bernstein, A., Kiefer, C., and Reynolds, D. SPARQL basic graph pattern optimization using selectivity estimation. In: *Proc. 17th International Conference on World Wide Web (WWW)*, Beijing, China, April 2008, pp. 595–604, 2008.

W3C. Semantic web frequently asked questions. Available at http://www.w3.org/RDF/FAQ, 2009.

33 Cloud-Centric Assured Information Sharing for Social Networks

33.1 INTRODUCTION

The advent of *cloud computing* and the continuing movement toward SaaS (software as a service) paradigms has posed an increasing need for *assured information sharing* (AIS) as a service in the cloud. The urgency of this need was voiced in April 2011 by National Security Agency (NSA) Chief Information Officer Lonny Anderson in describing the agency's focus on a *cloud-centric* approach to information sharing with other agencies (Hoover, 2011). Likewise, the Department of Defense (DoD) has been embracing cloud computing paradigms to more efficiently, economically, flexibly, and scalably meet its vision of "delivering the power of information to ensure mission success through an agile enterprise with freedom of maneuverability across the information environment" (DoD, 2007, 2012). Both agencies, therefore, have a tremendous need for effective AIS technologies and tools for cloud environments. Furthermore, there is also an urgent need for those in different social circles within agencies to share the information in the cloud securely and in a timely manner. Therefore, extending the AIS tools to function in a cloud-centric social media environment is becoming a need for many organizations.

Although a number of AIS tools have been developed over the past 5 years for policy-based information sharing (Awad et al., 2010; Finin et al., 2009; Rao et al., 2008; Thuraisingham et al., 2008), to our knowledge none of these tools operate in the cloud and hence do not provide the scalability needed to support large numbers of users utilizing massive amounts of data such as social media users. Our recent prototype systems for supporting cloud-based AIS have applied cloud-centric engines that query large amounts of data in relational databases via non-cloud policy engines that enforce policies expressed in XACML (Thuraisingham et al., 2010, 2011). While this is a significant improvement over prior efforts (and has given us insights into implementing cloud-based solutions), it nevertheless has at least three significant limitations. First, XACML-based policy specifications are not expressive enough to support many of the complex policies needed for AIS missions like those of the NSA and DoD, as well as applications such as social networks. Second, to meet the scalability and efficiency requirements of mission-critical tasks, the policy engine needs to operate in the cloud rather than externally. Third, secure query processing based on relational technology has limitations in representing and processing unstructured data needed for command and control applications.

To share the large amounts of data securely and efficiently, there clearly needs to be a seamless integration of the policy and data managers for social media in the cloud. Therefore, to satisfy the cloud-centric AIS needs of the DoD and NSA, we need (i) a cloud-resident policy manager that enforces information-sharing policies expressed in a semantically rich language, and (ii) a cloud-resident data manager that securely stores and retrieves data and seamlessly integrates with the policy manager. To our knowledge, no such system currently exists. Therefore, our project has designed and developed such cloud-based assured information-sharing systems for social media users. Our policy engine as well as a data are represented using semantic web technologies, and therefore can represent and reason about social media data. That is, we have developed a cloud-centric policy manager that enforces policies specified in Resource Description Framework (RDF) and a

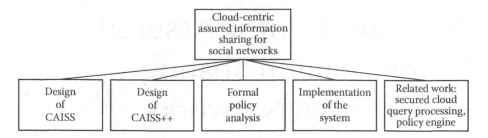

FIGURE 33.1   Cloud-centric assured information sharing for social networks.

cloud-centric data manager that will store and manage data, such as social graphs and associated data, also specified in RDF. This RDF data manager is essentially a query engine for SPARQL, a language widely used by the semantic web community to query RDF data. Furthermore, our policy manager and data manager will have seamless integration since they both manage RDF data.

To address the assured information-sharing requirements of various organizations, including social media users, we have designed and developed a series of cloud-based assured information-sharing systems. This chapter provides an overview of our design. The organization of this chapter is as follows. Our design philosophy is discussed in Section 33.2. Our system design will be discussed in Section 33.3. In particular, we will discuss the design and implementation of cloud-centric assured information sharing system (CAISS) in Section 33.3.1 and the design of CAISS++ in Section 33.3.2. Formal policy analysis and the implementation approach for CAISS++ will be provided in Sections 33.3.3 and 33.3.4, respectively. Related efforts are discussed in Section 33.4. Commercial developments are discussed in Section 33.5. Extending our approach to social media applications is discussed in Section 33.6. The chapter is concluded in Section 33.7. Figure 33.1 illustrates the contents of this chapter. Details of our work can also be found in Thuraisingham et al. (2012).

33.2   DESIGN PHILOSOPHY

Our design has proceeded in two phases. During phase 1, we have designed and implemented a proof-of-concept prototype of a CAISS that utilizes the technology components we have designed in-house as well as open source tools. CAISS consists of two components: a cloud-centric policy manager that enforces policies specified in RDF, and a cloud-centric data manager that will store and manage data also specified in RDF. This RDF data manager is essentially a query engine for SPARQL Protocol and RDF Query Language (SPARQL), a language widely used by the semantic web community to query RDF data. RDF is a semantic web language that is considerably more expressive than XACML for specifying and reasoning about policies. Furthermore, our policy manager and data manager will have seamless integration since they both manage RDF data. We have chosen this RDF-based approach for cloud-centric AIS during phase 1 because it satisfies the two necessary conditions stated in the previous paragraph, and we have already developed an RDF-based non-cloud-centric policy manager (Cadenhead et al., 2011a) and an RDF-based cloud-centric data manager for the Air Force Office of Scientific Research (AFOSR) (Husain et al., 2011). Having parts of the two critical components needed to build a useful cloud-centric AIS system puts us in an excellent position to build a useful proof-of-concept demonstration system, CAISS. Specifically, we are enhancing our RDF-based policy engine to operate on a cloud, extend our cloud-centric RDF data manager to integrate with the policy manager, and build an integrated framework for CAISS. Our goal is to extend CAISS for a social media environment.

While our initial CAISS design and implementation will be the first system supporting cloud-centric AIS, it will operate only on a single trusted cloud and will therefore not support information sharing across multiple clouds. Furthermore, while CAISS's RDF-based, formal semantics approach to policy specification will be significantly more expressive than XACML-based approaches; it will not support an enhanced machine interpretability of content since RDF does not provide a sufficiently rich vocabulary (e.g., support for classes and properties). Phase 2 will therefore develop a fully functional and robust AIS system called CAISS++ that addresses these deficiencies. The preliminary design for CAISS++ is completed and will be discussed later in this chapter. CAISS is an important stepping-stone toward CAISS++ because CAISS can be used as a baseline framework against which CAISS++ can be compared along several performance dimensions, such as storage model efficiency and Web Ontology Language (OWL)-based policy expressiveness. Furthermore, since CAISS and CAISS++ share the same core components (policy engine and query processor), the lessons learned from the implementation and integration of these components in CAISS will be invaluable during the development of CAISS++. Finally, the evaluation and testing of CAISS will provide us with important insights into the shortcomings of CAISS, which can then be systematically addressed in the implementation of CAISS++.

We will also conduct a formal analysis of policy specifications and the software-level protection mechanisms that enforce them to provide exceptionally high-assurance security guarantees for the resulting system. We envisage CAISS++ to be used in highly mission-critical applications. Therefore, it becomes imperative to provide guarantees that the policies are enforced in a provably correct manner. We have extensive expertise in formal policy analysis (Jones and Hamlen, 2010, 2011) and their enforcement via machine-certified, in-line reference monitors (Hamlen et al., 2006a,b; Sridhar and Hamlen, 2010). Such analyses will be leveraged to model and certify security properties enforced by core software components in the trusted computing base of CAISS++.

CAISS++ will be a breakthrough technology for information sharing because it uses a novel combination of cloud-centric policy specification and enforcement along with a cloud-centric data storage and efficient query evaluation. CAISS++ will make use of ontologies, a sublanguage of the OWL, to build policies. A mixture of such ontologies with a semantic web-based rule language (e.g., SWRL) facilitates distributed reasoning on the policies to enforce security. Additionally, CAISS++ will include an RDF processing engine that provides cost-based optimization for evaluating SPARQL queries based on information-sharing policies.

33.3 SYSTEM DESIGN

33.3.1 DESIGN OF CAISS

We are enhancing our tools developed for AFOSR on (i) secure cloud query processing with semantic web data, and (ii) semantic web-based policy engine to develop CAISS. Details of our tools are given in Section 33.4 (under related work). In this section, we will discuss the enhancements to be made to our tools to develop CAISS.

First, our RDF-based policy engine enforces access control, redaction, and inference control policies on data represented as RDF graphs. Second, our cloud SPARQL query engine for RDF data uses the Hadoop/MapReduce framework. Note that Hadoop is the Apache distributed file system and MapReduce sits on top of Hadoop and carries out job scheduling. As in the case of our cloud-based relational query processor prototype (Thuraisingham et al., 2010), our SPARQL query engine also handles policies specified in XACML and the policy engine implements the XACML protocol. The use of XACML as a policy language requires extensive knowledge about the general concepts used in the design of XACML. Thus, policy authoring in XACML requires a steep learning curve, and is therefore a task that is left to an experienced administrator. A second disadvantage of using XACML is related to performance. Current implementations of XACML require an access request to be evaluated against every policy in the system until a policy applies to the incoming request. This strategy is sufficient for systems with relatively few users and policies. However, for systems with a large number of users and a substantial number of access requests, the aforementioned strategy becomes a performance bottleneck. Finally, XACML is not sufficiently expressive to capture the semantics of information-sharing policies. Prior research has shown that semantic web-based policies are far more expressive. This is because semantic web technologies are based on description logic and have the power to represent knowledge as well as reason about knowledge. Therefore, our first step is to replace the XACML-based policy engine with a semantic web-based policy engine. Since we already have our RDF-based policy engine for the phase 1 prototype, we will enhance this engine and integrate it with our SPARQL query processor. Since our policy engine is based on RDF and our query processor also manages large RDF graphs, there will be no impedance mismatch between the data and the policies.

Enhanced Policy Engine. Our current policy engine has a limitation in that it does not operate in a cloud. Therefore, we will port our RDF policy engine to the cloud environment and integrate it with the SPARQL query engine for federated query processing in the cloud. Our policy engine will benefit from the scalability and the distributed platform offered by Hadoop's MapReduce framework to answer SPARQL queries over large distributed RDF triple stores (billions of RDF triples). The reasons for using RDF as our data model are as follows: (i) RDF allows us to achieve data interoperability between the seemingly disparate sources of information that are catalogued by each agency/organization separately; (ii) the use of RDF allows participating agencies to create data-centric applications that make use of the integrated data that is now available to them; and (iii) since RDF does not require the use of an explicit schema for data generation, it can be easily adapted to ever-changing user requirements. The policy engine's flexibility is based on its accepting high-level policies and executing them as query rules over a directed RDF graph representation of the data. While our prior work focuses on provenance data and access control policies, our CAISS prototype will be flexible enough to handle data represented in RDF and will include information-sharing policies. The strength of our policy engine is that it can handle any type of policy that could be represented using RDF and horn logic rules.

The second limitation of our policy engine is that it currently addresses certain types of policies, such as confidentiality, privacy, and redaction policies. We need to incorporate information-sharing policies into our policy engine. We have, however, conducted simulation studies for incentive-based AIS as well as AIS prototypes in the cloud. We have defined a number of information-sharing policies, such as "US gives information to UK provided UK does not share it with India." We specify such policies in RDF and incorporate them to be processed by our enhanced policy engine.

Enhanced SPARQL Query Processor. While we have a tool that will execute SPARQL queries over large RDF graphs on Hadoop, there is still the need for supporting path queries (i.e., SPARQL queries that provide answers to a request for paths in an RDF graph). An RDF triple can be viewed as an arc from the subject to object with the predicate used to label the arc. The answers to the SPARQL query are based on reachability (i.e., the paths between a source node and a target node). The concatenation of the labels on the arcs along a path can be thought of as a word belonging to the answer set of the path query. Each term of a word is contributed by some predicate label of a triple in the RDF graph. We have designed an algorithm to determine the candidate triples as an answer set in a distributed RDF graph. First, the RDF document is converted to an N-Triple file that is split based on predicate labels. A term in a word could correspond to some predicate file. Second, we form the word by tracing an appropriate path in the distributed RDF graph. We use MapReduce jobs to build the word and to get the candidate RDF triples as an order set. Finally, we return all of the set of ordered RDF triples as the answers to the corresponding SPARQL query.

Integration Framework. Figure 33.2 provides an overview of the CAISS architecture. The integration of the cloud-centric RDF policy engine with the enhanced SPARQL query processor must address the following. First, we need to make sure that RDF-based policies can be stored in the existing storage schema used by the query processor. Second, we need to ensure that the enhanced query processor is able to efficiently evaluate policies (i.e., path queries) over the underlying RDF storage. Finally, we need to conduct a performance evaluation of CAISS to verify that it meets the performance requirements of various participating agencies. Figure 33.3 illustrates the concept of operation of CAISS. Here, multiple agencies will share data in a single cloud. The enhanced policy engine and the cloud-centric SPARQL query processor will enforce the information-sharing policies. This proof-of-concept system will drive the detailed design and implementation of CAISS++.

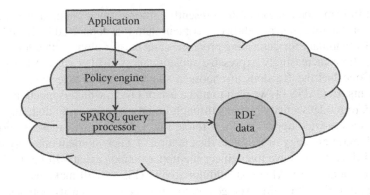

FIGURE 33.2 CAISS prototype overview.

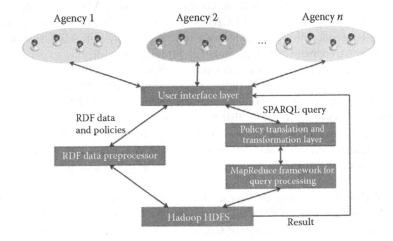

FIGURE 33.3 Operation of CAISS.

There are several benefits in developing a proof-of-concept prototype such as CAISS before we embark on CAISS++. First, CAISS itself is useful in sharing data within a single cloud. Second, we will have a baseline system that we can compare against with respect to efficiency and ease of use when we implement CAISS++. Third, this will give us valuable lessons with respect to the integration of the different pieces required for AIS in the cloud. Finally, by running different scenarios on CAISS, we can identify potential performance bottlenecks that need to be addressed in CAISS++.

33.3.2 Design of CAISS++

We have examined alternatives and carried out a preliminary design of CAISS++. On the basis of the lessons learned from the CAISS prototype and the preliminary design of CAISS++, we will carry out a detailed design of CAISS++ and subsequently implement an operational prototype of CAISS++ during phase 2. In this section, we will first discuss the limitations of CAISS and then discuss the design alternatives for CAISS++.

Limitations of CAISS.

i. *Policy engine*: CAISS uses an RDF-based policy engine that has limited expressivity. The purpose of RDF is to provide a structure (or framework) for describing resources. OWL is built on top of RDF and it is designed for use by applications that need to process the content of information instead of just presenting information to human users. OWL facilitates greater machine interpretability of content than that supported by RDF by providing additional vocabulary for describing properties and classes along with a formal semantics. OWL has three increasingly expressive sublanguages: OWL Lite, OWL DL, and OWL Full, and one has the freedom to choose a suitable sublanguage based on application requirements. In CAISS++, we plan to make use of OWL, which is much more expressive than RDF, to model security policies through organization-specific domain ontologies as well as a system-wide upper ontology. (Note that CAISS++ will reuse an organization's existing domain ontology or facilitate the creation of a new domain ontology if it does not exist. Additionally, we have to engineer the upper ontology that will be used by the centralized component of CAISS++.) Additionally, CAISS++ will make use of a distributed reasoning algorithm that will leverage ontologies to enforce security policies.

ii. *Hadoop storage architecture*: CAISS uses a static storage model wherein a user provides the system with RDF data only once during the initialization step. Thereafter, a user is not allowed to update the existing data. On the other hand, CAISS++ attempts to provide a flexible storage model to users. In CAISS++, a user is allowed to append new data to the existing RDF data stored in Hadoop Distributed File System (HDFS). Note that only allowing a user to append new data rather than deleting/modifying existing data comes from the append-only restriction for files that is enforced by HDFS.

iii. *SPARQL query processor*: CAISS only supports simple SPARQL queries that make use of basic graph patterns (BGPs). In CAISS++, support for other SPARQL query operators such as FILTER, GROUP BY, ORDER BY, etc., will be added. Additionally, CAISS uses a heuristic query optimizer that aims to minimize the number of MapReduce jobs required to answer a query. CAISS++ will incorporate a cost-based query optimizer that will minimize the number of triples that are accessed during the process of query execution.

Design of CAISS++. CAISS++ overcomes the limitations of CAISS. The detailed design of CAISS++ and its implementation will be carried out during phase 2. The lessons learned from CAISS will also drive the detailed design of CAISS++. We assume that the data is encrypted with appropriate DoD encryption technologies and therefore we will not conduct research on encryption in this project. The concept of operation for CAISS++ is shown in interaction with several participating agencies in Figure 33.4 where multiple organizations share data in a single cloud.

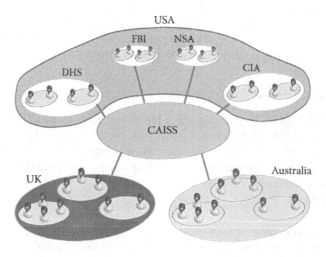

FIGURE 33.4   CAISS++ scenario.

The design of CAISS++ is based on a novel combination of an OWL-based policy engine with an RDF processing engine. Therefore, this design is composed of several tasks, each of which is solved separately, after which all tasks are integrated into a single framework. (i) *OWL-based policy engine*: The policy engine uses a set of agency-specific domain ontologies and an upper ontology to construct policies for the task of AIS. The task of enforcing policies may require the use of a distributed reasoner; therefore, we will evaluate existing distributed reasoners. (ii) *RDF processing engine*: The processing engine requires the construction of sophisticated storage architectures as well as an efficient query processor. (iii) *Integration framework*: The final task is to combine the policy engine with the processing engine into an integrated framework. The initial design of CAISS++ will be based on a trade-off between simplicity of design versus its scalability and efficiency. The first design alternative is known as centralized CAISS++ and it chooses simplicity as the trade-off, whereas the second design alternative (known as decentralized CAISS++) chooses scalability and efficiency as the trade-off. Finally, we also provide a hybrid CAISS++ architecture that tries to combine the benefits of both centralized and decentralized CAISS++. Since CAISS++ follows a requirements-driven design, the division of tasks that we outlined above to achieve AIS are present in each of the approaches that we present next.

Centralized CAISS++. Figure 33.5 illustrates two agencies interacting through centralized CAISS++. Centralized CAISS++ consists of shared cloud storage to store the shared data. All the participating agencies store their respective knowledge bases consisting of domain ontology with corresponding instance data. Centralized CAISS++ also consists of an upper ontology, a query engine, and a distributed reasoner. The upper ontology is used to capture the domain knowledge that is common across the domains of participating agencies, whereas domain ontology captures the knowledge specific to a given agency or a domain. Note that the domain ontology for a given agency will be protected from the domain ontologies of other participating agencies. Policies can either be captured in the upper ontology or in any of the domain ontologies depending on their scope of applicability. Note that the domain ontology for a given agency will be protected from domain ontologies of other participating agencies.

The design of an upper ontology as well as domain ontologies that capture the requirements of the participating agencies is a significant research area and is the focus of the ontology engineering problem. Ontologies will be created using suitable dialects of OWL that are based on description

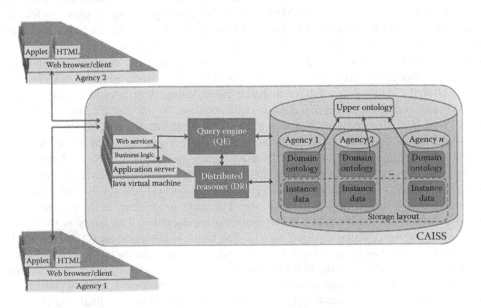

FIGURE 33.5 Centralized CAISS++.

logics (DL). Description logics are usually decidable fragments of first-order logic and will be the basis for providing sound formal semantics. Having represented knowledge in terms of ontologies, reasoning will be done using existing optimized reasoning algorithms. Query answering will leverage reasoning algorithms to formulate and answer intelligent queries. The encoding of policies in OWL will ensure that they are enforced in a provably correct manner. Later, we present an ongoing research project at The University of Texas at Dallas that focuses on providing a general framework for enforcing policies in a provably correct manner using the same underlying technologies. This work can be leveraged toward modeling and enforcement of security policies in CAISS++. The instance data can choose between several available data storage formats. The query engine receives queries from the participating agencies, parses the query, and determines whether the computation requires the use of a distributed reasoner. If the query is simple and does not require the use of a reasoner, the query engine executes the query directly over the shared knowledge base. Once the query result has been computed, the result is returned to the querying agency. If, however, the query is complex and requires inferences over the given data, the query engine uses the distributed reasoner to compute the inferences and then returns the result to the querying agency. A distributed DL reasoner differs from a traditional DL reasoner in its ability to perform reasoning over cloud data storage using the MapReduce framework. During the preliminary design of CAISS++ in phase 1, we will conduct a thorough investigation of the available distributed reasoners using existing benchmarks such as LUBM (Guo et al., 2005). The goal of this investigation is to determine if we can use one of the existing reasoners or whether we need to build our own distributed reasoner. In Figure 33.5, an agency is illustrated as a stack consisting of a web browser, an applet, and an HTML. An agency uses the web browser to send the queries to CAISS++, which are handled by the query processor.

The main differences between centralized CAISS++ and CAISS are as follows: (i) CAISS will use RDF to encode security policies, whereas centralized CAISS++ will use a suitable sublanguage of OWL that is more expressive than RDF and can therefore capture the security policies better. (ii) The SPARQL query processor in CAISS will support a limited subset of SPARQL expressivity; that is, it will provide support only for BGPs, whereas the SPARQL query processor in centralized CAISS++ will be designed to support maximum expressivity of SPARQL. (iii) The Hadoop storage architecture used in CAISS only supports data insertion during an initialization step. However, when data needs to be updated, the entire RDF graph is deleted and a new data set is inserted in its place. On the other hand, centralized CAISS++, in addition to supporting the previous feature, also opens up Hadoop HDFS's append-only feature to users. This feature allows users to append new information to the data that they have previously uploaded to the system.

Decentralized CAISS++. Figure 33.6 illustrates two agencies in interaction with decentralized CAISS++. Decentralized CAISS++ consists of two parts, namely global CAISS++ and local CAISS++. Global CAISS++ consists of a shared cloud storage that is used by the participating agencies to store only their respective domain ontologies and not the instance data unlike centralized CAISS++. Note that domain ontologies for various organizations will be sensitive; therefore, CAISS++ will make use of its own domain ontology to protect a participating agency from accessing other domain ontologies. When a user from an agency queries the CAISS++ data store, global CAISS++ processes the query in two steps. In the first step, it performs a check to verify whether the user is authorized to perform the action specified in the query. If the result of step 1 verifies the user as an authorized user, then it proceeds to step 2 of query processing. In the second step, global CAISS++ federates the actual query to the participating agencies. The query is then processed by the local CAISS++ of a participating agency. The result of computation is then returned to the global CAISS++, which aggregates the final result and returns it to the user. The step 2 of query processing may involve query splitting if the data required to answer a query spans multiple domains. In this case, the results of subqueries from several agencies (their local CAISS++) will need to be combined for further query processing. Once the results are merged and the final result is computed, the result is returned to the user of the querying agency. The figure illustrates agencies with a set

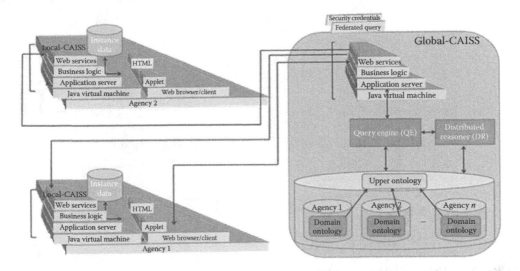

FIGURE 33.6   Decentralized CAISS++.

of two stacks, one of which corresponds to the local CAISS++ and the other consisting of a web browser, an applet, and an HTML, which is used by an agency to query global CAISS++. Table 33.1 shows the pros and cons of the centralized CAISS++ approach, while Table 33.2 shows the pros and cons of the decentralized CAISS++ approach.

Hybrid CAISS++. Figure 33.7 illustrates an overview of hybrid CAISS++, which leverages the benefits of centralized CAISS++ as well as decentralized CAISS++. The hybrid CAISS++ architecture is illustrated in Figure 33.8. It is a flexible design alternative as the users of the participating agencies have the freedom to choose between centralized CAISS++ or decentralized CAISS++. Hybrid CAISS++ is made up of global CAISS++ and a set of local CAISS++s located at each of the participating agencies. Global CAISS++ consists of a shared cloud storage that is used by the participating agencies to store the data they would like to share with other agencies.

TABLE 33.1

Pros and Cons of Centralized CAISS++

Pros	Cons
Simple approach	Difficult to update data. Expensive approach as data needs to be migrated to central storage on each update or a set of updates.
Ease of implementation	Leads to data duplication.
Easier to query	If data is available in different formats, it needs to be homogenized by translating it to RDF.

TABLE 33.2

Pros and Cons of Decentralized CAISS++

Pros	Cons
No duplication of data	Complex query processing
Scalable and flexible	Difficult to implement
Efficient	May require query rewriting and query splitting

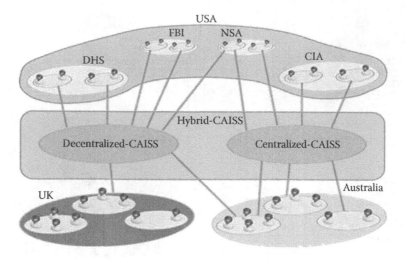

FIGURE 33.7 Hybrid CAISS++ overview.

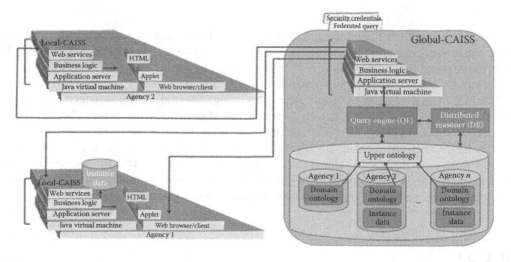

FIGURE 33.8 Hybrid CAISS++ architecture.

A local CAISS++ of an agency is used to receive and process a federated query on the instance data located at the agency. A participating group is a group composed of users from several agencies who want to share information with each other. The members of a group arrive at a mutual agreement on whether they opt for the centralized or the decentralized approach. Additional users can join a group at a later point in time if the need arises. Hybrid CAISS++ will be designed to simultaneously support a set of participating groups. Additionally, a user can belong to several participating groups at the same time. We describe a few use-case scenarios that illustrate the operation.

1. The first case corresponds to the scenario where a set of users who want to securely share information with each other opt for a centralized approach. Suppose users from agency 1 want to share information with users of agency 2 and vice versa, then both the agencies store their knowledge bases comprising domain ontology and instance data on the shared cloud storage located at global CAISS++. The centralized CAISS++ approach works by having the participating agencies arrive at mutual trust on using the central cloud storage. Subsequently, information sharing proceeds as in centralized CAISS++.

2. The second case corresponds to the scenario where a set of users opts for a decentralized approach. For example, agencies 3, 4, and 5 wish to share information with each other and mutually opt for the decentralized approach. All the three agencies store their respective domain ontologies at the central cloud storage, and this information is only accessible to members of this group. The subsequent information-sharing process proceeds in the manner described earlier for the decentralized CAISS++ approach.

3. The third case corresponds to the scenario where a user of an agency belongs to multiple participating groups, some of which opt for the centralized approach and others for the decentralized approach. Since the user is a part of a group using the centralized approach to sharing, he or she needs to make his or her data available to the group by shipping his or her data to the central cloud storage. Additionally, since the user is also a part of a group using the decentralized approach for sharing, he or she needs to respond to the federated query with the help of the local CAISS++ located at his or her agency.

Table 33.3 shows the trade-offs between the different approaches, and this will enable users to choose a suitable approach to AIS based on their application requirements. Next, we describe details of the cloud storage mechanism that makes use of Hadoop to store the knowledge bases from various agencies and then discuss the details of distributed SPARQL query processing over the cloud storage.

In Figure 33.9, we present an architectural overview of our Hadoop-based RDF storage and retrieval framework. We use the concept of a *Store* to provide data loading and querying capabilities on RDF graphs that are stored in the underlying HDFS. A store represents a single RDF data set and can therefore contain several RDF graphs, each with its own separate layout. All operations on an RDF graph are then implicitly converted into operations on the underlying layout, including the following:

- *Layout formatter*: This block performs the function of formatting a layout, which is the process of deleting all triples in an RDF graph while preserving the directory structure used to store that graph.
- *Loader*: This block performs loading of triples into a layout.
- *Query engine*: This block allows a user to query a layout using a SPARQL query. Since our framework operates on the underlying HDFS, the querying mechanism on a layout involves translating a SPARQL query into a possible pipeline of MapReduce jobs and then executing this pipeline on a layout.
- *Connection*: This block maintains the necessary connections and configurations with the underlying HDFS.
- *Config*: This block maintains configuration information such as graph names for each of the RDF graphs that make up a store.

TABLE 33.3

Comparison of the Three Approaches Based on Functionality of Hadoop Storage Architecture

Functionality	Centralized CAISS++	Decentralized CAISS++	Hybrid CAISS++
No data duplication	×	√	Maybe
Flexibility	×	×	√
Scalability	×	√	√
Efficiency	√	√	√
Simplicity—no query rewriting	√	×	×
Trusted centralized cloud data storage	√	×	×

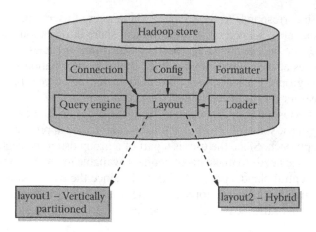

FIGURE 33.9   Hadoop storage architecture used by CAISS++.

   Since RDF data will be stored under different HDFS folders in separate files as a part of our storage schema, we need to adopt certain naming conventions for such folders and files.

   Naming Conventions. A Hadoop store can be composed of several distinct RDF graphs in our framework. Therefore, a separate folder will be created in HDFS for each such Hadoop store. The name of this folder will correspond to the name that has been selected for the given store. Furthermore, an RDF graph is divided into several files in our framework depending on the storage layout that is selected. Therefore, a separate folder will be created in HDFS for each distinct RDF graph. The name of this folder is defined to be *default* for the default RDF graph, while for a named RDF graph, the Uniform Resource Identifier (URI) of the graph is used as the folder name. We use the abstraction of a store in our framework for the reason that this will simplify the management of data belonging to various agencies. Two of the layouts to be supported by our framework are given below. These layouts use a varying number of HDFS files to store RDF data.

   Vertically Partitioned Layout. Figure 33.10 presents the storage schema for the vertically partitioned layout. For every unique predicate contained in an RDF graph, this layout creates a separate file using the name of the predicate as the file name, in the underlying HDFS. Note that only the local name part of a predicate URI is used in a file name, and a separate mapping exists between a file name and the predicate URI. A file for a given predicate contains a separate line for every triple that contains that predicate. This line stores the subject and object values that make up the triple. This schema will lead to significant storage space savings since moving the predicate name to the name of a file completely eliminates the storage of this predicate value. However, multiple occurrences of the same resource URI or literal value will be stored multiple times across all files as well

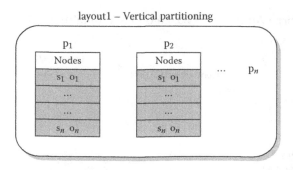

FIGURE 33.10   Vertically partitioned layout.

layout2 – Hybrid

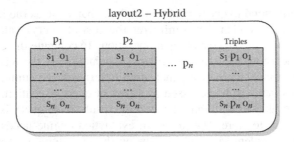

FIGURE 33.11 Hybrid layout.

as within a file. Additionally, a SPARQL query may need to look up multiple files to ensure that a complete result is returned to a user, for example, a query to find all triples that belong to a specific subject or object.

Hybrid Layout. Figure 33.11 presents the storage schema for the hybrid layout. This layout is an extension of the vertically partitioned layout, since in addition to the separate files that are created for every unique predicate in an RDF graph, it also creates a separate triples file containing all the triples in the SPO (subject, predicate, object) format. The advantage of having such a file is that it directly gives us all triples belonging to a certain subject or object. Recall that such a search operation required scanning through multiple files in the vertically partitioned layout. The storage space efficiency of this layout is not as good as the vertically partitioned layout due to the addition of the triples file. However, a SPARQL query to find all triples belonging to a certain subject or object could be performed more efficiently using this layout.

Distributed Processing of SPARQL. Query processing in CAISS++ comprises several steps (Figure 33.12). The first step is query parsing and translation where a given SPARQL query is first parsed to verify syntactic correctness, and then a parse tree corresponding to the input query is built. The parse tree is then translated into a SPARQL algebra expression. Since a given SPARQL query can have multiple equivalent SPARQL algebra expressions, we annotate each such expression with instructions on how to evaluate each operation in this expression. Such annotated SPARQL

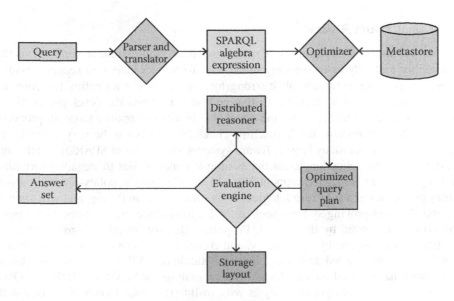

FIGURE 33.12 Distributed processing of SPARQL in CAISS++.

algebra expressions correspond to query-evaluation plans that serve as the input to the optimizer. The optimizer selects a query plan that minimizes the cost of query evaluation. To optimize a query, an optimizer must know the cost of each operation. To compute the cost of each operation, the optimizer uses a metastore that stores statistics associated with the RDF data. The cost of a given query-evaluation plan is alternatively measured in terms of the number of MapReduce jobs or the number of triples that will be accessed as a part of query execution. Once the query plan is chosen, the query is evaluated with that plan and the result of the query is output. Since we use a cloud-centric framework to store RDF data, an evaluation engine needs to convert SPARQL algebra operators into equivalent MapReduce jobs on the underlying storage layouts. Therefore, in CAISS++, we will implement a MapReduce job for each of the SPARQL algebra operators. Additionally, the evaluation engine uses a distributed reasoner to compute inferences required for query evaluation.

Framework Integration. The components that we have outlined that are a part of CAISS++ need to be integrated to work with another. Furthermore, this process of integration depends on a user's selection of one of the three possible design choices provided with CAISS++, namely, centralized CAISS++, decentralized CAISS++, or hybrid CAISS++. The integration of the various pieces of CAISS++ that have been presented thus far needs to take into account several issues. First, we need to make sure that our ontology engineering process has been successful in capturing an agency's requirements and, additionally, the ontologies can be stored in the storage schema used by the Hadoop storage architecture. Secondly, we need to ensure that the distributed SPARQL query processor is able to efficiently evaluate queries (i.e., user-generated SPARQL queries and SPARQL queries that evaluate policies) over the underlying RDF storage. Finally, we need to conduct a performance evaluation of CAISS++ to verify that it meets the performance requirements of various participating agencies as well as leads to significant performance advantages when compared with CAISS.

Policy Specification and Enforcement. The users of CAISS++ can use a language of their choice (e.g., XACML, RDF, and Rei) to specify their information-sharing policies. These policies will be translated into a suitable sublanguage of OWL using existing or custom-built translators. We will extend our policy engine for CAISS to handle policies specified in OWL. In addition to RDF policies, our current policy engine can handle policies in OWL for implementing role-based access control, inference control, and social network analysis.

33.3.3   FORMAL POLICY ANALYSIS

Our framework is applicable to a variety of mission-critical, high-assurance applications that span multiple possibly mutually distrusting organizations. To provide maximal security assurance in such settings, it is important to establish strong formal guarantees regarding the correctness of the system and the policies it enforces. To that end, we examined the development of an infrastructure for constructing formal, machine-checkable proofs of important system properties and policy analyses for our system. While machine-checkable proofs can be very difficult and time consuming to construct for many large software systems, our choice of SPARQL, RDF, and OWL as query, ontology, and policy languages opens unique opportunities to elegantly formulate such proofs in a logic programming environment. We will encode policies, policy-rewriting algorithms, and security properties as a rule-based, logical derivation system in Prolog, and will apply model-checking and theorem-proving systems such as ACL2 to produce machine-checkable proofs that these properties are obeyed by the system. Properties that we intend to consider in our model include soundness, transparency, consistency, and completeness. The results of our formal policy analysis will drive our detailed design and implementation of CAISS++. To our knowledge, none of the prior work has focused on such formal policy analysis for SPARQL, RDF, and OWL. Our extensive research on formal policy analysis with in-line reference monitors is discussed under related work.

33.3.4 IMPLEMENTATION APPROACH

The implementation of CAISS is being carried out in Java and is based on a flexible design where we can plug and play multiple components. A service provider or user will have the flexibility to use the SPARQL query processor as well as the RDF-based policy engine as separate components or combine them. The open source component used for CAISS will include the Pellet reasoner as well as our in-house tools such as the SPARQL query processor on the Hadoop/MapReduce framework and the cloud-centric RDF policy engine. CAISS will allow us to demonstrate basic AIS scenarios on our cloud-based framework.

In the implementation of CAISS++, we will again use Java as the programming language. We will use Protégé as our ontology editor during the process of ontology engineering, which includes designing domain ontologies as well as the upper ontology. We will also evaluate several existing distributed reasoning algorithms, such as WebPIE and QueryPIE, to determine the best algorithm that matches an agency's requirements. The selected algorithm will then be used to perform reasoning over OWL-based security policies. Additionally, the design of the Hadoop storage architecture is based on Jena's SPARQL database (SDB) architecture and will feature some of the functionalities that are available with Jena SDB. The SPARQL query engine will also feature code written in Java. This code will consist of several modules, including query parsing and translation, query optimization, and query execution. The query execution module will consist of MapReduce jobs for the various operators of the SPARQL language. Finally, our web-based user interface will make use of several components such as JBoss, EJB, and JSF, among others.

33.4 RELATED WORK

We will first provide an overview of our research directly relevant to our project and then discuss overall related work. We will also discuss product/technology competition.

33.4.1 OUR RELATED RESEARCH

Secure Data Storage and Retrieval in the Cloud. We have built a web-based application that combines existing cloud computing technologies such as Hadoop, an open source distributed file system, and Hive data warehouse infrastructure built on top of Hadoop with an XACML policy-based security mechanism to allow collaborating organizations to securely store and retrieve large amounts of data (Husain et al., 2011; Thuraisingham et al., 2010; University of Texas at Dallas [UTD] Secure Cloud Repository, http://cs.utdallas.edu/secure-cloud-repository/). Figure 33.13 presents the architecture of our system. We use the services provided by the HIVE layer and Hadoop, including the HDFS layer that makes up the storage layer of Hadoop and allows the storage of data blocks across a cluster of nodes. The layers we have implemented include the web application layer, the ZQL parser layer, the XACML policy layer, and the query-rewriting layer. The web application layer is the only interface provided by our system to the user to access the cloud infrastructure. The ZQL parser (http://zql.sourceforge.net/) layer takes as input any query submitted by a user, and either proceeds to the XACML policy evaluator if the query is success-fully parsed or returns an error message to the user. The XACML policy layer is used to build (XACML policy builder) and evaluate (XACML policy evaluation) XACML policies. The basic query-rewriting layer rewrites SQL queries entered by the user. The Hive layer is used to manage relational data that is stored in the underlying Hadoop HDFS (Thusoo et al., 2009). In addition, we have also designed and implemented secure storage and query processing in a hybrid cloud (Khadilkar et al., 2011).

Secure SPARQL Query Processing on the Cloud. We have developed a framework to query RDF data stored over Hadoop, as shown in Figure 33.14. We used the Pellet reasoner to reason at various stages. We carried out real-time query reasoning using the pellet libraries coupled with

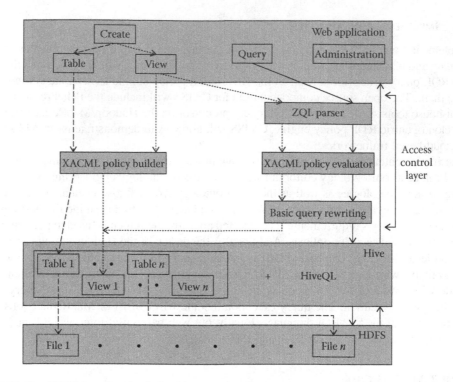

FIGURE 33.13   HIVE-based assured cloud query processing.

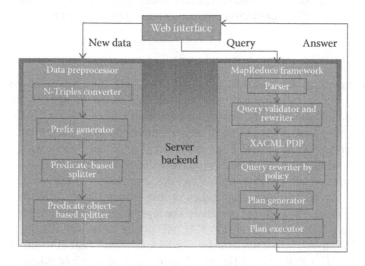

FIGURE 33.14   SPARQL-based assured cloud query processing.

Hadoop's MapReduce functionalities. Our RDF query processing is composed of two main steps: (i) preprocessing and (ii) query optimization and execution.

Preprocessing: To execute a SPARQL query on RDF data, we carried out data preprocessing steps and stored the preprocessed data in HDFS. A separate MapReduce task was written to perform the conversion of RDF/XML data into N-Triples as well as for prefix generation. Our storage strategy is based on predicate splits (Husain et al., 2011).

Query execution and optimization: We have developed a SPARQL query execution and optimization module for Hadoop. As our storage strategy is based on predicate splits, first, we examine the predicates present in the query. Second, we examine a subset of the input files that are matched with predicates. Third, SPARQL queries generally have many joins in them, and all of these joins may not be possible to perform in a single map–reduce job. Therefore, we have developed an algorithm that decides the number of jobs required for each kind of query. As part of optimization, we applied a greedy strategy and cost-based optimization to reduce query-processing time. We have also developed an XACML-based centralized policy engine that will carry out federated RDF query processing on the cloud. Details of the enforcement strategy are given in Husain et al. (2011), Khaled et al. (2010), and Hamlen et al. (2010a).

RDF Policy Engine. In our prior work (Cadenhead et al., 2011a), we have developed a policy engine to processes RDF-based access control policies for RDF data. The policy engine is designed with the following features in mind: scalability, efficiency, and interoperability. This framework (Figure 33.15) can be used to execute various policies, including access control policies and redaction policies. It can also be used as a testbed for evaluating different policy sets over RDF data and to view the outcomes graphically. Our framework presents an interface that accepts a high-level policy that is then translated into the required format. It takes a user's input query and returns a response that has been pruned using a set of user-defined policy constraints. The architecture is built using a modular approach; therefore, it is very flexible in that most of the modules can be extended or replaced by another application module. For example, a policy module implementing a discretionary access control could be replaced entirely by an RBAC module or we may decide to enforce all our constraints based on a generalized redaction model. It should be noted that our policy engine also handles role-based access control policies specified in OWL and SWRL (Cadenhead et al., 2010). In addition, it handles certain policies specified in OWL for inference control, such as association-based policies where access to collections of entities is denied, and logical policies where A implies B and if access to B is denied then access to A should also be denied (Cadenhead et al., 2010, 2011b; Carminati et al., 2009). This capability of our policy engine will be useful in our design and implementation of CAISS++ where information is shared across multiple clouds.

Assured Information-Sharing Prototypes. We have developed multiple systems for AIS at UTD. Under an AFOSR-funded project (between 2005 and 2008), we developed an XACML-based policy engine to function on top of relational databases and demonstrated the sharing of (simulated) medical data (Thuraisingham et al., 2008). In this implementation, we specified the policies in XACML and stored the data in multiple Oracle databases. When one organization requests data from another organization, the policies are examined and authorized data is released. In addition, we also conducted simulation studies on the amount of data that would be lost by enforcing the policies while information sharing. Under our MURI project, also funded by AFOSR, we conducted simulation studies for incentive-based information sharing (Kantarcioglu, 2010). We have also examined risk-based access control in an information-sharing scenario (Celikel et al., 2007). In addition to access control policies, we have specified different types of policies including need-to-share policies and trust policies (e.g., A shared data with B provided B does not share the data with

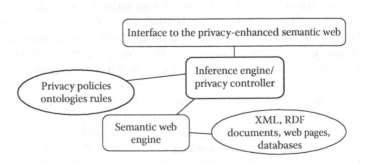

FIGURE 33.15 RDF policy engine.

C). Note that the 9/11 commission report calls for the migration from the more restrictive need-to-know to the less restrictive need-to-share policies. These policies are key to support the specification of directive concerning AIS obligations.

Formal Policy Analysis. By reducing high-level security policy specifications and system models to the level of the denotational and operational semantics of their binary-level implementations, our past work has developed formally machine-certifiable security enforcement mechanisms of a variety of complex software systems, including those implemented in .NET (Hamlen et al., 2006b), ActionScript (Sridhar and Hamlen, 2010), Java (Jones and Hamlen, 2010), and native code (Hamlen et al., 2010b). Working at the binary level provides extremely high formal guarantees because it permits the tool chain that produces mission-critical software components to remain untrusted; the binary code produced by the chain can be certified directly. This strategy is an excellent match for CAISS++ because data security specification languages such as XACML and OWL can be elegantly reflected down to the binary level of bytecode languages with XML-aware system APIs, such as Java bytecode. Our past work has applied binary instrumentation (e.g., in-lined reference monitoring) and a combination of binary type checking (Hamlen et al., 2006b), model checking (Sridhar and Hamlen, 2010), and automated theorem proving (e.g., via ACL2) to achieve fully automated machine certification of binary software in such domains.

33.4.2 OVERALL RELATED RESEARCH

While there are some related efforts, none of the efforts have provided a solution to AIS in the cloud, nor have they conducted such a formal policy analysis.

Secure Data Storage and Retrieval in the Cloud. Security for cloud has received recent attention (Talbot, 2009). Some efforts on implementing at the infrastructure level have been reported (O'Malley et al., 2009). Such development efforts are an important step toward securing cloud infrastructures but are only in their inception stages. The goal of our system is to add another layer of security above the security offered by Hadoop (UTD Secure Cloud Repository, http://cs.utdallas.edu/secure-cloud-repository/). Once the security offered by Hadoop becomes robust, it will only strengthen the effectiveness of our system. Similar efforts have been undertaken by Amazon and Microsoft for their cloud computing offerings (Amazon Web Services, 2015; Marshall et al., 2010). However, this work falls in the public domain, whereas our system is designed for a private cloud infrastructure. This distinguishing factor makes our infrastructure *trusted* over public infrastructures where the data must be stored in an encrypted format.

SPARQL Query Processor. Only a handful of efforts have been reported on SPARQL query processing. These include BioMANTA (http://www.itee.uq.edu.au/eresearch/projects/biomanta) and SHARD (scalable, high-performance, robust, and distributed; Zeyliger, 2010). BioMANTA proposes extensions to RDF Molecules (Ding et al., 2005) and implements a MapReduce-based molecule store (Newman et al., 2008). They use MapReduce to answer the queries. They have queried a maximum of 4 million triples. Our work differs in the following ways: First, we have queried 1 billion triples. Second, we have devised a storage schema that is tailored to improve query execution performance for RDF data. To our knowledge, we are the first to come up with a storage schema for RDF data using flat files in HDFS, and a MapReduce job determination algorithm to answer a SPARQL query. SHARD is an RDF triple store using the Hadoop Cloudera distribution. This project shows initial results demonstrating Hadoop's ability to improve scalability for RDF data sets. However, SHARD stores its data only in a triple store schema. It does no query planning or reordering, and its query processor will not minimize the number of Hadoop jobs. None of the efforts have incorporated security policies.

RDF-Based Policy Engine. There exists prior research devoted to the study of enforcing policies over RDF stores. These include the work in Carminati et al. (2004), which uses RDF for policy specification and enforcement. In addition, the policies are generally written in RDF. Jain and Farkas (2006) proposed an access control model for RDF. Their model is based on RDF data semantics and incorporates RDF and RDF Schema (RDFS) entailments. Here, protection is provided at the resource level, which adds granularity to their framework. Other frameworks enforcing policies over RDF/OWL include those of Uszok et al. (2004) and Kagal (2002). Uszok et al. (2004) described KAoS, a policy and domain services framework that uses OWL, both to represent policies and domains. Kagal (2002) introduced Rei, a policy framework that is flexible and allows different kinds of policies to be stated. Extensions to Rei have been proposed recently (Khandelwal et al., 2010). The policy specification language allows users to develop declarative policies over domain-specific ontologies in RDF, DAML+OIL, and OWL. Reddivari et al. (2005) also introduced a prototype, RAP, for implementation of an RDF store with integrated maintenance capabilities and access control. These frameworks, however, do not address cases where the RDF store can become very large or the case where the policies do not scale with the data. Under an Intelligence Advanced Research Projects Activity-funded project, we have developed techniques for very large RDF graph processing (UTD Semantic Web Repository, http://cs.utdallas.edu/semanticweb/).

Hadoop Storage Architecture. There has been significant interest in large-scale distributed storage and retrieval techniques for RDF data. The theoretical designs of a parallel processing framework for RDF data are presented in the work done by Castagna et al. (2009). This work advocates the use of a data distribution model with varying levels of granularity such as triple level, graph level, and data set level. A query over such a distributed model is then divided into a set of subqueries over machines containing the distributed data. The results of all subqueries will then be merged to return a complete result to a user application. Several implementations of this theoretical concept exist in the research community. These efforts include the work done by Choi et al. (2009) and Abraham et al. (2010). A separate technique that has been used to store and retrieve RDF data makes use of peer-to-peer systems (Aberer et al., 2004; Cai and Frank, 2004; Harth et al., 2007; Valle et al., 2006). However, there are some drawbacks with such systems as peer-to-peer systems need to have super-peers that store information about the distribution of RDF data among the peers. Another disadvantage is a need to federate a SPARQL query to every peer in the network.

Distributed Reasoning. The InteGrail system uses distributed reasoning, whose vision is to shape the European railway organization of the future (InteGrail, 2009). Urbani et al. (2009) have shown a scalable implementation of RDFS reasoning based on MapReduce that can infer 30 billion triples from a real-world data set in less than 2 hours, yielding an input and output throughput of 123,000 triples/second and 3.27 million triples/second, respectively. They have presented some nontrivial optimizations for encoding the RDFS ruleset in MapReduce and have evaluated the scalability of their implementation on a cluster of 64 compute nodes using several real-world data sets.

Access Control and Policy Ontology Modeling. There have been some attempts to model access control and policy models using semantic web technologies. Cirio et al. (2007) have shown how OWL and DL can be used to build an access control system. They have developed a high-level OWL DL ontology that expresses the elements of a role-based access control system and have built a domain-specific ontology that captures the features of a sample scenario. Finally, they have joined these two artifacts to take into account attributes in the dentition of the policies and in the access control decision. Reul et al. (2010) first presented a security policy ontology based on DOGMA, which is a formal ontology engineering framework. This ontology covers the core elements of security policies (i.e., condition, action, resource) and can easily be extended to represent specific security policies, such as access control policies. Andersen and Neuhaus (2009) present an ontologically motivated approach to multilevel access control and provenance for information systems.

33.5 COMMERCIAL DEVELOPMENTS

33.5.1 RDF Processing Engines

Research and commercial RDF processing engines include Jena by HP Labs, BigOWLIM, and RDF-3X. Although the storage schemas and query-processing mechanisms for some of these tools are proprietary, they are all based on some type of indexing strategy for RDF data. However, only a few tools exist that use a cloud-centric architecture for processing RDF data and, moreover, these tools are not scalable to a very large number of triples. In contrast, our query processor in CAISS++ will be built as a planet-scale RDF processing engine that supports all SPARQL operators and will provide optimized execution strategies for SPARQL queries and can scale to billions of triples.

Semantic Web-Based Security Policy Engines. As stated in Section 33.2, the current work on semantic web-based policy specification and enforcement does not address the issues of policy generation and enforcement for massive amounts of data and support large number of users.

Cloud. To the best of our knowledge, there is no significant commercial competition for cloud-centric AIS. Since we have taken a modular approach to the creation of our tools, we can iteratively refine each component (policy engine, storage architecture, and query processor) separately. Because of the component-based approach we have taken, we will be able to adapt to changes in the platforms we use (e.g., Hadoop, RDF, OWL, and SPARQL) without having to depend on the particular features of a given platform.

33.6 EXTENSIONS FOR SOCIAL MEDIA APPLICATIONS

There are several variations of the designs discussed in this chapter that we can adapt for social media applications. First, members of a network may want to share data. Therefore, they could implement the information-sharing policies with each member having his or her own data store. In the second design, the members could use a shared space or a cloud to store the data and the policies and share the data securely.

The member could also belong to multiple social networks. That is, one person could belong to more than one network or a person could belong to just one network. In this case, a member could share more data with the members of his or her network while sharing limited data with members of another network. Also, different networks may use heterogeneous technologies for representation. Therefore, the heterogeneous representations have to be resolved. One could also develop a logical representation of the multiple networks and have mapping to the individual networks.

Some of the chapters in this book have discussed social network integration (e.g., Chapters 30 and 34). For example, for the system discussed in Chapter 30, we have carried out entity resolution for multiple social networks such as LinkedIn and Google+. For the social network discussed in Chapter 34, we have investigated privacy aspects for integration. There are several challenges that need to be investigated for not only social network integration, but also security and privacy for such integration when sharing information.

33.7 SUMMARY AND DIRECTIONS

This chapter has described our design and implementation of a cloud-based information-sharing system called CAISS. CAISS utilizes several of the technologies we have developed as well as open source tools. We also described the design of an ideal cloud-based assured information-sharing system called CAISS++.

We have developed a proof-of-concept prototype of both CAISS and CAISS++. In the implementation of CAISS, we utilized our SPARQL query processor with the policies specified in XACML. This is more or less the system described in Chapter 25. In the second prototype, we specified policies in RDF, developed the policy engine in the cloud, and integrated it with the data engine. This system is discussed in Cadenhead et al. (2012a,b). In the future, we will continue to enhance our prototype by implementing more complex policies. Our policies include both access control policies as well as information-sharing policies. We will also carry out a formal analysis of the execution of the policies.

REFERENCES

Aberer, K., Cudré-Mauroux, P., Hauswirth, M., and Van Pelt, T. GridVine: Building Internet-scale semantic overlay networks. In: *Proceedings of International Semantic Web Conference*, Hiroshima, Japan, 2004.

Abraham, J., Brazier, P., Chebotko, A., Navarro, J., and Piazza, A. Distributed storage and querying techniques for a semantic web of scientific workflow provenance. In: *Proceedings IEEE International Conference on Services Computing (SCC)*, Miami, FL, 2010.

Amazon Web Services. Overview of security processes. Available at: https://d0.awsstatic.com/whitepapers/security/aws_security_whitepaper, 2015.

Andersen, B. and Neuhaus, F. An ontological approach to information access control and provenance. In: *Proceedings of Ontology for the Intelligence Community*, Fairfax, VA, October 2009.

Awad, K. and Thuraisingham, B.M. Policy enforcement system for inter-organizational data sharing. *Journal of Information Security and Privacy* 4(3): 22–39, 2010.

Cadenhead, T., Kantarcioglu, M., and Thuraisingham, B. Scalable and efficient reasoning for enforcing role-based access control. In: *Proceedings of Data and Applications Security and Privacy XXIV*, 24th Annual IFIP Working Group 11.3 Working Conference, Rome, Italy, pp. 209–224, 2010.

Cadenhead, T., Khadilkar, V., Kantarcioglu, M., and Thuraisingham, B. Transforming provenance using redaction. In: *Proceedings of ACM Symposium on Access Control Models and Technologies (SACMAT)*, Innsbruck, Austria, pp. 93–102, 2011a.

Cadenhead, T., Khadilkar, V., Kantarcioglu, M., and Thuraisingham, B. A language for provenance access control. In: *Proceedings of ACM Conference on Data Application Security and Privacy (CODASPY)*, San Antonio, TX, pp. 133–144, 2011b.

Cadenhead, T., Khadilkar, V., Kantarcioglu, M., and Thuraisingham, B.M. A cloud-based RDF policy engine for assured information sharing. In: *Proceedings of ACM Symposium on Access Control Models and Technologies (SACMAT 2012)*, Newark, NJ, pp. 113–116, 2012a.

Cadenhead, T., Kantarcioglu, M., Khadilkar, V., and Thuraisingham, B.M. Design and implementation of a cloud-based assured information sharing system. In: *Proc. of Intl. Conf. on Mathematical Methods, Models and Architectures for Computer Network Security*, St. Petersburg, Russia, pp. 36–50, 2012b.

Cai, M. and Frank, M. RDFPeers: A scalable distributed RDF repository based on a structured peer-to-peer network. In: *Proceedings ACM World Wide Web Conference (WWW)*, New York, 2004.

Carminati, B., Ferrari, E., and Thuraisingham, B.M. Using RDF for policy specification and enforcement. In: *Proc. of Intl. Workshop on Database and Expert Systems Applications*, Zaragoza, Spain, pp. 163–167, 2004.

Carminati, B., Ferrari, E., Heatherly, R., Kantarcioglu, M., and Thuraisingham, B.M. Design and implementation of a cloud-based assured information sharing system. In: *Proc. of ACM Symposium on Access Control Models and Technologies*, Stresa, Italy, pp. 177–186, 2009.

Castagna, P., Seaborne, A., and Dollin, C. A parallel processing framework for RDF design and issues. Technical report, HP Laboratories, HPL-2009-346, 2009.

Celikel, E., Kantarcioglu, M., Thuraisingham, B., and Bertino, E. Managing risks in RBAC employed distributed environments. In: *On the Move to Meaningful Internet Systems 2007: CoopIS, DOA, ODBASE, GADA, and IS*. Volume 4804 of Lecture Notes in Computer Science, Springer, New York, pp. 1548–1566. 2007.

Choi, H., Son, J., Cho, Y., Sung, M., and Chung, Y. SPIDER: A system for scalable, parallel/distributed evaluation of large-scale RDF data. In: *Proceedings of ACM Conference on Information and Knowledge Management (CIKM)*, Hong Kong, China, pp. 2087–2088, 2009.

Cirio, L., Cruz, I., and Tamassia, R. A role and attribute based access control system using semantic web technologies. In: *IFIP Workshop on Semantic Web and Web Semantics*, Vilamoura, Algarve, Portugal, 2007.

Department of Defense. DoD information enterprise strategic plan, 2010–2012. Available at: http://dodcio.defense.gov/Portals/0/Documents/DodIESP-r16.pdf, 2012.

Department of Defense. Department of Defense information sharing strategy, 2007. Available at: http://www.defense.gov/releases/release.aspx?releaseid=10831, 2007.

Ding, L., Finin, T., Peng, Y., da Silva, P., and McGuinness, D. Tracking RDF graph provenance using RDF molecules. In: *Proc. International Semantic Web Conference*, Galway, Ireland, 2005.

Finin, T., Joshi, J., Kargupta, H., Yesha, Y., Sachs, J., Bertino, E., Li, N. et al. Assured information sharing life cycle. In: *Proc. Intelligence and Security Informatics*, Dallas, 2009.

Guo, Y., Pan, Z., and Heflin, J. LUBM: A benchmark for OWL knowledge base systems. *Web Semantics* 3(2,5): 158–182, October 2005.

Hamlen, K., Morrisett, G., and Schneider, F. Computability classes for enforcement mechanisms. *ACM Transactions on Programming Languages and Systems* 28(1): 175–205, 2006a.

Hamlen, K., Morrisett, G., and Schneider, F. Certified in-lined reference monitoring on .NET. In: *Proc. ACM Workshop on Programming Language and Analysis for Security*, Ottawa, Canada, pp. 7–16, 2006b.

Hamlen, K., Kantarcioglu, M., Khan, L., and Thuraisingham, B. Security issues for cloud computing. *Journal of Information Security and Privacy* 4(2), 2010a.

Hamlen, K., Mohan, V., and Wartell, R. Reining in Windows API abuses with in-lined reference monitors. Tech. Rep. UTDCS-18-10, Computer Science Department, The University of Texas at Dallas, Dallas, 2010b.

Harth, A., Umbrich, J., Hogan, A., and Decker, S. YARS2: A federated repository for searching and querying graph structured data. In: *Proceedings of International Semantic Web Conference*, Busan, Korea, 2007.

Hoover, J.N. NSA pursues intelligence-sharing architecture. *InformationWeek*. Available at http://www.infor mationweek.com/news/government/cloud-saas/229401646, 2011.

Husain, M., McGlothlin, J., Masud, M., Khan, L., and Thuraisingham, B. Heuristics-based query processing for large RDF graphs using cloud computing. *IEEE Transactions on Knowledge and Data Engineering* 23: 1312–1327, 2011.

InteGrail. Distributed reasoning: Seamless integration and processing of distributed knowledge. Available at: http://www.integrail.eu/documents/fs04.pdf, 2009.

Jain, A. and Farkas, C. Secure resource description framework: an access control model. In: *Proceedings of ACM Symposium on Access Control Models and Technologies (SACMAT)*, Lake Tahoe, CA, 2006.

Jones, M. and Hamlen, K. Disambiguating aspect-oriented security policies. In: *Proc. 9th Intl. Conference on Aspect-Oriented Software Development*, Rennes and St. Malo, France, pp. 193–204, 2010.

Jones, M. and Hamlen, K. A service-oriented approach to mobile code security. In: *Proc. 8th Intl. Conference on Mobile Web Information Systems (MobiWIS)*, Niagara Falls, Ontario, Canada, 2011.

Kagal, L. Rei: A policy language for the me-centric project. HPL-2002-270. Accessible online http://www.hpl .hp.com/techreports/2002/HPL-2002-270.html, 2002.

Kantarcioglu, M. Incentive-based assured information sharing. *AFOSR MURI Review*, October 2010.

Khadilkar, V., Kantarcioglu, M., Thuraisingham, B., and Mehrotra, S. Secure data processing in a hybrid cloud. In: *Proc. Computering Research Repository (CoRR)*. abs/1105.1982, 2011.

Khaled, A., Husain, M., Khan, L., Hamlen, K., and Thuraisingham, B. A token-based access control system for RDF data in the clouds. In: *Proceedings of CloudCom*, Indianapolis, IN, 2010.

Khandelwal, A., Bao, J., Kagal, L., Jacobi, I., Ding, L., and Hendler, J. Analyzing the AIR language: A semantic web (production) rule language. In: *Proceedings of International Web Reasoning and Rule Systems*, Bressanone, Brixen, Italy, pp. 58–72, 2010.

Marshall, A., Howard, M., Bugher, G., and Harden, B. Security best practices in developing Windows Azure applications. Microsoft Corp., Redmond, WA, 2010.

Newman, A., Hunter, J., Li, Y., Bouton, C., and Davis, M. A scale-out RDF molecule store for distributed processing of biomedical data. In: *Semantic Web for Health Care and Life Sciences Workshop, World Wide Web Conference (WWW)*, Beijing, China, 2008.

O'Malley, D., Zhang, K., Radia, S., Marti, R., and Harrell, C. Hadoop security design. Available at: https:// issues.apache.org/jira/secure/attachment/12428537/security-design.pdf, 2009.

Rao, P., Lin, D., Bertino, E., Li, N., and Lobo, J. EXAM: An environment for access control policy analysis and management. In: *Proc. of IEEE Workshop on Policies for Distributed Systems and Networks (POLICY)*, Palisades, NY, 2008.

Reddivari, P., Finin, T., and Joshi, A. Policy-based access control for an RDF store. Policy management for the web. In: *Proc. of Intl. Joint Conference on Artificial Intelligence Workshop (IJCAI)*, Edinburgh, Scotland, UK, 2005.

Reul, Q., Zhao, G., and Meersman, R. Ontology-based access control policy interoperability. In: *Proc. 1st Conference on Mobility, Individualisation, Socialisation and Connectivity (MISC)*, London, 2010.

Sridhar, M. and Hamlen, K. Model-checking in-lined reference monitors. In: *Proc. 11th Intl. Conference on Verification, Model Checking, and Abstract Interpretation*, Madrid, Spain, pp. 312–327, 2010.

Talbot, D. How secure is cloud computing? *Computing News*. Available at http://www.technologyreview.com /computing/23951/, 2009.

Thuraisingham, B., Kumar, Y.H., and Khan, L. Design and implementation of a framework for assured information sharing across organizational boundaries. *Journal of Information Security and Privacy* 2(4): 67–90, 2008.

Thuraisingham, B., Khadilkar, V., Gupta, A., Kantarcioglu, M., and Khan, L. Secure data storage and retrieval in the cloud. In: *CollaborateCom*, Chicago, 2010.

Thuraisingham, B. and Khadilkar, V. Assured information sharing in the cloud. UTD Tech. Report, September 2011.

Thuraisingham, B.M., Khadilkar, V., Rachapalli, J., Cadenhead, T., Kantarcioglu, M., Hamlen, K.W., Khan, L., and Husain, M.F. Cloud-centric assured information sharing. In: *Proceedings of the Pacific Asia Workshop on Intelligence and Security Informatics (PAISI)*, Kuala Lumpur, Malaysia, pp. 1–26, 2012.

Thusoo, A., Sharma, J., Jain, N., Shao, Z., Chakka, P., Anthony, S., Liu, H., Wyckoff, P., and Murthy, R. Hive—A warehousing solution over a map-reduce framework. In: *Proceedings of VLDB Endowment*, 2009.

Urbani, J., Kotoulas, S., Oren, E., and van Harmelen, F. Scalable distributed reasoning using MapReduce. In: Bernstein, A., Karger, D.R., Heath, T. et al., editors. *Proceedings of the International Semantic Web Conference 2009*, Lecture Notes in Computer Science, vol. 5823, Springer, Berlin, 2009.

Uszok, A., Bradshaw, J., Johnson, M., Jeffers, R., Tate, A., Dalton, J., and Aitken, S. KAoS policy management for semantic web services. *IEEE Intelligent Systems* 19(4): 2004, 32–41.

Valle, E., Turati, A., and Ghioni, A. AGE: A distributed infrastructure for fostering RDF-based interoperability. In: *Proceedings of Distributed Applications and Inter-Operable Systems (DAIS)*, Bologna, Italy, 2006.

Zeyliger, P. How Raytheon BBN Technologies researchers are using Hadoop to build a scalable, distributed triple store. Available at http://blog.cloudera.com/blog/2010/03/how-raytheon-researchers-are-using-hadoop-to-build-a-scalable-distributed-triple-store/, 2010.

34 Social Network Integration and Analysis with Privacy Preservation

34.1 INTRODUCTION

Social networks have drawn substantial attention in recent years owing to the advancement of Web 2.0 technologies. Aggregating social network data becomes easier through crawling user interactions on the Internet (Adibi et al., 2004). Social network analysis discovers knowledge hidden in the structure of social networks that is useful in many domains such as marketing, epidemiology, homeland security, sociology, psychology, and management. Social network data is usually owned by an individual organization or government agency. However, each organization or agency usually has a partial social network from the data aggregated in their own source. Knowledge cannot be extracted accurately if only partial information is available. Sharing of social networks between organizations enables knowledge discovery from an integrated social network obtained from multiple sources. However, the information sharing between organizations is usually prohibited owing to the concern of privacy preservation; especially, a social network often contains sensitive information of individuals. Early research on privacy preservation focuses on relational data, and some recent research extends it to social network data. Techniques such as *k-degree anonymity* and *k-anonymity* achieved by edge or node perturbation are proposed. However, the anonymized social network is designed for studying global network properties. It is not applicable for integration of social networks or other social network analysis and mining tasks such as identifying the leading person or gateway. A recent study has also shown that a substantial distortion to the network structure can be caused by perturbation. Such distortion may cause errors in social network analysis and mining. In this chapter, we discuss aspects of sharing insensitive and generalized information to support social network analysis and mining while preserving privacy at the same time.

We will motivate the problem with the following scenario. Consider two local law enforcement units A and B that have their own criminal social networks, G_A and G_B. Each of these criminal social networks is a partial network of the regional criminal social networks covering the areas policed by A and B. The criminal intelligence officer of A may not be able to identify the close distance between suspects i and j by analyzing G_A because i and j are connected through k in G_B but k is not available in G_A. Similarly, the criminal intelligence officers of B may not be able to determine the significance of suspect k by conducting centrality analysis on G_B because k makes little influence on the actors in G_B but has substantial influence on the actors in G_A. By integrating G_A and G_B, the criminal intelligence officers of A and B are able to discover the knowledge that otherwise they cannot.

In this chapter, we will discuss our generalization approach for integrating social networks with privacy preservation. In Section 34.2, we will first provide some information on the application of social network for terrorism analysis and the need for privacy. The limitation of current approaches will be discussed in Section 34.3. Our approach is discussed in Section 34.4. Directions are discussed in Section 34.7. The work discussed in this chapter is by Yang and Thuraisingham (2014), with many of the ideas emanating from Yang. Figure 34.1 illustrates the contents of this chapter.

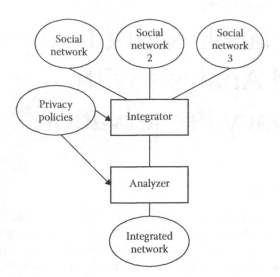

FIGURE 34.1 Social network integration and analysis with privacy preservation.

34.2 SOCIAL NETWORK ANALYSIS

A *social network* is a network of actors with the edges corresponding to their ties. A social network is represented as a graph, $G = (V, E)$, in which V is a set of nodes corresponding to actors and E is a set of edges $(E \subseteq V \times V)$ corresponding to the ties of the respective actors.

Many *social network analysis techniques* have been investigated in the literature. *Centrality measures* and *similarity measures* are two popular measurements. In general, centrality measures determine the relative significance of a node in a social network. In centrality measures, degree centrality, closeness centrality, and betweenness centrality are the typical measures. The degree centrality of a node (u) measures the ratio of the degree of u and the number of nodes other than u in the network. The closeness centrality of u measures the inverse of the total distance between u and all other nodes in the network. The betweenness centrality of u measures the number of shortest paths between any two nodes in the network that passes through u out of all the shortest paths between any two nodes. In general, centrality measures determine the relative significance of a node in a social network. Similarity measures compute the similarity between two subgroups within a social network. L1-Norm, L2-Norm, mutual information, and clustering coefficient are some common measures in similarity measures.

Recent development in *link mining* (Getoor and Diehl, 2005) of social networks focuses on *object ranking* (Bhattacharya and Getoor, 2004; Kleinberg, 1999; Page et al., 1998), *object classification* (Brickell and Shmatikov, 2005; Himmel and Zucker, 1983; Lafferty et al., 2001; Lu and Getoor, 2003; Oh et al., 2000), *group detection* (Adibi et al., 2004; Kubica et al., 2002, 2003; Newman, 2004; Tyler et al., 2003; Wasserman and Faust, 1994), *entity resolution* (Bhattacharya and Getoor, 2004, 2005; Dong et al., 2005), *link prediction* (Craven et al., 2000; Leroy et al., 2010; Leung et al., 2010; Liben-Nowell and Kleinberg, 2003; O'Madadhain et al., 2005), *subgraph discovery* (Ketkar et al., 2005; Kuramochi and Karypis, 2001; Yan and Han, 2002), *graph classification* (Gartner, 2002, 2003), and *graph generative models* (Gartner, 2002; Watts and Strogatz, 1998). Object ranking utilizes the link structure of a network to prioritize the objects that are represented as nodes in a network. The PageRank and HITS are the most prominent algorithms of link-based object ranking applied in web information retrieval. Object classification (Brickell and Shmatikov, 2005; Himmel and Zucker, 1983; Lafferty et al., 2001; Lu and Getoor, 2003; Oh et al., 2000) aims at labeling nodes of a social network from a set of categorical values by exploiting the correlation of related objects. Group detection (Adibi et al., 2004; Kubica et al., 2002, 2003; Newman, 2004; Tyler et al., 2003;

Wasserman and Faust, 1994) clusters nodes of a social network into distinct groups that share common characteristics using techniques such as graph partitioning (Newman, 2004), agglomerative clustering, edge betweenness (Tyler et al., 2003), and stochastic modeling (Wasserman and Faust, 1994). Entity resolution (Bhattacharya and Getoor, 2004, 2005; Dong et al., 2005) determines the identity of a node that it is referred to in the real world. Such techniques are widely used in co-reference resolution, object consolidation, and deduplication. Link prediction (Craven et al., 2000; Leroy et al., 2010; Leung et al., 2010; Liben-Nowell and Kleinberg, 2003; O'Madadhain et al., 2005) tries to predict the existence of a link between two nodes in a social network based on the attributes of the nodes and other related links. For example, it has been utilized to predict the potential interaction between actors in a social event, such as blogs and forums. Subgraph discovery (Ketkar et al., 2005; Kuramochi and Karypis, 2001; Yan and Han, 2002) recognizes interesting subgraphs with specific patterns in a set of social networks. Graph classification (Gartner, 2002, 2003) determines if a social network is a positive or negative example of a specific class of network. Graph generative modeling (Gartner, 2002; Watts and Strogatz, 1998) develops different random graph distributions to study the structural properties of social networks such as the World Wide Web, communication networks, citation networks, and biological networks.

Some recent applications in epidemiology, expert identification, criminal/terrorist social network, academic social network, and social network visualization are found in the literature. For example, several models of social networks have been applied in epidemiology (Morris, 2004). Population in an epidemiology social network can be divided into four groups: susceptible (S), exposed (E), infected (I), and recovered (R). The SIR and SEIR models try to map bond percolation onto a social network. The SIS model is used to model diseases where a long-lasting immunity is not present. Expert identification (Ahmad and Srivastava, 2008) develops mechanisms to identify experts in a social network, and route queries to the identified experts. A criminal/terrorist social network (Xu and Chen, 2005; Yang et al., 2006; Yang and Ng, 2007; Yang, 2008) aims at identifying the roles of terrorists and criminals by mining the patterns in a social network. Academic social network (Tang et al., 2008) models provide topical aspects of publications, authors, and publication venues, and is also a search service of experts and their associations. Co-authorship and co-citations networks are the typical networks in this study (Chau and Yang, 2008; Huang et al., 2010). Social network visualization (Yang and Sageman, 2009) provides network visualization techniques to analyze the dynamic interactions of individuals in a network.

In the work of Chris Yang and colleagues, they have demonstrated how to utilize social network analysis to identify the leaders, terrorist subgroups, or gatekeepers between two or more subgroups (Yang et al., 2006, 2007; Yang and Ng, 2007, 2008; Yang, 2008). Such analysis is beneficial to law enforcement and crime intelligence agencies in their investigations. Visualization tools were also developed to explore the details in social networks and support the investigators in determining the path between any two actors of interest. For example, Figure 34.2 illustrates the two subgroups led by John and Mary, and the connecting paths and gateways between the two leaders. Without this social network analysis and these visualization tools, the huge volume of aggregated data may not be meaningful to the agencies for their tasks. In their work, Yang and Sageman (2009) gives a real-world example of a similar situation where the social network associated with Osama bin Laden and Fateh was visualized.

34.3 LIMITATIONS OF CURRENT APPROACHES FOR PRIVACY-PRESERVING SOCIAL NETWORKS

As discussed in Section 34.2, social network analysis is powerful in discovering embedded knowledge in the social network structure. However, extracting knowledge from a partial social network will indeed misinform us about the importance of actors or relationships between actors because of the missing information in the incomplete social network. Several attempts have been made to publish social network data for analysis. However, the k-anonymity approach to be discussed later does

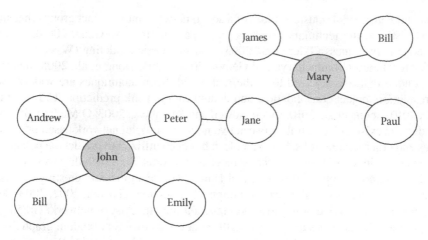

FIGURE 34.2 Illustration of social network analysis and visualization. (From Yang, C.C. and Sageman, M., *J. Inf. Sci.*, 35, 299, 2009.)

not allow social network integration so that social network analysis can be conducted on a global social network incorporating multiple social networks from different sources and yet preserve the privacy.

In our approach, we do not intend to publish individual social networks with privacy preservation. Instead, our objectives are generalizing the individual social networks so that sensitive information is preserved and multiple generalized social networks are integrated as a global social network. In this case, social network analysis can be conducted on the integrated social network that combines the generalized information of multiple social networks. The result of analyzing the integrated social network will be more accurate, and knowledge on the global network can be discovered.

34.3.1 PRIVACY PRESERVATION OF RELATIONAL DATA

There is a desire to publish an anonymized version of relational data owned by an organization to the public so that data mining and analytics can be conducted while the identity of individuals cannot be determined so that no one can recognize the sensitive attribute values of a particular record. Privacy preservation is important in data publishing. A simple approach to privacy preservation of relational data is removing attributes that uniquely identify a person, such as names and identification numbers. It is a typical approach of de-identification. However, given the knowledge of some private information of the person, such as a harmless set of attributes including age, gender, and zip code, a trivial linking attack can identify this person again even if the names and identification numbers are removed. This set of attributes supporting a linking attack is known as quasi-identifiers. Below is an illustration of the linking attack.

Charles is a registered voter. Table 34.1 shows the medical records in a hospital and the voter registration records in the state. Both records include Charles. If the medical records are de-identified, we will not be able to tell that Charles has HIV (human immunodeficiency virus), which is considered as sensitive and private information. However, the voter registration records are not de-identified. If a hacker conducts a linking attack and cross checks both the medical records and the voter registration records, he will be able to find that there is one person who has the same values in the set of quasi-identifiers, [Age = 29, Sex = M, Location = 35667], and therefore, he is able to conclude that Charles has HIV.

A number of approaches for *privacy preservation of relational data* have been developed, for example, *k*-anonymity (Tai et al., 2010), *l*-diversity (Machanavajjhala et al., 2006), *t*-closeness (Li

TABLE 34.1

Medical Records and Voter Registration Records in Information Sharing Using Attribute Removal

Medical Records—Removing Names

Name	Age	Sex	Location	Disease
Peter	8	M	00330	Viral infection
Paul	14	M	01540	Viral infection
Andrew	18	M	18533	Viral infection
Stephen	20	M	14666	Viral infection
Charles	29	M	35667	HIV
Gordon	30	M	43986	Cancer
Linda	35	F	31147	Cancer
Mary	39	F	45246	Cancer
Stella	45	F	85103	Heart disease
Angel	51	F	96214	HIV

Quasi-identifiers

Voter Registration Records

Name	Age	Sex	Location
Charles	29	M	35667
Paul	14	M	01540
David	25	M	00338
...			

and Li, 2007), m-invariance (Xiao and Tao, 2007), δ-presence (Nergiz et al., 2007), and k-support anonymity (Tai et al., 2010).

34.3.2 k-ANONYMITY

k-Anonymity (Sweeney, 2002) is the first attempt at privacy preservation of relational data by ensuring at least k records with respect to every set of quasi-identifier attributes are indistinguishable. If every record in a table is indistinguishable from at least $k - 1$ other records with respect to every set of quasi-identifier attributes, this table satisfies the property of k-anonymity. Table 34.2 illustrates the de-identified medical records with k-anonymity. There are three quasi groups. In each quasi group, the age and location are generalized. For example, Age in quasi group A is generalized to [5,20], Age in quasi group B is generalized to [20,40], and Age in quasi group C is generalized to [41,60]. Similarly, Location in these quasi groups is also generalized to a range of values. In this case, if a hacker knows the age of a person in the voter registration records, he will not be able to link to a particular person in the medical records because there are $k - 1$ other persons who has the age in the same range. However, k-anonymity fails when there is a lack of diversity in the sensitive attributes. For example, there is a lack of diversity of the attribute values of disease in the quasi group with Age = [5,20] and Location = [00300, 02000]. One can see that all the values of the attribute Sex are M and all the values of the attribute Disease are *Viral infection* in this quasi group. As a result, a hacker is able to link Paul (Age = 14, Location = 00332) to quasi group A and determine that Paul has viral infection.

TABLE 34.2

Medical Records and Voter Registration Records Using
***k*-Anonymity**

Medical Records—*k*-Anonymity

Age	Sex	Location	Disease	
[5,20]	M	[00300,02000]	Viral infection	
	M		Viral infection	Quasi group *A*
	M		Viral infection	
	M		Viral infection	
[20,40]	M	[20001,50000]	HIV	
	M		Cancer	Quasi group *B*
	F		Cancer	
	F		Cancer	
[41,60]	F	[80000,99999]	Heart disease	Quasi group *C*
	F		HIV	

Voter Registration Records

Name	Age	Sex	Location
Peter	29	M	35667
Paul	14	M	00332
David	25	M	00338
...			

34.3.3 *l*-DIVERSITY

l-Diversity (Machanavajjhala et al., 2006) ensures that there are at least *l* well-represented values of the attributes for every set of quasi-identifier attributes. The weakness is that one can still estimate the probability of a particular sensitive value. *m*-Invariance (Xiao and Tao, 2007) ensures that each set of quasi-identifier attributes has at least *m* tuples, each with a unique set of sensitive values. There is at most $1/m$ confidence in determining the sensitive values. Others enhanced the techniques of *k*-anonymity and *l*-diversity with personalization, such as personalized anonymity (Xiao and Tao, 2006) and (α,k)-anonymity (Wong et al., 2006), allowing users to specify the degree of privacy protection or specify a threshold α on the relative frequency of sensitive data. Versatile publishing (Jin et al., 2010) anonymizes subtables to guarantees privacy rules.

Privacy preservation of relational data has also been applied in statistical databases. *Query restriction* (Kenthapadi et al., 2005; Nabar et al., 2006), *output perturbation* (Blum et al., 2005; Dinur and Nissim, 2003; Dwork et al., 2006), and *data modification* (Agrawal et al., 2005; Muralidhar and Sarathy, 1999; Xiao and Tao, 2008) are three major approaches. Query restriction (Kenthapadi et al., 2005; Nabar et al., 2006) rejects certain queries when a leak of sensitive values is possible by combining the results of previous queries. Output perturbation (Blum et al., 2005; Dinur and Nissim, 2003; Dwork et al., 2006) adds noise to the result of a query to produce a perturbed version. Data modification (Agrawal et al., 2005; Muralidhar and Sarathy, 1999; Xiao and Tao, 2008) prepares an adequately anonymized version of relational data to a query. The cryptography approach of privacy preservation of relational data aims to develop a protocol of data exchange between multiple private parties. It tries to minimize the information revealed by each party. For example, top-*k* search (Vaidya and Clifton, 2005) reports the top-*k* tuples in the union of the data in several parties. However, the techniques on preserving the privacy of relational data cannot be directly applied on social network data. In recent years, these techniques were extended for preserving the privacy of social network data.

34.4   PRIVACY PRESERVATION OF SOCIAL NETWORK DATA

The current research on privacy preservation of social network data (or graphs) focuses on the purpose of data publishing. A naïve approach is removing the identities of all nodes but only revealing the edges of a social network. In this case, the global network properties are preserved for other research applications assuming that the identities of nodes are not of interest in the research applications. However, Backstrom et al. (2007) proved that it is possible to discover whether edges between specific targeted pairs of nodes exist or not by active or passive attacks. On the basis of the uniqueness of small random subgraphs embedded in a social network, one can infer the identities of nodes by solving a set of restricted isomorphism problems. Active attacks refer to planting well-structured subgraphs in a published social network and then discovering the links between targeted nodes by identifying the planted structures. Passive attacks refer to identifying a node by its association with neighbors and then identifying other nodes that are linked to this association. Such attacks can also be considered as neighborhood attacks.

To tackle active and passive attacks and preserve the privacy of node identities in a social network, there are several anonymization models proposed in the recent literature: k-candidate anonymity (Hay et al., 2007), k-degree anonymity (Liu and Terzi, 2008), and k-anonymity (Zhou and Pei, 2008). Such anonymization models are proposed to increase the difficulty of being attacked based on the notion of k-anonymity in relational data. k-Candidate anonymity (Hay et al., 2007) defines that there are at least k candidates in a graph G that satisfies a given query Q. k-Degree anonymity (Liu and Terzi, 2008) defines that, for every node v in a graph G, there are at least $k-1$ other nodes in G that have the same degree as v. k-Anonymity (Zhou and Pei, 2008) has the strictest constraint. It defines that, for every node v in a graph G, there are at least $k-1$ other nodes in G such that their anonymized neighborhoods are isomorphic. Zheleva and Getoor (2007) proposed an edge anonymization model for social networks with labeled edges rather than labeled nodes.

The technique to achieve the above anonymities is edge or node perturbation (Hay et al., 2007; Liu and Terzi, 2008; Zhou and Pei, 2008). By adding and/or deleting edges and/or nodes, a perturbed graph is generated to satisfy the anonymity requirement. Adversaries can only have a confidence level of $1/k$ of discovering the identity of a node by neighborhood attacks.

Since the current research on privacy preservation of social network data focuses on preserving the node identities in data publishing, the anonymized social network can only be used to study the global network properties but may not be applicable to other social network analysis tasks. In addition, the sets of nodes and edges in a perturbed social network are different from the set of nodes and edges in the original social network. As reported by Zhou and Pei (2008), the number of edges added can be as high as 6% of the original number of edges in a social network. A recent study (Ying and Wu, 2008) has investigated how edge and node perturbation can change certain network properties. Such distortion may cause significant errors in certain social network analysis tasks, such as centrality measurement, although the global properties can be maintained. In this research, we not only preserve the identities of nodes but also the social network structures (i.e., edges).

The limitations of current social network privacy preservation techniques include the following: (i) it preserves the identities of nodes in a social network but it does not preserve the network structure (i.e., edges) of a social network; (ii) the anonymization approach prohibits the integration of social networks; (iii) the perturbation changes the connectivity of nodes, and it can significantly distort the social network analysis result; (iv) the existing privacy preservation techniques have not considered the application of social network analysis.

Another approach to privacy-preserving social network analysis is secure multiparty computation (SMC) (Yao, 1982). In SMC, there is a set of functions that multiple parties wish to jointly compute, and each party has its own private inputs (Lindell and Pinkas, 2009). By preserving the private inputs, SMC uses cryptography technology to compute the joint function (Brickell and Shmatikov, 2005; Frikken and Golle, 2006; Kerschbaum and Schaad, 2008; Sakuma and Kobayashi, 2009). However, there are disadvantages of the cryptography approach. The encrypted data can be attacked and recovered by the malicious party. The complexity of SMC is high, which may not be computationally feasible for large-scale social network data.

34.5 APPROACH BY YANG AND THURAISINGHAM

Instead of using edge or node perturbation or SMC approaches, we propose to use a subgraph generalization approach to preserve the sensitive data and yet share the insensitive data. The social network owned by each party will be decomposed to multiple subgraphs. Each subgraph will be generalized as a probabilistic model depending on the sensitive and insensitive data available, as well as the objective of the social network analysis and mining tasks. The probabilistic models of the generalized subgraphs from multiple sources will then be integrated for social network analysis and mining. Social network analysis and mining will be conducted on the global and generalized social network rather than the partial social network owned by each party. The knowledge that cannot be captured in individual social networks will be discovered in the integrated global social network.

Using such an approach will overcome the limitations of the errors produced by the perturbation approach and yet allow the integration of multiple social networks. It also avoids the attack on the encrypted data in the SMC approach because the shared data are insensitive. The complexity of this approach will also be reduced substantially.

34.5.1 OUR DEFINITION OF PRIVACY

Given two or more social networks $(G_1, G_2, ...)$ from different organizations $(O_1, O_2, ...)$, the objective is achieving more accurate social network analysis and mining results by integrating the shared crucial and insensitive information between these social networks and at the same time preserving the sensitive information with a prescribed level of privacy leakage tolerance. Each organization O_i has a piece of social network G_i, which is part of the whole picture—a social network G constructed by integrating all G_i. Conducting the social network analysis task on G, one can obtain the exact social network analysis result from the integrated information. However, conducting the social network analysis task on any G_i, one can never achieve the exact social network analysis result because of missing information. By integrating G_i and some generalized information of G_j, O_i should be able to achieve more accurate social network analysis results, although it is not the exact social network analysis result. That means if O_i can obtain generalized information from all other organizations, O_i will be able to obtain a social network analysis result much closer to the exact social network analysis result than that obtained from G_i alone.

The adversary attack can be active or passive. Active attacks refer to planting well-structured subgraphs in a social network and then discovering the links between targeted nodes by identifying the planted structures. Passive attacks refer to identifying a node by its association with neighbors and then identifying other nodes that are linked to this association. Such attacks can also be considered as neighborhood attacks.

The generalized information in our approach is a probabilistic model of the general property of a social network. As a result, it does not release the sensitive information of a particular social network. In addition, not all information is useful for a particular social network analysis task. To determine how to generate the generalized information, one may decide what the crucial information for the designated social network analysis task is.

Integration points are crucial to integrate the probabilistic models of multiple social networks. These integration points must be insensitive information to the parties that are involved in the process. A piece of information is not sensitive when it is known to both parties; however, other information that is related to such insensitive information is still considered sensitive. For example, when a suspect is referred from a law enforcement unit to another law enforcement unit, the identity of this suspect is insensitive to both units but the identities of other acquaintances who are associated with this suspect are sensitive. A piece of information can also be known to both parties when such information is available from a common source. For example, when a suspect is reported in the national news or his identity is available in a national database, the identity of this suspect is known to all law enforcement units.

Any generalized information is still subject to privacy leakage depending on the background knowledge owned by the other parties. As a result, we need to ensure that a specified tolerance of privacy leakage is satisfied. The measure of privacy leakage must be independent from the techniques in generating and integrating generalized information of social networks. Privacy means that no party should be able to learn anything more than the insensitive information shared by other parties and the prescribed output of the social network analysis tasks. If any adversary attack can be applied to learn any private and sensitive data, there is a privacy leakage. In this problem, the shared insensitive information is the generalized information and the identity of the insensitive nodes, which are the integration points. The prescribed outputs of the social network analysis tasks are the centrality measures or similarity measures, such as the closeness centrality of a node.

The leakage of private information includes the identities of sensitive nodes and the adjacency (i.e., edges) of any two nodes regardless of whether any of these nodes are sensitive or insensitive. If any of the active or passive attacks can be applied to the generalized information or the output of the social network analysis tasks to learn the above-mentioned private information, there is a privacy leakage. Any privacy preservation technique should protect the exact identity of sensitive nodes or the adjacency between any two nodes. Table 34.3 presents the definitions of the tolerance of privacy leakage on a sensitive node, on the adjacency between an insensitive node and a sensitive node, and on the adjacency between two sensitive nodes.

Most attacks cannot discover the exact identity or adjacency given a reasonable privacy preservation technique. However, many attacks are able to narrow down the identity to a few possible known identities. Ideally, a privacy-preserving technique should achieve a tolerance where no attack can find a clue of the possible identity of a sensitive node. In reality, it is almost impossible to achieve such tolerance because of the background knowledge possessed by the adversaries. However, a good privacy-preserving technique should reduce privacy leakage as much as possible, which means achieving a higher value of τ in privacy leakage.

The generalized information in this problem is the probabilistic models of the generalized social networks instead of a perturbed model using the k-anonymity approach. As a result, the τ-tolerance of privacy leakage is independent to the generalization technique. In addition, it preserves both the identities and network structures. By integrating the probabilistic models of multiple generalized social networks, the objective is achieving a better performance of social network analysis tasks. At the same time, neither the probabilistic models nor the social network analysis results should release private information that may violate the prescribed τ-tolerance of privacy leakage when it is under adversary attacks.

TABLE 34.3

Definitions of τ-Tolerance of Privacy Leakage

τ-Tolerance of privacy leakage on a sensitive node:
1. The identity of a sensitive node cannot be identified as one of τ or fewer possible known identities.

τ-Tolerance of privacy leakage on the adjacency between an insensitive node and a sensitive node:
1. The identity of an insensitive node is known but its adjacency with other sensitive nodes is not known.
2. The adjacent nodes cannot be identified as one of τ or fewer possible sensitive nodes.

$\tau_1\tau_2$-Tolerance of privacy leakage on the adjacency between two sensitive nodes:
1. The identity of a sensitive node A cannot be identified as one of τ_1 or fewer possible known identities.
2. The adjacent node of this sensitive node A cannot be identified as one of τ_2 or fewer possible known identities.

34.6 FRAMEWORK OF INFORMATION SHARING AND PRIVACY PRESERVATION FOR INTEGRATING SOCIAL NETWORKS

In this chapter, we use the framework of information sharing and privacy preservation for integrating social networks as shown in Figure 34.3.

34.6.1 SHARING INSENSITIVE INFORMATION

Assume organization P (O_P) and organization Q (O_Q) have social networks G_P and G_Q, respectively, and O_P needs to conduct a social network analysis task but G_P is only a partial social network. If there are no privacy concerns, one can integrate G_P and G_Q to generate an integrated G and obtain a better social network analysis result. If there are privacy concerns, O_Q cannot release G_Q to O_P but can only share the generalized information of G_Q to O_P. At the same time, O_P does not need all data from O_Q but only those that are critical for the social network analysis task. The objectives are maximizing the information sharing that is useful for the social network analysis task but preserving the sensitive information to satisfy the prescribed τ-tolerance of privacy leakage and achieve more accurate social network analysis results.

Thuraisingham (1994, 2008) discussed a coalition of dynamic data sharing in which security and integrity policies are enforced. As reported in the *Washington Post* in September 2008 (Nakashima, 2008), there was no systematic mechanism for sharing intelligence between private companies, or between companies and the government. It also emphasized that the government should take action on developing a mechanism to share unclassified information while some information should remain classified. Without information sharing, the United States developed products and technology that could be easily stolen with little effort. The key point is differentiating sensitive and insensitive information to permit necessary information sharing while protecting privacy. A well-developed privacy policy provides a mechanism to determine what information should be shared on the basis of the information needs and the trust degree of the information-requesting party.

In our framework as presented in Figure 34.3, we propose that the information shared between two parties should be based on the *information needs* to satisfy the social network analysis task, the *identification of insensitive information* between the two parties, and the *information available* in the social network. When we perform social network data sharing, we need to consider what kinds of information have the highest utility to accomplish a particular social network analysis task. We need to determine the insensitive data to be shared and serve as the integration points between two social networks so that the generalized information can be integrated.

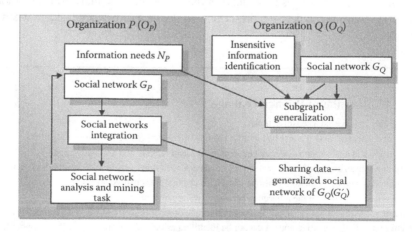

FIGURE 34.3 Framework of information sharing and privacy preservation for integrating social networks.

In our research problem, both identities and network structure are considered sensitive but only generalized information is shared. However, we also consider that a small number of identities are insensitive. The identities of these nodes are known to the public or insensitive to both organizations that are sharing the information. We define the sensitivity of an identity u between two organizations O_p and O_q as sensitivity(u, O_p, O_q):

$$sensitivity(u, O_p, O_q)$$

$$= \begin{cases} 0 & \text{if } Refer_{O_p}(u, O_q) = 1, Refer_{O_q}(u, O_p) = 1, \text{or } Source_{O_p O_q}(u) = 1 \\ 1 & \text{else} \end{cases}$$

where $Refer_x(u, y) = 1$ when x makes a referral of u to y and $Source_{x,y}(u) = 1$ when u can be obtained from a common source of x and y.

In this work, we focus on the fundamental centrality analysis. To compute different centrality measures, attributes such as the degree of nodes and the shortest distance between nodes (Gao et al., 2010; Gubichev et al., 2010) have high utilities. When information is shared with another organization, some sensitive information must be preserved but the generalized information can be released so that more accurate estimation of the required information for centrality measures can be obtained. Attributes for consideration in generalization include the number of nodes in a subgroup, the diameter of a subgroup, the distributions of node degrees, and the eccentricity of insensitive nodes.

34.6.2　GENERALIZATION

A subgraph generalization generates a generalized version of a social network, in which a connected subgraph is transformed as a *generalized node* and only *generalized information* will be presented in the generalized node. The generalized information is the probabilistic model of the attributes. A subgraph of $G = (V, E)$ is denoted as $G' = (V', E')$ where $V' \subset V$, $E' \subset E$, $E' \subseteq V' \times V'$. G' is a connected subgraph if there is a path for each pair of nodes in G'. We only consider a connected subgraph when we conduct subgraph generalization. The edge that links from other nodes in the network to any nodes of the subgraph will be connected to the generalized node. The generalized social network protects all sensitive information while releasing the crucial and nonsensitive information to the information-requesting party for social network integration and the intended social network analysis task. A mechanism is needed to (i) identify the subgraphs for generalization, (ii) determine the connectivity between the set of generalized nodes in the generalized social network, and (iii) construct the generalized information to be shared.

The constructed subgraphs must be mutually exclusive and exhaustive. A node v can only be part of a subgraph but not any other subgraphs. The union of nodes from all subgraphs $V_1', V_2', \dots, V_n'$ should be equal to V, the original set of nodes in G. To construct a subgraph for generalization, there are a few alternatives, including n-neighborhood and k-connectivity.

1. *n-Neighborhood*: For a node $v \in G$, the ith neighbor of v is $N_i(v) = \{u \in G : d(u,v) = i\}$, where $d(u,v)$ is the distance between u and v. Given a target node, v, which can be an insensitive node, the n-neighborhood graph of v is denoted as n-neighbor(v, G). n-Neighbor$(v, G) = (V^i, E^i)$ such that $V^i = \{u \in G : d(u,v) \leq n\}$ and $E^i \subset E$, $E^i \subseteq V^i \times V^i$.
2. *k-Connectivity*: The connectivity $\kappa(G)$ of a graph G is the minimum number of nodes whose removal results in a disconnected graph. The edge connectivity $\kappa'(G)$ of a graph G is the minimum number of edges whose removal results in a disconnected graph. A graph is k-connected if $\kappa(G) \geq k$ and it is k-edge connected if $\kappa'(G) \geq k$. If a graph is k-edge

connected, two or more connected subgraphs (components) that are disconnected from each other are created after removing the k edges. Subgraphs can further be generated if the subgraphs being created are also k-edge connected.

We illustrate the subgraph generalization using the K-nearest neighbor (KNN) method. Let $SP^D(v, V_i^c)$ be the distance of the shortest path between v and $v_i^c v_i^c$. When v is assigned to the subgraph G_i in subgraph generation, $SP^D(v, V_i^c)$ must be shorter than or equal to $SP^D(v, V_i^c)$ where $j = 1, 2,.., K$ and $j \neq i$. Secondly, an edge exists between two generalized nodes G_i and G_j in the generalized graph G' if and only if there is an edge between any two nodes in G such that one from each generalized node, G_i and G_j.

The KNN subgraph generation algorithm is presented below:

```
1: length = 1;
2: V = V − {v₁ᶜ, v₂ᶜ,..., vₖᶜ};
3: While V ≠ Ø
4:     For each vⱼ ∈ V
5:         For each i = 1 to K
6:             IF (SPᴰ(vⱼ, Vᵢᶜ) == length);
7:                 Vᵢ = Vᵢ + vⱼ;
8:                 V = V − vⱼ;
9:         End For;
10:    End For;
11: length++;
12: End While
13: For each (vᵢ,vⱼ) ∈ E
14:     IF(Subgraph(vᵢ) == Subgraph(vⱼ))
15:     //Subgraph(vᵢ) is the subgraph such that vᵢ ∈ Subgraph(vᵢ)
            Gₖ = Subgraph(vᵢ)
16:         Eₖ = Eₖ + (vᵢ,vⱼ)
17:     ELSE
18:         Create an edge between Subgraph(vᵢ) and Subgraph(vⱼ) and add it to E′
19: End For
```

Figure 34.4 illustrates the subgraph generation by the KNN method. G has seven nodes including v_1 and v_2. If we take v_1 and v_2 as the insensitive nodes and we are going to generate two subgraphs by the KNN method, all other nodes will be assigned to one of the two subgraphs depending on their shortest distances with v_1 and v_2. Two subgraphs, G_1 and G_2, are generated as illustrated in Figure 34.4.

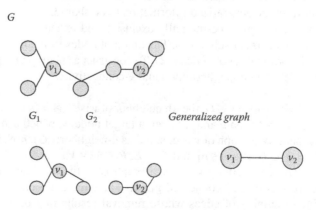

FIGURE 34.4   Illustrations of generating subgraphs.

The KNN subgraph generation algorithm creates K subgraphs $G_1, G_2, \ldots, G_K$ from G. Each subgraph, G_i, has a set of nodes, V_i, and a set of edges, E_i. Edges between subgraphs, E', are also created. A generalized graph, G', is constructed where each generalized node corresponds a subgraph G_i and labeled by the insensitive node, v_i^C.

34.6.3 Probabilistic Model of Generalized Information

For each generalized node $v_j' \in V_i'$, we determine the generalized information to be shared. The generalized information should achieve the following objectives: (i) is useful for the social network analysis task after integration, (ii) preserves the sensitive information, and (iii) is minimal so that unnecessary information is not released. The generalized information of V_i' can be the probabilistic model of the distance between any two nodes v_j and v_k in V_i', $P(\text{Distance}(v_j, v_j) = d)$, $v_j, v_k \in V_i'$ (Yang and Tang, 2009). The construction of subgraphs plays an important role in determining the generalized information to be shared and the usefulness of the generalized information.

In addition to the utility of the generalized information, the development of the subgraph construction algorithms must take the privacy leakage into consideration. By taking the generalized subgraphs and the generalized information of each subgraph, attacks can be designed to discover identities and adjacencies of sensitive and insensitive nodes.

34.6.4 Integrating Generalized Social Network for Social Network Analysis Task

Figure 34.5 presents the overview of the subgraph generalization approach. Taking the generalized social network from the multiple organizations, we need to develop techniques to make use of the shared data with the existing social network to accomplish the intended social network analysis task, as illustrated in Figure 34.5. For example, if the social network analysis task is computing the closeness centrality, we need to develop a technique to make use of the additional information from the generalized nodes to obtain accurate estimations of the distances between nodes in a social network (Gao et al., 2010; Gubichev et al., 2010).

The result of a social network analysis task is denoted as $\Im(G)$, where G is a social network. The social network analysis result of organization P is $\Im(G_P)$. If organization Q shares its social network, G_Q, with organization P, P can integrate G_P and G_Q to G and obtain a social network analysis result $\Im(G)$. The accuracy of $\Im(G)$ is much higher than that of $\Im(G_P)$; however, Q cannot share G_Q with P owing to privacy concerns but only the generalized social network, G_Q'. The integration technique here should be capable of utilizing the useful information in G_Q' and integrate with G_P, which is denoted as $I(G_P, G_Q')$. The accuracy of $\Im(I(G_P, G_Q'))$ should be close to $\Im(G)$ and significantly better than $\Im(G_P)$.

We have conducted an experiment using the Global Salafi Jihad terrorist social network (Yang and Sageman, 2009). There are 366 nodes and 1275 ties in this network with four major terrorist

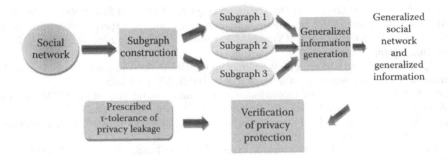

FIGURE 34.5 Framework of subgraph generalization approach.

groups including Central Staff of al Qaeda, Core Arab, Southeast Asia, and Maghreb Arab. We have applied the KNN subgraph generalization technique and utilized the closeness centrality as the social network analysis task. It was found that using the generalization approach can improve the performance of closeness centrality by more than 35%. This result shows that the proposed approach of integrating social networks is promising.

34.7 SUMMARY AND DIRECTIONS

Social network analysis is very useful in discovering the embedded knowledge in social network structures, which is applicable in many practical domains, including homeland security, public safety, epidemiology, public health, electronic commerce, marketing, and social science. However, social network data is usually distributed and no single organization is able to capture the global social network. For example, a law enforcement unit in region A has the criminal social network data of the region; similarly, another law enforcement unit in region B has another criminal social network data of region B. Unfortunately, owing to privacy concerns, these law enforcement units may not be allowed to share the data, and therefore, neither of them can benefit from analyzing the integrated social network that combines the data from the social networks in region A and region B. In this chapter, we discussed aspects of sharing the insensitive and generalized information of social networks to support social network analysis while preserving the privacy at the same time. We discussed the generalization approach to construct a generalized social network in which only insensitive and generalized information is shared. We also discussed the integration of the generalized information and how it can satisfy a prescribed level of privacy leakage tolerance, which is measured independently of the privacy-preserving techniques.

Social network analysis is important for extracting hidden knowledge in a community. It is particularly important for investigating terrorist and criminal communication patterns and the structure of their organization. Unfortunately, most law enforcement and intelligence units only own a small piece of the social network. Owing to privacy concerns, these pieces of data cannot be shared among the units. Therefore, the utility of each piece of information is limited. In this chapter, we also introduced a generalization approach for preserving privacy and integrating multiple social networks. The integrated social network will provide better information for us to conduct social network analysis, such as computing the centrality. In addition, we discussed the τ-tolerance, which specifies the level of privacy leakage that must be protected. Our experimental result also shows that the generalization approach and social network integration produce promising performance.

REFERENCES

Adibi, A., Chalupsky, H., Melz, E., and Valente, A. The KOJAK group finder: Connecting the dots via integrated knowledge-based and statistical reasoning. In: *Innovative Applications of Artificial Intelligence Conference*, San Jose, CA, 2004.

Agrawal, R., Srikant, R., and Thomas, D. Privacy preserving OLAP. In: *ACM SIGMOD'05*, Chicago, 2005.

Ahmad, M.A. and Srivastava, J. An ant colony optimization approach to expert identification in social networks. In: Liu, H., Salerno, J.J., and Young, M.J., editors. *Social Computing, Behavioral Modeling, and Prediction*, Springer, Berlin, 2008.

Backstrom, L., Dwork, C., and Kleinberg, J. Wherefore art thou R3579X? Anonymized social networks, hidden patterns, and structural steganography. In: *WWW'07* Banff, Alberta, Canada, 2007.

Bhattacharya, I. and Getoor, L. Iterative record linkage for cleaning and integration. In: *SIGMOD'04 Workshop on Research Issues on Data Mining and Knowledge Discovery*, Paris, France, 2004.

Bhattacharya, I. and Getoor, L. Entity resolution in graphs. Technical Report 4758, Computer Science Department, University of Maryland, 2005.

Blum, A., Dwork, C., McSherry, F., and Nissim, K. Practical privacy: The SuLQ framework. In: *ACM PODS'05*, Baltimore, 2005.

Brickell, J. and Shmatikov, V. Privacy-preserving graph algorithms in the semi-honest model. In: *Proceedings of ASIACRYPT*, Chennai, India, pp. 236–252, 2005.

Chau, A.Y.K. and Yang, C.C. The shift towards multi-disciplinarily in information science. *Journal of the American Society for Information Science and Technology* 59(13): 2156–2170, 2008.

Craven, M., DiPasquo, D., Freitag, D., McCallum, A., Mitchell, T., Nigam, K., and Slattery, S. Learning to construct knowledge bases from the world wide web. *Artificial Intelligence* 118: 69–114, 2000.

Dinur, I. and Nissim, K. Revealing information while preserving privacy. In: *ACM PODS'03*, 2003.

Dong, X., Halevy, A., and Madhavan, J. Reference reconciliation in complex information spaces. In: *ACM SIGMOD International Conference on Management of Data*, San Diego, CA, 2005.

Dwork, C., McSherry, F., Nissim, K., and Smith, A. Calibrating noise to sensitivity in private data analysis. In: *TCC'06*, New York, 2006.

Frikken, K.B. and Golle, P. Private social network analysis: How to assemble pieces of a graph privately. In: *The 5th ACM Workshop on Privacy in Electronic Society (WPES'06)*, Alexandria, VA, 2006.

Gao, J., Qiu, H., Jiang, X., Wang, T., and Yang, D. Fast top-k simple shortest discovery in graphs. In: *ACM CIKM*, Toronto, Ontario, 2010.

Gartner, T. Exponential and geometric kernels for graphs. In: *NIPS Workshop on Unreal Data: Principles of Modeling Nonvectorial Data*, Whistler, BC, Canada, 2002.

Gartner, T. A survey of kernels for structured data. In: *ACM SIGKDD Explorations*, vol. 5, pp. 49–58, 2003.

Getoor, L. and Diehl, C.P. Link mining: A survey. In: *ACM SIGKDD Explorations*, vol. 7, pp. 3–12, 2005.

Gubichev, A., Bedathur, S., Seufert, S., and Weikum, G. Fast and accurate estimation of shortest paths in large graphs. In: *ACM CIKM*, Toronto, Ontario, 2010.

Hay, M., Miklau, G., Jensen, D., Weis, P., and Srivastava, S. Anonymizing social networks. Technical Report 07-19, University of Massachusetts, Amherst, 2007.

Himmel, R. and Zucker, S. On the foundations of relaxation labeling process. In: *IEEE Transactions on Pattern Analysis and Machine Intelligence*, pp. 267–287, 1983.

Huang, J., Sun, H., Han, J., Deng, H., Sun, Y., and Liu, Y. SHRINK: A structural clustering algorithm for detecting hierarchical communities in networks. In: *ACM CIKM*, Toronto, Ontario, 2010.

Jin, X., Zhang, M., Zhang, N., and Das, G. Versatile publishing for privacy preservation. In: *ACM KDD*, Washington, DC, 2010.

Kenthapadi, K., Mishra, N., and Nissim, K. Simulatable auditing. In: *PODS'05*, Baltimore, 2005.

Kerschbaum, F. and Schaad, A. Privacy-preserving social network analysis for criminal investigations. In: *Proceedings of the ACM Workshop on Privacy in Electronic Society*, Alexandria, VA, 2008.

Ketkar, N., Holder, L., and Cook, D. Comparison of graph-based and logic-based multi-relational data mining. In: *ACM SIGKDD Explorations*, vol. 7, December 2005.

Kleinberg, J. Authoritative sources in a hyperlinked environment. *Journal of the ACM* 46: 604–632, 1999.

Kubica, J., Moore, A., Schneider, J., and Yang, Y. Stochastic link and group detection. In: *National Conference on Artificial Intelligence*. American Association for Artificial Intelligence, Edmonton, Alberta, Canada, 2002.

Kubica, J., Moore, A., and Schneider, J. Tractable group detection on large link data sets. In: *IEEE International Conference on Data Mining*, Melbourne, FL, 2003.

Kuramochi, M. and Karypis, G. Frequent subgraph discovery. In: *IEEE International Conference on Data Mining*, San Jose, CA, 2001.

Lafferty, L., McCallum, A., and Pereira, F. Conditional random fields: Probabilistic models for segmenting and labeling sequence data. In: *International Conference on Machine Learning*, Williamstown, MA, 2001.

Leroy, V., Cambazoglu, B.B., and Bonchi, F. Cold start link prediction. In: *ACM SIGKDD*, Washington, DC, 2010.

Leung, C.W., Lim, E., Lo, D., and Weng, J. Mining interesting link formation rules in social networks. In: *ACM CIKM*, Toronto, Ontario, 2010.

Li, N. and Li, T. t-Closeness: Privacy beyond k-anonymity and l-diversity. In: *ICDE'07*, Istanbul, Turkey, 2007.

Liben-Nowell, D. and Kleinberg, J. The link prediction problem for social networks. In: *International Conference on Information and Knowledge Management (CIKM'03)*, New Orleans, LA, 2003.

Lindell, Y. and Pinkas, B. Secure multiparty computation for privacy-preserving data mining. *The Journal of Privacy and Confidentiality* 1(1): 59–98, 2009.

Liu, K. and Terzi, E. Towards identity anonymization on graphs. In: *ACM SIGMOD'08*, ACM Press, Vancouver, BC, Canada, 2008.

Lu, Q. and Getoor, L. Link-based classification. In: *International Conference on Machine Learning*, Washington, DC, 2003.

Machanavajjhala, A., Gehrke, J., and Kifer, D. L-diversity: Privacy beyond k-anonymity. In: *ICDE'06*, Atlanta, GA, 2006.

Morris, M. *Network Epidemiology: A Handbook for Survey Design and Data Collection.* Oxford University Press, London, 2004.

Muralidhar, K. and Sarathy, R. Security of random data perturbation methods. *ACM Transactions on Database Systems* 24: 487–493, 1999.

Nabar, S.U., Marthi, B., Kenthapadi, K., Mishra, N., and Motwani, R. Towards robustness in query auditing. *VLDB*, Seoul, Korea, 151–162, 2006.

Nakashima, E. Cyber attack data-sharing is lacking, Congress told. *Washington Post*, September 19, 2008, p. D02. Available at http://www.washingtonpost.com/wp-dyn/content/article/2008/09/18/AR2008091803730.html, 2008.

Nergiz, M.E., Atzori, M., and Clifton, C. Hiding the presence of individuals from shared database. In: *SIGMOD'07*, Beijing, China, 2007.

Newman, M.E.J. Detecting community structure in networks. *European Physical Journal B* 38: 321–330, 2004.

Oh, H.J., Myaeng, S.H., and Lee, M.H. A practical hypertext categorization method using links and incrementally available class information. In: *International ACM SIGIR Conference on Research and Development in Information Retrieval*, Athens, Greece, 2000.

O'Madadhain, J., Hutchins, J., and Smyth, P. Prediction and ranking algorithms for even-based network data. *ACM SIGKDD Explorations*, vol. 7, Chicago, December 2005.

Page, L., Brin, S., Motwani, R., and Winograd, T. The PageRank citation ranking: Bringing order to the web. Technical Report, Stanford University, 1998.

Sakuma, J. and Kobayashi, S. Link analysis for private weighted graphs. In: *Proceedings of ACM SIGIR'09*, Boston, pp. 235–242, 2009.

Sweeney, L. *K*-anonymity: A model for protecting privacy. In: *International Journal of Uncertainty Fuzziness Knowledge-Based Systems* 10: 557–570, 2002.

Tai, C., Yu, P.S., and Chen, M. *k*-Support anonymity based on pseudo taxonomy for outsourcing of frequent itemset mining. In: *ACM SIGKDD*, Washington, DC, 2010.

Tang, J., Zhang, J., Yao, L., Li, J., Zhang, L., and Su, Z. ArnetMiner: Extraction and mining of academic social networks. In: *ACM KDD'08*. ACM Press, Las Vegas, NV, 2008.

Thuraisingham, B. Security issues for federated databases systems. In: *Computers and Security*, North Holland, Amsterdam, 1994.

Thuraisingham, B. Assured information sharing: Technologies, challenges and directions. In: Chen, H. and Yang, C.C., editors, *Intelligence and Security Informatics: Techniques and Applications*, Springer, Berlin, 2008.

Tyler, J.R., Wilkinson, D.M., and Huberman, B.A. Email as spectroscopy: Automated discovery of community structure within organizations. In: *Communities and Technologies*, pp. 81–96. Kluwer, Dordrecht, 2003.

Vaidya, R.J. and Clifton, C. Privacy-preserving top-*k* queries. In: *International Conference of Data Engineering*, Tokyo, Japan, 2005.

Wasserman, S. and Faust, K. *Social Network Analysis: Methods and Applications.* Cambridge University Press, Cambridge, 1994.

Watts, D.J. and Strogatz, S.H. Collective dynamics of "small-world" networks. *Nature* 339: 440–442, 1998.

Wong, R.C., Li, J., Fu, A., and Wang, K. (α,k)-Anonymity: An enhanced *k*-anonymity model for privacy-preserving data publishing. In: *SIGKDD*, Philadelphia, PA, 2006.

Xiao, X. and Tao, Y. Personalized privacy preservation. In: *SIGMOD*, Chicago, 2006.

Xiao, X. and Tao, Y. *m*-Invariance: Towards privacy preserving re-publication of dynamic datasets. In: *ACM SIGMOD'07*, ACM Press, Beijing, China, 2007.

Xiao, X. and Tao, Y. Dynamic anonymization: Accurate statistical analysis with privacy preservation. In: *ACM SIGMOD'08*, ACM Press, Vancouver, BC, Canada, 2008.

Xu, J. and Chen, H. CrimeNet explorer: A framework for criminal network knowledge discovery. *ACM Transactions on Information Systems* 23: 201–226, 2005.

Yan, X. and Han, J. gSpan: Graph-based substructure pattern mining. In: *International Conference on Data Mining*, Mabachi City, Japan, 2002.

Yang, C.C., Liu, N., and Sageman, M. Analyzing the terrorist social networks with visualization tools. In: *IEEE International Conference on Intelligence and Security Informatics*, San Diego, CA, 2006.

Yang, C.C. and Ng, T.D. Terrorism and crime related weblog social network: Link, content analysis and information visualization. In: *IEEE International Conference on Intelligence and Security Informatics*, New Brunswick, NJ, 2007.

Yang, C.C., Ng, T.D., Wang, J., Wei, C., and Chen, H. Analyzing and visualizing gray web forum structure. In: *Pacific Asia Workshop on Intelligence and Security Informatics*, Chengdu, China, 2007.

Yang, C.C. Information sharing and privacy protection of terrorist or criminal social networks. In: *IEEE International Conference on Intelligence and Security Informatics*, Taipei, Taiwan, pp. 40–45, 2008.

Yang, C.C. and Ng, T.D. Analyzing content development and visualizing social interactions in web forum. In: *IEEE International Conference on Intelligence and Security Informatics*, Taipei, Taiwan, 2008.

Yang, C.C. and Sageman, M. Analysis of terrorist social networks with fractal views. *Journal of Information Science* 35: 299–320, 2009.

Yang, C.C. and Tang, X. Social networks integration and privacy preservation using subgraph generalization. In: *Proceedings of AMC SIGKDD Workshop on CyberSecurity and Intelligence Informatics*, Paris, France, June 28, 2009.

Yang, C. and Thuraisingham, B. A generalized approach for social network integration and analysis with privacy preservation. In *Data Mining and Knowledge Discovery for Big Data: Methodologies, Challenge and Opportunities*, Springer-Verlag, Berlin, 2014, 259–280.

Yao, A. Protocols for secure computations. In: *Proceedings of the Annual IEEE Symposium on Foundations of Computer Science*, Chicago, p. 23, 1982.

Ying, X. and Wu, X. Randomizing social networks: A spectrum preserving approach. In: *SIAM International Conference on Data Mining (SDM'08)*, Atlanta, GA, 2008.

Zheleva, E. and Getoor, L. Preserving the privacy of sensitive relationships in graph data. In: *First ACM SIGKDD International Workshop on Privacy, Security, and Trust in KDD (PinKDD'07)*, San Jose, CA, 2007.

Zhou, B. and Pei, J. Preserving privacy in social networks against neighborhood attacks. In: *IEEE International Conference on Data Engineering*, Cancun, Mexico, 2008.

35 Attacks on Social Media and Data Analytics Solutions

35.1 INTRODUCTION

We are hearing about attacks to computer systems, networks, and critical infrastructures almost daily. More recently, we are also hearing about social networks being attacked. Furthermore, these social networks are being used to attack computer systems, networks, and critical infrastructures. Therefore, one of the areas that we can expect to get increasing attention is that of attacks on social media and the solution to handle such attacks. That is, these social networks are being infiltrated with malware.

Malware is the term used for malicious software. Malicious software is developed by hackers to steal data and cause harm to computers, networks, and infrastructures, and deny legitimate services to users, among others. Malware has plagued society and the software industry for around four decades. Some of the early malware include the Creeper Virus of 1970 and the Morris Worm of 1988.

As computers became interconnected, the amount of malware increased at an alarming rate in the 1990s. Today, with the World Wide Web and so many transactions and activities being carried out on the Internet, the malware problem is causing chaos among computer and network users.

There are various types of malware, including viruses, worms, time and logic bombs, Trojan horses, and spyware. Preliminary results from Symantec published in 2008 suggest that "the release rate of malicious code and other unwanted programs may be exceeding that of legitimate software applications" (http://en.wikipedia.org/wiki/Malware). CME (Common Malware Enumeration) was "created to provide single, common identifiers to new virus threats and to the most prevalent virus threats in the wild to reduce public confusion during malware incidents" (http://cme.mitre.org/).

In this chapter, we discuss the attacks on social networks and discuss some potential solutions. First, we provide an overview of the various types of malware discussed in the literature. Then, we discuss some of the attacks being carried out on social networks, including the recent attack published by the *Financial Times* on July 30, 2015, on hackers using Twitter images to attack the computing resources of the members of the network (Jones, 2015). Some solutions using data analytics for detecting malware are discussed next. Finally, some other aspects of security concerns in social networks are discussed.

The organization of this chapter is as follows. In Section 35.2, we discuss the various types of malware, including virus, worms, and botnets, among others. Attacks on social media are discussed in Section 35.3. Data mining solutions are discussed in Section 35.4. The experimental cloud-based data mining system we have developed that can be used to detect suspicious activity in streaming Twitter messages is discussed in Section 35.5. The chapter is summarized in Section 35.6. Figure 35.1 illustrates the concepts discussed in this chapter.

35.2 MALWARE AND ATTACKS

35.2.1 TYPES OF MALWARE

Malware is a potent vehicle for many successful cyber attacks every year, including data and identity theft, system and data corruption, and denial of service; it therefore constitutes a significant security threat to many individuals and organizations. The average direct malware cost

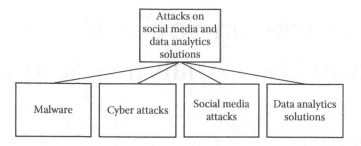

FIGURE 35.1 Attacks on social media.

damages worldwide per year from 1999 to 2006 have been estimated at US$14 billion (Computer Economics Inc., 2007), and several billion more today. This includes labor costs for analyzing, repairing, and disinfecting systems; productivity losses; revenue losses due to system loss or degraded performance; and other costs directly incurred as the result of the attack. However, the direct cost does not include the prevention cost, such as antivirus software, hardware, and IT (information technology) security staff salary, etc. Aside from these monetary losses, individuals and organizations also suffer identity theft, data theft, and other intangible losses due to successful attacks.

Malware includes viruses, worms, Trojan horses, time and logic bombs, botnets, and spyware. A number of techniques have been devised by researchers to counter these attacks; however, the more successful the researchers become in detecting and preventing the attacks, the more sophisticated malicious code appears in the wild. Thus, the arms race between malware authors and malware defenders continues to escalate. One popular technique applied by the antivirus community to detect malicious code is *signature detection*. This technique matches untrusted executables against a unique telltale string or byte pattern known as a *signature*, which is used as an identifier for a particular malicious code. Although signature detection techniques are widely used, they are not effective against zero-day attacks (new malicious code), polymorphic attacks (different encryptions of the same binary), or metamorphic attacks (different code for the same functionality) (Crandall et al., 2005). There has, therefore, been a growing need for fast, automated, and efficient detection techniques that are robust to these attacks. Below, we elaborate on the various types of malware. Figure 35.2 illustrates the various types.

Virus. Computer viruses are malware that piggyback onto other executables and are capable of replicating. Viruses can exhibit a wide range of malicious behaviors, ranging from simple annoyance (such as displaying messages) to widespread destruction such as wiping all the data on the hard drive (e.g., CIH virus). Viruses are not independent programs. Rather, they are code fragments that *exist on* other binary files. A virus can infect a host machine by replicating itself when it is brought

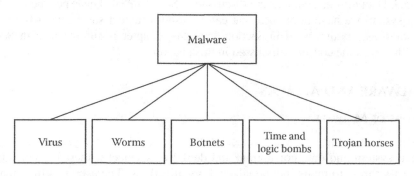

FIGURE 35.2 Types of malware.

in contact with that machine, such as via a shared network drive, removable media, or e-mail attachment. The replication is done when the virus code is executed and it is permitted to write in the memory.

There are two types of viruses based on their replication strategy: *nonresident* and *resident*. The nonresident virus does not store itself on the hard drive of the infected computer. It is only attached to an executable file that infects a computer. The virus is activated each time the infected executable is accessed and run. When activated, the virus looks for other victims (e.g., other executables) and infects them. Conversely, resident viruses allocate memory in the computer hard drive, such as the boot sector. These viruses become active every time the infected machine starts.

The earliest computer virus dates back to 1970 with the advent of *Creeper* virus, detected on ARPANET (Kaspersky Lab, 2011). Since then, hundreds of thousands of different viruses have been written, and corresponding antivirus have also been devised to detect and eliminate the viruses from computer systems. Most commercial antivirus products apply a signature-matching technique to detect virus. A *virus signature* is a unique bit pattern in the virus binary that can accurately identify the virus (PCMag Digital Group, n.d.). Traditionally, virus signatures are generated manually. However, automated signature generation techniques based on data mining have been proposed recently (Masud et al., 2007, 2008b).

Worms. Computer worms are malware but unlike viruses, they need not attach themselves to other binaries. Worms are capable of propagating themselves to other hosts through network connections. Worms also exhibit a wide range of malicious behavior such as spamming, phishing, harvesting, and sending sensitive information to the worm writer; jamming or slowing down network connections; deleting data from hard drive; and so on. Worms are independent programs, and reside in the infected machine by camouflage. Some of the worms open a *backdoor* in the infected machine, allowing the worm writer to control the machine and making it a zombie (or bot) for its malicious activities.

The earliest computer worm dates back to 1988, programmed by Robert Morris, who unleashed the *Morris Worm*. It infected 10% of the then Internet, and his act resulted in the first conviction in the United States under the Computer Fraud and Abuse Act (Dressler, 2007). One of the six authors of this book was working in computer security at Honeywell Inc. in Minneapolis at that time, and vividly remembers what happened that November day.

Other infamous worms since then include the Melissa worm unleashed in 1999 that crashed servers; Mydoom worm released in 2004, which was the fastest spreading e-mail worm; and SQL Slammer worm founded in 2003 that caused a global Internet slow down.

Commercial antivirus products also detect worms by scanning worm signatures against the signature database. However, although this technique is very effective against regular worms, it is usually not effective against zero-day attacks (Frei et al., 2008), polymorphic attacks, and metamorphic worms. However, recent techniques for worm detection address these problems by automatic signature generation techniques (Kim and Karp, 2004; Newsome et al., 2005). Several data mining techniques also exist for detecting different types of worms (Masud et al., 2007, 2008b).

Trojan Horse. Trojan horses have been studied within the context of multilevel databases. They covertly pass information from a high-level process to a low-level process. A good example of a Trojan horse is the manipulation of file locks. Now, according to the Bell and La Padula security policy discussed in Chapter 38, a *Secret* process cannot directly send data to an unclassified process, as this will constitute a write down. However, a malicious Secret process can covertly pass data to an unclassified process by manipulating the file locks as follows. Suppose both processes want to access, say, an unclassified file. The secret process wants to read from the file while the unclassified process can write into the file. However, both processes cannot obtain the read and write locks at the same time. Therefore, at time T1, let us assume that the Secret process has the read lock while the unclassified process attempts to get a write lock. The unclassified process cannot obtain this lock. This means a one-bit information, say 0, is passed to the unclassified process. At time T2, let us assume that the situation does not change. This means a one-bit information of 0 is passed.

However, at time T3, let us assume the Secret process does not have the read lock, in which case the unclassified process can obtain the write lock. This time, a one-bit information of 1 is passed. Over time, a classified string of 0011000011101 could be passed from the Secret process to the unclassified process.

A Trojan horse (http://en.wikipedia.org/wiki/Trojan_horse_(computing)) is software that appears to perform a desirable function for the user but actually carries out a malicious activity. In the above example, the Trojan horse does have read access to the data object. It is reading from the object on behalf of the user. However, it also carries out malicious activity by manipulating the locks and sending data covertly to the unclassified user.

Time and Logic Bombs. In the software paradigm, time bomb refers to a computer program that stops functioning after a prespecified time/date has reached. This is usually imposed by software companies in beta versions of software so that the software stops functioning after a certain date. An example is the Windows Vista Beta 2 that stopped functioning on May 31, 2007 (Microsoft Corporation, 2007).

A logic bomb is a computer program that is intended to perform malicious activities when certain predefined conditions are met. This technique is sometimes injected into viruses or worms to increase the chances of survival and spreading before getting caught.

An example of a logic bomb is the Fannie Mae bomb in 2008 (Claburn, 2009). A logic bomb was discovered at the mortgage company Fannie Mae on October 2008. An Indian citizen and IT contractor, Rajendrasinh Babubhai Makwana, who worked in Fannie Mae's Urbana, Maryland, facility, allegedly planted it, and it was set to activate on January 31, 2009, to wipe all of Fannie Mae's 4000 servers. As stated in Claburn (2009), Makwana's employment had been terminated around 1:00 pm on October 24, 2008, and planted the bomb while he still had network access. He was indicted in a Maryland court on January 27, 2009, for unauthorized computer access.

Botnet. Botnet is a network of compromised hosts or *bots*, under the control of a human attacker known as the *botmaster*. The botmaster can issue commands to the bots to perform malicious actions, such as recruiting new bots, launching coordinated DDoS (distributed denial-of-service) attacks against some hosts, stealing sensitive information from the bot machine, sending mass spam e-mails, and so on. Thus, botnets have emerged as an enormous threat to the Internet community.

According to Messmer (2009), more than 12 million computers in the United States are compromised and controlled by the top 10 notorious botnets. Among them, the highest number of compromised machines is due to the Zeus botnet. Zeus is a kind of Trojan (a malware), whose main purpose is to apply key-logging techniques to steal sensitive data such as log-in information (password, etc.), bank account and credit card numbers. One of its key-logging techniques is to inject fake HTML forms into online banking log-in pages to steal log-in information.

The most prevalent botnets are the IRC (Internet Relay Chat) botnets (Saha and Gairola, 2005), which have a centralized architecture. These botnets are usually very large and powerful, consisting of thousands of bots (Rajab et al., 2006). However, their enormous size and centralized architecture also make them vulnerable to detection and demolition. Many approaches for detecting IRC botnets have been proposed (Goebel and Holz, 2007; Karasaridis et al., 2007; Livadas et al., 2006; Rajab et al., 2006). Another type of botnet is the peer-to-peer (P2P) botnet. These botnets are distributed and much smaller than IRC botnets. Therefore, they are more difficult to locate and destroy. Many works have analyzed the characteristics of P2P botnets (Grizzard et al., 2007; Lemos, 2006; LURHQ Threat Intelligence Group, 2004).

Spyware. Spyware (http://en.wikipedia.org/wiki/Spyware) is a type of malware that can be installed on computers, which collects information about users without their knowledge. For example, spyware observes the websites visited by the user, the e-mails sent by the user, and, in general, the activities carried out by the user on his or her computer. Spyware is usually hidden from the user. However, sometimes employers can install spyware to find out the computer activities of employees.

An example of spyware is keylogger (also called keystroke logging) software. Keylogging (http://en.wikipedia.org/wiki/Keystroke_logging) is the action of tracking the keys struck on a keyboard, usually in a covert manner so that the person using the keyboard is unaware that their actions are being monitored. Another example of spyware is adware, when advertisement pops up on the computer when the person is doing some usually unrelated activity. In this case, the spyware monitors say the websites surfed by the user and carries out targeted marketing using adware.

35.2.2 THREATS TO CYBERSECURITY

While the previous section discussed the various types of malware, in this section, we discuss some of the threats to cybersecurity. These include cyberterrorism, identity theft, and malicious intrusions. Figure 35.3 illustrates the various cybersecurity threats.

Cyberterrorism. Cyberterrorism is one of the major terrorist threats posed to our nation today. As we have mentioned earlier, there is now so much information available electronically and on the web. An attack on our computers as well as networks, databases, and the Internet could be devastating to businesses. It is estimated that cyberterrorism could cost businesses billions of dollars. For example, consider a banking information system. If terrorists attack such a system and deplete accounts of their funds, then the bank could lose millions and perhaps billions of dollars. By crippling the computer system, millions of hours of productivity could be lost, and that equates to money in the end. Even a simple power outage at work through some accident could cause several hours of productivity loss, and as a result, a major financial loss. Therefore, it is critical that our information systems be secure. We discuss various types of cyberterrorist attacks. One is spreading viruses and Trojan horses that can wipe away files and other important documents; another is intruding in computer networks.

Note that threats can occur from outside or inside of an organization. Outside attacks are attacks on computers and networks from someone outside the organization. We hear of hackers breaking into computer systems and causing havoc within an organization. There are hackers who start spreading viruses, and these viruses cause great damage to the files in various computer systems. But a more sinister problem is the insider threat. Just like non-information-related attacks, there is the insider threat with information-related attacks. There are people inside an organization who have studied the business practices and develop schemes to cripple the organization's information assets. These people could be regular employees or even those working at computer centers. The problem is rather serious as someone may be masquerading as someone else and causing all kinds of damage. In the next few sections, we will examine how data mining could detect and perhaps prevent such attacks.

Malicious Intrusions. Malicious intrusions may include intruding in networks, the web clients and servers, the databases, and operating systems. Many cyberterrorism attacks are due to malicious intrusions. We hear much about network intrusions. What happens here is that intruders try to tap into the networks and get the information that is being transmitted. These intruders may be human intruders or Trojan horses set up by humans. Intrusions could also occur on files. For example, one can masquerade as someone else and log into someone else's computer system and access the files.

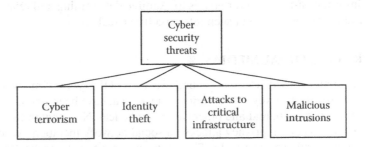

FIGURE 35.3 Cybersecurity threats.

Intrusions can also occur on databases. Intruders posing as legitimate users can pose queries such as SQL queries and access the data that they are not authorized to know.

Essentially, cyberterrorism includes malicious intrusions as well as sabotage through malicious intrusions or otherwise. Cybersecurity consists of security mechanisms that attempt to provide solutions to cyber attacks or cyberterrorism. When we discuss malicious intrusions or cyber attacks, we may need to think about the non-cyber world, that is, non-information-related terrorism, and then translate those attacks to attacks on computers and networks. For example, a thief could enter a building through a trap door. In the same way, a computer intruder could enter the computer or network through some sort of a trap door that has been intentionally built by a malicious insider and left unattended through perhaps careless design. Another example is a thief entering the bank with a mask and stealing the money. The analogy here is an intruder masquerades as someone else, legitimately enters the system, and takes all the information assets. Money in the real world would translate to information assets in the cyber world. That is, there are many parallels between non-information-related attacks and information-related attacks. We can proceed to develop countermeasures for both types of attacks.

Credit Card Fraud and Identity Theft. We are hearing a lot these days about credit card fraud and identity theft. In the case of credit card fraud, others get hold of a person's credit card and make all kinds of purchases; by the time the owner of the card finds out, it may be too late. The thief may have left the country by then.

A more serious theft is identity theft. Here, one assumes the identity of another person, say by getting hold of the social security number and essentially carrying out all the transactions under the other person's name. This could even involve selling houses and depositing the income in a fraudulent bank account. By the time the owner finds out, it will be far too late. It is very likely that the owner may have lost millions of dollars due to the identity theft.

We need to explore the use of data mining both for credit card fraud detection as well as for identity theft. There have been some efforts on detecting credit card fraud (Chan et al., 1999). We need to start working actively on detecting and preventing identity theft.

Attacks on Critical Infrastructure. Attacks on critical infrastructure could cripple a nation and its economy. Infrastructure attacks include attacking the telecommunication lines, electronic power supplies, gas reservoirs, water supplies, food supplies, and other basic entities that are critical for the operation of a nation.

Attacks on critical infrastructures could occur during any type of attack whether they are non-information-related, information-related, or bioterrorism attacks. For example, one could attack the software that runs the telecommunications industry and close down all the telecommunication lines. Similarly, software that runs the power and gas supplies could be attacked. Attacks could also occur through bombs and explosives. That is, the telecommunication lines could be attacked through bombs. Attacking transportation lines such as highways and railway tracks are also attacks on infrastructure.

Infrastructure could also be attacked by natural disasters such as hurricanes and earthquakes. Our main interest here is attacks on infrastructure through malicious attacks, both information-related and non-information-related. Our goal is to examine data mining and related data management technologies to detect and prevent such infrastructure attacks.

35.3 ATTACKS ON SOCIAL MEDIA

While the previous section provided a more general overview of the types of malware and threats, in this section we will provide a survey of the various attacks that have been uncovered on social networks. Some of these attacks are real and others are hypothetical. Note that in Section IV, we have already discussed some potential privacy attacks on social network members. Below, we will discuss some other security and privacy attacks. These are various types of attacks. One is to attack the social media and the other is to attack the computer systems, networks, and infrastructure through

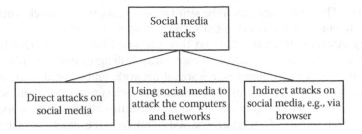

FIGURE 35.4 Social media attacks.

social media. The third group consists of attacks specially formulated for social media systems. We illustrate both types of attacks in Figure 35.4.

De-Anonymization Attacks. In their paper on "A practical attack to de-anonymize social network users," Wondracek et al. (2010) discussed a de-anonymization attack where the hackers can exploit the group membership information about the members of networks and subsequently identify the members. The authors stated that the "group information is available on social networking sites." Specifically, they used web browser attacks to obtain group membership information. When a member of a group and the social network visits a malicious website, the website will carry out the de-anonymization attack formulated by the hacker. They then provide the experimental results.

Seven Deadly Attacks. In their article on the seven deadly social media attacks, Timm and Perez (2010) discussed seven attacks that could occur, including malware attacks, phishing attacks, and identity theft. For example, for malware attacks, they stated that there are two ways the malware can compromise the network. One is a virus that will infect the system, and the other is a malware such as a Trojan horse that could conceal information. They also explain the cross-site scripting (XSS) attack where the malware will enable the user's browser to execute the attacker's code and cause a compromise to the network.

COMBOFIX List of Attacks. The COMBOFIX website lists several attacks to social media (Combofix, n.d.). These include the following. The *Bad SEO* attack attracts the user to a website that contains the malware. The users are also lured to fake websites. The *Pornspace* malware was a worm that utilized a flaw in the security mailing list of MySpace and stole the profiles of the users and then sent porn-based spam. In the *Over the Rainbow* malware attack, the hackers embedded JavaScript code into Twitter messages that can retweet. The user as well as the members of his or her network could be directed to porn sites. In the *Dislike Scam on Facebook* attack, the users were given bogus surveys and once they filled the surveys, they were attacked by malware.

Top Ten Attacks in Social Media. At the RSA conference in 2014, Gary Bahadur (2014), the CEO of KRAA Security, described various attacks on Facebook, Twitter, LinkedIn, and some other social media attacks. For example, he explained how an Android malware attack spread through Facebook. This attack showed that the gadgets we use to connect to a social network site can cause a serious attack to the site.

Top Nine Social Media Threats of 2015. The Zerofox (2015) website published the top nine social media threats, including executive impersonations, corporate impersonations, account takeover, customer scams, and phishing attacks. An account takeover attack in 2015 was especially sinister as it affected the US Central Command (CENTCOM).

***Financial Times* Report.** On July 30, 2015, the *Financial Times* reported that hackers are using Twitter to conceal intrusions (Jones, 2015). For example, the hackers used Twitter images to conceal malware, and from there attacked the computers they wanted to compromise. This attack appears to be similar to a stenographic attack where suspicious messages are embedded into a medium such as images and video.

Link Privacy Attacks. In their article on link privacy, Effendy et al. (2012) discussed a version of the link privacy attack. It is essentially bribing or compromising some of the members (usually a small number) in a social network, and using this to obtain the link details (i.e., who their friends are) of those members who are not compromised. They also discussed the term *degree inference* and showed that this attack can be made more effective using such inference. They also discussed solutions to the attack. Note that this type of attack is specific to a social network.

As the reader can see, the list goes on, and it is not possible for us to list all of the attacks that have occurred or could occur. However, the list of such diverse attack shows that users of a social media site must be aware of how the network can be compromised, and exercise caution when using such sites. Even though it is impossible to handle all types of threats, proper social media use and the solutions the cybersecurity technologists are developing could alleviate the problems a great deal.

35.4 DATA ANALYTICS SOLUTIONS

35.4.1 OVERVIEW

Now that we have discussed the various types of malware and threats as well as social media attacks, in this section we will examine how data analytics solution (e.g., data mining techniques) may be applied to handle the attacks. Data mining has shown a lot of promise to detect attacks on computers and networks. We believe that similar techniques have to be deployed to handle malware attacks on social networking sites. In this section, we will discuss how data mining techniques may be applied for malware detection in general, and how we can deploy them for social networking sites.

Ensuring the integrity of computer networks, both in relation to security and with regard to the institutional life of the nation in general, is a growing concern. Security and defense networks, proprietary research, intellectual property, and data-based market mechanisms, which depend on unimpeded and undistorted access, can all be severely compromised by malicious intrusions. We need to find the best way to protect these systems. In addition, we need techniques to detect security breaches.

Data mining has many applications in security, including in national security (e.g., surveillance) as well as in cybersecurity (e.g., virus detection). The threats to national security include attacking buildings or destroying critical infrastructures such as power grids and telecommunication systems (Bolz et al., 2005). Data mining techniques are being investigated to find out who the suspicious people are and who is capable of carrying out terrorist activities. Cybersecurity involves protecting the computer and network systems against corruption due to Trojan horses and viruses. Data mining is also being applied to provide solutions such as intrusion detection and auditing. In this chapter, we will focus mainly on data mining for cybersecurity applications.

To understand the mechanisms to be applied to safeguard the nation and the computers and networks, we need to understand the types of threats. In Thuraisingham (2003), we described both real-time and non-real-time threats. A real-time threat is a threat that must be acted upon within a certain time to prevent some catastrophic situation. Note that a non-real-time threat could become a real-time threat over time. For example, one could suspect that a group of terrorists will eventually perform some act of terrorism. However, when we set time bounds such as a threat will likely occur, say, before July 1, 2004, then it becomes a real-time threat and we have to take action immediately. If the time bounds are tighter such as "a threat will occur within 2 days," then we cannot afford to make any mistakes in our response.

There has been a lot of work on applying data mining for both national security and cyber-security. Much of the focus of our previous book was on applying data mining for national security (Thuraisingham, 2003). In this section, we will discuss data mining for cybersecurity and then explore how the techniques could be applied for attacks on social networks.

35.4.2 Data Mining for Cybersecurity

Data mining is being applied for problems such as intrusion detection and auditing. For example, anomaly detection techniques could be used to detect unusual patterns and behaviors. Link analysis may be used to trace the viruses to the perpetrators. Classification may be used to group various cyber attacks and then use the profiles to detect an attack when it occurs. Prediction may be used to determine potential future attacks depending, in a way, on information learned about terrorists through e-mail and phone conversations. Also, for some threats, non-real-time data mining may suffice, while for certain other threats such as for network intrusions, we may need real-time data mining. Many researchers are investigating the use of data mining for intrusion detection. While we need some form of real-time data mining, that is, the results have to be generated in real time, we also need to build models in real time. For example, credit card fraud detection is a form of real-time processing. However, here, models are usually built ahead of time. Building models in real time remains a challenge. Data mining can also be used for analyzing web logs as well as analyzing the audit trails. On the basis of the results of the data mining tool, one can then determine whether any unauthorized intrusions have occurred or whether any unauthorized queries have been posed.

Other applications of data mining for cybersecurity include analyzing the audit data. One could build a repository or a warehouse containing the audit data and then conduct an analysis using various data mining tools to see if there are potential anomalies. For example, there could be a situation where a certain user group may access the database between 3 and 5 am. It could be that this group is working the night shift, in which case there may be a valid explanation. However, if this group is working between, say, 9 am and 5 pm, then this may be an unusual occurrence. Another example is when a person accesses the databases always between 1 and 2 pm, but for the last 2 days he has been accessing the database between 1 and 2 am. This could then be flagged as an unusual pattern that would need further investigation. It should be noted that owing to the vast number of members of the popular social networks, the audit data could be massive. Therefore, we need scalable solutions to analyze such massive amounts of data.

Insider threat analysis is also a problem both from a national security and from a cybersecurity perspective. That is, those working in a corporation who are considered to be trusted could commit espionage. Similarly, those with proper access to the computer system could plant Trojan horses and viruses. Catching such terrorists is far more difficult than catching terrorists outside of an organization. One may need to monitor the access patterns of all the individuals of a corporation even if they are system administrators, to see whether they are carrying out cyberterrorism activities.

Another application of data analytics solutions for social media is in the area of social media forensics. Once it is determined that the social media systems have been attacked, then the forensics examiner will have to collect the various evidence data and apply analytics solutions. It should be noted that social media forensics can help toward analyzing the communication and behavior patterns of the members. For example, the data they post could be analyzed in the case of, say, a homicide to determine whether a member has carried out any suspicious activity.

While data mining can be used to detect and possibly prevent cyber attacks, data mining also exacerbates some security problems such as the inference and privacy problems. With data mining techniques, one could infer sensitive associations from the legitimate responses. For more details on a high-level overview of data mining applications for cybersecurity, we refer to Thuraisingham (2004, 2005). Note that Sections IV and V also discussed the privacy violations that could occur in social media due to data mining.

We are developing a number of tools on data mining for cybersecurity applications at The University of Texas at Dallas. In a previous book, we discussed one such tool for intrusion detection (Awad et al., 2009). An intrusion can be defined as any set of actions that attempt to compromise the integrity, confidentiality, or availability of a resource. As systems become more complex, there are always exploitable weaknesses due to design and programming errors, or through the use of various *socially engineered* penetration techniques. Computer attacks are split into two categories, host-based attacks and network-based attacks. Host-based attacks target a machine and try to gain access to privileged services or resources on that machine. Host-based detection usually uses routines that obtain system call data from an audit process that tracks all system calls made on behalf of each user.

Network-based attacks make it difficult for legitimate users to access various network services by purposely occupying or sabotaging network resources and services. This can be done by sending large amounts of network traffic, exploiting well-known faults in networking services, overloading network hosts, etc. Network-based attack detection uses network traffic data (i.e., tcpdump) to look at traffic addressed to the machines being monitored. Intrusion detection systems are split into two groups: anomaly detection systems and misuse detection systems.

Anomaly detection is the attempt to identify malicious traffic based on deviations from established normal network traffic patterns. Misuse detection is the ability to identify intrusions based on a known pattern for the malicious activity. These known patterns are referred to as signatures. Anomaly detection is capable of catching new attacks. However, new legitimate behavior can also be falsely identified as an attack, resulting in a false positive. The focus with the current state of the art is to reduce the false-negative and false-positive rates.

Our tools include those for e-mail worm detection, malicious code detection, buffer overflow detection, and botnet detection, as well as analyzing firewall policy rules. Figure 35.5 illustrates the various tools we have developed. Some of these tools were discussed in Sections II through VII of this book. For example, for e-mail worm detection, we examine e-mails and extract features such as *number of attachments*, and then train data mining tools with techniques such as SVM (support vector machine) or naïve Bayesian classifiers and develop a model. Then, we test the model and determine whether the e-mail has a virus/worm or not. We use training and testing data sets posted on various websites. Similarly, for malicious code detection, we extract *n*-gram features both with assembly code and binary code. We first train the data mining tool using the SVM technique and then test the model. The classifier will determine whether the code is malicious or not. For buffer overflow detection, we assume that malicious messages contain code while normal messages contain data. We train SVM and then test to see if the message contains code or data. Figure 35.6 illustrates data mining applications in cybersecurity.

35.4.3 MALWARE DETECTION AS A DATA STREAM CLASSIFICATION PROBLEM

While we have provided some general information on data mining for malware detection in the previous section, in this section we describe one such technique, and that is classification. The problem

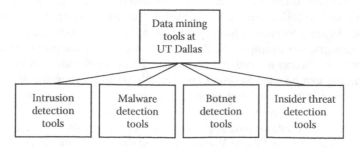

FIGURE 35.5   Data mining tools at UT Dallas.

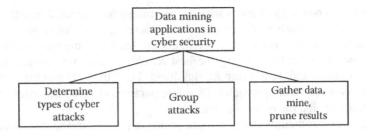

FIGURE 35.6   Data mining applications in cybersecurity.

of detecting malware by using data mining (Kolter and Maloof, 2004; Masud et al., 2008a; Schultz et al., 2001) involves classifying each executable as either *benign* or *malicious*. Most past works have approached the problem as a static data classification problem, where the classification model is trained with fixed training data. However, the escalating rate of malware evolution and innovation is not well suited to static training. Detection of continuously evolving malware is better treated as a *data stream* classification problem. In this paradigm, the data stream is a sequence of executables in which each data point is one executable. The stream is *infinite length*. It also observes *concept drift* as attackers relentlessly develop new techniques to avoid detection, changing the characteristics of the malicious code. Similarly, the characteristics of benign executables change with the evolution of compilers and operating systems.

Data stream classification is a major area of active research in the data mining community. It is especially relevant to social media data, as certain social media systems such as Twitter include streaming data. The data stream classification problem requires surmounting at least three challenges: first, the storage and maintenance of potentially unbounded historical data in an infinite-length, concept-drifting stream for training purposes is infeasible; second, the classification model must be adapted continuously to cope with concept drift; and third, if there is no predefined feature space for the data points in the stream, new features with high discriminating power must be selected and extracted as the stream evolves, which we call *feature evolution*.

Solutions to the first two problems are related. Concept drift necessitates refinement of the hypothesis to accommodate the new concept; most of the old data must be discarded from the training set. Therefore, one of the main issues in mining concept-drifting data streams is the selection of training instances adequate to learn the evolving concept. Solving the third problem requires a feature selection process that is ongoing, since new and more powerful features are likely to emerge and old features are likely to become less dominant as the concept evolves. If the feature space is large, then the running time and memory requirements for feature extraction and selection becomes a bottleneck for the data stream classification system.

One approach to addressing concept drift is to select and store the training data that are most consistent with the current concept (Fan, 2004). Other approaches, such as Very Fast Decision Trees (VFDTs) (Domingos and Hulten, 2000), update the existing classification model when new data appear. However, past work has shown that ensemble techniques are often more robust for handling unexpected changes and concept drifts (Kolter and Maloof, 2005; Scholz and Klinkenberg, 2005; Wang et al., 2003). These maintain an ensemble of classifiers and update the ensemble when new data appear.

We design and develop a multipartition, multichunk ensemble classification algorithm that generalizes existing ensemble methods. The generalization leads to significantly improved classification accuracy relative to existing *single-partition, single-chunk* (SPC) ensemble approaches when tested on real-world data streams. The ensemble in our approach consists of Kv classifiers, where K is a constant and v is the number of partitions, to be explained shortly.

Our approach divides the data stream into equal sized *chunks*. The chunk size is chosen so that all data in each chunk fits into the main memory. Each chunk, when *labeled*, is used to train classifiers. Whenever a new data chunk is labeled, the ensemble is updated as follows. We take the r most recent labeled consecutive data chunks, divide these r chunks into v *partitions*, and train a classifier with each partition. Therefore, v classifiers are trained using the r consecutive chunks. We then update the ensemble by choosing the best Kv classifiers (based on accuracy) among the newly trained v classifiers and the existing Kv classifiers. Thus, the total number of classifiers in the ensemble remains constant. Our approach is therefore parameterized by the number of partitions v, the number of chunks r, and the ensemble size K.

Our approach does not assume that new data points appearing in the stream are immediately labeled. Instead, it defers the ensemble updating process until labels for the data points in the latest data chunk become available. In the meantime, new unlabeled data continue to be classified using the current ensemble. Thus, the approach is well suited to applications in which misclassifications solicit corrected labels from an expert user or other source. For example, consider the online credit card fraud detection problem. When a new credit card transaction takes place, its class (*fraud* or *authentic*) is predicted using the current ensemble. Suppose a fraudulent transaction is misclassified as *authentic*. When the customer receives the bank statement, he or she identifies this error and reports it to the authority. In this way, the actual labels of the data points are obtained and the ensemble is updated accordingly.

35.5 CLOUD-BASED MALWARE DETECTION FOR EVOLVING DATA STREAMS

35.5.1 CLOUD COMPUTING FOR MALWARE DETECTION

Some of the social media systems have nearly a billion users. Furthermore, systems such as Twitter have streaming data. Therefore, we need to apply stream mining techniques to determine suspicious activity. Furthermore, owing to the vast number of users and billions of messages being sent or posted every day, we need scalable techniques for determining suspicious behavior. We believe that cloud computing tools would be very useful in developing such scalable analytics solutions. In this section, we describe one such cloud computing tool we have developed for malware detection for evolving data streams. In particular, we describe a data mining technique that is dedicated to the automated generation of signatures to defend against these kinds of attacks. Owing to the need for near real-time performance of the malware detection tools, we have developed our data mining tool in the cloud.

If the feature space of the data points is not fixed, a subproblem of the classification problem is the extraction and selection of features that describe each data point. As in prior work (e.g., Kolter and Maloof, 2004), we use binary n-grams as features for malware detection. However, since the total number of possible n-grams is prohibitively large, we judiciously select n-grams that have the greatest discriminatory power. This selection process is ongoing; as the stream progresses, newer n-grams appear that dominate the older n-grams. These newer n-grams replace the old in our model in order to identify the best features for a particular period.

Naïve implementation of the feature extraction and selection process can be both time intensive and storage intensive for large data sets. For example, our previous work (Masud et al., 2008a) extracted roughly a quarter billion n-grams from a corpus of only 3500 executables. This feature extraction process required extensive virtual memory (with associated performance overhead), since not all of these features could be stored in main memory. Extraction and selection required about 2 hours of computation and many gigabytes of disk space for a machine with a quad-core processor and 12 GB memory. This is despite the use of a purely static data set; when the data set is a dynamic stream, extraction and selection must recur, resulting in a major bottleneck. In this chapter, we consider a much larger data set of 105,000 executables for which our previous approach is insufficient.

We therefore design and develop a scalable feature selection and extraction solution that leverages a cloud computing framework (Dean and Ghemawat, 2008). We show that depending on the availability of cluster nodes, the running time for feature extraction and selection can be reduced by a factor of m, where m is the number of nodes in the cloud cluster. The nodes are machines with inexpensive commodity hardware. Therefore, the solution is also cost-effective as high-end computing machines are not required.

Our Contributions. Our contributions can therefore be summarized as follows. We design and develop a generalized multipartition, multichunk ensemble technique that significantly reduces the expected classification error over existing SPC ensemble methods. A theoretical analysis justifies the effectiveness of the approach. We then formulate the malware detection problem as a data stream classification problem and identify the drawbacks of traditional malicious code detection techniques relative to our data mining approach.

We design and develop a scalable and cost-effective solution to this problem using a cloud computing framework. Finally, we apply our technique to synthetically generated data, as well as real botnet traffic and real malicious executables, achieving better detection accuracy than other stream data classification techniques. The results show that our ensemble technique constitutes a powerful tool for intrusion detection based on data stream classification.

Related Work. Our work is related to both malware detection and stream mining. Both are discussed in this section. Traditional *signature-based* malware detectors identify malware by scanning untrusted binaries for distinguishing byte sequences or *features*. Features unique to malware are maintained in a *signature database*, which must be continually updated as new malware is discovered and analyzed. Traditionally, signature databases have been manually derived, updated, and disseminated by human experts as new malware appears and is analyzed. However, the escalating rate of the appearance of new malware and the advent of self-mutating, polymorphic malware over the past decade have made manual signature updating less practical. This has led to the development of automated data mining techniques for malware detection (e.g., Hamlen et al., 2009; Kolter and Maloof, 2004; Masud et al., 2008a; Schultz et al., 2001) that are capable of automatically inferring signatures for previously unseen malware.

Data mining-based approaches analyze the content of an executable and classify it as malware if a certain combination of features are found (or not found) in the executable. These malware detectors are first trained so that they can generalize the distinction between malicious and benign executables, and thus detect future instances of malware. The training process involves feature extraction and model building using these features. Data mining-based malware detectors differ mainly on how the features are extracted and which machine learning technique is used to build the model. The performance of these techniques largely depends on the quality of the features that are extracted.

In the work reported in Schultz et al. (2001), the authors extracted DLL call information (using *GNU binutils*) and character strings (using *GNU strings*) from the headers of Windows PE executables, as well as 2-byte sequences from the executable content. The DLL calls, strings, and bytes are used as features to train models. Models are trained using two different machine learning techniques, RIPPER (Cohen, 1996) and naïve Bayes (NB) (Michie et al., 1994), to compare their relative performances. Kolter and Maloof (2004) extracted binary n-gram features from executables and applied them to different classification methods, such as k nearest neighbor (KNN) (Aha et al., 1991), NB, SVM (Boser et al., 1992), decision trees (Quinlan, 2003), and boosting (Freund and Schapire, 1996). Boosting is applied in combination with various other learning algorithms to obtain improved models (e.g., boosted decision trees). Our previous work on data mining-based malware detection (Masud et al., 2008a) extracts binary n-grams from the executable, assembly instruction sequences from the disassembled executables, and DLL call information from the program headers. The classification models used in this work are SVM, decision tree, NB, boosted decision tree, and boosted NB.

Hamsa and Polygraph (Li et al., 2006; Newsome et al., 2005) apply a simple form of data mining to generate worm signatures automatically using binary n-grams as features. Both identify a collection of n-grams as a worm signature if they appear only in malicious binaries (i.e., positive samples) and never in benign binaries. This differs from the traditional data mining approaches already discussed (including ours) in two significant respects: First, Polygraph and Hamsa limit their attention to n-grams that appear only in the malicious pool, whereas traditional data mining techniques also consider n-grams that appear in the benign pool to improve the classification accuracy. Second, Polygraph and Hamsa define signature matches as simply the presence of a set of n-grams, whereas traditional data mining approaches build classification models that match samples based on both the presence and absence of features. Traditional data mining approaches therefore generalize the approaches of Polygraph and Hamsa, with corresponding increases in power.

Almost all past works have approached the malware detection problem as a static data classification problem in which the classification model is trained with fixed training data. However, the rapid emergence of new types of malware and new obfuscation strategies adopted by malware authors introduces a dynamic component to the problem that violates the static paradigm. We therefore argue that effective malware detection must be increasingly treated as a data stream classification problem in order to keep pace with attacks.

Many existing data stream classification techniques target infinite-length data streams that exhibit concept drift (Aggarwal et al., 2006; Fan, 2004; Gao et al., 2007; Hashemi et al., 2009; Hulten et al., 2001; Kolter and Maloof, 2005; Wang et al., 2003; Yang et al., 2005; Zhang et al., 2009). All of these techniques adopt a one-pass incremental update approach, but with differing approaches to the incremental updating mechanism. Most can be grouped into two main classes: single-model incremental approaches and hybrid batch-incremental approaches.

Single-model incremental updating involves dynamically updating a single model with each new training instance. For example, decision tree models can be incrementally updated with incoming data (Hulten et al., 2001). In contrast, hybrid batch-incremental approaches build each model from a batch of training data using a traditional batch learning technique. Older models are then periodically replaced by newer models as the concept drifts (Bifet et al., 2009; Fan, 2004; Gao et al., 2007; Wang et al., 2003; Yang et al., 2005). Some of these hybrid approaches use a single model to classify the unlabeled data (e.g., Chen et al., 2008; Yang et al., 2005), while others use an ensemble of models (e.g., Scholz and Klinkenberg, 2005; Wang et al., 2003). Hybrid approaches have the advantage that model updates are typically far simpler than in single-model approaches; for example, classifiers in the ensemble can simply be removed or replaced. However, other techniques that combine the two approaches by incrementally updating the classifiers within the ensemble can be more complex (Kolter and Maloof, 2005; Wang et al., 2003).

Accuracy weighted classifier ensembles (AWE) (Scholz and Klinkenberg, 2005; Wang et al., 2003) are an important category of hybrid-incremental updating ensemble classifiers that use weighted majority voting for classification. These divide the stream into equal-sized chunks, and each chunk is used to train a classification model. An ensemble of K such models classifies the unlabeled data. Each time a new data chunk is labeled, a new classifier is trained from that chunk. This classifier replaces one of the existing classifiers in the ensemble. The replacement victim is chosen by evaluating the accuracy of each classifier on the latest training chunk. These ensemble approaches have the advantage that they can be built more efficiently than a continually updated single model, and they observe higher accuracy than their single-model counterparts (Tumer and Ghosh, 1996).

Our ensemble approach is most closely related to AWE, but with a number of significant differences. First, we apply multipartitioning of the training data to build v classifiers from that training data. Second, the training data consists of r consecutive data chunks (i.e., a multichunk approach) rather than from a single chunk. We have proved both analytically and empirically that both of these enhancements, that is, multipartitioning and multichunk, significantly reduce ensemble classification error (Masud et al., 2011). Third, when we update the ensemble, v classifiers in the ensemble are replaced by v newly trained classifiers. The v classifiers that are replaced may come from different chunks; thus, although some classifiers from a chunk may have been removed, other classifiers from that chunk may still remain in the ensemble. This differs from AWE, in which removal of a classifier means total removal of the knowledge obtained from one whole chunk. Our replacement strategy also contributes to error reduction. Finally, we use simple majority voting rather than weighted voting, which is more suitable for data streams, as shown in Gao et al. (2007). Thus, our multipartition, multichunk ensemble approach is a more generalized and efficient form of that implemented by AWE.

Our work extends our previously published work (Masud et al., 2009). Most existing data stream classification techniques, including our previous work, assume that the feature space of the data points in the stream is fixed. However, in some cases, such as text data, this assumption is not valid. For example, when features are words, the feature space cannot be fully determined at the start of the stream since new words appear frequently. In addition, it is likely that much of this large lexicon of words has low discriminatory power, and is therefore best omitted from the feature space. It is therefore more effective and efficient to select a subset of the candidate features for each data point. This feature selection must occur incrementally as newer, more discriminating candidate features arise and older features become outdated. Therefore, feature extraction and selection should be an integral part of data stream classification. In this chapter, we describe the design and implementation of an efficient and scalable feature extraction and selection technique using a cloud computing framework (Dean and Ghemawat, 2008; Zhao et al., 2009). This approach supersedes our previous work in that it considers the real challenges in data stream classification that occur when the feature space cannot be predetermined. This facilitates the application of our technique to the detection of real malicious executables from a large, evolving data set, showing that it can detect newer varieties of malware as malware instances evolve over time.

35.5.2 DESIGN AND IMPLEMENTATION OF THE SYSTEM ENSEMBLE CONSTRUCTION AND UPDATING

Our *extended, multipartition, multichunk* (EMPC) ensemble learning approach maintains an ensemble $A = \{A_1, A_2, ..., A_{Kv}\}$ of the most recent, best Kv classifiers. Each time a new data chunk D_n arrives, it tests the data chunk with the ensemble A. The ensemble is updated once chunk D_n is labeled. The classification process uses simple majority voting.

The ensemble construction updating process is illustrated in Figure 35.7 and summarized in Algorithm 35.1. Lines 1 through 3 of the algorithm compute the error of each classifier $A_i \in A$ on chunk D_n, where D_n is the most recent data chunk that has been labeled. Let D be the data of the most recently labeled r data chunks, including D_n. Line 5 randomly partitions D into v equal parts $\{d_1, ..., d_v\}$ such that all the parts have roughly the same class distributions. Lines 6 through 9 train a new batch of v classifiers, where each classifier A^n is trained with data set $D - d_j$. The error of each classifier $A^n \in A^n$ is computed by testing it on its corresponding test data. Finally, line 10 selects the best Kv classifiers from the $Kv + v$ classifiers in $A^n \cup A$ based on the errors of each classifier computed in lines 2 and 8. Note that any subset of the nth batch of v classifiers may be selected for inclusion in the new ensemble. Figure 35.7 illustrates the ensemble construction.

Error Reduction Analysis. As explained in Algorithm 35.1, we build ensemble A of Kv classifiers. A test instance x is classified using a majority vote of the classifiers in the ensemble. We use simple majority voting rather than weighted majority voting (refer to Wang et al., 2003), since simple majority voting has been theoretically proven to be the optimal choice for data streams (Gao et al., 2007). Weighted voting can be problematic in these contexts because it assumes that

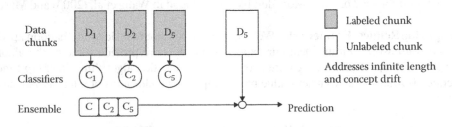

FIGURE 35.7 Ensemble construction.

the distributions of training and test data are the same. However, in data streams, this assumption is violated because of concept drift. Simple majority voting is therefore a better alternative. Our experiments confirm this in practice, obtaining better results with simple rather than weighted majority voting.

We have shown in Masud et al. (2011) that EMPC can further reduce the expected error in classifying concept-drifting data streams compared with SPC approaches, which use only one data chunk for training a single classifier (i.e., $r = v = 1$). Intuitively, there are two main reasons for the error reduction. First, the training data per classifier is increased by introducing the multichunk concept. Larger training data naturally lead to a better-trained model, reducing the error. Second, rather than training only one model from the training data, we partition the data into v partitions, and train one model from each partition. This further reduces error because the mean expected error of an ensemble of v classifiers is theoretically v times lower than that of a single classifier (Tumer and Ghosh, 1996). Therefore, both the multichunk and multipartition strategies contribute to error reduction.

Algorithm 35.1: Updating the Classifier Ensemble

Input: $\{D_{n-r+1},...,D_n\}$: the r most recently labeled data chunks
A: the current ensemble of best Kv classifiers
Output: an updated ensemble A
1: **for** each classifier $A_i \in A$ **do**
2: $e(A_i) \leftarrow$ *error of* A_i *on* D_n// test and compute error
3: **end for**
4: $D \leftarrow \bigcup_{j=n-r+1}^{n} D_j$
5: Partition D into equal parts $d_1, d_2,...,d_v$
6: **for** $j = 1$ to v **do**
7: $A_j^n \leftarrow n$ newly trained classifier from data $D - d_j$
8: $e(A_j) \leftarrow$ error of A_j on d_j// test and compute error
9: **end for**
10: $A \leftarrow$ best Kv from $A^n \cup A$ *based on computed error* $e(.)$

Empirical Error Reduction and Time Complexity. For a given partition size v, increasing the window size r only yields reduced error up to a certain point. Thereafter, increasing r actually hurts the performance of our algorithm. The upper bound of r depends on the magnitude of drift ρ_d. We have shown in Masud et al. (2011) the relative error E_R for $v = 2$, and different values of ρ_d, for increasing r. It is clear from the graph that for lower values of ρ_d, increasing r reduces the relative error by a greater margin. However, in all cases after r exceeds a certain threshold, E_R becomes greater than 1. Although it may not be possible to know the actual value of ρ_d from the data, we may determine the optimal value of r experimentally. In our experiments, we found that for smaller chunk sizes, higher values of r work better, and vice versa. However, the best performance–cost trade-off is found for $r = 2$ or $r = 3$. More details can be found in Wang et al. (2003) and Masud et al. (2008b).

Hadoop/MapReduce Framework. We used the open source Hadoop (hadoop.apache.org) MapReduce framework to implement our experiments. We here provide some of the algorithmic details of the Hadoop MapReduce feature extraction and selection algorithm. The *Map* function in a MapReduce framework takes a key–value pair as input and yields a list of intermediate key–value pairs for each.

$$\text{Map: } (MKey \times MVal) \rightarrow (RKey \times RVal)*$$

All the Map tasks are processed in parallel by each node in the cluster without sharing data with other nodes. Hadoop collates the output of the Map tasks by grouping each set of intermediate values $V \subseteq$ RVal that share a common intermediate key $k \in$ RKey. The resulting collated pairs (k, V) are then streamed to Reduce nodes. Each reducer in a Hadoop MapReduce framework therefore receives a list of multiple (k, V) pairs, issued by Hadoop one at a time in an iterative fashion. *Reduce* can therefore be understood as a function having signature

$$\text{Reduce: (RKey} \times \text{RVal*)*} \to \text{Val}$$

Codomain Val is the type of the final results of the MapReduce cycle.

In our framework, Map keys (MKey) are binary file identifiers (e.g., file names), and Map values (MVal) are the file contents in bytes. *Reduce* keys (RKey) are n-gram features, and their corresponding values (RVal) are the class labels of the file instances whence they were found.

Algorithm 35.2 shows the feature extraction procedure that Map nodes use to map the former to the latter.

Lines 5 through 10 of Algorithm 35.3 tally the class labels reported by Map to obtain positive and negative instance counts for each n-gram. These form a basis for computing the information gain of each n-gram in line 11. Lines 12 through 16 use a min-heap data structure h to filter all but the best S features as evaluated by information gain. The final best S features encountered are returned by lines 18 through 20.

The q reducers in the Hadoop system therefore yield a total of qS candidate features and their information gains. These are streamed to a second reducer that simply implements the last half of Algorithm 35.3 to select the best S features.

Algorithm 35.2: Map(file_id, bytes)

Input: file ID with content bytes
Output: list of pairs (g, l), where g is an n-gram and l is file ID's label
1: $T \leftarrow \varnothing$
2: **for all** n-grams g in bytes **do**
3: $\quad T \leftarrow T \cup \{g, \text{labelof(file id)}\}$ $\{(g, \text{labelof(fil\_id)})\}$
4: **end for**
5: **for all** $(g, l) \in T$ **do**
6: $\quad$ **print** (g, l)
7: **end for**

Algorithm 35.3: Reduce$_{p,t}(F)$

Input: list F of (g, L) pairs, where g is an n-gram and L is a list of class labels; total size t
$\quad$ of original instance set; total number p of positive instances
Output: S pairs (g, i), where i is the information gain of n-gram g
1: **heap** $h/$* empty min-heap */
2: **for all** (g, L) in F **do**
3: $\quad t' \leftarrow 0$
4: $\quad p' \leftarrow 0$
5: $\quad$ **for all** l in L **do**
6: $\quad\quad t' \leftarrow t' + 1$
7: $\quad\quad$ **if** $l = +$ **then**
8: $\quad\quad\quad p \leftarrow p + 1$
9: $\quad\quad$ **end if**

```
10: end for
11: i ← Ĝ(p′,t′,p,t)
12: if h.size < S then
13:    h.insert(i_g)
14: else if (h.root < i) then
15:    h.replace(h.root, i_g)
16: end if
17: end for
18: for all i_g in h do
19: print (g, i)
20: end for
```

35.5.3 MALICIOUS CODE DETECTION

Malware is a major source of cyber attacks. Some malware varieties are purely static; each instance is an exact copy of the instance that propagated it. These are relatively easy to detect and filter once a single instance has been identified. However, a much more significant body of current-day malware is polymorphic. Polymorphic malware self-modifies during propagation so that each instance has a unique syntax but carries a semantically identical malicious payload. The antivirus community invests significant effort and manpower toward devising, automating, and deploying algorithms that detect particular malware instances and polymorphic malware families that have been identified and analyzed by human experts. This has led to an escalating arms race between malware authors and antiviral defenders, in which each camp seeks to develop offenses and defenses that counter the recent advances of the other. With the increasing ease of malware development and the exponential growth of malware variants, many believe that this race will ultimately prove to be a losing battle for the defenders.

The malicious code detection problem can be modeled as a data mining problem for a stream having both infinite length and concept drift. Concept drift occurs as polymorphic malware mutates, and as attackers and defenders introduce new technologies to the arms race. This conceptualization invites application of our stream classification technique to automate the detection of new malicious executables.

Feature extraction using n-gram analysis involves extracting all possible n-grams from the given data set (training set), and selecting the best n-grams among them. Each such n-gram is a feature. That is, an n-gram is a sequence of n bytes. Before extracting n-grams, we preprocess the binary executables by converting them to hexdump files. Here, the granularity level is 1 byte. We apply the UNIX hexdump utility to convert the binary executable files into text files (*hexdump files*) containing the hexadecimal numbers corresponding to each byte of the binary. This process is performed to ensure safe and easy portability of the binary executables. In a nondistributed framework, the feature extraction process consists of two phases: feature extraction and feature selection, described shortly. Our cloud computing variant of this traditional technique is presented in this chapter.

Nondistributed Feature Extraction and Selection. In a nondistributed setting, feature extraction proceeds as follows. Each hexdump file is scanned by sliding an n-byte window over its content. Each n-byte sequence that appears in the window is an n-gram. For each n-gram g, we tally the total number t_g of file instances in which g appears, as well as the total number $p_g \leq t_g$ of these that are positive (i.e., malicious executables).

This involves maintaining a hash table T of all n-grams encountered thus far. If g is not found in T, then g is added to T with counts $t_g = 1$ and $p_g \in \{0, 1\}$ depending on whether the current file has a negative or positive class label. If g is already in T, then t_g is incremented and p_g is conditionally incremented depending on the file's label. When all hexdump files have been scanned, T contains all the unique n-grams in the data set along with their frequencies in the positive instances and in total.

It is not always practical to use all n-gram features extracted from all the files corresponding to the current chunk. The exponential number of such n-grams may introduce unacceptable memory overhead, slow the training process, or confuse the classifier with large numbers of noisy, redundant, or irrelevant features. To avoid these pitfalls, candidate n-gram features must be sorted according to a selection criterion so that only the best ones are selected.

We choose *information gain* as the selection criterion because it is one of the most effective criteria used in literature for selecting the best features. Information gain can be defined as a measure of the effectiveness of an attribute (i.e., feature) for classifying the training data. If we split the training data based on the values of this attribute, then information gain measures the expected reduction in entropy after the split. The more an attribute reduces entropy in the training data, the better that attribute is for classifying the data.

We have shown in Masud et al. (2011) that as new features are considered, their information gains are compared against the heap's root. If the gain of the new feature is greater than that of the root, the root is discarded and the new feature inserted into the heap. Otherwise, the new feature is discarded and feature selection continues.

Distributed Feature Extraction and Selection. There are several drawbacks related to the non-distributed feature extraction and selection approach just described.

- The total number of extracted n-gram features might be very large. For example, the total number of 4-grams in one chunk is around 200 million. It might not be possible to store all of them in main memory. One obvious solution is to store the n-grams in a disk file; however, this introduces unacceptable overhead due to the cost of disk read/write operations.
- If colliding features in hash table T are not sorted, then a linear search is required for each scanned n-gram during feature extraction to test whether it is already in T. If they are sorted, then the linear search is required during insertion. In either case, the time to extract all n-grams is worst-case quadratic in the total number N of n-grams in each chunk, an impractical amount of time when $N \approx 10^8$. Similarly, the nondistributed feature selection process requires a sort of the n-grams in each chunk. In general, this requires $O(N \log N)$ time, which is impractical when N is large.

To efficiently and effectively tackle the drawbacks of the nondistributed feature extraction and selection approach, we leverage the power of cloud computing. This allows feature extraction, n-gram sorting, and feature selection to be performed in parallel, utilizing the Hadoop MapReduce framework.

MapReduce (Dean and Ghemawat, 2008) is an increasingly popular distributed programming paradigm used in cloud computing environments. The model processes large data sets in parallel, distributing the workload across many nodes (machines) in a share-nothing fashion. The main focus is to simplify the processing of large data sets using inexpensive cluster computers. Another objective is ease of usability with both load balancing and fault tolerance.

MapReduce is named for its two primary functions. The Map function breaks jobs down into subtasks to be distributed to available nodes, whereas its dual, Reduce, aggregates the results of completed subtasks. We will henceforth refer to nodes performing these functions as *mappers* and *reducers*, respectively. In this section, we give a high-level overview of the approach.

Each training chunk containing N training files is used to extract the n-grams. These training files are first distributed among m nodes (machines) by the Hadoop Distributed File System (HDFS) (Figure 35.8, step 1). Quantity m is selected by HDFS depending on system availability. Each node then independently extracts n-grams from the subset of training files supplied to the node using the technique (Masud et al., 2011) (Figure 35.8 step 2). When all nodes finish their jobs, the n-grams extracted from each node are collated (Figure 35.8, step 3).

For example, suppose node 1 observes n-gram abc in one positive instance (i.e., a malicious training file), while node 2 observes it in a negative (i.e., benign) instance. This is denoted by pairs abc, $+$ and abc, $-$ under nodes 1 and 2, respectively, in Figure 35.8. When the n-grams are combined, the labels of instances containing identical n-grams are aggregated. Therefore, the aggregated pair for abc is abc, $+ -$. The combined n-grams are distributed to q reducers (with q chosen by HDFS based on system availability). Each reducer first tallies the aggregated labels to obtain a positive count and

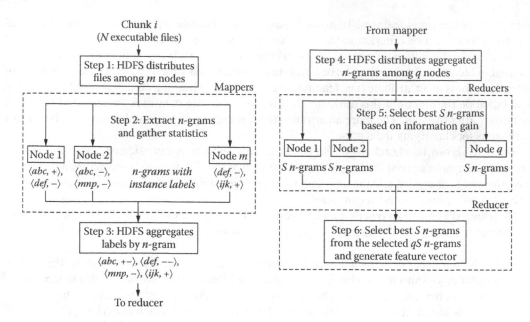

FIGURE 35.8 Distributed feature extraction and selection.

a total count. In the case of n-gram abc, we obtain tallies of $p_{abc} = 1$ and $t_{abc} = 2$. The reducer uses these tallies to choose the best S n-grams from the subset of n-grams supplied to the node (Figure 35.8, step 5). This can be done efficiently using a min-heap of size S; the process requires $O(W \log S)$ time, where W is the total number of n-grams supplied to each reducer. In contrast, the nondistributed version requires $O(W \log W)$ time. Thus, from the q reducer nodes, we obtain qS n-grams. From these, we again select the best S by running another round of the MapReduce cycle in which the Map phase does nothing but the Reduce phase performs feature selection using only one node (Figure 35.8, step 6). Each feature in a feature set is binary; its value is 1 if it is present in a given instance (i.e., executable) and 0 otherwise. For each training or testing instance, we compute the feature vector whose bits consist of the feature values of the corresponding feature set. These feature vectors are used by the classifiers for training and testing.

35.5.4 Experiments

We evaluated our approach on synthetic data, botnet traffic generated in a controlled environment, and a malware data set. The results of the experiments are compared with several baseline methods.

Data Sets

Synthetic data set: To generate synthetic data with a drifting concept, we use a moving hyperplane, given by $\sum_{i=1}^{d} a_i x_i = a_0$ (Wang et al., 2003). If $\sum_{i=1}^{d} a_i x_i \leq a_0$, then an example is negative; otherwise, it is positive. Each example is a randomly generated d-dimensional vector $\{x_1,\ldots,x_d\}$, where $x_i \in [0, 1]$. Weights $\{a_1,\ldots,a_d\}$ are also randomly initialized with a real number in the range $[0, 1]$. The value of a_0 is adjusted so that roughly the same numbers of positive and negative examples are generated. This can be done by choosing $a_0 = \frac{1}{2}\sum_{i=1}^{d} a_i$. We also introduce noise randomly by switching the labels of p percent of the examples, where $p = 5$ in our experiments. There are several parameters that simulate concept drift. We use parameters identical to those in Wang et al. (2003).

In total, we generate 250,000 records and four different data sets having chunk sizes 250, 500, 750, and 1000, respectively. Each data set has 50% positive instances and 50% negative.

Botnet data set: Botnets are networks of compromised hosts known as *bots*, all under the control of a human attacker known as the *botmaster* (Barford and Yegneswaran, 2006). The botmaster can issue commands to the bots to perform malicious actions, such as launching DDoS attacks, spamming, spying, and so on. Botnets are widely regarded as an enormous emerging threat to the Internet community. Many cutting-edge botnets apply P2P technology to reliably and covertly communicate as the botnet topology evolves. These botnets are distributed and small, making them more difficult to detect and destroy. Examples of P2P bots include Nugache (Lemos, 2006), Sinit (Stewart, 2003), and Trojan.Peacomm (Grizzard et al., 2007).

Botnet traffic can be viewed as a data stream having both infinite length and concept drift. Concept drift occurs as the bot undertakes new malicious missions or adopts differing communication strategies in response to new botmaster instructions. We therefore consider our stream classification technique to be well suited to detecting P2P botnet traffic.

We generate real P2P botnet traffic in a controlled environment using the Nugache P2P bot (Lemos, 2006). The details of the feature extraction process are discussed in Masud et al. (2008b). There are 81 continuous attributes in total. The whole data set consists of 30,000 records, representing 1 week's worth of network traffic. We generate four different data sets having chunk sizes of 30, 60, 90, and 120 minutes, respectively. Each data set has 25% positive (botnet traffic) instances and 75% negative (benign traffic).

Malware data set: We extract a total of 38,694 benign executables from different Windows machines, and a total of 66,694 malicious executables collected from an online malware repository VX Heavens (2010), which contains a large collection of malicious executables (viruses, worms, Trojans, and backdoors). The benign executables include various applications found at the Windows installation folder, as well as other executables in the default program installation directory.

We select only the Win32 Portable Executables (PE) in both cases. Experiments with the ELF executables are a potential direction of future work. The collected 105,388 files (benign and malicious) form a data stream of 130 chunks, each consisting of 2000 instances (executable files). The stream order is chosen by sorting the malware by version and discovery date, simulating the evolving nature of Internet malware. Each chunk has 1500 benign executables (75% negative) and 500 malicious executables (25% positive). The feature extraction and selection process for this data set is described in earlier sections.

Note that all these data sets are dynamic in nature. Their unbounded (potentially infinite-length) size puts them beyond the scope of purely static classification frameworks. The synthetic data also exhibits concept drift. Although it is not possible to accurately determine whether the real data sets have concept drift, theoretically the stream of executables should exhibit concept drift when observed over a long period of time. The malware data exhibits feature evolution as evidenced by the differing set of distinguishing features identified for each chunk.

Baseline Methods. For classification, we use the Weka machine learning open-source package (Hall et al., 2009). We apply two different classifiers: J48 decision tree and Ripper. We then compare each of the following baseline techniques to our EMPC algorithm.

BestK: This is an SPC ensemble approach, where an ensemble of the best K classifiers is used. The ensemble is created by storing all the classifiers seen thus far, and selecting the best K based on expected error on the most recent training chunk. An instance is tested using simple majority voting.

Last: In this case, we only keep the classifier trained on the most recent training chunk. This can be considered an SPC approach with $K = 1$.

AWE: This is the SPC method implemented using accuracy-weighted classifier ensembles (Wang et al., 2003). It builds an ensemble of K models, where each model is trained from one data chunk. The ensemble is updated as follows. Let C_n be the classifier built on the most recent training chunk. From the existing K models and the newest model C_n, the K best models are selected based on their error on the most recent training chunk. Selection is based on weighted voting where the weight of each model is inversely proportional to the error of the model on the most recent training chunk.

All: This SPC uses an ensemble of all the classifiers seen thus far. The new data chunk is tested with this ensemble by simple voting among the classifiers. Since this is an SPC approach, each classifier is trained from only one data chunk.

We obtain the optimal values of r and v to be between 2 and 3, and between 3 and 5, respectively, for most data sets. Unless mentioned otherwise, we use $r = 2$ and $v = 5$ in our experiments. To obtain a fair comparison, we use the same value for K (ensemble size) in EMPC and all baseline techniques.

Hadoop Distributed System Setup. The distributed system on which we performed our experiments consists of a cluster of 10 nodes. Each node has the same hardware configuration: an Intel Pentium IV 2.8 GHz processor, 4 GB main memory, and 640 GB hard disk space. The software environment consists of an Ubuntu 9.10 operating system, the Hadoop-0.20.1 distributed computing platform, the JDK 1.6 Java development platform, and a 100 MB LAN network link.

Discussion. Our work considers a feature space consisting of purely syntactic features: binary n-grams drawn from executable code segments, static data segments, headers, and all other content of untrusted files. Higher-level structural features such as call- and control-flow graphs, and dynamic features such as runtime traces, are beyond our current scope. Nevertheless, n-gram features have been observed to have very high discriminatory power for malware detection, as demonstrated by a large body of prior work as well as our experiments. This is, in part, because n-gram sets that span the entire binary file content, including headers and data tables, capture important low-level structural details that are often abstracted away by higher-level representations. For example, malware often contains a handwritten assembly code that has been assembled and linked using nonstandard tools. This allows attackers to implement binary obfuscations and low-level exploits not available from higher-level source languages and standard compilers. As a result, malware often contains unusual instruction encodings, header structures, and link tables whose abnormalities can only be seen at the raw binary level, not in assembly code listings, control-flow graphs, or system API call traces. Expanding the feature space to include these additional higher-level features requires an efficient and reliable method of harvesting them and assessing their relative discriminatory power during feature selection, and is reserved as a subject of future work.

The empirical results reported in Masud et al. (2011) confirm our analysis that shows that multipartition, multichunk approaches should perform better than single-chunk, single-partition approaches. Intuitively, a classifier trained on multiple chunks should have better prediction accuracy than a classifier trained on a single chunk because of the larger training data. Furthermore, if more than one classifier is trained by multipartitioning the training data, the prediction accuracy of the resulting ensemble of classifiers should be higher than a single classifier trained from the same training data because of the error reduction power of an ensemble over single classifier. In addition, the accuracy advantages of EMPC can be traced to two important differences between our work and that of AWE. First, when a classifier is removed during ensemble updating in AWE, all information obtained from the corresponding chunk is forgotten; however, in EMPC, one or more classifiers from an earlier chunk may survive. Thus, EMPC ensemble updating tends to retain more information than does AWE, leading to a better ensemble. Second, AWE requires at least Kv data chunks, whereas EMPC requires at least $K + r - 1$ data chunks to obtain Kv classifiers. Thus, AWE tends to keep much older classifiers in the ensemble than EMPC, leading to some outdated classifiers that can have a negative effect on the classification accuracy.

However, the higher accuracy comes with an increased cost in running time. Theoretically, EMPC is at most rv times slower than AWE, its closest competitor in accuracy. This is also evident in the empirical evaluation, which shows that the running time of EMPC is within five times that of AWE (for $r = 2$ and $v = 5$). However, some optimizations can be adopted to reduce the runtime cost. First, parallelization of training for each partition can be easily implemented, reducing the training time by a factor of v. Second, classification by each model in the ensemble can also be done in parallel, thereby reducing the classification time by a factor of Kv. Therefore, parallelization of training and classification should reduce the running time at least by a factor of v, making the runtime close to that of AWE. Alternatively, if parallelization is not available, parameters v and r can be lowered to sacrifice prediction accuracy for lower runtime cost. In this case, the desired balance between runtime and prediction accuracy can be obtained by evaluating the first few chunks of the stream with different values of v and r and choosing the most suitable values.

35.6 SUMMARY AND DIRECTIONS

In this chapter, we have provided an overview of malware (also known as malicious software). We discuss various types of malware such as virus, worm, time and logic bombs, Trojan horse, botnet, and spyware. As we have stated, malware is causing chaos in society and in the software industry. Malware technology is getting more and more sophisticated. Malware is continuously changing patterns so as not to get caught. Therefore, developing solutions to detect and/or prevent malware has become an urgent need. In some of our previous books, we provided a sample of the tools we have developed. More details can be found in Awad et al. (2009) and Masud et al. (2011). Next, we discussed the various types of attacks, including attacks on social media. This was followed by a discussion of data mining for cybersecurity problems, including malware detection, and then described the prototype stream of a cloud computing tool that can detect malware in data streams, which includes Twitter data streams.

Data mining for national security as well as for cybersecurity is a very active research area. Various data mining techniques, including link analysis and association rule mining, are being explored to detect abnormal patterns. Because of data mining, users can now make all kinds of correlations. This also raises privacy concerns. More details on privacy can be obtained in Thuraisingham (2002). Many intrusion detection problems can be formulated as classification problems for infinite-length, concept-drifting data streams. Concept drift occurs in these streams as attackers react and adapt to defenses. We formulated both malicious code detection and botnet traffic detection as such problems, and introduced EMPC, a novel ensemble learning technique for automated classification of infinite-length, concept-drifting streams. Applying EMPC to real data streams obtained from polymorphic malware and botnet traffic samples yielded better detection accuracies than other stream data classification techniques. This shows that the approach is useful and effective for both intrusion detection and more general data stream classification.

EMPC uses generalized, multipartition, multichunk ensemble learning. Both theoretical and empirical evaluation of the technique show that it significantly reduces the expected classification error over existing SPC ensemble methods. Moreover, we show that EMPC can be elegantly implemented in a cloud computing framework based on MapReduce (Dean and Ghemawat, 2008). The result is a low-cost, scalable stream classification framework with high classification accuracy and low runtime overhead.

At least two extensions to our technique offer promising directions for future work. First, our current feature selection procedure limits its attention to the best S features based on information gain as the selection criterion. The classification accuracy could potentially be improved by leveraging recent work on supervised dimensionality reduction techniques (Rish et al., 2008; Sajama and Orlitsky, 2005) for improved feature selection. Second, the runtime performance of our approach could be improved by exploiting additional parallelism available in the cloud computing architecture. For example, the classifiers of an ensemble could be run in parallel as mappers in a MapReduce framework, with reducers that aggregate the results for voting. Similarly, the candidate classifiers for the next ensemble could be trained and evaluated in parallel. Reformulating the ensemble components of the system in this way could lead to significantly shortened processing times, and hence opportunities to devote more processing time to classification for improved accuracy.

REFERENCES

Aggarwal, C.C., Han, J., Wang, J., and Yu, P.S. A framework for on-demand classification of evolving data streams. *IEEE Transactions on Knowledge and Data Engineering* 18(5): 577–589, 2006.

Aha, D.W., Kibler, D., and Albert, M.K. Instance-based learning algorithms. *Machine Learning* 6: 37–66, 1991.

Awad, M., Khan, L., Thuraisingham, B., and Wang, L. *Design and Implementation of Data Mining Tools*, CRC Press, Boca Raton, FL, 2009.

Bahadur, G. Top attacks in social media. In: *RSA Conference 2014*. Available at http://www.rsaconference.com/writable/presentations/file_upload/hum-f03a-top-attacks-in-social-media_v2.pdf, 2014.

Barford, P. and Yegneswaran, V. An inside look at botnets. In: Christodorescu, M., Jha, S., Maughan, D., Song, D., and Wang, C., editors. *Malware Detection, Advances in Information Security*, Springer, Heidelberg, pp. 171–192, 2006.

Bifet, A., Holmes, G., Pfahringer, B., Kirkby, R., and Gavalda, R. New ensemble methods for evolving data streams. In: *Proceedings of the 15th ACM International Conference on Knowledge Discovery and Data Mining (KDD)*, Paris, France, pp. 139–148, 2009.

Bolz, F., Dudonis, K., and Schulz, D. *The Counterterrorism Handbook: Tactics, Procedures, and Techniques,* Third Edition. CRC Press, Boca Raton, FL, 2005.

Boser, B.E., Guyon, I.M., and Vapnik, V.N. A training algorithm for optimal margin classifiers. In: *Proceedings of the 5th ACM Workshop on Computational Learning Theory*, Pittsburgh, PA, pp. 144–152, 1992.

Chan, P., Fan, W., Prodromidis, A., and Stolfo, S. Distributed data mining in credit card fraud detection. *IEEE Intelligent Systems* 14(6): 67–74, 1999.

Chen, S., Wang, H., Zhou, S., and Yu, P.S. Stop chasing trends: Discovering high order models in evolving data. In: *Proceedings of the 24th IEEE International Conference on Data Engineering (ICDE)*, Cancun, Mexico, pp. 923–932, 2008.

Claburn, T. Fannie Mac contractor indicted for logic bomb. Available at http://www.informationweek.com/news/security/management/showArticle.jhtml?articleID=212903521, 2009.

Cohen, W.W. Learning rules that classify e-mail. In: *Proceedings of the AAAI Spring Symposium on Machine Learning in Information Access*, Portland, Oregon, pp. 18–25, 1996.

Combofix. List of malware attacks on the social networking sites. Available at http://www.combofix.org/list-of-malware-attacks-on-the-social-networking-sites.php, n.d.

Computer Economics Inc. Malware report: The economic impact of viruses, spyware, adware, botnets, and other malicious code. Available at http://www.computereconomics.com/article.cfm?id=1225, 2007.

Crandall, J.R., Su, Z., Wu, S.F., and Chong, F.T. On deriving unknown vulnerabilities from zero-day polymorphic and metamorphic worm exploits. In: *Proceedings of the 12th ACM Conference on Computer and Communications Security (CCS'05)*, Alexandria, VA, pp. 235–248, 2005.

Dean, J. and Ghemawat, S. MapReduce: Simplified data processing on large clusters. *Communications of the ACM* 51(1): 107–113, 2008.

Domingos, P. and Hulten, G. Mining high-speed data streams. In: *Proceedings of the 6th ACM International Conference on Knowledge Discovery and Data Mining (KDD)*, Boston, pp. 71–80, 2000.

Dressler, J. United States v. Morris. *Cases and Materials on Criminal Law*. Thomson/West, St. Paul, MN, 2007.

Effendy, S., Yap, R.H.C., and Halim, F. Revisiting link privacy in social networks. In: *Proceedings IEEE/ACM Conference on Social Networks, Istanbul, Turkey*, August 2012.

Fan, W. Systematic data selection to mine concept-drifting data streams. In: *Proceedings of the 10th ACM International Conference on Knowledge Discovery and Data Mining (KDD)*, Seattle, WA, pp. 128–137, 2004.

Frei, S., Tellenbach, B., and Plattner, B. 0-Day patch—Exposing vendors (in)security performance. techzoom.net publications. Available at http://www.techzoom.net/publications/0-day-patch/index.en, 2008.

Freund, Y. and Schapire, R.E. Experiments with a new boosting algorithm. In: *Proceedings of the 13th International Conference on Machine Learning*, Bari, Italy, pp. 148–156, 1996.

Gao, J., Fan, W., and Han, J. On appropriate assumptions to mine data streams: Analysis and practice. In: *Proceedings of the 7th IEEE International Conference on Data Mining (ICDM)*, Omaha, NE, pp. 143–152, 2007.

Goebel, J. and T. Holz. Rishi: Identify bot contaminated hosts by IRC nickname evaluation. In: *Usenix/Hotbots '07 Workshop*, Cambridge, MA, 2007.

Grizzard, J.B., Sharma, V., Nunnery, C., Kang, B.B., and Dagon, D. Peer-to-peer botnets: Overview and case study. In: *Proceedings of the 1st Workshop on Hot Topics in Understanding Botnets (HotBots)*, Cambridge, MA, pp. 1–8, 2007.

Hall, M., Frank, E., Holmes, G., Pfahringer, B., Reutemann, P., and Witten, I.H. The WEKA data mining software: An update. *ACM SIGKDD Explorations Newsletter* 11(1): 10–18, 2009.

Hamlen, K.W., Mohan, V., Masud, M.M., Khan, L., and Thuraisingham, B.M. Exploiting an antivirus interface. *Computer Standards and Interfaces* 31(6): 1182–1189, 2009.

Hashemi, S., Yang, Y., Mirzamomen, Z., and Kangavari, M.R. Adapted one-versus-all decision trees for data stream classification. *IEEE Transactions on Knowledge and Data Engineering* 21(5): 624–637, 2009.

Hulten, G., Spencer, L., and Domingos, P. Mining time-changing data streams. In: *Proceedings of the 7th ACM International Conference on Knowledge Discovery and Data Mining (KDD)*, San Francisco, pp. 97–106, 2001.

Jones, S. Russia's cyber warriors use Twitter to hide intrusions. *Financial Times*, July 29, 2015. Available at http://www.ft.com/intl/cms/s/0/74d964a2-3606-11e5-b05b-b01debd57852.html#axzz3hgh2V1T8, 2015.

Karasaridis, A., Rexroad, B., and Hoeflin, D. Wide-scale botnet detection and characterization. In: *Usenix/Hotbots '07 Workshop*, Cambridge, MA, 2007.

Kaspersky Lab. Securelist.com threat analysis and information. Available at http://www.securelist.com/en /threats/detect, 2011.

Kim, H.A. and Karp, B. Autograph: Toward automated, distributed worm signature detection. In: *Proc. of the 13th Usenix Security Symposium (Security 2004)*, Boston, pp. 271–286, 2004.

Kolter, J. and Maloof, M.A. Learning to detect malicious executables in the wild. In: *Proceedings of the 10th ACM International Conference on Knowledge Discovery and Data Mining (KDD)*, Seattle, WA, pp. 470–478, 2004.

Kolter, J.Z. and Maloof, M.A. Using additive expert ensembles to cope with concept drift. In: *Proceedings of the 22nd International Conference on Machine Learning (ICML)*, Bonn, Germany, pp. 449–456, 2005.

Lemos, R. Bot software looks to improve peerage. *SecurityFocus*. Available at www.securityfocus.com/news /11390, 2006.

Li, Z., Sanghi, M., Chen, Y., Kao, M.-Y., and Chavez, B. Hamsa: Fast signature generation for zero-day polymorphic worms with provable attack resilience. In: *Proceedings of the IEEE Symposium on Security and Privacy (S&P)*, Oakland, CA, pp. 32–47, 2006.

Livadas, C., Walsh, B., Lapsley, D., and Strayer, T. Using machine learning techniques to identify botnet traffic. In: *2nd IEEE LCN Workshop on Network Security (WoNS'2006)*, Les Ménuires, France, November 2006.

LURHQ Threat Intelligence Group. Sinit P2P Trojan analysis. LURHQ. Available at http://www.lurhq.com /sinit.html, 2004.

Masud, M., Khan, L., and Thuraisingham, B. E-mail worm detection using data mining. *International Journal of Information Security and Privacy* 1(4): 47–61, 2007.

Masud, M.M., Gao, J., Khan, L., Han, J., and Thuraisingham, B. Mining concept-drifting data stream to detect peer to peer botnet traffic. Tech. rep. UTDCS-05-08, The University of Texas at Dallas, Richardson, TX, 2008a.

Masud, M., Khan, L., and Thuraisingham, B. A scalable multi-level feature extraction technique to detect malicious executables. *Information System Frontiers* 10(1): 33–45, 2008b.

Masud, M.M., Gao, J., Khan, L., Han, J., and Thuraisingham, B.M. A multi-partition multi-chunk ensemble technique to classify concept-drifting data streams. In: *Proceedings of the 13th Pacific-Asia Conference on Advances in Knowledge Discovery and Data Mining*, Bangkok, Thailand, 2009.

Masud, M.M., Al-Khateeb, T., Hamlen, K.W., Gao, J., Khan, L., Han, J., and Thuraisingham, B.M. Cloud-based malware detection for evolving data streams. *ACM Transactions on Management Information Systems*. 2(3): 16, 2011.

Messmer, E. America's 10 most wanted botnets. *Networkworld*. Available at http://www.networkworld.com /news/2009/072209-botnets.html, July 22, 2009.

Michie, D., Spiegelhalter, D.J., and Taylor, C.C., editors. *Machine Learning, Neural and Statistical Classification*. Ellis Horwood Series in Artificial Intelligence. Morgan Kaufmann, San Mateo, CA, pp. 50–83, 1994.

Microsoft Corporation. Windows Vista home page. Available at http://windows.microsoft.com/en-us/windows -vista/products/home, 2007.

Newsome, J., Karp, B., and Song, D. Polygraph: Automatically generating signatures for polymorphic worms. In: *Proceedings of the IEEE Symposium on Security and Privacy (S&P)*, Oakland, CA, pp. 226–241, 2005.

PCMag Digital Group. Definition of: Virus signature. *PC Magazine Encyclopedia*. Available at http://www .pcmag.com/encyclopedia_term/0,2542,t=virus+signature&i=53969,00.asp, n.d.

Quinlan, J.R. *C4.5: Programs for Machine Learning*, 5th Ed. Morgan Kaufmann, San Francisco, CA, 2003.

Rajab, M.A., Zarfoss, J., Monrose, F., and Terzis, A. A multifaceted approach to understanding the botnet phenomenon. In: *Proc. of the 6th ACM SIGCOMM on Internet Measurement Conference (IMC)*, Rio de Janeiro, Brazil, 2006.

Rish, I., Grabarnik, G., Cecchi, G.A., Pereira, F., and Gordon, G.J. Closed-form supervised dimensionality reduction with generalized linear models. In: *Proceedings of the 25th ACM International Conference on Machine Learning (ICML)*, Helsinki, Finland, pp. 832–839, 2008.

Saha, B. and Gairola, A. Botnet: An overview. CERT-In White Paper CIWP-2005-05, 2005.

Sajama and Orlitsky, A. Supervised dimensionality reduction using mixture models. In: *Proceedings of the 22nd ACM International Conference on Machine Learning (ICML)*, Bonn, Germany, pp. 768–775, 2005.

Scholz, M. and Klinkenberg, R. An ensemble classifier for drifting concepts. In: *Proceedings of the 2nd International Workshop on Knowledge Discovery in Data Streams (IWKDDS)*, pp. 53–64, 2005.

Schultz, M.G., Eskin, E., Zadok, E., and Stolfo, S.J. Data mining methods for detection of new malicious executables. In: *Proceedings of the IEEE Symposium on Security and Privacy (S&P)*, Oakland, CA, pp. 38–49, 2001.

Stewart, J. Sinit P2P Trojan analysis. Available at www.secureworks.com/research/threats/sinit, 2003.

Thuraisingham, B. Data mining, national security, privacy and civil liberties. *SIGKDD Explorations Newsletter* 4(2): 1–5, 2002.

Thuraisingham, B. *Web Data Mining Technologies and Their Applications in Business Intelligence and Counter-terrorism*. CRC Press, Boca Raton, FL, 2003.

Thuraisingham, B. In: Kumar, V., Srivastava, J., and Lazarevic, A., editors. *Managing Threats to Web Databases and Cyber Systems, Issues, Solutions and Challenges*, Kluwer, Waltham, MA, p. 3, 2004.

Thuraisingham, B. *Database and Applications Security*. CRC Press, Boca Raton, FL, 2005.

Timm, C. and Perez, R. Seven deadliest social network attacks. Available at: http://www.sciencedirect.com/science/article/pii/B9781597495455000112?np=y, 2010.

Tumer, K. and Ghosh, J. 1996. Error correlation and error reduction in ensemble classifiers. *Connection Science* 8(3): 385–404.

VX Heavens. VX Heavens 2010. Available at vx.heaven.org, 2010.

Wang, H., Fan, W., Yu, P.S., and Han, J. Mining concept-drifting data streams using ensemble classifiers. In: *Proceedings of the 9th ACM International Conference on Knowledge Discovery and Data Mining (KDD)*, Washington, DC, pp. 226–235, 2003.

Wondracek, G., Holz, T., Kirda, E., and Kruegel, C. A practical attack to de-anonymize social network users. In: *IEEE Symposium on Security and Privacy*, Oakland, CA. Available at: https://www.iseclab.org/papers/sonda-TR.pdf, 2010.

Yang, Y., Wu, X., and Zhu, X. Combining proactive and reactive predictions for data streams. In: *Proceedings of the 11th ACM International Conference on Knowledge Discovery and Data Mining (KDD)*, Chicago, pp. 710–715, 2005.

Zerofox. Top 9 social media threats of 2015. Available at https://www.zerofox.com/whatthefoxsays/top-9-social-media-threats-2015/, 2015.

Zhang, P., Zhu, X., and Guo, L. Mining data streams with labeled and unlabeled training examples. In: *Proceedings of the 9th IEEE International Conference on Data Mining (ICDM)*, Miami, FL, pp. 627–636, 2009.

Zhao, W., Ma, H., and He, Q. Parallel *K*-means clustering based on MapReduce. In: *Proceedings of the 1st International Conference on Cloud Computing (CloudCom)*, Beijing, China, pp. 674–679, 2009.

CONCLUSION TO SECTION VIII

While Sections VI and VII discussed our experimental social media analytics systems and applications, in Section VIII we discussed our experimental secure social media systems. In particular, we discuss secure query-processing systems as well as assured information sharing systems.

In Chapter 31, we presented a system that allows cooperating organizations to securely share large amounts of data. We ensured that the organizations have a large common storage area by using Hadoop. Furthermore, we used Hive to present users of our system with a structured view of the data and to also enable them to query the data with an SQL-like language. In Chapter 32, we described an access control system for Resource Description Framework data that incorporates a token-based mechanism. In Chapter 33, we described our design and implementation of a cloud-based information sharing system called CAISS. CAISS utilizes several of the technologies we have developed as well as open source tools. We also described the design of an ideal cloud-based assured information sharing system called CAISS++. In Chapter 34, we discussed a generalized social network in which only insensitive and generalized information is shared. We also discussed the integration of the generalized information and how it can satisfy a prescribed level of privacy leakage tolerance that is measured independently of the privacy-preserving techniques. In Chapter 35, we discussed attacks on social networks and then described a cloud-based malware detection data mining system that could be used to detect suspicious activity in Twitter data streams.

Section IX

Secure Social Media Directions

INTRODUCTION TO SECTION IX

Now that we have described the various concepts and provided an overview of the systems we have developed on analyzing and securing social media, we will now describe our exploratory work as well as provide directions. In particular, we will describe (i) a unifying framework for social media, (ii) integrity and provenance, (iii) multilevel secure online social networks (MLS/OSNs), and (iv) an educational infrastructure.

Section IX consists of four chapters: Chapters 36 through 39. Chapter 36 will essentially integrate much of the design and implementation of the systems discussed in Sections II and III, as well as some of the novel methods discussed in Section IV, and will describe a unifying framework. The framework includes components both for access control and inference control, as well as information-sharing control. In Chapter 37, we will provide an overview of data integrity, which includes data quality and data provenance. We will discuss the applications of semantic web technologies for data integrity, as well as discuss integrity for social media systems represented using semantic web technologies. Chapter 38 will provide an overview of mandatory access control and policies for multilevel database management systems (MLS/DBMSs), as well as describe a taxonomy for the designs of MLS/DBMSs. We will then discuss ways of adapting the developments in MLS/DBMSs to MLS/OSNs. In Chapter 39, we will describe the secure cloud infrastructure we have developed, and provide an overview of our strategy for education in analyzing and securing social media. Some of the courses we will discuss have already been offered, while some others are in progress. We are utilizing the infrastructure we have developed for the cloud for our course programming projects.

36 Unified Framework for Analyzing and Securing Social Media

36.1 INTRODUCTION

In this chapter, we integrate the various parts of a social media system into an automatic framework for carrying out analytics but at the same time for ensuring security. In particular, we integrate the analytics techniques in Section III with the privacy and security techniques discussed in Sections IV and V. We preserve features such as scalability, efficiency, and interoperability in developing this framework. This framework can be used to execute various policies, including access control policies, redaction policies, filtering policies, and information-sharing policies as well as inference strategies. Our framework can also be used as a testbed for evaluating different policy sets over social media graphs. Our recent work discussed in Thuraisingham et al. (2014) and Cadenhead et al. (2011) proposes new mechanisms for developing a unifying framework of data provenance expressed as Resource Description Framework (RDF) graphs. These methods can be applied for social media systems represented using semantic web technologies.

The framework we present in this chapter is in the design stages. Specifically, we give guidelines for policy processing for social media data as well as metadata that includes data provenance for access control, inference control, and information sharing. We can integrate features such as risk-based access control and inference into such a framework. In addition, we can also incorporate privacy-aware data analytics for social media. Our ultimate goal is to develop a social media system that not only carries out access control and inference control but also information-sharing and risk-based policy processing as well as privacy-aware analytics.

The organization of this chapter is as follows. In Section 36.2, we discuss our framework. Aspects of what we call our global inference controller will be discussed in Section 36.3. Such an inference controller will handle unauthorized inference during access control as well as during data sharing. The chapter is summarized in Section 36.4. Figure 36.1 illustrates the contents of this chapter.

36.2 DESIGN OF OUR FRAMEWORK

The final architecture for our provenance manager is extended to include an inference controller, as well as a data sharing manager and a risk manager. This enables us to add the risk-based mechanism into our framework. Our architecture takes a user's input query and returns a response that has been pruned using a set of user-defined policy constraints. We assume that a user could interact with our system to obtain both traditional data and provenance. In our design, we will assume that the available information is divided into two parts: the actual data and provenance. Both the data and provenance are represented as RDF graphs, but they are not limited to any data format since tools can map existing formats to RDF (Bizer, 2003).

The architecture is built using a modular approach; therefore, it is very flexible in that most of the modules can be extended or replaced by another application module. For example, an application user may substitute a policy parser module that handles the parsing of high-level business policies to low-level policy objects, or replace or extend one policy layer without changing the inner workings of the other policy layer modules. This substitution or replacement of modules would

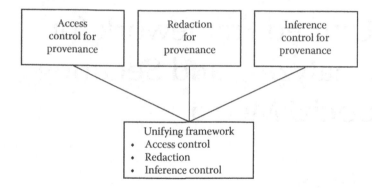

FIGURE 36.1   Unified framework for analyzing and securing social media.

allow the application user to continue using high-level business policies independent of our software implementation.

A user application can submit a query for access to the data and its associated provenance, or vice versa. Figure 36.2 shows the design of our framework. All of the modules that comprise this framework make up our inference controller. We call this the global inference controller as it handles inference control for access control and information sharing. We now present a description of the modules in Figure 36.2. Some aspects of our global inference controller will be discussed in Section 36.3.

Data Controller. The data controller is a suite of software programs that store and manage access to data, which, in this case, is social media data. The data could be stored in any format, such as in a relational database, in XML files, or in an RDF store. The controller accepts requests for information from the policy manager (or the inference engine layer) if a policy allows the requesting user access to the data item. This layer then executes the request over the stored data and returns

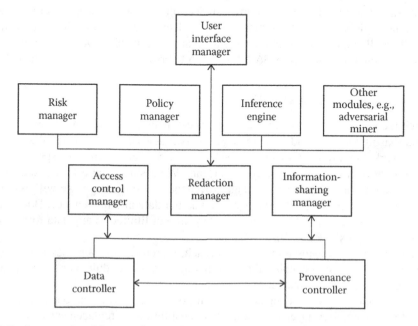

FIGURE 36.2   Integrated architecture for a social media system.

results back to the policy layer (or the inference engine layer) where it is reevaluated on the basis of a set of policies.

Provenance/Metadata Controller. The provenance/metadata controller is used to store and manage provenance/metadata information that is associated with data items that are present in the data controller. In the case when we select a graph representation of provenance, the provenance controller stores information in the form of logical graph structures in any appropriate data representation format. This controller also records the ongoing activities associated with the data items stored in the data controller. This controller takes as input a graph query and evaluates it over the provenance information. This query evaluation returns a subgraph back to the inference controller layer where it is reexamined using a set of policies.

User Interface Manager. The user interface module provides a layer of abstraction that allows a user to interact with the system. The user interacts with the system via a user interface layer. This layer accepts a user's credentials and authenticates the user. Our interface module hides the actual internal representation of our system from a user by providing a simple question–answer mechanism. This mechanism allows the user to pose standard provenance queries such as why a data item was created, where in the provenance graph it was generated, how the data item was generated, and when and what location it was created. This layer also returns results after they have been examined against a set of policies. Essentially, the user interface manager is responsible for processing the user's requests, authenticating the user, and providing suitable responses back to the user. The interface manager also provides an abstraction layer that allows a user to interact with the system. A user can therefore pose either a data query or a provenance/metadata query to this layer. The user interface manager also determines whether the query should be evaluated against the traditional data or provenance.

Policy Manager. The policy module is responsible for enforcing any high-level policy defined by a high-level application user or administrator. The policies are not restricted to any particular security policy definition, model, or mechanism. In fact, we can support different access control policies, for example, role-based access control (RBAC), access control based on context such as time (TRBAC), location (LBAC), and others. Besides the traditional and well-established security models built on top of access control mechanisms, we also support redaction policies that are based on sharing data for the ongoing mutual relationships among businesses and stakeholders. The policy layer also interacts with any reasoners in the inference layer, which offer further protection against inference attacks. The inference layer enforces policies that are in the form of Description Logic (DL) constraints, Web Ontology Language (OWL) restrictions, or Semantic Web Rule Language rules. We also observe that some of the access control policies can be expressed as inference rules or queries via query rewrite or views. Our policy module, therefore, has many layers equipped with security features, thus ensuring we are enforcing the maximal protection over the underlying provenance store. The policy module also handles the information-sharing policies.

Essentially, the policy manager is responsible for ensuring that the querying user is authorized to use the system. It evaluates the policies against a user's query and associated query results to ensure that no confidential information is released to unauthorized users. The policy manager may enforce the policies against the traditional data or against the provenance data. Each data type may have its own policy manager; for example, the traditional data may be stored in a different format from the provenance data. Hence, we may require different implementations for each policy manager.

Inference Engine. The inference engine is the heart of the inference controller described in Section V. The engine is equipped to use a variety of inference strategies that are supported by a particular reasoner. Since there are many implementations of reasoners available, our inference controller offers an added feature of flexibility, whereby we can select from among any reasoning tool for each reasoning task. We can improve the efficiency of the inference controller since each inference strategy (or a combination of strategies) could be executed on a separate processor. An inference engine typically uses software programs that have the capability of reasoning over some data representation, for example, a relational data model or an RDF graph model representation.

The inference problem is an open problem, and a lot of research has been pivoted around its implementation based on traditional databases (Hinke et al., 1997; Marks, 1996). However, since provenance has a logical graph structure, it can also be represented and stored in a graph data model; therefore, it is not limited to any particular data format. Although our focus in this chapter is on building an inference controller over the directed graph representation of provenance, our inference controller could be used to protect the case when provenance is represented and stored in a traditional relational database model. Also, the use of an RDF data model does not overburden our implementation with restrictions, since other data formats are well served by an RDF data model. Furthermore, there are tools to convert, say, relational data into RDF and vice versa (e.g., D2RQ Platform, http://d2rq.org/).

Query Manager. The query-processing module is responsible for accepting a user's query, parsing it, and submitting it to the provenance knowledge base. After the query, results are evaluated against a set of policies; it is returned to the user via the user interface layer. The query-processing module can accept any standard provenance query as well as any query written in the SPARQL format. The querying user is allowed to view the errors that are due to the syntax of a query, as well as the responses constructed by the underlying processes of the inference controller.

Information-Sharing Manager. The information-sharing manager will implement the information-sharing policies. For example, if organization A wants to share data with organization B, then the information-sharing controller will examine the policies via the policy manager, determine whether there are any unauthorized inferences by communicating with the inference engine, and determine whether data is to be given to organization B.

Access Control Manager. This access control module is responsible for determining whether the user can access the data. The access control policies are obtained via the policy manager. The inference engine will determine whether any unauthorized information will be released by carrying out reasoning. The results are given to the user via the user interface manager.

Redaction Manager. This module will determine which data has to be redacted before it is given to the user. It operates in conjunction with the access control manager. It also examines the information that has been released previously and determines whether the new information obtained as a result of executing the query should be given to the user.

Risk Analyzer. The risk analyzer will compute the risks for releasing the information and makes a determination whether the information should be released to the user. It interacts with other modules, such as the access control manager, the redaction manager, and the information-sharing manager, in making this determination. The results of the risk manager are then given to the access control manager, the redaction manager, and the information-sharing manager to execute the results.

Adversarial Data Miner. This module will implement the strategies to mine the adversary to see what his or her motives are. An adversary could be a human or some malicious code. In particular, such a data miner will determine how to thwart the adversary as well as apply game theoretic reasoning in determining what information is to be released to the user. It will work jointly with the inference engine.

36.3   GLOBAL SOCIAL MEDIA SECURITY AND PRIVACY CONTROLLER

Our global controller should determine unauthorized inference during access control, redaction, and information sharing, as well as determine whether privacy violations have occurred through data mining. It has to compute the risks in disclosing the information as well as apply novel strategies such as adversarial monitoring to be ahead of the adversary. In this section, we will discuss some of the key points of such an inference controller.

Our prior work has developed models that can be used to determine the expected risk of releasing data and metadata. We need to extend such models to determine whether the addition of social media data influences security and privacy. The extended models would typically incorporate inference tools into the architecture.

Inference Tools. Newly published data, when combined with existing public knowledge, allows for complex and sometimes unintended inferences. Therefore, we need semiautomated tools for detecting these inferences before releasing provenance information. These tools should give data owners a fuller understanding of the implications of releasing the provenance information, as well as help them adjust the amount of information they release in order to avoid unwanted inferences (Staddon et al., 2007). The inference controller is a tool that implements some of the inference strategies that a user may utilize to infer confidential information that is encoded into a provenance graph. Our inference controller leverages from existing software tools that perform inferencing, for example, Pellet (Sirin et al., 2007), Fact++ (Tsarkov and Horrocks, 2006), Racer (Haarslev and Möller, 2001), Hermit (Shearer et al., 2008), and Closed World Machine (http://www.w3.org/2001/sw/wiki/CWM). Therefore, we can add more expressive power by replacing the default base engine of our inference controller with a more powerful reasoner. Furthermore, since there is a trade-off of expressivity and decidability, an application user has more flexibility in selecting the most appropriate reasoner for his or her application domain.

For our default reasoner, we employ the services of Pellet (Sirin et al., 2007). Pellet has support for OWL-DL (SHOIN(D)) and is also extended to support OWL 2 specification (SROIQ(D)). The OWL 2 specification adds the following language constructs:

- Qualified cardinality restrictions
- Complex subproperty axioms (between a property chain and a property)
- Local reflexivity restrictions
- Reflexive, irreflexive, symmetric, and antisymmetric properties
- Disjoint properties
- Negative property assertions
- Vocabulary sharing (punning) between individuals, classes, and properties
- User-defined data ranges

In addition, Pellet provides all the standard inference services that are traditionally provided by DL reasoners. These are

- Consistency checking

  This ensures that an ontology does not contain any contradictory facts. The OWL 2 Direct Semantics provide the formal definition of ontology consistency used by Pellet.
- Concept satisfiability

  This determines whether it is possible for a class to have any instances. If a class is unsatisfiable, then defining an instance of that class will cause the whole ontology to be inconsistent.
- Classification

  This computes the subclass relations between every named class to create the complete class hierarchy. The class hierarchy can be used to answer queries such as getting all or only the direct subclasses of a class (Sirin et al., 2007).
- Realization

  This finds the most specific classes that an individual belongs to; that is, realization computes the direct types for each of the individuals. Realization can only be performed after classification since direct types are defined with respect to a class hierarchy (Sirin et al., 2007). Using the classification hierarchy, it is also possible to get all the types for each individual.

The global inference controller has to reason with big data. Its operation has to be timely. Therefore, we propose a cloud-based implementation of such an inference controller. In Chapter 33, we discussed our initial implementation of policy-based information sharing in a cloud. Our ultimate goal is to implement the entire inference controller in the cloud.

36.4   SUMMARY AND DIRECTIONS

This chapter has essentially integrated much of the design and implementation of the systems discussed in Sections II and III, as well as some of the novel methods discussed in Section IV, and described a unifying framework. The framework includes components both for access control and inference control, as well as information-sharing control. Our framework can also include the modules for risk and game theoretic approaches for access and inference control. We discussed the modules of the framework as well as building of the global inference controller.

Our framework is in the design stages. Essentially, we have provided guidelines toward implementing such a framework. We can essentially plug and play various modules in order to develop such a framework. We believe that a cloud-based implementation of such a framework can provide scalability and efficiency. Our ultimate goal is to develop our global inference controller in the cloud so that it can handle inferences for big data.

REFERENCES

Bizer, C. D2R MAP-A database to RDF mapping language. In: *WWW Posters*, Budapest, Hungary, 2003.

Cadenhead, T., Khadilkar, V., Kantarcioglu, M., and Thuraisingham, B.M. A language for provenance access control. In: *CODASPY*, San Antonio, TX, pp. 133–144, 2011.

Haarslev, V. and Möller, R. RACER system description. In: *IJCAR*, pp. 701–706, 2001.

Hinke, T.H., Delugach, H.S., and Wolf, R.P. Protecting databases from inference attacks. *Computers & Security* 16(8): 687–708, 1997.

Marks, D.G. Inference in MLS database systems. *IEEE Transactions on Knowledge and Data Engineering* 8(1): 46–55, 1996.

Shearer, R., Motik, B., and Horrocks, I. HermiT: A highly-efficient OWL reasoner. In: Ruttenberg, A., Sattler, U., and Dolbear, C., editors. *Proc. of the 5th Int. Workshop on OWL: Experiences and Directions (OWLED 2008 EU)*, Karlsruhe, Germany, October 26–27, 2008.

Sirin, E., Parsia, B., Grau, B.C., Kalyanpur, A., and Katz, Y. Pellet: A practical OWL-DL reasoner. *Web Semantics: Science, Services and Agents on the World Wide Web* 5(2), 2007.

Staddon, J., Golle, P., and Zimny, B. Web-based inference detection. In: *Proceedings of 16th USENIX Security Symposium*, Boston, 2007.

Thuraisingham, B., Cadenhead, T., Kantarcioglu, M., and Khadilkar, V. *Secure Data Provenance and Inference Control with Semantic Web Technologies*, CRC Press, Boca Raton, FL, 2014.

Tsarkov, D. and Horrocks, I. FaCT++ description logic reasoner: System description. In: *IJCAR*, pp. 292–297, 2006.

37 Integrity Management and Data Provenance for Social Media

37.1 INTRODUCTION

In this chapter, we will discuss integrity management for social media. Integrity includes several aspects. In the database world, integrity includes concurrency control and recovery as well as enforcing integrity constraints. For example, when multiple transactions are executed at the same time, the consistency of the data has to be ensured. When a transaction aborts, it has to be ensured that the database is recovered from the failure into a consistent state. Integrity constraints are rules that have to be satisfied by the data. Rules include "salary value has to be positive" and "age of an employee cannot decrease over time." More recently, integrity has included data quality, data provenance, data currency, real-time processing, and fault tolerance.

Integrity management is essential for social media to provide accurate and timely information to its users. For example, when users want to share information with their friends, they may want to share a certain version or the most recent version of the data. Furthermore, the member of the network may copy data from other sources and post it on their social media pages. In such situations, it would be useful to provide the sources of the information as well as from where the information was derived.

In this chapter, we discuss aspects of integrity for social media as well as implementing integrity management as cloud services. For example, how do we ensure the integrity of the data and the processes? How do we ensure that data quality is maintained? Some aspects of integrity are already being investigated by researchers, and some other aspects are yet to be investigated. The organization of this chapter is as follows. In Section 37.2, we discuss aspects of integrity, data quality, and provenance. In particular, integrity aspects will be discussed in Section 37.2.1. Data quality and provenance will be discussed in Section 37.2.2. Cloud services and integrity management are discussed in Section 37.3. In particular, data integrity and provenance as a cloud service for social media systems will be discussed in Section 37.3.1. Data integrity for social media will be discussed in Section 37.3.2. The chapter is concluded in Section 37.4.

37.2 INTEGRITY, DATA QUALITY, AND PROVENANCE

37.2.1 ASPECTS OF INTEGRITY

There are many aspects to integrity. For example, concurrency control, recovery, data accuracy, meeting real-time constraints, data accuracy, data quality, data provenance, fault tolerance, and integrity constraint enforcement are all aspects of integrity management. This is illustrated in Figure 37.1. In this section, we will examine each aspect of integrity.

Concurrency Control. In data management, concurrent control is about transactions being executed at the same time and ensuring consistency of the data. Therefore, transactions have to obtain locks or utilize time stamps to ensure that the data is left in a consistent state when multiple transactions attempt to access the data at the same time. Extensive research has been carried out on concurrency control techniques for transaction management both in centralized as well as in distributed environments (Bernstein et al., 1987).

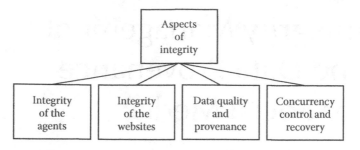

FIGURE 37.1   Aspects of integrity.

Data Recovery. When transactions abort before they complete execution, the database should be recovered to a consistent state such as it was before the transaction started execution. Several recovery techniques have been proposed to ensure the consistency of the data.

Data Authenticity. When the data is delivered to the user, its authenticity has to be ensured. That is, the user should obtain accurate data and the data should not be tampered with. We have conducted research on ensuring authenticity of XML (eXtensible Markup Language) data during third-party publishing (Bertino et al., 2004).

Data Completeness. Data that a user receives should not only be authentic but also be complete. That is, everything that the user is authorized to see has to be delivered to the user.

Data Currency. Data has to be current. That is, data that is outdated has to be deleted or archived, and the data that the user sees has to be current data. Data currency is an aspect of real-time processing. If a user wants to retrieve the temperature, he or she has to be given the current temperature, not the temperature 24 hours ago.

Data Accuracy. The question is, how accurate is the data? This is also closely related to data quality and data currency. That is, accuracy depends on whether the data has been maliciously corrupted or whether it has come from an untrusted source.

Data Quality. Is the data of high quality? This includes data authenticity, data accuracy, and whether the data is complete or certain. If the data is uncertain, then can we reason with this uncertainty to ensure that the operations that use the data are not affected? Data quality also depends on the data source.

Data Provenance. This has to do with the history of the data; that is, from the time the data originated, such as emanating from the sensors, until the present time when it is given to the general user. The question is, who has accessed the data? Who has modified the data? How has the data traveled? This will determine whether the data has been misused.

Integrity Constraints. These are rules that the data has to satisfy, such as the age of a person cannot be a negative number. This type of integrity has been studied extensively by the database and artificial intelligence communities.

Fault Tolerance. As in the case of data recovery, the processes that fail have to be recovered. Therefore, fault tolerance deals with data recovery as well as process recovery. Techniques for fault tolerance include check pointing and acceptance testing.

Real-Time Processing. Data currency is one aspect of real-time processing where the data has to be current. Real-time processing also has to deal with transactions meeting timing constraints. For example, stock quotes have to be given within, say, 5 minutes. If not, it will be too late. Missing timing constraints could cause integrity violations.

37.2.2   INFERENCING, DATA QUALITY, AND DATA PROVENANCE

Some researchers feel that data quality is an application of data provenance. Furthermore, they have developed theories for inferring data quality. In this section, we will examine some of the developments, keeping in mind the relationship between data quality, data provenance, and the semantic cloud services.

Data quality is about accuracy, timeliness, and dependability (i.e., trustworthiness) of the data. It is, however, subjective and depends on the users and the domains. Some of the issues that have to be answered include the creation of the data; that is, where did it come from and why and how was the data obtained? Data quality information is stored as annotations to the data and should be part of data provenance. One could ask the question as to how we can obtain the trustworthiness of the data. This could depend on how the source is ranked and the reputation of the source.

As we have stated, researchers have developed theories for inferring data quality (Pon and Cárdenas, 2005). The motivation is because data could come from multiple sources, it is shared and prone to errors. Furthermore, data could be uncertain. Therefore, theories of uncertainty such as statistical reasoning, Bayesian theories, and the Dempster–Shafer theory of evidence are being used to infer the quality of the data. With respect to security, we need to ensure that the quality of the inferred data does not violate the policies. For example, at the Unclassified level, we may say that the source is trustworthy; however, at the Secret level, we know that the source is not trustworthy. The inference controllers that we have developed could be integrated with the theories of interceding developed for data quality to ensure security.

Next, let us examine data provenance. For many of the domains including medical and health care as well as defense, where the accuracy of the data is critical, we need to have a good understanding as to where the data came from and who may have tampered with the data. As stated in Simmhan et al. (2005), data provenance, a kind of metadata, sometimes called *lineage* or *pedigree*, is the description of the origin of a piece of data and the process by which it arrived in a database. Data provenance is information that helps determine the derivation history of a data product, starting from its original source.

Provenance information can be applied to data quality, auditing, and ownership, among others. By having records of who accessed the data, data misuse can be determined. Usually, annotations are used to describe the information related to the data (e.g., who accessed the data? where did the data come from?) The challenge is to determine whether one needs to maintain coarse-grained or fine-grained provenance data. For example, in a course-grained situation, the tables of a relation may be annotated, whereas in a fine-grained situation every element may be annotated. There is, of course, the storage overhead to consider for managing provenance. XML, Resource Description Framework (RDF), and Web Ontology Language (OWL) have been used to represent provenance data, and this way the tools developed for the semantic web technologies may be used to manage the provenance data.

There is much interest in using data provenance for misuse detection. For example, by maintaining the complete history of data, such as who accessed the data, or when and where the data was accessed, one can answer queries such as "who accessed the data between January and May 2010?". Therefore, if the data is corrupted, one can determine who corrupted the data or when the data was corrupted. Figure 37.2 illustrates the aspects of data provenance. We have conducted

```
                    ┌──────────────────────────────────────────┐
                    │            Data provenance               │
                    │                                          │
                    │   Who created the data?                  │
                    │   Where has the data come from?          │
                    │   Who accessed the data?                 │
                    │   What is the complete history of the data? │
                    │   Has the data been misused?             │
                    └──────────────────────────────────────────┘
```

FIGURE 37.2   Data provenance.

extensive research on representing and reasoning about provenance data and policies represented using semantic web technologies (Cadenhead et al., 2011a,b; Thuraisingham et al., 2014).

37.3 INTEGRITY MANAGEMENT, CLOUD SERVICES, AND SOCIAL MEDIA

37.3.1 CLOUD SERVICES FOR INTEGRITY MANAGEMENT

There are two aspects here. One is that integrity management may be implemented with cloud services, and the other is ensuring that the cloud services have high integrity. For implementing integrity management as cloud services, the idea is to invoke cloud services to ensure data quality, as well as the integrity of the data and the system. Figure 37.3 illustrates implementing integrity management as a cloud service.

Like confidentiality, privacy, and trust, semantic web technologies such as XML may be used to specify integrity policies. Integrity policies may include policies for specifying integrity constraint as well as policies for specifying timing constraints, data currency, and data quality. Here are some examples of the policies.

Integrity Constraints. Age of an employee has to be positive. In a relational representation, one could specify this policy as

```
EMP.AGE>0
```

In XML, this could be represented as

```
<Condition Object="//Employe/Age">
    <Apply FunctionId="greater-than">
        <AttributeValue DataType="http://www.w3.org/2001/
XMLSchema#integer">0
        </AttributeValue>
    </Apply>
</Condition>
```

Data Quality Policy. The quality of the data in the employee table is LOW. In the relational model, this could be represented as

```
EMP.Quality=LOW
```

In XML, this policy could be represented as

```
<Condition Object="//Employe/Quality">
    <Apply FunctionId="equal">
        <AttributeValue
DataType="http://www.w3.org/2001/XMLSchema#string">LOW
        </AttributeValue>
    </Apply>
</Condition>
```

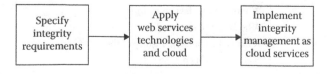

FIGURE 37.3 Cloud service for integrity management.

Data Currency. An example is as follows: The salary value of EMP cannot be more than 365 days old. In a relational representation, this could be represented as

```
AGE (EMP.SAL) <=365 days
```

In XML, this is represented as

```
<Condition Object="//Employe/Salary">
   <Apply FunctionId="AGE">
      <Apply FunctionId="less-than-or-equal">
         <AttributeValue
DataType="http://www.w3.org/2001/XMLSchema#integer">365
         </AttributeValue>
      </Apply>
   </Apply>
</Condition>
```

The above examples have shown how certain integrity policies may be specified. Note that there are many other applications of semantic web technologies to ensure integrity. For example, to ensure data provenance, the history of the data has to be documented. Semantic web technologies such as XML are being used to represent, say, the data annotations that are used to determine the quality of the data or whether the data has been misused. That is, the data captured is annotated with metadata information such as what the data is about, when it was captured, and who captured it. Then, as the data moves from place to place or from person to person, the annotations are updated so that at a later time, the data may be analyzed for misuse. These annotations are typically represented in semantic web technologies such as XML, RDF, and OWL.

Another application of semantic web technologies for integrity management is the use of ontologies to resolve semantic heterogeneity. That is, semantic heterogeneity causes integrity violations. This happens when the same entity is considered to be different at different sites, and therefore compromises integrity and accuracy. Through the use of ontologies specified in, say, OWL, it can be expressed that ship in one site and submarine in another site are one and the same.

Semantic web technologies also have applications in making inferences and reasoning under uncertainty or mining (Thuraisingham et al., 2014). For example, the reasoning engines based on RDF, OWL, or, say, rules may be used to determine whether the integrity policies are violated. We have discussed inference and privacy problems and building inference engines in earlier chapters. These techniques have to be investigated for violation of integrity policies.

37.3.2 INTEGRITY FOR SOCIAL MEDIA

While integrity management can be provided as cloud services for social media and other systems, we ensure that the social media data has high integrity. The idea here is to not only ensure that the data shared by the social media members are accurate and current, but it is also important to ensure that the social media system is not malicious and does not corrupt the data or other services. Figure 37.4 illustrates integrity management for social media systems.

Since many of the social media systems that we have developed utilize semantic web technologies for data resonation and reasoning, we need to ensure that integrity is maintained for semantic web technologies. Annotations that are used for data quality and provenance are typically represented in XML or RDF documents. These documents have to be accurate, complete, and current. Therefore, integrity has to be enforced for such documents. Another aspect of integrity is managing databases that consist of XML or RDF documents. These databases have all of the issues and challenges that are present for, say, relational databases. That is, the queries have to be optimized

FIGURE 37.4 Integrity for social media systems.

and transactions should be executed concurrently. Therefore, concurrency control and recovery for XML and RDF documents become a challenge for managing XML and RDF databases. This is yet another aspect of integrity for semantic web documents.

The actions of the agents that make use of the semantic services to carry out operations such as searching, querying, and integrating heterogeneous databases, as well as information sharing in social media systems, have to ensure that the integrity of the data is maintained. These agents cannot maliciously corrupt the data. They have to ensure that the data is accurate, complete, and consistent. Finally, when integrating heterogeneous databases, semantic web technologies such as OWL ontologies are being used to handle semantic heterogeneity. These ontologies have to be accurate and complete and cannot be tampered with.

In summary, for the social media systems to be useful to their members, they have to enforce data, system, and process integrity. Since many of the systems we have developed utilize semantic web technologies, we need to ensure that integrity is enforced on the semantic web database.

37.4 SUMMARY AND DIRECTIONS

In this chapter, we have provided an overview of data integrity, which includes data quality and data provenance. We discussed the applications of semantic web technologies for data integrity as well as discussed integrity for social media systems represented using semantic web technologies.

Data provenance and data quality, while important, are only recently receiving attention. This is because there are vast quantities of information stored in the cloud. Furthermore, massive amounts of data and information are managed and shared by members of a social media system. Therefore, it is important to know the extent to which such data and information are accurate. In addition, members need to know whether the data is copied and/or plagiarized. We also need to have answers to questions such as who owns the data or has the data been misused. Therefore, data provenance is important in determining the security of social media data.

Social media systems should have high integrity. Furthermore, integrity techniques can be implemented as cloud services. Semantic web technologies provide a way to represent and store data quality and provenance data. As we make progress with these technologies, we will have improved solutions for data quality and data provenance management. Essentially, data quality and data provenance are part of data security, and semantic web technologies are very useful in managing data quality and data provenance information. In Chapter 35, we addressed an aspect of integrity in social media systems, and that is on the malicious attacks to such systems.

REFERENCES

Bernstein, P., Hadzilacos, V., and Goodman, N. *Concurrency Control and Recovery in Database Systems*. Addison-Wesley, Boston, 1987.
Bertino, E., Carminati, B., Ferrari, E., and Thuraisingham, B. Secure third party publication of XML documents. *IEEE Transactions on Knowledge and Data Engineering* 16(10): 1263–1278, 2004.
Cadenhead, T., Khadilkar, V., Kantarcioglu, M., Thuraisingham, B.M. A language for provenance access control. In: *CODASPY*, San Antonio, TX, pp. 133–144, 2011a.

Cadenhead, T., Khadilkar, V., Kantarcioglu, M., and Thuraisingham, B.M. Transforming provenance using redaction. In: *SACMAT*, pp. 93–102, 2011b.

Pon, R.K. and Cárdenas, A.F. Data quality inference. UCLA Report, 2005.

Simmhan, Y.L., Plale, B., and Gannon, D. A survey of data provenance in e-Science. Indiana University Technical Report, also in *SIGMOD Record* (34): 3, 2005.

Thuraisingham, B., Cadenhead, T., Kantarcioglu, M., and Khadilkar, V. *Secure Data Provenance and Inference Control with Semantic Web Technologies*. CRC Press, Boca Raton, FL, 2014.

38 Multilevel Secure Online Social Networks

38.1 INTRODUCTION

In this chapter, we continue with the discussion of exploratory ideas on social networks/media. In particular, we will discuss aspects of developing multilevel social networks (MLS/OSNs) following along the lines of the definition of multilevel database management systems (MLS/DBMSs) designed and developed mainly in the 1980s. In an MLS/DBMS, users are cleared at different clearance levels, such as Unclassified, Confidential, Secret, and TopSecret. Data is assigned different sensitivity levels, such as Unclassified, Confidential, Secret, and TopSecret (Thuraisingham, 2005). Similarly, we have defined an MLS/OSN that enables users cleared at different security levels to access and share information at different sensitivity levels with their peers or friends also cleared at different security levels.

MLS/DBMSs have evolved from the developments in multilevel secure operating systems such as MULTICS and SCOMP (see, e.g., IEEE Computer, 1983) and the developments in database systems. A major initiative and summer study by the Air Force was convened (Air Force Studies Board, 1983). This summer study marks a significant milestone in the development of MLS/DBMSs. Various designs of MLS/DBMSs were proposed in the 1980s, and prototypes and products have been developed on the basis of these designs. In addition, multilevel data models have also been developed mainly on the basis of the relational data model. Following along the lines of these designs and models, in this chapter we will explore the design of MLS/OSNs.

The organization of this chapter is as follows. In Section 38.2, we will discuss the various designs of MLS/DBMSs, including the integrity lock and the single-kernel approach. Multilevel relational data models are also discussed. In Section 38.3, we will explore the application of the designs and models for MLS/DBMSs for MLS/OSNs. We believe that while it is possible to develop such MLS/OSNs, the question of whether such networks are realistic remains to be answered. The chapter is summarized in Section 38.4. Figure 38.1 illustrates the concepts discussed in this chapter.

38.2 MULTILEVEL SECURE DATABASE MANAGEMENT SYSTEMS

38.2.1 MANDATORY SECURITY

Multilevel Operating Systems versus Multilevel Database Systems. While DBMSs must deal with many of the same security concerns as trusted operating systems (identification and authentication, access control, and auditing), there are characteristics of DBMSs that introduce additional security challenges. For example, objects in DBMSs tend to be of varying sizes and can be of fine granularity, such as relations, attributes, and elements. This contrasts with operating systems where the granularity tends to be coarse, such as files or segments. Because of the fine granularity in MLS/DBMSs, also often called trusted database systems (TDBMSs), the objects on which mandatory access control (MAC) and discretionary access control (DAC) are performed may differ. In MLS operating systems, also called *trusted operating systems*, MAC and DAC are usually performed on the same object such as a file.

There are also some functional differences between operating systems and DBMSs. Operating systems tend to deal with subjects attempting to access some object. DBMSs are employed for sharing data between users, and to provide users with a means to relate different data objects. Also,

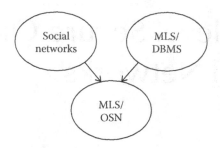

FIGURE 38.1 Toward multilevel secure online social networks.

DBMSs are generally dependent on operating systems to provide resources such as interprocess communication and memory management. Therefore, trusted DBMS designs often must take into account how the operating systems deal with security.

The differences between DBMSs and operating systems discussed above mean that the traditional approaches utilized in developing secure systems need to be adapted for trusted DBMSs. Currently, there is no standard architectural approach in the development of MLS/DBMSs. A variety of approaches to designing and building MLS/DBMSs have been proposed. Taxonomies for MAC have been proposed by Hinke and Graubart, among others (see Graubart, 1989; Hinke, 1989). Some information on these approaches is also given in Thuraisingham (2005) and Ferrari and Thuraisingham (2000).

MAC Policies. MAC policies specify access that subjects have to objects. Many of the commercial DBMSs are based on the Bell and LaPadula (1973) policy specified for operating systems. In the Bell and LaPadula security model, subjects are assigned clearance levels, and they can operate a level up to and including their clearance levels. Objects are assigned sensitivity levels. The clearance levels as well as the sensitivity levels are called security levels. The set of security levels forms a partially ordered lattice with Unclassified < Confidential < Secret < TopSecret. The following are the two rules of the policy.

> *Simple security property:* A subject has read access to an object if its security level dominates the level of the object.
> **-Property (read star property):* A subject has write access to an object if the subject's security level is dominated by that of an object.

These properties apply for database systems also. However, for database systems, the *-property is usually modified to read as follows:

> *A subject has write access to an object if the subject's level is that of the object.*

This means that a subject can modify relations at its level.

Note that other mandatory policies include the noninterference policy by Goguen and Meseguer (1982). However, these policies are yet to be investigated fully for DBMSs, although the LOCK Data Views project did some preliminary investigation (see Stachour and Thuraisingham, 1990). Figure 38.2 illustrates a mandatory policy for DBMSs.

38.2.2 SECURITY ARCHITECTURES

Figure 38.3 illustrates the various security architectures for designing a MLS/DBMS. They are integrity lock architecture, operating system enforcing mandatory security architecture, kernel extensions architecture, trusted subject architecture, and the distributed architecture. Note that distributed architecture is divided further on the basis of the partitioned approach and the replication approach.

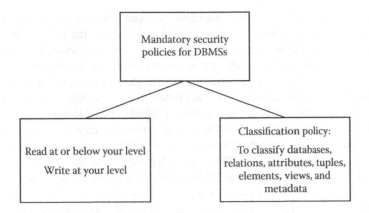

FIGURE 38.2   Mandatory policy for DBMSs.

> **Taxonomy/security architectures for MLS/DBMSs:**
>
> - Integrity lock
> - Trusted subject
> - Operating system providing mandatory access control
> - Distributed: partitioned and replicated kernel extensions

FIGURE 38.3   Security architectures/taxonomy.

Integrity Lock. This approach utilizes an untrusted back-end DBMS with access to the data in the database, an untrusted front-end that communicates with the user, and a trusted front-end that makes use of encryption technology. The untrusted components are isolated from each other so that there is no communication between the two without the mediation of the trusted filter (also called the trusted front-end). The back-end DBMS is maintained at system high, which is the highest level supported by the system. Multiple instantiations of the front-end are maintained. There is one instantiation for each user level. The trusted filter is also maintained at system high.

Under this approach, every tuple that is inserted into the database has associated with it a security label (also called a sensitivity label) and a cryptographic checksum that depends on the data content and the security label. The checksums are computed by the trusted filter on insertions and recomputed during retrieval. For insertions, the trusted filter computes the checksum, and the untrusted back-end DBMS takes the data (i.e., the tuple) and associated label and checksum, and stores them in the database. On retrieval, the back-end retrieves the data tuples and passes them to the trusted filter that recomputed the checksum on the basis of the tuple and label retrieved. If the trusted filter determines that the data has not been tampered with, then it passes the data to the user via the untrusted front-end (Burns, 1986; Graubart, 1984).

Operating System Providing Access Control. This approach, also known as the Hinke–Schaefer approach (Hinke and Schaefer, 1975), utilizes the underlying trusted operating system to perform the access control mediation. No access control mediation is performed by the DBMS. The DBMS objects (e.g., tuples) are aligned with the underlying operating system objects (e.g., files). Thus, Secret tuples are stored in Secret files and TopSecret tuples are stored in TopSecret files. With this approach, there is no single DBMS that has access to the data in the database. There is an instantiation of the DBMS for each security level. The advantage of this approach is that it is simple and secure. The disadvantage is that performance will increase with the number of security levels (see Graubart, 1989; Hinke, 1989). Note that this approach is also called the single-kernel approach.

Kernel Extensions Architecture. This approach is an extension to the single-kernel approach. The underlying operating system is utilized to provide the basic MAC and DAC mediation. However, the MLS/DBMS will supplement this access mediation by providing some additional access control mediation. For example, the MLS/DBMS might provide context-dependent DAC on views. This approach differs from the trusted subject approach because the policies enforced by the MLS/DBMS do not depend on those of the operating system. This approach has the same performance problems associated with the single-kernel approach. However, because it provides more sophisticated access control mechanisms, it could address some real-world access control needs (Thuraisingham, 2005).

Trusted Subject Architecture. This approach, also sometimes called dual kernel-based architecture, does not rely on the underlying operating system to perform access control mediation. The DBMS performs its own access mediation for objects under its control. Thus, access to DBMS records is mediated by the trusted DBMS. The architecture is referred to as a trusted subject approach because the DBMS is usually a trusted subject (or process) hosted on top of the operating system. Essentially, the DBMS has access to the data in the database. The advantage of this architecture is that it can provide good security, and its performance is independent of the number of security levels involved. The disadvantage is that the DBMS code that performs access mediation must be trusted. This means that a large amount of trusted code may be needed for this approach (Thuraisingham, 2005).

Distributed Architecture. In this approach, there are multiple untrusted back-end DBMSs and a single trusted front-end DBMS. Communication between the back-end DBMSs occurs through the front-end DBMS. There are two main approaches to this architecture. In one approach, each back-end DBMS has data at a particular level and operates at that level. That is, the back-end DBMS at the Secret level will manage the Secret data, while the back-end DBMS at the TopSecret level will manage the TopSecret data. We will refer to this as the partitioned approach. With the second approach, lower-level data is replicated at the higher levels. Thus, the Secret DBMS will manage the secret data, the confidential data, and the unclassified data. The confidential DBMS will manage the confidential data and the unclassified data. We will refer to this second approach as the replicated approach.

With the partitioned approach, the trusted front-end is responsible for ensuring that the query is directed to the correct back-end DBMS as well as for performing joins on the data sent from the back-end DBMSs. Because the query itself could contain information classified higher than the back-end DBMSs (such as the values in the *where* clause of the query), this approach suffers from a potentially high signaling channel. This is because queries are sent to the DBMSs that are operating at levels lower than the user.

For the replicated approach, the trusted front-end ensures that the query is directed to a single DBMS. Because only the DBMSs operating at the same level as the user are queried, this approach does not suffer from the signaling channel of the first approach. Furthermore, this approach does not require front-end DBMS to perform the join operations. However, because the data is replicated, the trusted front-end must ensure consistency of the data maintained by the different DBMSs (Costich et al., 1994).

38.2.3 MULTILEVEL SECURE RELATIONAL DATA MODEL

In this section, we will discuss aspects of developing a multilevel secure relational data model and then discuss extensions for a multilevel social network model. The first step toward developing an

MLS/RDBMS is developing a multilevel secure relational data model. In the late 1980s and early 1990s, there were several efforts on multilevel relational data models. Notable among these efforts are those of Sea View (Denning and Lunt, 1987; Lunt et al., 1990), LOCK Data Views (Stachour and Thuraisingham, 1990), SWORD (Wiseman, 1993), and the work of Jajodia and Sandhu (Jajodia and Sandhu, 1990). Furthermore, ASD-Views also developed a multilevel relational data model where the granularity of classification is based on views (Garvey and Wu, 1988). There were also efforts on developing a standard multilevel relational data model (Thuraisingham, 1993). In this section, we discuss some of the essential points on multilevel relational data models. Note that we do not discuss each multilevel relational data model. We have given many references so that the interested reader can follow up on the various efforts. Our goal is to explain the major issues and constructs. Figure 38.4 illustrates the various multilevel relational data models discussed in the literature.

Granularity of Classification. The granularity of classification in a relational database system could be at the database level, attribute level, tuple level, or even at the element level. Furthermore, one could also assign security levels to views as well as to collections of attributes. Essentially, security levels are assigned on the basis of what we have called security constraints, and these constraints classify data on the basis of content, context, association, and events. We discuss classifying databases, relational, tuples, attributes, and elements, which are the components of the relational data model in Thuraisingham (2005). Figure 38.5 illustrates element level classification.

Polyinstantiation is the technique used in relational databases to represent the fact that users at different levels have different views of the same entity. For example, at the TopSecret level, John's salary would be $70K while at the Secret level it would be $60K, at the Confidential level it would be $50K, and at the Unclassified level it would be $40K. In the case of Jane's salary at the Unclassified and Confidential levels it would be $0K, while at the Secret and TopSecret level it would be $0K.

> **Multilevel relational data model:**
>
> - Classifying databases, relations, attributes, tuples, elements, metadata, and views
> - Polyinstantiation
> - Security constraints
> - Normal forms and theory for multilevel relations

FIGURE 38.4 Multilevel relational data models.

EMP

SS#:	Ename:	Salary	D#:
1, S	John, U	20K, C	10, U
2, S	Paul, U	30K, S	20, U
3, S	Mary, U	40K, S	20, U

DEPT

D#: U	Dname: U	Mgr: S
10, U	Math, U	Smith, C
20, U	Physics, U	Jones, S

U = Unclassified
C = Confidential
S = Secret

FIGURE 38.5 Classifying elements.

EMP

SS#	Ename	Salary	D#	Level
1	John	20K	10	U
2	Paul	30K	20	S
3	Mary	40K	20	TS
3	Mary	10K	20	U
3	Mary	30K	20	S
3	Mary	20K	20	C
2	Paul	15K	20	U

U = Unclassified
C = Confidential
S = Secret
TS = TopSecret

FIGURE 38.6 Polyinstantiated relation.

Polyinstantiation is illustrated in Figure 38.6 Note that in this figure, we have multiple entries for Mary and Paul. For Mary, we have four entries as her salary is different at different levels. For Paul, we have two entries as the users cleared at the Secret level will read the Secret and the unclassified value, and those cleared at the unclassified level will read only the unclassified value.

The question that has been asked often is, why do we need polyinstantiation? The answer is to avoid signaling and covert channels. For example, if we are to have only one answer for John's and Jane's salaries, and if they are to be the actual values, then John's salary will be 70K and Jane's salary will be 90K. If a user at the Unclassified, Confidential, or Secret level queries for John's salary, then he or she will not get any answer. Similarly, if a user at the Unclassified and Confidential level asks for Jane's salary, he or she will not get an answer. By not giving an answer, we have caused a signaling channel. That is, some information at the higher level has interfered with the lower level world. If there are malicious processes that collude, they could insert/delete values at the higher level and exploit the signaling channel so that it becomes more of a covert channel over time.

38.3   MULTILEVEL ONLINE SOCIAL NETWORKS

As stated in Section 38.1, following along the lines of the definition of a MLS/DBMS, we have defined an MLS/OSN that enables users cleared at different security levels to access and share information at different sensitivity levels with their peers or friends also cleared at different security levels. If the *read at or below* your security level and *write at* your security level policy is enforced, then a user can read all the information posted at security levels below his or her level and update social networks at his or her level. Furthermore, a user can also share data and information at his or her level. Typically, an MLS/OSN can be hosted as applications of an MLS/DBMS or directly on top of a secure operating system.

Next, let us examine the architectures for an MLS/OSN. With the integrity lock approach, all the information that a person posts is encrypted and stored in the OSN database together with his or her security level. A checksum is computed that is based on the data and the security level and stored with the data. When the data is shared and/or queried, the checksum is recomputed and if the new checksum matches with the old checksum, then the data is shared with the user. With the operating system providing access control approach, there is an OSN instance at each level and runs as an untested application. The MAC (as well as sharing of the data) is carried out by the moderating system. In the trashed subject approach, some trust is placed on the OSN for data query, update, and sharing operations. With the distributed architecture approach, all access is carried out via the trusted front-end. Finally, with the extended kernel approach, functions such as inference control are carried out by developing extensions to the security kernel.

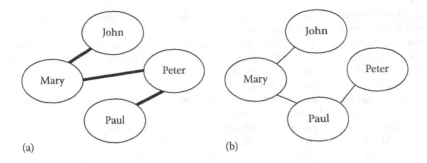

FIGURE 38.7 Multilevel online social network.

MLS/OSNs can also handle polyinstantiation. In such a situation, different users of the OSN have different views of the data. For example, we illustrate a multilevel social networking in Figure 38.7. At the Secret level, illustrated by a thicker line, there is a friendship between Mary and Peter, while this is not the case at the unclasped level.

While in theory, it is possible to develop MLS/OSNs following along the lines of MLS/DBMSs, whether this is realistic in practice is the main question. How can we envisage in the real world for different countries to form partnerships and coalitions at different security levels and share data? These partnerships can be represented as multilevel graphs. These graphs are, in turn, stored in multilevel RDF data stores. We have discussed aspects toward developing multilevel semantic webs in Thuraisingham (2007). Such an approach has to be examined for developing MLS/OSNs.

38.4   SUMMARY AND DIRECTIONS

This chapter has provided an overview of MAC and policies for MLS/DBMSs, as well as described taxonomy for the designs of MLS/DBMSs. We first described the differences between access control in operating systems and access control in DBMSs. Then, we provided an overview of the Bell and LaPadula security policy and its adaptation for MLS/DBMSs. Finally, we provided an overview of various security architectures for MLDS/DBMSs. We also discussed aspects of a multilevel relational data model. Finally, we discussed ways of adapting the developments in MLS/DBMSs to MLS/OSNs.

As we have discussed in this book, social networks are exploding. Analyzing and securing social networks have become a major aspect of the developments of such networks. However, there is no discussion as of yet on developing MLS/OSNs. One can envisage humans and organizations operating at different security levels forming social networks at multiple security checks. Furthermore, we believe that it is possible to develop such networks. However, the question of whether such networks are realistic is yet to be answered.

REFERENCES

Air Force Studies Board, Committee on Multilevel Data Management Security. *Multilevel Data Management Security*. National Academy Press, Washington, DC, 1983.

Bell, D. and LaPadula, L. *Secure Computer Systems: Mathematical Foundations and Model, M74-244*. The MITRE Corporation, Bedford, MA, 1973.

Burns, R. Integrity lock DBMS. In: *Proceedings of the National Computer Security Conference*, Gaithersburg, MD, September 1986.

Costich, O., Kang, M.H., and Froscher, J.N. The SINTRA data model: Structure and operations. In: *Proceedings of the IFIP Database Security Conference*, Huntsville, AL, 1993. Formal proceedings published by North Holland, Amsterdam, 1994.

Denning, D. and Lunt, T. A multilevel rational data model. In: *Proceedings of the IEEE Symposium on Security and Privacy*, Oakland, CA, 1987.

Ferrari, E. and Thuraisingham, B. Secure database systems. In: Piatini, M. and Diaz, O., editors. *Advances in Database Management.* Artech House, London, 2000.

Garvey, C. and Wu, A. Views as the security objects in a multilevel secure relational database management system. In: *Proceedings of the IEEE Symposium on Security and Privacy*, Oakland, CA, 1988.

Goguen, J. and Meseguer, J. Security policies and security models. In: *Proceedings of the IEEE Symposium on Security and Privacy*, Oakland, CA, 1982.

Graubart, R. The integrity-lock approach to secure database management. In: *Proceedings of the IEEE Symposium on Security and Privacy*, Oakland, CA, April 1984.

Graubard, R. A comparison of three secure DBMS architectures. In: *Proceedings of the IFIP Database Security Conference*, Monterey, CA. North Holland, Amsterdam, 1989.

Hinke, T. DBMS trusted computing base taxonomy. In: *Proceedings of the IFIP Database Security Conference*, Monterey, CA. North Holland, Amsterdam, 1989.

Hinke T. and Schaefer, M. Secure data management system. System Development Corp., Tech. Rep. RADC-TR-75-266, November 1975.

IEEE Computer. *Computer Security Technology* 16(7), 1983.

Jajodia, S. and Sandhu, R. Polyinstantiation, integrity in multilevel relations. In: *Proceedings of the IEEE Symposium on Security and Privacy*, Oakland, CA, 1990.

Lunt, T., Denning, D.E., Schell, R.R., Heckman, M., and Shockley, W.R. The SeaView security model. *IEEE Transactions on Software Engineering* 6(6): 593–607, 1990.

Stachour, P. and Thuraisingham, B. Design of LDV: A multilevel secure relational database management system. *IEEE Transactions on Knowledge and Data Engineering* 2(2): 190–209, 1990.

Thuraisingham, B. Towards the design of a standard multilevel relational data model. *Computer Standards and Interface Journal* 15(1), 1993.

Thuraisingham, B. *Database and Applications Security: Integrating Information Security and Data Management.* CRC Press, Boca Raton, FL, 2005.

Thuraisingham, B. *Building Trustworthy Semantic Webs.* CRC Press, Boca Raton, FL, 2007.

Wiseman, S. Using SWORD for the military aircraft command example database. In: *Proceedings of the IFIP Database Security Conference*, Vancouver, BC. North Holland, Amsterdam, 1993.

39 Developing an Educational Infrastructure for Analyzing and Securing Social Media

39.1 INTRODUCTION

Online social networks are online applications that allow their users to connect by means of various link types. Since their inception in the mid- to late-1990s, social networks have provided a way for users to interact, reflective of social networks or social relations among, for example, people who share interests or activities. Initially, critics regarded social media as a fad, a temporary fashion. However, today, social media has demonstrated exponential growth, making it the most popular activity on the World Wide Web. As the increase in popularity of social networking is on a constant rise, new uses for the technology are frequently being observed. As a result of the proliferation of these social networks, there is a critical need to securely store, manage, share, and analyze massive amounts of complex (e.g., semistructured and unstructured) social media data to determine patterns and trends in social communication, to better safeguard the nation and improve the quality of health care. The emerging cloud computing model attempts to handle massive amounts of data. Facebook has developed the Hive cloud-based relational data management framework, and Google has introduced the MapReduce framework for processing large amounts of data on commodity hardware. Furthermore, Apache's Hadoop Distributed File System (HDFS) is emerging as a superior software component for cloud computing, combined with integrated parts such as MapReduce. However, state-of-the-art social media do not provide adequate security mechanisms to protect sensitive data and provide defenses against malicious attacks. Two major areas that are at the forefront of the social media revolution are the development of (i) data analytics technologies for analyzing these networks and extracting useful information such as location, demographics, and sentiments of the participants of the network, and (ii) security and privacy technologies that ensure the privacy of the participants of the network, as well as providing controlled access to the information posted and exchanged by the participants.

To address the limitations of current social media platforms, at The University of Texas at Dallas (UTD) we have utilized state-of-the-art hardware, software, and data components based on Hadoop and MapReduce technologies, and are developing a secure cloud-based social media computing framework for multiple agencies including the Air Force Office of Scientific Research. In conjunction with the research, we have also established a strong education program in cybersecurity (CyS) since 2004 at UTD. We were designated a National Security Agency/Department of Homeland Security Center for Excellence in Education in 2004 and for Research in 2008, and have received multiple recertifications as well as multiple National Science Foundation Scholarship for Service (NSF SFS) awards to train students. Our course offerings include systems security, network security, data/applications security, cryptography, digital forensics, secure cloud, and analyzing/securing social media.

Our capacity-building project leverages the extensive investments we have made in assured cloud-based social media research and CyS education at UTD to develop courses in analyzing and securing social media. In particular, we will develop a comprehensive course related to analyzing and securing social media, as well as enhance our existing courses on data and applications security, big data analytics, and secure cloud. We will also enhance the current cloud-based social computing framework

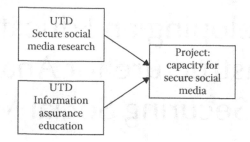

FIGURE 39.1 Educational infrastructure for analyzing and securing social media.

that we have developed so that students can (i) utilize this framework for their course projects and (ii) build features to this framework as part of their class programming projects. As illustrated in Figure 39.1, our research in secure social media as well as our education program in cybersecurity will be integrated to build a strong capacity for secure social computing education at UTD.

The organization of this chapter is as follows. In Section 39.2, we will describe our current capabilities with respect to CyS education. Our education program in analyzing and securing social media will be described in Section 39.3. The chapter is summarized in Section 39.4. We have included this chapter in this book so that those who want to use our book as a reference for their courses will be able to get some insights from what we have presented in this chapter.

39.2 CYBERSECURITY EDUCATION AT UTD

One of the strengths of our CyS program is its strong foundations in computer science (CSci) with a diverse curriculum. This has enabled us to offer graduate degrees in multiple concentration areas, including one in information assurance/CyS. During the past decade, there has been a significant increase in the number of new course offerings in CyS especially at the graduate level. The current CyS courses are discussed below. Note that the courses in bold are those directly influenced by our research and education on analyzing and securing social media.

Graduate-Level Core Courses
System Security and Binary Code Analysis; Information Security
Data and Application Security; Network Security; Introduction to Cryptography
Recently Offered Graduate-Level Elective Courses
Security of Critical Infrastructures; Cybersecurity Essentials
Analyzing and Securing Social Networks; **Developing and Securing the Cloud**
Secure Cloud Data Storage; Language-Based Security
Operating System Security; Information Theoretic Cryptography
Trusted and Secure Integrated Circuits and Systems; **Big Data Analytics**
Undergraduate-Level Elective Courses
Computer and Network Security, **Data and Applications Security**, **Digital Forensics**

We are continuously evaluating our courses and adding new courses to our curriculum. In addition to the above CSci courses, the School of Management and the School of Economics, Policy, and Political Sciences at UTD offer a number of courses that are related to management, policy, and criminal aspects of CyS. A significant accomplishment is the development of an interdisciplinary graduate-level certificate program in CyS. In addition, we also have multiple certificates in CyS available at both the graduate and undergraduate levels.

Our education program is also funded by multiple grants, including our NSF SFS program, Department of Defense scholarship grants, as well as the capacity-building grants NSF Capacity

Building in Cloud Computing and IBM Faculty Award in Cybersecurity. These grants help us organize and enhance special courses in CyS, such as Developing and Securing the Cloud. Our goal is to obtain funding for specialized courses such as Analyzing and Securing the Cloud, Secure Mobile Computing, and Securing Social Media. We have also built a software tool to facilitate creation and running of CyS competitions, and have been using it for running CyS competitions at UTD. These grants together with some supplementary NSF grants have helped us support students from other higher-education institutions in Texas to participate in our annual Texas Security Awareness Week (TexSAW) event since 2011. Our CSG (Computer Security Group), which consists of students interested in CyS, includes activities that are an integral part of our hands-on educational activities in CyS. These include semester crash courses on hands-on CyS topics, weekly hands-on training classes, participation in various CyS competitions, and running weekly CyS challenges. In these activities, students are exposed to various software tools that are typically used in the industry, for example, Wireshark, Metasploit, IDAPro (licensed version), and Hexrays (licensed version).

39.3 EDUCATION PROGRAM IN ANALYZING AND SECURING SOCIAL MEDIA

39.3.1 ORGANIZATION OF THE CAPACITY-BUILDING ACTIVITIES

Our capacity-building project will utilize the extensive research we have carried out in analyzing and securing social media (discussed in Sections III through VIII of this book) as well as the CyS education discussed in Section 39.2. Our project consists of two major components: (i) curriculum development and (ii) laboratory development. A capstone project course around social media security is one of the major outcomes of this effort. Social media systems are comprehensive systems including different layers making up a fairly complex and critical computing resource. Securing a social media system involves different aspects of security, all the way from data security to access control to defense against attacks to system-level security to network security to the use of various security technologies (firewall systems, intrusion detection systems, etc.). Our course will emphasize how the principles of social media and CyS come together to build a secure social media system. In particular, we will use knowledge of known security vulnerabilities of distributed systems and known and new ways to address those vulnerabilities in the context of securing a social media system.

Our research in secure social media as well as our strong education program in CyS puts us in a unique position to develop the capacity for secure social media. Our current secure social media framework, illustrated in Figure 39.2, includes secure cloud virtual machine, secure cloud data management, and secure cloud storage. This framework will be utilized for both instructing and

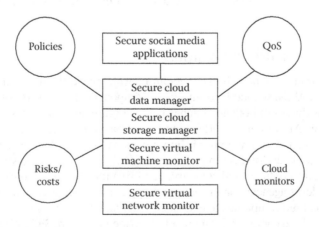

FIGURE 39.2 Our current secure social media framework.

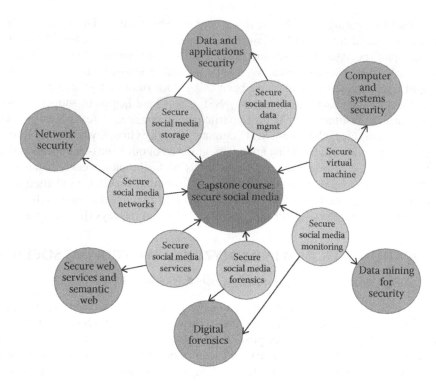

FIGURE 39.3   Social media capstone course plan.

experimentation. The second part of the proposed capacity project is to build a realistic instructional cloud-based social media system with all the necessary components and develop necessary curriculum around it to teach various aspects of CyS as it relates to securing such large-scale social media systems. Our system will be open to other institutions for similar educational purposes, and we will share the curriculum material and the use of our instructional social media system in their curriculum in accordance with the UTD and Facebook policies and procedures. Our proposed curriculum will be discussed in Section 39.3.2. Proposed programming projects for students will be discussed in Section 39.3.3. Paper presentations on analyzing and securing social media will be discussed in Section 39.3.4 and instructional cloud computing facility will be discussed in Section 39.3.5. Evaluation will be discussed in Section 39.3.6. Figure 39.3 illustrates the course plan.

39.3.2   CURRICULUM DEVELOPMENT ACTIVITIES

We will take a two-pronged approach to curriculum development: the first is a capstone course on secure social media and the second is to introduce components into several of our key courses in CyS. We will discuss details of both approaches below. Figure 39.3 illustrates our approach.

Capstone Course. At present, we offer a course in analyzing and securing social media. We are enhancing this course and developing it into a capstone course. Our capstone course is motivated by (i) research and development in social media; (ii) emerging secure social media research, prototypes, commercial products, and standards; and (iii) the research and experimentation UTD is conducting for federal agencies on (a) data and applications security and privacy, (b) big data analytics, (c) assured cloud computing, and (d) social media. Our secure social media course will be based on our assured cloud computing framework described in Figure 39.2. We are also planning to develop the course with inputs from social media companies. In particular, our course will include the following components.

1. *Analyzing and securing social media*: This is our capstone course on secure social media. Students are first introduced to social networks, CyS, and data analytics. The first part of the course will be on analyzing social networks. Students apply various tools to determine whether private information can be revealed in social networks. The second part of the course will address access control and trust management in social networks. The third part of the course will focus on privacy. The last part of the course focuses on attacks to social networks as well as explores forensics issues.

Component Insertion into Existing Courses. As illustrated in Figure 39.3, several of the components that we will introduce into our capstone course will fit nicely into our current courses in CyS. We describe the enhancements to our current courses.

2. *Data and applications security*: In this course, we introduce policy management in databases, multilevel secure data management, inference problem, secure objects and multimedia systems, assured information sharing, secure information integration, secure data warehousing, privacy-preserving data mining, secure social networks, secure knowledge management, and attacks to databases. We will incorporate additional modules into this course that are based on secure social data management, such as secure query optimization and query rewriting and secure indexing.
3. *Big data analytics*: Students are introduced to a variety of data mining techniques and then explore how cloud computing tools may be used to manage large databases. Students build data analytics tools. We will introduce a new module that will discuss how cloud computing can be used for secure scalable social media. In addition, we will also examine how data mining may be used to analyze social media and determine whether privacy violations could occur.
4. *Developing and securing the cloud*: Students are introduced to web services, semantic web, and cloud computing, as well as security issues for these technologies. In particular, policy enforcement as well as various cloud security standards for web services are discussed. We will introduce modules that will enable the students to experiment with cloud-based assured information sharing and social networking.
5. *Digital forensics*: Students are introduced to digital forensics concepts, including file systems forensics, network forensics, mobile system forensics, e-mail forensics, and other application forensics. We will introduce a module on social media attacks as well as explore how forensics may be carried out for social media.

39.3.3 COURSE PROGRAMMING PROJECTS

As part of the courses that we have described in Section 39.2.2, students can carry out a number of programming projects that will enhance their skills in secure social media. The following are some sample programming projects for our students.

Analytics for Social Media. We will conduct sentiment analysis from the postings in social media such as Facebook and Twitter. Sentiment analysis will be carried out at the user level and individual posting level in a group on a particular social media system. This task will be carried out in the context of postings having more than one language. For sentiment analysis, semisupervised learning will be utilized. For feature extraction, bag of keywords and advanced natural language processing (NLP) techniques will be utilized.

By implementing this programming project, students will learn various data mining techniques and NLP techniques as applied to social media.

Scalable Techniques for Anomaly Detection in Social Media. Spamming is prevalent in social media. In this project, we will identify this type of anomalous behavior that deviates from the normal/benign case. At the same time, we will carry out this task in real time with high accuracy and a low false-positive rate. For this, we will utilize unsupervised/semisupervised learning to model benign characteristics in a big data framework (i.e., SPARK, Cassandra, etc.). By carrying out the project, students will learn about various attacks to social media systems.

Access Control Policy Enforcement for Social Media. Most users have problems in understanding the basic access control features on social network sites such as Facebook. In this programming project, students will be asked to develop a Facebook application (app) that will analyze the user's privacy and access control settings, and notify users automatically about the information that they are sharing with friends and family. Furthermore, the students will be asked to develop simple post analysis tools to see whether a user is disclosing sensitive information about their activities to unwanted people. Finally, the app may suggest users to create certain groups (e.g., close family friends) to enable more fine-grained access control.

Privacy Violation Detection for Social Media. In our previous work, we developed a private information disclosure analysis tool that can analyze whether the information disclosed on Facebook can be used to infer further undisclosed but potentially private information such as sexual orientation. In this project, the students will be asked to develop basic data mining-based prediction tools to analyze the user profiles and warn users about potential private information disclosure and privacy violations.

Trust Management in Social Media. In this project, the students will be asked to develop tools to analyze the trustworthiness of the posts by others based on the trustworthiness of the post owner's identity (e.g., trustrank of the user) and the trustworthiness of the post (e.g., for outside links, pagerank of the website). This project will allow students to learn basic concepts such as pagerank and apply them in the context of social media.

Cloud-Based Secure Social Media. We have developed many tools for secure information sharing and data analytics. In particular, we have developed a secure cloud computing framework as well as multiple secure cloud query-processing systems. Our framework uses Hadoop to store and retrieve large numbers of RDF triples by exploiting the cloud computing paradigm, and we have developed a scheme to store Resource Description Framework (RDF) data in an HDFS. We implemented XACML as well as RDF-based policy management and integrated it with our query-processing strategies. For secure query processing with relational data, we utilized the Hive framework. We have also developed demonstration systems. The first demonstration illustrates how information may be shared in our cloud, based on policies specified in XACML. In the second demonstration, we have implemented a semantic web-based policy engine. As part of our proposed project, students will carry out projects that enable multiple social networks to share information on our cloud.

Social Media Attacks and Forensics. We have carried out extensive research in malware attacks and also offer a course in digital forensics. We will introduce modules on social media attacks and social media forensics in the capstone course. In addition, we will also include these modules in our data and applications security as well as forensic courses. For the programming project, students will try to penetrate social media as well as carry out forensics for social media. We will work with the social media companies in developing such programming exercises.

39.3.4 Paper Presentations on Analyzing and Securing Social Media

While the first part of the capstone course will include lectures that will essentially consist of much of the material discussed in this book as well as material from several other papers and books, the students will also read papers from important social media and CyS conferences and present papers in class during the second part of the course. The papers will be on analyzing or securing social media and include papers from recent conferences such as the ASONAM (Advances in Social Network Analysis and Mining) conference series. These papers help the students utilize the knowledge gained during the first half of the course. In addition, the papers also help them with the programing projects that they will carry out as part of the course. These projects include the ones we have discussed in Section 39.3.3, as well as other projects that the students may formulate.

36.3.5 Instructional Cloud Computing Facility for Experimentation

We will use various open source tools to help students become familiar with the basic cloud computing concepts that are useful for conducting experiments in social media. For large-scale social media analysis in the cloud, we will dedicate part of our research cloud infrastructure consisting of a Hadoop cluster. Students will conduct programming projects using this cluster. In addition, students will have hands-on experience using Hadoop for the various activities we have described in the previous section. For example, for the data and applications security class, the students can use this infrastructure to carry our programming assignments for assured information sharing for social media. Students will be divided into groups. Each group will act as a coalition partner, and will design their policies for the other groups and will store the policies with the data in the cloud. These policies will be enforced when a group wants to access the data. For example, group A devises a set of policies for group B and a different set of policies for group C. Appropriate policies will be executed against the data when a group (e.g., B or C) wants to access the data placed by group A. In addition to structured data, the students also experiment with unstructured data (e.g., text or image). We are creating a second cloud cluster to be used entirely for educational purposes. With this cluster, we will conduct social media penetration and forensics exercises as part of the capstone course as well as the digital forensics, network systems, and data security courses. We are also planning to develop detailed instructional material that will include lecture notes as well as laboratory exercises that we will design and place on the project web site. In addition, user manuals will be developed.

36.3.6 Evaluation Plan

The best evaluators of our courses and experiments are our students. We are obtaining detailed evaluations from our students and discussing with them how we can enhance the courses. We also get inputs from our partners and use these inputs to improve our courses. On the basis of the inputs we get, we will also produce user manuals for the course so that students from around the country can log into our system and learn how to use our cloud for their education and experiments.

We propose three broad stages of program evaluations: (i) effectiveness of the project implementation, (ii) meeting our goals and objectives, and (iii) the overall impact of the program. First, the processes to evaluate are made of two major parts. Formative evaluation will be conducted to monitor activities that involve project implementation for further refinements and continual improvement. The purpose of this stage of evaluation is to document successes and challenges, as well as lessons learned from the implementation stages and to monitor status of project activities. Secondly, summative evaluation will be conducted for meeting our program goals and objectives, impact of our program on student learning, and improvement of secure social media education.

39.4　SUMMARY AND DIRECTIONS

In this chapter, we have built on the secure cloud infrastructure discussed in our previous book (Thuraisingham, 2014), and presented our strategy for education in analyzing and securing social media. Some of the courses we have discussed have already been offered, while some others are in progress. We are utilizing the infrastructure we have developed for the cloud for our course programming projects. Many of our students have become experts on programming with the Hadoop/ MapReduce framework. At present, we are offering a new course on big data analytics in the cloud, which will involve the implementation of various data mining algorithms in the cloud. In addition, our data and applications security course discusses details on access control and malware attacks. Furthermore, we offer a course on developing and securing the cloud. Several of these courses will include modules on analyzing and securing social media.

We will continue to enhance both our cloud computing framework as well as the courses we offer. For example, during the spring semester of 2013 (January through May 2013), we offered our first course on analyzing and securing social networks. This course utilized our cloud infrastructure for the programming projects. Students were also given some background information on social media systems represented using semantic web technologies (Mika, 2007). This course was offered in fall 2015 (August through December 2015). For the new class, we will expand on the work on SNODSOC as well as the other systems we have discussed in this book with security features as part of the class projects. That is, we will develop techniques to mine various social network data (e.g., Twitter, YouTube, etc.), enforce security and privacy policies, and implement the techniques in the cloud (e.g., use of Storm). We believe that as the need for big data analytics increases, so does the need for better cloud infrastructures as well as more courses on assured cloud computing and social networking. Security will be a major aspect with respect to the infrastructures developed as well as the courses offered about analyzing and securing social media.

REFERENCES

Mika, P. *Social Networks and the Semantic Web*. Springer, New York, 2007.
Thuraisingham, B. *Developing and Securing the Cloud*. CRC Press, Boca Raton, FL, 2014.

CONCLUSION TO SECTION IX

The chapters in this section have described our exploratory work, including an education infrastructure for analyzing and securing social media. We also discussed integrity and provenance, as well as aspects on developing multilevel secure online social networks (MLS/OSNs).

Chapter 36 essentially integrated much of the design and implementation of the systems discussed in Sections II and III, as well as some of the novel methods discussed in Section IV, and described a unifying framework. The framework includes components both for access control and inference control, as well as information-sharing control. In Chapter 37, we provided an overview of data integrity, which includes data quality and data provenance. We discussed the applications of semantic web technologies for data integrity, and also discussed integrity for social media systems represented using semantic web technologies. Chapter 38 provided an overview of mandatory access control and policies for multilevel database management systems (MLS/DBMSs), as well as describing a taxonomy for the designs of MLS/DBMSs. We then discussed ways of adapting the developments in MLS/DBMSs to MLS/OSNs. In Chapter 39, we described the secure cloud infrastructure we have developed, and provided an overview of our strategy for education in analyzing and securing social media. Some of the courses we have discussed have already been offered, while some others are in progress. We are utilizing the infrastructure we have developed for the cloud for our course programming projects.

40 Summary and Directions

40.1 ABOUT THIS CHAPTER

This chapter brings us to a close of *Analyzing and Securing Social Networks*. We discussed several aspects, including social media analytics, security for social networks, privacy aspects of social networks, and experimental social media systems, as well as attacks on social media systems. The topics discussed included location mining for social media access control and privacy-preserving social media integration. In addition, we also discussed the emerging technologies for social media systems. The experimental systems are the ones that we have developed at The University of Texas at Dallas, and include secure cloud query processing for social media and cloud-based assured information sharing systems for social media.

The organization of this chapter is as follows. In Section 40.2, we give a summary of this book. This summary has been taken from the summaries of each chapter. In Section 40.3, we discuss directions for analyzing and securing social media. In Section 40.4, we share our goals for analyzing and securing social media. In Section 40.5, we give suggestions as to where to go from here.

40.2 SUMMARY OF THIS BOOK

We summarize the contents of each chapter, essentially taken from the summary and directions section of each chapter. Chapter 1 provided an introduction to the book. We first provided a brief overview of the supporting technologies for cloud computing, which included information security, as well as data, information, and knowledge management. Then, we discussed various topics addressed in the book, including secure web services and secure semantic web, which are at the heart of secure cloud computing. We also discussed cloud computing and secure cloud computing. Our framework is a nine-layer framework, and each layer was addressed in each main section of this book. This framework was illustrated in Figure 1.4. We replicate this framework in Figure 40.1.

The book is divided into nine main sections. Section I, which described supporting technologies, consisted of four chapters: Chapters 2 through 5. Chapter 2 provided an overview of the various social networks that have emerged during the past decades. We then selected a few networks (e.g., Facebook, LinkedIn, Google+, and Twitter) and discussed some of their essential features. In Chapter 3, we provided an overview of discretionary security policies in database systems. We started with a discussion of access control policies, including authorization policies and role-based access control. Then, we discussed administration policies. We briefly discussed identification and authentication. We also discussed auditing issues and views for security. In Chapter 4, we first provided an overview of the various data mining tasks and techniques, and then discussed some of the popular techniques such as neural networks, support vector machines (SVM), and association rule mining (ARM). Chapter 5 introduced the notion of the cloud and semantic web technologies. We first discussed concepts in cloud computing, including aspects of virtualization. Next, we discussed technologies for the semantic web including eXtensible Markup Language (XML), Resource Description Framework (RDF), ontologies, and Web Ontology Language (OWL). This was followed by a discussion of security issues for the semantic web. Finally, we discussed cloud computing frameworks based on semantic web technologies.

Section II, which described aspects of analyzing and securing social media, consisted of three chapters: Chapters 6 through 8. Chapter 6 gave the reader a feel for the various applications of social media analytics. These applications ranged from detecting communities of interest to determining political affiliations. We also addressed security and privacy aspects. Chapter 7 discussed aspects of

Developing an Educational Infrastructure for Analyzing and Securing Social Media	Layer 9
Multilevel Secure Online Social Networks	Secure Social
Integrity Management and Data Provenance for Social Media	Media Directions
Unified Framework for Analyzing and Securing Social Media	

Attacks on Social Media and Data Analytics Solutions	
Social Network Integration and Analysis with Privacy Preservation	Layer 8
Cloud-Centric Assured Information Sharing for Social Networks	Secure Social
Secure Cloud Query Processing for Semantic Web-Based Social Media	Media Systems
Secure Cloud Query Processing with Relational Data for Social Media	

Stream Data Analytics for Multipurpose Social Media Applications	Layer 7
Social Media and Bioterrorism	Social Media
Temporal Geosocial Mobile Semantic Web	Application
Graph Mining for Insider Threat Detection	Systems

Social Networking in the Cloud	Layer 6
Experimental Cloud Query Processing System for Social Networks	Social Media
Semantic Web-Based Social Network Integration	Integration and Analytics
Social Graph Extraction, Integration, and Analysis	Systems

Implementing an Inference Controller for Social Media Data	Layer 5
Inference Control for Social Media	Access Control
Implementation of an Access Control System for Social Networks	and Inference for
Access Control for Social Networks	Social Networks

Sanitization of Social Network Data for Release to Semitrusted Third Parties	Layer 4
Social Network Classification through Data Partitioning	Social Network
Extending Classification of Social Networks through Indirect Friendships	Analytics and
Classification of Social Networks Incorporating Link Types	Privacy
Our Approach to Studying Privacy in Social Networks	Considerations

Understanding News Queries with Geo-Content Using Twitter	Layer 3
Tweeque: Identifying Social Cliques for Location Mining	Techniques
Tweecalization: Location Mining Using Semisupervised Learning	and Tools
TweetHood: A Social Media Analytics Tools	for Social Network
Developments and Challenges in Location Mining	Analytics

Confidentiality, Privacy, and Trust for Social Media Data	Layer 2
Semantic Web-Based Social Network Representation and Analysis	Aspects of Analyzing and
Analyzing and Securing Social Networks	Securing Social Networks

Cloud Computing and Semantic Web Technologies	Layer 1
Data Mining Techniques	Supporting
Data Security and Privacy	Technologies
Social Networks: A Survey	

FIGURE 40.1 Layered framework for analyzing and securing social media.

representing and reasoning about social networks represented as RDF graphs. Chapter 8 discussed confidentiality, privacy, and trust for social networks. Confidentiality policies will enable the members of the network to determine what information is to be shared with their friends in the network. Privacy policies will determine what a network can release about a member provided these policies are accepted by the member. Trust policies will provide a way for members of a network to assign trust values to the others.

Section III, which described social network analytics, consisted of five chapters: Chapters 9 through 13. Chapter 9 discussed aspects of location mining for social networks. Such approaches would enable, say, law enforcement to determine where the users are if they have committed a crime. On the other hand, we may want to protect the location of the innocent users. We first discussed the importance of location mining and then provided an overview of the related efforts on this topic. This was followed by a discussion of the challenges in location mining. Some aspects of geospatial proximity and friendship were then discussed. Finally, we provided an overview of our contributions to location mining. Chapter 10 described TweetHood, an algorithm for agglomerative clustering on fuzzy k closest friends with variable depth. Graph-related approaches are the methods that rely on the social graph of the user while deciding on the location of the user. We described three such methods that show the evolution of the algorithm currently used in TweetHood. These algorithms are (i) a simple majority algorithm with variable depth, (ii) k closest friends with variable depth, and (iii) fuzzy k closest friends with variable depth. We have also provided experimental results for the algorithms. In Chapter 11, we argued that the location data of users on social networks is a rather scarce resource and only available to a small portion of the users. This creates a need for a method that makes use of both labeled and unlabeled data for training. In this case, the location concept serves the purpose of class label. Therefore, our problem is a classic example of the application of semisupervised learning algorithms. We described a semisupervised learning method for label propagation, which we call Tweecalization. Chapter 12 described the effects of migration and proposed a set of algorithms that we call Tweeque. In particular, we discussed the effect of migration and temporal data mining aspects. Then, we discussed social clique identification algorithms and provided our experimental results. Chapter 13 described an application of our location mining work, and we describe the development of a system that focuses on understanding the intent of a user search query. In particular, we discussed a system called TWinner that examines the application of social media in improving the quality of the web.

Section IV, which described privacy aspects of social media, consisted of five chapters: Chapters 14 through 18. Chapter 14 began with a discussion of one of the early full-scale analyses of social networks with a focus on privacy. We provided several major insights that contributed to the overall concept. We showed that based on simple, preexisting relational classifiers, we are able to use specific information about link types that had previously been ignored and use this to increase our ability to determine hidden information. Chapter 15 presented, for ease of comparison, a summary of all of our experiments. We believe that it shows that our enhancements to the traditional relational Bayes classifier, which we call link-type rBC and weighted link-type rBC, are both successful extensions to the well-researched area of classification in social networks. We showed how our extensions have improved on the implementation of the traditional relational Bayes classifier on our data set, and how the overall accuracy compares to similar experiments done on a similar data set in other research work. In Chapter 16, we showed that by intelligently choosing *important* nodes in a subgraph, one is able to increase classification accuracy on real-world social network data. We presented a method of selecting nodes by using weighted graph metrics and a programmatically determinable threshold parameter. Furthermore, we showed that our τ threshold is a useful tool for determining the general increase in graph size versus a desired amount of classification accuracy, and that it may be possible to determine a beneficial value of τ through calculation of the chosen degree metric. In Chapter 17, we discussed that information gain-based partitioning methods may be used to efficiently divide and then classify the data in a social network. In Chapter 18, we addressed various issues related to private information leakage in social networks. For unmodified social network graphs, we showed that using details alone, one can predict class values more accurately than using friendship links alone. We further showed that using both friendship links and details together gives better predictability than details alone. In addition, we explored the effect of removing details and links in preventing sensitive information leakage. In the process, we discovered situations in which collective inferencing does not improve on using a simple local classification method to identify nodes. When we combined the results from the collective inference implications with the individual results, we began to see that removing details and friendship links together is the best way to reduce classifier accuracy.

Section V, which described experimental access and inference control for social networks, consisted of four chapters: Chapters 19 through 22. In Chapter 19, we proposed an extensible fine-grained online social network access control model based on semantic web tools. In addition, we discussed authorization, administration, and filtering policies that are modeled using OWL and Semantic Web Rule Language (SWRL). The architecture of a framework in support of this model was also presented. In Chapter 20, we described the implementation of an extensible fine-grained online social network access control model based on semantic web tools. In particular, we discussed the implementation of the authorization, administration, and filtering policies that are modeled using OWL and SWRL. That is, we discussed the implementation of a version of the framework described in Chapter 19, and presented experimental results for the length of time access control that can be evaluated using this scheme. In Chapter 21, we first described the design of an inference controller that operates over a semantic web-based provenance graph and protects important provenance information from unauthorized users. Since our social networks discussed in Chapters 19 and 20 are also represented by semantic web technologies, the techniques we have developed apply for such social media data. We used RDF as our data model, as it supports the interoperability of multiple databases having disparate data schemas. In addition, we expressed policies and rules in terms of semantic web rules and constraints, and we classified data items and relationships between them using semantic web software tools. In Chapter 22, we described the implementation of an inference controller for data provenance discussed in Chapter 21. The inference controller is built using a modular approach; therefore, it is very flexible in that most of the modules can be extended or replaced by another application module.

Section VI, which described experimental social media analytics systems, consisted of four chapters: Chapters 23 through 26. Chapter 23 provided some basics on the use of semantic web technologies for representing and reasoning about social networks. We first discussed aspects of entity representation and integration with semantic web. Next, we discussed heuristic reasoning for RDF graphs. Third, we discussed the analysis of RDF graphs that represent social networks. Finally, we discussed ways of managing very large RDF graphs. In Chapter 24, we first described aspects of social network integration and explained the use of semantic web technologies for this purpose. We then discussed three separate experimental cloud-based semantic web data management systems for social network integration. In Chapter 25, we presented a Hadoop-based framework capable of handling enormous amounts of RDF data that can be used to represent social networks. We described a schema to store RDF data, an algorithm to determine a query-processing plan whose worst-case is bounded, to answer a SPARQL query, and a simplified cost model to be used by the algorithm. Chapter 26 described the design of SNODSOC (stream-based novel class detection for social network analysis). SNODSOC will be a great asset to the analysts who have to deal with billions of blogs and messages. For example, by analyzing the behavioral history of a particular group of individuals, analysts will be able to predict behavioral changes in the near future and take necessary measures.

Section VII, which described experimental social media application systems, consisted of four chapters: Chapters 27 through 30. Chapter 27 discussed our approach to insider threat detection. We represent the insiders and their communication as RDF graphs, and then query and mine the graphs to extract the nuggets. Chapter 28 described the challenges for developing a system for stabilization and reconstruction operations (SARO). In particular, we discussed the design of a temporal geospatial mobile social semantic web that can be utilized by military personnel, decision makers, and local/government personnel to reconstruct after a major combat operation. In Chapter 29, we discussed our approach to enhancing the susceptible, infected, and recovered (SIR) model through epidemiology approximation. Our model is based on social interactions. We have created a hybridized model that balances the simplicity of the original with an approximation of what more complex agent-based models already offer, with an emphasis on the exploration of large search spaces. In Chapter 30, we have described the design of InXite. InXite will be a great asset to the analysts who have to deal with massive amounts of data streams in the form of billions of blogs and messages, among others. For example, by analyzing the behavioral history of a particular group of individuals as well as details of concepts such as events, analysts will be able to predict behavioral changes in the near future and take necessary measures.

Section VIII, which described experimental secure social media application systems, consisted of five chapters: Chapters 31 through 35. In Chapter 31, we presented a system that allows cooperating organizations to securely share large amounts of data. We ensured that the organizations have a large common storage area by using Hadoop. Furthermore, we used Hive to present users of our system with a structured view of the data and to also enable them to query the data with an SQL-like language. In Chapter 32, we described an access control system for RDF data that incorporates a token-based mechanism. In Chapter 33, we described our design and implementation of a cloud-based information sharing system called CAISS. CAISS utilizes several of the technologies we have developed as well as open source tools. We also described the design of an ideal cloud-based assured information sharing system called CAISS++. In Chapter 34, we discussed a generalized social network in which only insensitive and generalized information is shared. We also discussed the integration of the generalized information and how it can satisfy a prescribed level of privacy leakage tolerance, which is measured independently of the privacy-preserving techniques. Finally, in Chapter 35, we addressed one of the most important directions in social media research, and that is on attacks on social media systems.

Section IX, which described our exploratory work, consisted of four chapters: Chapters 36 through 39. Chapter 36 essentially integrated much of the design and implementation of the systems discussed in Sections II and III, as well as some of the novel methods discussed in Section IV, and described a unifying framework. The framework includes components both for access control and inference control, as well as information-sharing control. In Chapter 37, we provided an overview of data integrity, which includes data quality and data provenance. We discussing the applications of semantic web technologies for data integrity, as well as discussing integrity for social media systems represented using semantic web technologies. Chapter 38 provided an overview of mandatory access control and policies for multilevel database management systems (MLS/DBMSs), and also described taxonomy for the designs of MLS/DBMSs. We then discussed ways of adapting the developments in MLS/DBMSs to multilevel social networks (MLS/OSNs). In Chapter 39, we described the secure cloud infrastructure we have developed and provide an overview of our strategy for education in analyzing and securing social media. Some of the courses we have discussed have already been offered, while some others are in progress. We are utilizing the infrastructure we have developed for the cloud for our course programming projects.

This book has one Appendix. In this appendix, we provide the broad picture of how all the books we have written relate to one another. There are many developments in the field of social media analytics and security, and it is impossible for us to list all of them. We have provided a broad but fairly comprehensive overview of the field. The book is intended not only for technical managers as well as technologists who want to get a broad understanding of the field but also for those who want to learn some of the details. It is also intended for students who wish to pursue research in data and applications security, in general, and secure social media, in particular.

40.3   DIRECTIONS FOR ANALYZING AND SECURING SOCIAL MEDIA

There are many directions for social media analytics as well as for social media security. We discuss some of them for the topics addressed in this book. Figure 40.2 illustrates the directions and challenges.

As discussed in Chapter 6, in the area of social media analytics, several problems are being studied. These include extracting demographics (including location), sentiment analysis, detecting communities of interest, determining leaders, detecting persons of interest, determining political affiliation, as well as other aspects such as determining gender biases, detecting suspicious behavior, and even predicting future events. These social network analysis techniques use various analytics tools that carry out association rule mining, clustering, classification, and anomaly detection, among others. The challenge we have is to develop techniques that have high accuracy and low false positives and negatives. Furthermore, these techniques have to be scalable for massive amounts of social media data. For example, parallelization of the various analytics techniques needs to be examined. The data also has to be cleansed, as it may be incomplete and/or uncertain. We also need to develop techniques that can reason under uncertainty.

Without a doubt, social media analytics is something that will be extremely useful for developing and managing useful social media systems. However, a major challenge is the violation of privacy. Our work has shown how privacy could be violated for various social media analytics techniques. Therefore, we need to develop privacy-preserving social media analytics techniques as well as reasons about the information posted by the members of the network, and advise them not to post data that could potentially violate their privacy. With respect to the confidentiality of the social networks, we need to develop suitable access control models. We have discussed some directions in Section V of this book. However, the numerous access control models that have been developed in the literature need to be examined for social media, and the scalability of these models have to be studied. Finally, we need to develop techniques that can detect and prevent attacks on social networks. This is one of the most challenging directions we are faced with today. In addition, we also need to explore areas such as identity management, handling identity threats, as well as auditing and forensics for social media systems.

Another closely related research area is big data analytics, security, and privacy. Big data analytics techniques are needed for cybersecurity applications, including determining when the social networks have been attacked. Because systems such as Facebook have close to a billion active daily users, we need big data analytics techniques to monitor the activity and determine suspicious behavior. Furthermore, social media data, which is essentially a type of big data that includes not only text but also photos, images, video, audio, and animation data, has to be secure. That is, we

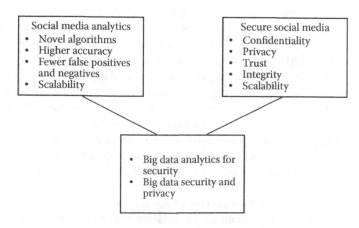

FIGURE 40.2   Directions and challenges in analyzing and securing social media.

need appropriate policies for such data. In addition, we need to develop models that take into consideration utility, cost, and privacy.

40.4 OUR GOALS FOR ANALYZING AND SECURING SOCIAL MEDIA

While we have discussed many concepts on analyzing and securing social media such as location mining and privacy aspects, much of our research has focused on secure social media data management. Therefore, one of the major goals for us is to continue to develop systems in secure social media data storage, secure social media data management, as well as implementing applications such as malware detection, insider threat detection, and assured information sharing for social media.

The major aims of our research are to (i) extract entities and relationships between the entities from the numerous data sources, both structured and unstructured; (ii) build networks from the extracted entities and relationships between the entities; and (iii) analyze the networks and extract the nuggets from the networks that will be useful for the analyst. Our goal is to implement the social networking systems that we are developing in the cloud. Furthermore, as we make progress with security and privacy for social networks, we will also implement the secure social networks in the cloud.

Our team at The University of Texas at Dallas is also conducting extensive research on secure cloud virtualization, cloud forensics, and formal policy analysis for the cloud. Therefore, we will continue to explore the fundamental issues surrounding social media systems utilizing the cloud. Figure 40.3 illustrates our goals on analyzing and securing social media.

40.5 WHERE DO WE GO FROM HERE?

This book has focused on analyzing and securing social media. We have stated many concepts, challenges, and solutions. We need to continue with research and development efforts if we are to make progress in this very important area.

The question is where do we go from here? First of all, those who wish to work in this area must have a good knowledge of the supporting technologies including social media, data analytics, and security and privacy. For example, it is important to understand the technologies that comprise the semantic web, and how they are used to represent and reason about social media.

Next, since the field is expanding rapidly and there are many developments in the field, the reader has to keep up with developments, including reading about the commercial products and prototypes as well as the emerging systems. Finally, we encourage the reader to experiment with the products and also develop security tools. This is the best way to become familiar with a particular field. That is, work on hands-on problems and provide solutions to get a better understanding. The developers should be familiar with technologies such as Hadoop, MapReduce, HBase, and Storm. The cloud will continue to have a major impact on handling massive amounts of data and processing for social media, and therefore security for the cloud will be an important aspect. Finally, social media systems are considered to be part of big data systems, and therefore big data analytics, security, and privacy are also major areas for further work. Finally, the importance of work in attacks on social networks and developing solutions cannot be stressed enough.

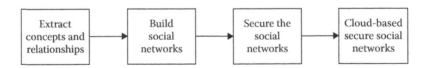

FIGURE 40.3 Our goals on analyzing and securing social media.

We need research and development support from the federal and local government funding agencies. Agencies such as the National Science Foundation, National Security Agency, the US Army, Navy, Air Force, the Defense Advanced Research Projects Agency, the Intelligence Advanced Research Projects Activity, and the Department of Homeland Security are funding research in security. The Air Force is focusing a great deal on securing the cloud. We also need commercial corporations to invest research and development funds so that progress can be made in industrial research and allow the transfer of the research to commercial products. We also need to collaborate with the international research community to solve problems and promote standards that are not only of national interest but also of international interest. In summary, we need public/private/academic partnerships to develop breakthrough technologies in the very important area of analyzing and securing social media.

Appendix: Data Management Systems: Developments and Trends

A.1   OVERVIEW

The main purpose of this appendix is to set the context of the series of books we have written in data management, data mining, and data security. Our series started back in 1997 with our book on *Data Management Systems: Evolution and Interoperation* (Thuraisingham, 1997). Our subsequent books have evolved from this first book. We have essentially repeated the Chapter 1 of our first book in the Appendix of our subsequent books. The purpose of this appendix is to provide an overview of data management systems and to show how the field has evolved over the years: from data to information to knowledge and now to big data. We will then discuss the relationships between the books we have written.

As stated in our series of books, the developments in information systems technologies have resulted in the computerization of many applications in various business areas. Data have become a critical resource in many organizations, and therefore, efficient access to data, sharing the data, extracting information from the data, and making use of the information have become urgent needs. As a result, there have been several efforts on integrating the various data sources scattered across several sites. These data sources may be databases managed by database management systems or they could simply be files. To provide the interoperability between the multiple data sources and systems, various tools are being developed. These tools enable users of one system to access other systems in an efficient and transparent manner.

We define data management systems to be systems that manage the data, extract meaningful information from the data, and make use of the information extracted. Therefore, data management systems include database systems, data warehouses, and data mining systems. Data could be structured data such as that found in relational databases or it could be unstructured such as text, voice, imagery, and video. There have been numerous discussions in the past to distinguish between data, information, and knowledge. For our purposes, data could be just bits and bytes or it could convey some meaningful information to the user. We will, however, distinguish between database systems and database management systems. A database management system is that component which manages the database containing persistent data. A database system consists of both the database and the database management system.

A key component to the evolution and interoperation of data management systems is the interoperability of heterogeneous database systems. Efforts on the interoperability between database systems have been reported since the late 1970s. However, it is only recently that we are seeing commercial developments in heterogeneous database systems. Major database system vendors are now providing interoperability between their products and other systems. Furthermore, many of the database system vendors are migrating toward an architecture called the client–server architecture, which facilitates distributed data management capabilities. In addition to efforts on the interoperability between different database systems and client–server environments, work is also directed toward handling autonomous and federated environments.

The organization of this appendix is as follows. Since database systems are a key component of data management systems, we first provide an overview of the developments in database systems. These developments are discussed in Section A.2. Then, we provide a vision for data management systems in Section A.3. Our framework for data management systems is discussed in Section A.4. Note that data mining, warehousing, and web data management are components of this framework.

Building information systems from our framework with special instantiations is discussed in Section A.5. The relationship between the various texts that we have written (or are writing) for CRC Press is discussed in Section A.6. This appendix is summarized in Section A.7.

A.2   DEVELOPMENTS IN DATABASE SYSTEMS

Figure A.1 provides an overview of the developments in database systems technology. While the early work in the 1960s focused on developing products based on the network and hierarchical data models, much of the developments in database systems took place after the seminal paper by Codd (1970) describing the relational model (see also Date, 1990). Research and development work on relational database systems was carried out during the early 1970s, and several prototypes were developed throughout the 1970s. Notable efforts include IBM's (International Business Machine Corporation's) System R and University of California at Berkeley's INGRES. During the 1980s, many relational database system products were being marketed (notable among these products are those of Oracle Corporation, Sybase Inc., Informix Corporation, INGRES Corporation, IBM, Digital Equipment Corporation, and Hewlett Packard Company). During the 1990s, products from other vendors emerged (e.g., Microsoft Corporation). In fact, to date, numerous relational database system products have been marketed. However, Codd has stated that many of the systems that are being marketed as relational systems are not really relational (see, e.g., the discussion in Date, 1990). He then discussed various criteria that a system must satisfy to be qualified as a relational database system. While the early work focused on issues such as data model, normalization theory, query processing and optimization strategies, query languages, and access strategies and indexes, later the focus shifted toward supporting a multiuser environment. In particular, concurrency control and recovery techniques were developed. Support for transaction processing was also provided.

Research on relational database systems as well as on transaction management was followed by research on distributed database systems around the mid-1970s. Several distributed database system prototype development efforts also began around the late 1970s. Notable among these efforts include IBM's System R*, DDTS (Distributed Database Testbed System) by Honeywell Inc., SDD-I and Multibase by CCA (Computer Corporation of America), and Mermaid by SDC

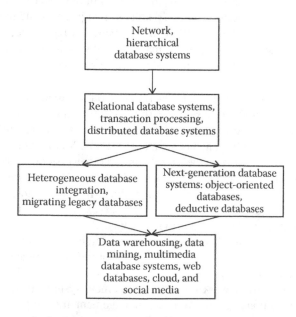

FIGURE A.1   Developments in database systems technology.

(System Development Corporation). Furthermore, many of these systems (e.g., DDTS, Multibase, and Mermaid) function in a heterogeneous environment. During the early 1990s, several database system vendors (such as Oracle Corporation, Sybase Inc., and Informix Corporation) provided data distribution capabilities for their systems. Most of the distributed relational database system products are based on client–server architectures. The idea is to have the client of vendor A communicate with the server database system of vendor B. In other words, the client–server computing paradigm facilitates a heterogeneous computing environment. Interoperability between relational and nonrelational commercial database systems is also possible. The database systems community is also involved in standardization efforts. Notable among the standardization efforts are the ANSI/SPARC 3-level schema architecture, the IRDS (Information Resource Dictionary System) standard for Data Dictionary Systems, the relational query language SQL (Structured Query Language), and the RDA (Remote Database Access) protocol for remote database access.

Another significant development in database technology is the advent of object-oriented database management systems. Active work on developing such systems began in the mid-1980s, and they are now commercially available (notable among them include the products of Object Design Inc., Ontos Inc., Gemstone Systems Inc., and Versant Object Technology). It was felt that new-generation applications such as multimedia, office information systems, CAD/CAM, process control, and software engineering have different requirements. Such applications utilize complex data structures. Tighter integration between the programming language and the data model is also desired. Object-oriented database systems satisfy most of the requirements of these new-generation applications (Cattell, 1991).

According to the Lagunita report published as a result of a National Science Foundation (NSF) workshop in 1990 (see Kim, 1990; Silberschatz et al., 1990), relational database systems, transaction processing, and distributed (relational) database systems are stated as mature technologies. Furthermore, vendors are marketing object-oriented database systems and demonstrating the interoperability between different database systems. The report goes on to state that as applications are getting increasingly complex, more sophisticated database systems are needed. Furthermore, since many organizations now use database systems, in many cases of different types, the database systems need to be integrated. Although work has begun to address these issues and commercial products are available, several issues still need to be resolved. Therefore, challenges faced by the database systems researchers in the early 1990s were in two areas. One was next-generation database systems and the other was heterogeneous database systems.

Next-generation database systems include object-oriented database systems, functional database systems, special parallel architectures to enhance the performance of database system functions, high-performance database systems, real-time database systems, scientific database systems, temporal database systems, database systems that handle incomplete and uncertain information, and intelligent database systems (also sometimes called logic or deductive database systems). Ideally, a database system should provide the support for high-performance transaction processing, model complex applications, represent new kinds of data, and make intelligent deductions. While significant progress has been made during the late 1980s and early 1990s, there is much to be done before such a database system can be developed.

Heterogeneous database systems have been receiving considerable attention during the past decade (March, 1990). The major issues include handling different data models, different query processing strategies, different transaction processing algorithms, and different query languages. Should a uniform view be provided to the entire system, or should the users of the individual systems maintain their own views of the entire system? These are questions that have yet to be answered satisfactorily. It is also envisaged that a complete solution to heterogeneous database management systems is a generation away. While research should be directed toward finding such a solution, work should also be carried out to handle limited forms of heterogeneity to satisfy the customer needs. Another type of database system that has received some attention lately is a federated database system. Note that some have used the terms heterogeneous database system and federated

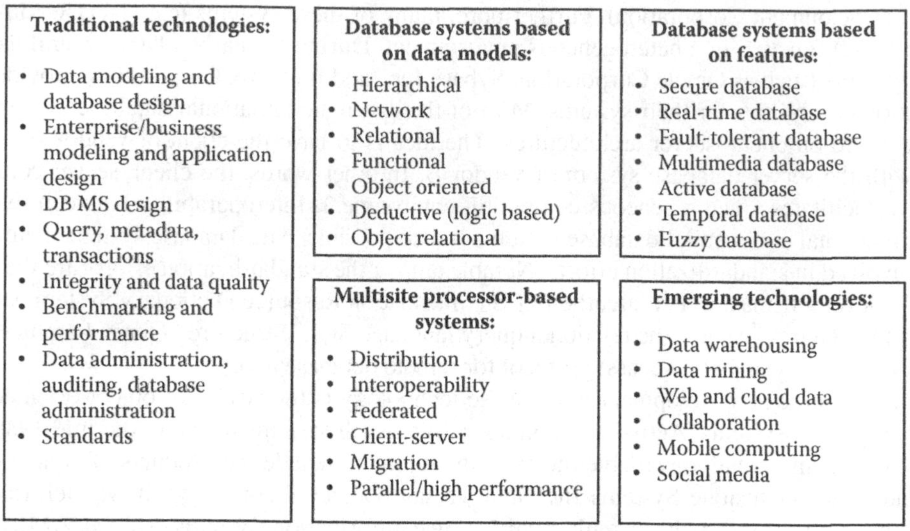

Traditional technologies:	Database systems based on data models:	Database systems based on features:
• Data modeling and database design • Enterprise/business modeling and application design • DB MS design • Query, metadata, transactions • Integrity and data quality • Benchmarking and performance • Data administration, auditing, database administration • Standards	• Hierarchical • Network • Relational • Functional • Object oriented • Deductive (logic based) • Object relational	• Secure database • Real-time database • Fault-tolerant database • Multimedia database • Active database • Temporal database • Fuzzy database
	Multisite processor-based systems:	**Emerging technologies:**
	• Distribution • Interoperability • Federated • Client-server • Migration • Parallel/high performance	• Data warehousing • Data mining • Web and cloud data • Collaboration • Mobile computing • Social media

FIGURE A.2   Comprehensive view of data management systems.

database system interchangeably. While heterogeneous database systems can be part of a federation, a federation can also include homogeneous database systems.

The explosion of users on the web as well as developments in interface technologies has resulted in even more challenges for data management researchers. A second workshop was sponsored by NSF in 1995, and several emerging technologies have been identified to be important as we go into the twenty-first century (Widom, 1996). These include digital libraries, managing very large databases, data administration issues, multimedia databases, data warehousing, data mining, data management for collaborative computing environments, and security and privacy. Another significant development in the 1990s is the development of object-relational systems. Such systems combine the advantages of both object-oriented database systems and relational database systems. Also, many corporations are now focusing on integrating their data management products with web technologies. Finally, for many organizations, there is an increasing need to migrate some of the legacy databases and applications to newer architectures and systems such as client–server architectures and relational database systems. We believe there is no end to data management systems. As new technologies are developed, there are new opportunities for data management research and development.

A comprehensive view of all data management technologies is illustrated in Figure A.2. As shown, traditional technologies include database design, transaction processing, and benchmarking. Then, there are database systems based on data models such as relational and object oriented. Database systems may depend on features they provide, such as security and real-time performance. These database systems may be relational or object oriented. There are also database systems based on multiple sites or processors, such as distributed and heterogeneous database systems, parallel systems, and systems being migrated. Finally, there are the emerging technologies such as data warehousing and mining, collaboration, and the web. Any comprehensive text on data management systems should address all of these technologies. We have selected some of the relevant technologies and put them in a framework. This framework is described in Section A.5.

A.3   STATUS, VISION, AND ISSUES

Significant progress has been made on data management systems. However, many of the technologies are still stand-alone technologies, as illustrated in Figure A.3. For example, multimedia systems

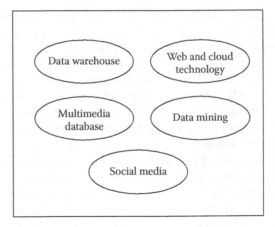

FIGURE A.3 Stand-alone systems.

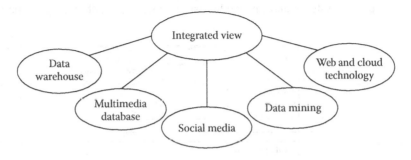

FIGURE A.4 Vision.

are yet to be successfully integrated with warehousing and mining technologies. The ultimate goal is to integrate multiple technologies so that accurate data, as well as information, are produced at the right time and distributed to the user in a timely manner. Our vision for data and information management is illustrated in Figure A.4.

The work discussed in Thuraisingham (1997) addressed many of the challenges necessary to accomplish this vision. In particular, integration of heterogeneous databases, as well as the use of distributed object technology for interoperability, was discussed. While much progress has been made on the system aspects of interoperability, semantic issues still remain a challenge. Different databases have different representations. Furthermore, the same data entity may be interpreted differently at different sites. Addressing these semantic differences and extracting useful information from the heterogeneous and possibly multimedia data sources are major challenges.

A.4 DATA MANAGEMENT SYSTEMS FRAMEWORK

For the successful development of evolvable interoperable data management systems, heterogeneous database systems integration is a major component. However, there are other technologies that have to be successfully integrated with each other to develop techniques for efficient access and sharing of data, as well as for the extraction of information from the data. To facilitate the development of data management systems to meet the requirements of various applications in fields such as medical, financial, manufacturing, and military, we have proposed a framework, which can be regarded as a reference model, for data management systems. Various components from this framework have to be integrated to develop data management systems to support the various applications.

Figure A.5 illustrates our framework, which can be regarded as a model for data management systems. This framework consists of three layers. One can think of the component technologies, which we will also refer to as components, belonging to a particular layer to be more or less built on the technologies provided by the lower layer. Layer I is the Database Technology and Distribution Layer. This layer consists of database systems and distributed database systems technologies. Layer II is the Interoperability and Migration Layer. This layer consists of technologies such as heterogeneous database integration, client–server databases, and multimedia database systems to handle heterogeneous data types and migrating legacy databases. Layer III is the Information Extraction and Sharing Layer. This layer essentially consists of technologies for some of the newer services supported by data management systems. These include data warehousing, data mining (Thuraisingham, 1998), web databases, and database support for collaborative applications. Data management systems may utilize lower-level technologies such as networking, distributed processing, and mass storage. We have grouped these technologies into a layer called the Supporting Technologies Layer. This supporting layer does not belong to the data management systems framework. This supporting layer also consists of some higher-level technologies such as distributed object management and agents. Also, shown in Figure A.5 is the Application Technologies Layer. Systems such as collaborative computing systems and knowledge-based systems, which belong to the Application

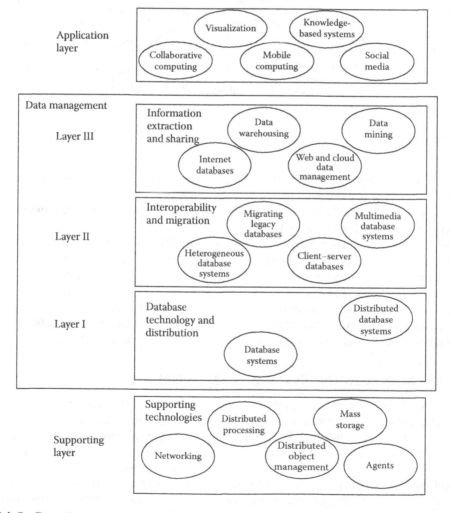

FIGURE A.5   Data management systems framework.

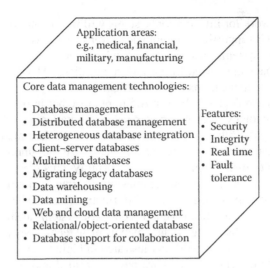

FIGURE A.6   Three-dimensional view of data management.

Technologies Layer, may utilize data management systems. Note that the Application Technologies Layer is also outside of the data management systems framework.

The technologies that constitute the data management systems framework can be regarded to be some of the core technologies in data management. However, features like security, integrity, real-time processing, fault tolerance, and high-performance computing are needed for many applications utilizing data management technologies. Applications utilizing data management technologies may be medical, financial, or military, among others. We illustrate this in Figure A.6, where a three-dimensional view relating data management technologies with features and applications is given. For example, one could develop a secure distributed database management system for medical applications or a fault-tolerant multimedia database management system for financial applications.

Integrating the components belonging to the various layers is important to developing efficient data management systems. In addition, data management technologies have to be integrated with the application technologies to develop successful information systems. However, at present, there is limited integration between these various components. Our books have addressed concepts related to the various layers of this framework.

Note that security cuts across all the layers. Security is needed for the supporting layers such as agents and distributed systems. Security is needed for all of the layers in the framework, including database security, distributed database security, warehousing security, web database security, and collaborative data management security.

A.5   BUILDING INFORMATION SYSTEMS FROM THE FRAMEWORK

Figure A.5 illustrated a framework for data management systems. As shown in that figure, the technologies for data management include database systems, distributed database systems, heterogeneous database systems, migrating legacy databases, multimedia database systems, data warehousing, data mining, web databases, and database support for collaboration. Furthermore, data management systems take advantage of supporting technologies such as distributed processing and agents. Similarly, application technologies such as collaborative computing, visualization, expert systems, and mobile computing take advantage of data management systems.

Many of us have heard of the term *information systems* on numerous occasions. This term has sometimes been used interchangeably with *data management systems*. In our terminology, information systems are much broader than data management systems, but they do include data management systems. In fact, a framework for information systems will include not only the data management system layers, but also the supporting technologies layer as well as the application technologies layer. That is, information systems encompass all kinds of computing systems. It can be regarded as the finished product that can be used for various applications. That is, while hardware is at the lowest end of the spectrum, applications are at the highest end.

We can combine the technologies of Figure A.5 to put together information systems. For example, at the application technology level, one may need collaboration and visualization technologies so that analysts can collaboratively carry out some tasks. At the data management level, one may need both multimedia and distributed database technologies. At the supporting level, one may need mass storage as well as some distributed processing capability. This special framework is illustrated in Figure A.7. Another example is a special framework for interoperability. One may need some visualization technology to display the integrated information from the heterogeneous databases. At the data management level, we have heterogeneous database systems technology. At the supporting technology level, one may use distributed object management technology to encapsulate the heterogeneous databases. This special framework is illustrated in Figure A.8.

Finally, let us illustrate the concepts that we have described above by using a specific example. Suppose a group of physicians/surgeons want a system where they can collaborate and make

```
┌──────────────────────────────┐
│  Collaboration, social media, │
│             and               │
│        visualization          │
└──────────────────────────────┘

┌──────────────────────────────┐
│     Multimedia database,      │
│  distributed database systems │
└──────────────────────────────┘

┌──────────────────────────────┐
│        Mass storage,          │
│     distributed processing    │
└──────────────────────────────┘
```

FIGURE A.7   Framework for multimedia data management for collaboration.

```
┌──────────────────────────────┐
│                              │
│        Visualization         │
│                              │
└──────────────────────────────┘

┌──────────────────────────────┐
│        Heterogeneous         │
│           database           │
│          integration         │
└──────────────────────────────┘

┌──────────────────────────────┐
│          Distributed         │
│            object            │
│          management          │
└──────────────────────────────┘
```

FIGURE A.8   Framework for heterogeneous database interoperability.

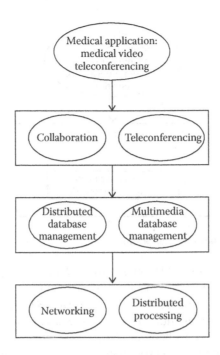

FIGURE A.9 Specific example.

decisions about various patients. This could be a medical video teleconferencing application. That is, at the highest level, the application is a medical application and, more specifically, a medical video teleconferencing application. At the application technology level, one needs a variety of technologies, including collaboration and teleconferencing. These application technologies will make use of data management technologies such as distributed database systems and multimedia database systems. That is, one may need to support multimedia data such as audio and video. The data management technologies, in turn, draw upon lower-level technologies such as distributed processing and networking. We illustrate this in Figure A.9.

In summary, information systems include data management systems as well as application-layer systems such as collaborative computing systems and supporting-layer systems such as distributed object management systems. While application technologies make use of data management technologies and data management technologies make use of supporting technologies, the ultimate user of the information system is the application itself. Today, numerous applications make use of information systems. These applications are from multiple domains such as medical, financial, manufacturing, telecommunications, and defense. Specific applications include signal processing, electronic commerce, patient monitoring, and situation assessment. Figure A.10 illustrates the relationship between the application and the information system.

A.6   RELATIONSHIP BETWEEN THE TEXTS

We have published two book series. The first series is mainly for technical managers, while the second series is for researchers and developers. This book is the tenth in the first series. Our previous nine books are *Data Management Systems: Evolution and Interoperation* (Thuraisingham, 1997), *Data Mining: Technologies, Techniques, Tools and Trends* (Thuraisingham, 1998), *Web Data Management and Electronic Commerce* (Thuraisingham, 2000), *Managing and Mining Multimedia Databases for the Electronic Enterprise* (Thuraisingham, 2001), *XML, Databases and the Semantic Web* (Thuraisingham, 2002), *Web Data Mining and Applications in Business Intelligence and*

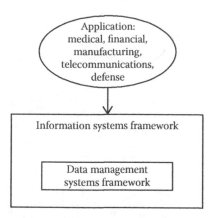

FIGURE A.10   Application–framework relationship.

Counter-terrorism (Thuraisingham, 2003), *Database and Applications Security: Integrating Data Management and Information Security* (Thuraisingham, 2005), *Building Trustworthy Semantic Webs* (Thuraisingham, 2007), and *Secure Semantic Service-Oriented Systems* (Thuraisingham, 2010). Our last book in these series, titled *Developing and Securing the Cloud* (Thuraisingham, 2013), has evolved from our previous book on *Secure Semantic Service-Oriented Systems*. All of these books have evolved from the framework that we illustrated in this appendix and address different parts of the framework. The connection between these texts is illustrated in Figure A.11.

We have published three books in the second series. The first is titled *Design and Implementation of Data Mining Tools* (Awad et al., 2009) and the second is titled *Data Mining Tools for Malware Detection* (Masud et al., 2011). Our book, *Secure Data Provenance and Inference Control with Semantic Web* (Thuraisingham et al., 2014) was the third in these series. Our current book, *Analyzing and Securing Social Media*, is the fourth in these series (Abrol et al., 2015). The relationship between these books as well as with our previous books is illustrated in Figures A.12 and A.13.

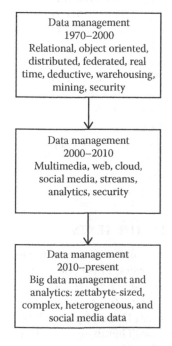

FIGURE A.11   From data to big data.

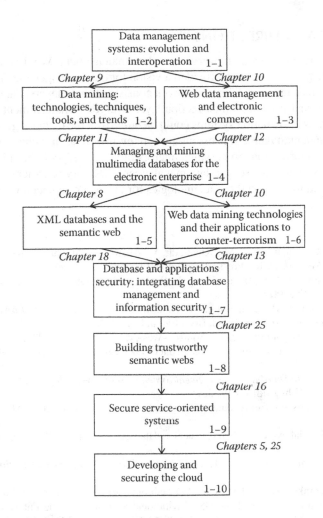

FIGURE A.12 Relationship between texts—series I.

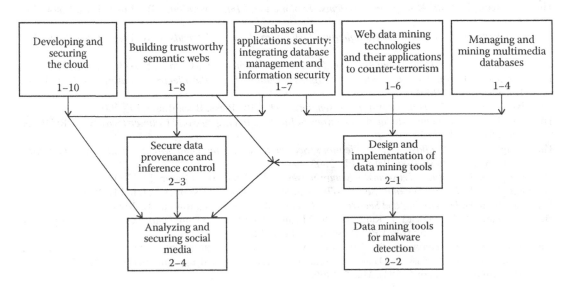

FIGURE A.13 Relationship between texts—series II.

A.7 SUMMARY AND DIRECTIONS

In this appendix, we have provided an overview of data management. We first discussed the developments in data management and then provided a vision for data management. Then, we illustrated a framework for data management. This framework consists of three layers: database systems layer, interoperability layer, and information extraction layer. Web data management belongs to layer 3. Finally, we showed how information systems could be built from the technologies of the framework.

We believe that data management is essential to many information technologies including data mining, multimedia information processing, interoperability, and collaboration and knowledge management. This appendix stresses on data management. Security is critical for all data management technologies, and we rely on these technologies for our work on social media systems.

REFERENCES

Abrol, S., Heatherly, R., Kantarcioglu, M., Khadilkar, V., Khan, L., and Thuraisingham, B. *Analyzing and Securing Social Networks*. CRC Press, Boca Raton, FL, 2015.

Awad, M., Khan, L., Thuraisingham, B., and Wang, L. *Design and Implementation of Data Mining Tools*. CRC Press, Boca Raton, FL, 2009.

Cadenhead, T., Thuraisingham, B., Kantarcioglu, M., and Khadilkar, V. *Secure Data Provenance and Inference Control with Semantic Web*. CRC Press, Boca Raton, FL, 2013.

Cattell, R. *Object Data Management Systems*. Addison-Wesley, Reading, MA, 1991.

Codd, E.F. A relational model of data for large shared data banks. *Communications of the ACM* 13(6): 377–387, 1970.

Date, C.J. *An Introduction to Database Management Systems*. Addison-Wesley, Reading, MA, 1990 (6th edition published in 1995 by Addison-Wesley).

Kim, W., editor. Directions for future database research & development. *ACM SIGMOD Record* 19(4), December 1990.

March, S.T., editor. Special issue on heterogeneous database systems. *ACM Computing Surveys* 22(3), September 1990.

Masud, M., Thuraisingham, B., and Khan, L. *Data Mining Tools for Malware Detection*. CRC Press, Boca Raton, FL, 2011.

Silberschatz, A., Stonebraker, M., and Ullman, J.D., editors. Database systems: Achievements and opportunities. The "Lagunita" report of the NSF Invitational Workshop on the Future of Database Systems Research, February 22–23, Palo Alto, CA (TR-90-22), Department of Computer Sciences, University of Texas at Austin, Austin, TX, 1990. Also in *ACM SIGMOD Record*, December 1990.

Thuraisingham, B. *Data Management Systems: Evolution and Interoperation*. CRC Press, Boca Raton, FL, 1997.

Thuraisingham, B. *Data Mining: Technologies, Techniques, Tools and Trends*. CRC Press, Boca Raton, FL, 1998.

Thuraisingham, B. *Web Data Management and Electronic Commerce*. CRC Press, Boca Raton, FL, 2000.

Thuraisingham, B. *Managing and Mining Multimedia Databases for the Electronic Enterprise*. CRC Press, Boca Raton, FL, 2001.

Thuraisingham, B. *XML, Databases and the Semantic Web*. CRC Press, Boca Raton, FL, 2002.

Thuraisingham, B. *Web Data Mining Applications in Business Intelligence and Counter-terrorism*. CRC Press, Boca Raton, FL, 2003.

Thuraisingham, B. *Database and Applications Security: Integrating Data Management and Information Security*. CRC Press, Boca Raton, FL, 2005.

Thuraisingham, B. *Building Trustworthy Semantic Webs*. CRC Press, Boca Raton, FL, 2007.

Thuraisingham, B. *Secure Semantic Service-Oriented Systems*. CRC Press, Boca Raton, FL, 2010.

Thuraisingham, B. *Developing and Securing the Cloud*. CRC Press, Boca Raton, FL, 2013.

Thuraisingham, B., Cadenhead, T., Kantarcioglu, M., and Khadilkar, V. *Secure Data Provenance and Inference Control with Semantic Web*. CRC Press, Boca Raton, FL, 2014.

Widom, J., editor. *Proceedings of the Database Systems Workshop*. Report published by the National Science Foundation, 1995. Also in Database research: Achievements and opportunities into the 21st century. *ACM SIGMOD Record* 25 (1), March 1996.

Index

Page numbers followed by f and t indicate figures and tables, respectively.